A+ Certification Study System

A+ CERTIFICATION STUDY SYSTEM

Michael A. Pastore
and Bill Karow,
with Candy Paape,
Randall Thomas,
and John Glassman

IDG Books Worldwide, Inc.

An International Data Group Company

Foster City, CA ● Chicago, IL ● Indianapolis, IN ● New York, NY

A+ Certification Study System

Published by
IDG Books Worldwide, Inc.
An International Data Group Company
919 E. Hillsdale Blvd., Suite 400
Foster City, CA 94404
www.idgbooks.com (IDG Books Worldwide Web site)

Library of Congress Catalog Card Number: 98-071152
ISBN: 0-7645-3166-2
Printed in the United States of America
10 9 8 7 6 5 4 3 2 1
1B/RQ/QT/ZZ/FC
Distributed in the United States by IDG Books Worldwide, Inc.

Distributed by CDG Books Canada Inc. for Canada; by Transworld Publishers Limited in the United Kingdom; by IDG Norge Books for Norway; by IDG Sweden Books for Sweden; by Woodslane Pty. Ltd. for Australia; by Woodslane (NZ) Ltd. for New Zealand; by TransQuest Publishers Pte Ltd. for Singapore, Malaysia, Thailand, Indonesia, and Hong Kong; by ICG Muse, Inc. for Japan; by Norma Comunicaciones S.A. for Colombia; by Intersoft for South Africa; by Le Monde en Tique for France; by International Thomson Publishing for Germany, Austria and Switzerland; by Distribuidora Cuspide for Argentina; by Livraria Cultura for Brazil; by Ediciones ZETA S.C.R. Ltda. for Peru; by WS Computer Publishing Corporation, Inc., for the Philippines; by Contemporanea de Ediciones for Venezuela; by Express Computer Distributors for the Caribbean and West Indies; by Micronesia Media Distributor, Inc. for Micronesia; by Grupo Editorial Norma S.A. for Guatemala; by Chips Computadoras S.A. de C.V. for Mexico; by Editorial Norma de Panama S.A. for Panama; by American Bookshops for Finland. Authorized Sales Agent: Anthony Rudkin Associates for the Middle East and North Africa.

For general information on IDG Books Worldwide's books in the U.S., please call our Consumer Customer Service department at 800-762-2974. For reseller information, including discounts and premium sales, please call our Reseller Customer Service department at 800-434-3422.

For information on where to purchase IDG Books Worldwide's books outside the U.S., please contact our International Sales department at 317-596-5530 or fax 317-596-5692.

For consumer information on foreign language translations, please contact our Customer Service department at 800-434-3422, fax 317-596-5692, or e-mail rights@idgbooks.com.

For information on licensing foreign or domestic rights, please phone +1-650-655-3109.

For sales inquiries and special prices for bulk quantities, please contact our Sales department at 650-655-3200 or write to the address above.

For information on using IDG Books Worldwide's books in the classroom or for ordering examination copies, please contact our Educational Sales department at 800-434-2086 or fax 317-596-5499.

For press review copies, author interviews, or other publicity information, please contact our Public Relations department at 650-655-3000 or fax 650-655-3299.

For authorization to photocopy items for corporate, personal, or educational use, please contact Copyright Clearance Center, 222 Rosewood Drive, Danvers, MA 01923, or fax 978-750-4470.

ABOUT IDG BOOKS WORLDWIDE

Welcome to the world of IDG Books Worldwide.

IDG Books Worldwide, Inc., is a subsidiary of International Data Group, the world's largest publisher of computer-related information and the leading global provider of information services on information technology. IDG was founded more than 30 years ago by Patrick J. McGovern and now employs more than 9,000 people worldwide. IDG publishes more than 290 computer publications in over 75 countries. More than 90 million people read one or more IDG publications each month.

Launched in 1990, IDG Books Worldwide is today the #1 publisher of best-selling computer books in the United States. We are proud to have received eight awards from the Computer Press Association in recognition of editorial excellence and three from Computer Currents' First Annual Readers' Choice Awards. Our best-selling *...For Dummies®* series has more than 50 million copies in print with translations in 31 languages. IDG Books Worldwide, through a joint venture with IDG's Hi-Tech Beijing, became the first U.S. publisher to publish a computer book in the People's Republic of China. In record time, IDG Books Worldwide has become the first choice for millions of readers around the world who want to learn how to better manage their businesses.

Our mission is simple: Every one of our books is designed to bring extra value and skill-building instructions to the reader. Our books are written by experts who understand and care about our readers. The knowledge base of our editorial staff comes from years of experience in publishing, education, and journalism — experience we use to produce books to carry us into the new millennium. In short, we care about books, so we attract the best people. We devote special attention to details such as audience, interior design, use of icons, and illustrations. And because we use an efficient process of authoring, editing, and desktop publishing our books electronically, we can spend more time ensuring superior content and less time on the technicalities of making books.

You can count on our commitment to deliver high-quality books at competitive prices on topics you want to read about. At IDG Books Worldwide, we continue in the IDG tradition of delivering quality for more than 30 years. You'll find no better book on a subject than one from IDG Books Worldwide.

John Kilcullen
Chairman and CEO
IDG Books Worldwide, Inc.

Steven Berkowitz
President and Publisher
IDG Books Worldwide, Inc.

*Eighth Annual
Computer Press
Awards ≥1992*

*Ninth Annual
Computer Press
Awards ≥1993*

*Tenth Annual
Computer Press
Awards ≥1994*

*Eleventh Annual
Computer Press
Awards ≥1995*

IDG is the world's leading IT media, research and exposition company. Founded in 1964, IDG had 1997 revenues of $2.05 billion and has more than 9,000 employees worldwide. IDG offers the widest range of media options that reach IT buyers in 75 countries representing 95% of worldwide IT spending. IDG's diverse product and services portfolio spans six key areas including print publishing, online publishing, expositions and conferences, market research, education and training, and global marketing services. More than 90 million people read one or more of IDG's 290 magazines and newspapers, including IDG's leading global brands — Computerworld, PC World, Network World, Macworld and the Channel World family of publications. IDG Books Worldwide is one of the fastest-growing computer book publishers in the world, with more than 700 titles in 36 languages. The "...For Dummies®" series alone has more than 50 million copies in print. IDG offers online users the largest network of technology-specific Web sites around the world through IDG.net (http://www.idg.net), which comprises more than 225 targeted Web sites in 55 countries worldwide. International Data Corporation (IDC) is the world's largest provider of information technology data, analysis and consulting, with research centers in over 41 countries and more than 400 research analysts worldwide. IDG World Expo is a leading producer of more than 168 globally branded conferences and expositions in 35 countries including E3 (Electronic Entertainment Expo), Macworld Expo, ComNet, Windows World Expo, ICE (Internet Commerce Expo), Agenda, DEMO, and Spotlight. IDG's training subsidiary, ExecuTrain, is the world's largest computer training company, with more than 230 locations worldwide and 785 training courses. IDG Marketing Services helps industry-leading IT companies build international brand recognition by developing global integrated marketing programs via IDG's print, online and exposition products worldwide. Further information about the company can be found at www.idg.com. 1/24/99

CREDITS

ACQUISITIONS EDITOR

Tracy Thomsic

DEVELOPMENT EDITORS

Martin V. Minner
Jennifer Rowe

TECHNICAL EDITORS

Ray Mosley
Ron Millione

COPY EDITORS

Jennifer H. Mario
Nicole Fountain
Lauren Kennedy

PROJECT COORDINATOR

Tom Debolski

BOOK DESIGNER

Kurt Krames

GRAPHICS AND PRODUCTION SPECIALISTS

Stephanie Hollier
James Kussow

GRAPHIC TECHNICIANS

Sarah Barnes
Linda Marousek

QUALITY CONTROL SPECIALISTS

Mick Arellano
Mark Schumann

ILLUSTRATOR

Jesse Coleman

PROOFREADING AND INDEXING

York Production Services

PACKAGING COORDINATOR

Constance Petros

ABOUT THE AUTHORS

Michael Pastore has been in the computer field for more than 20 years. He is an A+ technician, a Microsoft Certified Professional (MCP), and the president of IBID Publishing, which specializes in computer-training products. He has written eight books on computers and has an MA in leadership, a BS in business administration, and an AA in electronics engineering. Pastore writes about and teaches computer-related topics throughout the United States, and is a faculty member of the Information Systems Department at the City University in Bellevue, Washington. He welcomes comments from his readers and can be contacted via the Internet at mikepast@aol.com.

Bill Karow received a BS in business administration from the University of Florida and an MBA in finance from the Crummer Graduate School of Business. He has worked as a financial analyst, a computer industry analyst, and a trumpet player. He is currently manager of systems development for a large entertainment company in Orlando, Florida.

PREFACE

Welcome to the *A+ Certification Study System*! This book will to help you acquire the knowledge and skills you'll need to pass the A+ exam and work competently as a computer technician or computer support professional. It is designed to be the only book you'll need to prepare for the A+ exam and covers the material in more depth than you need to pass the exam.

HOW THIS BOOK IS ORGANIZED

This book is organized into three major parts, followed by supplemental appendixes and a CD-ROM. Each section contains several related chapters. The three sections are *Introduction to A+ Certification*, *Core Components*, and *DOS/Windows Systems*.

Each chapter is designed to build on the previous one. At the end of each chapter you'll find a series of multiple-choice and fill-in-the-blank exercises. Following the exercises, most chapters include one or more labs designed to help reinforce the key concepts in the chapter. If you perform the labs, do the exercises, and read the chapters, you should be able to pass the A+ Certification exam.

The parts of this book are as follows:

o **Part I: Introduction to A+ Certification.** This part discusses the challenges you will encounter and the study methods you can use as you prepare for the exam. It also covers career opportunities for an A+ certified technician.

o **Part II: Core Components.** This part examines in detail the technical concepts you need to understand the test materials. This section helps you understand how the components interact and work together, and presents concepts about computer systems, monitors, printers, and the various peripherals and components that make up a modern PC system.

o **Part III: DOS/Windows Systems.** This part covers the key information you need to install, configure, and maintain computer systems. Here, you gain an in-depth understanding of a practicing technician's concerns, including safety, electrical concepts, construction, and assembly techniques. This section addresses the conceptual parts of an operating system, as well as its features and capabilities and covers the exam you are required to pass for A+ certification.

HOW TO USE THIS BOOK

This book can be used by individuals or as part of a classroom experience. We recommend that you develop a plan of attack to complete the book and pass the exam.

After reading each chapter, study the Key Point Summary section at the end. Then go back and quickly reread the chapter itself, scanning for information that helps you understand the material more completely. Go back and review the Key Point Summary section again. Answer the Instant Assessment questions and score yourself. Review, in the chapter, the answers for each question. This may sound repetitive, but you will retain almost all of the material if you do this.

Progress through each chapter in this manner until you have completed the entire book. After you have done this, get a spiral-bound notebook, start at the beginning of the book, and write down all of the key points from each chapter. This will reinforce your learning.

Five days before you are scheduled to take the exam, go through the notebook and quickly review everything you wrote down. If you are unclear about a point, go back into the book and quickly review that section.

The night before you take the exam, review all of the material one last time before you go to bed. Don't worry about it after that — you will, undoubtedly, do fine on the exam.

PREREQUISITES

This book assumes that you have very limited knowledge of computer technology. You, however, should have the following knowledge or abilities:

o A working user-level knowledge of computer equipment.

- Basic computer skills, including the ability to use a mouse, pointer, and other devices.

- The desire to become an A+ certified technician. (We can provide you the knowledge, but only you can provide the desire to learn.)

THE HARDWARE AND SOFTWARE YOU'LL NEED

You will need access to various hardware and software to complete the Hands-on Lab Exercises in this book. It is extremely important that you perform these labs. If you don't have the specific hardware we use in the labs, feel free to substitute hardware when it is appropriate.

Hardware Requirements

The minimum hardware requirements are as follows:

- Intel-based computer 486/66 processor, 16MB RAM, and 500MB of available hard disk space

- CD-ROM drive

- Mouse

- VGA monitor and graphics card

Optional hardware includes the following:

- Additional computer (for assembly and disassembly)

- Network adapter

- Printer

- Modem and Internet connection

Software Requirements

The minimum software requirements are as follows:

- Microsoft Windows 95

- Microsoft DOS 6.0 or above

ICONS USED IN THIS BOOK

Several different icons are used throughout this book to draw your attention to matters that deserve a closer look:

 **Be careful here! This icon points out information that can save you a lot of grief. It's often easier to prevent tragedy beforehand than to fix it afterward.**

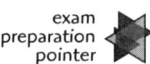 **This icon identifies important advice as you study to pass the A+ Certification exam.**

 This icon points out an interesting or a helpful fact, or some other comment that deserves emphasis.

 This icon offers a little piece of friendly advice, a shortcut, or a bit of personal experience that might be of use to you.

ACKNOWLEDGMENTS

Putting together a book like this is a huge undertaking that requires many individuals working many long and hard hours. Several very important people were essential to the completion of this book. I'd like to take a minute and recognize some of those people personally for their help.

To Randall Thomas, A+ for your work and diligence in pulling together the middle chapters. Your work on photography and animation was essential. I would also like to thank Don Drumheller for his outstanding work with photography and with the various other things he worked on when needed. Candy Paape was instrumental in putting together the Windows/DOS section, performing editing, and giving input on the book. Thanks to Russ Albright, MA, and John Glassman, JD, for their help with content and writing.

The IDG Book Worldwide team has been super to work with, especially acquisitions editor Tracy Thomsic and lead development editor Jennifer Rowe — thank you. Thanks to Marty Minner, development editor, who worked countless hours reviewing chapters. Also thanks to copy editors Jennifer Mario and Nicole Fountain, and technical editors Ray Mosley and Ron Millione. All of these people helped make the final product well-polished. And thanks to the production team for their efforts.

My family and coworkers have been extremely supportive throughout this project and deserve special recognition. First, my wife Sheryl, who always had a good word to say (even when she didn't mean it). My kids, Erin, John, and Mark for their patience with me. Nancy DeChenne and Heath Tonack for bearing with me through all this.

— *Michael Pastore*

I would like to thank the following people for their assistance and support while I worked on this project: Suzanne Kincaid, Mike Beltrano, Frankie Borison, Mike Failla, Joe Gruber, Brian Hentschel, Tyson Heyn, Peter Hipson, Janice Kiesel, Myra Monahan, Barry and Marcia Press, Colleen Railey, and Paul Sullivan.

I'd also like to thank Tracy Thomsic, acquisitions editor, and Jennifer Rowe, development editor, because without their patience and assistance this book would never have survived. And I apologize in advance for almost certainly missing someone!

— *Bill Karow*

CONTENTS AT A GLANCE

CONTENTS

Introduction to A+ Certification

The A+ Exam

About Chapter 1

This chapter introduces you to a method for demonstrating your skills as a qualified computer technician — A+ certification. This chapter describes the process of preparing for and taking the A+ exam. It also provides an overview of the information needed to pass this exam.

By the end of this chapter you will have a clearer sense of what you need to know to become an A+ Certified technician, as well as how to pursue the testing process itself. Your pursuit of A+ certification will help you improve your technical expertise and show others your commitment to the computer profession.

OVERVIEW OF A+ CERTIFICATION

The A+ certification is designed to measure the ability of computer technicians to install, troubleshoot, and support computer systems. The exam is designed to assure employers and customers that you have demonstrated competence in computer systems issues and are able to deal with the variety of technical issues you will likely encounter in the workplace.

The A+ credential is maintained by an organization called CompTIA (The Computing Technology Industry Association). CompTIA, along with its supporters and members, maintain this certification to ensure that it represents what is needed in the industry for computer technicians and support personnel.

CompTIA has recruited over 7,500 companies and organizations that support and hire A+ certified professionals. Over 65,000 people have been A+ certified since 1993. Compaq, Microsoft, Hewlett Packard, Dell, Toshiba, Apple, Digital Equipment, and thousands of other computer manufacturing, support, and service organizations have come to rely on the A+ certified professional for technical support. These companies know that someone with the skills and expertise demonstrated by A+ certification can have a significant bottom-line impact. The CompTIA Web site (www.comptia.org) contains a great deal of information on the A+ certification standards as well as other CompTIA certifications.

While the A+ certification program does not address every issue in the computer field, it provides a solid foundation on how computers operate and how they're installed and serviced. You learn the skills needed to perform quick and efficient system repairs in the field. Time is one of the most critical elements in the computer business. The ability to diagnose, repair, and put a computer back in service quickly and correctly pays big benefits to both the user and the technician.

concept link **Make sure you read the section titled "How to Use This Book," in the Preface. It offers helpful tips on how best to take advantage of this book as a study guide for the A+ Certification exam.**

The A+ certification is a lifetime certification, according to CompTIA. Once you have passed the exam, you are not required to take it again. However, CompTIA and other organizations are adding new certifications and programs on an almost daily basis. We discuss them later in this chapter under "Trends in Certification."

A CompTIA committee consisting of industry and educational experts monitors the exam requirements and certification standards. The exams go through a periodic review and update to reflect the latest practices and technologies in the industry.

A+ certification requires the successful completion of the Core Module and the Windows/DOS elective exam. The Core test measures your knowledge and comprehension in the following areas:

- Installation, configuration, and upgrading computer systems
- Diagnosing and troubleshooting computer systems
- Safety and preventative maintenance
- Motherboards, processors, memory
- The Windows and DOS operating system and related components
- Printers
- Portable systems
- Basic networking
- Customer satisfaction issues

The DOS/Windows exam measures your ability to install, configure, and troubleshoot DOS- and Windows-related software. As an A+ certified technician you will almost certainly be required to repair DOS- and Windows-based computers.

The exam is divided into sections that measure expertise in the following areas:

- Function, structure, operation, and file management
- Memory management
- Installation, configuration, and upgrading operating systems
- Troubleshooting operating systems problems
- Network and software configuration

The next two sections describe the Core and Windows/DOS modules in more detail.

CORE MODULE

The A+ Certification exam was completely rewritten and went live in July of 1998. The descriptions provided in this section are derived from the most current A+ exam objectives as published by CompTIA. The Core exam covers eight content areas.

Content Area 1: Installation, Configuration, and Upgrading

Here you are tested on your knowledge and skills pertaining to installation, configuration, and upgrading of microcomputer components and peripherals. You are required to have an understanding of software and configuration concerns, such as IRQ's, DMA's, and I/O addresses. You are expected to know how to configure switches and set jumpers.

This section of the exam tests you on the following tasks:

- Identify basic terms, concepts, and functions of system modules, including how each module should work during normal operations.
- Identify basic procedures for adding and removing field replaceable modules.
- Identify IRQ's, DMA's, and I/O addresses and procedures for setting switches and configuring jumpers.
- Identify common peripheral ports, cabling, and connectors.
- Install and configure IDE/EIDE devices.
- Install and configure SCSI devices.
- Configure and install peripherals.
- Use appropriate tools to repair and replace components.
- Identify methods for improving system performance.

Content Area 2: Diagnosis and Troubleshooting

You are responsible for knowing how to diagnose and troubleshoot common systems problems in this section. Based on the symptoms described by end users and visual observation, you make the appropriate component replacements to restore system operation.

This section of the exam tests you on the following tasks:

- Identify common symptoms and problems; troubleshoot and isolate problems.
- Use basic troubleshooting procedures and practices to clarify customers' descriptions of symptoms.

Content Area 3: Safety and Preventative Maintenance

In the course of working with computer systems you will be exposed to potentially harmful voltages and lasers. You are required to demonstrate the knowledge of safe and prudent practices. You are also required to know how to dispose of used chemicals and components safely (for instance, batteries).

You are also expected to be able to minimize the risk of component damage from electrostatic discharge (ESD).

This section of the exam tests you on the following tasks:

- Identify the various types of preventative maintenance products and when and how to use them.
- Identify the procedures and devices used to protect systems from environmental hazards.
- Identify potential hazards and use proper safety procedures around high voltage and lasers.
- Identify and properly dispose of items that require special environmental handling.
- Identify electrostatic discharge precautions and procedures. Know how to use the common ESD protection devices.

Content Area 4: Motherboards/ Processors/Memory

You are required to know and understand terms and technologies pertaining to computer system components, such as motherboards, processors, and memory.

This section of the exam tests you on the following tasks:

- Identify various CPU chips and their characteristics.
- Identify the different types of random access memory (RAM) and their physical characteristics.
- Identify the popular types of motherboards, as well as associated components and architectures used in systems.
- Identify the purposes of complementary metal-oxide semiconductors (CMOS) and how and how they affect systems parameters and operations.

Content Area 5: Printers

You are expected to have a basic understanding of printers and printing devices. You must demonstrate your knowledge of how they work, how to maintain them, and how to repair common problems.

This section of the exam tests you on the following tasks:

- Understand basic printer operation and identify field replaceable units on primary printer types.
- Provide diagnosis and solutions for common printer problems.
- Identify the common printer connections and configurations.

Content Area 6: Portable Systems

Here you must demonstrate your knowledge of portable computer systems and how they differ from desktop and other systems.

This section of the exam tests you on the following tasks:

- Identify the components of a portable system.
- Understand the unique problems of portable systems.

Content Area 7: Basic Networking

Networking is an important aspect of the technician's job; therefore, you need to know about basic networking components. You are expected to determine if and how a computer is connected to a network. Your knowledge of network components is tested, and you must know how to configure and install network cards.

This section of the exam tests you on the following tasks:

- Explain basic networking concepts and how networks work.
- Identify the procedures for replacing and configuring NICs (network interface cards).
- Explain possible ramifications involved with network repair.

Content Area 8: Customer Satisfaction

As a successful technician you need more than technical knowledge — you need to work well with people. This section measures your ability to interact with customers. You are expected to know how to question customers to gain information in a sensitive manner. You must know how to build rapport with customers and conduct yourself professionally in dealing with them.

This section of the exam focuses on a single task:

- Identifying and differentiating between effective and ineffective behaviors towards customers to maximize productivity and achieve customer satisfaction.

DOS/WINDOWS EXAM

The DOS/Windows exam is required along with the A+ core hardware exam to become an A+ certified technician. Here, you are expected to install, configure, and troubleshoot Windows and DOS-related problems. This exam covers both Windows 95 and Windows 3.x (which refers to Windows 3.1, Windows 3.11, and Windows for Workgroups 3.11). You need to understand the concepts behind DOS and Windows systems, as well as how to support them in the real world. You must also be able to explain the options available to configure and manage peripherals, such as disk drives.

Many situations in the real world will require you to repair both hardware and software problems. This might include replacing drivers, installing software patches, and performing maintenance upgrades to operating systems. This section evaluates your ability to perform these tasks. The DOS/Windows exam covers five content areas.

Content Area 1: Operating System's Functions, Structure, and File Management

The exam evaluates your knowledge of DOS, Windows 3.x, and Windows 95 systems. You need to know the structure, functions, and capabilities of these systems, as well as how to manage files and directories. You need to know how to run both DOS- and Windows-based programs.

This section of the exam tests you on the following tasks:

o Identify operating system functions, structure, and file systems.

o Identify ways to navigate the operating system and acquire technical information on the system.

o Identify the basic concepts and procedures for file and directory creation and management in DOS and Windows.

o Identify the methods for viewing and changing file attributes; understand the security issues associated with file attributes.

o Identify basic disk management procedures.

o Identify operating system storage and file allocation methods.

Content Area 2: Memory Management

You must be able to differentiate between the types of memory technologies used by DOS and Windows and how to rectify memory address conflicts, should they occur.

This section of the exam tests you on the following tasks:

o Differentiate between the types of memory used by DOS and Windows.

o Correct memory conflicts and optimize memory usage.

Content Area 3: Installation, Configuration and Upgrading

The exam also tests your ability to upgrade and configure DOS, Windows 3.x and Windows 95 systems.

This section of the exam tests you on the following tasks:

o Identify the procedures to install DOS, Windows 3.x, and Windows 95 operating systems. This includes disk and driver management.

- Identify needed steps to upgrade operating systems.
- Explain the boot sequences for DOS, Windows 3.*x* and Windows 95 systems.
- Know how to use alternative boot methods.
- Identify and explain Plug and Play.
- Use and follow instructions to load/add devices and update systems software.
- Change configuration options using Windows printing subsystem.
- Launch Windows and non-Windows applications.
- Identify and edit AUTOEXEC.BAT and CONFIG.SYS files and options.

Content Area 4: Diagnosing and Troubleshooting

You must be able to troubleshoot and repair common problems in the operating systems. You are expected to understand normal operations and to identify symptoms of common problems.

This section of the exam tests you on the following tasks:

- Recognize and interpret common error codes, startup messages, and icons from boot sequences.
- Correct startup or boot problems.
- Create and maintain an emergency boot disk using systems utilities.
- Recognize, troubleshoot, and repair printer problems.
- Recognize and categorize common systems problems and identify possible causes.
- Use various DOS- and Windows-based utilities to troubleshoot and repair problems.
- Install, configure, and troubleshoot DOS applications in Windows 95.
- Identify and remove viruses from a computer system.

Content Area 5: Networks

In this section you are tested on your basic knowledge of networking capabilities in DOS and Windows. You need to know how to connect to networks, including the Internet.

This section of the exam tests you on the following tasks:

o Identify the networking capabilities of DOS and Windows systems.

o Identify the concepts and capabilities of Internet access using Windows.

WHAT YOU NEED TO KNOW TO TAKE THE EXAM

As you can see, the A+ Certification exam is very comprehensive. It covers most of the material that an experienced computer repairperson needs to know. Before you throw up your hands in desperation, the core exam consists of 57 questions and the DOS/Windows module contains 45 questions. You are allotted a total of two hours and fifteen minutes for both sections, which is ample time if you are fully prepared.

 If you complete the chapter readings, Instant Assessment Questions, and lab exercises in this book, you should not have any difficulty passing this exam on the first attempt.

Passing scores for the exam are as follows:

o 72% for the Core exam

o 69% for the DOS/Windows exam

The cost for these exams is broken down into two categories: one for members and one for nonmembers. If your organization is a CompTIA member, you receive other membership benefits. Currently, the pricing is as shown in Table 1-1.

TABLE 1-1 A+ CERTIFICATION EXAM PRICING		
TEST(S)	COMPTIA MEMBERS	NONMEMBERS
Any Module	$85	$120
Core + 1 Module	$140	$215

 Be sure to check with CompTIA for the most current pricing of A+ Certification exams.

To register for a test, call Sylvan Prometric at 1-800-776-4276. They will help you find the closest test center and arrange a time to take the test. You are encouraged to arrive at the testing center 15 minutes early. You will need two pieces of identification: one with a photo and one other major piece of identification. You will be signed in and, when it is time, taken to your workstation.

The only materials you can take into the test room are those given to you by the test proctor. You will be under video camera surveillance during the test.

After you have completed the test, you are permitted to leave the test room. Make sure to get a printout with your test results from the proctor. If you pass the exam at that point — congratulations. If not, you can try again after reviewing the areas with which you had difficulty.

The next two sections fill you in on the growing importance of certification, and its benefits.

TRENDS IN CERTIFICATION

Without question, the industry is moving towards certification as a way to measure competence. The computer field has had certification and training programs for many years, and the trend toward certification is even stronger today. Many manufacturers of computer equipment have certified service technicians ready to repair customer-owned equipment. Companies such as IBM, DEC, and HP have extensive certification programs that require months of study to pass. These certified technicians are capable of repairing and maintaining these companies' highly proprietary systems. To become a certified service technician for one of these companies is no small accomplishment, especially today. Some of the certification programs for minicomputer and mainframe technicians are done at company-owned training centers. As few as ten years ago, it would not be unusual for a service technician to spend one to two months learning how to repair a new computer system. The larger scale systems sold by mainframe manufacturers still rely on this type of technical training for service technicians today.

As computer technology matured, companies moved away from the expensive dinosaurs of the past. Instead, they have come to rely on desktop computer systems that cost between one and three thousand dollars. Usually when a desktop PC has a hardware-related problem, the component can be repaired quickly and easily. While years ago a computer technician might only be able to service and support a handful of systems, today that same technician can support thousands of computer systems.

Newer technologies have integrated a larger number of components into smaller packaging. This makes the hardware in most situations less complicated and more reliable. At the same time, most of the newer computer systems allow for the addition of custom video boards and other devices. This can make configuration and software installation software more complicated; thus, qualified technicians are needed more than ever.

In order to minimize travel time and other expenses, most computer manufacturers use telephone support professionals to provide support and diagnose problems. As you can imagine, the person providing this technical support must be both a competent technician and an effective communicator.

The A+ certification provides a way to show your prospective employers that you have made the grade. It may not make you a seasoned professional in the field, but it will certainly show that you know the basics and have made a commitment to the computer profession.

After you have completed the A+ certification, many other professional development options await you. Many of the major hardware and software manufacturers provide certification programs that measure specific knowledge about their products. These certifications are much more advanced and challenging.

Microsoft, for example, has a certification program leading to the Microsoft Certified Systems Engineer (MCSE) designation, while Novell has the Certified Network Engineer (CNE). Other companies, such as Oracle and Adobe, provide certification programs specific to programming, and development or administration of their systems.

The entire computer industry seems to have jumped on the certification bandwagon. Obtaining the A+ certification will bring you a great deal of credibility and employability. You also have a great opportunity to broaden your knowledge, and to experience a different aspect of the computer business.

My advice is simple: GO FOR IT!

A+ CERTIFICATION BENEFITS

A+ certification benefits the employee, the employer, and the end user in several ways. This section briefly discusses these benefits.

Benefits to the Employee

The employee gains several things from A+ certification. First, the employee receives recognition from a nationally recognized certification program. This certification, while not as rigorous as a CPA or bar exam, provides positive recognition and professional credentials.

The A+ certification is a great way to build self-confidence in demonstrating your level of technical knowledge. For a person entering the field, A+ certification provides a stepping stone to higher-paying computer positions.

Most computer professionals are well compensated and work in relatively comfortable environments. The initial positions that A+ helps qualify you for open a world of opportunity in network engineering, administration, service, and support positions.

Benefits to the Employer

Many organizations embrace the certification process because it can greatly affect the bottom line. When a workstation or server goes down, it can cost a company hundreds or even thousands of dollars per hour in lost productivity. Having a highly trained technician on the scene with the right tools and knowledge outweighs the costs associated with the certification.

In many companies, senior computer professionals, such as IS managers, computer programmers, and software developers are doing work that can be accomplished by less-experienced individuals. In many organizations, a large percentage of the employees own computers and putter around with them at home. Giving these people the opportunity to train and become certified computer technicians offers them new skills, reinforces existing skills, and increases the overall technological competency of the workforce. This equates to serious cost advantages.

Another way to look at this is how much it costs when you permit untrained people to repair a computer. PCs are a significant cost to most employers, email and online downtime can wreak havoc, and it goes without saying that data stored on networks and hard drives is priceless. A certified professional is a valuable insurance policy.

Benefits to the End-User

Ultimately, A+ certification is about serving the end user. When your computer goes down you can't access important data, do your work, or meet deadlines. You need a qualified technician who knows how to get the job done and treats you with respect. A+ certification training provides technicians with both the technical knowledge and the customer relations skills to make the end user's life easier.

Many people pawn themselves off as computer experts and build systems for friends and neighbors. This is a great way to build experience, but it leaves enormous gaps in that individual's knowledge. Frequently these untrained enthusiasts are hired as computer technicians for small- and medium-sized companies. A computer technician with inadequate training on installation techniques, static electricity, and other computer-related areas could wreak havoc on standard computer systems. The end user pays for that in the form of higher maintenance costs and lower reliability. A+ certification ensures that the people you are working with are competent.

The net result of A+ certification is improved quality of service for everyone concerned. Vendors, resellers, end users, and corporate users can be more productive knowing that the person about to dive into that $5,000 computer system has the knowledge to repair it. You wouldn't let just anybody work on your car — why would you let just anyone repair or install your computer system?

KEY POINT SUMMARY

The computer industry is growing at an incredible rate and creating a need for people who can troubleshoot, repair, and install computer systems. This is why the A+ certification is the perfect place to enter the market.

- Employers and customers want to be sure that the people they are working with are capable and competent. Certification programs provide proof of your competence and expertise.

- Computer technicians should be able to work with the computer technology, and also to work effectively with customers. In this book we look at both the technical knowledge and the customer relations skills needed to be an effective A+ certified technician.

Self Motivation and Study Skills

About Chapter 2

The decision to become certified is a major one. One of the biggest difficulties you will face is sticking with the training program day after day. Having worked for almost 15 years with adult learners who are using independent study to advance their careers, we'd like to share some pointers on how to achieve this certification.

This chapter gives you the tools to help you stay on target. To begin with, you made a strong statement of your intent by starting to read this book. Don't be afraid to set high goals for yourself. Start here. Start today. Start now!

If you are like most people, you have a full life with very busy days. If you haven't started a professional development program for a while, this is a great way to begin. Throughout this chapter, you have the opportunity to answer some questions. This exercise is important and we encourage you to spend a few minutes on it. These questions help you stay focused and will set you on a path that leads to great rewards.

In the process of becoming A+ certified you have to make changes in your use of time. Time is your best friend and your worst enemy. One of the most common excuses is a shortage of time. Let us set the record straight: nobody is more capable than you are.

GOALS

All great things start with rather humble beginnings. When considering your goals for becoming A+ certified, we want you to take a few minutes to answer some simple questions. Answering these questions will help you express your motivations and desires for achieving A+ certification. (Don't be afraid to mention more money, a better house, and so on.)

1. Why do you want to be certified as an A+ technician?

2. What will you do differently once you are A+ certified?

3. What support and assistance will you need to become an A+ technician?

4. How will you adjust your schedule to fit study time into your day?

5. What will you do after you have accomplished the A+ certification?

All of your motivations are real and you must acknowledge them. If your goal is to become a more professional you — go for it. It is not for us, or anyone else, to determine your goals. They are *your* goals.

 note **Most people get in trouble with this type of exercise because they answer the questions with answers they don't believe. So, be honest.**

TIME MANAGEMENT

It is important to learn how to manage your time efficiently. Human beings by nature are creatures of habit, and habits can be both good and bad. If you have the habit of exercising, you know that you won't feel good about yourself if you let a few days go by without a workout. As with daily physical exercise, you need to get in the habit of giving your brain a regular workout by studying and preparing for the A+ Certification exam.

We encourage you to use a calendar and a time planner to schedule your study time. Set aside at least 30 minutes to study every day. Make no exceptions.

If you set aside a regular time to study, every day, you will proceed through this material much faster than you might expect. Plan for this to take a few months. Think about this as an investment, one that you need to make on a regular basis, with a commitment to achieving the final goal: your certification.

Remember that by making a commitment to study for and pass the A+ Certification exam, you are making the best investment you can make. You are investing in yourself.

Try to keep this process fun! Enjoy learning. If you go beyond the boundaries of this book, you will learn a great deal about this industry. Become involved in professional organizations, such as the Association of Information Technology Professionals (AITP) (www.aitp.org) and Computing Technology Industry Association (CompTIA) (www.comptia.org). Read industry publications such as *Datamation, Windows NT Magazine,* and *Microsoft Certified Professional Magazine.* Network with your peers in technical associations and local users groups. A great group to become involved in is the Help Desk Institute (www.helpdeskinst.com).

You can accomplish these things with a minimum investment in time and provide yourself with the most up-to-date education possible. If you live in an area that does not have many groups such as these, start one. You can visit some of the computer stores in your area and invite one of the technicians out for coffee. Spend a few minutes discussing what your career goals are and ask if they have any suggestions on how to accomplish them. Many more experienced professionals in the field will be happy to offer you suggestions and advice that could save you a great deal of time and energy on your journey into the computer field. After all, they all had to start somewhere.

Most major metropolitan areas have one or more computer users groups that address any number of issues. A good place to start your search is on the Yahoo! Web site at www.yahoo.com/Computers_and_Internet/Organizations/

How to Use This Book

Your attempt to achieve certification requires both practical experience and book learning. To get a well-rounded education, we suggest you use this book as the basis for your study and follow up with hands-on practice.

To get the most from this book, follow these steps:

1. Skim the book from cover to cover. The beginning of each chapter includes an overview of the information contained in the chapter. Become familiar with the chapter contents. This helps you organize your thoughts on how to tackle this book.

2. Read the review section of each chapter. The end of each chapter contains a review section that outlines the important components of every chapter. Take a quick look at these to learn the highlights of each chapter. This helps you find the key points of the material in the book.

3. Take a quick look at the lab exercises at the end of each chapter. This shows you some practical applications of the material covered in the book.

4. Now read the chapters. Start at Chapter 1 and work your way through the book. Each chapter is designed to build on the previous chapter.

5. Create flash cards or memory aids based on the important information in each chapter. These cards are useful in preparing for the test. Keep the cards with you and review them when you have a few minutes.

6. Answer the review questions. Review each of the areas associated with those questions. Don't worry about memorizing these questions, but learn the concepts. Don't just know the right answer — be able to explain *why* an answer is correct.

7. Mark the book with a highlighter or pencil. When you finish, you can quickly scan the important comments you made. You paid good money for this book — don't be afraid to wear it out!

8. Do the laboratory exercises in each chapter. Get a small spiral notebook and make notes to yourself about what you've learned. Review these periodically to see how you are progressing.

This may sound like a lot to do but, in reality, it adds only a few minutes to each lesson. By doing this, your retention of the material is much greater than if you just read straight through the book.

Hands-on Exercises

Each hands-on exercise in this book is designed to help you grasp an important concept or principle. Don't be afraid to do the exercises. In addition, don't be afraid to talk to your friends, coworkers, or others who might be expert in this field. Most people, especially computer people, are flattered when you ask them technical questions. Remember that you are learning, and it is okay to ask a question that you might think is dumb. Many computer technicians may chuckle and remember when they asked that same dumb question.

If you are having a problem getting something to work, don't be afraid to take your computer to a service center and have them explain what's wrong. If you tell them you are working on a certification course, they may be willing to answer your questions.

As you move toward becoming a qualified professional, be prepared to build a set of experiences. Every experienced computer technician has been where you are. When you make a mistake, take your lumps and learn from it. Don't be afraid to fail.

If you're reluctant to take the family or office PC apart to perform the labs, go to a local computer store and buy the components to build a system. You can buy almost all of the system components we present in this book for less than $1,000. Find out whether any of your friends, neighbors, or coworkers are in the market for a computer. Offer to build one for them — they'll save some money, and you'll get valuable experience.

Preparing for the Test

By creating the study aids suggested earlier in this chapter, you have a very short preparation time. Take your notes, flash cards, and other comments and review them once a day during the week before you take the exam. Make a point to review your notes completely at least three times in each review session. Reread each of the chapter review sections and all of the questions.

The day before the exam, take one last look at your notes and put them away. Spend no more than a half-hour doing your review. Relax, take it easy, and don't get stressed out. Many people (including us) tend to get excited the night before an exam. We don't recommend that you cram the night before — it's a better idea to get a good night's sleep. You'll want to be energized when you take the exam.

We suggest that you take your test early in the day. Most people are more alert in the morning, and you won't have all day to worry about it. Have a nice breakfast, spend just 10 or 15 minutes reviewing for the exam, and then go for it. Plan to arrive at the testing center 15 minutes early.

You will know within minutes after you complete the exam whether you passed or not. If you passed — congratulations! You are now an A+ technician. If you didn't pass, don't be discouraged. Take the feedback sheet and hit the books again. You'll get it next time.

Good luck!

KEY POINT SUMMARY

Chapter 2 introduced the concepts of self motivation and creating a professional development program so as you study for A+ certification you can set realistic goals, manage your time wisely, and use various means of support and assistance.

- When you explore the reasons why you want to be an A+ certified technician, and evaluate career opportunities, you'll discover hidden motivations that will vitalize your learning process.

- With a calendar and a time planner, you can schedule study time that suits your lifestyle and learning pace. By planning objectives, and making a commitment to achieving certification, you are able to accomplish your goals with a minimum investment of time.

- Review the study skills outlined in this chapter to get the most from this book. This book, with its straightforward layout and presentation, is designed to help you easily retain the material.

Core Components

System Components

About Chapter 3

This chapter explores the components of a modern computer system. We'll discuss the motherboard—the area of the computer where the main components can be found—and look at important components such as the central processing unit (CPU), memory, ports, and disk controllers. We'll look at stored programs and computer performance, two important concepts that will help you understand how computer systems work. Then we'll look more closely at various types of CPUs and memory. Finally, the lab section at the end of the chapter will guide you through the process of building your own computer system.

INTRODUCTION TO COMPUTER SYSTEMS

Modern computer systems are made up of a large number of components that must all work together. In this chapter, you'll learn the basic relationships between those components.

The chapter will focus primarily on the motherboard and the main system components. The chapters that follow, which cover communications, storage, and input/output devices, will build upon the information you'll learn here. Figure 3-1 shows several types of system units. These system units contain the motherboard and other components.

FIGURE 3-1 Notebook and mid-tower systems

THE MOTHERBOARD

A computer's *motherboard* contains the *central processing unit* (CPU), memory, and most of the computer's control and expansion slots. It is called the motherboard because the expansion boards are typically plugged into these slots. The motherboard is also sometimes called the *systems board* or *planar board*. Figure 3-2 depicts a typical motherboard with expansion slots, memory slots, and disk controllers built onto it. Depending on the case configuration, some motherboards have riser cards plugged into them, and expansion boards are then plugged into this riser card (see Figure 3-3).

 note **The motherboard is also known as the systems board or planar board.**

FIGURE 3-2 A typical motherboard for a Pentium II PC system

The next several sections will examine the major components of the motherboard and how each component interacts with the others. We'll discuss the CPU, memory, ports, and disk controllers. We'll also look at number systems, stored programs, and other concepts that will help you to understand the components found on the motherboard.

FIGURE 3-3 A motherboard with riser card configuration (photo courtesy of Intel Corporation)

The CPU

Every organization needs a leader — someone who directs the principal activities. The *central processing unit* (CPU) serves that function for the computer system. The CPU is generally mounted on the motherboard on most systems. Most modern personal computer systems utilize a single integrated circuit as the CPU. This *integrated circuit* (IC) is called a *microprocessor*.

The CPU must work with both programs and data. To accomplish this, the CPU has a *Control Unit* (CU), registers, and the *Arithmetic Logic Unit* (ALU). *Data* is the information that is processed by the computer program. Examples of data include financial information that is needed for the accounting department, or perhaps the commands to destroy the enemy's starbase in a computer game. *Programs,* on the other hand, are the instructions that the computer follows to manipulate data.

The parts of the CPU accomplish the following functions:

- The Control Unit is responsible for receiving instructions from the program and seeing that they are carried out. This process of receiving and carrying out instructions is carried out millions of times per second. The program may instruct the CPU to get data from a disk location and store it in memory, or it may direct output to a printer or other device.

- The Arithmetic Logic Unit is concerned with arithmetic and logical operations. The ALU performs mathematical operations such as addition and subtraction, as well as logical operations such as "greater than," "less than," or "equal to."

- Registers are storage places in the CPU that can be manipulated by the CU and the ALU.

 **The CPU is the nucleus of the PC. All devices are connected to the CPU through controllers and ports.**

Let's look more closely at the parts of the CPU. One of the key components in the process of understanding how computer programs work is a location in the CPU called a register. A register is a storage location that enables data to be manipulated. This enables computer programs to manipulate and change data values; for instance, changing the number 4 to the number 5. Registers differ from memory because data in memory cannot be manipulated, whereas data in a register can be.

Most CPUs have a small amount of internal memory for caching, temporary storage, and other purposes. *Caching* is a memory process that stores the most frequently used instructions and data into a limited amount of extremely high-speed memory designed for quick access by the CPU. Caching is explained in more detail later in this chapter. However, the bulk of memory locations are outside the CPU, on the motherboard. Registers receive the instructions to be performed from the computer program. These instructions are transferred into the registers from the CU, which then decodes and executes them. Figure 3-4 illustrates a typical computer organization showing the CU, registers, and ALU. The register can contain instructions from the computer program such as describing where to retrieve the next instruction, or to add a number to a register. If the number is retrieved from cache instead of from memory, it is available more quickly to the CPU.

Registers are almost always internal to the microprocessor chip. They are generally accessible only by the Control Unit and Arithmetic Logic Unit. The register is also the only area of memory where values can be manipulated arithmetically. This is covered in more detail in the "Stored Programs" section later in this chapter.

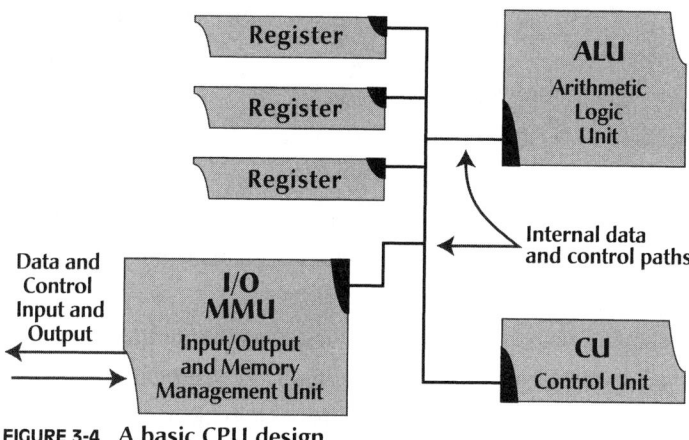

FIGURE 3-4 A basic CPU design

The control unit receives instructions from the program, decodes it, and then instructs each appropriate resource to accomplish the task. Most tasks, at their most basic level, involve an arithmetic or logical operation such as Add or Subtract, and logical operations such as "And," "Or," and "Not."

These three basic logical operators can be used to make extremely complex decisions. For example, the And operator says that in order for the output to be true, all of the inputs must be true. Assume we have two inputs, A and B. So if the input is A and B, then both A and B must be true for the output to be true. The Or operator requires that for the output to be true, one or more inputs must be true. So if the inputs are A Or B, then either A, B, or both A and B must be true for the output to be true. The Not operator is merely the inverse of the input, so if A is true then the output is false, and vice versa.

The CU directs the ALU to accomplish or execute the instruction. The ALU then performs the operation and deposits the results into a register that is accessible to the CU to process. The *Input/Output* (I/O) unit shown in Figure 3-4 manages and moves data between other areas of the computer unit and the CU. The CU controls both the ALU and the I/O unit.

note **The motherboard—also known as the system board or planar board—houses the central processing unit (CPU), read-only memory (ROM), and random-access memory (RAM).**

Microprocessor-based systems utilize a manufacturing process called *Very Large Scale Integration* (VLSI) or *Ultra Large Scale Integration* (ULSI). VLSI and

ULSI manufacturing enables the high-density packaging of computer circuitry. This packaging enables the CPU and corresponding support chips to reside in one big package or chip. This package contains most of the circuitry for the computer to function. This chip is in turn connected through a series of wires or embedded circuitry to the rest of the computer components.

A motherboard is typically organized into areas that perform certain functions, such as power management, memory management, CPU and support chips, and expansion slots.

Figure 3-5 shows the expansion slots on the motherboard. The long slots in the lower right corner are called *Industry Standard Architecture* (ISA) or *Advanced Technology* (AT) bus expansion slots. ISA slots are 16 bit and in widespread use today. ISA slots are typically used to hold modem cards, sound cards, or other similar devices. Older computer systems could manipulate and work with 16 bits of data at a time; newer systems such as 80486 and Pentium processors are able to work with 32 or even 64 bits of data at a time.

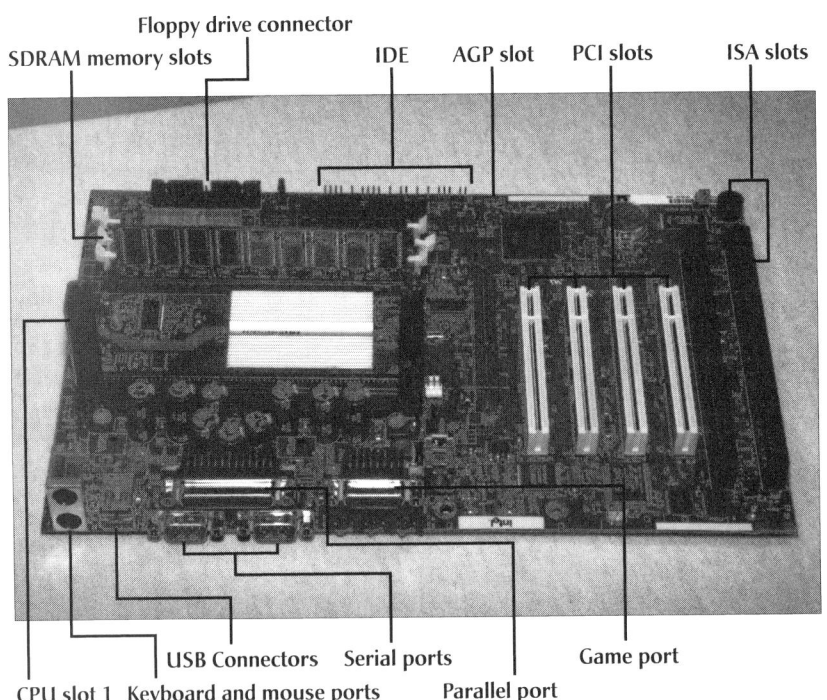

FIGURE 3-5 Expansion slots on a motherboard

The smaller expansion slots to the left of the ISA slots are called *Peripheral Component Interconnect* (PCI) expansion slots. The PCI bus is a 64-bit bus that supports 32-bit data for processors such as the 80486. PCI devices are very fast and typically more expensive than the ISA bus devices. PCI slots are typically used for video cards, some newer network cards, and other higher-performance devices.

The single slot to the left of the PCI slots is an *Accelerated Graphics Port* (AGP) expansion slot. AGP is supported on Pentium II systems, and offers significantly enhanced transfer speed. PCI bus slots can provide up to 133Mbps bandwidth, whereas AGP can provide bandwidth of over 500Mbps, which is required by the latest generation of video accelerator cards.

A Pentium II chip appears in Figure 3-6. The socket 3 holds a 486 CPU. Some versions of the Intel i386 and i486 families also have a separate math coprocessor. The math coprocessor provides higher-performance hardware-based math operations instead of software-based operations provided by the CPU.

FIGURE 3-6 **Pentium II going into a Slot 1 (photo courtesy of Intel Corporation)**

Early microprocessor systems included a separate math coprocessor that greatly sped up the execution of some mathematical operations. The Intel 8088, 80286, 80386, and some 80486 systems needed separate math coprocessors to perform certain mathematical operations efficiently.

When Intel introduced the 80386 to the market, the response was incredible. Almost overnight, all new systems were being built with this new, more powerful chip. This chip was later renamed the 80386DX when Intel introduced the 80386SX. The 80386SX chip, though faster than the 80286 chip, was somewhat slower than the 80386DX. The main advantage of the 80386SX chip was its ability to work in 16-bit hardware environments, whereas the 80386DX worked in 32-bit hardware environments. These coprocessors are designated as i80387, i80387SX, and i486SX, respectively.

The Pentium family integrated the math coprocessor into the CPU chip itself, as have most other CPU chips now in production.

As the capability of microprocessors increased, the number of pins necessary to connect the microprocessor to the systems board increased. A number of packaging schemes were introduced to enable higher-density, or more tightly packaged, chips to be installed. The major mechanism to connect microprocessors and other similar chips to the systems unit used either the *Pin Gate Array* (PGA), *Staggered Pin Gate Array* (SPGA), or the *Plastic Quad Flat Package* (PQFP). The newer Pentium II chip from Intel uses a new packaging scheme called Socket 1, which is a radical departure from the flat chip installation methods previously mentioned. Some of the more common pin configurations are illustrated in Figure 3-6. Each successive generation of CPU chip seems to create another socket or pin configuration. In some cases, standard Pentium chips are interchangeable. Usually, the CPU chips of more modern computer systems use a larger number of pins.

Many of the modern CPU chips are installed using a Zero Insertion Force, or ZIF, socket. It's called a ZIF socket because the chip can be inserted into the socket using very little force, if any. The chip is secured in the socket by a locking mechanism. The locking mechanism enables the chip to be easily inserted and mechanically fastened to the motherboard.

Socketed chips are relatively easy to replace in the field, whereas soldered chips can't be replaced without special tools and training. Most PC systems, with the exception of portables, use ZIF or other socket systems for easy replacement on the motherboard. Soldered chips, with rare exception, for all practical purposes, are not field replaceable.

Many of the newer chips generate a great amount of heat. To keep your CPU warranty in force, a mini-fan attached to the CPU chip is required. Mini-fans cost only a few dollars and provide much-needed airflow to the CPU chip. With higher clock speeds, a fan can greatly improve the lifespan and stable operation of the chip.

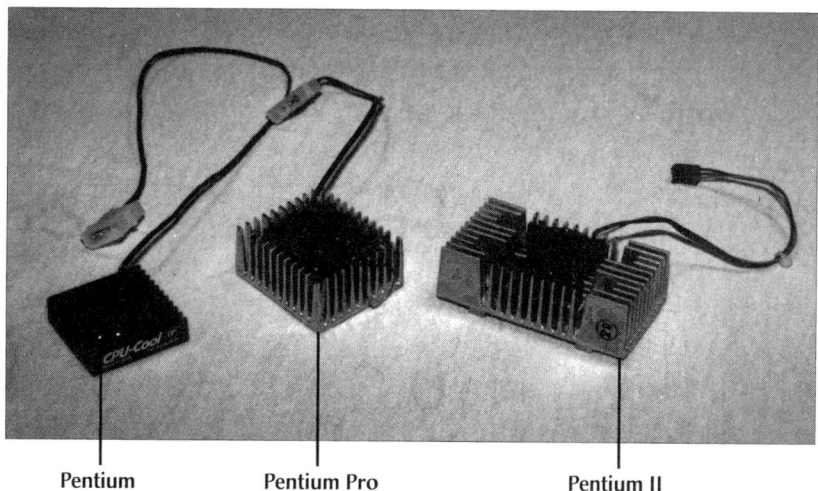

Pentium   Pentium Pro   Pentium II

FIGURE 3-7 CPU cooling fans for the Pentium, Pentium Pro, and Pentium II (photo courtesy of PC Power and Cooling)

Memory

The CPU chip typically includes the internal support circuitry needed to access and manage memory. This circuitry is called a *memory management unit* (MMU). External memory is usually installed in an area similar to the labeled slots in Figure 3-5. The motherboard shown in the illustration uses a type of memory chip known as *Synchronous Dynamic Random Access Memory* (SDRAM). The SDRAM module is a very compact high-density storage module used on newer Pentium II-based motherboards. We'll discuss SDRAM and other types of memory later in this chapter in the "Computer Memory" section.

Early motherboards required the installation of individual groups of memory chips either directly on the motherboard or on an expansion board that filled one of the ISA expansion slots. Modern memory expansion modules, however, plug directly into the motherboard.

Ports

For a computer to be useful, it must have the ability to communicate with the outside world. This is accomplished with *ports*. In this section, "ports" refers to these external connections made between the motherboard and the outside world. When we discuss computer programs later in this book, you will see that "ports" will take on a slightly different meaning — that of physical addresses used by the CPU.

Simply put, a port is a type of connection, either internal or external, that enables a device or systems component to be connected to the CPU for communications and control purposes. These ports can include a *serial* port, which can be used for computer-to-computer communications. A printer or higher speed *Input/Output* (I/O) device can also use *parallel* ports. Serial ports process one character at a time. Parallel ports, on the other hand, break data into multiple streams that are processed simultaneously. Typically, a connection is provided for the keyboard, mouse, and in many newer computer motherboards, integrated ports for disk drives, network connections, and modems. Examples of these ports are illustrated in Figure 3-5. This motherboard is built in the ATX form factor, and connectors for the different ports are connected directly to the motherboard. Other motherboards use a series of wires and ribbon connectors to attach the ports to the illustrated connectors. The ports are then installed on the back panel of the system unit. This enables the end user to access these connections easily. Most computers provide one or more serial and parallel ports on the back of the system unit.

Disk Controllers

Disks provide the computer with the ability to store information, and several standards exist for this storage. Many motherboards provide support for the direct attachment of floppy drives, hard drives, and CD-ROM drives directly to the motherboard through a controller. Hard drives and CD-ROM drives are usually attached using a standard design called *Integrated Device Electronics* (IDE). The IDE bus was first made available for the IBM PC/AT bus. This has become a carry-over from the IBM PC/AT bus. The IDE standard is also called the ATA interface. The ATA designation was created to indicate that this was an IBM PC/AT, or Advanced Technology Attachment. Examples of these controllers and connectors are in Figure 3-5.

Computer systems manufactured before the 1990s were plagued with incompatibilities. Two manufacturers might both make 20MB or 40MB hard drives that were not interchangeable. This may have seemed like a good marketing ploy, but in reality it created a nightmare for manufacturers and service personnel alike. Seagate Technologies, a large disk manufacturer, created and offered a standard called the ST506 interface. This interface provided a common connection for disk drives and helped create an entire movement within the industry toward standardized interfaces. The ATA and IDE are two of the more prevalent interfaces in the market today.

STORED PROGRAMS

A *program* gives a computer the ability to execute instructions to accomplish work. A program is simply a set of recorded or stored steps that tell the computer how to accomplish a task. Programs are generally defined as either systems level or applications level. Systems-level programs include such things as the operating system of the computer. Applications-level programs include program compilers, word processors, and other similar applications that enable end users to manipulate data and create output.

Programs at the end user level are written in languages such as BASIC, FORTRAN, COBOL, and C. These programs get translated by software — again stored programs — into a language that the CPU can understand. Programs that are written in computer languages such as BASIC are processed through another program called a *compiler*. A compiler takes the English-like instructions that the programmer typed into the computer and translates or compiles them into machine language, or binary language. The final result of this process is a program that the computer can load and understand. Unfortunately, as smart as modern computer systems appear to be, a computer can only perform instructions that have been programmed into it, in an understandable fashion, using a programming language and compiler.

Computer-level instructions are stored and executed in a number system called *binary*. Binary is the base 2 number system. You can get more experience with binary mathematics from electronics math books or by taking a course in digital electronics from a local community college or trade school. Table 3-1 shows the binary number system and the equivalent base 10 number. The binary number columns represent, from right to left, 1, 2, 4, 8, and so on. Each subsequent column is simply the one that precedes it, doubled. The binary system works like a simple light switch. The basic concept is fairly easy: If the switch is closed, the light goes on. If the switch is open, the light is off. Any light that is on is a 1 and any light that is off is a 0. The actual implementations of binary can become quite complex, but for this book and exam, this explanation should be adequate for you to understand the concepts involved in binary.

TABLE 3-1 BINARY REPRESENTATION

BASE 10	BASE 2
DECIMAL	BINARY
0	0000
1	0001
2	0010
3	0011
4	0100
5	0101
6	0110
7	0111
8	1000
9	1001
10	1010
11	1011
12	1100
13	1101
14	1110
15	1111

Digital computers work only in binary. Think of it this way: binary represents one of two possible values — 0 or 1. From these humble beginnings, a complete number system can be created. Binary digits (0 or 1) are also called bits (BInary digiTS). With decimal, or base 10, when a number reaches the largest in a given place — for example 9 — the next number is a 10, which is in reality a 0, carrying the 1 into the next position. With binary, the largest number in a place is one, so in the case of a counting situation, the next largest number is a 0, carry the one. In the case of a base 10 number, the positions or places are 1, 10, 100, 1000, 10000, and so on. A number like 954 really means 9 x100 + 5x10 + 4x1, for a total of 954. In binary, a number such as 10110 really means 1x16+0x8+1x4+1x2+0x1, or 10110, which is represented as 22 in base 10. If these examples seem confusing, remember that familiarity with binary math just takes practice. Believe it or not, this is how computer systems work with numbers. While this may seem like an enormously painful way for us to think, computers, which are digital, can process millions of these types of additions per second.

The binary digits are usually organized into units of 8. This smallest storage unit is called a byte, for By Itself. This grouping of 8 bits, or a byte, provides an easy way for standard notations and computer architecture to be used. The largest number that a computer can store in one byte is 255 (base 10). Addition and subtraction is simpler for a computer using byte representation than in base 10, as is typically used by humans. As the size of processors increased, first two and then four bytes became a word. A word is simply two or more bytes that form a single number or instruction. In the case of a 16-bit computer, two bytes would form a word, whereas in the case of a 32-bit computer, four bytes would constitute a word.

As you can see, binary numbers can be hard to remember and keep straight. Computer scientists agreed to organize this data into groups of three. Initially, this system used one number to represent three binary digits. This number system was called *octal*, or base 8. In octal, the largest number is 7. When an octal number exceeds 7, a carry occurs like the one between 9 and 10 in base 10.

The next logical grouping of bits was to that of four. This system is called hexadecimal, hex, or base 16. The hexadecimal equivalent of the value 10 is now represented as the letter A, B is 11, and so on until the letter F. The letter F represents a single location that can store a value of up to 15, which is the largest number that can be stored in 8 bits. Table 3-2 illustrates how these numbers are represented. In debugging computer problems, it is not uncommon for a technician to be asked to work with hexadecimal. Don't panic — it just takes a little practice. Modern diagnostic and troubleshooting equipment often provides status codes or results in hexadecimal. These codes provide information about the status of a problem or program. When Windows systems malfunction, they often print out or display the registers in hexadecimal format. A software technician at the manufacturer can use this information to identify the true nature of the problem, and how to resolve it.

TABLE 3-2 NUMBER SYSTEM COMPARISON

DECIMAL	OCTAL	HEX
0	0	0
1	1	1
2	2	2
3	3	3
4	4	4
5	5	5
6	6	6
7	7	7
8	10	8
9	11	9
10	12	A
11	13	B
12	14	C
13	15	D
14	16	E
15	17	F
16	20	10
17	21	11
18	22	12
19	23	13
20	24	14
21	25	15
22	26	16
23	27	17
24	30	18
25	31	19
26	32	1A
27	33	1B
28	34	1C
29	35	1D

DECIMAL	OCTAL	HEX
30	36	1E
31	37	1F
32	40	20

When we were children, we were told that we used the base 10 number system because that's how many fingers we have. The base 10 number system really has a range of 10 numbers from 0 to 9. We tend to forget about the 0, which is a very critical number. When you're working with number systems, it's critical to remember that the reference to a base is always one larger than the largest number you can use. For example, base 8 uses 0 through 7, base 10 uses 0 through 9, and base 16 uses 0 through F.

Regardless of the particular number system used, these bits are read or transferred from memory into the CU and decoded. The reading process brings the data stored at a certain memory address into a register. The decoding process performed by the CU on the data stored in the register determines what will happen with that data. The CU then either executes the instruction or directs the appropriate resources to deal with it. A typical program may contain several thousand instructions.

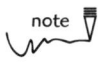 note

When bytes are formed together and signify alphabetic text, they are called *character strings*. An example of alphabetic text is the sentence you are reading right now. Most word processors specialize in processing alphabetic text.

The CPU typically reads an instruction or data from memory and follows the instructions that are contained in its operation code (or opcode). Data is loaded from memory into a register, processed, and then stored back to memory. The CPU does not manipulate memory except to load or store values directly to specified locations. All value or data manipulations occur in registers contained in the CPU. The MMU is responsible for moving data to and from memory into registers. *Manipulations* refers to the ability of the registers' values to be changed by the CU. A typical case in point is that the value of a given register can be changed from a value of 4 to a value of 6. This changed register value can then be stored or saved to a memory address.

An additional register that is essential in computer systems is called the *program counter,* or PC. The program counter is responsible for tracking the location of memory that will next be read into the register from memory. The PC always contains or points to a memory address from the program executed. For example, in a particular program, the program counter or PC always points at the next program instruction. In many situations where the computer stops functioning, called a system crash, the PC may offer the only useful indication of where the manufacturer should begin troubleshooting.

COMPUTER PERFORMANCE

People used to brag about the size of a car's engine, but today computer power has become the thing to brag about. Many automobile enthusiasts use the car's horsepower to represent its capability, but in reality, sheer horsepower is only one measure of a car's potential. Cornering, braking, and comfort all play a role in defining the performance of the car. An equivalent use of computer power measurements can be similarly misleading, because many factors influence overall computer system performance. Many manufacturers and resellers attempt to persuade customers to purchase computer equipment based on performance alone.

One of the early measurements of computer power was the measurement of Millions of Instructions Per Second, or MIPS, the measure of how many instructions can be performed in a given second.

Microprocessor speeds are usually expressed in hundreds of MIPS. The MIPS measurement describes only the raw horsepower of the CPU, and may or may not reflect the actual performance of the overall computer system. Envision a 500-horsepower engine installed on a skateboard. The engine is big and powerful, but unless wheels, transmission, and other necessary components matched to the power of the engine are added, all that will happen is a lot of noise and maybe some teeny tires melting very, very quickly. In the computer arena, after all the noise, if the system does not have a good bus, fast peripherals, and the other things it needs to operate quickly, the system will not perform significantly faster than a system with a slower processor.

Another common measure of computer performance is clock speed. Clock speed is expressed in megahertz. Megahertz (MHz) refers to the millions of cycles a processor can process per second, and is considered the unit of measurement for clock speeds and performance. Early microcomputers frequently had clock speeds of 1 to 10MHz. In those days, they were considered to be quite fast. The first IBM PC had a clock speed of 4.77MHz. The IBM PC/AT had a clock speed of a whopping 8MHz. The top-of-the-line PC available today has clock speeds in excess of 400MHz. These speeds offer performance on the order of hundreds of times the performance and four or more times the bit width of the early microprocessor-based computers.

 note **Megahertz is the unit of measurement for clock speeds and performance.**

Of course, in the final analysis, the only performance measurement that matters is that of the person who has to accomplish work using the computer. It is almost a running joke that if someone buys a computer system today, the focus will initially be on the CPU speed instead of some of the other equally important considerations, like memory and storage capacity. If a fast computer system has inadequate disk storage, or not enough memory, the system will eventually become unusable or extremely slow because it has no space left with which to accomplish meaningful work.

CPU FAMILIES

Much of the current commotion in the computer industry is focused on the relative power of the different microprocessors. This seems to be the proverbial "my chip is bigger than yours" duel. Traditionally, the measures of speed and power have focused on the number of bits width and the clock speed of the chip. The CPU chip is changing in capability at such an incredible pace that it is sometimes hard to remember how this all started. This section will briefly introduce you to the Intel and Motorola families of CPU chips and show you how they evolved.

Early microcomputers were produced by one of several manufacturers — Intel, Motorola, Texas Instruments, and others. The early Intel processors were based upon a fixed-memory architecture. The primary limitation of this approach was the constraint on how memory could be processed and accessed. Motorola, on the other hand, took the approach that all devices on the system could be accessed as memory. These two approaches formed the basis for two different schools of thought on computer design. Over time, the two approaches have somewhat merged in implementation in both types of environments.

Most IBM-compatible CPUs are derivatives of the Intel 8080 family of microprocessors. The 8080 CPU, primitive by today's standards, was considered a top-of-the-line CPU in the mid-1970s.

The 8080 was the basis of evolution leading to the standard for the majority of the microprocessor systems in the market today. The Zilog Z80 was later offered by Zilog Computers as a more capable or faster alternative to the 8080 and was offered in computers made by Radio Shack and other manufacturers. The Z80 was anywhere from fifty to one hundred percent faster than equivalent 8080 microprocessors. The 8080 family of chips laid the groundwork for the high-speed, high-performance chips in use today, such as the 80486 and Pentium. These early processors set the groundwork for what was to become one of the fastest-growing industries in the world today — the personal computer market.

Early Systems

The original computers and operating systems were optimized for 8-bit operations. The operating system that most of these early microprocessors used was called *Control Program/Monitor*, or *Control Program for Microcomputers* (CP/M). CP/M provided a very rudimentary set of commands and capabilities. Nevertheless, many small businesses were able to accomplish word processing, accounting, and other tasks quite effectively on these little systems. These early CP/M machines had a memory limit of 64K, which by modern standards is miniscule. The CP/M environment was used during the late 1970s and early 1980s.

Companies such as Microsoft, Lotus (now owned by IBM), Ashton-Tate (owned by Borland for a while and sold again), and WordPerfect (owned by Novell for a while and sold to Corel) entered the market on these small computer systems. At that time, they provided a powerful alternative to many of the dedicated word processing systems and computational machines used by many businesses. Dedicated word processing systems were the predecessors to word processing software. These systems were generally only capable of text manipulation and document creation. But they were considerably faster than the electric typewriter and more productive.

Several companies that produced dedicated word processors immediately switched away from the proprietary or private architectures they had been using.

IBM, for example, made a word processing system called a DisplayWriter. The DisplayWriter was a desktop microcomputer that was primarily oriented toward word processing. Tens of thousands of office workers were experts with DisplayWriters. Shortly after IBM introduced the PC, they introduced DisplayWrite software for the PC. Most companies that were using DisplayWriters immediately switched to the PC and surplused these older but still usable systems. Frequently, in order to provide compatibility with existing systems and to maintain product consistency, they would not tell their customers what they had done. Most of these manufacturers assumed that the customer would not want to know anything technical about those systems, but would trust the manufacturer to provide support and other services.

Apple developed its own standard of disk operating system, originally called AppleDos, later upgraded to ProDos. This DOS was designed to work with the 5.25-inch floppies used in Apple II computers. The Apple II used a chip called the 6502, which was loosely related to the 6800 CPU. The Apple family of computers made a dramatic jump from the 6502 family of processors to the 6800 family of superchips when Apple introduced the Macintosh family of computers. These computers used a version of the Macintosh operating system (Mac O/S) that provided the user with a graphical interface. A graphical interface is a method whereby users can manipulate a pointing device (mouse) or other similar technology to manipulate characters and programs directly on the screen. This is supposed to be more productive than a strictly keyboard-oriented approach, and it is definitely more intuitive for new users.

Derivatives of this operating system still exist today, and considerable enhancements have been made to it. The newest version of the Macintosh uses a *Reduced Instruction Set Computer* (RISC) chip that enables extremely fast processor operations. The Macintosh has a number of technological firsts associated with it, including being the first truly 32-bit desktop computer. Prior to the introduction of the Macintosh computer, 32-bit computers were largely limited to minicomputers and mainframes. The Macintosh, and later the PC, provided capabilities to end users that were unknown before the advent of the 32-bit microprocessor. Windows NT, a Microsoft operating system for larger computer systems, also runs on RISC chips such as the Alpha processor manufactured by Digital Equipment Corporation.

The PC Revolution

The Intel 8088 changed everything for the computer industry. All of a sudden, a higher-powered 16-bit CPU chip came on the market. The 8088 computer was considered a 16-bit CPU with an 8-bit data bus. Depending upon whose version of history you choose to believe, some stories claim that the 8-bit data bus was used primarily for compatibility purposes with the older 8080-based systems. Other versions of history maintain that the 8088 chip was used because it was cheaper to implement, using then-available technology. From a performance perspective, the wider the number of bits, the greater the performance of the processor. A 16-bit computer is capable of processing twice as many instructions in the same amount of time as an 8-bit processor if they operate at the same speed.

In 1978, a new chip was introduced: the 8086. The 8086 chip implemented the same architecture as the 8088, but with a 16-bit bus. Both of these chips had a memory limitation of 1MB. This was quite a step up from the earlier chips, which had a memory limitation of 64K. The 8086 and 8088 were significantly more powerful than the 8080 and Z80.

These processors accessed memory in what is now referred to as real mode. Real mode describes the ability of the CPU to access only the memory below 1MB. Upper memory boundary is the highest address of memory that can be accessed by the CPU. All the Intel-based processors provide real mode even to this day, which enables compatibility to older operating systems and applications. Real mode is the mode in which MS-DOS operates. MS-DOS set up a limit to applications and data of 640K. It was assumed that this would be adequate for any application for quite some time. It made ten times more memory available for applications and data than had ever been made available to computer programmers.

The memory areas above 640K but below 1MB were available for use, but could not be accessed by applications programs. These areas were used as systems areas for video, BIOS, and other functions. As memory technology improved and larger areas of memory became available for use by the operating system, this area of memory became available for use with utilities and programs that were designed to manage this area. (Figure 3-8 illustrates these memory areas.) The area above 640K later came to be called expanded memory and extended memory. Several memory management schemes were introduced to manage this space and make it usable for programs and data. This will be covered in greater detail in Part III of this book, "DOS/Windows Systems."

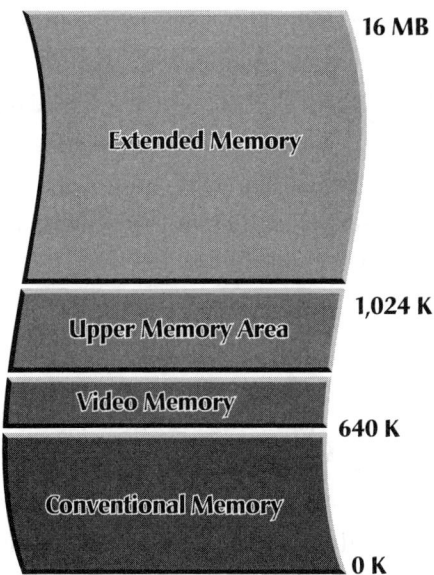

FIGURE 3-8 The original memory implementation used in MS-DOS was based upon an available memory maximum of 640K. Later versions of MS-DOS utilized the memory above 640K.

The 80286 Chip

The 80286 chip brought the industry forward into the beginning 16-bit arena. The performance improvement of the 80286 over the 8086 and 8088 chips was, to say the least, astounding. The chip was three or more times faster, could access larger amounts of memory, and could outwork an 8088 chip in virtually any capacity. One of the early 286-based systems was the IBM PC/AT. The first 80286s were usually equipped with a 10MB hard drive and 512K of memory. These systems were at least two or three times faster than the systems previously available.

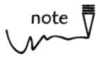 **The 80286 computer is the first place that the AT bus was used. When people refer to the AT bus, they are referring to the bus used on the first IBM 80286 systems.**

The 80286 supported two types, or modes, of addressing: protected and real mode. Real mode was provided so that it could perform tasks identically to the 8088 and 8086. In real mode, the 80286 was quite a bit faster than the previous generation of chips.

Protected mode provided the ability of the 80286 to address up to 16MB of memory. It is the same addressing method used by 8088- and 8086-based systems. This capability outstripped the ability of MS-DOS, which still used real mode. With additional systems memory management software, this memory was made available to applications, and provided considerable performance improvements. Protected mode is currently used by most non-DOS environments such as Windows 95, Windows NT, UNIX, OS/2, and others.

The 80386 Chip

The 80386 chip provided a huge increase in performance over the 80286 and the ability to access over 4GB of data. The prefix giga- stands for one billion. The 80386 provided 32-bit data and address space. Data and address space refer to the ability of the processor to work with 32-bit addresses and data. This is in marked contrast to the 80286, which was limited to 16-bit operation. It was the first of the "monster processors" available to developers. The 80386 provided on a desktop the equivalent of a minicomputer or even a mainframe. The 80386 architecture is very similar to virtually all large-scale computer system architectures used by IBM mainframes, DEC VAX systems, and other 32-bit based computer systems.

The 80386 was introduced with two major variants: the 80386DX and the 80386SX. The 80386, later renamed the 80386DX, used a 32-bit external bus. The SX processor provided an external bus that was 16 bits wide instead of 32 bits. The 80386 chip also required a math coprocessor chip called an 80387 if high-speed calculations were required. The SX variant was considerably less expensive and was used in low-end computers. The DX version of the 80386 provides the ability to use a 32-bit data bus. The SX chip was less expensive than the 80386 DX chip.

The i486DX or 80486 Chip

The top of the line of chips that were based around the 8086 was the 80486. This chip provided considerable performance improvements over the 80386 processor. Its processor cycle was more efficient and enabled frequently used instructions to be executed two or three times faster than a corresponding instruction on an 80386. The 80486 provided additional internal memory to improve high-speed data transfer. The 80486 was also introduced in two versions: the 80486DX and the 80486SX. The 80486 DX included a math coprocessor in the chip, whereas the

80486SX had a disabled math coprocessor. An external math coprocessor was made available for 80486SX computers. The 80486 is downward compatible with the 80386 and supports the real mode of the 8086. Manufacturers use the term "downward compatible" to mean that a microprocessor can run the instructions and programs from earlier microprocessors.

The 80486 also provided clock speeds approaching 100MHz. This blazing speed gave graphic-intensive applications a great performance surge. Unfortunately, MS-DOS is unable to take advantage of this capability, primarily because it is still based around the concept of a 640K applications limit. Many graphics packages may require twenty or thirty million bytes of memory to process a single image. MS-DOS was not originally designed to work with these types of memory requirements.

The introduction of the 80486 made more powerful operating systems such as Windows NT viable on the desktop. Windows NT can really begin to harness the power of this type of processor with its sophisticated capabilities. Windows NT uses a memory management model that is extensively based upon the concept of virtual memory. Virtual memory, covered later in this chapter, describes the capability of the operating system, once physical memory is full, to use hard disk space as a replacement for memory. From the programmer's perspective, this virtual memory can be addressed and treated like RAM memory. Since hard drive access is much slower, there is a significant performance penalty attached to the use of virtual memory, but it is a far better solution than allowing the program to crash once RAM memory is full.

The i486 family of chips provided computer users the ability to have either an SX or DX package, like the 80386 user had. Many manufacturers offered i486SX packaging as a way to provide low-cost systems that still had most of the functionality and speed of the i486DX chip.

The Pentium or P5 Chip

The Pentium chip was a radical departure from the older 8086 line. The Pentium architecture is based upon a 64-bit model, enabling a huge performance increase. A Pentium running at 200MHz provides 330 *Million Instructions Per Second* (MIPS), whereas an i486Dx2-66 provides 54 MIPS. The Pentium chip also takes advantage of a different approach in design called *Reduced Instruction Set Computing* (RISC). RISC architecture is based on the concept that a smaller number of opcodes can be highly optimized for speed of execution, making the design simpler. In return, these instructions can operate at least twice as fast as microcoded instructions.

Most of the chips like the 80486 use many self-contained internal programs to perform tasks. For example, the 80486 may use a small program to perform addition. This small program, usually burned into the chip, is called microcode. Microcoding enables a single microprocessor to have hundreds of program instructions with very little internal hardware. The tradeoff in this situation is that the microcoded programs must be loaded and executed, whereas the RISC instructions in a RISC chip are always immediately available.

The Pentium provides improved caching and a number of other technologically advanced features. Early versions of the Pentium had clock speeds of 60MHz and 66MHz. These chips used a higher voltage power supply and thus generated more heat. These early Pentium chips cannot be used in later versions of Pentium motherboards. The early Pentium chips had different voltage requirements than later Pentium chips. Using an older style Pentium chip in a newer motherboard may require board reconfiguration or it could cause catastrophic damage to the older Pentium chip.

note   **Not all computers require a heat sink. A *heat sink* is a device that gets mounted on the chip to carry heat away from the hardware. Many 8080, 80286, 80386, and some 80486 chips did not require heat sinks. Almost all newer chips require a heat sink. Nonetheless, it has been good practice since at least the days of the 486-66 to use CPU fans as a cheap insurance policy against premature heat-related chip failure.**

Pentium Pro

The top of the line in the Intel family prior to the introduction of the Pentium II Xeon was the Pentium Pro. The Pentium Pro was designed to give the power user a tremendous performance improvement over previous chips. The Pro provides a huge cache as well as a hardware *floating point unit* (FPU). The FPU is special computer circuitry that specializes in arithmetic operations. This enables the microprocessor to perform some math operations extremely quickly.

The architecture of the Pentium Pro is somewhat different from the P5. The Pentium Pro has a 36-bit address bus that enables 64GB of physical addressing, fast caching, and overall better performance architecturally than the P5. The Pentium Pro chip is also configured differently and requires a different connector and support circuitry and motherboard.

MMX Technology

In 1996, Intel announced the availability of multimedia extensions, or MMX, technology. MMX technology enables significant performance enhancement in applications that use graphics and multimedia (audio and video). These applications, when designed with MMX enhancements, have the ability to operate more than twenty percent faster than non-MMX equipped systems. Most of the newer systems designed for home use are now equipped with MMX extensions. All Pentium II CPUs include MMX technology.

Pentium II

The newest member of the Intel family is the Pentium II. This chip uses a different socket configuration as well as improved caching and a top speed (as this is written) of 450MHz. This chip screams. Fundamentally, though, the Pentium II is a new generation of chip with significant performance improvements over the Pentium P5. Intel has announced that all new developments in Pentium processor speeds will use the Pentium II architecture. This leaves the Pentium P5 with a top speed of 233MHz as of the writing of this book.

AMD K6

The AMD K6 is a rival Pentium type chip; it is seen as a direct competitor in the market for the P5 and sometimes the Pentium II chip. It is slightly less expensive than the P5, while providing arguably better performance. The K6 is pin compatible with the P5 and includes support for applications. Field tests of the K6 show that it performs virtually identically to a similar P5 with MMX technology for slightly less money.

Motorola 680x0

This chip was one of the first commercially available 32-bit microprocessors. The 680x0 included advanced memory management capabilities as well as the full capabilities of large memory addressing. The 680x0 family has been used in Macintosh computers since their inception. The latest generation of the 680x0 family is the 68040, which is considered the technological end of that family. Apple is moving its higher performance systems to a relatively new chip technology, which accomplishes work using RISC technology.

PowerPC P601 and P604 RISC

The P601 RISC chip is part of the current family of microprocessor chips used in Macintosh computers. IBM, Motorola, and Apple jointly created these chips. These chips provide a virtually unlimited growth path similar to that of the Pentium family. The current version of Mac O/S forces the PowerPC chip to emulate a Motorola 68040, which slows the processor down considerably. Version 8.0 of Mac O/S provides native mode support, which enables the PowerPC to operate at its full capabilities. Native mode support means that the operating system is designed to take full advantage of the PowerPC architecture, rather than internally emulating the previous chip type through which instructions must pass before accessing the PowerPC chip. This second scenario is emulation, and carries a significant performance penalty. This change from emulation mode to native mode significantly enhances the speed and performance of PowerPC-based systems. It is rumored that the P615 will be pin compatible with the Pentium socket, in that it can be plugged into an Intel Pentium socket directly and operate as a Pentium chip.

The potential of these newer processors in the form of processing power is incredible. The only drawback is that most operating systems and applications cannot truly take advantage of these capabilities. Newer operating systems such as Windows 95 and Windows NT take this capability for granted but still do not utilize the potential of these systems to the fullest. Primarily, the software development technologies used by most software development organizations lag several years behind the capabilities of the hardware. Additionally, software companies are in the business of selling as many copies of their product as possible, and they target the largest installed base of users, not the small number of leading-edge high performance systems.

COMPUTER MEMORY

A simple way to conceptualize memory and memory organization is to take a look at this book. This book is organized into chapters, sections, pages, paragraphs, sentences, and words. You can also think of each page being a collection of rows and columns, rows being each line in the book, and columns being each character position in the line. For example, we could ask you to open the book to page 30 and look in the second line at the fourth letter and you could tell us what that letter was. You could not necessarily modify that letter in the book, but you could take that letter, write it onto another sheet of paper, and turn it into a smiley-faced animal. In a nutshell, this is how computer memory works.

The hardware components of computer memory think in terms of pages, rows, and columns, while the software part of the computer may think in the additional concept of sentences. All this really does for the computer is provide it with a way to store and retrieve information from memory very quickly and in a consistently organized manner.

The primary unit of storage is called memory. Memory in modern computer systems is composed of memory chips arranged in banks. The banks are typically the data width or number of bits of the microprocessor. If a microprocessor is 32-bit, the memory would typically be 32 bits wide. Memory is measured in bytes in virtually all applications. The standard measurement of memory is the megabyte, or MB. Because binary numbers are base 2, the closest round number to a million is 1024K, or 1.02 million. Memory is typically organized into banks. These banks roughly equate to a page in a book. Each location of memory has a unique address that is accessed by a row and column method shown in Figure 3-9. Access to these unique locations is done by a row and column organization of the banks. The rows and columns equate roughly to the locations on a page where data can be accessed. In short, if we were to ask you to open the book to any page and get the information stored in row 3, column 2, you would be able to tell us the value that was printed in that location.

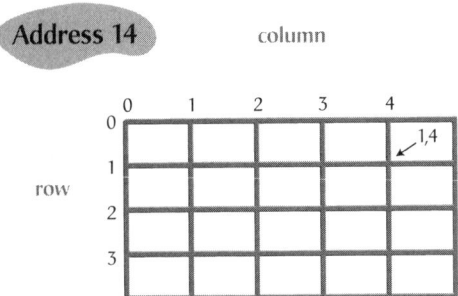

FIGURE 3-9 A typical memory-addressing scheme used in memory chips

Computer memory comes in two primary types: *Random Access Memory* (RAM) and *Read Only Memory* (ROM). Random Access Memory enables information to be stored and retrieved by the CPU. The contents of a RAM location can be altered. If the power is shut off from the computer system, RAM will be erased. RAM memory is usually considered *volatile*. Volatility refers to the inability of memory to retain the information it stores. Volatile memory is said to be temporary, in that if the power is removed, the data will be lost. Data and information are refreshed by the memory controller circuitry to retain information. Most RAM memory is actually dynamic RAM, or DRAM.

Another form of memory that is occasionally used is called *static RAM*. Static RAM stores the data statically in the memory chip. The data is not periodically refreshed like the dynamic RAM process. It is not very likely that you will encounter static RAM in newer computers, but it is still manufactured. Static RAM memory is typically faster access than dynamic RAM, but is more expensive, requires more power, and generates more heat.

 Memory enables the microprocessor to process its program instructions and data. Data and programs are read from and stored to memory, enabling the CPU to quickly manipulate data.

Memory functions are accessed via a set of data, address, and control signals. This is normally performed by a DRAM controller. A DRAM controller controls the address, data, and control lines. The DRAM controller is a part of the CPU support chip set or is built into the CPU chip itself. The design of the memory boards involved usually provides eight, sixteen, or thirty-two of these chips in parallel across the data and address bus. Figure 3-10 depicts a logical layout of a typical computer memory chip. This chip might be a 16MB chip, meaning that it has the ability to store and retrieve 16 million elements of data. Many of the chips can store four or more bits at a time. This enables the chip to store 4 x 16MB or more bits simultaneously. Newer chip technologies enable even higher density to be stored on a single memory board.

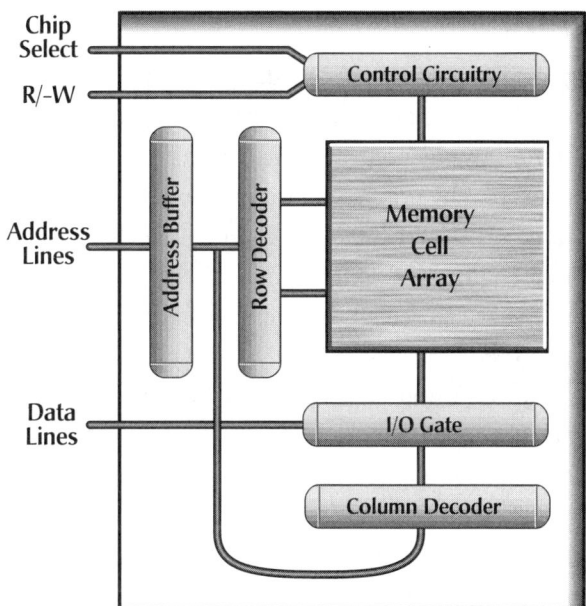

FIGURE 3-10   The layout of a typical memory chip is based upon storage of data in rows and columns. Control lines enable the access and storage of data to a specific location.

Control of memory chips is also accomplished by a chip select control line and a read/write function line. When a specific address needs to be accessed, the address is presented to the chip bank or row using the address lines. The appropriate address is decoded by the row and column decoder, which finds the specific cell or location in memory. The appropriate chip is enabled using the chip select signal line. If the R/-W line is set to a binary 1 or high, the data presents itself through the I/O gate to the data lines. This data can then be transferred to the memory management unit for use by the CPU.

In the case where data is to be written to the cell, the appropriate address and chip is enabled in the manner described above. The R/-W line will be set to low or 0, which means that the data presented by the memory management unit to the data lines will be loaded to that location.

This is how data is updated on a memory chip; the process occurs millions of times per second.

ROM Memory

ROM memory provides computer system designers with the opportunity to store critical configuration and start-up programs on the motherboard with relative ease. Early computers would frequently have banks of switches that would have to be set to load software. The process of loading these switches was called *booting the system*. In large systems, it could take several hours to load all of the switches and get the computer running. ROM memory technology enabled those switch settings to in essence be stored on the computer motherboard. This may enable the storage of the *Basic Input Output System* (BIOS), which causes the motherboard to boot from disk and load the operating system. The BIOS contains machine-specific information such as programs and instructions on how to access the keyboard, disk drives, how to organize memory, and other necessary initial systems information. The specifics of this will be covered in later chapters.

ROM memory is normally burned or programmed at the manufacturer. Some technologies actually burned the program into the chip using high voltage that opens the wires in the chip, setting that location to high or binary 1; an area that has not been burned open is set at a binary 0. This process still exists today. If a bug was found in the programs contained in the ROM, or an upgrade was required, a technician removed and replaced the old ROM chips with a new set. ROM manufacture is very cost effective for large-scale, high-volume situations.

PROM

The PROM is another technology based upon ROM technology. The PROM functions identically to ROM, with the exception that a PROM chip can be programmed using a PROM programmer, or burner unit. This programmer can produce one or a small number of PROM chips. PROMS are also extensively used in prototype or customized systems. Once the PROM chip is burned, it has characteristics similar to a ROM chip from all operational aspects. The programming, once loaded or burned on a PROM, is permanent.

In most cases, you would not be expected to use a PROM programmer, as it is primarily used by software engineers to make changes to low-level programs. However, you may be required to change PROMs in some systems.

EPROM

The Erasable PROM, or EPROM, chip enables technicians to make corrections to the programming, rather than throwing the chip away. An EPROM chip is programmed using a device similar to the PROM burner described above. The EPROM chip contains thousands of miniature fuses that store the program loaded from the EPROM programmer. The chip, for all practical purposes, behaves like a normal ROM chip from that point forward. The only way to erase the chip is to use a high-voltage *ultraviolet* (UV) light. The chips have a window of clear plastic or glass on the top that is covered by electrical tape or a sticker. To erase the chip, you remove the tape from the top and put it in a special UV light eraser for several minutes. The chip, when removed, would be blank at that point. It is very important to cover the window, as exposure to sunlight causes the information on the chip to be slowly erased.

 **EPROMs are used almost exclusively in software development and system prototype environments. Most likely, all you will need to do with EPROMs is replace them.**

EEPROM

The *Electrically Erasable PROM* (EEPROM or flash memory) is a technology that enables the contents of the ROM chip to be erased and reprogrammed using electrical impulses. Many computer manufacturers are now using flash memory instead of ROM devices so that they can be upgraded in the field. Flash memory is a type of EPROM that can be reprogrammed in place. They operate identically to ROM chips once programmed in that they can be accessed as regular memory. The term *flash memory* was first used by Toshiba to identify the chip's ability to be reprogrammed in a flash. Several manufacturers allow for BIOS upgrades to occur online. BIOS upgrading enables the addition of new software and program fixes to occur without taking the computer out of service or requiring any special support from a service technician. This eliminates BIOS problems and simplifies maintaining legacy (older) computer systems.

RAM Memory

RAM, or Random Access Memory, is the memory used in virtually all computers for the temporary storage of data and programs. This memory, as previously explained, can be accessed by the CPU very quickly as compared to disk access. This memory is typically stored in banks or memory boards that can be connected to the computer's motherboard using an edge connector or memory socket.

RAM refers to DRAM or dynamic RAM in this section. RAM memory capabilities, densities, and costs seem to be changing on an almost daily basis. RAM chips started out able to hold only 200 to 500 instructions a few years ago. The new RAM chips contain more than 200 million transistors and components and can store 32 million or more bytes of data. All of the components in a RAM chip are stored in a device smaller than a U.S. postage stamp. Most modern operating systems' performance today can be improved by adding more memory. Many current desktop applications, including word processors and spreadsheets, will not even start running well until more than 16MB of RAM is available. This growth is remarkable considering that in the 1980s, if you had more than 2MB of RAM, you were probably wealthy, given the cost of memory.

 I recommend that a workstation being used for word processing, networking, and other functions, including modem communications, have no less than 16MB of RAM running Windows 95 and no less than 32MB running Windows NT Workstation.

Early motherboards frequently had banks of open chip slots that could be populated two or four banks at a time. This sometimes required a special tool called a chip insertion tool to insert them into the socket without bending them (see Figure 3-11). The penalty for plugging a chip in backwards was the instantaneous destruction of that chip upon power-up. End users often bent leads, incorrectly inserted, or otherwise messed up memory installation, causing much consternation for technicians in the field.

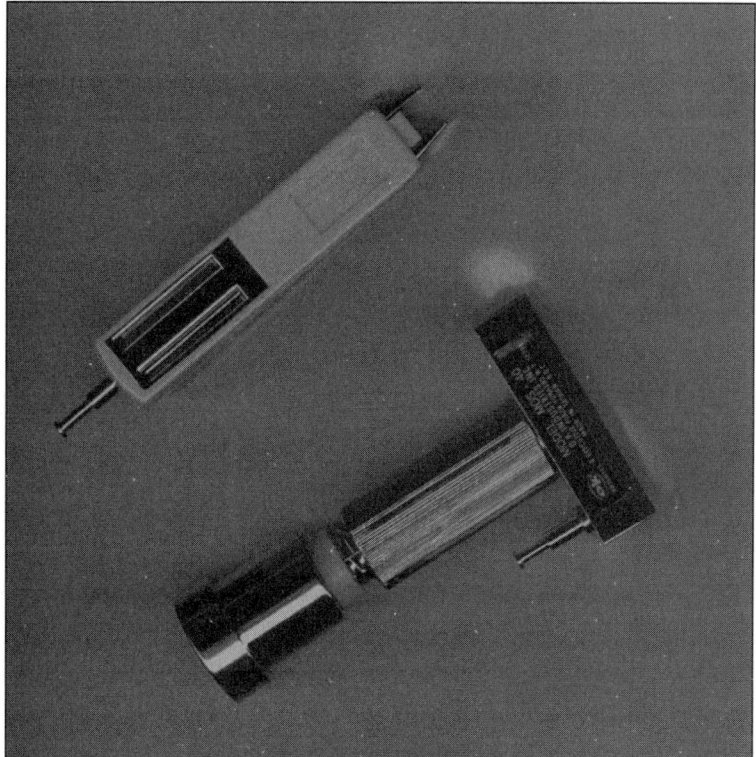

FIGURE 3-11 Memory chip insertion tool

Technology put more transistors in the chips, thus making memory even smaller. Companies like IBM, Compaq, and others started creating memory modules. The evolution of these memory modules was from the SIPP to the EDO memory. Figure 3-12 illustrates several of these memory technologies. SIPP modules, or Single In-line Pin Package modules, were one of the early efforts to create a modular memory system. One of the most current memory modules, the EDO, or Extended Data Out RAM, is in high use in modern computer systems. EDO RAM is being replaced by SDRAM or Synchronous Dynamic RAM modules because they are faster than EDO RAM.

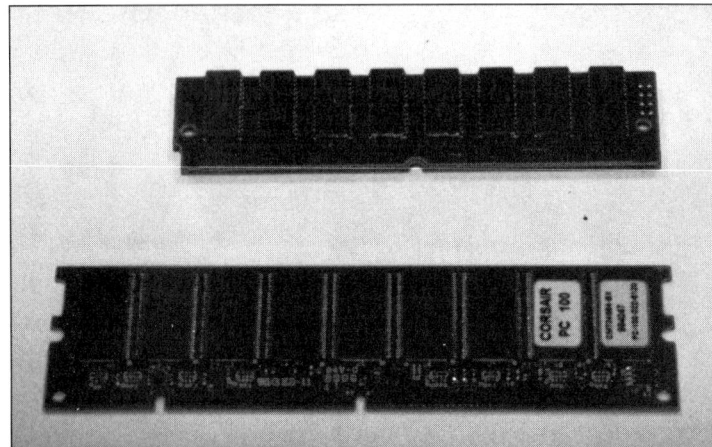

FIGURE 3-12   16MB SIMM and 64MB SDRAM module

SIPP

SIPP, or Single In-line Pin Package, sometimes called SIPP memory, is a 30-pin memory board, which has pins that must be inserted into holes. This unit is then snapped into a socket mechanism that holds the module onto the board. SIPP chips are only used on very old systems and replacements are hard to find. SIPP boards each provide storage for 8 bits.

30-pin SIMM memory

SIMM, or Single In-Line Memory Module, is a 30-pin memory module that enables easy installation of memory using an edge connector. The edge connector provides 30 pin connections to the motherboard. SIMM memory modules provide data for 8 bits. Thirty-pin SIMM memory is not used in most current motherboards. SIMM memory is frequently used in intelligent peripherals like printers, fax machines, and scanners.

72-pin SIMM memory

The 72-pin SIMM provides the capability of storing an entire 32 bits of data on a single memory chip. Functionally, it works like the 30-pin SIMM, but enables wider storage on a single module.

DIMM memory

DIMM, or Dual In-line Memory Module, is a type of packaging similar to SIMM, only much more dense. DIMM memory enables 168 pins to be accessed, allowing for 64-bit storage, required by most Pentium motherboards. DIMM memory provides two rows of connectors on the memory module for connection to the computer. Most of the memory provided for Pentium processors is DIMM memory.

 note **SIMM and DIMM refer only to the packaging of the memory chip and not the capability or speed of that memory. We have heard many computer salespeople explain this to customers incorrectly.**

EDO memory

EDO, or Extended Data Out Memory, is a new memory technology that enables fast memory transfers between the CPU and memory unit. It is typically provided in DIMM modules for installation into the computer. EDO, when used in properly configured systems, does not require the CPU to wait for data transfer. This memory is so fast that it may be faster than some older motherboards were designed to use. The newer motherboards enable faster transfers than is typically available using standard Dynamic RAM.

SDRAM

SDRAM, or Synchronous DRAM, is a new player in the memory arena. SDRAM is synchronized to the clock speed of the computer. This enables memory transfers that exceed the current speeds of most computer buses. Today, the maximum speed available to the system unit bus is 100MHz. SDRAM has the ability to match this performance, making it the upcoming favorite memory standard.

Cache Memory

Speed is an important factor in today's computer systems. The CPU is typically the fastest device in any computer system. Every time the CPU has to wait for something to be found, moved, or put back, time is lost.

Cache memory is a special memory that is dedicated to the high-speed transfer of information. Caching provides a temporary storage area where commonly used instructions can be accessed for instant recall.

If a microprocessor is operating at 335 Million Instructions Per Second or MIPS, delays in memory transfer could cause twenty to thirty percent of the system's performance to be lost while the CPU retrieves information from memory. Most architecture has implemented high-speed, on-board memory that is used for caching. This cache enables the CPU to work on functions while information is being processed. Cache memory speeds are typically two or three times faster than RAM memory. The CPU typically has a cache controller that manages that cache for the CPU.

note   **The larger the cache memory, the faster a processor can run.**

The 80486 and Pentium processors provide support for two levels of caching: Level 1 (L1) and Level 2 (L2). Figure 3-13 portrays the layout of a cache system on a typical CPU. The L1 cache is usually internal to the microprocessor and extremely fast; the L2 cache is usually "close" to the microprocessor chip and provides additional caching for performance.

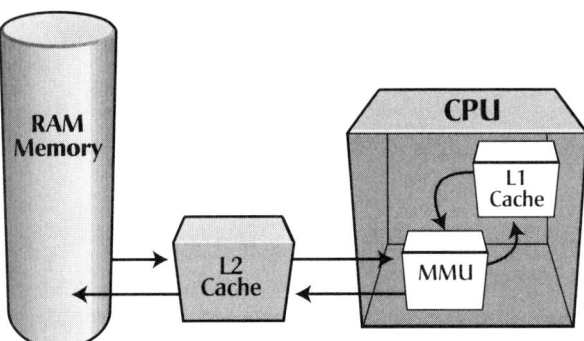

FIGURE 3-13   The cache system on a CPU

L1 cache

L1 caching is the on-chip cache. L1 cache is part of the microprocessor chip. The amount of L1 cache on 80486es and Pentiums is 8K. This cache is extremely fast and is managed using a *last recently used* (LRU) algorithm. LRU is also a most recently addressed approach. If data in the cache is not used in a specified amount of time, it is replaced by data that is more frequently used. This process enables frequently used information in the cache to be updated quickly.

L2 cache

L2 cache is the cache memory that is next closest to the CU of the microprocessor. Normally, it is not a part of the microprocessor chip, but is a dedicated memory area designed to supplement the L1 cache. This memory is accessed first after L1. If the information is not contained in the L1 cache, the CPU issues an L2 cache request. Information is moved from main memory into the L2 cache, thus freeing up the L1 cache to store frequently used information. Most of the motherboards in production today seem to provide either 256K or 512K of L2 cache.

Virtual Memory

Most computer systems provide the ability for the operating system and applications to use more memory than is physically installed in the computer. This is useful in a number of situations where large amounts of data must be accessed. Typically, this virtual memory uses an area on disk. This area is called a *swapping* or *page* file. A page is a unit of storage that can be brought into or put into the paging file at once, rather than sequentially.

Most of this virtual memory is organized into pages, which can be paged in or out depending upon program requirements. This lets the program become considerably larger than did older methods of memory management. Virtual memory has been available in microprocessors since the implementation of the 80286 microprocessor and since the first version of the Macintosh. Windows 95 uses virtual memory to a certain extent, and the Windows NT memory management scheme is based on virtual memory. In Figure 3-13, the real memory is the memory that is closest in attachment to the CPU, whereas the virtual memory is all of the memory resources including the page or swap file.

When the processor issues a request for a page of information, the memory management software checks the existing real memory, and if sufficient memory is available, it transfers it to the cache area. If the requested information is not in real memory, it is paged from virtual memory. This process occurs thousands of times per second. Each time a requested memory is paged, a page fault is generated. Page faults are neither good nor bad — they merely measure the number of times the disk has been searched in disk memory. Excessive page faults degrade performance of the CPU. The solution to excessive page faults is usually to add more memory.

KEY POINT SUMMARY

Chapter 3 introduced the systems unit and all of the components associated with the CPU. This unit also introduced the concepts of stored programs, number systems, memory, and the various types of computer processors in use today.

- The systems unit consists of the motherboard and all internal devices, including the power supply.

- The CPU consists of the *Arithmetic Logic Unit* (ALU), the *Control Unit* (CU), registers, and support circuitry. The CU directs the entire operation and controls how information is processed.

- Most motherboards produced today support ISA, or AT and PCI slots for expansion.

- Computers represent data in a series of ones and zeros using a binary numbering system. Programmers and systems professionals usually convert these into numbering systems such as octal or hexadecimal, base 8 and base 16 respectively.

- Computer performance is measured in Millions of Instructions Per Second, or MIPS. The power of a computer is usually measured by the number of bits that the processor can process simultaneously. Pentium processors process 64 bits at a time. Clock speed or megahertz is frequently used to measure processor or peripheral speeds and transfer rates.

- The Pentium family of chips is the current release of chips manufactured by Intel. The PowerPC family of RISC chips is currently used in Macintosh and some IBM computers.

- Memory configurations include SIMM, for Single In-line Memory Module, or DIMM, for Dual In-line Memory Modules. DIMM chips are more prevalent in Pentium and Motorola-based processors produced today.

- Computer memory is either RAM or ROM. RAM memory is usually dynamic and loses its information when the power is turned off. ROM is permanent memory that in some cases can be altered in the field.

- ROM memory types include PROM, EPROM, and EEPROM. EPROM and EEPROM (more commonly called flash memory) can be programmed in the field using special equipment called burners or EEPROM programmers.

- Memory modules come in several configurations. Older styles of memory modules include the SIPP and SIMM memory. Current memory modules typically use the DIMM design. EDO and SDRAM are the fastest RAM technologies available in the market today for PC and Macintosh users.

- Cache memory helps the processor not waste processor time. Cache memory helps the CPU by keeping frequently used information close to the CPU. Most CPUs either have or work with a cache controller for high performance. Two types of cache are usually referenced: L1 and L2 cache. L1 cache is the cache inside the CPU, and L2 cache is the cache immediately outside the CPU chip.

- Virtual memory is an approach to memory management that enables the CPU to access more memory than is physically present. This is accomplished by using disk space for memory storage. The memory is broken down into smaller units called pages, which can be written or read to the disk file.

APPLYING WHAT YOU'VE LEARNED

This chapter has covered a lot of important material that will help you prepare for the A+ exam and be an excellent computer technician. Take a few minutes and work through the questions in the Instant Assessment, then review your notes and see how you did.

The Hands-on lab will also help you build your comfort level with the hardware as well as reinforce the readings from this chapter.

Instant Assessment

Multiple choice

Choose the best answer(s). There may be more than one correct answer for each question.

1. The microprocessor chip can be inserted into a:

   A. Zip drive

   B. ZIF socket

   C. Expansion slot

   D. Power supply

2. Which of the following pin counts is an option for SIMM?

   A. 30

   B. 16

   C. 78

   D. 24

3. The Intel Pentium processor is a:

   A. CISC-based chip

   B. DISC-based chip

   C. RISC-based chip

   D. POKER-based chip

4. ROM memory is which type of memory?

   A. Volatile memory

   B. Non-volatile memory

   C. RISC memory

   D. CISC memory

5. Level 1 or L1 caching is the caching that resides:

   A. On the RAM board

   B. On the systems board

   C. In the CPU chip

   D. On the virtual memory management chip

6. Computer power is measured in several ways, including:

   A. MOPS

   B. FLPS

   C. MMUS

   D. MIPS

7. The 80386 processor is an early example of a(n):

A. 8-bit processor

B. 16-bit processor

C. 32-bit processor

D. 18-bit processor

8. The Pentium processor is an example of a(n):

A. 16-bit processor

B. 64-bit processor

C. 8-bit processor

D. 128-bit processor

9. Real mode is a memory mode in which:

A. Memory is accessed below 250K

B. MS-DOS cannot operate efficiently

C. MS-DOS must operate

D. MS-DOS machines can access 16MB of RAM

10. EPROM memory is memory that:

A. Must be programmed at the factory

B. Can only be erased at the factory

C. Can be erased and reprogrammed in the field

D. Is designed to be used as an alternative to cache memory

Fill in the blank

1. Modern computer systems have the ability to appear to use more RAM memory than is physically installed. This is called

_____.

2. The Pentium microprocessor is a _____-based CPU.

3. The _____ cache memory is located inside the CPU.

4. The _____ is responsible for logic and arithmetic operations.

5. Memory that is considered volatile is called _____.

6. The original 8080 and 6800 microprocessors were _____-bit machines.

7. The Pentium processor is a _____-bit microprocessor.

8. A typical value for L2 caching is _____.

9. The _____ contains all of the system and control circuitry.

10. The _____ Unit is concerned with memory resources and allocation.

Hands-on Lab Exercise

During the course of the labs in this book, we are going to be assembling and disassembling a PC system. If you are comfortable working on the system that you use for other things, it is certainly okay to take that machine apart. On the other hand, if you have a system put together by one of the major manufacturers, taking it apart may void your warranty.

Almost every town has a store that specializes in creating customized systems. We suggest that you visit one of these stores and talk to the manager about what you are trying to accomplish. You might offer to assist putting together a few systems, or maybe you want to take a crack at building one for somebody you know.

Have no fear — if you got through the first part of this book, and you can use a screwdriver and follow reasonable directions, then you can easily accomplish these tasks. If you buy a system from a computer parts store, you can always take it into the store and ask for help if you are stuck.

Virtually everybody in this field started out by doing what we are talking about. Many newly minted A+ technicians will find this kind of work very informative and fun.

So, let's begin.

Lab 3.1 *Assembling a PC system*

Getting organized

The system we are building will be based on an Intel 440BX motherboard. Many manufacturers, including ASUS, SuperMicro, and Micronics, make motherboards.

Our system will have the following components installed in it:

- Systems unit (which typically includes the power supply and disk cables)

- Intel Seattle motherboard with integrated sound (440BX chipset)
- 400MHz Pentium II processor
- Mid-tower case
- 275-watt Silencer ultra-quiet power supply
- CPU-Cool K1 Pentium II cooling fan
- Bay-Cool extra cooling fan kit (previous four items from PC Power and Cooling Corp.)
- 64MB of PC100-compliant SDRAM
- Toshiba DVD-ROM Player
- Toshiba 32X SCSI CD-ROM drive
- 4.5GB UW SCSI hard drive
- 3.5-inch floppy disk
- ATI All-in-Wonder Pro AGP video card
- Adaptec 2940U2W SCSI Controller card
- Microsoft IntelliMouse
- Microsoft Natural Keyboard Elite
- ViewSonicG790 19-inch monitor

All of these components can be ordered from mail order in the back of most computer magazines, or from computer stores that specialize in computer components. Competitive pricing information can be found at www.pricewatch.com.

With the exception of the DVD player, this is a high-end machine that you may encounter in offices this year. In most office settings, you will find a CD-ROM player instead of a DVD player.

Tools required

- A Static Strap, available from most electronic supply houses or by mail order.
- A screwdriver (probably a #2 Phillips head is all you will require).

These tools can be purchased at electronic supply houses such as Radio Shack.

We will be using a table to lay all of the components out. This will help us build this system with a minimum of fuss and aggravation. As you can see in Figure 3-14, we have pretty well taken over the table.

 tip **Always use a fan on the CPU chip. This will prevent the premature destruction of the chip. The surface temperature of a Pentium II CPU can exceed 200 degrees without a fan.**

FIGURE 3-14 The computer system laid out in pieces

General procedures

The following paragraphs briefly explain the steps we will be performing during the installation. The specific steps we will take are shown later in the lab.

The first step in this process is mounting the motherboard to the systems unit. The PC Power and Cooling mid-tower case opens from both sides, but only the left side (looking at the case from the front) needs to be removed to mount the motherboard. Later, when we're installing drives in the drive bays, the right side of the case can be removed to mount the right side of the drives. Figure 3-15 shows the motherboard mounted into the case. Notice that in the middle right of the motherboard is the Pentium II CPU chip with a clip-mounted fan. Pentium II chips generate a great deal of heat and require a fan. If you forget this, then in all probability, your CPU chip will melt itself and you will have to get a new one. Failure to use a CPU fan voids nearly all CPU warranties.

FIGURE 3-15 **The motherboard being mounted into the systems case**

Mounting the Intel motherboard requires a series of metallic and plastic standoff spacers. The metallic standoffs are used on the holes in the motherboard that are ringed with metal — in this case, all but two of the mounting holes. In addition to serving as a sturdy base for the motherboard, these metallic standoffs also act as a ground and ensure that the board will be shielded. Shielding is important to help ensure the motherboard does not generate *electromagnetic interference* (EMI) in nearby electronic equipment.

This motherboard is designed to support Pentium II CPUs in a wide range of speeds, from the early 233MHz models up to the current fastest model, the 450MHz. Many boards require jumper settings to adjust the board's operating speed and CPU voltage to the levels for a particular CPU speed. The Seattle automatically senses the CPU's speed and adjusts itself accordingly. Be sure to read the manual that comes with your motherboard *before* powering anything up!

Notice also that the memory chips have been inserted into the board in the top right. The connectors to the left are for the keyboard, mouse, and *Universal Serial Bus* (USB) devices. Below these connectors are the PCI slots, and finally the ISA slots. To the right of the memory are the onboard drive connectors, for EIDE drives as well as the floppy drive. Through the course of assembling this system, we will also be connecting wires to power the speaker, fan, and other indicators and controls.

As you can see, most of the motherboards today accomplish a great deal with very few parts. There are really only a half-dozen or so chips on the motherboard. Older PCs might have had thirty or forty chips on the motherboard. The chip in the middle is the ROM that contains the BIOS. The battery (the round object in the lower right corner) provides power to the motherboard, which enables it to remember the date and firmware or permanent systems settings.

The advantage of this type of design (from a technical support perspective) is that very few things can be replaced in the field. Most of the time, a technician will carry a motherboard, a spare CPU chip, and just a few other parts.

Part 1: Installing the motherboard

By mounting the motherboard against the wall of the case, we've accomplished our first step — to mount the motherboard into the system unit. Notice in Figure 3-16 that the expansion slots are close to the openings on the left side of the picture (or back of the systems unit). In the upper left-hand corner of the motherboard is a connector into which the keyboard is plugged. The U-shaped brackets above the motherboard are used for mounting disk drives. These brackets can be easily removed and reinstalled, making access to the motherboard simple. At this time, you will want to install the CPU and fan and check and configure systems jumpers (if needed) per your installation manual.

Mate the connectors with the openings in the back of the case

FIGURE 3-16 Motherboard and systems unit mating ritual

Part 2: Installing cables and jumpers

The next step in our process is to install cables. The first cable we are going to install is very easy to identify because it's the biggest, longest cable in the system. This cable connects the motherboard to the power supply. On our motherboard, it plugs into the motherboard in the top right corner (Figure 3-17).

FIGURE 3-17   Power connector connected to the motherboard

Part 3: Installing systems unit cables

The next step is to plug all of the case wires into the motherboard. Figure 3-18 shows the area that these wires are plugged into. Typically, the disk activity light, power light, the reset button, and system speaker are plugged into these jumpers. Some cases provide a turbo light on the case and a jumper for it. This is a carryover from the 80486 and earlier systems, which frequently had a switch that allowed for the clock speed to be reduced in the event of applications timing problems. Thankfully, most systems manufacturers have figured out how to have things work at one speed.

Front panel control and light wiring

FIGURE 3-18 The front panel's controls and lights are connected to the motherboard.

Part 4: Installing keyboard, monitor, and video card

At this point, we are almost ready to apply power and test the motherboard. To do this, we will have to connect the keyboard, a video card, and the power cord. The video card goes into the AGP slot on this system. On the Intel 440BX motherboard, the AGP slot (to be explained in Chapter 7) is the first slot below the CPU. The keyboard plugs into the connector on the back of the system unit.

With the monitor, keyboard, and power cord all connected, it is time to turn the machine on for the first time. Turn your monitor on first to give it a few seconds to warm up.

Part 5: Powering on the system

Turning on the power is a real treat. If everything is working, the system will beep and the screen will display information on its BIOS. At this point, if everything is working, you can turn the machine off and continue installation.

Congratulations, break open the champagne! A new computer is born! Anybody got a cigar?

If for some reason you have encountered a problem with your machine, only a few things could be wrong:

1. Check your power cables (both ends).
2. Check all of the jumpers on the motherboard to verify they are configured correctly.
3. Replace the CPU chip.
4. Replace the motherboard.
5. Check the power supply voltage settings.
6. Replace the power supply.

In most cases, you can take the system and CPU back to the place you purchased them and ask for a replacement. Most reputable computer shops will gladly do this for you. If that does not solve the problem, it may be worth it to have them repair the system and show you what you might have done wrong.

Disk and Tape Storage Components

About Chapter 4

This chapter explores the different types of magnetic data storage available in a modern computer system. It covers hard drives, floppy drives, and tape standards. We'll introduce the different types of magnetic storage devices, and some of their physical characteristics. Then we'll explore how they interact with the motherboard and the software. Finally, this chapter is designed to help you evaluate configuration types and options and decide which are most appropriate in various situations.

DISK STORAGE CONCEPTS

With the possible exception of highly specialized network terminals, most computer systems in today's office environment have some form of integrated disk storage capability. This allows the end user to store and retrieve information easily and efficiently. This section identifies the types of disk storage available (see Figure 4-1), and some of the physical methods for storing and retrieving information.

No matter how much storage your computer system has, it never seems to be enough. Several years ago, hard drives were measured in megabytes. A 20MB or 40MB hard drive was considered the top of the line. Today, a normal computer system will be equipped with no less than 2GB of hard drive space and probably more. An application suite that includes a word processor, spreadsheet, graphics program, and a database program might require in excess of 200MB just to be installed. Typical operating systems in use today frequently require over 100MB. As you can see, more than a third of that minimal disk configuration is utilized before anybody has even started working with the computer.

FIGURE 4-1 **Storage devices, including hard disk drive,**
floppy drive, and CD-ROM

DIGITAL STORAGE CONCEPTS

The basic storage technology of digital signals on disk drives is magnetic. Simply put, three magnetic states can exist: positive polarity, negative polarity, and no polarity. A positively charged piece of metal could represent a binary 1, whereas a negatively charged piece of metal could represent a binary 0, and a piece of metal with no charge could be an unused piece of metal (available for storage). If you lined up millions of these metal bars side by side and read them with a small compass, you could store information almost indefinitely on those magnetic bars. Figure 4-2 illustrates how this looks. Each of the bars with a + on the top is said to be positively charged — this would represent the equivalent of a binary 1. Each of the bars with a negative symbol at the top would have a reverse charge, which would be a binary 0.

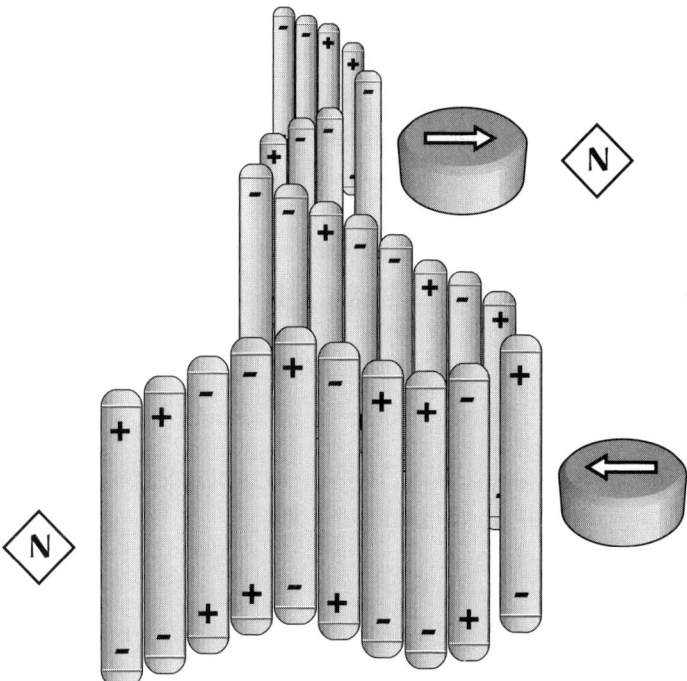

FIGURE 4-2 The magnetic bars on the figure represent a binary 1 when polarized in one direction and a binary 0 when polarized in the other.

The magnetic bars represent the storage media, and the compass represents the read head — the head that is used to read data from the media. As you can imagine, this would not be a very space-efficient way of storing information simply because in our example, you would not be able to separately magnetize the individual bars. Nevertheless, this is how magnetic storage works. Instead of the data being stored in metal bars in a straight line, they are stored on a round flat piece of metal with many millions of these metal bars on the surface, as shown in Figure 4-2. Modern disk drives also do not move the head; instead, they move the media past the head by spinning the disk. The head, while stationary on one axis, has the ability to move in and out along the radius of the disk. This allows information to be stored in bands or tracks that can be accessed individually.

In the case of a floppy disk, this equates to approximately 17,000 bits per inch of media. This media is typically broken down into bands called tracks. Tracks and other units of data organization are covered later in this chapter. The important thing to remember is that virtually all disk storage uses magnetically based media.

Disk Drive Architecture

Most of the storage available on standard computers today is based on disk drive storage technology. Many of the disk drives in the market exceed six billion bytes of storage. This storage is organized into an easy-to-understand structure. The sections below provide you with a comprehensive understanding of the technology.

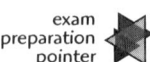
exam preparation pointer

A double-sided, double-density (DSDD) 5.25-inch diskette can be formatted to a maximum of 360KB.

Floppy disks usually use both sides of the disk for information storage. Larger disk drives have multiple platters connected together into a spindle. The section on cylinders illustrates this in detail. Each platter has its own read/write head, which transfers information to and from the platter. These heads are mounted on an arm that reaches into the inner tracks and out to the outer tracks.

Tracks

Floppy disk storage typically provides between 40 and 80 *tracks* (low-density versus high-density), whereas a hard disk has hundreds or even thousands of tracks. Figure 4-3 shows a track on a disk drive. Between each of the tracks is an area that is not magnetized, providing a dead zone between tracks. This dead zone makes it easy for the disk drive electronics to determine when one track ends and another begins. As manufacturing tolerances have improved over time, the area between tracks has shrunk at the same time magnetic density per page is skyrocketing.

Sectors

If the disk drive were sliced into even "pie slices," each of the slices would include several tracks. Each pie slice, as shown in Figure 4-3, is called a *sector*. The sectors provide an easy way for the information to be organized. Each sector is uniquely numbered, starting with sector one. Typically, a sector stores 512 bytes of data. A floppy disk drive might typically have anywhere from 9 to 36 sectors per track.

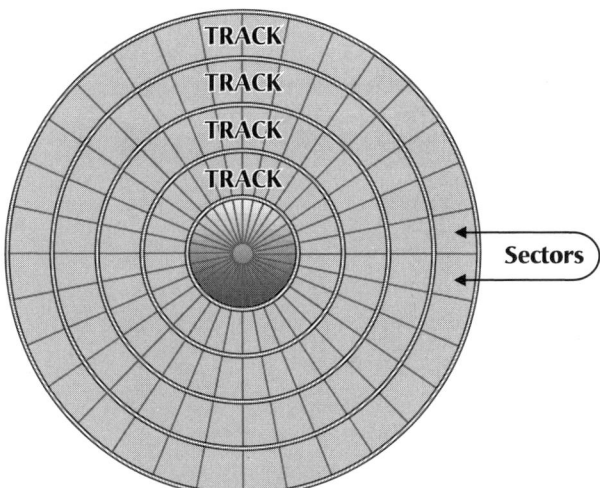

FIGURE 4-3 **A disk drive showing tracks and sectors**

Clusters

Clusters are a logical grouping of sectors. Clusters allow multiple sectors to be transferred onto and off the disk drive. Floppy disks typically have a cluster size of two, which means they have two sectors per cluster. Larger hard disks can have sector sizes of up to 64. If a cluster size on a drive were 16, then each cluster would contain 16 x 512 bytes, or 8,192 bytes.

Cylinders

A *cylinder* is a collection of tracks across one or more platters. The area defined by all tracks above and below one another is called a cylinder (see Figure 4-4). Cylinders provide a way for a larger amount of information to be accessed at one time. Since all of the heads of a disk drive travel together on the same arm, this gives the drive the ability to address big blocks of data.

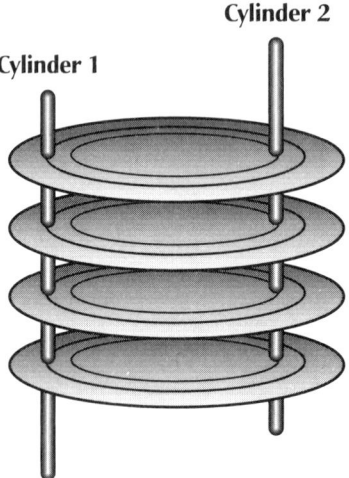

Cylinder 1

Cylinder 2

FIGURE 4-4   A disk drive showing the parts of a cylinder

Blocks

A disk *block* is another unit of storage. Typically, a block is a consecutive collection of storage areas, usually 256. A block of data is primarily a logical or programming construct, as opposed to a hardware construct. The smallest unit of data that a programming language usually works with is a disk block, when performing input and output to disks.

As a technician, you will likely encounter people talking about bad blocks of data on their hard disk. In reality, it is usually a sector, track, or other physical measurement of data that has gone bad, not a block.

The quantity of disk storage available today is growing at an exponential rate. A few years ago, a 1GB hard drive would have been considered the ultimate storage unit, and would have cost thousands of dollars. Today you can purchase a 6GB hard drive for less than $300 over the counter at a computer store.

This is both a blessing and a curse. The blessing is that more information can be stored online less expensively than was ever dreamed of a few years ago. The curse is that now so much information is online and easily accessible that some people are truly overwhelmed with information.

These large disk drives can store an organization's entire history, and if the computer system fails, or the hard drive crashes, then huge amounts of valuable data could be irretrievably lost to the organization. It is critical that organizations schedule regular backups of data. The implications of not backing up data can be disastrous.

File Systems

File systems are the organizational systems that computers use to manage, manipulate, and store information on disks or other storage media. *Files* are groupings of data that are managed as a unit. Files are considered logical groupings, whereas clusters and sectors are considered physical groupings.

Files contain one or more blocks of data. A computer program typically opens a file for reading or writing, which informs the operating system that the blocks identified or associated with this file are in use. The program, when it reads or writes information to the files, reads and writes blocks of data.

Operating systems such as Windows 95 and Mac O/S have implemented methods of file management that we'll discuss briefly here and in the relevant operating systems sections.

To manage these files, the operating system creates a file system. Like a filing cabinet, a file system usually includes a way to organize data into drawers and cabinets. Figure 4-5 illustrates the logical construction of a file system.

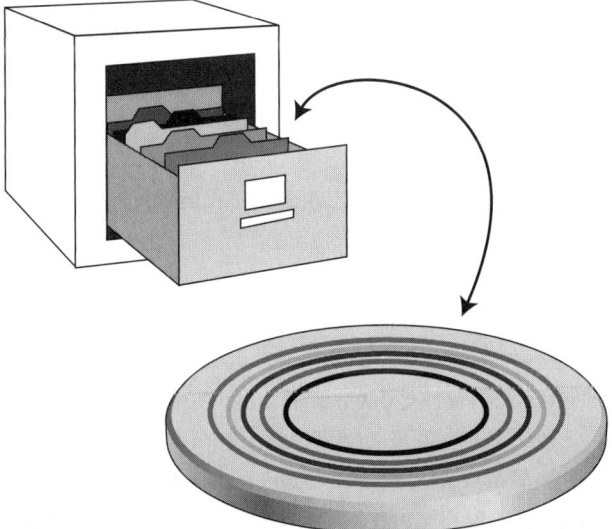

FIGURE 4-5 A filing cabinet with drawers and folders, the equivalent disk system

The importance of a file system is that the operating system takes over the responsibility for file maintenance. The operating system is also responsible for access and management. Most operating systems accomplish this management using a file called a *file allocation table* (FAT).

File Allocation Table

The *file allocation table* (FAT) is a list or file that maintains information about the free and occupied areas of the disk. The FAT maintains this information by creating a table of allocated space. Each time a file area is allocated, an entry is made to the FAT file indicating that the space is no longer available. Think of it like a library. If the library were interested in managing shelf space each time a book was taken out, a card could be removed and stored in a folder. This folder would tell the librarian which areas in the bookshelf were empty. Those empty areas could then be used for other purposes.

MS-DOS and Windows 95 use the FAT file system. Recently, Microsoft shipped Windows 95 systems with a file system called the FAT32 file system. The FAT32 system is relatively new and will not be supported by Microsoft's Windows NT until the release of NT 5.0. This system solves a problem that wasted a great deal of hard drive space called cluster slop. Under the FAT system, the hard drive is divided into chunks called clusters that are a defined size, based on the size of the hard drive partition. Under FAT16, disks between 1,024MB and 2,048MB have a cluster size of 32K. This means that all files use a minimum 32K of disk space, regardless of their size. Small files like Windows 95 shortcuts (1K each) still take up 32K of drive space. This difference is cluster slop, and it can cause a significant portion of hard drive space to be wasted. FAT32 minimizes cluster slop by allowing much smaller clusters on any sized partition.

File Access

Disk drives are random access devices. The disk drive can immediately go to any location on the disk and read or write data without having to move sequentially to that new location. This allows quick and efficient ways to access data. Technologies such as magnetic tape and punch cards, on the other hand, used an access method called sequential access. Sequential access requires the information be read from beginning to end. For example, to access a card somewhere deep in a card deck, each card had to be fed through a card reader machine one after another. This process was extremely fast if the information was close to the front of the deck, but slow if the data you wanted was at the end. Imagine a deck of playing cards and you were looking for the queen of spades. You would have to evaluate each card to determine if that was it or not, and continue on in order until you found the queen. Sequential access can be painfully slow in large files with many pieces of data.

In summary, random access allows for a piece of information to be accessed quickly, whereas sequential access requires data to be evaluated from the beginning to the end until the desired information is found.

In order for random access to work, the data must be organized in an orderly manner. For example, assume a customer file is organized alphabetically. In a sequential file, you would need to read all of the cards from beginning to end in order to find the customer record for Zigfield Zimmerman. This process could be extremely slow and might require reading many cards.

In a random access environment, however, you could read the cards halfway in the file. After evaluating the name, you would conclude that Zigfield's record was after Michael Morris. You could then read a card halfway between Michael Morris and the end of the file. You would then, for example, find you were looking at Terry Thomas, again not Zigfield. You can keep doing this, each time halving the distance from the current location until the name you read is past or beyond the name you are looking for. At that point, you could start reading the file backwards until you found Zigfield's record. This process would make the task of finding Zigfield's record much quicker than reading the customer deck from one end to the other. This type of lookup process is called a binary search and is one of the most fundamental or common random access processes used.

As file systems grew, and the need to add and remove information grew, it became more difficult to keep the information in alphabetical order. To accomplish data access, a second file called an *index file* is created to keep track of the individual records in the primary, or data, file. Since the index contains only the information about the name or key and the record number, a binary search similar to what was described in the previous paragraph would be very fast. The index file enables rapid searching of information to take place, as well as adding and deleting information. The index file concept is used by most database management systems as the primary building block for information access.

Partitions

The final disk concept that we'll discuss in this section is the *disk partition*. Large disk drives can be broken down into smaller units, or partitions. This is called partitioning. In the current versions of MS-DOS, partitions can be 2GB. This is a considerable increase from earlier versions of MS-DOS partition sizes of 32MB. Recently, Microsoft released a new version of the FAT system, which was first included in Windows 95 OEM Service Release 2 (OSR2). FAT32 allows access of disk space up to 2 terabytes in size.

Each of the partitions is treated by the operating system as a separate drive in most instances. These logical drives are still parts of the one physical hard drive, but they are partitioned into smaller, more manageable disk storage units or drives. Our computer, for instance, has two hard drives on it. One of the drives is 6.2GB, and the other is 2.1GB. The smaller drive is partitioned into one drive labeled drive E; the 6.2GB drive is partitioned into three 2GB hard drives. In this manner, we can store different versions of the operating system on each of the drives. These drives are labeled C, D, and F. The net effect of this is the creation of three partitions from the large 6.2GB disk drive.

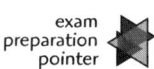

exam
preparation
pointer

DOS 3.3 does not recognize a partition beyond 32MB.

Disk Formatting

Disk formatting prepares the disk to accept the operating system. Most operating systems provide a utility to format the drive. In the MS-DOS and Windows 95 environment, this utility is called *Format*. The Format program typically carries out the task of creating the tracks and sectors on the drive as well as initializing the disk blocks to prepare them for storage. Put simply, formatting is the process whereby a magnetic storage media is prepared by the operating system to be used for storage.

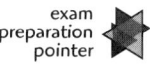

exam
preparation
pointer

The capacity of a 5.25-inch high-density diskette is 1.2MB.

Two different types of formatting must be performed on most disk drives. The first, typically performed by the disk manufacturer, is called low-level formatting. Low-level formatting prepares the drive to be electronically organized. This includes setting up the tracks, sectors, cylinders, and other parameters necessary for the drive to be installed on a computer system.

High-level formatting establishes the storage organization of the drive. For example, high-level formatting creates the file system and establishes size and storage conventions. In most cases, the operating system establishes the requirements for a high-level format. For example, Windows 95 OSR2 (also referred to as Windows 95B) amd Windows 98 allow for two different formats to be used: FAT and FAT32. The FAT file system has a maximum limit of 2GB per disk partition, whereas FAT32 has a virtually unlimited partition size capability. For the disk to be FAT32, it must be formatted as such under OSR2 or Windows 98.

Occasionally, if a hard disk develops a malfunction and a high-level format does not fix it, a low-level format may be required to reestablish the disk layout. Normally, the disk manufacturer provides a utility program for this purpose.

DIGITAL TAPE STORAGE

If any technology has evolved and changed with the times, it is magnetic tape. Most users will encounter only cartridge, QIC, and DAT formats, but longtime users of computer systems inevitably worked with reel-to-reel tape. Two common types of tape cartridges are QIC, for Quarter Inch Committee, and DAT, for Digital Audio Tape. The QIC and DAT formats are explained in greater detail later in this chapter.

The fundamental concepts of magnetic tape are similar to those of audio-cassette. The data is read or written to the tape via a magnetic head. In most tape storage mechanisms, the tape is pulled across stationary recording/play heads. An additional head is typically provided, which is a formatting or magnetic head. Figure 4-6 illustrates the process of magnetic tape uses.

Magnetic tape technology uses a series of channels to store information. These channels are parallel to each other on the tape and have their own read/write heads. The heads are usually combined into a single unit or head assembly, which is replaced or serviced all at one time to maintain the precise alignment of its components. Many reel-to-reel and data tape systems are organized into eight or sixteen channels. These channels are also referred to as *tracks*.

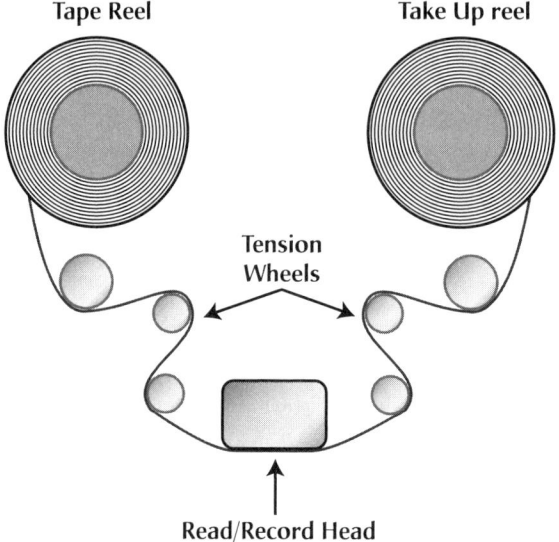

Tension Wheels

Tape Reel

Take Up reel

Read/Record Head

FIGURE 4-6 A reel-to-reel magnetic tape drive system

Data accuracy is a major consideration for data storage. To ensure that information is stored and retrieved correctly, most tape systems include an additional channel for parity or *Error Correction Code* (ECC). This ninth channel is usually not referred to in the channel count. ECC allows for information on the tape to be verified for accuracy by the tape drive. Tapes using an ECC method are usually more reliable. Parity uses that extra or ninth track to store information about the other eight tracks.

Reel-to-Reel

Early tape users used a reel-to-reel model of tape. This process provided a way to store large amounts of data off-line that could be retrieved and read easily. Even though this technology is very old, it provides the baseline for many technologies, such as cassette, DAT, and other channel-oriented technologies.

The tape reel that contains the tape is loaded onto the tape drive. The tape is wound through a series of pulleys and vacuum chambers and then loaded onto a take-up reel. The tape drive then winds the tape across the tape heads for reading and recording. These tapes were very slow and could contain typically anywhere from 200MB to 400MB of information. The tape drives typically cost tens of thousands of dollars and the tapes cost anywhere from $20 to $30. A system operator's worst nightmare was to drop one of these tapes. They had a tendency to unwind and were easily damaged. Typically, a tape reel contained 2,400 feet of tape. The data storage density of a typical early tape drive was 800 *bits per inch* (BPI). Technology pushed this limit upward to 6,250 BPI. Only large information technology shops use this type of technology, and then primarily to address legacy or downward-compatibility concerns.

The early advantages of tape drive storage included the cost effectiveness of storage compared to the cost of disk storage. To a certain extent, this gap is closing, but tape backup schemes still provide a reliable way to store large amounts of information. Most of the newer technologies utilize a data cartridge that contains all of the rollers and take-up reel.

Cassette

Audiocassette technology brought a wealth of new and relatively inexpensive technology to the computer field. The audiocassette was developed by Phillips as a way to replace reel-to-reel audiotape. Audiocassette is rugged and very compact for the amount of information that it can store. Many of the original computers included an audiotape port that programs were loaded and saved to. These cassettes never really caught on for computer use and are seldom encountered.

QIC Format

The next iteration of the audiocassette is the quarter-inch cartridge named QIC, after the Quarter Inch Committee. The QIC Consortia is a non-profit industry association that developed a standard for tape storage for the PC industry. The consortia includes members such as Sony, Verbatim, Hewlett-Packard, and others concerned with magnetic tape storage. For information on the standard, see their Web site at www.qic.org. The QIC tape is a rugged package that looks similar to a VHS cassette, but smaller. The 3M Corporation originally produced these cartridges, and they are currently available from a variety of vendors.

Early QIC tape drives were connected to the floppy drive controller and could store 40MB of data. Current cartridges can store over 2.1GB of data. The drive designations also represent the storage capacity. For example, a QIC-120 stores 120MB of data, and the QIC-500 stores 500MB of data. Travan tapes, the latest variation on QIC technology, can hold multiple gigabytes of data.

DAT Tape

Digital Audio Tape, or DAT, is a relatively new standard that takes a slightly different approach to magnetic storage. In DAT storage, the recording/writing heads are attached to a cylindrical drum. The drum contains four sets of read/write heads. Figure 4-7 shows a picture of the rotating head and R/W heads. This technology is very similar in principle to how the read/write heads on a VCR operate. The advantage of DAT is that it is very high density for a small physical tape package. DAT tape has virtually replaced the reel-to-reel technology that was so prevalent in computer centers.

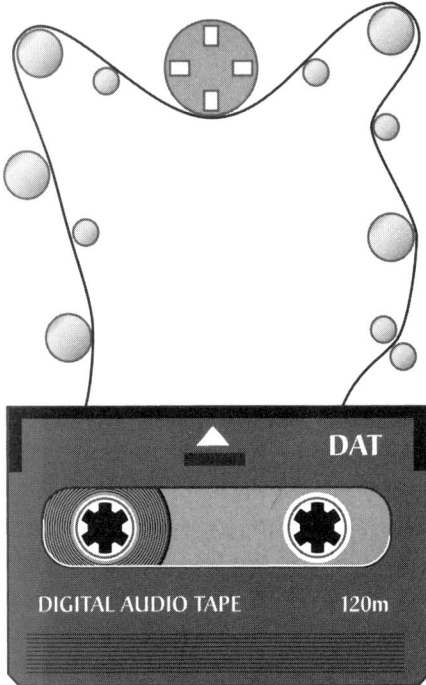

FIGURE 4-7   A DAT tape cartridge

Current DAT technology uses either 4 or 8mm media. Current 8mm DAT storage allows for 10GB of storage per cartridge. Current 4mm DAT drives with DDS-3 technology have a capacity of 20MB, or up to 40MB with hardware compression.

DAT technology is based upon a helical scan pattern. The tape head is slightly off center by 6 to 8 degrees. This puts the data at a slight angle (or azimuth angle). Figure 4-8 illustrates this. The tape head spins at approximately 2,000 rpm. DAT tape drives are considerably more complex than traditional tape drives, but are extremely reliable in most settings.

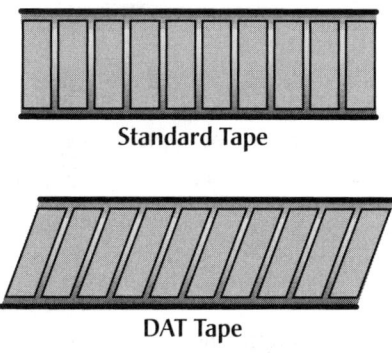

Standard Tape

DAT Tape

FIGURE 4-8 Azimuth angle of a tape

Preventative maintenance on a DAT drive can be a little complicated. The tolerances involved can require precision tools and calibration procedures. With DAT technology, the tape cartridges are relatively inexpensive, as the tight tolerances are built into the tape unit itself. In contrast, Travan (QIC) tapes are significantly more expensive, as the tight tolerances must be built into the tape cartridge itself because the tape drive operates at much looser tolerances. Most DAT systems provide a usage counter. This usage counter indicates when it is time to clean the drive. Our DAT drive manufacturer provided a cleaning cassette and solvent to be used along with it. Every few hundred times we load a tape into the drive, it lets us know that it is time to clean the drive. Beyond this cleaning cartridge, little more can be done by the end user.

Tape technology is the oldest method of magnetic storage. This technology continues to evolve and grow with the industry. Even so, tape technology is slowly being replaced by other technologies such as CD-R and DVD technology. It is highly unlikely that tape technologies will continue to serve reliably for many more years.

FLOPPY DISK STORAGE

Floppy disk storage provides a convenient way to move small amounts of data between computers. At present, two standards exist for computer disks: 5.25-inch and 3.5-inch disk drives, though the 5.25-inch standard is rapidly waning in popularity. The first floppy disks were 8 inches and could contain approximately 160K of information. These disks were somewhat delicate, but were extensively used in early 8088 computers.

Standard floppy storage capabilities are outlined in Table 4-1. One of the major advantages of the 3.5-inch drive is that the spindle, or center, is a rigid connection. The center area on a 5.25-inch drive, on the other hand, is a tension press when it is inserted in the drive. These floppies had a large amount of mechanical slop in them. In some cases, if a floppy wasn't working, you could rotate the floppy and try moving the center position. This often fixed the problem long enough to get the data off the floppy. The 3.5-inch high-density disk is currently the standard configuration delivered on most computer systems today, though its capacity of 1.44MB is inadequate for many file transfers, especially sound and graphics files.

The write protect on 3.5-inch drives is enabled by pushing a small tab on the back corner of the disk. On 5.25-inch drives, you have to use a piece of tape or a write-protect sticker to cover the notch. Most systems today are equipped only with a 3.5-inch drive.

TABLE 4-1 COMMON FLOPPY DISK STORAGE CAPABILITIES		
DISK TYPE	*CAPACITY*	*TRACKS PER INCH (TPI)*
5.25-inch double-density	360K	48
5.25-inch high-density	1.2MB	96
3.5-inch double-density	720K	135
3.5-inch high-density	1.44MB	135

The floppy disk drive mechanism is straightforward and consists of two heads. Most floppy disks in use today are two-sided. The speed that the floppy disk

rotates and the distance that the head travels are the primary mechanical considerations of the disk. The head moves in and out between tracks of the drive, controlled by a stepper motor.

Floppy drives have changed little in the last few years and are primarily used
to store small amounts of data or information. Floppy technology will be around
for many more years. For a technician, floppies are at times the most troublesome
component of the computer system. Floppy disks must be kept clean and free of
contamination. Though they look almost indestructible, a small speck of dirt or
dust can ruin them. Usually, a good cleaning using one of several cleaning kits will
restore operation of the contaminated floppy disk drive back to nominal levels.

Several other removable storage devices are available, though the market
hasn't clearly established which will ultimately replace the 3.5-inch floppy disk.
Iomega's Zip drive holds 100MB on a disk not much larger than a standard
3.5-inch floppy disk. The Zip drive is available in both internal and external models. The downside to the Zip drive is that it does not read standard 3.5-inch floppies, and thus can't serve as a complete replacement unit. On the other hand, the
Zip drive is widely popular. More Zip disks have been sold than any other high-
capacity removable disk.

Also popular is the LS-120 drive. The LS-120 drive, while not as widely used
as the Zip drive, holds 120MB per disk and can also read standard 3.5-inch floppy
disks. The most common determining factor in selecting between these drives is
determining what is in use at your destination. If you're submitting graphics to a
service bureau, you may be more likely to find Zip drives in use since they have
been available longer. Conversely, if you're simply trying to put as much information on a disk as possible to take home, and you'll buy whatever drive you need to
match the one at your office, the LS-120 may better suit your needs given the
thinner, higher capacity disks it uses.

Bridging the gap between floppy and hard drives is the Iomega Jaz drive. The
Jaz drive offers removable disks, slightly larger than a boxed CD-ROM, that are
available in one or two GB capacities. These replacement Jaz disks are competitive in price per MB to standard hard drives, and can be removed for security or
portability.

HARD DRIVE STORAGE

Hard drives are the backbone of information storage for most computer systems. The earlier sections of this chapter covered the theoretical considerations of disk storage. This section covers the various technologies currently in use. The cost of hard disk storage continues to keep falling. A few years ago, it would have cost you more than $1,000 for a 100MB hard drive. Recently, we purchased a 6.4GB disk drive for a little less than $300. With the addition of *disk compression software*, this drive could store almost 10GB.

Disk compression software enables the data to be organized or compressed more efficiently. This compression allows for anywhere from 1.25 to 2 times more efficient storage of disk information. The major drawback of disk compression is that the compression process requires additional computer power (for the data to be compressed and uncompressed) and the need for special utilities to repair and access compressed disk files. Given the extremely low cost of hard drive space today and the unnecessary complexity added by compression utilities, use of compression is less common now than it was a few years ago.

HDA

The *Hard-Disk Assembly* (HDA) includes the mechanical components of the hard drive: the spindle, heads, stepper motor, and drive electronics. The majority of the mechanical and electronic components are mounted in an airtight unit. This unit allows for constant air pressure and atmospheric conditions. Floppy disk and hard disk storage methods are almost identical.

One major difference, however, is the fact that the heads on a hard disk are not supposed to come into contact with the surface of a hard disk. The heads on a hard disk usually "fly" over the surface of the disk within a few thousands of an inch. This is caused by a small air current created by the turning disk. If the heads come into contact with the media, that is called a *disk crash*. It typically causes the destruction of the drive and the data it contains. In general, when that happens, all you can do is replace the drive. Proper operations of the systems, i.e., minimizing vibration, and proper startup and power down procedures, minimize the risk of a disk crash.

Disk assemblies are designed to fit into the drive bays of system units. The typical sizes of disk drives are 5.25 inches, 3.5 inches, and in the case of many laptop computers, 2.5 inches. These units are either attached to the side rails of the expansion units, in hangers, or directly onto the chassis of the unit. Figure 4-9 shows the most common mounting method used in PCs today. Many computer systems use standard disk units and install them with proprietary mounting hardware.

Figure 4-9 shows a case with several different types of mounting areas for disk drives. The computer case has steel cradles for 3.5-inch and 5.25-inch drives. Drives are slid into these openings, bolted to the sides, and if necessary (as for CD-ROMs and floppy drives), the drive bay cover is removed from the front of the case to expose the drive. This case also has slots for mounting five devices in the front. We prefer mid-tower and tower cases for their ease in adding and replacing drives — with the side of the case open, access is easy.

In general, drives are either snapped in or screwed in. A number of manufacturers, such as Compaq, require special mounting kits that must be purchased from an authorized Compaq dealer or mail order from Compaq.

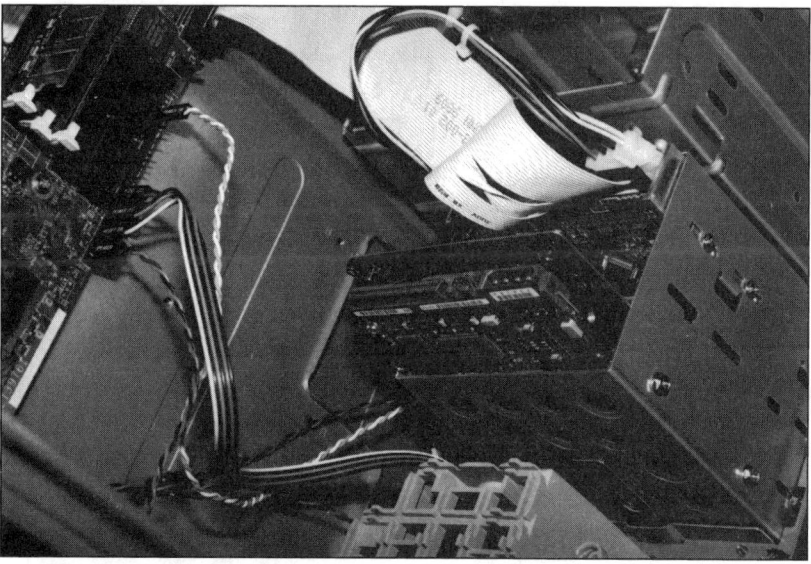

FIGURE 4-9 Hard drive mounting

Storage Formats

Disk drives store information in one of two formats today: RLL or MFM format. RLL stands for Run Length Limited, and MFM stands for Modified Frequency Modulation. MFM format is derived from the FM or Frequency Modulation method. FM stores information by changing the frequency of the signal. MFM format allows for better density of data storage than the older FM standard. Most of the new high-density drives use RLL format. Early drive storage methods for personal computers were built around the MFM format.

Drive Logic and Cabling

Disk drives are usually connected to the computer via a data and control cable. The data cable provides the connection to the controller board or circuitry, which connects the drive to the computer systems. Many motherboards include all of the necessary circuitry to directly connect the disk drive to the motherboard with no separate controller card needed. These motherboards are said to have an *integrated controller*. If the motherboard does not include the controller, add-on controllers can be purchased and installed in an expansion slot.

Disk drives are connected to the disk controller via a disk interface (see Figure 4-10). An early PC-based disk interface standard is called the ST-506 disk interface. The ST-506 was pioneered by Seagate Technologies. The ST-506 was adequate for slower 8-bit and early 16-bit computers. Now, however, new standards exist, such as the no longer common *Enhanced Small Device Interface* (ESDI), and the current *Integrated Drive Electronics* (IDE), and *Small Computer Systems Interface* (SCSI). The SCSI interface can function in much larger roles than the disk controller and will be covered in greater depth in Chapter 11. SCSI drives are considered the fastest and most expensive compared to IDE drives.

IDE allows you to connect up to two disk drives. The IDE drive interface was first introduced with the PC/AT computer system and is called the AT bus interface. IDE drives contain a great deal of the intelligence necessary to operate on the drive. This allows the disk drive to be highly optimized, which enables higher speeds of operation.

Most motherboards provide two connectors for hard drives and one for floppy drives. Some older systems may require a separate controller for IDE drives. Either way, the drive is still connected with a cable. The hard drive connectors are labeled *primary* and *secondary* IDE connectors. Normally, you should connect a drive to each of these cables before connecting them together. By doing this, you are able to take advantage of the speed of having the drives on both channels. However, in the case where a CD-ROM drive is connected to a secondary drive controller, you'll get better performance by putting two hard drives on the primary controller than by sharing the secondary between the CD-ROM and a hard drive.

IDE Connector   SCSI drive

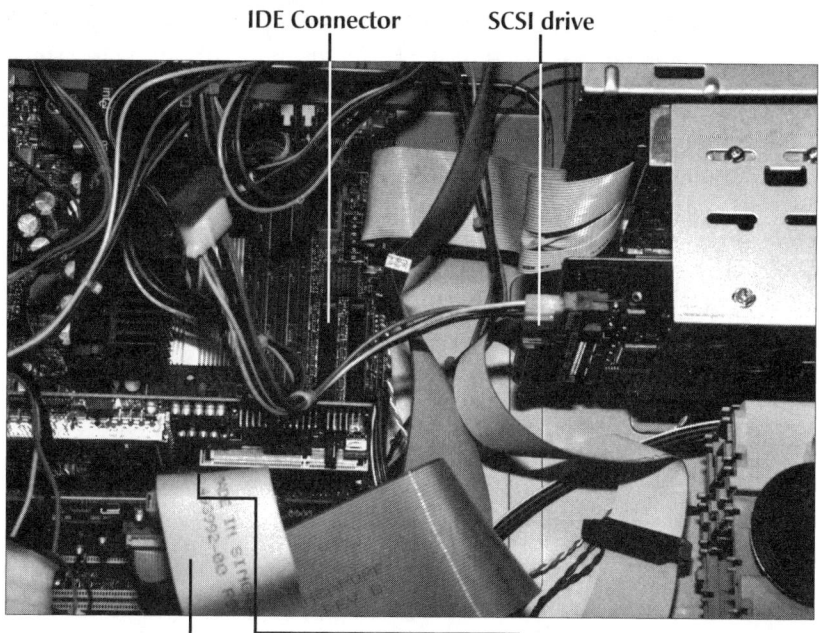

SCSI Adapter Card   SCSI Connector on adapter card

FIGURE 4-10 Disk drive interface

Newer motherboards are being shipped with a relatively new standard called the UltraATA interface. This interface is designed to take advantage of the newer high-speed drives. It seems that almost every year, a new or improved standard becomes available to end users.

DATA TRANSFER RATE

Disk speed is one of the critical factors most computer people use to measure performance, because virtually everything involved with end-user applications requires disk access. Several different measurements determine disk speed. This section briefly outlines those specifications and describes the impact they have on performance.

Access time is one of the terms you will hear used to describe disk performance. This term can have four different meanings: track-to-track, position, random, and full stroke. Full *track-to-track* access refers to the time it takes for the head to move from one track to an adjacent track. *Position* refers to the time it takes for the head to move from the current track to a randomly selected track. *Random* refers to the time it takes for the head to position to a completely random location anywhere on the disk. Random differs from position in that position starts from the current position, whereas random moves to a different "random" position and then repositions. *Full-stroke* time refers to the time it takes to move from track 0 to the maximum cylinder number, or the reverse.

The data transfer rate is also an essential component in the disk performance equation. Many computer manufacturers use a *burst rate* for data transfer rates. Burst rate refers to a situation where data is already on the disk cache and can be transmitted to main memory via the controller. This may not always be realistic. Here's a simple formula to explain this:

Internal data transfer rate = <u>Sectors/track * bytes/sector * rpm</u>

Interleave

Interleave refers to how the sectors are organized and used on the disk drive. In previous sections, we demonstrated that sector two follows sector one, and so on. This is true logically, but on a disk that is spinning at over 3,600 rpm, sector one is offset enough so that it can be read "sequentially" by the disk controller. This interleave is usually established and preformatted by the disk manufacturer for optimum performance.

Figure 4-11 illustrates the principle of interleaving. It takes a certain amount of time for the disk controller to finish reading the first sector and prepare to read the second. Interleaving provides a mechanism whereby the sectors appear to be next to each other, but are slightly offset using what is called the interleave. Interleaving is established during the low-level format, and the manufacturer provides optimum interleaving parameters. Many modern drives such as IDE have an interleave factor of 1:1, which means no offset. The IDE controller that is integrated on the drive assembly manages this offset.

As you can see from the formula above, the data transfer rate will be reasonably consistent for virtually any given situation, as opposed to a burst mode transfer rate which doesn't maintain a constant transfer rate.

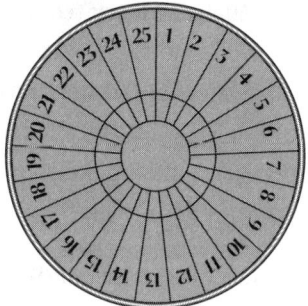

1:1 Interleave

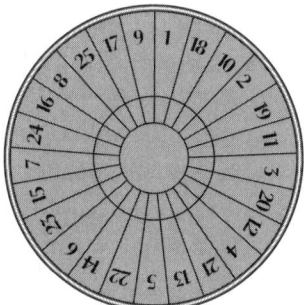

1:3 Interleave

FIGURE 4-11   An example of interleaving

Reliability

Reliability of hard disks is a major concern. If the hard drive for a computer fails, it virtually guarantees that work will stop. The most common measurement of reliability is Mean Time Between Failure, or MTBF. MTBF is the average number of hours between failures of a given device. Typically for hard drives, the MTBF should be measured in terms of years! A hard drive generally will not fail quickly once it has been burned in, unless something in the environment changes, such as power or vibration. In most cases, you can assure customers that a hard drive should offer at least three years of uninterrupted service, though the likelihood that a drive will last is inversely proportional to how frequently it is backed up — if you have a current backup, the drive never seems to fail. It has been our experience that computers that are left running usually have higher levels of reliability than computers that are turned on and off each day. Power-on/power-off cycles can be very traumatic on the motors and actuators associated with hard drives. Power surges and other power-related anomalies could also cause problems.

Disk storage options today provide the capability for redundancy. The systems we have described to this point have dealt with what is called a *SLED*, or single large expensive disk. The next section deals with an alternative technology called Redundant Array of Inexpensive Disks, or RAID.

exam
preparation
pointer

The RAID Advisory Board has adopted nine levels of RAID technology.

RAID

Disk storage technology is typically very reliable. When higher reliability of disk storage is required, devices called RAID drives, or Redundant Array of Inexpensive Disks, offer higher reliability and fault tolerance. RAID drives are usually special hardware units that can be used in place of a large single disk drive. Many servers use RAID technology for both performance and reliability purposes. Some operating systems such as Windows NT Server provide software RAID implementations. Most RAID environments, however, implement hardware-level RAID. Hardware RAID systems are simply plugged into the system and perform like any other drive, from the operating system's perspective. Software RAID is accomplished by providing utilities and interface mechanisms in the system. Hardware RAID is almost always faster, because the RAID controller manages all disk access to the RAID Array.

exam
preparation
pointer

The term RAID stands for Redundant Array of Inexpensive Disks.

The RAID Advisory Board, an industry board that sanctions or identifies standard RAID implementations, has adopted nine levels of RAID implementation. These levels of implementation start with RAID 0. Table 4-2 outlines some of the more popular RAID levels. Most hardware manufacturers use the RAID recommendations as the basis for their RAID implementations. While there are nine levels of RAID, most manufacturers have only implemented three or four of the RAID levels.

TABLE 4-2 CURRENT COMMONLY IMPLEMENTED RAID LEVELS	
RAID LEVEL	*NAME*
0	Disk Striping
1	Data Mirroring
3	Disk Striping by Byte with Error Correction
5	Disk Striping with Parity

RAID 0, or Disk Striping, is the process whereby data is spread out across multiple disk drives. RAID 0 is primarily a performance improvement rather than a fault tolerance mechanism, because a single drive failure will have the same consequences as a stand-alone drive failure.

RAID 1, or Disk Mirroring, is a mechanism whereby a second drive is added that is an exact copy of the primary disk. Disk Mirroring can either happen on the same controller or across multiple controllers. If the mirror disk is on a different controller, that is referred to as *Disk Duplexing*.

RAID 3, or Disk Striping by Byte with Error Correction, is an extremely fast method of redundancy for large files. RAID 3 is extremely popular in large file applications.

RAID 5, or Disk Striping with Parity, writes parity across all of the disks as well as the data.

In RAID 1, 3, and 5, if a drive malfunctions in the RAID array, the drive can be replaced with no data loss. This is not true in RAID 0.

Error Recovery Strategies

Over time, all disks go bad. As the old saying goes, "It isn't a matter of whether or not you will have a disk failure, but when!" Anybody who has worked in this industry has many horror stories to share about how they lost weeks of work, months of work, or even years of work. The plain and simple fact is, you will eventually have to deal with disk failures and you have limited options, period.

The first line of defense against disk failures is a backup scheme. Data files should be backed up on a regular basis and stored off the machine. Tape backup, or even floppy backup of critical information can accomplish this.

The second line of defense against disk failures is to run whatever diagnostic programs are included with your operating system on a regular basis. If you notice that you are consistently logging disk errors, this might be a strong indication that a failure is imminent. Most disk drives give you plenty of warning before they become inoperable.

The third line of defense is to purchase a data recovery tool. There are several in the market and to a certain extent they all work.

The last line of defense is to send a failed disk out to a data recovery center to attempt to read the data from this disk. We have had to do this several times in the last few years, with mixed results. Recognize that in this situation, you may be spending thousands of dollars to recover the information on the disk, with no guarantee that it will work. One company we worked with had a complete electronic scrub room in which drives were disassembled and reassembled, in an attempt to recover data. We only pray that you will never have to face this situation, because it is literally like watching a hospital soap opera, complete with high-voltage machines.

RAID technology is to a certain extent able to minimize data loss in servers and other mission-sensitive computer systems. For most end users, though, it is prohibitively expensive. The simplest and most cost effective way to protect your data is to do regular backups.

 A good rule of thumb is to back up often, store copies away from your computer, and do it regularly. Back up, back up, back up.

KEY POINT SUMMARY

Chapter 4 introduced the components of magnetic storage. Most computer systems today and into the future will use some form of disk storage mechanism. Many different options exist today, with more coming.

o Disk drives work by moving a disk read/write head in and out on a moving surface called a platter. The head in most disk drives does not make contact with the surface of the disk. When this happens unintentionally, this is called a *head crash* or *disk crash* and it usually destroys the disk and its data.

o Data on disk drives is oriented in storage units called *tracks, sectors, clusters,* and *cylinders.* These units allow the disk drive hardware and software to move larger amounts of data at one time and allow for data organization. These parameters are usually configured when the disk is first prepared for usage (low-level format).

o Data on disks is usually organized into units called *blocks* and *files.* Files, file names, and addresses are usually managed by the operating system. Blocks refer to the amount of data that is physically read into or written from memory at one time.

o File access is accomplished using either *sequential* or *random access* techniques. Sequential access techniques are similar to how an audiocassette is played, from start to end. Random access is more representative of how a music CD can be used, as the user can quickly jump around to any track they choose.

o The mechanism for breaking a single large disk down into smaller logical disks is called *partitioning.* Most operating systems allow big drives to be partitioned into one or more smaller drives.

exam
preparation
pointer  **Most versions of DOS prior to release 4.0 support a maximum partition size of 32MB.**

o Digital tape provides a mechanism for high volumes of data to be stored and removed from the computer system. This may be valuable for backup purposes or for archival purposes. Data is read to and written from this type of media sequentially.

o QIC format is an analog storage mechanism used by many inexpensive tape formats. QIC followed by a number (for example, QIC-120) indicates the storage amount of the tape. The number 120 represents approximately 120MB of data. Current limits of QIC tape is slightly more than 2GB of data.

o DAT format is a digital tape standard that allows for higher volumes of storage on a DAT tape. DAT tapes are more complex and some units can store upwards of 20GB of data on a single tape.

o Removable disks such as floppy disks allow for small amounts of data to be stored or transferred. The current standard used by most computers is the 3.5-inch high-density 1.44MB floppy disk.

o The two standard formats of hard disk storage are MFM and RLL. RLL is used in most drives available today. The current interfaces used by many disk manufacturers today are IDE and SCSI.

o *Data transfer rate* and *reliability* are two of the primary means for measuring disk performance. Data transfer rates are evaluated using criteria that include full-stroke, track-to-track, position, or random. Reliability is measured in hours in the form of MTBF.

o RAID storage systems provide redundancy by enabling multiple disk drives to store data. Another method of preventing data loss is called a backup plan. Critical files and information should always be backed up onto another drive or tape, in case of a disk error.

APPLYING WHAT YOU'VE LEARNED

This chapter has covered a lot of important material that will help you prepare for the A+ exam and be a competent technician. Take a few minutes and work through the Instant Assessment questions, review your notes, and see how you did.

The Hands-on lab will also help build your comfort level with the hardware, as well as reinforce the readings from this chapter.

Instant Assessment

Multiple choice

Choose the best answer(s). There may be more than one correct answer for each question.

1. The component of a disk drive that reads and writes data to the disk is called a(n):

A. Spindle

B. Idler arm

    C. Access mechanism

    D. Head

2. Disk drive technology is based upon the following principle:

    A. Magnetism

    B. Capacitance

    C. Transductance

    D. Luminescence

3. Data is organized using the following organization mechanisms:

    A. Tracks, drums, sectors clusters

    B. Tracks, sectors, clusters, cylinders

    C. Heads, tracks, sectors, rings

    D. Phalanx mechanism, cylinders, clusters, rings

4. A disk block is one of the following:

    A. A logical grouping of heads

    B. A physical collection of devices

    C. The area of data that is contained in one cylinder

    D. A logical gathering of information

5. A logical grouping of information that is stored on a disk is called a(n):

    A. Input device

    B. Floppy disk

    C. File

    D. I/O unit

6. Disks can be broken down into areas called _____ that look like different drives:

    A. Sectors

    B. File Allocation Tables

    C. Terabytes

    D. Partitions

7. Reel-to-reel devices read data:

    A. Randomly

    B. Serially

    C. Sequentially

    D. Sporadically

8. Two types of common tape formats are:

    A. Stringy and analog

    B. DAT and QIC

    C. Floppy and variable

    D. Fixed and variable

9. RAID is an acronym for:

    A. Redundant Array of Inexpensive Disks

    B. Really Awful Individual Diets

    C. Replacement Assistance for Independent Drives

    D. Rapid Access Intermediate Device

10. One of the best mechanisms for preventing data loss is:

    A. Disk swapping

    B. Parity stripping

    C. Tape backup

    D. Quantum Data Replacement, or QDR

Fill in the blank

1. Digital storage technology stores data using _____ and _____ magnetic polarities.

2. Disk drive platters rotate on a _____.

3. A cylinder is a collection of _____ across one or more platters.

4. The _____ maintains information on available and used areas on a disk.

5. _____ tape units have heads attached in a cylindrical drum.

6. The current 3.5-inch floppy used in PCs can store _____of data.

7. The two common storage formats used in disks are _____ and _____.

8. An early standard for storage is the _____ disk interface.

9. Reliability is measured using _____.

10. RAID disk storage provides data redundancy by using _____ disk drives in parallel.

Hands-on Lab Exercise

This lab will demonstrate the installation of disk drives and cables into the system we started building. At the end of this lab, you should be able to install and configure your hard disks.

caution

It is very important, when working with the types of cables we will be working with, that you do not force them onto the pins. They have a tendency to bend and are a pain to straighten.

Let's get going!

Lab 4.2 *Installing a hard drive*

We are going to be installing a hard drive with an Adaptec 2940U2W controller card and a floppy drive onto the motherboard's floppy interface.

Tools required

- Phillips Head screwdriver
- Static strap

Operating system

Decide where to mount the drive. As a convention, the floppy drive gets mounted in the topmost available bay that it will fit, which in our case is the top of the 3.5-inch bays in the lower part of the case. We will mount the hard drive in the lowest 3.5-inch bay, leaving space between it and the floppy drive to help airflow and cooling. Figure 4-12 shows the Adaptec SCSI card. The Adaptec card is slid gently into the top available PCI slot, and its bracket screwed down. We will connect the cables with the red stripe being on Pin 1. This is a convention that we will follow from here on out.

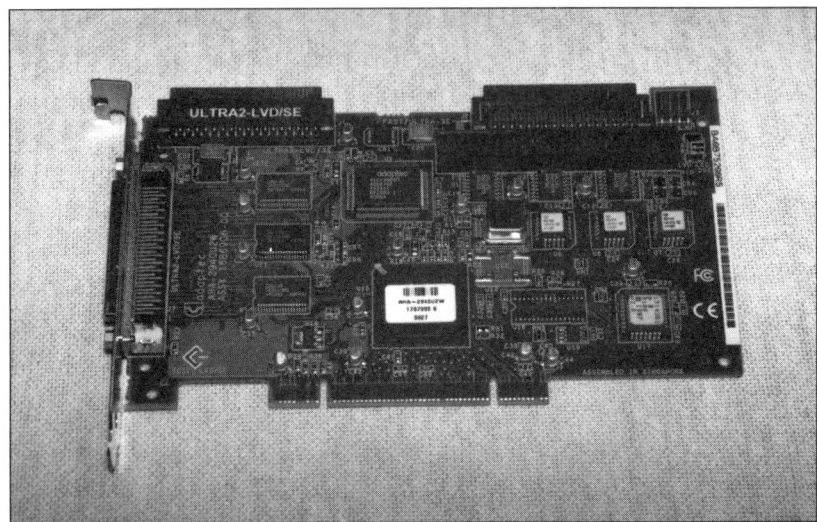

FIGURE 4-12 Adaptec 2940U2W SCSI controller card

The floppy drive connector is immediately next to the power connector shown in Chapter 3.

We will be connecting the hard drive to the Adaptec card. The power supply for the hard drive must also be connected to the drive. The power cord is a four-wire connector that plugs into the back of the drive. You will have your choice of two different types of connectors. Pick the one that works with each device and plug them in.

The hard drive will also require some configuration in order to work properly. First we have to ensure that the SCSI ID jumpers on the back of the drive are configured properly. We will configure this drive to be SCSI ID 0, which is reserved for boot drives. The Seagate Cheetah drive is shipped set to ID 0 as a default, so no change was needed.

Figure 4-13 is a photo of the back of the Seagate Cheetah drive. As you can see, you must connect the power supply, the SCSI cable, and the jumper for the configuration. The jumper configurations for your drive will be explained in the instruction manual that comes with the drive. If you get stuck with this, don't be afraid to ask the person you purchased it from.

Earlier in this chapter you saw a floppy disk drive being mounted into one of the slots, so we won't waste your time by showing you again.

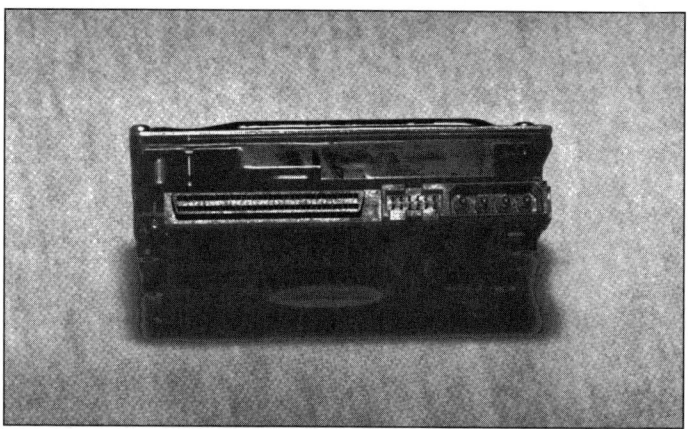

FIGURE 4-13 The back of a disk drive for configuration and cables

At this point, your system should have a floppy disk, a hard disk, a keyboard, memory, and a video board connected to it. You have a system that should be functionally ready to be powered up and the hard disk formatted.

When you turn your system on, the start screen should indicate what devices are present on your computer. After a moment, the light on the floppy drive should go on. It should then go off, as no operating system is loaded.

We are going to go ahead and put the boot floppy in drive A. This will bring up the setup and installation program for Windows 95. We will need to perform an FDISK on our hard drive to partition it and make it ready. FDISK is the disk utility program that partitions and allocates storage units on Windows 95 systems. This is explained in the DOS sections in greater detail in Chapters 17 through 19 of this book.

We will also need to format the hard disk to get it ready for installation. The format program prepares the disk for the storage of data on a Windows 95 system. This is covered in greater detail in Chapters 17 through 19 of this book.

If for some reason you are having problems with your system, check the most common and obvious areas:

1. Are all the cables plugged in and oriented correctly? Remember, Pin 1 will always be what you orient your cables with. The red stripe or band on your cable should always be on Pin 1.

2. Check the SCSI ID jumpers on the hard drive. Are they set to zero?

If you are still having problems, review your BIOS manual and ensure that all of the parameters are configured properly. Again, don't be afraid to call the place where you bought the motherboard and ask for their help.

Good luck and congratulations on completing this lab!

Optical Storage, CD-ROMs, and Multimedia Components

About Chapter 5

This chapter explores optical storage technologies available to PC users today. It covers CD-ROMs, optical disks, and a relatively new technology, the DVD (which stands for either Digital Versatile Disk or Digital Video Disk, depending on whose story you're listening to). First we introduce optical and laser storage technologies and look at the two primary technologies used today. Then we discuss multimedia and multimedia file types. This chapter also explores the various physical characteristics or properties of the various storage media. Finally, we look at configuration and evaluation options.

OPTICAL STORAGE TECHNOLOGIES

Optical storage technologies use light or heat to store information on a physical disk or media. Even though we will be presenting them in the same chapter, CDs are not the same as other optical disks. CD-ROMs are, with the exception of the CD-Recordable (or CD-R), read-only devices, whereas most of the optical disk types can be recorded and re-recorded.

The most common optical storage technologies you will encounter are optical disk, CD-ROM, and DVD. Optical disk is the oldest of the technologies, but CD-ROM is the most commonly used technology for both computer and entertainment purposes. The DVD is the newest of the disk storage technologies available and provides all of the capabilities of the CD-ROM as well as significantly larger storage capacity.

The two major types of optical drives are *optical* and *magneto-optical* drives. Optical drives fall into three general classes: erasable, write-once, and read-only. *Erasable* drives can be erased and recorded over again multiple times, whereas the *write-once* drive can have data written onto it once, but can be read many times. *Read-only* disks are written once, at the time of manufacturing, and can be read a virtually unlimited number of times.

Optical storage such as the CD-ROM are based on a laser light etching made into the media, where reflective surfaces, or flats, and non-reflective surfaces, or pits, contain the digital information. *Magneto-optical,* or MO, drives use magnetic recording technology coupled with laser technology. Lasers heat the storage media and polarize the storage locations. This makes the storage permanent until heat is applied to the media again. MO drives are covered in more detail in the next few paragraphs. Both optical and MO drives provide high-density storage that is difficult to achieve with purely magnetic drives. Virtually all optical media can be removed from the computer, as opposed to hard drives, which are typically non-removable.

Erasable optical disk systems use what is called *phase change*. Phase change technology uses a high-intensity laser at close range to alter the media. Magneto-optical drives are read magnetically, but are written with the use of a laser. Their magnetic state isn't easy to alter, unlike a floppy disk. The laser resets the magnetic properties of the rewritable disk to record new data. This resistance to alteration is a benefit of the MO disks, because they can be carried or stored with little concern for accidental data loss.

The primary advantage of MO media is its capacity for very high-density storage. The primary disadvantage is that MO technology is relatively slow, requiring two passes to rewrite a disk. In addition, after 500,000 erasures, the media may become unreliable. In a normal small office environment, this media life cycle is unlikely to be a huge issue. To overcome this minor drawback, the disk software drivers are designed to minimize repeated exposures and erasures of sectors. This spreads the write activity across the disk, thus reducing the potential for "bad spots" to appear on the disk or media.

The write-once, or WORM (Write Once Read Many), drive is designed for archiving or long-term information storage. WORM technology works on the principle that data can be stored on the disk once and read many times. This drive enables iterative versions of a document to be stored without overwriting the original, since WORM drives cannot overwrite previously recorded material. The WORM drive uses one of two technologies: *ablative WORM*, or *continuous composite write* (CCW).

- Ablative WORM, the traditional method of WORM storage, physically writes optical information to the drive. If the material needs updating, it must be read back into the computer from the disk, changed, and the updated information rewritten or stored to another location on disk.

- *Continuous composite write* (CCW) is a type of storage method that uses an MO drive to store information. The drive mechanism and controller make sure that valid information is not rewritten, making the drive appear to operate as a WORM drive.

Read-only storage refers to the fact that data or information cannot be altered or changed by the computer using the disk. For example, a movie could be stored on a disk. You would probably not want this movie to be altered by accident. By distributing the movie on read-only storage medium such as a CD-ROM, the movie or data would be read-only.

CD-ROM Storage

The CD-ROM (Compact Disk Read Only Memory) drive is standard equipment on almost all new computers sold today. CD-ROMs provide more than 600MB of storage in a small package, and they are relatively inexpensive to manufacture. The drive can be used to play standard audio CDs, as well as to store data or digital applications. Newer operating systems such as Windows NT all but require a CD, as do most of the new applications software packages. Given the sheer size of programs today, floppy disk installation of a program that requires 20 to 30 MB of hard drive space would require shuffling floppy disks for hours. Software is now distributed on CD, with allowances made for floppy disk distribution, but in many cases floppy disk versions of software cost more than CD-ROM versions. Given that CD-ROM drives can be purchased for under $50, we don't recommend that anyone do without a CD-ROM drive in their PC.

The CD-ROM was introduced as a replacement for the audiocassette and phonograph record in the early 1980s. CDs offer higher-quality sound and higher reliability than the cassette or LP, since the data is stored digitally and there is no physical contact with the player to wear out the recording medium. Many stereo manufacturers rapidly accepted this technology and made it available inexpensively on stereo systems. The computer industry quickly adopted CD-ROM technology because it was a relatively inexpensive information storage media.

CD-ROMs store information, whether music or data, in a digital format. Digital storage allows music recorded digitally to be static free, whereas analog storage devices such as audiocassette are prone to distortion and static.

CD-ROM Media

CD-ROM media is a read-only optical storage device. The CD, composed of a clear plastic disk with a layer of aluminum and a lacquer layer, stores information on the disc using flats and pits to reflect or disperse (respectively) the laser light shined on them by the player, as shown in Figure 5-1.

note **A single 5-inch diameter CD can store 650MB of data, or 74 minutes of audio.**

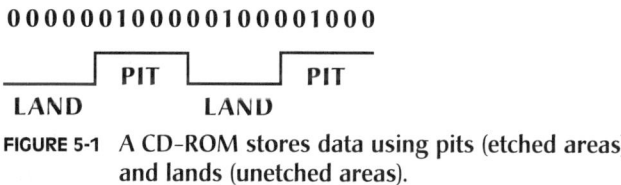

FIGURE 5-1 A CD-ROM stores data using pits (etched areas) and lands (unetched areas).

The data on a CD-ROM is organized into a single spiral from the outside of the disk to the inside. This spiral is organized into units of time such as minutes, seconds, and tenths of seconds instead of tracks and sectors, which is how magnetic media is organized.

A CD-ROM is mass-produced by creating a master CD on a copper or other photosensitive material. The data is burned onto the master by a laser beam. The master is then developed using photochemical processes. A *reverse disk* is pressed from this master, creating a disk with a series of pits and lands. This reverse disk is the equivalent of a photo negative. The reverse disk can then be pressed under high pressure against a blank CD, thus creating a "positive" CD. The new CD is then coated to protect it from scratches and dents. The aluminum layer is a reflective coating that returns the beam to the sensor. The polycarbonate layer of the CD-ROM is the center of the CD-ROM, which holds the aluminum layer and coatings. The mechanical strength of the CD-ROM comes from this polycarbonate layer.

The data on a CD-ROM can be stored almost indefinitely with little maintenance. CD-ROMs are not sensitive to moisture, weather conditions, or magnetism.

CD-ROMs are inexpensive to manufacture — in several thousand-unit quantities they can be produced for less than 50 cents per copy. A type of master disk called a *glass master* is a higher-quality master that costs a few hundred dollars to initially create, and is good for many thousands of copies.

CD-ROM Drive Types

CD-ROM drives connect to a controller card that looks like a disk drive. This controller card connects to the computer motherboard and interfaces the CD-ROM to the computer. Typically, the drive is connected via either a SCSI or IDE interface. SCSI, or Small Computer Systems Interface, is a high-performance standard and IDE, or Integrated Drive Electronics, is a connection standard used in many PCs today. Early CD-ROMs had a disk transfer speed of 150K. This speed was adequate for data access. Modern drives, however, have speeds in excess of ten times that 150K transfer rate. These drive speeds are represented by an X (which stands for *times*) designation, such as 2X, 4X, and so on. For most applications, a 2X or better drive is required.

CD-ROM drives accept media in one of two ways — with or without a caddy, or disk holder. Most of the early CD-ROM drives used a caddy, whereas most current drives work with a tray or are trayless. (Trayless drives simply have an opening, like a car CD player, into which you insert the CD.) The caddy is becoming increasingly rare in newer systems.

CD-ROM drives have a laser and a sensor. When the sensor reads a reflection, the drive outputs a 0; when a reflection does not occur, it is assumed that a 1 has been returned. The laser is very low power and works in the near-infrared wavelength. CD-ROM drives are highly reliable and require little maintenance.

CD-ROM drives can usually play audio recordings. Most CD-ROM drives have a separate connector for the audio output from the CD to the sound card multimedia board. Many computer manufacturers provide a set of software tools to play audio tracks on the system multimedia speakers or headsets; Windows 95 also includes this software. The CD-ROM audio is fed into a sound card via an analog cable on the back of the drive.

Several different types of CD audio cables are available, but the Multimedia PC, or MPC, standards defined by the Multimedia PC Marketing Council specify a four-wire cable connector. However, it is always a good idea to check this in the documentation, as not all CD drive manufacturers meet this standard. There are as many cable standards as there are CD drive manufacturers. Figure 5-2 shows a picture of this four-wire cable attached to the CD. If this cable is not attached to the sound card, the drive will support digital or data processing applications, but will not play audio CDs through the system. If equipped with a headphone jack (as many CD drives are), a CD player that isn't connected to the sound card can still be used to listen to music. External CD-ROMs do not usually support an audio connection, though they will work with headphones if equipped with a jack.

FIGURE 5-2 The small cable connection on the back of the CD-ROM drive connects the audio output of the CD-ROM to the computer's sound system.

In the audio world, CD players evolved into multiple CD players and CD changers. This changer concept is being adapted to computer applications. Changers can hold anywhere from 5 to 200 CDs. Unfortunately, only one CD can be used or accessed at a time. Many newer operating systems, including Windows 95, provide support for several types of CD changers. Changers can sometimes be chained together, allowing for access to more than one CD at a time.

CD players have seen major progress in speed and cost in a relatively short amount of time. Today, they cost less than $100 and are 12X their original speed or beyond. CDs have virtually replaced floppy disks for software and large-scale data distribution.

CD-Recordable (CD-R)

Recently, a new form of CD called a CD-R has entered the market. As its name suggests, the CD-R is a recordable media. These machines read CDs like a normal CD player. They differ in their construction, however, because of the addition of a dye layer (shown in Figure 5-3). The dye is clear until a laser strikes the dye. The laser beam darkens the dye, simulating a pit in the media. In essence, each CD-R becomes a master disk. The major disadvantage with CD-R technology is that the CD is relatively sensitive to light and has a tendency to wear out more quickly in comparison to regular CD-ROM or MO technologies. Additionally, some older CD-ROM players are not able to read CD-R media.

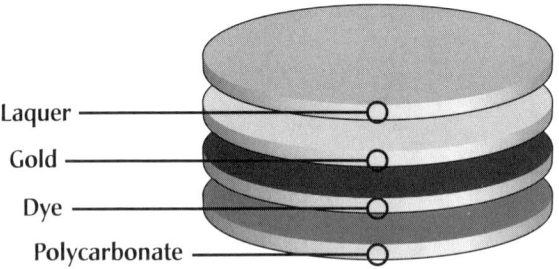

Laquer
Gold
Dye
Polycarbonate

FIGURE 5-3 Recordable CD-ROM with a dye layer

Despite these minor drawbacks, the CD-R process provides the ability to create a single copy relatively inexpensively and quickly. Thus, these drives are sometimes called *one-off* machines. CD-Rs are also useful for beta software distribution and low-quantity releases. The price of CD-R disks has fallen from more than $6 per CD to less than $2 as of this writing. A CD-R takes anywhere from 5 to 75 minutes to burn. The initial CD-R drives cost more than $1,200, but are now below $300, with $400 being about the middle of the line for quality.

CD-Rs are used extensively for testing and runs of less than 500 units of production. At those levels of production, it is inefficient and somewhat cost prohibitive to have a regular CD burn made. A large part of the expense associated would be in making the glass master and setup charges.

CD-ROM Standards

Several standards or specifications exist for CD-ROMs. Most of these standards are compatible with each other. Technicians generally are not required to know or use this information, as it mainly deals with standards and software/hardware design issues. Nevertheless, it may be helpful to know which documents form the basis for CD-ROM and multimedia standards. Documentation for CD formats exists in a series of books known by the color of their covers:

- The *Red Book* standard defines the layout of audio CDs. This is also called CD Digital Audio. The Red Book standard is also known as the ISO 10149 standard.

- The *Yellow Book*, in common use today, deals with CD-ROMs and includes the ISO 9660 format. ISO 9660 specifies the format of the directory structure, or the way information is stored and organized on a CD. The Yellow Book is also known as the High-Sierra format.

- The *Green Book*, or CD-I (CD-Interactive) format, is a standard put together by Philips and Sony. CD-I format requires a special player that is not compatible with normal CD players. CD-I allows for large amounts of data to be stored in a compressed format.

- The *White Book*, or Video CD format, is a standard for full-motion video. This format uses a compression scheme called *Moving Pictures Experts Group* (MPEG). MPEG-1 is the format used for Video CDs. Most Pentium computers work well with MPEG, though slower machines may require an MPEG board to keep the CPU from bogging down.

- The *Orange Book* deals with write-once technology and also covers the photo CD that was a standard used by Kodak to digitize 35mm slides or negatives onto CD. Early photo CDs had the ability to record only one session of films on the CD. Current CD-ROM drives can read multiple session of photos and are called multi-session drives. The Orange Book standard was developed jointly by Philips and Sony.

- The *Blue Book* covers multi-session CDs, which can hold music and data on one CD. It is currently being supported by Microsoft for video CDs as its CD-Plus format.

Installing and Configuring CD-ROM Drives

Installing CD-ROM drives is usually a straightforward process and is the subject of the lab at the end of this chapter. Typically, on the back of the drive you'll find a power cable, data cable, audio cable, and a series of jumpers. DVD, which is covered later in this chapter, can also be used to play CD-ROMs and is installed like a CD-ROM.

The CD-ROM, depending on the type of drive standard it adheres to, will either be installed into a SCSI chain using a connector on the SCSI cable or onto an IDE chain. As with other SCSI devices, which are covered more extensively in Chapter 7, you will need to specify the SCSI address. In the case of an IDE chain, you must determine whether the device is a Master or Slave drive. For IDE drives, this is usually the most difficult determination you will have to make.

A simple rule of thumb for IDE CD-ROMs is to configure them as a Slave on the IDE channel unless they are the only device on the IDE channel. Most motherboards manufactured provide dual IDE attachments. Each of these adapters can usually support two physical devices. If the CD-ROM is the only device on the attachment, set the CD-ROM as a Master. If it is sharing the attachment with a disk drive, set it as a Slave. If possible, attach the CD-ROM to the secondary IDE connector, since installing it as a Slave drive to a hard drive may adversely impact the performance of the hard drive.

The CD-ROM drive has a power connector that must be plugged into a power supply cable. The CD-ROM drive also provides a long connector with dual rows of pins that attaches to the IDE adapter. Generally, these cables are either keyed to prevent backwards installation, or have one wire that is color coded with a single color stripe to identify Pin 1. This cable will either be plugged into an IDE adapter on the motherboard or on an expansion card. The last connector present on most CD-ROMs is for connection to a multimedia or audio card. This connector, usually two- or three-wire, allows music and audio to be played on the computer systems sound card.

SCSI CD-ROM connections are virtually identical to the IDE connection, with the exception of the necessity to configure a unique address for the drive, either by setting the SCSI ID in software or with a jumper setting, as detailed in the manual provided with the SCSI device.

In other words, the installation and configuration of CD-ROMs is generally a quick and painless process. The major areas of difficulty in installing CD-ROMs revolve around the Master/Slave jumper or the Addressing jumper/switch. Plugging the data cable in backwards prevents the CD-ROM from operating, but will not damage the unit.

WORM Disk Storage

Optical disk storage is a broad topic that includes CD-ROMs and videodisks. However, when referring to optical disk, we're referring primarily to magneto-optical drives, the *Write Once Read Many* (WORM) technology, and the already discussed CD-R. Optical disks have greater disk storage capacity than do magnetic disk media. The higher-density storage potential exists because of the high precision of laser technology. Laser disks also have a 30-year life expectancy and are much less susceptible to heat and cold than magnetic disks.

The most common type of optical drive uses magneto-optical, or MO, technology. MO technology uses both magnetic and optical technology (see Figure 5-4). Writing is accomplished using a laser to heat a bit or binary digit and a magnet to align it. Reading is accomplished using a low-power laser similar to CD-ROM.

Writing to the disk is accomplished in two passes. The first pass or rotation sets the bits to zero, thus clearing it out. The second pass or rotation writes the data to the disk.

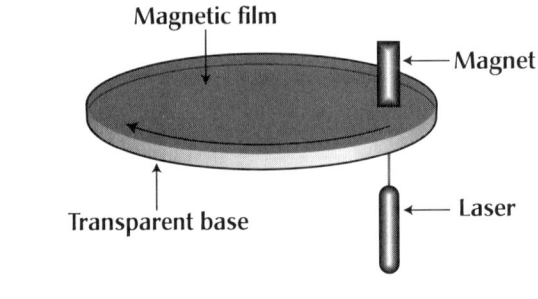

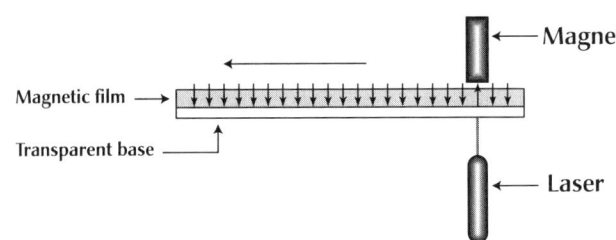

FIGURE 5-4 Reading and writing data on an MO drive

A new process changes the alignment or rotation of the magnetic data bit clockwise or counterclockwise. This process, called the Kerr effect, significantly speeds up the process of writing data.

Data transfer rates of optical disks are relatively poor when compared to magnetic drives. Typically, access time is 50 milliseconds for an optical disk, as opposed to 18 milliseconds for a magnetic drive. This transfer speed is made up for by the fact that an MO disk can accommodate 30,000 tracks. This allows for highly dense *tracks per inch* (TPI), as opposed to lower-density *bits per inch* (BPI), usually the measurement of magnetic disk storage. Optical disks can store anywhere from five to one hundred times the amount of data in the same storage area as a magnetic disk.

Much conjecture exists about the future of storage technology. Some people believe that the MO disk will eventually replace the magnetic disk, but this would require significant performance and cost improvements to MO drives.

DIGITAL VERSATILE DISK

A new type of disk has recently entered the market called the Digital Versatile Disk, or DVD. DVD uses a two-sided disk that looks almost identical to a CD-ROM. The exciting part of this new technology is the fact that a DVD can store in excess of 4.7GB of data.

Most DVD players can read CD-ROMs, and can replace a CD-ROM player in a computer system. It is important to note that in current DVD technology, the disk is two-sided and each side has two playback surfaces. In essence, the two-sided disk has four playing surfaces. This is accomplished by having the laser focus on one of two depths on the disk.

This four playing surface capability, coupled with other improvements, gives the disk the ability to store more than four times the amount of data of a typical CD-ROM. Table 5-1 shows the storage capacity and playing times of each of the various standards implemented in DVD today. Figure 5-5 shows the manner in which information is recorded on DVD disks. Because of the advances made with the laser manufacturing process, the storage density of DVD drives is very impressive.

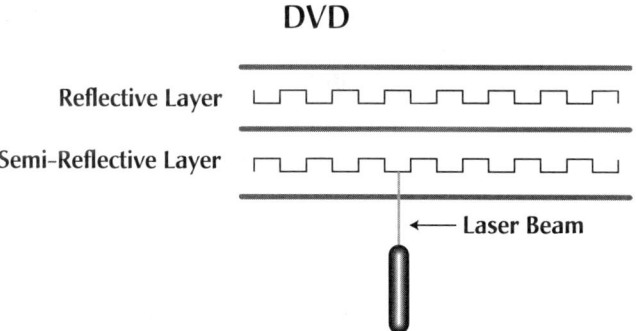

FIGURE 5-5   DVD uses both sides of the disk and two depths on each side. This gives DVD the capability to store massive amounts of data on a single disk.

TABLE 5-1 DVD Capacity and Playing Time				
Standard	*Capacity*	*Playing Time*	*Sides*	*Layers*
DVD-5	4.7GB	133 minutes	1	1
DVD-9	8.5GB	240 minutes	1	2
DVD-10	9.4GB	266 minutes	2	1
DVD-18	17.0GB	480 minutes	2	2

As you can see from the table, the DVD-5 standard playing time is roughly equivalent to a standard full-length movie. The original DVD-5 disk was designed for just that purpose. DVD has two additional important advantages over videotape. First, DVD signals and storage are digital and hence are largely immune to noise and distortion. Also, data on DVD can be accessed randomly instead of merely sequentially. This random access allows for instant access to any information stored on the DVD. The audio track on a typical movie DVD can also contain eight channels of audio, which allows for movie theater quality sound instead of just stereo (two-channel) sound. Most VCR tapes contain either two or four channels of audio. Many video stores and computer stores are starting to carry DVD disks of popular movies as an alternative to videotapes.

Sony, Philips, and Toshiba jointly developed DVD standards. Toshiba developed the actual disk technology, while Sony and Philips agreed upon the format. The significance of this union is that Sony was the creator of the Betamax standard and Philips is the spokesman for the VHS format. The VHS versus Betamax controversy in the videocassette market cost many consumers hundreds of dollars after Betamax players became obsolete and useless. In the DVD situation, the decision to implement a standard occurred before the product went to market, hopefully sparing consumers this type of difficulty again.

This agreement has a direct impact on the consumer, as it ensures that the format will have widespread acceptance in the industry. Internal DVD systems are available now for less than $300 and prices are expected to continue to fall sharply over the next two to three years.

DVD systems are now available as stand-alone units that can be directly connected to a television or monitor, or they can be an integral part of a computer system. The stand-alone DVD typically has a remote control similar to a VCR remote, and the computer-based unit will most likely have a series of programs that are designed to manage the player.

Optical Disk and CD-ROM Cleaning

In general, optical disk drives require little maintenance. If a sensor somehow becomes dirty, little can be done to remedy it beyond blowing it clean with compressed air except to replace it. To prevent the drive from becoming dirty, the CD or optical disk should be clean and dry before it is used. If the CD has smudges or scratches, the drive will be unable to read the information. Typically, the best way to clean a CD is to use a soft tissue or cloth. CDs can become scratched easily and care should be taken when handling them.

Here are some general guidelines for the care of CDs:

1. Always hold the CD on the edges. If your hand can't reach from edge to edge, use the center hole.

2. Use a soft cotton towel to clean smudges from a CD. Wipe the smudges from the center outwards to avoid scratching the disk.

3. Never use chemicals on a CD unless they are specifically designed for them. Do not use window cleaner, terminal cleaner, or any other abrasive cleaners on a CD. These types of cleaners can either scratch the protective coat or interact with the protective materials on the CD.

4. Don't stack CDs on top of each other — they can scratch each other and become ruined.

5. Do not leave CDs in direct sunlight. Sunlight can cause your disk to become unreadable.

6. Do not store CDs in areas of high heat. This can damage them, as CDs are somewhat heat sensitive.

7. Do not use labels or stickers on a CD unless they are designed specifically for CDs. The glue can interact with the protective cover and cause damage. In some CD-ROM players, the label may cause an imbalance, causing premature wear on the player.

In general, it is not feasible to repair a scratched or damaged CD. Normally, the only thing that can be done is to replace it. Early CDs had a tendency to fail often; this was called *CD rot* and was caused by a number of factors, including the interaction between the inks used and the media. Today, this should not be a problem.

Multimedia Cards

Early PCs had a simple speaker and tone generator. This speaker was frequently the only indicator that the computer was either functioning or malfunctioning. If you were lucky, you were blessed with a beep when you started your computer. This beep reassured you that the system was operating correctly and would probably start.

The speaker and tone generator could be manipulated to play music and make other sounds. Many early video games relied on this capability extensively. This created a market for improved sound capability for computer games and other applications. This was provided by add-on soundboards that were plugged into an expansion slot on the motherboard and could be used to manipulate several different types of files.

Computer audio is generally available in one of two forms: WAV (for Waveform audio) or *Musical Instrument Digital Interface* (MIDI). WAV is digital storage of an analog signal, which means that WAV files contain a digitized version of the audio signal. MIDI is a computer-synthesized music system. In the case of a WAV file, a microphone could be connected to the soundboard and the sound could be recorded. This sound could then be played back through the soundboard to a set of external speakers. These soundboards provide high-quality stereo sound that can rival the best stereo systems. WAV files can also be downloaded via the Internet and played on the computer.

The other format is MIDI. Most sound cards include a MIDI synthesizer, which enables the computer to play music. The MIDI synthesizer can include 32, 64, or more channels, each simulating a musical instrument. It is possible to play incredible synthesized music using the MIDI synthesizer. Most boards also include a MIDI connector that can be connected to a piano keyboard or other MIDI device.

The MIDI format enables the computer to act as conductor, sequencer, and editor, as well as perform other tasks associated with music production. Most MIDI circuitry was based upon the Roland MPU-401 adapter, an early MIDI interface. This has become the standard for MIDI, and most software requires MPU-401 software and hardware compatibility to operate correctly.

Most sound cards provide a series of connectors to attach devices to them. Typically, these connections include line-in, line-out, speaker-out, microphone-in, and MIDI connections. The line-out connection enables a device such as an external tape recorder to be connected for recording purposes. The line-in connection enables input from a tape recorder or similar device. The microphone-in connection allows for an external microphone to be connected to the sound card for audio or voice-processing applications. The MIDI/game port can be used to connect either a MIDI device or a joystick. The software that uses or accesses that port, such as a game or a music synthesizer, will know based on the data returned from the port whether the appropriate device is connected.

Two industry soundboard standards currently exist: Ad Lib and Sound Blaster. Ad Lib was the first soundboard in the market to gain wide acceptance. The Ad Lib standard provided the most basic hardware compatibility originally used with DOS games. Current standards for multimedia systems still require hardware compatibility with Ad Lib. Ad Lib will continue to be supported for years to come.

Creative Labs, a competitor of Ad Lib, entered the market and enhanced the Ad Lib board capabilities with its own design called the Sound Blaster. Early Sound Blaster cards provided a superset of features to the Ad Lib standard. The Sound Blaster is fully compatible with the Ad Lib board and provides considerably enhanced features. Current sound cards provided by most manufacturers are Ad Lib and Sound Blaster compatible. These manufacturers have then gone on to add 3D sound effects, advanced sound, and other features to improve capabilities for game and multimedia users.

Virtually all current sound cards, regardless of manufacturer, also provide Sound Blaster compatibility. These early 8-bit boards provided a considerable improvement over the speakers and amplifiers available to the average computer user. Later soundboards were introduced with 16-bit sound, 32-bit, and now 64-bit. At 16-bit sound levels, the audio quality of these systems rivals a traditional audio CD player. The limiting factor at that point becomes the speakers attached to the soundboard.

note **Eight-bit sound cards are capable of producing 256 tones**.

CD-ROM and DVD drives are connected to the soundboard by a four-wire cable. This enables audio signals to be sent directly to the sound card. Most sound cards have the capability for the volume, tone, and mixing to be controlled by a software application. This enables these and other parameters to be changed.

Installation and configuration of sound cards is usually quite straightforward. In most cases, newer boards can be installed directly into an expansion slot and the system configures the board automatically. If this is not possible, you can use the utility programs shipped with the boards to configure and test the boards. These utilities enable addressing and port information to be altered.

The popularity of sound cards is at an all-time high. Almost all computers being sold to consumers today include a CD-ROM player and a sound card. In some cases, the sound card is integrated onto the motherboard; in other cases, it is a separate card.

KEY POINT SUMMARY

Chapter 5 discussed the different types of optical technologies in use today, including CD-ROM and Digital Versatile Disk, or DVD. This chapter also introduced multimedia formats such as Musical Instrument Digital Interface, or MIDI, and WAV file conventions now in use.

- Optical disk technology includes CD-ROM, DVD, and laser disks. Most of these media are not erasable, although newer technologies such as DVD and CD-R are changing that.

- CD-ROM storage capacity exceeds 600MB. With the exception of CD-R technology, CD-ROMs are read-only. CD-R enables information to be recorded on the CD. CD-ROMS are not susceptible to magnetic interference, though some are sensitive to light.

- CD-R requires a special CD player/writer to make recordings. CD-Rs are relatively expensive to produce as compared to mass-recorded CDs, and are sensitive to erasure by exposure to light.

- CD-ROMs are installed in the same manner as hard drives, either on the IDE cable or on the SCSI cable. Most CD-ROMs are configured by the operating system and generally are accessed in a manner similar to a hard drive.

- Optical disks such as the Write Once Read Many, or WORM, drive enable one-time writing of data on the disk. Laser disks are similar in technology to WORM drives, though they are read-only. WORM drives are relatively expensive and not frequently encountered.

- DVD is a new technology that can store in excess of 4GB of data on a drive the size of a CD-ROM. DVD players can usually read CD-ROMs with no difficulty. CD-ROM players cannot read DVD drives, however. DVD players can be usually connected to A/V systems, resulting in full-featured digital enhanced video.

o Roland Ad Lib and Creative Labs Sound Blaster Standard are the two standard multimedia formats. Audio files that are stored on disk are called WAV files. Synthesized music files stored on disk are called MIDI files. A MIDI synthesizer processes MIDI files, while WAV files are actual recordings. WAV files can store and play back virtually any type of audio information.

APPLYING WHAT YOU'VE LEARNED

This chapter has covered a lot of important material that will help you prepare for the A+ exam and be a competent technician. Take a few minutes and work through the Instant Assessment, then review your notes and see how you did.

The Hands-on lab will also help you build your comfort level with the hardware, as well as reinforce the readings from this chapter.

Instant Assessment

Multiple choice

Choose the best answer(s). There may be more than one correct answer for each question.

1. The most common types of optical storage are:

   A. ROM, CD-ROM, and DVD

   B. CD-ROM, DVD, and laser disk

   C. Laser disk, DRV, and CD-ROM

      WORM, CD-R, and DVD

2. A CD-ROM can hold:

   A. Approximately 650MB of data

   B. Approximately 5.6GB of data

   C. Approximately 2.3TB of data

   D. Approximately 200MB of data

3. CD-ROM recording is accomplished by burning:

   A. Multiple tracks

   B. Pits and spirals

   C. Pits and flats

   D. Sectors and tracks

4. CD-ROMs, when stored properly, have a life expectancy of:

   A. one to two years

   B. seven to ten years

   C. Forever

   D. three to six months

5. Which of the following statements is true?

   A. CD-R media is sensitive to light

   B. CR-R technology has the same life expectancy for data storage as a normal CD-ROM

   C. CD-R media can be burned or programmed using a standard CD player

   D. CD-R media cannot be read on normal CD players

6. CD-ROMs are programmed to a series of standards known as:

   A. White papers

   B. Yellow pages

   C. ISO 9225.3 XT standard

   D. Books

7. Optical disk storage frequently includes the following technology:

   A. Optical landing zones

   B. Raster bias vectorization

   C. Magneto-optical

   D. Graham effect transfer

8. DVD is an acronym that stands for:

   A. Digital Video Disk

   B. Disk Viscosity Diameter

C. Data Video Disk

D. Digital Versatile Disk

9. WAV files are:

A. Digital storage of an audio signal

B. Synthesized 3D-FO files

C. Computer-generated music files

D. Operating systems swapping files

10. MIDI files are used to:

A. Reproduce voice conversations via telephone lines

B. Provide synthesized music using a MIDI chip

C. Manage memory

D. Simulate virtual reality

Fill in the blank

1. Optical disk drives are also called _____ drives.

2. CD-ROM is read-only data that is organized as a _____ on the CD-ROM.

3. CD-R storage uses _____ that is light sensitive for recording.

4. The book standard that covers the CD-ROM directory structure is the _____ book.

5. Optical disk drives have a life expectancy in excess of _____ years.

6. Data transfer rates on an optical disk are _____ than most magnetic drives.

7. DVD has the ability to store in excess of _____GB of data.

8. The device that enables higher-quality sounds to be generated by the computer are called _____ cards.

9. Virtually all multimedia cards are compatible with either the _____ or _____ multimedia card.

10. CD-ROMs and DVD are usually connected to the soundboard using a _____-wire cable.

Hands-on Lab Exercise

Lab 5-3 *Installing a DVD drive*

In the last two lab exercises, you installed the motherboard and peripherals, and verified the operation of the system unit. You also installed the hard drives and floppy disk drive. In this lab, we will install the DVD board and connect it to the DVD. The process of installing a DVD is virtually identical to the installation of a CD-ROM device. We will also install a multimedia board. This lab is a fairly short one.

The configuration will include the ability to listen to audio from the DVD through the sound system built into the Intel motherboard. DVD movies will be viewable on the monitor. The DVD will also operate as the system's CD-ROM player.

Materials required

- Static strap
- Phillips Head screwdriver
- DVD kit, including DVD drive and DVD board
- Multimedia card

Part 1: Laying out the DVD, controller, and cables

First, let's lay the pieces we will be installing on the table. The DVD drive looks exactly like a CD-ROM from the outside. The two boards we will be installing are the multimedia card — in this case an AWE64 Sound Blaster card — and a DVD DXR2 card. Figure 5-6 shows these cards and devices.

For the sake of this lab and to demonstrate the capabilities of this system, we are going to assume that we have already installed Windows 95. The specifics of how to install and configure this system will be covered later in the book, but for now assume that this system has Windows 95 installed on it.

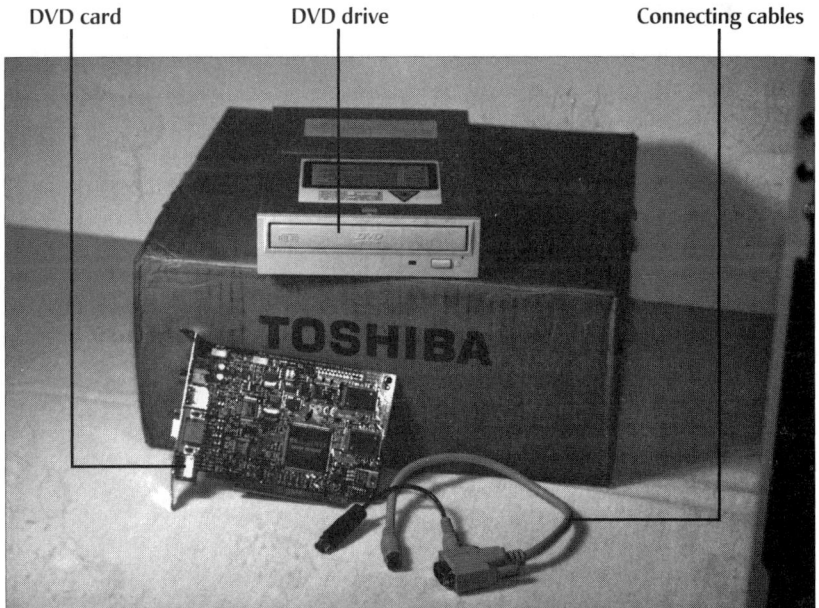

FIGURE 5-6 The components that will be installed into the systems unit

Part 2: Attaching cables

First, we are going to plug the IDE cable for the DVD into the secondary IDE port on the motherboard. Normally, the secondary IDE port will be a 50-pin connector near the disk drive cable on the motherboard. This gives us the primary port for the systems disk drive and the secondary port for the DVD. According to most manufacturers, this configuration provides the fastest access for both devices.

Part 3: Configuring the DVD drive

Configure the DVD drive as a Master. This is accomplished by ensuring that the jumper on the back of the DVD is set to Master. On an IDE port, one of the devices must be configured as a Master, while the other units must be configured as Slaves. This affects how the devices are accessed by the controller. If more than one device is configured as a Master on the motherboard, the IDE bus may hang, and all devices attached to that port will not work.

Part 4: Mounting the DVD

We will mount the drive (shown in Figure 5-7) onto the mounting rails provided for a large expansion slot. The DVD and rails can now be mounted and secured into the drive bay selected for it. The DVD cables will be connected between the DVD unit, the DVD card, and the Sound Blaster card. We will connect the power plug to the power cable. Most systems provide a few extra connectors for power supplies. If you run out of power supply cables, you can usually purchase power extender cables from a computer supply store. As an A+ technician, it is probably good to have a few extra splitter power cables in your toolbox. Connect a power cable to the drive.

IDE Connector   Sound Connector

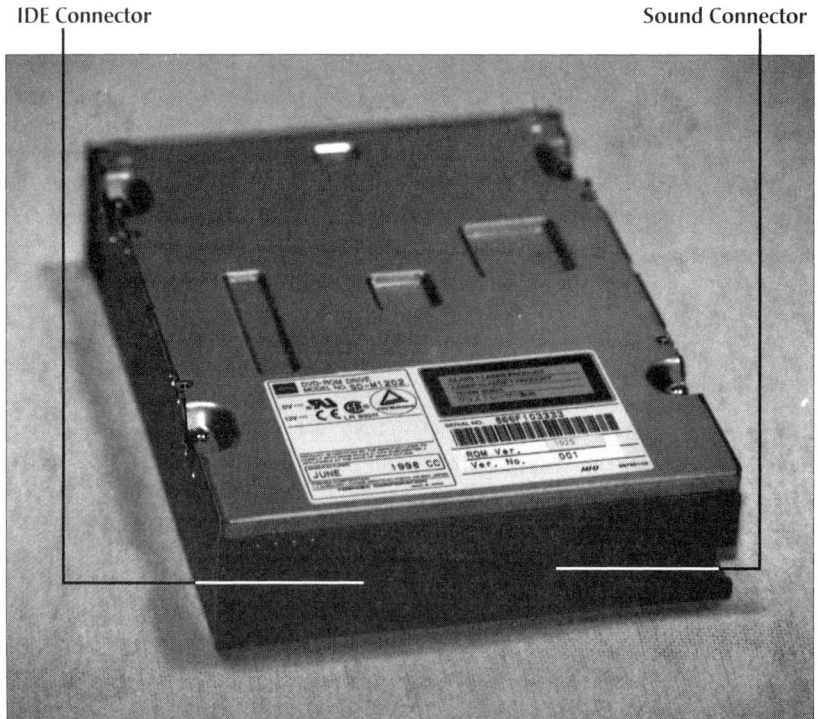

FIGURE 5-7 Installing the DVD drive into the systems unit

Part 5: Cabling the DVD cables to the motherboard

The signal and audio cable that comes with the DVD unit has a small notch in it that will not allow for an incorrect installation. Occasionally, you may encounter a cable without a notch or other type of keying mechanism — in these cases, a good rule of thumb is that the wire with the red marker is always installed closest to the power connector. At this point, we have the drive installed, the cables between the motherboard and the DVD connected, the power cable, and the audio connector on the DVD connected.

Part 6: Installing the DVD controller

The DVD board will be installed into one of the PCI slots closest to the disk connectors. The PCI slots are very fast and this subsystem will need it. After plugging in the card, we will connect the audio cable from the DVD to the connector on top of the board marked *In*.

Part 7: Attaching sound connections

Now move on to the sound system, built into the motherboard. All of the data transfer, with the exception of the analog or music cable, is handled through the IDE connector. Music is handled through that small cable connecting to the DVD card. This process is simple. Just connect the cable between the DVD and the sound port.

At this point, we are ready to power on the system and verify that devices are working. Installation and configuration are covered in more detail in Chapters 11, 12, and 13.

After installing the software per the manufacturer's instructions, we should be ready to rock and roll. The DVD comes with a number of demo programs and games designed to show the capabilities of this technology.

This device, when coupled with a good monitor and sound system, create an awesome workstation that can play movies and music, as well as accomplish meaningful work (almost all at the same time).

Connectivity

About Chapter 6

Ｔhis chapter explores how various connectivity options affect computer operation. This chapter also discusses networks, serial and parallel communications ports, and examines the Universal Serial Bus (USB) and modem communications. These ports and options are the primary mechanism by which computers connect to the outside world. All of the components covered here are designed for providing either input or output to the computer system. Some of the devices, such as the parallel port or the USB port, can accommodate a multitude of different devices, whereas a keyboard is exclusively an input device.

COMMUNICATIONS CONCEPTS

To be productive, a computer must have the capability to communicate with the outside world. Most input is captured from a number of devices such as the keyboard, mouse, modem, scanner, or other device. The two primary communications methods used are called *serial* or *parallel*. This section describes these two methods and some of the protocols that enable communications.

Communications Systems

Communications systems have three components. First, you have the sender. The sender attempts to convey some message across a medium to a receiver. The *medium* is the physical communications method through which the message is conveyed. In the case of conversation, the sender sends a message across a medium (air) to a receiver. For the purposes of our discussion, the *receiver* is a separate circuit that is independent of any other circuits. The three components can also be considered a *circuit*. This enables a simple description of a communications message to be processed, also known as a *transaction*. This one-way communication is called a *simplex circuit*.

A two-way connection that uses the same medium or wire is called *half-duplex* communication. Half-duplex communications resembles a polite conversation — when one side is finished talking, the other side can use the same medium. When people use two-way radios, they are almost always operating in half-duplex. When one of the parties finishes talking, the word *over* is used to indicate that the first side is finished talking. At that point, the circuit is open and the other person can start talking.

The third mechanism is called *duplex* or *full-duplex*. Full-duplex allows simultaneous transmission of data, regardless of flow from the other direction.

Circuits can be permanent or temporary. The simplest permanent connection is wire between two devices. An example of a temporary circuit would be a telephone call between two people. Large computer networks and telephone systems make thousands of different circuit connections per second, enabling efficient utilization of resources.

Serial Communications

The simplest method of communication is *serial communication*. This means that the information is passed sequentially, one character or information unit at a time. In serial communications, the data is encoded in a format that can be decoded by the other side. Most common for serial transmissions is simple *binary transfer*, where bits are sent one by one over the serial connection in a format negotiated by both parties.

Speed in serial applications is referred to as *bps*, or bits per second. Serial communication has the primary advantage of operating over an inexpensive transmission medium, the ubiquitous telephone wires. Additionally, serial communication operates over extended transmission distances. Most data communications involving telephone or radio frequencies utilize serial communications. The primary disadvantage of serial communication is the relatively slow speed. This is caused by the information traveling sequentially over the transmission medium.

Parallel Communications

Parallel communication differs from serial communication by sending all 8 bits in a byte at once. Remember that serial communication sends each bit, one after the other, until all eight are sent. Parallel communication requires eight parallel paths for data, and sends them simultaneously. You can see that parallel connections would be more expensive to manufacture, because they require more wiring in parallel than a serial connection. This enables much faster data transfer across the cable (hypothetically, eight times faster than a serial port). Typically, the parallel systems in use today include status, control, and synchronization signals. These signals help the computer and the device to communicate efficiently and quickly.

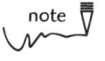 note ▐ **When data is transmitted from the parallel port, one byte is transmitted simultaneously as 8 bits, and 1 bit is sent on each wire.**

Generally, parallel speeds are measured in characters per second, or *CPS*. Parallel communication has the potential to be significantly faster than serial communication because of the simultaneous, rather than sequential, nature of the signal transmission. Parallel communications occur at a higher speed — therefore, interference such as crosstalk between wires becomes more of a problem; problems which go unnoticed at low speeds can cause data loss at higher speeds. Ribbon printer cables have ground wires between every data wire to reduce crosstalk. These problems are easier to control in serial communications because the data goes across one wire and one ground or return wire. Use of twisted pairs and proper termination virtually eliminate the above-mentioned interferences in serial applications. Most parallel systems have a much shorter distance capability — usually in the range of 12 to 15 feet — and are much more subject to electrical noise and interference. Also, parallel communication equipment usually costs more due to the added complexity. Nonetheless, most local devices like printers and scanners use some form of parallel communication today.

Asynchronous Protocols

Asynchronous, or *start/stop protocol*, is typically used to communicate between two serial devices. This data transmission is not rigidly timed. Data can be sent from the host at any time or any interval. Asynchronous transmission frames the bits in each transmitted byte with start and stop bits, because the signal is not dependent on any rigid timing or synchronization. A signal is sent back to the host from the other end, telling the host that it is clear to send (a CTS signal).

note ▐ **Asynchronous data transmission is characterized by irregular transmission times framed by start and stop bits.**

Synchronous Protocols

Synchronous transmission is built around a timing model. Synchronous transmission allows faster transmission times, because the receiver is not forced to sample the approximate middle of a bit to find out what bit it is. With accurate timing cycles, bits can occupy a very short space, and more bits can therefore be transmitted in the same amount of time. Synchronous communications depend on clock pulses for their timing.

Control lines and clock lines are used to synchronize both systems. Because each character is sent at a specific time or interval, if the frames or data carrier lose synchronization, the system will immediately generate a resynchronization process to bring the line back to synchronization. The control line will typically be used to pass information between the transmitter and receiver about the status of the system. As you may recall, in the asynchronous system, each character contained start and stop information. In synchronous transmission, this is accomplished by the synch frame.

At slower speeds, this overhead can be quite expensive in terms of throughput (overall data transfer), but in higher-speed applications, the data is guaranteed to arrive at the other end intact and with no errors, because retransmission of damaged frames or packets is automatic until it is received intact. This error checking and recovery process adds up to twenty percent overhead to the information being sent.

note   **Synchronous transmissions are synchronized by a shared clock, rather than by start bits.**

Half-Duplex and Full-Duplex Communication

Simplex transmission uses a pair of transmission lines that allow a data signal to travel one way. The transmission pair can send, but not receive. *Duplex* refers to a system where data signals may be both sent and received. This is achieved in several different ways. *Half-duplex* involves a pair of transmission wires alternately transmitting or receiving a data signal. *Hardware full-duplex* uses four wires, or two pairs in one system. One pair is used for data transmission, and the other pair is used for data receiving. This is the same as two simplex systems put together, and is typical of Ethernet network transmissions on twisted pair cabling, when duplexing is turned on.

Signal full-duplexing is more complicated. Signals from either transmitter are sent over one pair of wires, but use two different signal bands. The receiver at either end will receive both signals and needs to cancel out the signal that it sent, to clearly receive the other transmitter's data. Data transmission never occurs on one wire. Pairs of wires are always involved, and in the case of hardware duplexing, two pairs of wires are used. Half-duplexing uses only one signal wire pair.

Full-duplexing can result in faster communication, if both sides have equivalent amounts of information to send simultaneously. This is the whole issue of asymmetrical data transmission as currently exemplified by cable modems, because most transmissions occur somewhat unilaterally. Further, the cost of full-duplexing is a function of the cost of using four (two-pair) wire transmission systems. Though this is available in network cabling scenarios, modem transmissions are based largely on existing phone wiring and are thus constrained to a single wire pair.

note **A full-duplex modem allows data to be transmitted and received simultaneously.**

KEYBOARDS

The primary input device you use is the keyboard. Several different types of keyboards and connectivity options are available today. A keyboard helps you convert your thoughts into data or information that can be used by the computer to accomplish meaningful work (or meaningful play).

Keyboards are the part of a computer most subject to wear and debris, and as such can become damaged or worn out. Replacement is relatively easy, but be certain to get as close to an exact match to the original as possible. Some keyboards feature an L-shaped Enter key, whereas others use a single key-height Enter key. Replacing a touch typist's keyboard with an inexact match is a definite path to customer dissatisfaction.

Keyboard Designs

Keyboard layouts were derived from typewriters used almost 100 years ago. The basic layout specifies a row of keys that are depressed to create input. Normal keyboards have three rows of alphabetic characters, one row of numeric, and one or more rows of special keys. The first PC keyboard was the 83-key keyboard, which was replaced by the 84-key keyboard on the IBM AT. These keyboards can be identified easily by their absence of cursor keys between the alphabetic keys and the numeric keypad, and their location of the function keys to the left of the alphabetic characters ... or you could, of course, count the number of keys. Later versions of the AT included a 101-key keyboard, which changed the layout of the special keys significantly. Currently, a 104-key version is available, which includes three extra keys for Windows 95 operations. Figure 6-1 shows two types of 101- or 104-key keyboards used in PCs today. This 104-key keyboard is called a Windows 95 keyboard.

> note — **The keyboard is the most important input device on a PC.**

FIGURE 6-1 A conventional 101-key keyboard and a Microsoft Natural Elite keyboard

All of these keyboards are called *QWERTY* keyboards because of the key configuration—the keys start, upper left, with the letters QWERTY. It is an oft-repeated but undocumented legend that the QWERTY keyboard was deliberately laid out inefficiently to slow typists down. Early typing machines were mechanical wonders, but their mechanisms were much slower than the ability of skilled typists. The originator of the QWERTY keyboard was Christopher Scholes. Scholes left no notes about why he laid out the keyboard this way.

In the 1930s, an alternative keyboard layout was proposed called the *Dvorak* keyboard. This keyboard was supposed to be designed to make typing faster and more efficient. You will seldom if ever see these keyboards, but a driver to remap a standard QWERTY keyboard to this layout is included as an option in Windows 95 for the curious. Try to resist the temptation to secretly remap keyboards as an April Fool's joke.

Current versions of Windows and other operating systems can easily reprogram your keyboard to function like a Dvorak keyboard. Of course, unless you change the keycaps, your keys will be incorrectly marked. For someone using one computer system exclusively with no need to ever use another system, switching to a Dvorak key arrangement might make sense, though the evidence of the Dvorak layout's superiority is largely apocryphal. However, the inconvenience of learning the Dvorak system only to have to go back to QWERTY on every other system you encounter would surely outweigh any imagined advantage of the original swap.

PC keyboards with 101 and 104 keys have a series of function and control keys located above the alphanumeric keys. Some keyboards (the excellent models formerly made by Northgate, for example) featured these function keys to the left of the alphanumeric keys as well. 83- and 84-key keyboards offered these function keys only on the left side. Current keyboards include 12 function keys labeled F1 through F12 and editing or cursor movement keys — directional arrows, Home, End, Insert, Delete, Page up, and Page down. In addition, keyboards have a numeric keypad to the right of the other keys. All of these keys can be accessed by software to extend the function of the keyboard. For example, a common Windows convention defines F1 as the Help button.

Windows also offers *typematic*, or auto-repeat, capabilities. You can press and hold a specific character and after a configurable delay, it will start automatically repeating that character until the key is released. The speed and delay of the typematic function can be altered using the keyboard settings utility on most computers. In Windows 95, click Start ⇒ Settings ⇒ Control Panel ⇒ Keyboard. Repeat Rate and Repeat Delay are adjusted on the Speed tab.

Keyboard Input

Computers read the keyboard data via a serial cable that is attached to a keyboard connector. This connector usually has either five or six pins. The five-pin standard is a larger connector, and is the older standard. Most laptops and many newer computers use a six-pin mini-DIN connector. The five-pin and the six-pin are not interchangeable, though many of the keyboards that use the six-pin mini-DIN also include an adapter. These connectors are called *DIN connectors*, named after the

Deutsche Institut für Normung, the German equivalent of ANSI. Figure 6-2 shows a mini-DIN.

FIGURE 6-2   The keyboard mini-DIN connector

The computer's keyboard controller translates key presses into code the computer can process. The keyboard controller also controls the A20 gate (discussion of which is beyond our scope). This information is useful, because if a computer ever begins to return A20 gate errors when booting the system, this error is most often corrected with a new keyboard. Each key has a unique key number, as well as a unique make and break code. The make code is the number that the keyboard generates when the key is depressed, and the break code is the number the keyboard generates when the key is released.

Keyboards have three modes. Mode 1 keyboards were the original 83-key keyboard used on the first PCs. Mode 2 were the 84-key keyboards used on the Original PC AT. Mode 3 is the advanced and Windows keyboard mode provided by most keyboard and manufacturers.

The most common designs for keyboard manufacturers are *capacitive* and *hard contact*. Capacitive keyboards use the electrical property of capacitance to accomplish input. The keys when depressed provide a small change in the electrical charge of the key. This change is amplified by the electronics on the keyboard and converted into a "sharp" transition. The hard contact method uses a switch to alter electrical flow. A majority of the keyboards made today are contact based.

Contact keyboards have shorter lifespans, but they are relatively inexpensive to replace. Three primary technologies used in contact keyboards today are:

- Mechanical switch keyboards
- Rubber dome keyboards
- Membrane keyboards

Mechanical switches use a switch to make and break contact. The keys in many mechanical keyboards can be replaced easily. The switch contacts are made of gold or other similar metals. These switches use springs to return the key to the upright position. Many mechanical switch keyboards can be repaired in the field by replacing the switch. In most cases, however, they are simply replaced with a new keyboard.

Rubber dome keyboards use a contact switch like the mechanical switch, wrapped in a rubber dome. The dome is shaped into a dimple under the keycap. Depressing the keycap pushes the dimple down, causing the top and bottom of the dimple to make contact. This is the equivalent of a switch contact being made.

Membrane keyboards are like rubber domes, except they use thin plastic sheets. This plastic sheet or membrane is manufactured with small conductive traces on them. This membrane can be sealed inside a plastic dimple, which closes on contact. Membrane keys are used in many peripherals such as printers and auxiliary keypads. These keys are very inexpensive to manufacture and are nearly impervious to dirt, contaminants, and liquid. They are seldom used for primary keyboards, however, because they require additional mechanisms to emulate how keyboards travel and feel.

Keyboard problems can plague users. It is important to emphasize that keyboards should be kept free of contamination. A single cup of coffee or soft drink spilled into a keyboard can ruin it. Maintenance that can be performed on a keyboard includes cleaning off the keycaps with a damp cloth, and spills can occasionally be successfully dried out. Keycaps frequently pop off, depending on the keyboard, and this type of keyboard can be cleaned of excess lint and hair. Keep in mind, though, that keyboards are relatively inexpensive, and the time you spend on maintenance can quickly exceed the cost of a replacement.

Mice

First originated at the Xerox *Palo Alto Research Center* (PARC) and brought to widespread use by the Apple Macintosh, the mouse has provided an alternative to the keyboard for commands and input. The mouse provides a point-and-click capability that has become a major selling point to end users. The mouse remains an area of contention for some older computer professionals, however. These professionals learned to use Function and Alt key shortcut combinations before the widespread acceptance of the mouse, and some feel that the mouse actually slows them down. You be the judge, but realize that the mouse radically changed the computer business and is implemented in virtually all modern computer programs.

The original mice were based on a small ball that was mounted upside-down in a small soap bar shaped device. The ball can be rotated on a surface in any direction. The mouse has sensors to manage two axes, X and Y. This positioning information is managed by the operating system. Most operating systems that support mice make positioning information available to the application through a driver.

Optical mice were a widely promoted alternative to the mechanical mouse. This technology provided a light beam to detect motion across a special pad. Optical mice are not in much use today, but the optical feature has been co-opted in a combination device known as an *opto-mechanical* mouse.

Mice typically have two or more buttons. Macintosh computers use a single button mouse (the purist version). Most PCs provide either a two- or three-button mouse. In a two-button mouse, the left button usually activates a button on the screen. In older applications, the right button was either not used, or specially defined per application. In new applications for Windows 95, however, the right button brings up a menu of context-sensitive special options. Some programs, including Windows 3.*x* and Windows 95, allow the mouse buttons to be reversed for left-handed operations. Many new devices include a rotating wheel that enables scrolling of windows onscreen without requiring the user to pinpoint the tiny vertical scrolling button. Most new mouse devices can be reprogrammed with new functions for each button.

Trackballs are similar to a mouse turned upside down. The ball is manipulated by finger movement. Functionally, they are identical in operation to the mouse, except the ball is controlled by fingers instead of dragging. They can either be free-standing units, or integrated into a keyboard.

Drawing tablets are another technology that utilizes the x/y coordinate process. Drawing tablets can be used by art and drawing packages to provide drawing input to the computer, and usually resemble a pen that can be traced over a gradated smooth surface.

These devices are typically connected to the computer in one of the following ways:

○ Serial port

○ Bus mouse port (no longer common)

○ Mini-DIN mouse port (most common)

○ *Universal Serial Bus* (USB) port (rapidly growing in popularity)

FIGURE 6-3 Mouse and mini-DIN connector

The *serial mouse* utilizes a standard serial port, such as COM1 or COM2. These mice operate on the hardware level as an RS-232C or standard serial port device. Usually a driver is loaded by the operating system that translates the serial input into mouse input for use by the software. The RS-232C port will be covered in detail later in this chapter.

The *bus mouse* uses a dedicated controller to interact with the mouse. This frees up a serial port, but at the cost of filling one ISA slot. In the past, a few video card manufacturers offered a bus mouse connector on their video card, but this is no longer offered. Bus mice are no longer widely available.

Most computer manufacturers provide the *mini-DIN mouse port*. These built-in mouse ports allow the mouse to plug into the motherboard with no impact on system ports. Many of the newer motherboards include this as a standard feature.

SERIAL PORTS

The serial port most commonly used in computers today is the RS-232C port. The RS-232C port is a standard port defined by the *Electronics Industry Association* (EIA), and is the lowest common denominator to virtually all computer systems. This port, referred to as the *asynchronous data communications port* or the *communications port*, has since become known in the PC environment as the *COM port*. The RS-232 port has a limit of approximately 115,200, or 115K bits. Available speed settings COM ports are 110, 300, 600, 1200, 2400, 4800, 9600, 19200, 38400, 56600, or 115200bps. The ability of the serial port to provide these upper-end speeds depends upon the hardware used by computer manufacturers. Most computers sold in the past few years use a 16550AFN *universal asynchronous receiver transmitter* (UART) chip to control the COM port, and this UART easily handles the high speeds. For computers without a 16550AFN, high-speed serial port cards are available.

The standard connector for the RS-232C connection is a DB-25 connector. With the advent of the PC AT, a new connector was added as an alternative to the DB-25, the DB-9 connector. The RS-232C port only used ten pins. Of these pins, two were used for ground. The DB-9 eliminates the chassis ground and uses the other eight for signals. Figure 6-4 shows the DB-25 and DB-9 connectors.

The switch to the DB-9 enables the PC to have two connectors mounted in one slot opening. Today, standard COM ports on PCs are generally DB-9. Cables can be purchased to connect from DB-9 to DB-25 and vice versa.

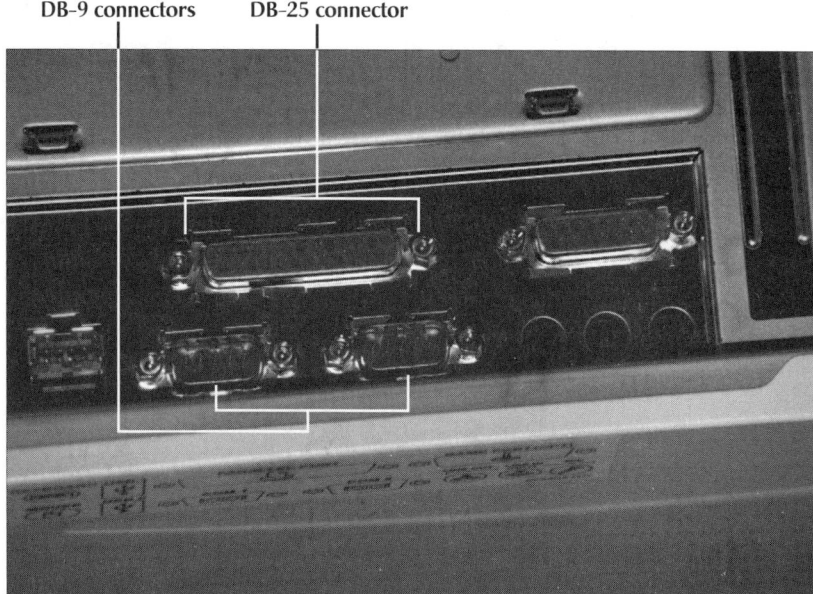

FIGURE 6-4 DB-25 and DB-9 connectors

The signals on the RS-232 connection provide a wealth of control signals for device control. Besides Pin 2 and 3 for receive and transmit, the port provides for six control lines. These pins will be briefly explained here:

o *Data Terminal Ready* (DTR): DTR is used by a data terminal (or serial port) to indicate it is ready to communicate. The DTR line is held high by applying a positive voltage to the line to show it is ready.

o *Data Set Ready* (DSR): DSR is used by the device to indicate it is ready to participate. The data set (device communicating over the serial port) sets the DSR line to high. A serial port will not send out data unless it receives the DSR signal.

o *Request to Send* (RTS): RTS is sent by the data terminal, indicating it is on and ready to send data. This signal is used in flow control. Flow control refers to the capability of the data terminal to manage data flow from the data set (or device communicating over the serial port).

- *Clear to Send* **(CTS):** CTS is sent by the device when it is ready to receive data. If the CTS signal is off, the data terminal will stop receiving information. If the terminal is full, it can turn off CTS, thus stopping data transmission at the other end.

- *Carrier Detect* **(CD):** CD is used by modems and other devices to indicate that a connection has been negotiated, and the device is now able to communicate. CD is most frequently used in dial-up situations. External modems that show the status of a call will show CD as one of the earliest signal lights.

- *Ring Indicator* **(RI):** RI indicates that the modem or device has detected an incoming phone call. Typically used in modem applications, the receiving equipment will indicate an RI when the phone is connected.

- *Signal Ground* **:** Signal ground provides a return path for electrical flow. If ground is not established, the connection will not function.

- *Chassis Ground* **:** Chassis ground provides ground connection between the hardware systems. In older technology, the chassis and signal grounds were kept separate and isolated. This was done to prevent ground loops — to equalize potential between equipment set up on different electrical grounds. This ground is now virtually always connected to the signal ground or eliminated. Many cables sort Pins 1 and 7 together in a DB-25 situation. IBM removed this pin because it is not needed for equipment plugged into the same electrical circuit, which includes most computer equipment. Hence, the DB-9 connector fits most data applications perfectly.

Modems

Modulator-demodulators, or *modems*, are devices that allow two computers to communicate across remote distances. Modems work over telephone lines. Original modems were relatively unsophisticated, quite bulky, and expensive. Prior to the divestiture of AT&T in the United States, you were virtually required to lease them from the telephone company. Modems were in most cases beyond the reach of an average home computer user (although not that much of a home computer market existed in those days).

Modem Technology

An important method of communicating among data devices is a method called *frequency shift keying*, or FSK. FSK is based upon the premise that binary ones could be represented as one frequency, while binary zeros could be another frequency. FSK is a derivative of *frequency modulation* (FM). Early modems that adhered to the Bell 103 standard used two frequencies to modulate a carrier. The first carrier was at 1200Hz and the other was at 2200Hz.

One frequency was used for receiving and one for transmitting. These frequencies were increased in frequency by 150Hz for a mark and down 150Hz for a space. This enabled the encoding of data and reliable transmission at the 300-baud rate. As speeds become faster, it is harder for the modem to detect and react to the rapid frequency changes; thus, FSK becomes hard to use at higher bandwidths.

Phase modulation is a mechanism whereby two signals are sent simultaneously along the media. These signals are either *in phase* — reaching peaks and valleys in the signal simultaneously — or *out of phase*. As the modulated wave is compared to the carrier wave, a shift of phase can be seen. This shift of phase can be converted into four possible states: in-phase, 90, 180, or 270 degrees. This process enables information to be rapidly and compactly transmitted over a relatively narrow bandwidth. The major drawback to this type of system is the requirement for clean phone lines. Static can cause huge amounts of data loss because of the amount of information squeezed into the data signal.

Current technologies are pushing the bandwidth of analog modems to the 56Kbps range, though the very upper speeds are only possible if one side of the connection is not using an analog-to-digital converter, such as when calling an Internet service provider from home. The limiting factor of these higher-speed modems is available bandwidth in the existing telephone wiring systems, and the noise-level quality of that bandwidth.

Modem Standards

For two modems to communicate with each other, they must first go through a handshaking process. The two devices negotiate a connection at the highest speed supported by both units given the line quality. Line noise can have a big impact on high-speed modem connections. This process is usually automatic and the user has very limited interaction until the session has been established, though the process can be altered for special circumstances. A number of handshaking standards have been created to confuse end users and mystify technicians. Some of the more common standards have been defined by the Comité Consultatif International Télégraphique et Téléphonique, or CCITT, the International Telecommunications Union, or ITU, the Microcom Networking Protocol, or MNP, and Bell Laboratories.

Designations that start with the letter v, such as v.22 or v.32 indicate origination from the CCITT or ITU. The v.34 standard is very common in computer modems today, indicating a speed as fast as 33,600bps. Many new standards are being proposed almost every day, but most of the newer high-speed modems seem to be able to communicate in v.34 mode. Two new modem protocols that can operate upwards of 56Kbps are designated as *K56flex* and *x2*. Both of these formats are proprietary, but the new v.90 standard has been released that is the international standard for 56Kbps connectivity. Manufacturers of K56flex and x2 modems are offering ways to upgrade their modems to the new standard from their proprietary protocol. The MNP standards provide a set of guidelines about different operating characteristics of the modem equipment. For example, MNP Class 5 is a data-compression protocol that allows for highly efficient data transfer.

Bell Laboratories begat the modem. The basic standards still in use today are the Bell 103 standard, which is a 300bps standard, and the Bell 212A standard, which is a 1200bps standard. Most modems on the market today still support the 103 and 212 standards. Internationally, the v.22 standard was equivalent to the Bell 212A standard.

Modem Lines

A number of telephone services exist today to provide users with data communications. Data communication can be done on anything from a local telephone line all the way up to a high-speed dedicated connection like a T1 or T3, and maximum speed is reflected by the costs of the different services along the spectrum.

Telephone lines come in one of two flavors: analog or digital. Analog lines, used by conventional analog modems, are relatively slow. The trade-off for using *plain old telephone service* (POTS) is a relative lack of speed—current maximum of 33.6 or 56Kbps—and lower reliability of connection. Though most telephone companies work very hard to provide noise reduction, it is sometimes difficult to track down and repair noisy circuits in a phone system. Digital lines, on the other hand, are virtually guaranteed a bandwidth as part of the service. Table 6-1 shows the more common services available to computer users.

TABLE 6-1 COMMON SERVICES FOR DATA COMMUNICATIONS

STANDARD	CONNECTION	SPEED
POTS	Analog	Up to 56Kbps (Plain Old Telephone Service)
v.34	Analog	33.6Kbps (a modem communications standard)
ISDN	Digital	128Kbps
T1	Digital	1.544mbps

Many other services are available, but these three represent what you will probably run across in the field. ISDN is an excellent choice for small offices that need a relatively inexpensive line to a central computer. ISDN can handle connectivity for several users in a small office. T1 is generally used between large business units or enterprises. Hundreds of simultaneous sessions can occur using this standard. ISDN is a variant of frame relay, a totally digital line that runs into the home or office using standard twisted pair wiring. Most higher-speed lines beyond ISDN are unswitched or dedicated lines.

In *unswitched* digital circuits, equipment called *Data Send Unit* (DSU) and *Channel Service Unit* (CSU) is used. The DSU connects to the customer equipment such as the computer systems and the CSU connects to the line. The DSU transmits the data and provides buffering and flow control. The CSU manages the connection to the Telco network, provides troubleshooting, and is the terminus of the digital line. Most network providers have the ability to poll and troubleshoot the line by communicating with the CSU. Most, if not all, modern equipment manufacturers have integrated the CSU and DSU into a single box.

Modem Equipment

Modems come as either external or internal units. External units are connected to the computer via a serial cable to an RS-232C port. These modems also require a separate power supply. Internal modems are installed into one of the expansion slots on the computer's motherboard. Many manufacturers now include the modem as an integral part of the motherboard, making an additional modem unnecessary. Figure 6-5 shows an external modem. The modem is connected to the telephone lines, typically using an RJ-11 modular jack. The RJ-11 is a four-wire push fit connector Although only two wires are used per phone line, the fit connector is used in virtually all telephone installations in the United States. Though the connector can hold four wires, only two wires are actually used in the RJ-45 connection. Other standards exist throughout the world, and several manufacturers provide international kits to connect to telephone lines.

As a word of caution, unless a modem is approved by the regulatory equivalent of the *Federal Communications Commission* (FCC) in a foreign country, hooking a non-approved modem to a phone system is considered a criminal act in many countries.

In many cases, the approved modem is identical to the one in your computer, but if the stamp is not there, you could face serious consequences hooking up a foreign modem to a telephone line.

FIGURE 6-5 External US Robotics Dual Standard modem

External modems usually provide a set of indicator lights on the front panel that are helpful for troubleshooting. Many computer manufacturers also provide software that can monitor the status of the modem. The status lights provided on most modems are briefly described in Table 6-2.

TABLE 6-2 SIGNALS USED IN MOST MODEMS

HS	High speed	Shows modem at highest speed
AA	Auto answer	Indicates that modem will answer the phone if called
CD	Carrier detect	Indicates remote connection is in effect
OH	Off hook	Modem is using phone line
RD	Receive data	Modem is receiving data
SD	Send data	Modem is sending data
TR	Terminal ready	PC is able to communicate
MR	Modem ready	Modem is ready to communicate

Fortunately today, modems are an "off the shelf" item. They are inexpensive and extremely reliable. Most manufacturers offer long warranties on them, making service simple. The biggest challenge in working with modems is their initial installation. Many modems use one of the available communications ports available on the PC. Newer modems utilize a feature in Windows called Plug and Play to be automatically configured in the PC. This feature will be covered more extensively in the Windows section of this book.

Modem Commands

Hayes Microcomputer Products developed a set of communications modems in the late 1970s, which became the standard for the industry. These modems were called *smart modems* because they could be configured through the serial port. They could be reset, make calls, change modes, or make any number of other changes by using the AT command set. Most modems manufactured today are Hayes-compatible. Three commands you should know about are:

- **ATZ:** This resets the modem to its normal state
- **ATH:** This hangs up the telephone line
- **ATDT <number>:** This dials a number (touch tone dialing) and attempts to make a connection

These three commands are very valuable for troubleshooting modem problems. If you can't get the modem to respond to an ATZ or an AT command, you probably have a sick modem on your hands. To get to these commands, you would use a terminal emulation program and connect directly to your modem. You would then press the Esc key or the + key several times to get its attention, then enter the command. If the operation was successful, the modem sends an OK back to you. Windows 95 also has modem diagnostics built in — click Start ⇒ Settings ⇒ Control Panel ⇒ Modems, then select the modem and click on the Diagnostics tab.

Modem Speeds

Speed in modems is measured using *bits per second*, or bps. A 14.4Kbps modem is capable of transmitting roughly 1,400 characters per second. In text mode, this equates to about a second per screen. In graphically oriented modes, 14.4Kbps modems can feel very slow, with almost painful lags in screen performance.

With data compression, a 14.4Kbps modem can have a character transmission of 28.8Kbps, though the Internet is rarely surfed in text-only mode. Current modems claim speeds of 56Kbps. Unfortunately, a 56Kbps signal cannot go through analog-to-digital converters, and cannot go through analog amplifiers common to phone lines in residential areas. The modem has to be relatively close to the telephone company (also referred to as Telco). A 56Kbps connection is more likely to be somewhere between 33.6Kbps and 45Kbps in reality. Over the next few years, you will see other options, such as ISDN and cable modems, becoming more cost effective for home users.

PARALLEL PORTS

Most printers communicate with the computer using a *parallel port*. The standard interface for the parallel port in use today is the 25-pin parallel port, whereas most parallel cables connect to the printer through what is called the *Centronics parallel interface*. The Centronics interface is a 36-wire standard that allows for fast data transfer. Many motherboards provide an integrated parallel port along with the serial port. Add-on boards can also be purchased that use an expansion slot on the motherboard.

Standards

Several standards are in use today both for the interface protocols and the cabling. Some of the most common standards include the *Institute of Electrical and Electronics Engineers* (IEEE), IEEE 1284 compatible and compliant ports, the *Extended Capabilities Port* (ECP), and the *Enhanced Parallel Port* (EPP). Early computer printers operated in what was called *nibble mode* and *byte mode*. Nibble and byte modes were a relatively slow means of using a parallel port for reverse data transfer. Most of the early parallel ports could be tricked into becoming bi-directional by redefining signals. Nibble mode is a 4-bit transfer scheme, whereas byte mode transfers 8 bits at a time. Byte mode required special hardware. To further complicate the issue, a number of connections are available to connect the different types of devices. Some of the more common connectors used today are the DB-25 Female or IEEE 1284 A connector, the 36-pin ribbon jack or IEEE 1284 B connector, and the 36-pin IEEE 1284 C connector. This section will briefly cover these differing standards and provide a means to help you identify them.

Currently these standards allow for a maximum length of 30 feet for printer cables. Printer cables may work at a longer length, but they should always work at least to 30 feet. If a manufacturer indicates that a cable is IEEE 1284 compliant, they are stating that they warrant the cable to meet the standards. Several manufacturers sell cables that are IEEE 1284 *compatible*, but these cables, though pin-for-pin compatible with the IEEE 1284 standard, may not meet the quality standards and be unable to operate at the speeds and distances of the compliant cable. A compatible cable may work fine for years, or might be susceptible to interference from the other wires in the cable (called crosstalk) or from external interference such as lights or power lines. The difference in cost is usually only a few dollars, and over time, not a significant factor. In our experience with cabling, this is an area where cutting corners is not a good idea.

Connectors

Initial parallel connections used by computer manufacturers were big square screw-on connectors that may have had dozens of wires in them. These connectors were typically highly proprietary and forced the computer user to purchase computer printers only from the computer manufacturers. Several manufacturers of larger systems touted the speed and capabilities of their printers, which would run only on their computer. In the early days of the microcomputer field, several manufacturers, including Apple and Radio Shack, provided low-cost, low-end printers that would only work with their computer system. Initially, given the high cost of other printers, this was received with great success.

A printer manufacturer by the name of Centronics introduced a series of dot-matrix printers in the early 1970s that worked with a simple interface that could be added to most minicomputers and microcomputers. This parallel standard quickly became available to most computer users. The connector used to connect the device to the printer was a parallel cable that had 36-pin Centronics connectors on both ends. This connector is now referred to as the IEEE 1284 B connector. It is still in use today on most printers.

The major disadvantage of this type of connector is that it is quite large. When IBM wanted to introduce the PC, the back of the computer where IBM wanted to mount the printer interface was not big enough to contain it. Early PCs provided a display adapter and printer port on the same expansion board. To accommodate the connector, IBM rewired the 36 pins into 25 on the PC end and introduced the computer with a DB-25 female connector. This connector has been adopted by most of the manufacturers and is now the standard for printer connections on the computer end. This connector is the IEEE-1284 type A connector.

The IEEE 1284-C, or C connector, is a relatively new standard that is supposed to replace the B connector in the near future. The C connector is smaller and fits into the size of an A connector, thus solving the original space problem IBM had. Table 6-3 shows the C connector pin outs.

TABLE 6-3 TYPE C WIRING CONNECTIONS

A CONNECTOR	B CONNECTOR
1	Busy
2	Select
3	Ack
4	Fault
5	Error
6	Data 0
7	Data 1
8	Data 2
9	Data 3

A CONNECTOR	B CONNECTOR
10	Data 4
11	Data 5
12	Data 6
13	Data 7
14	Init
15	Strobe
16	Select
17	AutoFD
18	Host logic high
19	Gnd Busy
20	Gnd Select
21	Gnd Ack
22	Gnd Fault
23	Gnd Error
24	Data 0
25	Gnd Data 1
26	Gnd Data 2
27	Gnd Data 3
28	Gnd Data 4
29	Gnd Data 5
30	Gnd Data 6
31	Gnd Data 7
32	Gnd Init
33	Gnd Strobe
34	Gnd Select
35	Gnd AutoFeed
36	Peripheral logic high

By now you have probably wondered how the 25-pin connector gets connected to the 36-pin connector. This is accomplished by rewiring one end of the connector to accommodate the 36-pin expansion. Table 6-4 shows a pin-for-pin connection chart of the A connector to the B connector. Table 6-5 shows a pin connection chart for the A connector to C connector, and finally, Table 6-6 shows a pin connection for a C to B connection. As you can see, many of the signal names are identical and their purpose is self-evident.

TABLE 6-4 A TO B CONNECTOR ADAPTER WIRING CONNECTIONS

A Connector	*B Connector*
1	1
2	2
3	3
4	4
5	5
6	6
7	7
8	8
9	9
10	10
11	11
12	12
13	13
14	14
15	32
16	31
17	36
18	19
19	20 and 21
20	22 and 23
21	24 and 25
22	26 and 27
23	29
24	28
25	30

TABLE 6-5 A TO C CONNECTOR ADAPTER WIRING CONNECTIONS

A Connector	*C Connector*
1	15
2	6
3	7
4	8
5	9
6	10
7	11
8	12
9	13
10	3
11	1
12	5
13	2
14	17
15	4
16	14
17	16
18	33
19	24 and 25
20	26 and 27
21	28 and 29
22	30 and 31
23	19 and 22
24	20, 21 and 23
25	32, 34 and 35

TABLE 6-6 C TO B CONNECTOR ADAPTER WIRING CONNECTIONS

C CONNECTOR	B CONNECTOR
1	11
2	13
3	10
4	32
5	12
6	2
7	3
8	4
9	5
10	6
11	7
12	8
13	9
14	31
15	1
16	36
17	14
18	not used
19	29
20	28
21	28
22	29
23	28
24	20
25	21
26	22
27	23
28	24
29	25
30	26

C CONNECTOR	B CONNECTOR
31	27
32	30
33	19
34	30
35	20
36	18

Printer Port Modes

Printer ports operate in several modes. These modes are *EPP, ECP, nibble,* and *byte*. Performance in parallel port data transfers have increased to a level that exceeded what was originally intended for printer applications. A software developer discovered how to use this port for bidirectional communications. Early bidirectional applications worked in nibble mode. This mode allowed for the transfer of 4 bits at a time across the line back to the computer. The byte mode was an improvement that enabled 8 bits to be transferred.

Nibble mode used four of the status lines that fed printer status back to the computer. Four-bit transfer, though slow, was still faster than most serial ports were able to communicate. Programs such as Lap Link could connect computers to each other for high-speed file transfers.

Byte mode was an upgrade to the port that enabled data to be transferred both ways. This was effectively twice the speed of nibble mode, and could run at the native speed of both devices. Native speed refers to the normal or default speeds at which a device operates.

EPP was a standard promoted by Zenith, Xircom, and Intel. EPP streamlined the data transfer process, making information transfer faster. The timing signals were changed to make them more precise, enabling data transfer speed increases. This standard was at best a compromise and did not provide the speeds that were needed for high-volume data transfers.

ECP is a standard created by Hewlett-Packard and Microsoft. Most computer systems shipped today include ECP as a mode on the parallel port. ECP adds functionality to the EPP concept, as well as higher speed and data compression. ECP can query an ECP device on the other end and configure printer drivers accordingly.

The IEEE 1284 standard implements both ECP and EPP modes, as well as formalizes the specifications for serial port communications. IEEE 1284 specifies five modes, which help standardize the environment. The five modes are: compatibility mode, nibble mode, byte mode, EPP mode, and ECP mode. *Compatibility mode* refers to the original mode supported by Centronics parallel ports.

Pins and Definitions

This section outlines the different signals specified by IEEE 1284 and what they do. This is intended to provide you with an understanding of how data is passed in parallel ports. These signals and lines provide you with the basics of how a parallel port operates and the signals necessary to keep things in synch:

- **Data 1 through Data 8:** The eight data lines carry the data between the two devices.
- **Strobe line:** The strobe line signals the other end that data is ready to be sent across. The strobe is a pulse sent by one end, indicating the data on the data lines is valid.
- **Busy line:** The busy line tells your computer that the device is unable to accept any additional data. The sender will stop sending data until the busy line clears.
- **Acknowledge or ACK:** The ACK line sends a signal back to the sender that the information has been received.
- **Select:** The select line tells the sender that the device is online and ready to work. If the select signal is not present, the device is assumed to be offline.
- **Paper Empty or pError:** This control line indicates the printer has run out of paper.
- **Fault or nFault:** Fault is a signal that the printer has malfunctioned. It is a general-purpose indicator that might include low ink, paper jam, or another mechanical problem.
- **Initialize printer:** Initialize printer sends a prime or reset to the printer that returns it to its default state.
- **Select input or nSelectIn:** Select input is a signal that your PC can use to switch a printer online or offline.
- **Autofeed or nAutoFd:** Autofeed enables the computer to specify how to advance the carriage. For instance, the printer could advance the carriage one line when a carriage return was encountered.

As you can see, parallel port communications are a little more complicated than the serial port from a control perspective, but the parallel port can provide speeds thousands of times faster than what is currently available in serial port technology. A high-speed parallel port can send more than 100,000 characters per second, which is far beyond the performance of most serial transfers.

USB

The *Universal Serial Bus* (USB) is a relatively new arrival to the computer industry. It overcomes one of the largest shortcomings of traditional serial and parallel ports: available addresses and slots. A USB hub can support up to 127 devices. Figure 6-6 shows a sample USB port on the back of a PC. The four-wire USB connection is similar to a telephone modular jack.

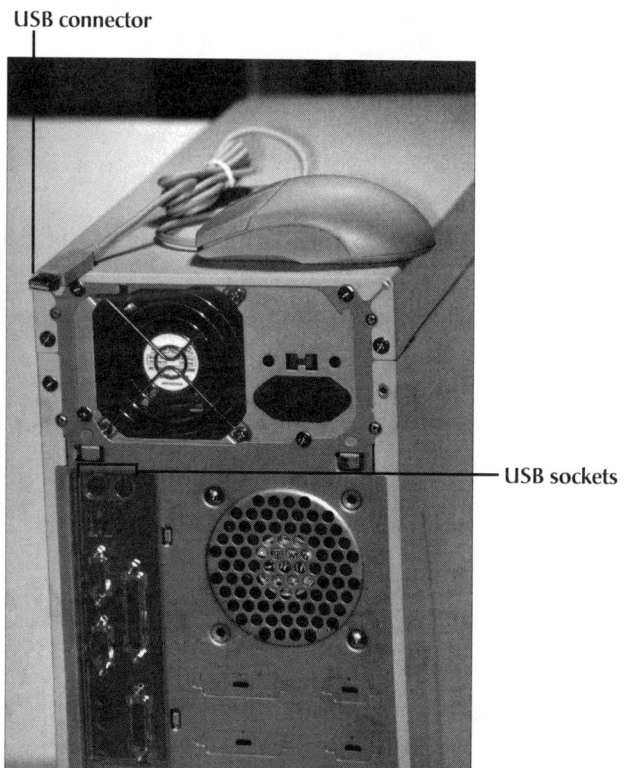

FIGURE 6-6 USB port on the back of a computer. The USB mouse is on top.

The USB scheme is hierarchical in nature. The PC system is called the *host*. The two types of devices that can be attached to a host are the *hub* and the *individual devices*. The hub is a device that provides jacks into which you can plug devices. Devices can be plugged into the hub or directly into the host. Hubs can also be plugged into other hubs, creating a root structure similar to a tree, with the only requirement being the avoidance of cabling loops. Figure 6-7 shows a typical USB configuration.

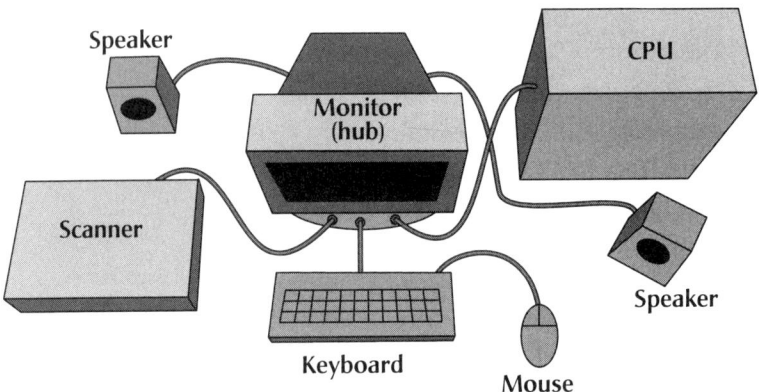

FIGURE 6-7   A typical USB configuration

The circuitry in the PC controls the host hub and is called the *bus controller*. USB systems can have only one bus controller.

Two great things about the USB are the speed at which it operates and the fact that the function hardware configuration is handled entirely by the USB system. USB technology provides a signaling rate of 12Mbits per second in high-speed mode and 1.2Mbits per second in low-speed mode. The maximum length of USB cables is 5 meters. Hubs regenerate the signal, enabling longer lengths of daisy-chained devices. USB is a very new technology that is only now beginning to be available in peripherals.

Two challenges exist for USB: first is the relative lack of hardware and software that is available for USB, but this is changing daily. Second, rival protocols such as FireWire are gaining acceptance, but at a significantly higher cost per device. FireWire is being targeted at higher-speed devices such as disk drives. Microsoft and its Windows 98 specifications require that a PC have a USB port.

NETWORKING CONCEPTS

Volumes have been written about networking. As an A+ technician, you will be expected to know how to install and configure networking cards, install cables, and troubleshoot network configurations. This section will briefly describe the concepts of a network and how to isolate problems.

Network Topologies

How a network is laid out is called its *topology*. Fundamentally, three topologies exist for networking: *bus*, *star*, and *ring*. In practical use, these three are sometimes combined in different network segments. Figure 6-8 shows these three topologies. Fundamentally, the bus network is the easiest to implement, the star is the easiest to troubleshoot, and the ring is the most reliable.

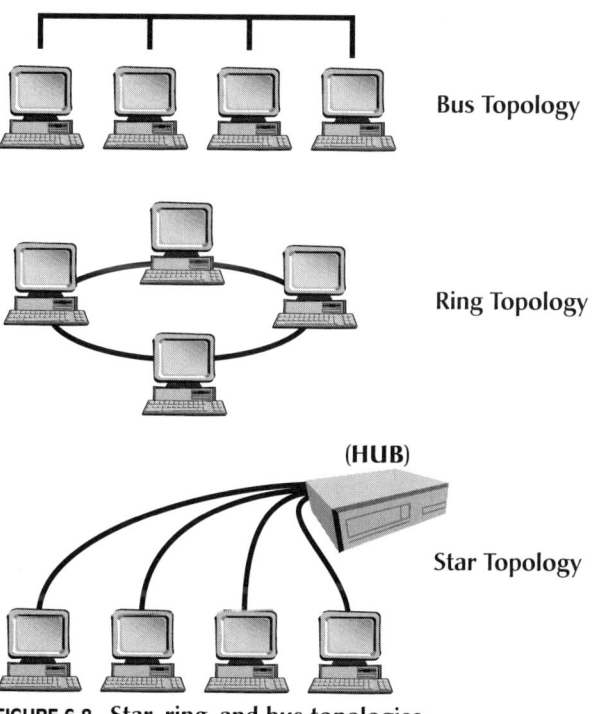

FIGURE 6-8 Star, ring, and bus topologies

The bus topology is implemented by running a data cable from computer to computer in a daisy-chain manner. Each workstation is connected to the bus in series. Each end of the bus must be terminated with some form of termination device to prevent malfunctions. The Ethernet network is based on the bus network model. Any computer or station on the network can broadcast information onto the bus for all other computers to see. The broadcast contains the address of the destination as well as the message. The appropriate station receives and processes the data.

The ring topology is similar to the bus, with the exception that the system is closed — one end is connected to the other end. Rings frequently use the *token system*. The token is sent prior to any data, and possession of the token gives the computer the right to send data on the network. Think of it like the passing of a baton in a relay race. This token is read by each workstation on its way to the destination. When the receiving station processes the token, it releases it to the network for use by another system.

The third topology is the most common today — the star topology. The star topology is constructed by connecting all workstations to a central device called a *hub*. This hub provides the only network connection between stations. Hubs can be connected to each other for network expansion. This allows for virtually unlimited growth of the network.

Connecting a computer to a network is accomplished by a *Network Interface Card* (NIC). The NIC is usually plugged into the system's PCI or ISA slots. Like the other devices we have discussed, NICs must have the proper IRQ, DMA, and memory addresses configured. Most of the newer cards are Plug and Play and require very little configuration support. If the card comes with a configuration program, it must be run and the options set before the system can power up.

The most common types of problems you will encounter with a network involve loose or broken cables, or malfunctioning network cards. In a bus network, stations are added using BNC-T connectors. These connectors can usually be purchased at almost any computer store. It is critical in a bus network that both ends of the network have a terminator of some sort attached. These terminators prevent stray signals from entering the network and also prevent signals on the network from bouncing back and causing interference.

Network Types

The most common type of networks are the 10Base networks. The *10* refers to the fact that the network has a data rate of 10Mbps. The *Base* refers to the fact that the network is a *baseband network*, which means the signal is transmitted without a carrier signal. Standard 10Base standards include the 10BaseT, 10Base5, and 10Base2. Table 6-7 shows the more common 10Base networks and the lengths associated with them.

 **exam preparation pointer** **A simple way to remember the lengths of a network is by the name. The maximum length of a 10Base2 network is 185 meters, the 10Base5 is 500 meters, and the 10BaseT is 100 meters.**

TABLE 6-7 THE THREE MOST COMMON BASEBAND NETWORKS

CONFIGURATION	TECHNOLOGY	LENGTH
10Base2	Thinnet	185 meters
10Base5	Thicknet	500 meters
10BaseT	Twisted pair	100 meters

The other type of network that you may encounter is called a *broadband network*. The difference conceptually is fairly simple. A broadband network is the computer equivalent of a TV cable system. The cable is broken down into separate channels that can be "tuned-into" depending on the requirements. Broadband networks are capable of handling enormous amounts of information when coupled with microwave or satellite technologies. Capacity in a baseband network is a function of the speed of the cable. Capacity in a broadband network, however, is a function of the number of available channels and the speed of each of those channels. A 100BaseT system is ten times faster than a 10BaseT network.

 **exam preparation pointer** **A simple way to remember the relationship between baseband and broadband is to remember that a broadband carries basebands.**

Cabling Types

The last part of this section briefly discusses the various types of cabling used in networks. Primarily, two types are used: *twisted pair* and *coaxial*. Twisted pair is primarily used today in higher-speed, higher-bandwidth networks. Figure 6-9 shows the two types of cabling discussed in this section. Most office environments use some form of twisted pair wiring.

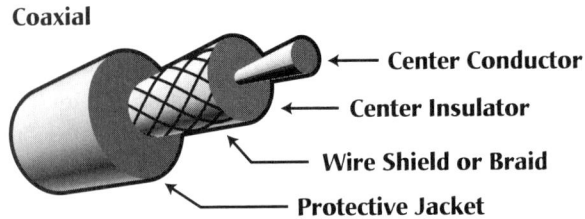

Coaxial

← **Center Conductor**
← **Center Insulator**
Wire Shield or Braid
Protective Jacket

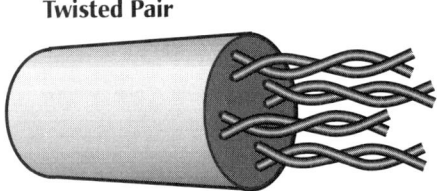

Twisted Pair

FIGURE 6-9   The two common types of cables involved in networking systems

Twisted pair uses a differential signal with noise cancellation to fight noise and interference. Coaxial cable uses the outer braid to carry the signal return, and can be very susceptible to noise and interference. Coaxial cable has one wire, whereas twin-axial has two. Coaxial type cables can also be run for longer lengths because they do not suffer as badly from *attenuation*. Attenuation is a characteristic of electricity and radio frequency, where the strength of the signal decreases over length. At some point, the signal and the noise level become indistinguishable from each other. Amplifiers and repeaters can increase signal strength and overcome attenuation in many environments. Coaxial cabling can cost substantially more than twisted pair wiring to install, and has been largely replaced by twisted pair.

Twisted pair wiring is an adaptation from the telephone industry. Wires are twisted around each other in a manner that helps them minimize interference. This type of cable can either be *unshielded* or *shielded*. Unshielded twisted pair is referred to as *UTP*, and shielded twisted pair is called *STP*.

The third type of cabling that you will encounter is *fiber optic*. Fiber optic cables send information by using light impulses instead of voltage. The advantage to fiber cables is their ability to send large amounts of data at very high speed. Fiber optic systems require special cabling, tools, and installation procedures, and are relatively expensive to install. Fiber optic cable has the ability to exceed 100Mbps bandwidth. Many large networks use fiber optic cabling to connect between smaller networks. This interconnection is called a *backbone network* and allows for the most cost-effective use of the fiber medium.

KEY POINT SUMMARY

Communications systems require several components to function: a sender, a receiver, a medium or way to send the message, and the message.

- Serial communication involves sending each information unit in sequence, one behind the other. Parallel communication systems involve sending more than one information unit simultaneously, along separate channels. Most computer parallel communication ports work with 8-bit data and send this all at one time.

- Data is sent either asynchronously or synchronously. Asynchronous information involves the message containing timing information, such as start and stop bits along with the message. Synchronous protocol is timed by one end or the other and the data is framed into channels. Synchronous protocol enables higher-speed data transmission than does asynchronous transmission.

- Information that can be sent and received at the same time is called full-duplex. If only one direction can be active at a time, that is called half-duplex. Most communications on serial ports today is full-duplex.

- The keyboard is the primary input device for most computers. Information is scanned into the CPU from keystrokes on the keys. The keys of most keyboards are composed of one of the following technologies: mechanical switch, rubber dome, or membrane key switch.

o The mouse provides point-and-click operation to most computer systems on the market today. The mouse uses a small ball that is rolled across a surface. The motion of the ball is translated into a coordinate system that positions the cursor on the screen. Most mice have one, two, or three buttons that activate commands in the program.

o Serial ports use a series of signaling wires to indicate status of the lines. Common lines include DTR, DSR, and RTS. All serial cables require that a return line be provided between the two systems.

o A modem is a device that allows computers to use telecommunications networks to transfer information. Modems typically use either AM or FSK frequency modulation. Higher-speed modems usually use some form of FSK for data transmission.

o A CSU/DSU differs from a modem because it is designed to be used in digital circuits, whereas the modem is designed for analog circuits. Digital communications such as ISDN or T1 provide faster information transfer because they use a wider bandwidth.

o Most printers today use the parallel port for communications. Data transfer rates on the parallel port can far exceed serial communication speeds. Typically, a parallel port uses a 36-pin connector at the printer for communications. This connector is referred to as a Centronics connector. IBM adapted the Centronics port to fit on a 25-pin connector to the system, thus saving space on the system unit. This has become a standard for most PC systems.

o Several standards exist for parallel cabling today. The most common standard that you will encounter is called the IEEE 1284 standard. This standard lays out signal handling characteristics of printer cables. Whenever possible, use this standard for cabling.

o Printer ports can operate in several modes. The most common mode is called the ECP mode. This mode is bidirectional and extremely fast. ECP enables automatic configuration of devices on the cable.

o A relatively new standard being released is called the USB. USB connections promise to be fast and easy. Several other proposed standards are being tried that may make USB obsolete before it is even fully implemented. Most current motherboards provide integrated USB support.

APPLYING WHAT YOU'VE LEARNED

This chapter has covered a lot of important material that will help you prepare for the A+ exam and be a competent technician. Take a few minutes and work through the Instant Assessment questions, review your notes, and see how you did.

The Hands-on lab will also help build your comfort level with the hardware, as well as reinforce the readings from this chapter.

Instant Assessment

Multiple choice

Choose the best answer(s). There may be more than one correct answer for each question.

1. Serial communication involves moving the data:

  A. In reverse byte swapping down the line

  B. In a sequential stream

  C. Across multiple lines simultaneously

  D. From the receiver to the sender

2. Asynchronous transmission involves the following:

  A. Sending information using a start/stop protocol

  B. Sending information using external clocking

  C. Sending data using mechanical feeder protocol

  D. Receiving information from the sender in time clocked order

3. Synchronous communications involves information transfer using:

  A. Start/stop bits

B. Xon/Xoff protocol

C. *Random Frame Generation* (RFM)

D. Synchronizing clock signals

4. Data that can be sent and received simultaneously is called:

   A. Full-duplex

   B. Half-duplex

   C. Frequency modulation

   D. Phase shift keying

5. Keyboards use which of the following methods (select all that apply):

   A. Mechanical switch

   B. Electro-static capacitance

   C. Rubber dome

   D. Membrane

6. The most common serial port standard is:

   A. IEE-488

   B. RS-232C

   C. HP-IB

   D. DTR

7. Modems translate what types of data (select all that apply):

   A. AC to DC

   B. Analog to digital

   C. Digital to analog

   D. Phase shift to multiplexed

8. A standard parallel port used for printers is:

   A. IEEE 1284

   B. IEEE RS-488

   C. IEEE PC-AI

   D. ANSI X36.V

9. The standard connector used on printers to connect them to computers is:

   A. 36-pin B connector

B. 25-pin A connector

C. 36-pin D connector

D. 25-pin B connector

Fill in the blank

1. Synchronous transmission requires a _____ level of administrative overhead.

2. Keyboards are connected to the systems unit using a _____ connector.

3. Keyboard input data is _____ by the BIOS and sent to the operating system.

4. The two standard connectors used for serial communications are the _____ and _____.

5. The CSU/DSU is used for _____ circuits.

6. Parallel ports on most computers today provide support for the _____ mode.

7. The USB port uses a _____ method for device interconnection.

Hands-on Lab Exercise

Lab 6-4 *Installing serial and parallel port cables, the mouse port, modem card, and network card*

In the last three lab exercises, you installed the motherboard and peripherals, and verified the operation of the system unit. You also installed the hard drives, and if you were industrious, you read ahead into the later chapters about how to configure your hard drives and your CD-ROM player. In this lab, you are going to install the serial and parallel port cables, the mouse port, modem card, and a network card.

Materials required

- Static strap
- Phillips-head screwdriver

- Parallel/serial connector kit
- Modem card
- Network card

In this lab, we will install a modem and a 3Com 10BaseT NIC (network interface card).

Laying the system on its side, we will choose an available ISA slot for the modem. We will also choose a PCI slot for the network card. The modem we will be installing is a 56K modem and the network card we are installing is a 100/10Mbit network card.

Let's get the modem card installed into the computer system.

This modem is Plug and Play, and will be configured by the operating system on startup. We will also install the NIC into an available PCI slot.

You will need to connect the modem into a modular telephone jack. For that, you will use what is called an RJ-11 connector. The RJ-11 is a four-wire system that most houses and offices have upgraded to. Several companies sell adapters for the wired wall plug to RJ-11 connector. If you have questions about how these work, take your phone jack apart and study how the wires are connected to the wall plate.

The network connector we will be connecting to what is called a *CAT-5 network*. CAT-5 refers to the bandwidth capabilities of a network. This network uses an STP eight-wire connector that is connected via an eight-wire jack called an *RJ-45*. These are standard cables and can be purchased at virtually any computer store. These systems are fairly simple to work with. Most residences have one- or two-wire cables pulled into a wiring jack. This allows for connection of multiple telephones to the Telco system.

Now it is time for you to take a field trip. Your organization, school, or church probably has a network and a complicated phone system. Go and ask one of the systems managers to give you a tour. Have them explain how the network functions, and the technologies used in that environment. You will probably find this to be fascinating and it will give you a chance to network with groups you may be interested in joining.

When you finish your field trip, write down the things you saw and answer these questions:

1. What type of network technology are they using?

2. Was the network you looked at part of a bigger network, such as the Internet, and how did they connect?

3. What type of network adapters and standards are they using?

4. How is network troubleshooting accomplished?

5. How many workstations are connected to the network?

6. Does the company allow end users to use modems on their computers?

7. How does their data communications system work and is it integrated with the voice system?

8. What was the most interesting thing you saw on the tour?

9. What did you learn about the industry?

Computer Buses

About Chapter 7

This chapter examines the types and contents of computer buses in use today. Specifically, this chapter covers the ISA, EISA, MCA, VLB, PCMCIA (PC Card), PCI, and AGP buses. The Small Computer Systems Interface (SCSI) bus, while technically an input/output (I/O) bus, offers many of the functions of a system-level bus, and is discussed in this chapter as well. We'll introduce bus concepts and then explore the differences between these buses.

The ISA, EISA, MCA, VLB, PCI, and AGP are computer buses, or data pathways, that reside on the motherboard and allow various types of controllers and physical devices to exchange data with the system's CPU and memory. Devices and controllers such as modems, disk controllers, and multimedia boards are connected to the computer by one of the computer buses mentioned here. The SCSI bus is designed to connect high-speed, high-performance peripherals and storage devices such as disk drives, tape drives, RAID arrays, and CDs to the system. Document scanners are also typically connected to the system unit via a SCSI interface, although manufacturers are now offering USB (Universal Serial Bus) scanners.

Bus Concepts

From a hardware perspective, a *bus* is a set of wires or copper traces that are used to interconnect devices on a computer system. This provides the electrical connection between multiple devices. Beyond this electrical connection, the bus must have a series of protocols or rules governing transmission of data over these connections so that multiple devices can use the pathway simultaneously without interfering with one another.

Early microcomputer buses were coupled directly to and managed by the CPU. Bus technology has evolved a great deal in the last 20 years, with more changes on the horizon. Most buses also provide power and status lines to power the devices that are plugged into it. The power and control schemes can be quite elaborate, as in the case of the PCI bus, or very simple, as indicated in Figure 7-1.

Picture the simplest of bus architectures — one data line with three devices sharing it. The bus also has two control lines — one for requests, and one for activity (busy or not busy signals). If device 1 has information it wants to transmit, it must send a request signal (on the request line). The bus controller acknowledges the request by setting the busy line to busy. When this happens, device 1 can send its data on the data line. If this data were of interest or concern to one of the other devices, it would be read and processed by that device as well. Once the data has been transmitted over the data line, device 1 drops its request flag on the request line, letting the bus controller know it's done with its transmission. After a reasonable amount of time has passed, the bus controller would then reset the busy line to not busy and await the next request.

In this simplified scenario, nothing occurs on the bus without the bus controller managing the dialogue. The bus controller serves as a bus master. If one of the three devices on the bus could perform this task, as well as its own individual task, this device would be called a *bus master device*. This model forms the basis for what is called bus mastering on computer buses.

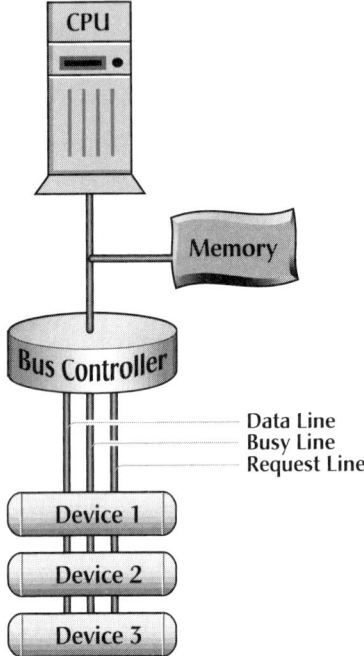

FIGURE 7-1 A conceptual bus

Bus Wars

Early personal computers had the CPU performing the role of bus controller as well as processing unit. This role, while allowing devices to be close to the CPU, also placed overhead requirements on the CPU, which reduced performance.

The early PCs were based on an 8-bit bus, which was called the *PC bus*. This bus was directly connected between the CPU and peripheral devices. The first PCs produced by IBM ran at 4.77MHz. All of the devices on the bus were also expected to run at that speed or slower. In reality, most of the devices operated considerably slower than that.

All boards on the PC ran no faster than the clock speed of the CPU and were limited to the data width of the CPU. The maximum bus speed was just slightly over 2MB per second. Main memory was connected to this bus using expansion cards. These machines were usually upgraded by someone similar in capability to an A+ technician. Each device on the bus required its own configuration jumpers for addresses, interrupts, and priority. These early PCs had a limit of 64K of memory on the motherboard, though it was possible to upgrade them to 256K. The more important limitation on the earliest PCs was the lack of BIOS calls to external BIOS chips, which prevented the use of hard drives. This became a factor for these earliest PCs after hard drives became more common and users were unable to upgrade their older PCs with a hard drive.

The overall effect of this was that since everything ran at the CPU speed, bus performance was seldom an issue. Of course, the downside of this mechanism was that any device on the bus had the undivided attention of the CPU whenever it needed it. This was often a detriment to system capabilities because of devices like printers, which were slow and required data transfer coordination from the CPU.

The 80286, or PC AT, introduced a change in the industry. Instead of a 16-bit microcomputer with 8-bit external data paths (like the 8088), the AT was a true 16-bit microprocessor. One of the first deficiencies of the PC bus was its limit of 8-bit width. In order to compensate for this, and to allow for future capabilities, IBM added a second connector to the bus. This contained 38 additional pins. These pins allowed a full 16-bit wide data space and a 24-address line capability. The 24-address line capability expanded the memory capability of the AT bus to address 16MB of data, and the 80286 could address up to 1GB of memory space by using virtual memory in protected mode.

The 8-bit portion of the connector enabled the addition of some older 8-bit boards into 16-bit slots. There were significant compatibility issues, however. Many older 8-bit boards would not run in an 8-bit AT slot, because they were designed to run at slower bus speeds. Further, there were distinct differences between 8- and 16-bit hard drive controllers. Many older 8-bit cards also had an "apron," which prevented its insertion into a 16-bit slot. This bus method became the *Industry Standard Architecture* (ISA) bus still in use today. Figure 7-2 shows a motherboard with ISA slots, as well as several others in use today.

note **The original IBM computer introduced the ISA bus.**

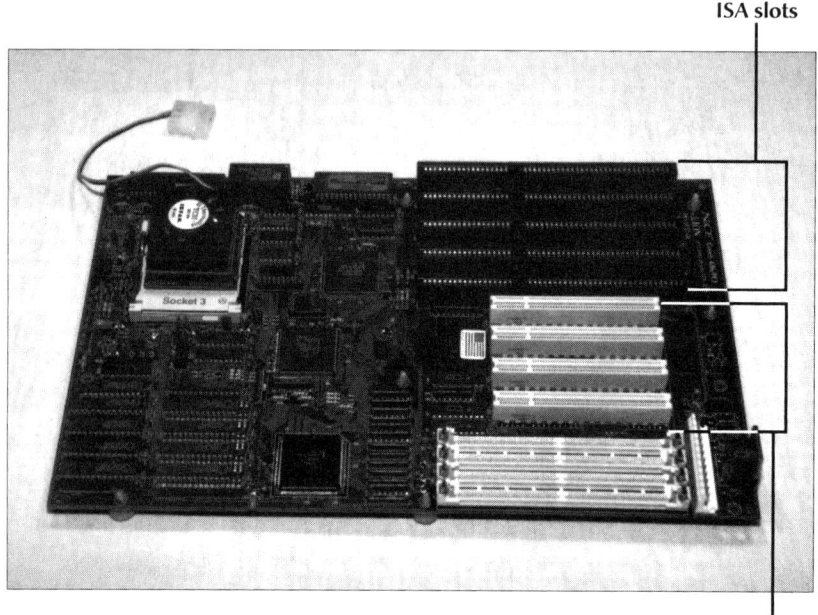

FIGURE 7-2 **Motherboard showing the different types of bus slots for expansion boards**

Expansion boards are available in several different configurations. You will notice in Figure 7-3 that the ISA board can be plugged into the EISA slot, whereas all the other architectures are deliberately incompatible so that cards cannot be inadvertently inserted into the wrong slot.

In the mid-1980s, Compaq Computer introduced a 12MHz 80286 system that was designed to outperform the 8MHz AT offered by IBM. This system introduced a new capability to the PC. In these Compaq systems, the CPU was able to run considerably faster than the expansion cards, which were designed to run at 8MHz. To counter this, Compaq introduced a second bus, or local bus, that could contain memory. This local bus worked at considerably faster speeds than the AT or ISA bus. Many ISA-based computer systems subsequently provided a similar high-speed memory board to accelerate CPU performance. This innovation by Compaq represented the first dual bus for a PC-based product.

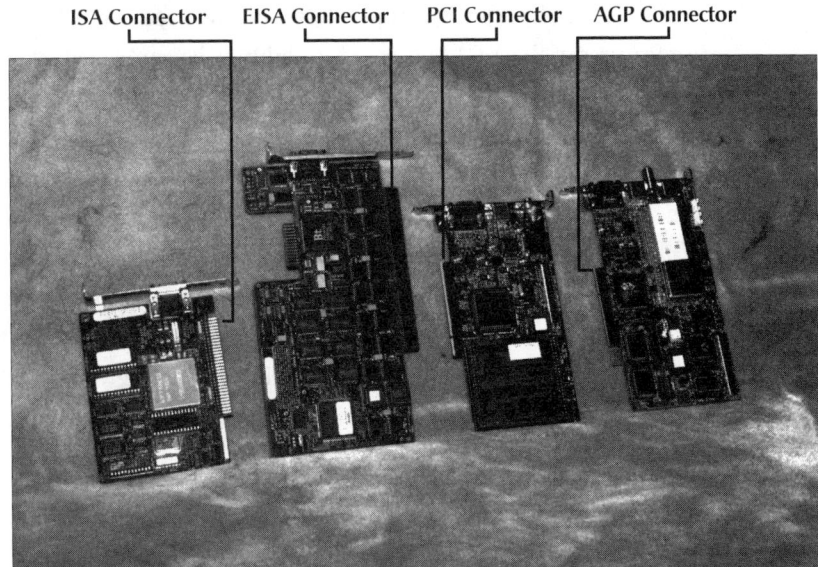

FIGURE 7-3 These cards – ISA, EISA, PCI, and AGP – are commonly used in PC computers today.

The PC AT bus eventually became recognized as the ISA bus by the IEEE. This standard is still being used today and most computer systems provide ISA slots that can be used to hook up lower-speed devices to the CPU.

Processor speeds and capabilities continued to accelerate through the late 1980s. IBM and others recognized the inherent limitations of the ISA bus and set about creating new standards that allowed for faster devices and higher throughput.

IBM introduced a new architecture called the *Micro Channel Architecture* (MCA) in 1987. The MCA, a clearly superior innovation for IBM, addressed many of the problems encountered by the PC and the ISA bus. The Intel 80386 was being released, which offered the promise of 16MHz throughput, 4GB memory storage, and a 32-bit data path. These new chips offered the potential to blow away the capabilities of the older 80286 systems. The major problem with this new technology was that it would have still been strapped to an 8-bit bus design that had been upgraded to 16-bit.

IBM set out to remedy this problem with the superior MCA bus. Some of the major features of the MCA bus were the ability to be controlled by a bus controller instead of the CPU. These bus controllers managed data traffic across the bus and were called *bus masters*. The Micro Channel bus also ran at 10MHz, a slight improvement over the 8MHz bus of the AT. However, MCA used a connector that was incompatible with the ISA bus, and IBM required manufacturers that wanted to manufacture add-in boards to pay a royalty and percentage for the right to use their proprietary standard. Many manufacturers had seen the benefit of truly standard PC components, not controlled by any one company, and they rebelled against this architecture, instead collaborating on another new standard. MCA has since been added to the list of technically superior but poorly marketed products in the historical boneyard.

note **IBM introduced the MCA bus on the PS/2 computer.**

In 1988, as a counter to IBM's MCA bus, a consortium of nine companies, including AST, Compaq, Epson, HP, NEC, Tandy, Wyse, and Zenith developed the Extended ISA, or EISA bus. EISA is similar in concept to Micro Channel but is really an enhancement of the ISA bus. EISA borrowed the best practices of the industry to create a "super-bus" that included bus mastering, automated setup, and interrupt sharing. EISA also added new data transfer modes that considerably sped up data transfer. The initial claims were that EISA would be fifty percent faster or more over MCA, but IBM responded and the net effect was that both bus architectures offered substantial speed improvements. The big advantage of EISA was that older ISA boards could be plugged into the EISA slots. EISA slots have two sets of connectors — one shallower, for ISA connectors, and one deeper within the slot, for EISA connectors. This, coupled with industry resentment of IBM's attempt to redefine and control an industry standard, led to EISA's more rapid acceptance.

Figure 7-4 shows a typical EISA board next to an ISA board. The board on the left (an 8-bit ISA card) has a connector that is exactly the same length as the bottom portion of the board to its right, the EISA board. This allows ISA boards to be used in EISA slots. Note the shorter length of the ISA connector — the EISA connector goes deeper into the EISA slot to a different set of connectors than the ISA board would.

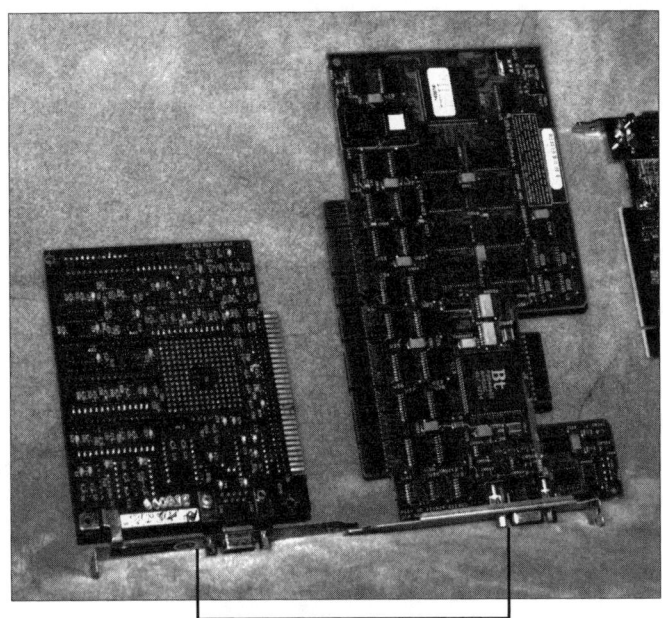

ISA and EISA Connectors side-by-side

FIGURE 7-4 ISA and EISA

Even now, the war rages on between IBM and the EISA group about performance. The major problem with these two architectures is the fact that they are very expensive and don't cause much of an apparent increase in system performance. This has hindered many people in embracing these technologies. At the same time, other technological breakthroughs such as VLB, PCI, and AGP have made it a moot point.

> note **EISA took the most popular features from other buses and expanded upon them.**

LOCAL BUSES

Many manufacturers recognized early on that the EISA-MCA war would do very little to provide high-speed performance to the newer generation of 80386 chips and beyond. This is caused by the fact that the bus speed is still under 10MHz in most examples. The relatively large amount of data required to drive video-intensive applications such as Windows 95 can effectively bring an ISA system to a grinding halt. In high-density video applications, it might take one to two seconds to fill a screen full of high-resolution graphics. Needless to say, while this was occurring, the system would be unable to accomplish any other work.

To solve this burgeoning performance problem, many manufacturers introduced a high-speed bus called a *local bus*. These local buses provided a high-speed slot that a video card could be inserted into. This capability gave video processors the opportunity to communicate at high speed with the CPU. Early versions of these local bus configurations were highly machine proprietary, and options were usually limited to the manufacturer's proprietary board.

The *Video Electronics Standards Association* (VESA) created the VESA Local Bus standard — the VL Bus. This standard was introduced in 1992. Most of the industry immediately accepted this standard and started creating products for it right away.

The VL Bus gave the industry a standard connection that allowed near CPU-speed access. The VL Bus controller is responsible for managing the VL Bus devices, as is the EISA/ISA bus controller.

note ▼ **The VL bus is another term for VESA Local Bus.**

In this arrangement, the VL Bus controller runs at the CPU clock speed up to a maximum of 66MHz, although the practical limit is 50MHz. Even at that speed, this is six times faster than a traditional ISA bus slot. However, very few machines built today include support for the VL Bus, having abandoned it for the superior PCI bus.

Intel introduced its version of a high-speed local bus, the PCI bus, which has proven to be a superior alternative to the VESA bus (see Figure 7-5). Although this bus was not originally designed as an alternative to the VL Bus, it has become the leader in the local bus arrangement. With burst rates of up to 133MB per second, it is quite formidable. The major advantage Intel brought to the table is a highly standardized chip set that could be rapidly integrated onto a motherboard, allowing systems designers and manufacturers to quickly implement a very stable PCI bus subsystem. Many peripheral cards are available in PCI, including coprocessed video and network cards. New sound cards and 3D graphics cards are also available that capitalize on the high speed of the PCI bus.

 note ▼ **The PCI bus is a local bus that provides performance in excess of 133MB in burst mode.**

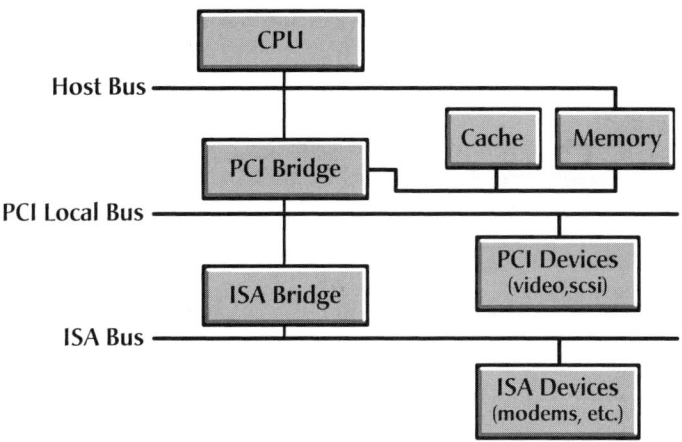

FIGURE 7-5 The functional subsystems in a PCI system

Notice the three buses referenced in Figure 7-5. The host bus is the fastest of the buses and can operate at speeds in excess of 500MB per second. The host bus is totally controlled by the CPU. Memory transactions such as caching, as well as all I/O transactions, occur on this bus. The PCI system manages memory access as well as certain cache operations. The PCI chip set also controls the PCI bus, which has a peak transfer rate of 133MB per second. The third bus is the ISA bus, which of course is the slowest bus of them all at 5 to 8MB per second.

All of these buses were designed with desktop and tower systems in mind. In those applications, ample space and power are available to the computer system. While these desktop systems were growing in capability, a great deal of change was occurring in the market for laptop and portable computer systems. These systems are constrained by physical size, weight, and power considerations.

PC CARD OR PCMCIA

PCMCIA stands for Personal Computer Memory Card International Association. This standard is now called the PC Card. The PC Card standard describes a four-size host socket that is usable by peripheral devices. The PC Card plugs into a 68-pin host socket. Currently, three size cards are specified. The cards are upward compatible in that a Type I card can fit in a Type II card slot, and a Type II card can fit in a Type III card, and so on. Table 7-1 shows the dimensions and typical usages of these cards according to PCMCIA.

note   **The PCMCIA or PC Card was designed for use in notebook and sub-notebook computers.**

TABLE 7-1 PC CARD DIMENSIONS AND USAGE

PC CARD	LENGTH	WIDTH	THICKNESS	TYPICAL USAGE
Type I	85.6 mm	54.0 mm	3.3 mm	Memory
Type II	85.6 mm	54.0 mm	5.0 mm	I/O
Type III	85.6 mm	54.0 mm	10.5 mm	Rotating mass storage

Most portable computer systems today provide ready access for multiple Type I and II cards or a single Type III card. Figure 7-6 shows a Type II card. The Type II card is a modem card that provides for an external connection. This connection is probably the weak link in the whole PC Card standard. If the wire is overstressed or bent, it has no mechanical strength to prevent it from breaking.

Socket connector

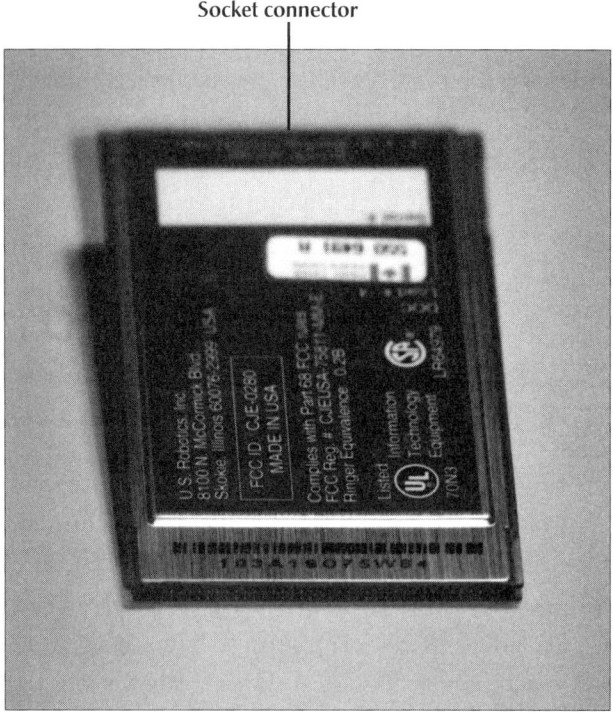

FIGURE 7-6 Enlarged socket connector on the edge of a PC Type II card

These cards add tremendous power to portable computers. The ability to mix and match components into portable computer systems enables users to have low-power consumption and plug-in capabilities. A typical laptop may include a hard drive and a floppy drive as standard equipment. If a CD-ROM is required, a separate PC Card may be required to interface to it. To add a modem, another PC Card can be added. However, if that same portable were to be used in the office, it may need connection to a network. In that case, it is possible to remove one of these PC Cards and add a network card. This process is easy and requires no special technical expertise on the part of the computer user.

The use of a standard connection enables inexpensive upgrades of the portable to occur. PC Card is only capable of a 16-bit width. This is usually adequate for any application. The card also has 24 address lines, which allows direct addressing of 64MB of RAM. Bear in mind that each PC Card is addressed separately and can manage its own 64MB of memory. Each card has the ability to store a second 64MB of data for attributes. These attributes might describe the card type, functions, and other information about the card. Most PC cards only use a few kilobytes of information for attributes, which enables the potential use of the attribute memory to be used as additional memory.

The configuration and programmability of PC Cards enables implementation of multiple peripheral options to be easy for the end user. The cards inform the computer what type they are, and most common portables maintain a database of device drivers that enable rapid configuration. In some cases, the cards can be removed and installed while the power is running, allowing for on-the-fly reconfiguration.

The following sections deal with some of the system specifics of the ISA, EISA, and the PCI bus. This information will be useful in helping you troubleshoot and repair problems that may occur with these buses. The EISA and PCI bus require little if any troubleshooting or configuration, whereas many devices that use the ISA bus still have jumpers and configuration options. Newer cards and software utilize one of several Plug and Play options that make installation and configuration easier.

THE ISA BUS

The *Industry Standard Architecture* (ISA) bus is probably the simplest bus on most computers systems today. The early ISA bus, as implemented on the original

IBM PC and compatibles, was an 8-bit bus. Most computer manufacturers today support a 16-bit, 8MHz bus. This bus utilizes 62 pins. The connector and socket have two sides, an A side and a B side. The edge connector is gold plated for a more reliable connection. Gold-plated connections will not corrode and are hard to scratch or damage. The 8-bit card is a single 62-pin connector and the 16-bit card uses the 62-pin plus the additional 38. Most 8-bit cards work properly when installed into the 62-pin socket of the 16-bit bus.

The ISA bus can address 16MB of memory because of its 24-bit address bus. Interrupt lines allow the boards to be configured according to priority. Interrupt ReQuest Assignments, or IRQs, are signal lines that connect between a device and the CPU. Many ISA boards required that the IRQ be configured by moving a jumper on the board. It is important to note that on an ISA bus, serious problems will occur if more than one device has the same IRQ. The bus may hang, making troubleshooting difficult, or the added device will not function. If a bus hangs, the system will not be able to communicate with the bus, which may cause the CPU to freeze. The solution to this is to attempt to change the interrupt to another number. Operating systems like Windows 95 will recognize that the device conflicts with another device and inform you which devices are conflicting.

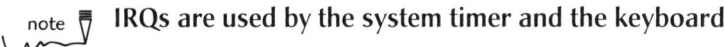 **IRQs are used by the system timer and the keyboard.**

Overall, the ISA bus is a relatively well-understood, easy-to-interface connection that allows low-speed devices to be configured on a PC. Many original expansion cards will still work on the ISA bus with no modifications. The major disadvantage of an ISA-based computer is the relatively slow speed offered to devices.

THE EISA BUS

The *Extended Industry Standards Architecture* (EISA) bus is a 32-bit bus designed to enhance performance of computer systems. It is a direct competitor to the PCI bus discussed in the next section. The EISA bus is most commonly found in servers. EISA configuration is performed with an EIS configuration utility provided by the system manufacturer. Because this configuration is system-specific, you'll need the system documentation. One of the interesting aspects of this bus is the fact that the EISA card has two levels of connectors that allow for connection of ISA cards into EISA slots. The EISA bus is faster than the ISA bus, but requires special cards to use that speed.

EISA allows for 4GB of memory, software device configuration, and no interrupts. These advantages and others were offset by the fact that though it is faster than the ISA or AT bus, it is still limited to 8MHz, making it extremely slow in comparison to the PCI bus.

THE PCI BUS

The first solution in the high-speed bus derby capable of supporting multiple PCI devices is the PCI bus. The PCI, or Peripheral Component Interconnect, is a high-speed bus that is standard on most motherboards available today. PCI is a standard developed originally by Intel for the 80486 and Pentium processor-based systems. Apple, DEC, and other non – Intel-based systems are now being released with PCI slots, allowing for larger availability and expansion options both for PCs and other systems.

The CPU and the bus talk to each other via a bridging circuit, which buffers the high-speed bus and CPU from the slower PCI bus. Intel manufactures chips that merely require CPU designers to interface to a standard signal and transfer protocol. Currently, PCI runs at 66MHz, making it the fastest of the PC buses. The effective throughput of this speed can be as high as 264Bps on a 64-bit board. We are talking about a huge amount of speed.

The connection between the CPU and the relatively slower devices is handled by a set of devices called a *bridging circuit*. The bridging circuit or Host-PCI bridge communicates with both memory and cache memory on behalf of the CPU. The PCI bridge provides a connection between the CPU and its memory via a bus.

This bus is called a host bus. It operates at very high speed and is difficult to interface with. The only things that connect with the host bus are memory, caching, and support chips necessary for the processor to operate. These chips are part of a chip set that Intel calls a PCI set. The chip set also maintains a connection to the PCI bus. This bus allows for the connection of PCI cards such as video or graphics cards, high-speed disk, video, or other types of cards that can handle those speeds.

The connection to the PCI bus uses a 124-pin socket. This socket also supports three different types of boards—3.3V, 5V, and universal adapter. These slots prevent the wrong board from being plugged into the slot, potentially frying the card. Most PCI cards today are of the universal type and will function properly in any PCI slot.

The PCI bus also allows for automated setup, which makes configuration easier. The sections on IRQs and Plug and Play outline this in greater detail. PCI seems to be the winner of the high-speed bus war and in the next several years, more devices will be available under the PCI configuration. Many of the newer motherboards have now expanded the number of PCI slots to five and reduced the number of ISA slots to one or two. These ISA slots are retained for compatibility purposes with older devices.

THE AGP Bus

The *Advanced Graphics Port* (AGP) connector was introduced soon after the Pentium II CPU (refer back to Figure 7-3). It allows a single AGP video card to connect to the host bus. Despite the huge performance gains offered by the PCI bus, graphics processing is extremely resource intensive. In very high-speed, high-resolution video applications — most notably games, as well as 3D animation programs and DVD playback — the PCI bandwidth is simply not fast enough for sufficient video data transfer. AGP offers a transfer speed faster than 500MB per second, more than four times that of the PCI bus. Current implementations provide only one AGP slot per system. Though AGP is the Next Big Thing right now, it's only a matter of time before demand forces the creation of yet another new, faster standard.

IRQs, DMA, and I/O Addresses

Systems configuration is accomplished using IRQs, DMA, and I/O addresses. In fact, for most installations, this is the hardest part of the process. This section will briefly explain these three terms and show you how you can make them work for you.

IRQs

Interrupt ReQuest Assignments, or IRQs, are signal lines that connect between a device and the CPU. All devices, such as COM ports, printer ports, modems, and disk controllers are assigned an IRQ. With little exception, two devices cannot share the same IRQ address.

The modern PC has the ability to support 16 IRQ assignments. The system will assign several of these lines to systems devices by default. The following descriptions define these systems IRQs and provide a brief explanation of them. In general, you cannot assign an expansion device to one of these IRQs, as havoc may erupt. This list shows the different IRQ assignments used in PC systems today. Note that these are the typical assignments, and can be overridden on a system-by-system basis.

- IRQ 0 is used for systems timing. This line is connected to the systems clock.
- IRQ 1 is used for the keyboard.
- IRQ 2 is used by a device called a *programmable interrupt controller* (PIC). The PIC supports the IRQ process.
- IRQ 3 is used for Serial Ports 2 and 4, or COM2 and COM4.
- IRQ 4 is used for Serial Ports 1 and 3, or COM1 and COM3.
- IRQ 5 is used for Parallel Port 2 or LPT2, sound cards, or network cards.
- IRQ 6 is used for the floppy disk controller.
- IRQ 7 is used for Parallel Port 1 or LPT1.
- IRQ 8 is used by the real-time clock.
- IRQ 9 is available for use by plug-in cards.
- IRQ 10 is available for use by plug-in cards.
- IRQ 11 is available for use by plug-in cards.
- IRQ 12 is used by an onboard or PS/2-type mouse.
- IRQ 13 is used by the math coprocessor.
- IRQ 14 is used by the primary IDE/ESDI disk controller.
- IRQ 15 is used by the secondary IDE/ESDI disk controller.

The IRQ line enables each device on the bus to be given a unique priority. Early PCs, with the 8-bit bus, only had the ability to manage eight interrupts. Computer technicians must become very comfortable with IRQ assignments because in new installations, this is typically a problem area for many computer systems.

 Debouncing **refers to cleaning up electrical signals generated by the keyboard.**

The largest difficulty in most systems today is the limited number of IRQ assignments available for expansion.

 Parallel and serial are the two options for connecting a printer to a stand-alone computer.

Early ISA systems required each device to be manually configured to operate correctly. It was not unusual for the proper configuration of a computer system to take days of time and frustration. Initially, it was almost impossible to determine the IRQ settings without physically inspecting each expansion card or buying an expensive diagnostic software package.

The PCI bus does not require the setting of IRQs, because it is handled differently. With the addition of the Plug and Play capabilities of newer computers, most end users will never need those types of tools. The PCI standard allows devices to share IRQ addresses, thus allowing for more expansion capabilities.

It is important to note that on computers that have both PCI and ISA buses, IRQ assignment cannot be shared across the two buses. For example, if an ISA device uses IRQ 7, a PCI device cannot use IRQ 7. On a PCI system, it is common practice to have multiple devices share a single IRQ. On our computer, a video card, DVD drive controller, and the USB port all share IRQ 9.

DMA

Direct Memory Access (DMA) is a process whereby devices can communicate with memory directly, rather than through the CPU. This direct communication offers faster systems performance. Sound cards and disk drives often have this capability. Windows 95 computer properties provide a button to view DMA addresses. This parameter does not need to be changed by an installer.

I/O Addresses

Hardware devices represent themselves as memory locations, which provides a standardized location for information to be transferred between devices and the CPU. These I/O addresses can identify standard places for communications between devices and the CPU. IBM recommends a standard set of addresses that are still in force today. Table 7-2 provides a subset of the standard address locations recommended by IBM.

TABLE 7-2 Using the Recommended Assignments Often Simplifies Systems Configurations

I/O Address		Recommended Assignment
Low	**High**	
0	1F	DMA controller number 1
20	3F	PIC number 1
40	5F	System timers
60	6F	Keyboard and speaker
70	7F	Real-time clock
80	9F	PIC number 2
C0	DF	DMA controller 2
200	20F	Game I/O (joystick)
360	36F	Network adapter card
378	37F	LPT1:
3F0	3EF	Floppy disk controller
3F8	3FF	COM1:

This is by no means a definitive list of the addresses, but as you can see, by sticking to this standard, it is likely that you will encounter little if any difficulty in installing legacy cards into a system. On a positive note, most of the newer operating systems and hardware make these decisions for you with no configuration required by the installer. This feature is called Plug and Play, and will be covered in the next section.

PLUG AND PLAY

The biggest difficulties most computer professionals encounter with PCs are installing and configuring expansion cards. Most controllers and expansion cards require an address, I/O port, and IRQ. Most computers have an abundance of available addresses and I/O ports, but a shortage of IRQs. Another important thing to remember with Plug and Play is that older motherboards will not support it unless the BIOS is upgraded.

Microsoft and Intel created a specification called *Plug and Play* (PNP) in 1993 that automatically gives the responsibility of configuring the card to the motherboard and the operating system. Windows 95 was the first operating system to provide support for Plug and Play.

PNP support is provided in the BIOS chip set for most newer mother boards. PNP-capable computers run through a checkup procedure each time they are booted up. This allows configurations to be changed easily. The reality of the PNP situation may be slightly different — if the boards that are being used are not PNP-capable, a combination of things will need to happen. Older motherboards may not be PNP-compatible, which may be correctable with a ROM or BIOS upgrade from the manufacturer. A good place to start is the appropriate manufacturer's Web site.

Expansion boards that are not PNP-capable must still be configured and installed in the computer expansion slots. These boards will require an IRQ, address, and I/O port configuration settings or jumpers to be set. Almost all newer PCI boards will be PNP, as will most of the newer ISA boards. With ISA boards, however, you must verify that the board indicates that it is Plug and Play compatible to be certain. These ISA boards are called legacy boards, according to the PNP specification.

When a PNP system is started, all the ISA cards not needed to boot up inactivate themselves. A typical device that is required for boot-up would be a disk controller. The PNP operating system tells the PNP cards what configuration they will be using. As you can see, this allows for a maximum of flexibility in that the card can be easily added and polled by the operating system.

PNP cards have four states in which they can exist:

o **Wait for key state**: The board will not respond to any signal on the ISA bus until they receive an initiation key. This key is generated by the operating system and BIOS and takes control of the card. This information is passed to the operating system, which makes configuration decisions.

o **Isolation mode**: Used by the card and the operating system to interact in a precisely defined manner. This manner is called an *isolation sequence*. The cards are addressed by using what is referred to as a *card select number* (CSN). This process allows each card to be assigned a unique CSN, which is passed to the operating system. The operating system then puts all of the cards back into sleep mode for further processing.

o **Configuration mode**: Used to read the card's resource requirements. Each card is switched by the BIOS or operating system individually. Only one card can be in configuration mode at a time. The configuration is then decided upon by the operating system, which activates that card and moves on to the next one.

o **Sleep mode**: Allows the card to exist on the bus and not interfere with the other cards that are being configured.

The hardest part of working with the PNP configuration deals with devices that are not PNP, but that coexist with boards that are. Many older boards have a limited number of options for configuration and may require juggling to fit in a single system.

For example, a typical PC has an ISA device that can exist only in IRQ 4, 5, and 6. Another device can only exist in IRQ 5 and 6, and a third device has an IRQ that can only exist in 4 and 5. For these three devices to work properly, device three could have IRQ 4, device two IRQ 5, and device one IRQ 6. This presents little problem, but limits options for expansion considerably. The PNP devices will examine the bus and fit themselves into locations that are not being used. Of course, PCI devices can share IRQs without any problems.

The biggest challenge in this environment remains integrating older or legacy cards into a newer system. Our recommendation is that if you are going to upgrade a system, you eliminate as many ISA devices as you can in favor of PCI devices.

SCSI Bus

The *Small Computer Systems Interface* (SCSI) is an all-purpose interface that allows for the connection of disks, scanners, and other devices to the computer system. Though technically an I/O bus rather than a system bus, SCSI's ability to control seven or fifteen high-performance devices with a single PCI controller effectively expands the system bus. Originally, SCSI was designed to provide a high-speed disk connection to a low-speed bus. SCSI interfaces and devices have become known for their speed and reliability.

 A SCSI interface supports a minimum of seven devices per controller card.

In fact, the SCSI interfaces available today are the fastest in the market available to computer users (of course, they also tend to be the most expensive). Early SCSI connections were not famous for ease of configuration or installation. Happily, this has changed in most situations and SCSI connections now provide no technological challenge to install or configure.

SCSI Hardware

In the early 1980s, an interface was created called *Shugart Associates Standard Interface* (SASI). Shugart and NCR proposed the SASI standard to ANSI, who issued the the SCSI standard in 1986. The SCSI interface offered a way for multiple types of devices to be hooked up to a single controller (considered by many to be a first). Up to this time, each physical device required its own separate interface standard. The major disadvantage of the SCSI interface is the potential incompatibility between devices. This is discussed later in this chapter.

The SCSI interface is a parallel interface, or bus. This bus is cable oriented and requires a termination on both ends. This termination can come in one of two forms — active or passive. SCSI controllers typically provide an internal connection port and an external connector. The internal connection is used to install drives in the systems unit, and the external connector can be used for external disks, scanners, and other peripherals. The internal connector is usually a 50-pin connector ribbon cable with one or more connections on it. Internal devices are attached to this ribbon cable. A terminator, such as a resistor pack contained in the device or a plug-in terminator, needs to be used on the device that is at the end of the chain.

The external connector may be one of several different types. Adaptec cards use small 50-pin or 68-pin connectors, whereas some lower-performance cards, like those used to connect scanners to PCs, use 25-pin connections. External devices are daisy chained, with the outermost connector device requiring a terminator. One of the major difficulties with SCSI is that cable length can become a challenge. SCSI cables must not exceed the lengths imposed by the standard, or be too short. The maximum length of the SCSI chain should not exceed 19 feet. Cables must also not be shorter in length than 13 inches.

Bus configurations such as SCSI typically require some form of termination. In the case of SCSI, both ends of the cable must be terminated. The SCSI interface serves as one end, while the last device on the other end is typically terminated in some manner. SCSI terminations can either be active or passive. The primary difference is in the manner that the termination is handled. Termination is critical because it keeps energy from reflecting or bouncing back toward the source. This reflection can interfere with the proper operation of the SCSI interface, which can lead to data loss or corruption.

Active terminators provide a power regulator that keeps voltage constant across all of the lines. Active termination results in quicker recovery time because it provides a constant voltage source that can provide additional current as necessary to drive the lines. Passive connectors derive power across a current-limiting resistor. The active terminator has a voltage regulator, whereas the passive has a pull-up circuitry. Resistors provide a mechanism to isolate power and limit current. The major difference is that the active circuit provides a given voltage to each line that is constant, whereas the passive terminator uses what is available.

Many devices, such as the Iomega Zip drive, have a terminator switch, which provides termination internally to the device. This type of situation does not require additional termination. Internal devices will usually be terminated at the last device in the chain.

Each device on a SCSI chain must have a unique address. These addresses are typically set by either a rotary-type switch on the back of the drive or by a set of jumpers on the drive. Most SCSI configurations on PC systems use address 7 as the default address for the controller. A recommended numbering assignment for a SCSI drive is illustrated in Table 7-3. This is not a requirement, but a recommended configuration.

TABLE 7-3 RECOMMENDED SCSI CONFIGURATION		
SCSI ID	*PRIORITY*	*USUAL ASSIGNMENT*
0	Lowest	Boot hard disk
1	Low	Additional hard drive
2-6	Higher	Removable media devices
7	Highest	SCSI host adapter

Our computer also has an IDE adapter that has a hard disk and a DVD installed on it. This configuration seems to work extremely well in the Windows NT environment, as well as under Windows 95. You will notice that the biggest drive is the closest address to the SCSI controller. This gives the fastest device on the bus the highest priority.

SCSI Standards

Three standards exist for SCSI. These are SCSI-I, SCSI-II, and SCSI-III. These standards represent an evolution in capabilities, as opposed to a revolution.

Early SCSI or SCSI-I devices were famous for being difficult to install and configure. Some SCSI devices might not work with other devices, and usually installation of SCSI devices was done by process of experimentation. This caused many manufacturers to offer "matching pairs," or sets of SCSI devices that could work together. It is very rare to encounter a SCSI-I device in retail distribution, and we recommend that you replace it with a newer device if possible.

The SCSI-II standard introduced a common command set that all devices on the bus understand. This virtually assures that all of the devices will work together. SCSI-II also provides wider data paths and faster I/O throughput. Most SCSI devices you will encounter today are SCSI-II devices.

The SCSI-III standard builds upon the SCSI-II standard and adds the capability to support a Serial SCSI, as well as faster technologies such as fiber-optic. Bandwidths of SCSI-III are similar to SCSI-II standards, but with the capability to support more devices. Table 7-4 presents these different standards and capabilities.

TABLE 7-4 SCSI CAPABILITIES

STANDARD	BUS WIDTH	MAX TRANSFER RATE	DEVICES
SCSI-I	8	5	8
SCSI-II	8	10	8
SCSI-II	16	20	8
SCSI-II	32	40	8
SCSI-III	8	10	8
SCSI-III	16	20	16
SCSI-III	32	40	32

Notice that SCSI-II and SCSI-III standards support 8-, 16-, and 32-bit modes.

During your evaluation of SCSI interfaces, you will encounter a number of industry buzzwords that may confuse you. Let's put them on the table here and make some sense of them.

- *Fast SCSI* is a method that adjusts the timing of the signals and allows for faster data transfers than were allowed under SCSI-I (5MB per second versus 10MB second).

- *Wide SCSI* refers to the width of the data signals (8 bits versus 16 bits). Lower-cost SCSI devices are not usually wide devices. Wide SCSI also enables 16 devices to be connected to the SCSI chain.

- *Twin Channel SCSI* refers to the ability of some SCSI controllers to manage more than one string of devices, appearing to operate like a wide controller. This method uses two separate buses that can each address seven devices plus the controller. This method gives the total ability to address 14 devices. This is usually less expensive than what is referred to as wide SCSI.

- *Ultra SCSI* is the highest transfer rate available on a practical basis. This Ultra SCSI refers to the 32-bit connection potential.

New SCSI devices are entering the market all the time. While this is exciting, it also creates opportunities for misunderstanding the capabilities of these devices. It is important to recognize that although a device is capable of a given mode, it may not work in that mode on a given SCSI chain. The following section will describe the cabling used in SCSI installations.

SCSI Cable Standards

We've discussed the different standards used in data transmission on the bus. As you might imagine, multiple cabling options exist as well. In this section, we will discuss the differing cable standards and when to use them. For starters, two fundamental SCSI bus standards are single-ended and differential.

Single-ended refers to the fact that a single wire is used for each signal. All of the signal wires use a common ground return. This is the typical environment used by most computer systems in offices and homes. The maximum length of a cable scheme of a single-ended system is 19 feet. Beyond 19 feet, the cables may become susceptible to external noise caused by lighting, electrical devices, and atmospheric conditions such as lightning.

Differential SCSI uses two wires for each signal. The difference in voltage between these two wires is how the signal state is determined. A simple way to keep this straight is to think of it this way: Anything that happens to one wire happens to another. Consequentially, the devices will ignore any noise or interference. This allows for fast data transfer and longer length. Differential SCSI enable lengths of up to 82 feet to be used. Most applications of SCSI are the single-ended SCSI configuration.

Cabling is a crucial part of high-performance SCSI devices. The quality of the cabling, both internal and external, can play a significant role in the performance you get. Adaptec offers a cable selector on their Web site (`www.adaptec.com`) — you pick the two connectors you're trying to attach and the length needed, and the selector offers a solution. Other manufacturers offer high-quality cables as well, so be sure to factor well-designed and manufactured cables into any SCSI installations you perform.

Internal devices use a 50-pin ribbon cable similar to what is used to connect disk drives under IDE. This last device should be internally connected to the farthest ends on the cable. This terminates that cable. External devices are typically connected using a 25-pin, 50-pin, or 68-pin connector. Early SCSI devices were usually connected using the 50-pin or A connector.

Apple computers use a 25-pin connector that resembles, but is not compatible with, a parallel port connector. This connector is called a *D-Shell* connector. Several manufacturers provide D-Shell connections as the primary connection. You can usually buy adapter cables to connect these devices to an A type connector.

Wide SCSI-II and SCSI-III devices use a 68-pin connector called a *B cable*. This B cable incorporates the additional 8 bits of data. Beyond the 16-bit standards, more than one cable is required for each device. These cables are called *P and Q cables*. The P cable provides data for the first 16 bits, while the Q cable provides the second 16 bits.

Most of the time, you will encounter only the A, D, and B connections. Most computer stores carry adapters to allow these different types of cables to be connected. From a practical standpoint, people generally hook the D cabled devices to the end of the string.

Configuring SCSI Devices

Configuring SCSI devices today usually only requires correct addressing. Most of the modern operating systems automatically configure the SCSI devices and allow them to start communicating. Several packages, such as Adaptec's EZ-SCSI software, make the process extremely easy. These utilities typically provide the ability to configure devices for proper operation. Adaptec provides an interface standard called the *Advanced SCSI Programming Interface* (ASPI), which allows programmers to write drivers for each device. ASPI drivers will usually be provided with the device. SCAM (SCSI Configured "AutoMagically," believe it or not) is a standard that, when used in conjunction with Plug and Play, enables connection without worrying about addresses or configuration options.

Many SCSI devices such as scanners provide a driver disk that allows the device to be installed on the SCSI chain. Windows 95, Windows NT, and Macintosh O/S provide comprehensive support for SCSI devices that eliminates the difficulty in installation and configuration.

Newer SCSI installations are generally pain-free and provide speed options that will please the most discerning computer users.

KEY POINT SUMMARY

The computer bus provides a mechanism for devices to be connected to the computer. The standard expansion buses are ISA, EISA, VLB, PCI, and AGP.

- The ISA bus is also referred to as the AT bus because it originated with the IBM PC/AT. ISA accepts either 8-bit or 16-bit expansion boards. The ISA bus is very slow and is being phased out in favor of faster bus architectures.

- The EISA bus is a slightly faster bus than the ISA bus, but is still very slow. IBM implemented its own version of an enhanced ISA bus and called it MCA. Computer manufacturers added a local bus called VL Bus, which allowed for a single video card to be connected. This improved video performance dramatically.

- The PCI bus is the current champion of general high-speed buses on PC and Macintosh computers. The PCI bus allows for data transfer rates in excess of 133MB per second. PCI is designed to be used in any number of different types of processor environments and is considered non-hardware specific.

- The AGP bus enables connection of a single video card to a very high-speed bus — up to four times faster than PCI.

- PC Cards, or PCMCIA cards, are plug-in cards that can be used to expand portable and handheld computer systems. Three types of cards are defined, with Type II and Type III as the most common. Type II cards are typically modem or expansion cards, whereas Type III cards are usually disk storage cards. PC Cards allow for easy connection to the portable and on-the-fly configuration.

- The ISA bus requires each device to have a unique interrupt, or IRQ. PCI bus allows devices to share the same IRQ. ISA and PCI devices on the same computer may not share the same IRQ.

- The hardware that connects differing buses together is called a bus-bridging circuit. Computers that support PCI and ISA expansion slots will have a PCI/ISA bridge. PCI systems also bridge between the PCI bus and the host bus. Intel makes a chip set that can be used by system manufacturers in any number of differing processor environments.

o IRQs are the signals that connect between a device and the CPU. Most computers today support up to 16 IRQ lines. Jumpers or software can configure either IRQ lines. Most computers today are facing a shortage of available IRQ lines.

o DMA is a process whereby devices can communicate directly with memory. This is faster than access involving the CPU. Many disk drives and sound cards use DMA for communications.

o I/O addresses provide a method for devices to be accessed by the CPU. Most PCs have a standard address list of devices such as keyboards, mouse, and video drivers. Other devices can occupy a variety of available address spaces.

o A new technology for PCs is called Plug and Play. Plug and Play allows the operating system to automatically configure all of the parameters a board needs to operate, such as IRQ, DMA, and I/O ports. Windows 95 uses the Plug and Play model.

o The SCSI bus is a high-performance bus that enables the connection of multiple devices to a single controller. SCSI data transfer rates are very fast compared to other disk transfer methods. The current SCSI standard is SCSI-III.

note **SCSI stands for Small Computer Systems Interface.**

o A single SCSI controller can traditionally manage up to seven devices. Newer SCSI controllers can manage seven or fifteen devices. Traditionally, the controller uses address 7. SCSI devices can include scanners, disks, and CD-ROMs. SCSI configuration was very difficult, but now is easy using the configuration tools available.

o SCSI devices are chained one after the other. The last device requires a terminator to prevent line noise from ruining the bus. Many different cable standards exist to connect SCSI devices. The most common is the 8-bit connection. Sixteen- and 32-bit connections are available, but require additional cabling.

APPLYING WHAT YOU'VE LEARNED

This chapter has covered a lot of important material that will help you prepare for the A+ exam and be an excellent computer technician. Take a few minutes and work through the assessments, review your notes, and see how you did.

The hands-on lab will also help you build your comfort level with the hardware as well as reinforce the readings from this chapter.

Instant Assessment

Multiple choice

Choose the best answer(s). There may be more than one correct answer for each question.

1. The ISA supports which of the following bus widths?

   A. 8

   B. 32

   C. 16

   D. 4

2. Which manufacturer introduced the MCA bus?

   A. Intel

   B. IBM

   C. Motorola

   D. Hewlett-Packard

3. The EISA bus operates at what clock speed?

   A. 6MHz

   B. 8MHz

   C. 33MHz

   D. 10MHz

4. What is the name of the bus introduced by Intel for high-speed local bus operations?

A. VESA bus

B. MESA bus

C. PCI bus

D. PIC bus

5. The PC Card bus is designed for which types of computer systems? (Select the best two.)

A. Desktop computers

B. Laptop computers

C. Palm computers

D. Servers

6. The PCI bus width that PCI is capable of supporting is:

A. 64-bit

B. 32-bit

C. 16-bit

D. 8-bit

7. The PCI bus communicates with other bus systems using what type of circuitry?

A. Packet-switching network

B. PIC bus-bridging circuitry

C. Data transfer register

D. Communications interface unit

8. Most PC systems can support how many IRQs?

A. 8

B. 16

C. 32

D. 4

9. Plug and Play is designed to automatically configure which resources? (Select all that apply.)

   A. IRQ

   B. DMA

   C. I/O addresses

   D. Virtual memory interfaces

10. A typical SCSI interface can support how many SCSI devices?

   A. 4

   B. 15

   C. 7

   D. 24

Fill in the blank

1. The _____ bus was an early attempt to remove high-speed devices such as a video card from the slower ISA bus.

2. The Microchannel bus runs at _____MHz.

3. The _____ is a CPU-independent high-speed bus.

4. The PCMCIA type 2 card is typically used for _____ and _____ devices.

5. The ISA bus was originally used on the _____ systems.

6. The 16-bit ISA bus can address up to _____MB of address space.

7. The standard IRQ for COM 1 and COM 3 is _____.

8. SCSI typically uses a _____-pin connector for internal use and a _____-, _____-, or _____-pin connector for external connections.

9. The SCSI bus requires _____ on each end of the cable.

10. Apple introduced a _____-pin standard for use on Macintosh computers.

Hands-on Lab Exercise

The previous chapters have addressed most of the issues about the systems unit and peripherals. In this chapter we will build a systems configuration design.

Lab 7-5 *Configuring and pricing computer systems*

Part 1

Configure and price a system for a customer. This system will be used by a graphic designer with several years of experience with PCs. She is very discerning about quality and wants a machine that will provide her with two or three years of service.

Her specifications for a system include:

- Pentium-II 450MHz
- Full-size case
- Keyboard and mouse
- Minimum 96MB RAM
- 12GB minimum Ultra SCSI disk drive configuration, minimum three disks
- 100MB Zip drive
- DAT tape backup unit
- CD-RW recorder
- Windows NT Workstation software
- Video card with minimum of 8MB of RAM
- Minimum 17-inch monitor
- Sound card, high-end with speakers
- Minimum 600 DPI flatbed scanner
- Floppy disk drive
- Laser printer

Research and price this system using top-of-the-line components, such as Sound Blaster Live sound card, HP laser printer, and so on. Which devices will be PCI, which will be ISA, and which will be SCSI? What IRQs must these components use to function correctly? Pick a case from the units available in the store and spec out where each device will go and how it will be mounted.

What components could be replaced with lower-cost components and still provide comparable performance? What would that system cost?

Part 2

Your manager has asked you to help him build a computer system. He has asked you to prepare pricing for a system that he can use at home. He is thinking about getting involved in digital photography, Web surfing, and other tasks such as home finance. He doesn't want to spend a lot of money, but wants a system that will hold up for two or three years. He would be comfortable spending between $600 and $1,000. Can you help him out?

Most cities have computer stores that specialize in selling individual components and parts for builders. Visit a couple of those shops and do your shopping there. You should plan on building both of these systems.

Have fun and happy shopping!

Printers

About Chapter 8

This chapter discusses the various types of printers you will encounter in the industry. Specifically, we cover dot matrix printers, thermal printers, line printers, ink jet printers, and laser printers. This chapter also explains and illustrates the printing process utilized by several of these printers.

Printers are an essential component of any workstation or office system. In most cases, the information or data being processed is printed in one of several forms. It is not uncommon to have several different printer technologies in use on a number of different media. For example, in the normal course of a day, our office may print out color overheads, computer reports, and in some cases, tee shirts with graphics on them.

Each of these types of printers places unique requirements on the printing systems in use in our office. Further, each of these printing subsystems must provide years of reliable maintenance and ease of use. Fortunately, the technologies available today have improved greatly in terms of reliability and cost. Nevertheless, as an A+ technician, you will be expected to provide preventative maintenance on these devices and in some cases, minor repairs.

TYPES OF PRINTERS

Despite the lip service paid to the concept of a paperless office, printed material is a significant part of everyday computer use. The ability to reliably and quickly generate printed output is crucial to most business and home computer users, making printer maintenance, diagnosis, and repair important skills to possess. The printer is one of the hardest-working devices in a computer system.

A number of different technologies are currently available to printer users, from the relatively inexpensive dot matrix or ink jet printers to the incredibly expensive and powerful document processors. Many things affect the cost and quality requirements of a modern printer. Printers, like other computer system components, have gone through a period of continuous improvements in performance and price. At the same time, advancements in high-end printer technology have greatly enhanced the capabilities available to small printing businesses and graphics shops.

Printers can be loosely categorized into four types of printer technology:

o *Impact printers* have elements that make a physical impact on the paper.

o *Thermal printers* use a print head, but use heat on specially treated paper instead of ink.

o *Ink jet* printers spray paint onto the paper.

o *Electrophotographic*, or *laser*, printers use a mechanical and electrical system to transfer images to the paper.

Printers can be broken down into several subsystems. These systems include the *electronic control unit* (ECU), the paper transport system, and the printing subsystem. Figure 8-1 illustrates these primary subsystems.

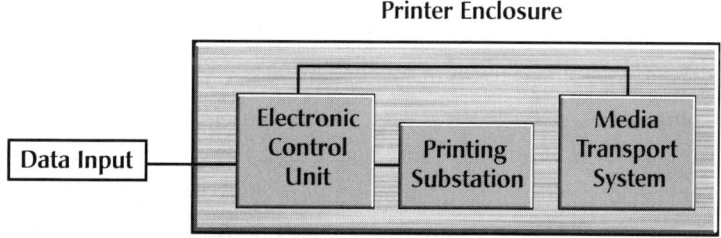

FIGURE 8-1 The major subsystems of a printer

The ECU manages printer status and controls the paper transport system, the printing subsystem, and the inking or transfer process. Printer status information includes information such as connection type, communications settings, and the health of the printer. In general, the ECU consists of a circuit board or boards, though in high-end printing systems, it can be a minicomputer or PC. Increasingly, ECUs contain a microprocessor and are highly configurable. Most modern printers can change printer parameters such as communications port settings, output resolution or print quality, and other such settings.

The inking, transfer, or ribbon system delivers the ink or other print medium to the process. In the case of a dot matrix printer, this includes advancing the ink ribbon, whereas in a laser printer, it may include the dispersion of toner.

The paper subsystem delivers the paper or print medium into the print area. This can involve feeding single sheets through a drum mechanism, pulling rolls of paper through a high-speed printer, or something in between.

In most cases, paper is the primary output of printer systems. A number of different types and grades of paper exist. Differentiating factors between paper types include the paper's surface quality, special purpose coatings, weave, and weight. It is critical to print quality and reliability that you use only the grades of paper that are specified by the printer manufacturer. If the wrong grade or finish of paper is used, poor print quality, excessive dust build-up, paper jams, or other problems can occur.

Most paper suppliers provide a multitude of paper qualities and grades for almost any application. Paper is usually measured or graded using five standard measurements: basis weight, caliper, smoothness, brightness, and opacity. Most printers provide specifications that help ensure that the proper grade of paper is used:

- *Basis weight* is the weight of a ream of paper (normally 500 sheets) cut in its basis size (17 inches by 22 inches). A ream of paper cut to basis size that weighs 30 pounds has a basis weight of 30 pounds. Higher basis weight generally indicates thicker paper.

- *Caliper* refers to the thickness of a sheet or stack of paper, expressed in thousandths of an inch. Most standard papers have a caliper of 4.2. If the caliper of the paper is outside of the specifications of the printer, the printer may jam or feed multiple sheets of paper through it simultaneously. For example, a typical paper that is 20 pounds has a caliper of 4.2, whereas a 24-pound paper has a caliper of 5.2.

- *Smoothness* refers to the surface characteristics of the paper. The rougher the paper, the less sharp the image and text will be, because the ink is absorbed into the fibers and is dispersed. Most standard papers have a smoothness of about 120. High-quality paper used for graphic applications has a smoothness of 50. This smoothness may require special inks or extra drying time.

- *Brightness* refers to the reflectivity of the paper. Most paper used in computer applications has a brightness of 93 or 94. Most applications can work with less bright paper, but it affects the way the paper reflects light.

- *Opacity* is the ability of the paper to inhibit show-through — the ability to see images or ink through the paper. You can witness show-through in double-sided printing or by putting a printed paper under a blank sheet. The more that shows through, the lower the opacity. Paper with a lower basis weight has lower opacity ratings.

Paper choices can become complicated because so many options exist. Paper can range from continuous sheet computer printout paper to very expensive parchment, as well as specially treated papers. It is critical for the health and well-being of the printer that only papers approved for a certain printer are used. If paper is rougher than specified for its use, premature wear of the paper feed mechanism can result. For example, early attempts at recycled paper for general laser printer use resulted in a paper that was too coarse and that contained particles that could damage laser printers. These issues have been addressed, and currently available recycled paper works well in a variety of printers.

Impact Printers

Impact printers are the backbone of large-scale printing. Impact technologies range from the dot matrix to large band printers. Impact technology goes back to the Gutenberg press. The basic process with these types of devices involves something physically impacting the paper or media with ink. Dot matrix printers (described in the following section) accomplish this by using a matrix of pins that press a printer ribbon onto paper. In larger or higher-speed printers, the pins strike a high-speed turning print band that then strikes the paper thousands of times per second. In the following sections, we'll discuss three types of impact printers: dot matrix printers, word processing printers, and line printers.

Dot matrix

The dot matrix printer is perhaps the oldest and least expensive printer technology available to PC users, though it has been largely replaced in all but highly specialized applications. The dot matrix name refers to the cluster of pins in the print head used to form images as the print head passes over the paper. These pins are fired out of the print head individually based on instructions from the computer. Usually either 9 or 24 pins are used by the printer to form letters and images on paper. The print quality of dot matrix output is limited by this matrix of pins — either the pin fires, leaving a dot on the paper, or it doesn't. The one thing all dot matrix printers have in common is that when they print, they make a dreadful racket. They sound like a dull razor blade being dragged across a pitted glass window, or maybe many, many fingernails across a BIG chalkboard. The printer prints by driving the pin into the printer ribbon, against the paper, and into some type of a backstop, usually metal. Hence the noise. One of the advantages of this technology is that dot matrix printers can print through multi-layer carbon or NCR type forms. This is also one of the last uses of the technology, given the drastic drop in laser printer prices and the drastic increase in laser printer speeds.

Components   The primary components of a dot matrix printer are the print head and the paper transport mechanism. The print head puts ink on the paper. Figure 8-2 shows an example of a print head and paper transport. Notice that the print head looks like a small box mounted on a sliding bar. This type of moving head printer is the most common dot matrix printer. It can print somewhere between 50 to 300 characters per second.

 Dot matrix impact printers most commonly have 9- and 24-pin configurations.

The 24-pin print head is able to produce letter-quality and graphics capabilities that make them attractive for applications that require a higher-quality output. These 24-pin printers are said to be *letter quality*. Letter quality usually refers to the ability of the reader to examine a sheet of paper and not be able to see the dots from the printer. The 9-pin printers can usually print at what is called *near letter quality*, or NLQ. This means that they are typically acceptable only for computer reports, point-of-sale terminals (such as cash registers), and other applications where print quality is not a major consideration.

FIGURE 8-2 Dot matrix printer

The printer ribbon roll or cassette provides an inked ribbon that is pressed by the print head onto the paper. A motor pulls the ribbon across the paper as each character is printed. The print head pin pushes the ribbon against the paper and transfers the ink from the ribbon onto the paper. These pins then retract back into the printer head.

The third component of a dot matrix printer system is the paper transport mechanism. Paper transport options for dot matrix printers typically include tractor-feed or friction-feed (single-sheet feed) options:

o *Tractor-feed* systems use rotating belts with external pins to pull paper with holes along its edges through the printer. The rotating belts, or tractors, are coupled to the motor that turns the print roller to advance the paper. The print head is pulled across the paper using either a belt-driven or pulley system. This system positions or steps the head to any horizontal position on the line that is being printed.

- *Friction-feed* uses the pressure from the platen or roller and the print carriage to provide tension to pull the paper through. The friction feed usually pulls single sheets of paper or single envelopes through the printer. Friction-feed systems are not suited to feed continuous sheets of paper. This task is better suited to tractor-feed systems, because even a slight amount of binding or misalignment of the paper in a friction-feed system can cause it to feed incorrectly.

note   **The print wire in a dot-matrix printer is fired by an electromagnet, forcing the print wire away from a permanent magnet in the print head, against the ink ribbon and paper.**

With proper maintenance, dot matrix systems last for years. It is not unusual for a print head to be rated for more than 200 million characters. Most light-duty users tire of the noise long before the printer typically wears out. Some printer manufacturers enclose the print head mechanism in a sound-reducing chamber, or even enclose the entire printer; this helps, but it can still be quite noisy.

Repair   The nice part about dot matrix printers is that mechanically, they are rather simple. The major issues with dot matrix printers revolve either around the print head, the paper feed mechanism, or the power supply. In a typical dot matrix printer, if the print head malfunctions, a new replacement may cost more than $135. It may be possible to find a rebuilt printer head that costs considerably less than the new head costs. Depending on the cost and availability of replacement print heads, repairing the printer may be less cost-effective than simply replacing the entire printer, especially if you can replace it for $200.

Friction is a major cause of wear on dot matrix printers. It is critical that the print head rail be kept clean and lubricated according to the manufacturer's specifications. If paper dust is allowed to build up, it will cause premature wear of the bar or bearings that the print head travels over. Figure 8-3 shows a typical cable and pulley mechanism used to move the print head in a dot matrix printer. The large black box, or carriage, contains the print head as well as the printer ribbon. The metal rod, or carriage rail, allows the carriage to move left and right across the paper. Notice that a motor, gear, and pulley mechanism move the carriage back and forth along a rail. Usually the belt requires no adjustments, but may require occasional replacement. This is a straightforward operation requiring only the loosening of a couple of screws and a few minutes of labor.

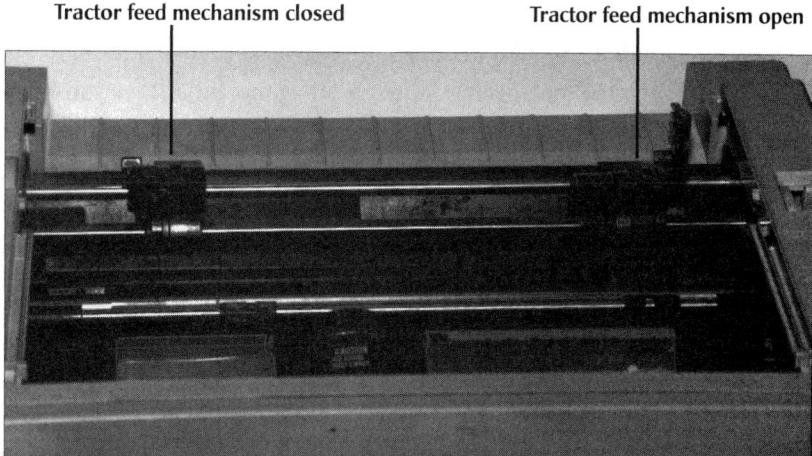

Tractor feed mechanism closed   Tractor feed mechanism open

FIGURE 8-3 Dot matrix printer carriage transport mechanism

Printer ribbons present another headache for some dot matrix printers. Better-quality printer ribbons provide a lubricant to help extend the life of the print head. Each time a pin contacts the ribbon, a small amount of cloth is removed from the ribbon. If a ribbon is overused, it will start to shred and generate excessive lint. This is typical with recycled or reused ribbons. When print quality starts to deteriorate, replace the ribbon immediately. If the ribbon starts to shed, the fibers can jam the print head, which eventually becomes damaged and requires replacement.

Small pieces of printer paper, labels, or dust may block a sensor, print element, or the paper feed path and cause the printer to stop printing or to jam. These types of problems can usually be quickly fixed. Be sure to check all parts of the paper transport path for debris when you're working on a printer. As a general rule, the only preventative maintenance you can perform on a print head is to replace it.

Word processing printers

IBM introduced a typewriter a number of years ago called the Selectric. This typewriter used a typing ball that traveled over the paper, in contrast with prior typewriter designs that moved the paper on a carriage past the area where the paper was struck by the keys. This technology was adapted to computer use by IBM and later Sony and provided truly letter-quality printing. In fact, the early IBM letter-quality printers used adapted Selectric components. NEC adopted this type of methodology as well in its Spinwriter family of letter-quality printers.

Another popular printer in the past was called a daisy wheel. Daisy wheel printers have not been produced for some time, and you probably will not encounter very many operational daisy wheels. The maintenance of these devices is similar to a typewriter: keep them clean, and keep them oiled. If they break, throw them out.

The daisy wheel print mechanism has a spoke shape. At the end of each spoke is a single character. The printer unit turns the wheel and a hammer pushes each individual character onto the paper. The print ball is mounted on a floating carriage that allows it to be rotated, twisted, and turned. The ball is then pushed against the paper to make an impression.

The typing ball and daisy wheel printers were excellent alternatives to the dot matrix systems of that time. However, they produced noise pollution as severe as that created by dot matrix printers. These printers have largely been replaced by laser or ink jet printers.

Line printers

The line printer remains the backbone printer for large, high-volume data processing applications. In general, line printers print a single line at a time. This enables line printers to print hundreds or even thousands of lines per minute. The most common line printer that you will encounter in the field is called a *band printer*. This type of printer uses a large metallic band that spins between two or more wheels along the paper. A hammer then strikes the band. Figure 8-4 shows a typical band printer. Notice that the physical impression of a band printer looks like a box with a window in it. Inside, however, is an extremely fast printing mechanism that enables high speed, volume, and reliability.

Components   The heart of a band printer is the print band, because it contains the entire character set. The advantage of this band is that when it wears out, or if a different typeface is required, you can easily change it. Figure 8-5 shows a typical band from a Dataproducts line printer. Notice that the print band edges are scalloped and that the individual characters are evenly spaced along the band. Many of these types of printers expose a huge section of the printer ribbon to the band, allowing many characters to strike at the same time while the ribbon is moving. This helps prevent ribbon wear in any one location.

FIGURE 8-4   Band printer used in larger computer system environments. This printer can print more than 200 lines per minute.

FIGURE 8-5   The print band containing all printable characters

Repair   Repairing these types of printers is usually left in the hands of a trained field service technician. These printers require cleaning on a regular basis, and beyond that, only scheduled service required by the manufacturer.

Ink Jet Printers

Ink jet printers are high-quality, inexpensive printers that can be used in the home as well as in the office. In principle, the process is simple. Ink is shot at the paper through small nozzles in the print head. The purchase price of ink jet printers is low, but ink jet printers can have a cost per page in excess of twenty cents due to the high cost of replacement ink cartridges and the specialized paper that is required for some printing tasks. This high cost of consumables makes them inefficient for larger-volume applications, but the low purchase price and versatility of the units make them quite practical for home use. Another advantage of ink jet printers is their low power consumption and relatively light weight, making them suitable for portability (see Figure 8-6).

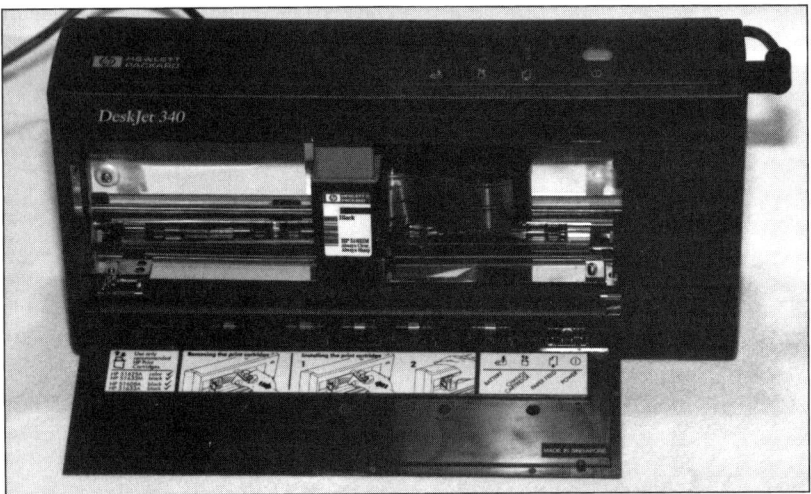

FIGURE 8-6   A portable ink jet printer

Most ink jet printers available today provide the ability to print in black ink as well as colored ink. Early ink jet printers only provided three-color cartridges, and black was created by mixing the colors. This was not an optimal solution, because the black was sort of a gray or olive drab in many cases. Newer ink jet printers have separate black cartridges in addition to the three-color cartridges, allowing replacement of either cartridge as needed. Each color is typically stored in a separate reservoir or cartridge. Most printers provide a black cartridge and a three-color print cartridge. This usually works fine, because virtually all color images involve combining the three colors in the color cartridge. Ink jet printers can cost anywhere from $100 to $900. This variation is due in part to the technologies used, as well as the duty cycle requirements.

note **The ink cartridge in an ink jet printer should be replaced with a new one rather than refilled. The ink used in ink jet cartridges is slightly abrasive and the nozzles, which are usually housed in the cartridge, are worn out by the time the cartridge runs out of ink.**

Hewlett Packard uses the *piezoelectric* approach in its DeskJet series of printers, whereas Canon uses *bubble pump* (Canon's version of bubble jet) technology. Both devices work very well and provide similar printing speeds and quality. Canon pioneered the bubble jet process, which heats the ink and causes it to jet out the nozzle. Figure 8-7 shows an ink jet cartridge with the nozzles exposed. In general, when you replace a printer cartridge, you are also replacing the nozzles. This replaces the part of the printer that is most susceptible to wear and clogging, which has the net effect of keeping the images sharp and clear.

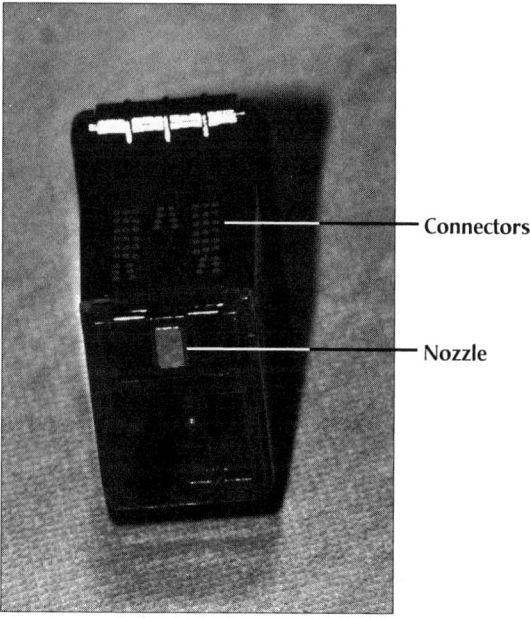

FIGURE 8-7 Ink jet cartridge

Ink jet output quality depends heavily on the type of paper used. Generally, ink jet printers require a slightly more expensive paper to provide high-quality images. If standard xerographic or laser paper is used, the images appear flat. This occurs because the paper is too porous, and the ink is absorbed too rapidly. Paper designed for ink jet printers provides exceptional-quality images that can approach photo quality. These special papers may include clay coating, which keeps the ink on the surface of the paper.

Components

The mechanics of ink jet printers are uncomplicated. The printer has a moving head, an ink cartridge, and electronics to drive the process. When the ink is used up, you replace the cartridge. If the jets become clogged and refuse to clear after usage or cleaning, you can replace the print head quickly. Most of the problems you will encounter with ink jet printers relate to print quality. The next section describes how to resolve print quality problems.

Repair

Ink jet printers are extremely reliable and mechanically simple. Usually the difficulties encountered in ink jet printers involve poor print quality. Print quality issues are usually caused by using the wrong type of paper, or by a clogged or empty printer cartridge. A common problem is that the output comes out striped, or it has large areas where printing is light or non-readable. This type of problem may be misdiagnosed as a printer problem, but in reality it usually indicates an empty ink cartridge. It is critical that the specified paper be used to produce the highest quality. In the case of an empty print cartridge, it can be replaced easily.

A clogged nozzle, however, may be a little more difficult to resolve. Most printers provide a mechanism to clean the jets, which may solve the problem. In many cases, it can take several attempts before this process works. A clear indication of a clogged nozzle is that the print quality improves after each cleaning. Remember that the ink dries when exposed to air. If it has dried, it may take several attempts at cleaning the nozzles before the problem goes away. If after this cleaning, the problem is not resolved, replace the printer cartridge. If the problem persists, you may have to replace either the head driver circuit card or the main logic circuit card.

Ink jet cartridges do not store well. Once they have been opened and installed on a printer, they begin to dry out. If a printer has been idle for a while, the printer will print poorly until the nozzles have cleared. In extreme cases, the print cartridge may need to be replaced. As a rule of thumb, any cartridge that has been installed for more than three or four months is a candidate for replacement.

Thermal Printers

The printers that we have examined up to this point force ink onto the paper with some sort of physical contact or ink transfer. Thermal printers, however, use a slightly different type of technology — heat. In a thermal printer, the paper is specially treated to respond to heat. This type of paper darkens when it encounters a high heat source. The net effect is a thermal image of the character caused by an alteration of the paper.

The advantages of this technology are reduced noise, size, and reliability. Thermal printers generally require little if any preventative maintenance, and are very inexpensive and lightweight. Many printers attached to calculators, medical instruments, mapping systems, and other types of portable devices use thermal printers because they are so light, and do not require printer ribbons to be changed. Hence, they are more reliable in situations where it is not convenient to carry supplies. The disadvantage of thermal printing is the limited life of the printouts. Thermal printing fades over time, and is sensitive to light exposure. The best advice for thermal printing is if you will need to refer back to your printouts in the future, make a photocopy of them on regular paper for storage.

Components

The mechanical components of a thermal printer are almost identical to that of an ink jet printer, only instead of an ink cartridge, chemically treated paper is used. The printer still uses a carriage feed system of some sort (typically friction feed), a cutter for the paper, and a motor for the print head.

 note **A disadvantage of thermal printers is that they require special heat-sensitive paper.**

Repair

In general, about the only maintenance required by thermal printers is to keep them clean and jam free. Normally, they can operate in harsh conditions and should periodically be vacuumed. Otherwise, it is outside a technician's scope to do anything but send it back to the factory for replacement.

Laser Printers

The laser printer has become the staple for most business and higher-end home users. The laser printer provides the absolute highest-quality printing available today. The technology has undergone a transformation from units that cost $10,000 to $20,000 to now, where laser printers cost just slightly more than an ink jet printer. Today, laser printers are available starting around $300 and can cost up to as much as several million dollars.

 note **In a laser printer, toner is moved to the print medium by the transfer roller.**

The laser printing process is complicated and power intensive. Laser printers tend to be quite heavy and somewhat complex. The laser printer market ranges from the HP6L, a small desktop laser printer, up to the Xerox Docutech setup. The Docutech is a monument to technology and includes a minicomputer to make it work. The Docutech can bind, print double-sided copies, collate, fold, staple, and almost anything else you can imagine. A Docutech can cost hundreds of thousands of dollars. Several companies including IBM also provide technology equivalent to the Docutech.

Many very large organizations use laser printers as an alternative to the printing press in small volumes. The neat part of this is that at the heart of these monsters is a technology similar to the $300 laser printer available at an office supply store. The bottom line is this: If you need true letter-quality black printing, no better option exists than a laser printer.

Laser chemicals use a dry toner process, which means that the chemical that is transferred to the paper is a fine non-toxic powder. If you open a printer cartridge, you can expect this powder to be everywhere. The best way to clean this up is with a specialized vacuum cleaner. You can purchase a special vacuum that uses a fine filtering system to capture the dust — we use a shop vacuum with water in my office. This toner powder seems to multiply — a little bit goes a long way. If you spill toner, clean it up immediately, as it will discolor almost anything.

Laser printers use high-voltage power supplies that can cause serious injury if you are exposed to them. If you open a laser printer, make sure that the power is turned off. Remove all jewelry from your hands and put one of your hands in your pocket. The one-hand rule prevents you from creating a closed circuit across your chest and keeps high voltage away from your heart, in case of a shock. The precautions you use with laser printers should be the same as with computer monitors.

 caution ▼ **Before diving into your laser printer, a few words of caution are in order. Laser printers use low-intensity laser beams that can cause eye damage if you stare at them. Beware of the laser mechanism and never stare into one either directly or with a mirror unless it is turned off.**

Here's one way of being extra cautious when working on a laser printer — assume that almost anything near the big drum in the middle of the printer can either shock you or burn you!

With that caveat in mind, let's take a look at the laser printing process. Laser printers go through a six-step process to create a document. This process is called the *ElectroPhoto*, or EP, process. The six steps of the EP process are cleaning, conditioning, writing, developing, transferring, and fusing. The next few paragraphs outline this process.

Components

The major components of a laser printer are shown in Figure 8-8. At the heart of the process is a large drum called an *Organic Photo Conductor* drum, or OPC drum. This drum carries the image onto the paper through a six-stage process. The OPC drum is made of a special material that stores an electrical charge for the printing process.

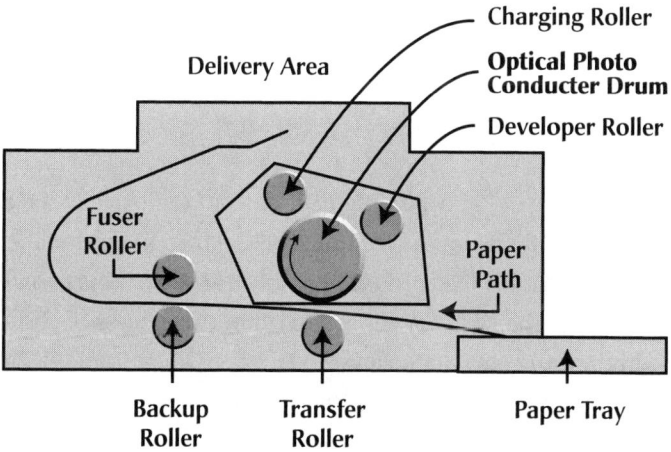

FIGURE 8-8 Major components of a laser printer with the OPC drum

In Figure 8-8, the paper enters the mechanism on the bottom right-hand corner. It immediately encounters the transfer roller and the OPC drum. From there, it continues out through the fuser and backup rollers. The transfer roller and OPC drum push the toner onto the paper. The transfer roller uses a high-voltage electrostatic charge to draw the toner off the OPC onto the paper. This charge is applied to the paper using a corona wire. The corona wire is attached to a high-voltage power supply to supply this charge that draws the toner onto the paper. Another charge system is located just past the transfer roller to discharge the paper after the particle transfer. The paper then goes through the fuser and backup roller, which heats the toner and melts it onto the paper. The paper then exits the printer complete.

One of the by-products of some laser printer systems is the creation of ozone by the corona wire systems. Since it has been hypothesized that ozone can cause health problems for some people, some printers now contain some type of ozone filtration. Many of the newer systems claim not to generate ozone and therefore do not include these filters.

You will notice that paper coming out of a laser printer is usually slightly warm, caused by the residual heat from the fuser roller. The fuser roller typically heats up to about 180 degrees Celsius (350 degrees Fahrenheit). This part of the process involves high voltage and high heat. In general, laser printers allow relatively easy access to both the transfer roller and the fuser circuitry.

 **In a laser printer, the corona wire applies a strong negative charge to the print media to attract the toner.**

The laser printer process, step by step

Step 1: Cleaning   The beginning of each print cycle involves cleaning leftover toner from the OPC drum. A cleaning blade, shown in Figure 8-9, accomplishes this task. The cleaning blade is usually rubber or some other form of soft cleaner. It is critical that the OPC not get scratched in the process of cleaning. A scratch on the drum results in a mark appearing on every item printed. The only thing to do when that happens is to replace the OPC drum.

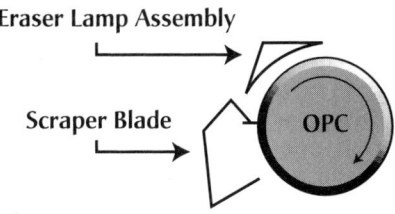

Debris Cartridge

FIGURE 8-9   The cleaning stage of the laser
printer process

Residual toner is dumped into a waste toner cavity (typically part of the printer cartridge). At the completion of this stage, the OPC drum section is clean and ready for the next step. Any residual charge is also removed from the drum at this stage using an erasure circuit, usually a corona wire.

Step 2: Charging or conditioning   The OPC drum is designed to retain a charge. A large charge (typically negative, but it depends on the printer) is applied to the surface of the drum (often higher than -600 V) via a wire called the *primary corona wire*. Figure 8-10 shows the charging circuitry in the process. This charge is uniformly applied across the drum. The charged section of the drum is now ready to proceed to the writing stage of the process.

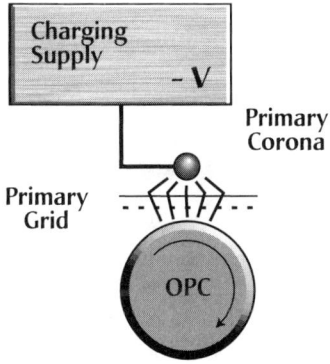

Surface of drum receives
a negative charge

FIGURE 8-10   The charging system

Step 3: Writing   The writing stage forms a latent or potential image on the drum. A laser beam shines on the OPC, effectively discharging the areas it meets. Two common technologies are available for laser printing.

The oldest method is the laser/scanning system. This system uses a fixed laser, a scanning mirror rotating at very high speed, and focusing lenses. Figure 8-11 shows a diagram of a laser/scanner system. The glass lenses and shock mountings make these printers bulky and expensive.

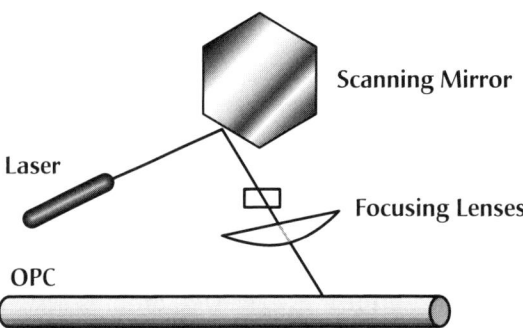

FIGURE 8-11   The laser, mirror, and lens assembly of a laser printer

The newer laser systems use a lower-powered laser *light-emitting diode* (LED) print assembly. The print assembly provides one LED for each print position. In short, this technology enables more than 2,000 LEDs to be mounted on a single 8-inch print bar. The light from these LEDs is then focused through a lens onto the paper. This capability enables a single line to be printed at one time. Figure 8-12 shows a print bar and focusing lens.

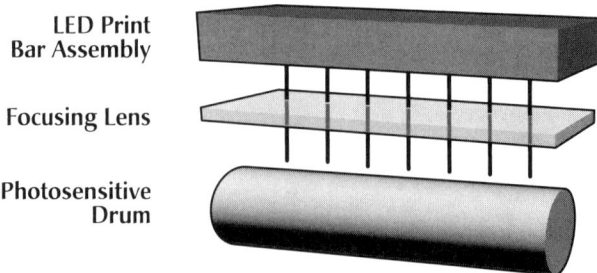

FIGURE 8-12   LED print assembly and focusing lens

note ✑ **A typical laser or electrophotographic printer cartridge may contain the toner roller, toner supply, debris cavity, primary corona, photosensitive blade, and cleaning blade assembly.**

Regardless of the technology, light is directed toward the OPC drum and neutralizes the charge where it hits. This creates a field that the toner, when applied, will not be attracted to.

Step 4: Developing   For the picture to be transferred onto the paper, some form of toner must be applied to the paper. This is accomplished in the developing stage. A fixed aperture in the toner cartridge allows the toner to be pulled or attracted to the OPC. The toner cartridge is also provided a small electrical charge that pushes toner onto the OPC and loose particles back into the toner cartridge. When this is done, toner is ready to be applied to the paper. Figure 8-13 shows the toner being grabbed by the highly charged areas on the OPC. The toner cartridge also maintains a small current charge to pull unused toner back into the cartridge.

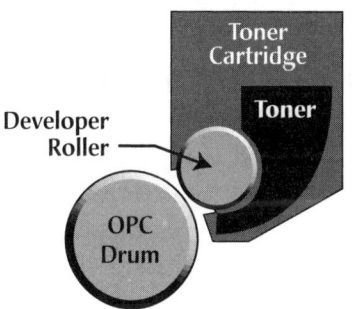

FIGURE 8-13   Toner being transferred onto the OPC drum

Step 5: Transferring   The transfer process moves the toner from the OPC drum to the paper. The paper is transported between the transfer corona wire and the OPC drum. This corona wire has an opposite charge on it, which pulls the toner off of the drum and onto the paper.

Beyond this point, a static eliminator neutralizes the charge on the paper. At this step, the paper has an opposite charge from the drum, so it tends to stick to the drum. Three common methods are used to separate the paper. One is a comb, or a separator, which peels the paper from the drum. Another method is a pick mechanism, such as a *pick tape*. This is more common on copiers, but is also used on laser printers. A corner of the paper is drawn underneath a plastic strip called a pick tape, and the paper proceeds to fall away from the drum from its own weight. A bad separator tape can cause paper jams. Finally, a corona wire is often used to reduce the static charge and allow the paper to separate from the drum.

note **In laser printers, toner is transferred from the drum to the print media by a strong negative charge on the corona wire.**

Step 6: Fusing   *Fusing* is the final stage in the process of creating a laser document. Two rollers are used in this process—the fusing roller and the pressure, or backup, roller. The fusing roller is heated by a quartz heating lamp that is temperature-controlled by a sensor. If the quartz lamp or sensor fails, the printer will not fuse the toner onto the paper. The fusing roller is usually treated with non-stick material such as Teflon to keep the toner from sticking to the roller. The paper with the toner is moved through the fusing unit, which heats the roller and melts the toner onto the paper. That sheet of paper is then fed out of the printer as a completed document.

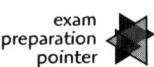 exam preparation pointer **Be sure to familiarize yourself with all six steps of this process. Exam questions frequently focus on details of this process.**

Repair

In spite of the complicated processes involved in a laser printer, they are actually very easy to repair and work on. Several common problems occur that can be repaired in the field. This section describes some of the more common failures and shows you how to repair them.

Printer jams are probably one of the most common problems encountered in laser printers. Many things can cause them. Some of the more common jams are caused by improper paper being used. If thick stock is used, it can become lodged in the feed roller area.

The best solution to this type of problem is to remove the paper tray and pull the paper out. If that does not work, you may need to open the printer and gain access to the feed roller assembly to dislodge the paper.

Normal wear of the paper feed system may reveal itself as smudged dark bands, called overprints. To repair this problem, you usually replace the pickup assembly and related components of the feed system.

Each of the printer trays usually has a coding sensor that identifies which paper tray is being used. This affects the width of the area used on the OPC drum. If the printer is indicating a problem with the tray, check that nothing is obstructing the sensor. The out-of-paper indicator is also a sensor that may need adjustment from time to time. This is an electro-mechanical switching system on an arm above the paper tray.

Laser printers contain a number of sensors that monitor internal circuitry as well as the open or closed status of its doors. Internal sensors include temperature, voltage, and motor controls. You will normally require additional documentation from the manufacturer to replace these sensors.

Motor problems can be caused by a number of different problems. The simple things to check are cable connections and circuit breakers or fuses if the printer is so equipped. Usually turning the power on will indicate some type of error. Without proper documentation, it is difficult to troubleshoot these types of problems.

The fans on laser printers should be checked for proper operation on a regular basis, as they can become clogged or dirty from paper dust from the paper. If left clogged or dirty, the fans can malfunction, causing the printer to overheat. Most printers today have temperature sensors that turn the printer off if it overheats, to prevent damage. Usually, cleaning or replacing a fan will solve these types of heat-related problems.

Occasionally a cartridge will malfunction. This may show up as poor print quality, dirty images on the paper, or other image-related problems. The simple approach is to first replace the cartridge with a known good unit and see if the problem persists.

Laser printer longevity can be greatly improved by preventative maintenance. In general, preventative maintenance should be performed when the printer cartridge is changed. Most manufacturers include a list of recommended maintenance steps. It is a good policy to save documentation for the various printers you most frequently encounter, so you can prepare for routine maintenance steps when you're called upon to check a printer. Here is a list of standard practices that might be relevant to your machine:

- Clean the transfer corona wire with a lint-free swab dipped in alcohol. Be gentle, as this wire is fragile. The corona wire tends to gather excess toner and paper dust on it. You may see a nylon filament wrapped around the corona wire — be careful not to break this. If this filament breaks, the printer will develop a strong tendency to jam. The monofilament line is there to keep the paper from being attracted into the corona case.

- Keep the transfer guides clean with a lint-free wipe dipped in "soft," or mineral-free water. This area is one of the spots on a laser printer that accumulates debris the fastest. As an alternative to a wipe, use a specially designed vacuum cleaner to remove any debris. Be careful, however — you may encounter toner dust in this area, and toner will damage vacuums that aren't specifically designed for this use.

- Brush clean the static eliminator teeth with a toothbrush or other cleaning type brush. This will ensure that paper passing by will be discharged. Again, be gentle when cleaning this area.

- Wipe the paper feed guide with a damp, clean, lint-free wipe.

- Replace the fuser-cleaning pad occasionally. If you see spotty images, this indicates that the fusing roller is dirty and requires cleaning. Typically, replacing the fuser-cleaning pad eliminates the problem.

As you can see, most of the maintenance and service involved with laser printers focuses on keeping the printer internals clean. Properly maintained laser printers can last a very long time.

KEY POINT SUMMARY

Printers can be broken down into several subsystems: the *electronic control unit* (ECU), the transport system, and the printing subsystem. The ECU manages the status and commands for the printer, the transport system moves the paper to and from the print system, and the print system makes an image on the paper or other print material.

- Impact printers physically strike the media with the ink using a hammer, band, or dot matrix print head. Hammer type print heads resemble electric typewriter technology. Band technology involves a high-speed band that spins between two pulleys. Dot matrix printers use a series of pins that press the ribbon onto the paper. Dot matrix printers usually use 9- or 24-pin configurations.

o Paper measurements describe a paper's weight, quality, and opaqueness. Basis weight is the measure of a ream of paper (500 sheets) cut in basis size (17 inches by 22 inches). Typical computer paper has a basis weight of between 20 and 24 pounds.

o Paper smoothness affects the ability of the paper to retain an image. The smoother the paper, the sharper the image will generally be. Overly smooth paper may not be able to hold the ink of certain types of printing.

o Ink jet and bubble jet printers provide high-quality printing for lower-volume applications at a low purchase price, but a slightly higher per-page cost than other alternatives. Ink jet printers use a cartridge, which contains nozzles that drop or spray ink onto the paper. These nozzles are controlled by electronic impulses from the printer's ECU.

o Thermal printers use a specially coated paper that does not require ink. Instead, the thermal printer heats up an area on the paper, which causes it to discolor. Thermal printers are typically used in environments where low maintenance is a critical characteristic. Output quality is lower than the other methods mentioned.

o Laser printers use a six-step process to create an image on paper. The six steps are cleaning, conditioning or charging, writing, developing, transferring, and fusing.

o Laser printers (sometimes known as electrophotographic printers) work by the principle of an Organic Photo Conductor, or OPC, drum transferring the image to the paper. The image is then fused, using heat on the paper.

o Laser printers either send a single laser beam through a mirror and lenses to create a scan line on the drum, or a series of LEDs through a lens to load the image onto the OPC.

o Toner cartridges contain the toner and other critical high-wear components. A toner cartridge is typically good for anywhere between 1,000 and 5,000 copies, depending on the type of cartridge and how it is used. Toner cartridges can either be recycled or thrown away when they are empty.

Applying What You've Learned

This chapter has covered a lot of important material that will help you prepare for the A+ exam and be an excellent computer technician. Take a few minutes and work through the assessments, review your notes, and see how you did.

The hands-on lab will also help you build your comfort level with the hardware as well as reinforce the readings from this chapter.

Instant Assessment

Multiple choice

1. Basis weight is the weight of which of the following?

    A. 500 sheets of 8.5 by 11-inch paper

    B. 1,000 sheets of 11 by 17-inch paper

    C. 500 sheets of 17 by 22-inch paper

    D. 500 sheets of 8.5 by 13-inch paper

2. As the smoothness of a computer paper goes down, which of the following may result (select the best two answers)?

    A. The images may be clean and crisp

    B. The images may be dull and fuzzy

    C. The print feed system may become more prone to jamming

    D. The print system may overheat and cause premature toner fusing

3. Impact printers strike the paper through:

    A. A paper guard

    B. A sheet feeder

    C. A striker bar

    D. Printer ribbon

4. Dot matrix printers usually come with which pin configurations (select the two best answers)?

A. 5-pin

B. 7-pin

C. 9-pin

D. 24-pin

5. Print bands are typically used in which type of printer?

A. Line printers

B. Dot matrix printers

C. Laser printers

D. Letter-quality printers

6. Thermal printers work by which process?

A. Specially treated paper that is heat sensitive

B. Ink ribbon passing through a printer ribbon

C. Dye emulsification caused by thermal dispersion

D. High-impact speed of the print head.

7. Ink jet printers spray the ink onto the paper using what technology?

A. Static bursts

B. Photoelectric transfer

C. Magnetic Concussion, or MC

D. Piezoelectric crystals ejecting ink

8. Choose the one that is *not* used in laser printers:

A. Cleaning

B. Developing

C. Inking

D. Fusing

9. Another word used instead of conditioning in laser printers is:

A. Cleaning

B. Charging

C. Clearing

D. Cohesion

10. Besides toner, the printer cartridge may contain which units?

A. The OPC drum

B. Corona wire

C. Feeder unit

D. Cleaning blade

Fill in the blank

1. The unit in a printer that controls the printing process is the _____.

2. Another name for a laser printer is _____.

3. _____ is the ability of paper to inhibit show-through.

4. Dot matrix printer ribbons may _____ when they approach the end of their life expectancy.

5. Nine-pin dot matrix printers are also referred to as _____-letter quality printers.

6. Daisy wheel and print ball printers have largely been replaced by _____ printers.

7. Two popular technologies exist to get ink onto the paper from ink jet printers; they are _____ and _____.

8. Many newer laser printers use _____ instead of lasers and optics.

9. A corona wire _____ the OPC drum.

10. Fusing occurs by passing the paper under the fusing roller and applying _____.

Hands-on Lab Exercise

The lab in this chapter focuses on preventative maintenance of printer units. Typically, the types of maintenance you can expect to perform involve changing the cartridge and cleaning paper and toner residue from printer areas. Most printers provide limited access to user or field technician repair.

LAB 8-6 *Changing the toner cartridge*

This lab involves replacing a toner cartridge in a laser printer.

Step 1: Opening the printer

On this printer, the release is on the front, as shown in Figure 8-14.

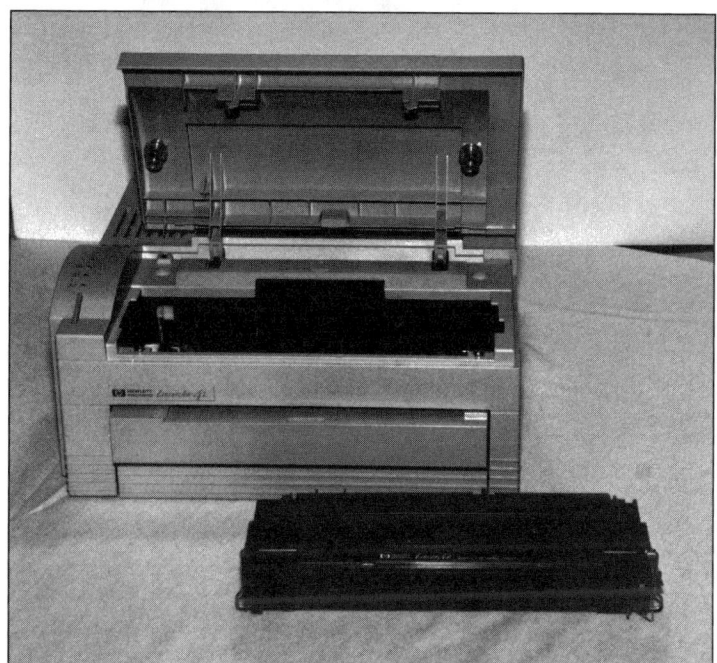

FIGURE 8-14 A laser printer with the cover open and the toner cartridge removed

Step 2: Removing the toner cartridge

The next step involves removing the toner cartridge and replacing it with a new one. Figure 8-15 shows the toner cartridge being replaced. Remember to follow the directions from the manufacturer regarding how to shake the toner in the cartridge before inserting it. This shaking ensures an even distribution of toner across the toner transfer area.

Release button

FIGURE 8-15   The new toner cartridge in the printer

Computer Monitors

About Chapter 9

In a graphical user interface (GUI) operating system like Windows, the monitor is your roadmap. You depend on the position of the cursor to allow you to control Windows in this graphical environment. Monitors have come a long way from the text monochrome models shipped with the first PCs, and as an A+ certified technician, you'll need an understanding of their evolution and the various monitor standards that have developed along the way.

This chapter addresses the evolution of computer video monitors from their inception until the present. This history will be helpful to you because you're likely to run into some older monitors during your career. We'll present the various types of monitors and their progression from monochrome to CGA, EGA, VGA, and SVGA, including principles of the cathode ray tube (CRT). Then we'll look at monitor controls and adjustments and provide a basic review of troubleshooting techniques.

VIDEO MONITOR BASICS

A computer monitor is the visual display portion of the computer system. It receives text and graphical information from the *central processing unit* (CPU) and outputs that information onto the screen. Figure 9-1 shows an example of a new computer monitor in use today. The computer monitor displays text and graphic information for the computer user to read and work with. The monitor typically has two inputs:

- AC power
- The video information from the computer

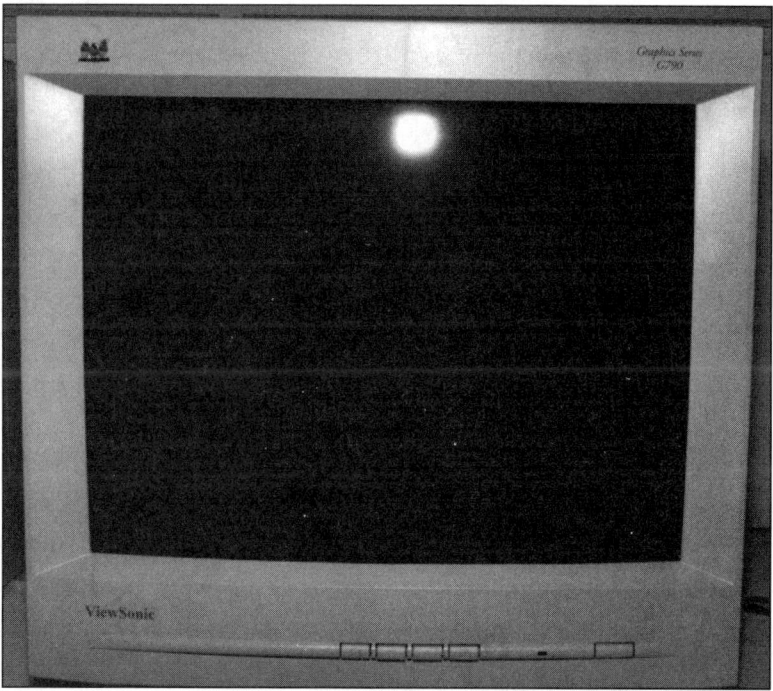

FIGURE 9-1 ViewSonic G790 monitor

Most monitors can handle common international power and frequency standards of 110 or 240 volts AC and 50 to 60Hz. You must, however, verify this by checking the data plate on the back of the monitor before you apply power. Some monitors still require the user to manually switch from 110 volts to 240 volts depending upon the power source available in the user's country. Because many older monitors still in use today work only on one voltage standard, it is important that you determine the characteristics of a monitor before using it by looking at the back of the monitor near the power cord connection. If you see a switch that is labeled for different voltages, then you may need to manually change the voltage setting.

The analog video information for most monitors is received at the monitor through a 15-pin male subminiature D connector, sometimes referred to as a D-sub connector (see Figure 9-2). This connection runs from the monitor to the video card.

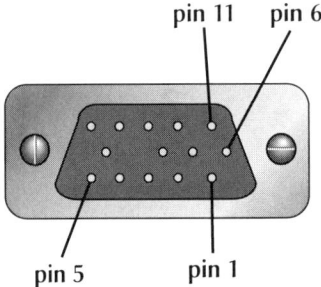

FIGURE 9-2 A 15-pin male D-sub connector

In video monitors used for TV playback as well as a computer display, the video inputs receive their signal through a BNC input, or a 9-pin D-sub connector. A BNC input is very similar in appearance to a connector on a TV that receives the cable TV signal.

Most monitors use a convection cooling design. This accounts for the grill-work on the top, sides, and bottom of a video monitor. It is important not to block this grillwork by setting books or papers on top of the video monitor. Blocking the grillwork can lead to overheating and possible premature monitor failure.

The monitor screen has two important characteristics:

○ Display size is measured diagonally across the full screen and is expressed in inches (i.e., 14-inch, 17-inch). In response to lawsuits, monitor manufacturers are now careful to give the nominal size (17-inch, for example) as well as the viewable screen area (15.9-inch or 16-inch) in the advertising.

- Dot pitch is measured in millimeters and gives the buyer a general idea of how well the monitor displays images. Dot pitch is the shortest diagonal distance between two phosphor dots of the same color on a screen. The smaller the dot pitch, the more dots that fit on the viewable surface, and thus the sharper the image. In other words, smaller is better when it comes to dot pitch. Dot pitch of .28" is good, while dot pitch much larger than that indicates a lower quality monitor you may want to avoid.

CRT Designs

Several types of CRT (cathode ray tube, or the actual picture tube itself) designs are used in monitors today. This section discusses them and gives you an overview of the basic differences. It is not paramount that you understand everything about the various types of CRTs. It is, however, important that you be able to distinguish them from one another so that you can consult the proper manufacturer's documentation if you should have to troubleshoot or replace one. The common types of CRTs in use today include the shadow-mask CRT, the aperture-grille CRT, the slot-mask CRT, and the liquid-crystal display. The most commonly used high-resolution PC monitor utilizes the shadow-mask CRT, in which the image on the monitor screen is made up of thousands of small circular dots, or *pixels*, of color phosphors. A *pixel* is the smallest visible image on the screen.

Shadow-mask

In a *shadow-mask* display, phosphors are grouped in triangles with a different color at each corner. The shadow mask is a screen used to separate the individual phosphor dots.

The advantages of the shadow-mask CRT are the clarity and sharpness in edges and diagonals resulting from the placement of the pixels. The shadow-mask configuration is good when text information is to be displayed on the monitor.

Aperture-grille

The *aperture-grille* CRT uses alternating red, green, and blue phosphor lines rather than individual dots. The lines are separated by a pattern of very thin wires called an aperture grille.

The advantage of this design is that brightness and contrast are better when compared to the shadow-mask design, without a decrease in the focus. The disadvantage in the aperture-grille design is that it must use several horizontal wires to keep the vertical wires stationary and secure. The shadows from these horizontal wires are sometimes visible when a brightly colored image is displayed on the monitor.

Due to the lack of horizontal delineation in this design, it is best suited for graphically intensive images such as gaming, image editing, and video applications. If you've ever noticed the flicker on your monitor when playing a graphically intense game, you've probably wondered why. This effect is due to horizontal delineation, a process by which the pixels are activated in a predefined order. The aperture-grille design all but eliminates this effect by its design. By lighting entire lines instead of individual pixels, it produces a smooth, almost flicker-free presentation, even in the most intense graphics applications.

Slot-mask

A variation of the aperture-grille design is the *slot-mask* CRT, a hybrid of the shadow-mask and aperture-grille technologies. This type of CRT is more common in TV sets than computer monitors.

This design uses a continuous series of oval-shaped phosphors. As in other designs, each series of three phosphors displays red, green, and blue. The elliptical-shaped phosphors give the slot-mask CRT the high vertical definition of the aperture-grille CRT, with improved horizontal definition that results from the shadow-mask CRT.

Liquid-crystal

Finally, the *liquid-crystal* (LCD) display utilizes a thin layer of material made from gel polymer or ferroelectric liquid crystals. These materials are fashioned into rectangular cells that effectively function like a pixel on a CRT type monitor. This type of design is unique from the others in that each cell borders the cell next to it without the incremental space that is present in the other designs. This ensures sharp, clear images.

The disadvantages of LCD monitors are twofold. First, the color is generally not as pronounced as those of CRT-type monitors and the design does not allow for quick transition from one image to another in a real-time environment. Additionally, the cost of an LCD display is currently three to four times that of similarly sized CRT monitors. Expect this price disparity to shrink as CRT monitors become more popular due to their small footprint (the amount of physical desk space they occupy), and lower heat production.

Screen Characteristics

The display has a ratio of width to height known as the *aspect ratio*. Two characteristics ensure a clear and crisp picture on the display screen. These are *resolution* and *dot pitch*.

- Resolution is the number of pixels displayed on the screen at a time. Resolution is expressed as a ratio of the horizontal pixels (total pixels in one line across the monitor) to the vertical pixels (total pixels in one line up and down the monitor surface) (for example, 640 x 480, or 1,024 x 768). This ratio is usually 4:3. The number of horizontal lines on a monitor is known as the *vertical resolution* and the number of pixels on one scan line is known as the *horizontal resolution*. A scan line is the total number of pixels in one line straight across the monitor surface. An additional external factor in resolution determination is the bandwidth, or volume of signal that can be sent to the monitor from the video adapter card. If the video card cannot send enough information to the monitor to activate all the pixels, then the resolution of the monitor is still the same; however, the viewable resolution will only be as much as the video card can support.

- The dot pitch is the diagonal measurement from one point on a pixel to the same point on a pixel of the same color adjacent to it; however, some manufacturers report the dot pitch as a horizontal or vertical measurement. Dot pitch is less than one millimeter and is expressed as a decimal (i.e., .28, .31). The same principle applies to stripe mask monitors, but the measurement is made horizontally instead of diagonally.

Most monitors in use today require a dot pitch of .28 or less to adequately portray graphical images. By comparison, television dot pitch is typically in the .75 to .80 range. Our eyes see these as comparable since we view TV from across the room, but view our monitor from arm's length.

The applicable features involved when the image changes on the monitor include a frame, the refresh rate, the scan rate, and interlacing. A *frame* is considered one complete scan updating the information on the screen. A *scan* is the process of updating the frame, and *interlacing* is the process of how the image is updated. The information is updated from left to right starting at the top and moving to the bottom. In some cases, the image is updated by drawing the even-numbered lines first, then drawing the odd-numbered lines to the screen separately. This is done because the video card may not support a high enough refresh rate to update all the lines sequentially.

This every-other-line refresh pattern is called interlacing because the odd lines join with the even lines to form an image. Interlaced screen refreshing can cause screen flicker, which occurs when non-refreshed lines fade before they are redrawn. When the monitor draws the complete image in one pass, starting at the first pixel of the frame and ending on the last pixel of the frame, the monitor is called *non-interlaced*.

The number of frames that are updated per second is known as the *vertical refresh rate*. The typical refresh rate of computer monitors is 60 to 72 Hz, but can go much higher. When refresh rates are decreased, the human eye can detect information being refreshed in the form of a flicker on the monitor. Depending on the individual and on office lighting, flicker can cause fatigue and eyestrain. Fluorescent lighting in an office can cause visible monitor flicker at rates of 60Hz or below, so it's best to choose a monitor and video card that enable a higher refresh rate. Screens are also updated left to right at the horizontal scan rate, which is expressed in kilohertz (kHz) since horizontal scan is so much faster than vertical refresh. Typical horizontal scan rates range from 20 to 100kHz.

Other advances in monitor technology include multiscan (multisync) and autoscan. *Multiscan* allows a monitor to synchronize its vertical and horizontal scan at set multiple speeds, increasing the refresh rate significantly. *Autoscan* is not limited to preset rates, but allows the monitor to synchronize to a wide range of scan rates for the best resolution.

VIDEO MONITOR STANDARDS

The first computer video monitor was the monochrome monitor, driven by its *monochrome display adapter* (MDA). As the name implies, the monochrome monitor (also referred to as *mono*) utilizes only a single color. The input signal was a digital video signal known as TTL (transistor-to-transistor logic). Typically, the display color was white, green, or sometimes orange. The monochrome monitor driven by the MDA was useful only for text, which became a problem for Lotus 123 users trying to display graphs. The *Hercules Graphics Card* (HGC) was introduced and enabled monochrome monitors to display graphics up to 720 x 350 resolution.

Still, the color graphics chase was on. Each succeeding generation of monitor incorporated more advanced technology that improved resolution and clarity. The earliest color monitor standard was the color graphics adapter, or CGA. Originally developed for IBM's line of personal computers, the CGA monitor could display either 40 or 80 columns and 25 lines of information. This format was known as 40 x 25 and 80 x 25. This color monitor was limited to 16 colors and had a resolution of either 320 x 200 or 640 x 200. This monitor has been obsolete for several years, but you may still run into them. Prepare for a headache — the resolution is too coarse to be of any real value. A monochrome monitor running a Hercules Graphics Card offered a much crisper graphical image.

The successor to the CGA monitor was the enhanced graphics adapter, or EGA. This monitor boosted resolution to 640 x 350. The EGA monitor is also obsolete. Both the CGA and EGA monitors used digital video inputs similar to the monochrome monitor.

The video graphics array monitor, or VGA, was the first monitor to use an analog video input. All monitor standards since the VGA use an analog video signal. By using a varying voltage to signify an intensity for each input instead of just on or off, the red, green, and blue color inputs may be varied throughout a wide range of colors. The VGA monitor received its unique name (*array* versus the earlier *adapter*) from IBM because it represented the first generation of monitors to offer a resolution that was suited to a graphically intense user environment.

The VGA monitor has a resolution of 640 x 480. This monitor became the *de facto* monitor of choice for several years and is still widely used today.

The *Super Video Graphics Array* (SVGA) monitor is the most recent generation of the graphics monitor. It has a typical resolution of 800 x 600, but may go as high as 1,600 x 1,200 or beyond. The adapter for Super Video Monitors was developed to the *Video Electronics Standards Association* (VESA) specifications, which were established in 1989.

PRINCIPLES OF THE CATHODE RAY TUBE

The *cathode ray tube* (CRT) is the screen used in monitors. The CRT receives instructions or data from the computer through the rear of the CRT, which are then displayed as images on a phosphor screen surface in front. The images are scanned onto the phosphor surface through deflection coils, which deflect the electron beam to the appropriate location on the screen.

In operation, the signal information sent from the video card travels through the monitor's circuitry, where it is translated into information the monitor can use, then to the back of the CRT, also known as the neck. This information is transferred to a heated electrode known as a cathode, or the "electron gun." When heated, the negatively charged electrons break loose from the cathode and are attracted to the positively charged anode. This electron beam was known as the cathode ray. Hence, the cathode ray tube, or CRT.

In monochrome monitors, one electron gun directs the video information toward the front of the CRT. Color monitors have three electron guns — one for the color red, one for the color green, and one for the color blue. The screen is covered with a material that radiates light when struck by the electrons. The amplitude with which the electrons strike the CRT's phosphor surface determines the intensity of the light radiated from the tube's surface.

This current is variable based on the voltage that has been applied to the electrons passing through voltage grids when they first break away from the cathode. The electron beam is directed to a specific spot on the tube's surface by deflection coils around the outside neck of the CRT. The deflection coils receive synchronization information from the horizontal and vertical information in the video input. The electron beam scans the complete screen surface from top to bottom in a horizontal direction. The *raster* includes the complete area of the phosphor surface that is scanned, not just the visible portion on the screen.

MONITOR CONTROLS AND ADJUSTMENTS

To ensure a crisp, clear image that fits the defined region of the monitor's screen, monitors have controls and adjustments. These controls and adjustments enable the user to fine-tune the image on the monitor. Earlier monitor designs included these controls as dials or knobs, but in modern monitors, these have generally been replaced by software or push button controls, or a combination of both. Table 9-1 lists some of the controls and adjustments normally provided on monitors. Horizontal size and position, vertical size and position, brightness, and contrast are the most common controls.

TABLE 9-1 MONITOR CONTROLS AND ADJUSTMENTS

CONTROL	ADJUSTMENTS
Horizontal Size	Adjusts the horizontal width in and out.
Horizontal Position	Adjusts the horizontal position to the left and right.
Vertical Size	Adjusts the vertical height up and down.
Vertical Position	Adjusts the vertical position to the top and bottom.
Brightness	Adjusts overall CRT or raster intensity.
Contrast	Adjusts balance between dark and light colors.
Pincushion	Compensates for the bow from distortion in the CRT.
Degauss	Discharges static magnetic fields that alter color.
Focus	Adjusts the picture clarity.

Horizontal size adjusts the width of the picture so as to fit within the defined limits of the screen on the left and right. Horizontal position works with horizontal size to center the picture on the screen. Vertical size adjusts the height of the picture to fit within the defined limits of the screen on the top and bottom. Vertical position works with vertical size the same way the horizontal position and horizontal size work together.

All monitors build up a magnetic field as a result of the high voltage and deflection coils around the yoke of the CRT. This may be evidenced by alterations in the colors on the monitor screen. Additionally, situating large-wattage multimedia speakers or mechanical devices (fans) next to a monitor will introduce magnetic fields to the CRT. The degauss function neutralizes this magnetic buildup. In general, you should degauss your monitor any time you notice warping or discoloration of your onscreen images.

The brightness control adjusts the overall light intensity of the monitor screen. It is useful when you're adjusting for different light settings wherever the computer is. The contrast control adjusts for differences between light and dark colors on the monitor. This adjustment is most profound in a non-graphic application such as DOS. Monitors with larger screens and more advanced features may include adjustments for rotation or tilt control. The tilt control adjustment helps to offset the distortion caused by the earth's magnetic field by allowing you to change the overall tilt of the image being displayed on the monitor screen.

TROUBLESHOOTING TECHNIQUES

Monitors stop working for a variety of reasons. Many of these reasons are not related directly to the monitor itself. Though it may seem obvious to investigate the simplest fix first, technicians often overlook the easiest solutions. Preventive maintenance is perhaps the single most important factor in extending the life of video monitors. Monitor users should keep monitors clean and dust free by wiping them down with a damp cloth — but remember, never allow water or cleaning solutions to get inside the case.

Having some basic ideas of video monitor operation is invaluable, as it will help the technician to isolate problems quickly and determine the most expedient means to repairing the problems. Before you assume the worst about a faulty monitor, you should check basic connections to ensure everything is properly connected. Ask yourself these questions:

1. Is the AC power applied to both the monitor and the computer?

2. Is the video connector secure at both the monitor and the computer?

3. Are both the monitor and computer turned on?

4. Are the brightness and contrast controls adjusted to midrange?

If the monitor is working, but the image is distorted, you can perform several simple checks that will eliminate most problems. A preliminary check of horizontal position and size, as well as vertical position and size controls would be appropriate. Selecting an incorrect scan rate or inaccurately setting up a video driver will result in either a distorted image or no image at all. If possible, check the monitor's setup to ensure that settings fall within the manufacturer's parameters for that monitor.

Although faulty monitors are often manifested through degraded images, CRT failure is one of the least common reasons for video monitor failures.

If repairs are required, you must understand that troubleshooting and repairing monitors are not for the faint of heart or for the untrained. Very real life-threatening dangers are present inside monitors that do not exist inside other parts of computer equipment. Electrical power inside monitors is sufficient to kill the novice or untrained technician.

caution **Without specific professional training, you should attempt no monitor repairs beyond troubleshooting. Under no circumstances should you ever open the monitor's case.**

KEY POINT SUMMARY

Chapter 9 explored the wide realm of video monitors available in the industry today and their history.

- The various types of monitors include CGA, EGA, VGA, SVGA and the cathode ray tube (CRT). In addition to detailed descriptions and troubleshooting techniques, you learned about monitors' controls and adjustments.

- The monitor's display size and dot pitch is important to the displayed image. Examples of CRT's that are used today include the shadow-mask, the aperture-grille, the slot-mask, and the liquid-crystal. Moreover, the screen's resolution depends on the dot pitch assigned to the monitor's display.

- The CRT receives data from the computer, and then these images are displayed on your screen.

- By adjusting your monitor's controls, you can achieve a clear image through horizontal and vertical positioning. In addition, you can set the brightness and contrast to obtain the best visual effect.

- Several questions were posed to help you shorten the troubleshooting cycle, and repair options were discussed.

- You had the opportunity to test your knowledge by answering questions in the instant assessment section. Finally, the hands-on lab exercises helped familiarize you with basic adjustments you can make without additional tools.

APPLYING WHAT YOU'VE LEARNED

This chapter has covered a lot of important material that will help you prepare for the A+ exam and be an excellent computer technician. Take a few minutes and work through the assessments, review your notes, and see how you did.

The hands-on lab will also help you build your comfort level with the hardware as well as reinforce the readings from this chapter.

Instant Assessment

Multiple choice

Choose the best answer(s). There may be more than one correct answer for each question.

1. Which of the following is not a monitor designation?

   A. VGA

   B. CGA

   C. Multiscan

   D. BGA

2. In a shadow-mask CRT design, dot pitch is measured:

   A. Horizontally

   B. Diagonally

   C. Vertically

   D. Overlaid

3. Dot pitch is the measurement of the distance between:

   A. Two adjacent pixels on the CRT

   B. A pixel and the location of the scanned electron beam

   C. Two adjacent pixels of the same color

   D. Horizontal pixels and vertical pixels

4. Which type of monitor does not utilize a CRT in its design?

   A. LCD

   B. Shadow-mask

   C. Aperture-grille

   D. Slotted-mask

5. Which feature does not contribute to a flicker-free appearance?

   A. Vertical refresh rate

   B. Phosphors persistence

   C. Dot pitch

   D. Brightness

6. The six most common controls and adjustments on video monitors are:

   A. Vertical size, vertical position, degauss, horizontal size, focus, brightness

   B. Brightness, horizontal position, vertical size, vertical position, contrast, horizontal size

   C. Contrast, focus, brightness, horizontal position, vertical position, degauss

   D. Vertical size, horizontal size, degauss, brightness, contrast, focus

7. The number of horizontal pixel lines on a CRT is known as:

   A. Vertical retrace

   B. Horizontal resolution

   C. Aspect ratio

   D. Vertical resolution

8. What aspect ratio is most commonly used at various standard video resolutions?

   A. 5:4

   B. 1:1

   C. 4:3

   D. 2:3

9. Monitor size is determined by measuring:

   A. The horizontal width and vertical length, and then adding them together

   B. The diagonal size of the screen

   C. The number of horizontal pixels versus vertical pixels

   D. Depth of the CRT from front to back

10. A *frame* is the measurement of:

    A. One scan of all the horizontal pixels in one line

    B. The horizontal refresh rate

    C. One scan of all pixels in the horizontal and vertical positions

    D. The vertical refresh rate

Fill in the blank

1. The two typical inputs to a video monitor are the _____ and _____.

2. Monitor size is measured _____ across the full screen.

3. The three colors used in monitors are _____, _____, and _____.

4. The CRT design that uses groups of small dots is called

   _____.

5. The monitor design that does not use conventional CRT design is the

   _____.

6. Typical _____ refresh rates are between 60 and 85Hz.

7. _____ is the method whereby first the even lines are refreshed, followed by the odd lines.

8. The _____ control demagnetizes built-up fields that may cause color distortion.

9. The _____ adjustments move the image on the CRT screen from left to right.

Hands-on Lab Exercises

For these lab exercises, you will need access to a complete computer system. The purpose of these exercises is to familiarize you with the essential adjustments that you can make in the field without additional tools.

Lab 9-9: *Adjusting a monitor*

Getting organized

Clear your work area of all non-essential items. You should be able to freely move the computer monitor on the work area without space constraints. For your safety, be sure that the computer and monitor are plugged in using three-prong power cords and that there is no water in or immediately around the work area. Also, as a point of general computer safety, keep soft drinks and coffee away from the computer and its peripherals. The computer and monitor will need to be turned on for these exercises.

 tip **On a wall outlet, the smaller of the two vertical slots is considered hot.**

Using a VGA or SVGA monitor, adjust the vertical and horizontal size of the screen using the controls on the monitor itself.

 note **Modern monitors can derive their power from the PC's power supply.**

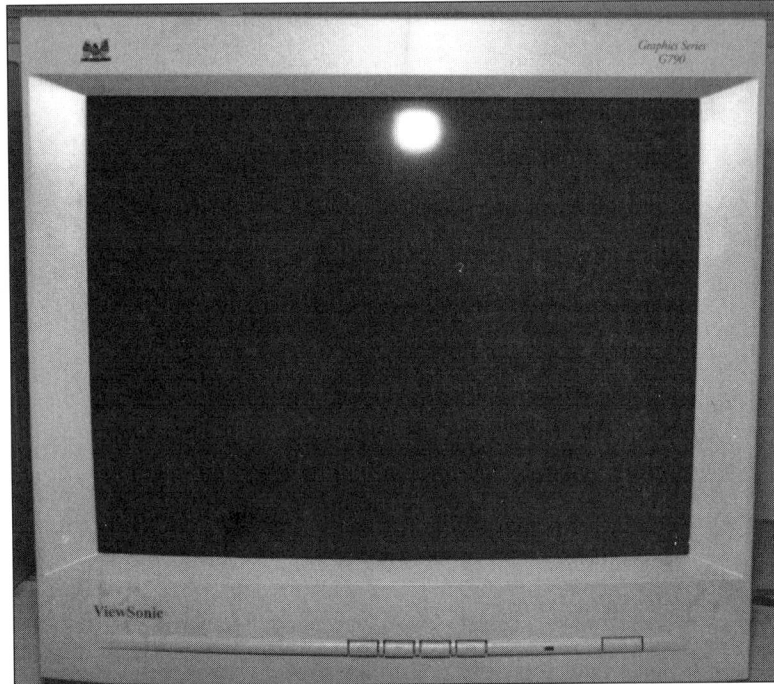

FIGURE 9-3 Monitor with normally sized picture

In Figure 9-3, you can see a properly sized display area. In the following illustrations, we will show you that it is possible to change both the horizontal and vertical display areas.

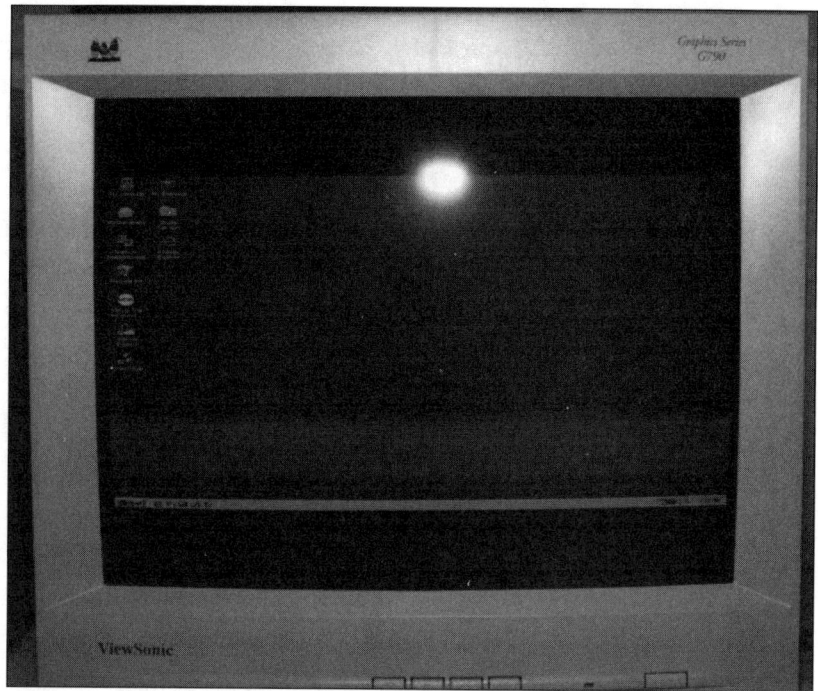

FIGURE 9-4 Monitor with improperly sized vertical image

In Figure 9-4, we have changed the vertical viewing size of the monitor. This is an essential skill to have when you're setting up a monitor for the first time. Not all monitors are preset with their optimum configuration from the factory. Each monitor is different, but the settings can be adjusted from the monitor's front panel. Throughout this exercise, try and set your monitor to match the figures, then reset it back to normal. You may need to refer to a monitor manual to ascertain exactly how each monitor is adjusted.

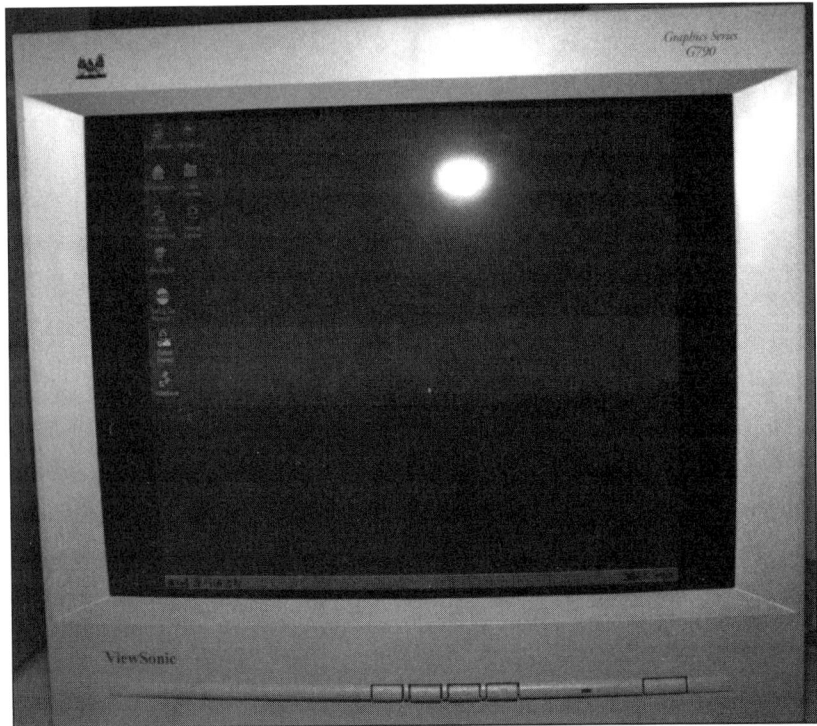

FIGURE 9-5 Monitor with improper horizontal sizing

In Figure 9-5, we have changed the horizontal viewing size of the monitor. Again, this is an essential skill when you're setting up a monitor for the first time. In addition to first-time setups, it is often the case that a customer having display problems actually has a problem with the adjustments of the monitor. The CRT can fail, but it is a rare occurrence within the first two years of a monitor's life.

Manual controls for the adjustment of the horizontal and vertical sizing can be in different places. Some monitors use knobs located at the base of the monitor in the front. Other monitors use push buttons, and still other monitors may need to be accessed from the back. These adjustments are the first thing you should check when diagnosing a monitor. Always check to be sure that the sizing adjustments are set before assuming there is something wrong inside the monitor itself.

About Chapter 10

In this chapter, we will discuss the interaction of the display adapter, or video card, and the computer monitor. The video card is a card that plugs into the computer bus and transfers information from the computer to the monitor. Then we'll look at the standards for video display and the basic principles behind the standards. This chapter is designed to give you a comprehensive understanding of PC video display adapters. This chapter will discuss common terms used in association with video cards. Many types of video cards are available, and in this chapter we'll cover the most common types you might encounter in the field. We'll also provide some historical information to give you an idea of the diverse functions these cards have served.

VIDEO ADAPTER BASICS

The earliest computers had switches for input, and blinking lights for output. Users meticulously entered their programs by flicking switches in a particular sequence, and were forced to start all over again in the event of any error. Output was limited to blinking lights. These computers were ideal for those enthralled with the idea of computers and programming, but they had little practical use. Until keyboards became available for easier input, and video displays for clear output as well as feedback during input, personal computers were little more than a proof of concept.

Computer monitors evolved from the days of those blinking lights to monitors that displayed only text, and only in a single color. This limitation led to the development of advancements allowing graphics on these same monitors. Further along the way, crude color monitors were introduced, and from this early development, we are today faced with large-screen monitors capable of breathtaking clarity. It is important for you to have a basic understanding of these various steps along the monitor's evolution, since you may find yourself face-to-face with a dinosaur of a monitor—and a request to fix the system.

We have now moved from blinking lights to visual representation of data. The monitor has made it possible for users to interpret information without having to know about the internal workings of their software. With the Altair computer, you needed to know what the blinking lights meant. Now, however, the computer is a tool used to make business decisions, and the availability of easy graphical depiction of data, such as charts in a spreadsheet, has made it unnecessary to know the inner machinations of the PC. This graphic depiction of data was made possible by a *video adapter*.

A video adapter is a circuit board that plugs into a computer to give it the capability of displaying the operations that are being performed by the computer in real-time. The display capabilities of a computer depend on the circuitry of the video adapter and the display capabilities of the monitor.

IBM developed the video display standards for the *monochrome display adapter* (MDA), *color graphics adapter* (CGA), *enhanced graphics adapter* (EGA), and the *video graphics array* (VGA). A consortium composed of monitor manufacturers and video display card manufacturers, jointly known as the *Video Electronics Standards Association* (VESA), used IBM's VGA standard to develop the *super video graphics array* (SVGA) standards. Several types of video adapters are available (see Figure 10-1). Although today's computers are usually equipped with the SVGA adapter and monitor, it is important that you be able to identify the different types of monitors and adapters in the field. This enables you to make determinations on the compatibility of systems and gives you the ability to upgrade or repair them in an efficient and cost-effective manner. For example, if an older system experienced irreparable monitor failure, your ability to determine system compatibility would enable you to find a suitable older monitor in the firm's PC boneyard.

AGP

FIGURE 10-1   An AGP video card

Different adapter types display images on the video monitor in distinct ways, which are referred to as *modes*. The two basic video modes are *text mode* and *graphics mode*. In text mode, a monitor displays only ASCII, the American Standard Code for Information Interchange. ASCII is a code for representing characters as numbers (see Figure 10-2). ASCII assigns each letter a number from 0 to 127.

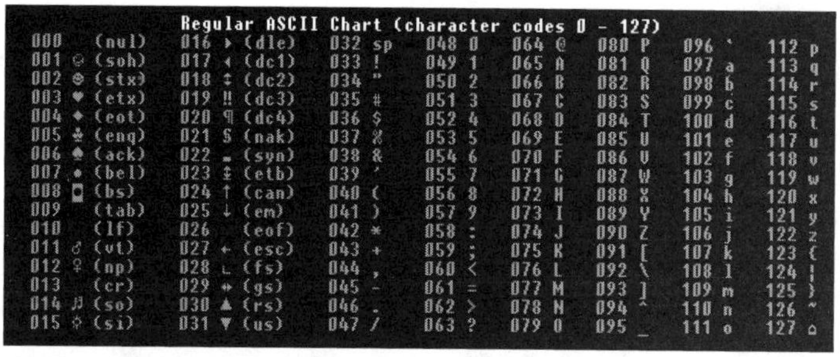

Regular ASCII Chart (character codes 0 - 127)

000 (nul)	016 ► (dle)	032 sp	048 0	064 @	080 P	096 `	112 p
001 ☺ (soh)	017 ◄ (dc1)	033 !	049 1	065 A	081 Q	097 a	113 q
002 ☻ (stx)	018 ↕ (dc2)	034 "	050 2	066 B	082 R	098 b	114 r
003 ♥ (etx)	019 ‼ (dc3)	035 #	051 3	067 C	083 S	099 c	115 s
004 ♦ (eot)	020 ¶ (dc4)	036 $	052 4	068 D	084 T	100 d	116 t
005 ♣ (enq)	021 § (nak)	037 %	053 5	069 E	085 U	101 e	117 u
006 ♠ (ack)	022 ▬ (syn)	038 &	054 6	070 F	086 V	102 f	118 v
007 • (bel)	023 ↨ (etb)	039 '	055 7	071 G	087 W	103 g	119 w
008 ◘ (bs)	024 ↑ (can)	040 (	056 8	072 H	088 X	104 h	120 x
009 (tab)	025 ↓ (em)	041)	057 9	073 I	089 Y	105 i	121 y
010 (lf)	026 (eof)	042 *	058 :	074 J	090 Z	106 j	122 z
011 ♂ (vt)	027 ← (esc)	043 +	059 ;	075 K	091 [	107 k	123 {
012 ♀ (np)	028 ∟ (fs)	044 ,	060 <	076 L	092 \	108 l	124 |
013 (cr)	029 ↔ (gs)	045 -	061 =	077 M	093]	109 m	125 }
014 ♫ (so)	030 ▲ (rs)	046 .	062 >	078 N	094 ^	110 n	126 ~
015 ☼ (si)	031 ▼ (us)	047 /	063 ?	079 O	095 _	111 o	127 ⌂

FIGURE 10-2 The ASCII character set

The ASCII character set uses 7 bits to represent each character. A bit can only represent the values 0 or 1. Combining bits creates larger units, and a byte, for example, is composed of 8 bits. In describing graphics, it is common to refer to the number of bits used. A monochrome image is referred to as a 1-bit image, a grayscale or 256-color image is referred to as an 8-bit image, a high-color image is referred to as a 16-bit image, and a true color image is referred to as a 24- or 32-bit image.

Other character sets exist as well. By using an 8-bit character set, for example, you can depict additional non-English characters, such as mathematical symbols. MS-DOS uses an enhanced version of ASCII to display information on the screen to the user. This character set is called *extended ASCII.*

Figure 10-3 shows an extended ASCII chart. DOS uses extended ASCII to display symbols, text, and graphics. In graphics mode, a monitor can display any image that is bit-mapped. A bit-map is a representation of columns and rows of dots. When a program displays a graphic, it sends a set of coordinates that are translated into a map, and then the map is displayed in bits.

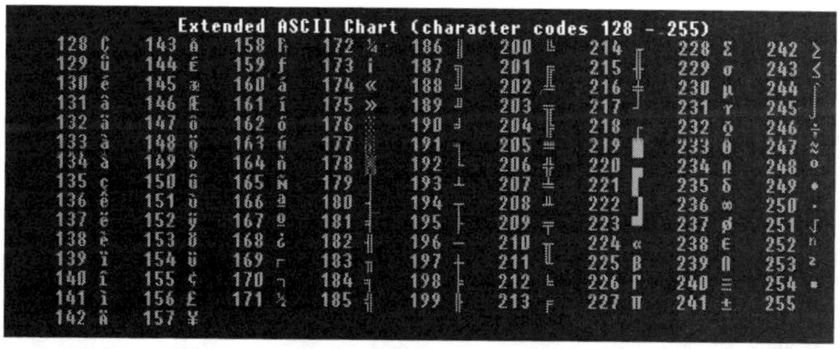

Extended ASCII Chart (character codes 128 - 255)

128 Ç	143 Å	158 ₧	172 ¼	186 ║	200 ╚	214 ╓	228 Σ	242 ≥
129 ü	144 É	159 ƒ	173 ¡	187 ╗	201 ╔	215 ╫	229 σ	243 ≤
130 é	145 æ	160 á	174 «	188 ╝	202 ╩	216 ╪	230 µ	244 ⌠
131 â	146 Æ	161 í	175 »	189 ╜	203 ╦	217 ┘	231 τ	245 ⌡
132 ä	147 ô	162 ó	176 ░	190 ╛	204 ╠	218 ┌	232 Φ	246 ÷
133 à	148 ö	163 ú	177 ▒	191 ┐	205 ═	219 █	233 Θ	247 ≈
134 å	149 ò	164 ñ	178 ▓	192 └	206 ╬	220 ▄	234 Ω	248 °
135 ç	150 û	165 Ñ	179 │	193 ┴	207 ╧	221 ▌	235 δ	249 ∙
136 ê	151 ù	166 ª	180 ┤	194 ┬	208 ╨	222 ▐	236 ∞	250 ·
137 ë	152 ÿ	167 º	181 ╡	195 ├	209 ╤	223 ▀	237 φ	251 √
138 è	153 Ö	168 ¿	182 ╢	196 ─	210 ╥	224 α	238 ε	252 ⁿ
139 ï	154 Ü	169 ⌐	183 ╖	197 ┼	211 ╙	225 ß	239 ∩	253 ²
140 î	155 ¢	170 ¬	184 ╕	198 ╞	212 ╘	226 Γ	240 ≡	254 ■
141 ì	156 £	171 ½	185 ╣	199 ╟	213 ╒	227 π	241 ±	255
142 Ä	157 ¥							

FIGURE 10-3 The extended ASCII character set

Dots are organized to create a picture on the screen. These pictures can be anything from photos to text to animations. Animations work in the same way as still graphics, but require the screen to be constantly updated. The color value of each dot is stored in one or more bits, depending on the number of colors being depicted. The more bits used, the more colors and shades can be displayed. The density of the dots on the screen is known as *resolution.*

Resolution determines the sharpness of the image; more dots add up to create better clarity and finer detail, and fewer dots produce a fuzzier, grainier appearance. Resolution is generally expressed in Dots Per Inch (DPI). To display an image on a monitor, the computer translates the bits and/or bytes into discrete groups of information displayed onscreen as *pixels*. These pixels collectively make up the pictures you see on a computer monitor. The translation of bits and bytes into pixels is called *bit-mapping*, and after it has occurred, the graphic is referred to as *bit-mapped.*

Different resolutions are available within the text and graphics modes. These resolutions are available based on which standard the text or graphics are being displayed in or with. For example, VGA has a resolution of 640 x 480 pixels for both text and graphics. SVGA (the current high-end standard) has a resolution of 800 x 600 for both text and graphics. In earlier standards, MDA had a resolution range of up to 700 x 320, and CGA had a maximum resolution of 640 x 200. Monitors themselves may also be capable of different resolutions below their maximum. For instance, an SVGA monitor is capable of displaying VGA text or graphics at 640 x 480 pixels, yet it can run at up to 800 x 600 pixels of resolution. Depending on the amount of video memory on the video adapter, monitors may be able to display more colors at lower resolutions.

Video adapters purchased today contain their own memory. The purpose of this video memory is to free up the computer's RAM so that it does not have to store the graphic images. Some types of video adapters have their own graphics coprocessor. This is a processing chip that makes calculations specifically for the video display. Without a coprocessor, the CPU would have to use a great deal of its resources to display data on the screen. The video coprocessor is designed to minimize the video overhead, or calculations, demanded from the CPU. An adapter that contains its own coprocessor is called a *graphics accelerator*. A video card can also be called a video adapter, video board, video display board, graphics card, graphics adapter, and VGA card. Each of these designations is correct, but for our purposes the name *video card* will be used in this book.

Monochrome Display and Color Graphics Adapters

In this section, we cover the basics of display and color graphics adapters that have led to today's SVGA standard. From the original PC monochrome monitor, resolution improvements have continued to more accurately represent color and text on the screen. This section gives you an overview of installing a display adapter and the considerations associated with the type of monitor you use.

MDA

The *Monochrome Display Adapter* (MDA) was the first of the IBM display adapters used in the personal computer. MDA offered a screen eighty characters wide by twenty-five lines high, and was designed to display the business-oriented software of the day—basic word processors and spreadsheets.

The MDA was great for most standard business and personal applications of the time. However, MDA could not display graphics. Even before color graphics became a consideration, the need to display graphics was apparent even to the average user. MDA had made it possible for the end user to see in real-time what the computer was doing and the result. MDA was able to display monochrome text at 720 x 350 pixels.

MDA was an excellent solution for word processing, spreadsheet, and database applications of the day. As the personal computer became more widely accepted, though, the power of the personal computer was becoming increasingly apparent. Businesses were using the computer to do the work of several people, and people were using the computer to do hour-long tasks in minutes. Users began to see the need for graphics beyond simple text. In response to this need for graphics, the Hercules Graphics adapter was created, which enabled the display of graphics images on a monochrome monitor. This was a substantial improvement for most users, but the desire for color displays kept innovation moving forward. The monochrome monitor and adapter were one of the most widely manufactured display systems ever for the personal computer. The MDA has not been made for years, but because of the sheer numbers that were produced, you may still run into this type of display from time to time.

CGA

IBM introduced the standard for CGA, or Color Graphics Adapter, in 1981. Like MDA, CGA was still based on a digital signal from the graphics adapter to the monitor, limiting the amount of variation possible in the signal. With its introduction, computer games and other software could be displayed in color for the first time. This greatly added to the value of the personal computer as a tool that could both work for and entertain you.

Though CGA was a huge leap forward in display technology, it fell short for both the personal and business user. End users required fonts to be displayed clearly, and CGA only had a maximum resolution of 640 x 200 pixels in two-color mode, displaying text less clearly than the MDA. This kept CGA from being accepted as a viable long-term color solution and as a result, it was primarily used for computer games.

EGA

IBM released the EGA, or Enhanced Graphics Adapter, in 1984. It was meant to display both graphics and text in a clear color format. Though it was certainly a large improvement over CGA in terms of both graphics quality and text display, it was still nowhere near meeting the demands of the business and personal user.

Fonts displayed by EGA still had that jagged-edged computer look and the graphics were still limited to computer-generated large dot images. This gave you an idea of the picture, but it just wasn't lifelike in appearance. EGA was still based on a digital signal from adapter to monitor, again limiting the variation capable in signal. EGA was not capable of making a word processing document on the screen look like what was being printed out on high-quality printers. The document onscreen might look fuzzy, but the actual text being printed was comparable to a typewriter.

EGA was capable of displaying 16 colors out of a 64-color palette at a resolution of 640 x 350 pixels. In graphics, the term *palette* is the set of available colors.

MDA, CGA, AND EGA INSTALLATION

The MDA, CGA, and EGA video cards used the standard ISA bus. To install the adapter card, the installer simply located a free ISA bus slot and inserted the display adapter. The technician had to be sure that the adapter was fully seated by visually inspecting the base where the adapter meets the bus and by applying gradual pressure downward along the length of the card. Because some of these adapters were designed for 8-bit bus slots, it was important to align the adapter to the back-most section of the ISA bus slot or use an 8-bit bus slot.

VGA

In 1987, IBM moved from digital signal display toward analog technology. That same year, IBM developed and released the *Video Graphics Array* (VGA) display for personal computers. VGA uses analog signals from the adapter to the monitor, whereas MDA, CGA, and EGA used digital signals. The significance of the analog signal is that it allows almost infinite variation in signal intensity, enabling the monitor to vary intensity or shading along a broad spectrum, rather than only two to sixteen colors, the previous limit.

VGA has become the base video standard for the IBM-compatible computer. All IBM-compatible PCs today support VGA at a minimum, making it the base video standard. The base VGA display can support resolution of 640 x 480 pixels in sixteen-color mode. The total palette of colors available in the VGA is 262,144.

For the first time, images could be rendered with a lifelike appearance and detailed photo-quality color. What You See Is What You Get (WYSIWYG) documents became a reality. Fonts were now able to be displayed the same onscreen as the printed output.

SVGA

SVGA is an acronym for Super Video Graphics Array. SVGA was designed to greatly enhance the capabilities of the VGA standard by providing higher resolutions and added color depth.

SVGA standards have been developed by a group of monitor and display card manufacturers called the *Video Electronics Standards Association* (VESA). All SVGA standards support 16.7 million colors. However, the number of colors that can be displayed at one time depends on the amount of video memory the adapter card has. Adding additional color depth, or enhancing resolution to a higher level, requires an increased amount of available video memory.

Although you may have an SVGA adapter, it is possible that you would only be able to display 256 colors or less at a time, again, depending on memory constraints and the resolution you're trying to display. It may be necessary to drop to the next lower resolution in order to increase the color depth to the desired level (see the upcoming "Video Memory" section for more details). The following resolutions are commonly supported by SVGA:

- 800 x 600 pixels
- 1,024 x 768 pixels
- 1,280 x 1,024 pixels
- 1,600 x 1,200 pixels

Video Accelerators

Video cards containing graphics coprocessors (graphics accelerators) are referred to as *accelerated video adapters*, or sometimes *video accelerators*. The main purpose of a video accelerator is to free up the computer processor from having to make complex graphics calculations. Most video adapter cards today are accelerated video adapters. In addition to freeing up resources of the computer's processor, doing the graphics calculations at the source increases the speed with which graphics can be displayed on the monitor. Aside from having a graphics processor, the other characteristics that differentiate graphics accelerators are:

- **Memory:** Graphics accelerators have their own memory.
- **Bus:** Most graphics accelerators are designed for the PCI bus or the newest standard, accelerated graphics port (AGP). These enhanced buses enable faster video data transmission.
- **Register width (a pointer to the data stored in memory):** The wider the register, the more data the processor can manipulate with each instruction.

Installation

Regular VGA adapter cards generally use the ISA bus and are installed in the same manner as described in the sidebar on MDA, CGA, and EGA installation. SVGA adapters with or without accelerators are primarily designed for the PCI Bus, although many were manufactured for the VL Bus. AGP cards for Pentium II systems are becoming more common.

 VL Bus **is another term for VESA Local Bus.**

VIDEO MEMORY

Several types of video memory are available. The manufacturer determines the type of memory a graphics display card uses. The manufacturer has many concerns, such as its intended purpose, target performance, and how much it will cost to make versus what it can be sold for. There is an adage in the industry that says, "Good, fast, or cheap. Pick any two." Added resolution capabilities require more video memory, as does the latest graphics coprocessor technology. Different types of memory have different characteristics, and may be better suited for different types of functions. As discussed earlier in this chapter, the amount of video memory determines the resolutions at which graphics are displayed (see Table 10-1).

TABLE 10-1 MEMORY REQUIREMENTS FOR VARIOUS MODES OF DISPLAY				
RESOLUTION	*16 COLORS (4-BIT)*	*256 COLORS (8-BIT)*	*65,000 COLORS (16-BIT)*	*16.7 MILLION COLORS (24-BIT, 32-BIT)*
640 x 480	512K	512K	1MB	2MB
800 x 600	512K	1MB	2MB	2MB
1,024 x 768	1MB	1MB	2MB	4MB
1,152 x 1,024	1MB	2MB	2MB	4MB
1,280 x 1,024	1MB	2MB	4MB	4MB
1,600 x 1,200	2MB	2MB	4MB	8MB

Following are the common types of memory used in video adapters:

o **DRAM:** Dynamic Random Access Memory

o **VRAM:** Video Random Access Memory

o **SRAM:** Static Random Access Memory

o **EDO DRAM:** Extended Data Out Dynamic Random Access Memory

o **WRAM:** Window Random Access Memory

o **RDRAM:** Rambus Dynamic Random Access Memory

o **SGRAM:** Synchronous Graphic Random Access Memory

This section covers each of these memory types in detail.

No matter what the acronym, RAM is either static or dynamic. Table 10-2 shows the relative access times of static versus dynamic memory. For more detail, see the following sections on different video memory types.

TABLE 10-2 TYPE AND ACCESS TIMES FOR RAM	
TYPE	*TYPICAL ACCESS TIMES*
Static RAM (SRAM)	10–50 nanoseconds
Dynamic RAM (DRAM)	50–150 nanoseconds

Top speed is an important issue; however, it is not the only consideration. When selecting an accelerator, the technology is as important as the RAM. In most cases, newer technology uses the fastest components, but this is not always true. Some graphics accelerator cards mix static and dynamic RAM. Some graphics accelerator cards use special technologies that give the RAM extended function characteristics, such as updating the state of an image at the same time they display their contents on the monitor.

Some graphics accelerators have a fixed speed at which they transfer data over the bus to the device, while others synchronize themselves to the CPU bus clock. It is possible to have slower RAM and still get display data to the monitor faster than an alternative design with faster RAM. Figure 10-4 illustrates how it is possible with slower RAM to update the display faster by increasing the speed at which the data arrives at its intended device.

In this illustration, the top line represents how long the data takes to get to its device at 33.3MHz over X period of time. The bottom line represents the time it takes the data to get to its device at 100MHz over X period.

note ✒ **Overall performance and speed can be measured in Megahertz.**

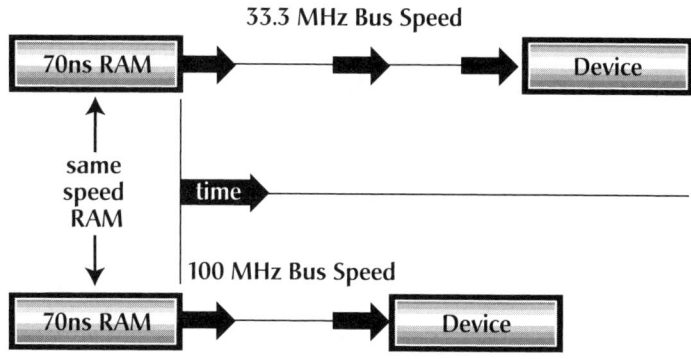

FIGURE 10-4 Bus speed vs. RAM speed

Figure 10-4 shows that it is not necessarily the speed of the RAM that determines the performance of the system. As you can see, the speed capability of the RAM is not the determining factor in getting the data displayed quickly—in this case, it's the bus speed that makes the difference.

Another way to think of this is to imagine yourself in the fastest type of car you know of. Although the car is very fast, you are restricted to traveling down the road at 33.3 miles per hour. Your friend, who is in a car nowhere near the speed capabilities of the car you're traveling in, is on a different road leading to the same place, but is able to go 100 miles per hour. If you're both going to the same place down the road, who gets there first?

Another consideration is the amount of data being delivered. This is where the amount of RAM is more of a consideration than the speed. Suppose you are now in a big truck. The objective now is to get the most payload to the destination—say for example, twenty tons of *Imaginary Random Access Memory* (IRAM). Let's say you are going down the road at 33.3 miles per hour with ten tons of IRAM. Your friend is going down the same road in a sports car and manages to cram one ton of IRAM in the car. Even with the sports car way overloaded, your friend manages to get the car to 100 miles per hour. Who will complete the objective first?

Since RAM speed isn't the only factor, video accelerators are designed for different uses. You may find that a video card that may not offer the best raw speed is, in fact, the card best suited for the tasks you do. In the remainder of this chapter, we will discuss the various types of RAM used in graphics accelerator adapters.

Dynamic Random Access Memory *(DRAM)*

The term *dynamic* indicates that the memory must be constantly refreshed or it will lose its contents. The cost and availability of DRAM makes this the most common type of RAM used in personal computers and peripherals. DRAM access times are typically between 50 to 150ns (nanoseconds). Other factors besides the access time determine how quickly the adapter displays its data on the screen. One such consideration is its ability to access ports. A port is an interface on the computer that is used to transfer data. In this case, the term *port* means an interface used to transfer video data from the display adapter to the monitor. Until VRAM was developed, RAM could only access and transfer data on one port. The term for this is *single ported*.

Video Random Access Memory *(VRAM)*

VRAM was designed specifically for use by video accelerator adapter cards. Two different devices can access VRAM simultaneously. This allows the monitor to access the VRAM for screen updates at the same time that a graphics processor updates the data. It is important to note that with VRAM, the data can be updated while the display is refreshed; however, no new data can be introduced while the monitor is accessing the VRAM. Typical access time for VRAM is 50 to 100ns.

To understand this technology better, think of an empty circle. Using VRAM, the accelerator can fill the circle with color, and the monitor can display the filled circle as the VRAM is updated. However, if the base shape of the image changed to a square, then the monitor would be interrupted while the new data was fed to the accelerator. The data would then be transferred to the VRAM, then on to the monitor. This whole process happens very quickly due to the speed of graphics accelerators and the speed at which the RAM can accept and transfer its data.

Static Random Access Memory *(SRAM)*

SRAM has faster access times than DRAM. This access time difference is due to its static nature, meaning that the information, once stored, remains stored until overwritten by another piece of information. SRAM does not need to be refreshed as often as DRAM, and therefore is interrupted less. This results in SRAM access times as low as 10ns. SRAM can perform the same functions of DRAM and do it faster, but it is much more expensive. This results in SRAM primarily being used as computer memory cache or as memory on high-end video accelerators.

Extended Data Out Dynamic Random Access Memory (EDO DRAM)

The main difference between DRAM and EDO DRAM is that DRAM only allows 1 byte to be read at a time. EDO DRAM, on the other hand, allows block transfer to its internal cache. A *block* is an entire group of data, rather than individual bytes. EDO DRAM also has internal multitasking capability, meaning that it can do more than one task at a time. The CPU or video accelerator is able to access the EDO cache while the memory collects another block of data. The term for this action is *pipeline burst*. Consequently, EDO DRAM only shows improved access times over conventional DRAM if the caching controller supports pipeline burst. It is important to note that simply because the graphics accelerator uses EDO DRAM, you may not get improved performance over an accelerator that uses standard DRAM. In most new computers, the pipeline burst function is controlled at the hardware level and requires no setup by the user; in other cases, pipeline burst can be enabled in the CMOS or by setting the jumpers on the device itself.

Window Random Access Memory (WRAM)

WRAM is similar to VRAM in that it performs caching and the image can be updated without interrupting the display. WRAM goes a step farther than VRAM, though, because WRAM can not only be accessed by two devices at a time, but it can also communicate with two ports at the same time without interrupting the process for new data to be introduced in memory. This means that while an image is being drawn or radically changed by the accelerator, it can be displayed on the screen. WRAM can do this because it can get new data at the same time it displays the data it has.

Rambus Dynamic Random Access Memory (RDRAM)

RDRAM gets its name from the developer of the technology, Rambus Incorporated. RDRAM, while not having faster access times than other dynamic RAM, can deliver its data to a device up to six times faster. RDRAM has not been widely available up until now; however, major corporations have expressed an interest in licensing the technology. If this happens, you're sure to see RDRAM in the near future.

Synchronous Graphic Random Access Memory (SGRAM)

SGRAM is probably the most common type of RAM you will encounter in newer video accelerator cards. SGRAM synchronizes itself with the CPU bus, meaning it automatically detects the bus speed and runs at that speed, and because of this, it can deliver its data at up to 100MHz. As with RDRAM, SGRAM is dynamic. Its speed comes from its ability to deliver data quickly to the device, rather than depending on a quick access time. SGRAM, like DRAM, is single ported; however, it uses several techniques that have the same net effect as increasing bandwidth, meaning that it can transfer more data as well as get it there fast. SGRAM also has the capability of opening two memory pages simultaneously. This capability approximates the function of WRAM's dual port capabilities; however, there is an interrupt process between the reading of the memory pages.

Upgrading Video Memory

As we discussed earlier, one of the characteristics of a video accelerator is that it has its own memory. This memory can sometimes be upgraded. When a manufacturer says that the adapter can be upgraded, they are talking about the *amount* of video memory, not the *type*. If your adapter uses DRAM and you want to upgrade the memory, you must use DRAM. Video memory upgrades are specific to the video card, and are available only from the manufacturer. Most commonly, they are fixed into some form of module that plugs directly into connectors on the video card. All video memory upgrade modules come with specific instructions, and these vary widely depending on the card's design.

 caution To prevent damage to computer components, you should use an ESD wrist strap when servicing computers. An ESD wrist strap is a device that keeps you grounded to prevent you from accidentally discharging harmful voltages into the computer's circuitry.

KEY POINT SUMMARY

In this chapter, we covered the function of video graphics adapters, the various types of video adapters available, and their evolution. We discussed the committees and companies that determine and set standards for the various types of video adapter cards. We covered installation of video adapters and the various types of memory used by video adapters. We also examined the difference between the bus types available for video adapters and learned to identify the correct bus type and slot to use during installation.

- Graphics adapters have gone through a history of change from the early MDA and Hercules models to CGA, EGA, VGA, and now SVGA. Each step along the way enhanced users' ability to more effectively display what they wanted as accurately as possible.

- Video cards are most commonly coprocessed to take a load off the CPU's processing. These coprocessed cards, like video cards in general, have their own memory on board. This memory can be one of many types, depending on the card design, the card cost, and its intended purpose.

APPLYING WHAT YOU'VE LEARNED

This chapter has covered a lot of important material that will help you prepare for the A+ exam and be an excellent computer technician. Take a few minutes and work through the assessments, review your notes, and see how you did.

The hands-on lab will also help you build your comfort level with the hardware as well as reinforce the readings from this chapter.

Instant Assessment

Multiple choice

Choose the best answer(s). There may be more than one correct answer for each question.

1. The main purpose of a video display adapter is to:

   A. Occupy space on the computer's bus and eat up system resources

   B. Provide an interface between the user and the keyboard

   C. Show in real-time what the computer is doing and allow user interaction

   D. Hook customers into buying upgrades

2. RAM, no matter what type, is basically either _____.

   A. Static or dynamic

   B. IBM or Mac

   C. Compressed or uncompressed

   D. Video or mainboard

3. In graphics mode, a monitor can display any:

   A. Color image

   B. Black and white image

   C. True color image

   D. Image that is bit-mapped

4. The purpose of video memory is:

   A. To free up the computer's RAM so that it does not have to store the graphics images

   B. To enable the monitor to display higher resolutions (DPI)

   C. To enable the CPU's coprocessor to store algorithms for graphics codes

   D. To enable the video card to store text, freeing up the computer's RAM

5. A video adapter that contains its own coprocessor is called a:

   A. Raster Graphics Compatible Display Adapter

   B. Vector Graphics Compatible Display Adapter

    C. Graphics Mode Enabled Display Adapter

    D. Graphics accelerator

6. The difference between an analog event and a digital event is that:

    A. A digital event can represent any increment, whereas an analog event is limited to a certain increment

    B. A digital event can represent only fixed increments, whereas analog can represent any increment

    C. An analog event is best thought of as a representation of a digital event

    D. A digital event can be described as a representation of an analog graphic

7. What is the base standard that was developed by IBM for video display?

    A. SVGA

    B. VGA

    C. VGA has become obsolete; only VESA compatible adapters are supported in IBM-compatible display adapters manufactured today

    D. Only IBM display adapters conform to VESA

8. The main change in adapter technology that allowed the display of sharp fonts in color was:

    A. Digital signal to analog signal

    B. Analog signal to digital signal

    C. Accelerated graphics adapters to warp field generators

    D. Dynamic RAM to static RAM

9. In the VGA palette, _____ colors are available.

    A. 16

    B. 256

    C. 262,144

    D. 16.7 million

10. The main determining factor in speed of display with a graphics accelerator is the:

    A. RAM access time

B. Coprocessor compile time

C. Type of RAM used

D. Speed the data travels along the busHands-

Lab Exercises

In this lab exercise, you will replace a video card. You'll need a computer, a screwdriver, and a video card suitable for your new system. It also makes sense for this card to offer better performance than what's currently installed — that way you don't have to remove it after the lab!

Lab 10-10 *Replacing a video card*

Getting organized

Clear your work area of all nonessential items. You should be able to freely move the computer around on the work area without space constraints. For your safety, unplug the system.

Remove the system cover for access to internal computer components. Certain screws on the back of the case enable removal of the cover, and others hold the power supply in place. Be sure to remove the right ones, which are typically right alongside the edge of the case cover.

In Figure 10-5, you can see that the system boards are held in place with screws and pressed into bus slots. The center card in this figure is the video card.

2. Remove the video card. Now unscrew the adapter card back plate. Once the back plate is free, pull up with just enough force to remove the adapter card. When you have finished, it will look like Figure 10-6.

Mounting hardware   Video card

FIGURE 10-5 Video card with mounting hardware

AGP slot

FIGURE 10-6 Empty bus slot

3. Insert a video card. In Figure 10-7, notice that the back plate is straight—this is important for proper seating of the card. Insert the card flush along the slot and apply only as much gentle force as is necessary to seat the card in the slot. Secure the card in the computer by screwing the back plate to the case.

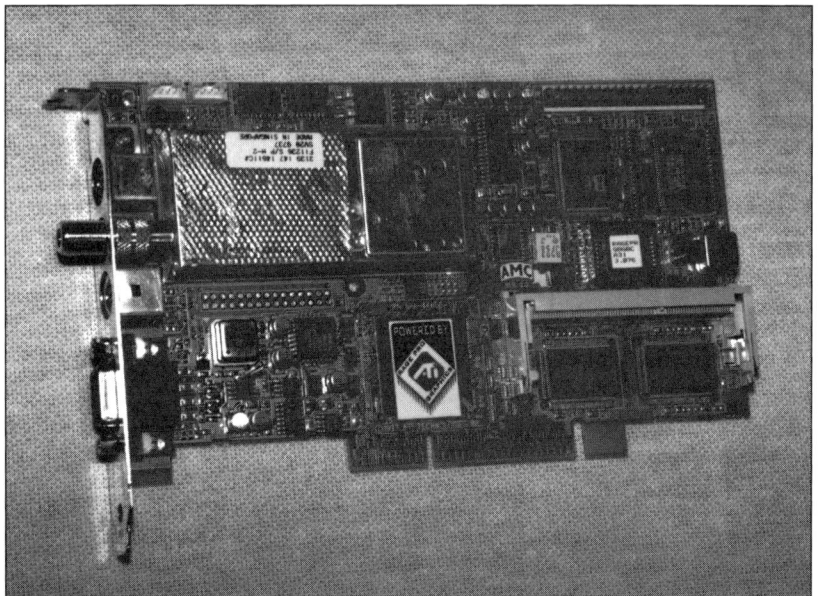

FIGURE 10-7 Side view of a video card

4. Replace the case cover. Be sure to line up the screw holes properly before tightening the case down, and be careful not to scratch the case with your screwdriver.

Configuration

About Chapter 11

In this chapter, we'll discuss configuration—the process of setting up hardware and software so the PC functions properly. This chapter discusses common terms used in association with configuring a PC, as well as some of the steps you'll need to follow when you configure a PC.

Some manufacturers build their PCs with everything the system is capable of supporting. These systems are called preconfigured—that is to say, the hardware and software are installed and should be ready to work out of the box. In the field, however, you may encounter customers who want to add on things such as sound cards, accelerated video adapters, and CD-ROM drives. These add-ons require configuration to function properly.

UNDERSTANDING CONFIGURATION

The word *configuration* comes from the root *configure*, which the Merriam Webster WWWebster Dictionary (at `http://www.m-w.com/dictionary.htm`) defines as "to set up for operation especially in a particular way." That's what you as an A+ certified technician will do for computer systems: set up both hardware and software in a particular way so that it all functions together properly.

If you've spent any time around the computing industry, you've probably heard people mention a system having an "old configuration." This generally means that the system was set up several years ago, and at that time it was a good system. However, computing technology changes so rapidly that a couple of years can make a good configuration completely useless if you're attempting to install recent hardware or software. For example, a typical configuration for a home PC in 1994 would have looked something like this:

- 8MB RAM
- 5.25-inch or 3.5-inch high-density floppy drive
- 500MB hard disk
- VGA monitor
- 1MB video adapter
- DOS and Windows 3.1

A more recent configuration might look like this:

- 32MB RAM
- 3.5" floppy drive
- Zip drive
- 2GB hard disk
- CD-ROM or DVD drive
- SVGA monitor
- 2MB accelerated video adapter
- Windows 98 or Windows NT 4.0

As you can see, the basic requirements for a reasonably well-configured PC have changed considerably.

Software products and operating systems have minimum system requirements that for the most part will dictate the minimum hardware configuration of the PC.

When you install a new piece of hardware, you generally must configure the resources it will use to communicate with other components in the system and with the system itself. For most components, you'll need to configure three things:

- *Input/Output port* (I/O port, or simply the port)
- *Interrupt Request Line* (IRQ)
- *Direct Memory Access Channel* (DMA Channel)

These are the basics of communication within a modern PC. To understand how these concepts relate to each other, consider a sound card as an example. Under normal conditions, all information flows between the CPU and the sound card through the I/O port. For the CPU to communicate with the sound card, though, it needs to know the address of the I/O port. Port addresses are generally expressed as a hexadecimal number. Once the CPU knows the address of the I/O port for the sound card, it can send and receive all the information it wants through that port.

However, in a typical computer, the CPU has a lot of things to do and can't pay attention to the sound card's I/O port all the time. If the sound card has some important information to send the CPU, it needs some way to tap it on the shoulder. This is what the IRQ is for. When the sound card needs the CPU's attention, it sends a signal on the CPU. This signal doesn't carry any information — it just lets the CPU know that some device needs its attention. Like the I/O port address, the CPU also needs to know which device will be using which IRQ, or it won't know which device is asking for attention when an IRQ signal comes in. If the CPU knows that the sound card uses IRQ 5, then whenever it receives a signal on IRQ 5, it can check the sound card's I/O port to see what the sound card needs.

This doesn't mean that the CPU will *always* respond to every IRQ signal. The idea behind the IRQ system is that several devices can be doing different things at the same time. When two devices try to signal the CPU at the same time, the CPU has to decide which has priority. To this end, the IRQs themselves have been set in a standard priority order that the CPU adheres to religiously. If the CPU is servicing a particular device and a signal comes in on a lower-priority IRQ, the CPU waits until it finishes what it's doing to handle the new request. On the other hand, if a signal comes in on a higher-priority IRQ, the CPU stops what it's doing immediately and handles that request.

DMA is similar to the I/O port in that data is transmitted through the DMA channel. The difference is that data travels directly from the device to memory over a DMA channel, whereas all data on I/O ports travels between the device and the CPU. If that data needs to be stored in memory, then the CPU must transfer it there, which requires an extra step, more processing overhead, and more time. Though the DMA transfer might require a computing cycle to get the information from the device to memory, overall system usage is lowered by using DMA rather than the standard I/O port for information bound for memory.

Configuring standard hardware usually consists of setting switches and jumpers to define the resources the device will use. This new hardware becomes part of the system's configuration.

These days, much of the hardware you'll install is *Plug and Play*, meaning that the hardware will attempt to automatically configure itself to work with the system it's installed in. Plug and Play devices tell the other pieces of the computer how to communicate with them in a way that does not conflict with the operation of the other devices on the PC. In many cases, Plug and Play works fine. Other times, these devices are the main reason you must have an understanding of how to configure devices on a PC. You can mix Plug and Play devices with jumper-configured devices; however, if you decide to do this, you will always have to have at least one standard I/O address and IRQ available for use by each Plug and Play device. Without understanding the concepts behind I/O and IRQs, you can't troubleshoot problems that occur when Plug and Play devices are competing for resources with legacy devices. For more information about IRQs and I/O addresses, see Chapter 7.

In the case of configuring software for use with the hardware, you will need to know what type of hardware is connected to the computer, and possibly what resources that hardware is using. When configuring operating systems, you also need to know which files and what commands to use to configure the operating environment. These commands can load drivers for the devices or tell the operating system which resources the devices are using. Typical files used in configuration are CONFIG.SYS or SYSTEM.INI. In the Macintosh operating systems, you configure the system through control panels.

COMMON CONFIGURATION CONCERNS

Before starting to configure a system, you need to find out how it will be used. The common concerns of configuration boil down to two questions: "What will the system be required to do?" and "What is the physical environment the system will be placed in?" Generally, you'll want to talk to the end user or the department manager to find out what the appropriate configuration will be. By determining what the user will be doing with the system, you can make reasonable and informed choices about what hardware and software should be installed and how to configure those components to best suit the task at hand.

Keep in mind that most customers are not technicians and can't talk to you about bits, bytes, gigs, IRQs drive controllers, and so on. You must thoroughly interview your customers to understand their true needs. It's generally a good idea to have a checklist of items that you can ask your customers about, since being non-technical people, they are not likely to know exactly what they need.

With that in mind, consider the following list of items:

- Will the customer be using the computer for graphics work? If not, then perhaps a smaller monitor and slightly slower system will be more cost-effective. However, if they'll be designing graphics on the system, then they'll probably need at least a 17-inch monitor and a reasonably fast accelerating graphics adapter. In particular, customers doing a good deal of 3D modeling or rendering will need a truly high-end system, including a fast processor and system bus, plenty of memory and drive space, and a state-of-the-art video system, including a fast 3D graphics accelerator and a large, high-resolution, high-refresh-rate monitor. High-end graphics work may also require specialized input devices such as pointing tablets, scanners, and digital cameras. Finally, graphics generally require a good deal of drive space — plan on a 9GB drive and perhaps a Jaz drive (a drive featuring removable 1- or 2GB cartridges) for backing up and transporting files.

- As for the operating system, many graphic designers still prefer Macintosh over Windows. The color management of a Macintosh is much more refined than that of Windows, and the interface is more intuitive to the creative, graphically inclined mind. However, many of the major graphics software packages these days are released for Windows first, then ported to

Macintosh afterward, simply because of the larger market and greater sales opportunity. If your customer wants the latest and greatest software at all times, then Windows may be the way to go.

- Will this system be running a database? Large databases benefit from as much processing power and memory as you can throw at them, so consider the fastest processor and system bus available, possibly even going with a multiprocessor system. Memory is relatively cheap these days, so suggest to the customer that adding as much memory as the system will accept will greatly improve performance. This is especially important if a large number of people will be accessing this database over a network. You may also want to suggest that in the case of a database server, a small monitor and modest video adapter will do, since no one should be working on the system for daily use. However, this system will require plenty of high-speed disk storage. Determine the amount of data they currently use, then triple or quadruple that amount, and consider a *Redundant Array of Inexpensive Disks* (RAID) storage system rather than a simple hard drive. You'll also want to include a large tape backup drive so that regular backups are easy and therefore more likely to be done.

- This type of system may be best served with a UNIX operating system due to its stability and security features. The drawback to UNIX is its reputation of being cryptic and difficult to use. If you're dealing with a non-technical customer who can't afford to hire a UNIX jockey to administer the database, then perhaps a Windows NT system running SQL Server or Oracle would be a better choice. Being comparatively new on the operating system scene, Windows NT doesn't have quite the stability or security of UNIX. The user interface, however, is much simpler, being basically the same as that of Windows 95/98. This doesn't necessarily make database administration a simple chore, but it smoothes the learning curve considerably for someone already familiar with Windows.

- Will someone be using this system on a regular basis for word processing, accounting, or other business tasks? This type of work will, of course, require a standard office productivity suite such as Microsoft Office or WordPerfect Office. A large monitor is a godsend to someone staring at a screen all day, but this type of system won't necessarily require the best video adapter available. A comfortable, ergonomic keyboard such as the Microsoft Natural keyboard will lower the risk of chronic wrist problems from prolonged typing, and a comfortable mouse should be considered, though you can probably skip the graphics tablet here. A reasonable processor, say a 233MHz Pentium, should be able to handle the tasks nicely, and most business applications run smoothly in 64 to 96MB of RAM. Depending upon the type of documents being used, you can probably install a 2- to 6GB hard drive without worrying about it filling up any time soon. You should also consider installing a Zip drive (an inexpensive add-on drive featuring 100MB removable disks) or some other mid-sized removable-media storage system so that users can transfer and back up multi-megabyte files without having to flip floppies, a tedious task at best.

- A system of this sort will most certainly be best off running a Windows operating system, either Windows 98 or Windows NT Workstation 4.0, due to the proliferation of software choices available for that platform. However, if the client is already proficient with the Macintosh interface, don't push too hard for the change; Macintosh users are very loyal to their favorite computer company!

- If the customer is a business with a network, then you'll need to install the appropriate network interface card.

- Rarely will you install a system these days that doesn't require a CD-ROM drive; nearly all applications are distributed on CD-ROM. The only consideration here is how fast a drive the customer is willing to pay for. However, if this system will be on a company network and all of the necessary applications will be installed from the network, then you may actually be able to get away without a CD-ROM.

- Similarly, if this computer won't be connected to a network, then you'll almost certainly need a modem. Determine how ("if" probably isn't the right question these days) this user will connect to the Internet and install the fastest modem that's compatible with the user's service provider, up to the customer's spending limit.

- Assess the space situation and then discuss whether the user would prefer to have the system in a desktop or tower case. You may need to explain that desktop systems take up more space on the desk, but if the CD-ROM or floppy drive will be used frequently, then having it on the desk makes it easier to access than a tower case on the floor.

While you're conducting the interview, keep in mind the customer's budget, but don't be afraid to press the customer to spend more on a system that will handle the necessary tasks better. Remind the customer that money spent on quality equipment now will save money and headaches down the road, both in support and upgrading costs. Whenever possible, configure a system so that it can be easily upgraded when necessary. For example, if the customer's budget necessitates a choice between a large monitor or 96MB of RAM, go with the large monitor and less memory, being sure to buy the memory in large units (two 32MB SIMMs instead of four 16MB SIMMs). That way, when the customer can afford to upgrade, you can insert two more 32MB SIMMs without losing anything. You just can't add 4 inches to a 15-inch monitor.

DISPLAYS

In this section, we discuss how to configure display monitors. There are several considerations common to configuring the display of a computer system:

- Configure the I/O port and IRQ for the adapter card.
- Make sure the adapter is properly connected to the computer.
- Make sure the monitor is properly connected to the adapter.
- Make sure the appropriate software drivers are installed on the computer.
- Make sure the monitor is turned on and properly adjusted.

In most cases, the video adapters you install will be preconfigured for the industry standard settings of I/O ports starting at A0000 and IRQ 9. However, on occasion you may run into an adapter card manufactured to be jumper configured. Consult the manufacturer's documentation for the settings of these jumpers. Most of the cards that required jumpers to be set only allowed you to change the IRQ from 9 to 10, 11, or 15. As a rule, stick with IRQ 9 for display.

In rare cases, you'll come across video adapters that also allow you to disable or enable the card's coprocessor or select the bus speed. Generally, you should enable the card's coprocessor, as very few systems have conflicts with a video adapter coprocessor. To enable the functions of the adapter, consult the owner's manual; see Chapter 10 for more information on this subject. As for the bus speed, the card's speed needs to be set the same as that of the system bus, which may or may not be the same as the speed of the CPU, as explained in Chapter 7. Check the documentation of the motherboard for the appropriate bus speed, then set the jumpers on the video adapter to match that speed.

The next two items (connecting the computer, adapter, and monitor together) are fairly self-explanatory. If the adapter is an expansion card, then you'll need to make sure that it is properly seated in its slot on the motherboard, as described in Chapter 10. On the other hand, if the adapter is built into the motherboard, then you can assume that it's properly connected, because modification of soldered motherboard components is beyond the realm of the A+ certified technician.

Once you have the video adapter attached to the computer properly, you need to plug the monitor into the adapter. You can then install the appropriate driver software. In many cases, the operating system will have drivers for your monitor and video adapter, though sometimes the hardware components come with a CD or set of diskettes that you should use to load the drivers. Generally, you'll be able to run the computer in a low-resolution video mode (probably 640 x 480, with 16 or 256 colors for Windows systems) while installing the drivers; this is very fortunate because loading drivers without being able to see what you're doing would be next to impossible.

Once the driver software is installed, you should set the resolution and color depth to the user's desired settings. Normally you do this via controls installed in the operating system. On Windows systems, you use the Display section of the Control Panel, while Macintosh users find these settings by clicking the Display option on the Apple menu. You'll either use the software provided with the video adapter or the specific application program (such as your word processor or graphics program) to configure the display on a DOS system. These configurations could vary widely, but the basic concepts should remain the same, covering such areas as color depth and display resolution. Refer to Chapters 9 and 10 for more information.

Having set the display to the desired resolution and color depth, your next step is to adjust the monitor to display the picture properly. Most monitors will have controls on them to adjust the configuration for optimum viewing. These are some of the more common controls on a computer monitor:

- **Horizontal Hold:** Just like on a television, this keeps the picture from disintegrating into horizontal lines.

- **Horizontal Position:** Adjusts the horizontal position of the information being displayed.

- **Vertical Hold:** Similar to Horizontal Hold, but for the vertical display.

- **Vertical Position:** Adjusts the vertical position of the information being displayed.

- **Brightness:** Controls the brightness of the display.

- **Contrast:** Controls the contrast of the display.

- **Height:** Controls the height of the information displayed on the monitor.

- **Width:** Controls the width of the information displayed on the monitor.

- **Pin Cushion:** This control lets you adjust the picture so that it is the same width from top to bottom, rather than being wider at the top and bottom than it is in the middle.

- **Tilt:** Lets you align the picture on the display so that it is straight up and down instead of tilted to one side.

STORAGE DEVICE CONFIGURATION

In this section, we discuss the various types of storage devices available to you, and how you can configure them. Storage device configuration is primarily driven by storage needs. For example, a company that does large volumes of database management would require more storage than an end user writing letters home.

Hard Drives

As discussed earlier in this book, a *hard drive* is a magnetic disk inside the computer that stores data. The term *hard* differentiates it from a floppy disk. Generally, hard disks hold more data and are faster than floppy disks. Hard disks vary in size from a few megabytes to several gigabytes — most floppies, on the other hand, have a storage capacity of 1.44MB or 2.88MB in most modern systems.

Hard disks are usually a collection of several platters. The data is stored on these platters, with two read/write heads for each platter. A platter requires two read/write heads because the data is stored on the top and bottom of the platter.

Read/write heads are attached to an access arm, which prevents the heads from moving independently. Within the hard drive, each platter has the same number of tracks, and cylinders — a track across all platters is called a *cylinder*.

When configuring the hard disk, it is important to remember that hard disks are not always permanently fixed to the computer — it is possible to use removable hard disks. Removable hard disks generally come in the form of disk packs or removable cartridges. Mounting kits are also available to turn standard hard drives into removable drives, which enables you to have different disks loaded with different operating systems. Shut the system down in Windows 98, swap hard drives, reboot, and you're in Windows 3.1, or whatever you choose. Generally, removable drives come with special software drivers that you'll need to install to allow the operating system to recognize the drive. Always read the manufacturer's documentation provided with any type of hard drive. Even though most systems today automatically detect and configure a hard drive, some hard drives work better with settings other than those chosen by the autodetection process. In the manufacturer's documentation, you will also find other helpful information.

SCSI Hard Drives

SCSI is an abbreviation for *Small Computer Systems Interface*. It's a protocol that allows up to seven (or up to fifteen, in the case of newer SCSI implementations) devices to be connected to the same expansion board plugged into the motherboard. A SCSI controller handles communications between devices and the CPU, and between the devices themselves, acting in a manner similar to that of a server on a local area network. The devices on the SCSI bus are daisy-chained together, so the cable goes from the adapter card to one drive, then to another drive until the end of the SCSI chain is reached. The last device in the chain must terminate the chain to route data back to the controller. Normally you'd do this by setting a jumper on the device or by plugging a terminator into the end of the SCSI cable.

SCSI interfaces generally provide faster data transmission rates (up to 80MB per second with Ultra2 SCSI) than IDE or EIDE interfaces. SCSI is an ANSI standard; however, many manufacturers use their own proprietary configurations, so two different SCSI controllers may not work together.

Whereas many Apple Macintoshes use SCSI as a standard drive interface, PCs generally use IDE or Enhanced IDE for their primary disk interface.

You attach a SCSI device to a PC by installing a SCSI controller (shown in Figure 11-1) in one of the system's available expansion slots.

Most high-end SCSI controllers have built-in utilities that enable you to perform basic configurations on the drive(s) attached. Some newer PCs come with a SCSI controller built in. The following varieties of SCSI are currently implemented:

- SCSI-I: 8-bit bus, 25-pin connector, data rates of 4MB per second
- SCSI-II: 8-bit bus, 50-pin connector, data rates of 10MB per second
- Fast SCSI: 8-bit bus, data rates of 10MB per second
- Ultra SCSI: 8-bit bus, data rates of 20MB per second
- Fast Wide SCSI: 16-bit bus, data rates of 20MB per second
- Ultra Wide/SCSI-III SCSI: 16-bit bus, data rates of 40MB per second
- Ultra 2 SCSI: 16-bit bus, data rates of 80MB per second

You attach the SCSI hard drive to the controller using a flat, wide, ribbon cable. It is inserted closest to Pin 1 (on both the card and the devices), as shown in Figure 11-2.

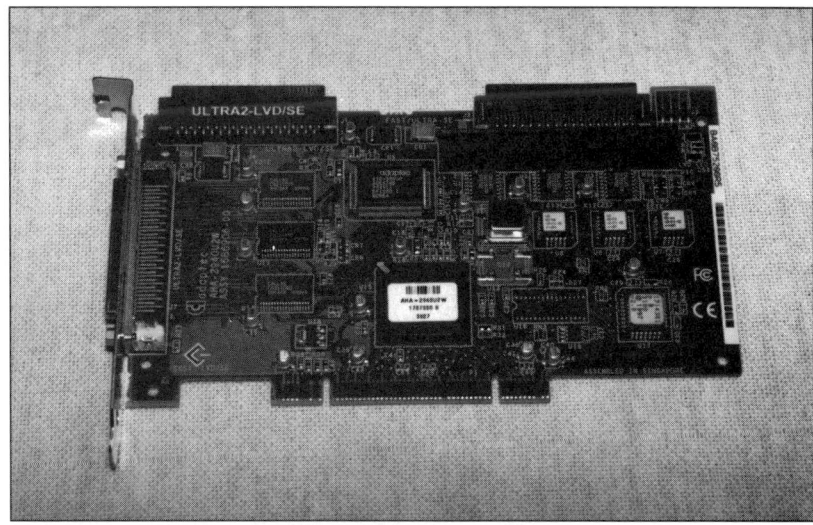

FIGURE 11-1 An Adaptec 2940U2W PCI SCSI controller card

Ribbon cable
connected to system board

Ribbon cable
connected to drive

FIGURE 11-2   Plugging the ribbon cable into the drive.

Once the adapter and the hard drive have been installed in the system, you must partition and format the drive. On the higher-end controllers, you'll commonly partition the drive with special drivers that load at boot-time; when the computer is booting, you'll see a message instructing you to press a special key combination to access the SCSI configuration program. On other controllers, you must install software to allow you access to the drive from the operating system so that you can partition and format it.

Regardless of what devices you attach to the SCSI controller, each requires a software driver to allow the operating system to communicate with it. Windows 95/98 and Windows NT ship with native drivers for many SCSI devices, though you may come across a device that needs special drivers provided by its manufacturer. To use SCSI devices with DOS-based systems, however, you'll need to rely on the drivers that ship with the device. Normally, these devices come with installation disks that automatically install the drivers for proper operation with DOS and Windows 3.1.

Configuring the drive is covered in the manufacturer's documentation. You will need to consult the controller documentation as well when dealing with SCSI devices. Keep in mind that though configuring a SCSI device is usually more time consuming and requires more specialized knowledge, the performance of a SCSI device is higher than the IDE or EIDE.

IDE/EIDE Hard Drives

In 1983, the IBM PC/AT computers had a Western Digital hard disk controller for connecting one or two hard disk drives to the PC/AT *Integrated System Attachment* (ISA) system bus. Five years later, the whole controller was integrated into a single chip and placed in the hard drive that could be connected directly to the ISA bus. Hence, the term *Integrated Device Electronics,* or IDE, disk drive was coined. Eleven years later, the same IDE hard disk controller technology is still being used by ninety percent of the PCs whose processors are one hundred times faster than their counterparts. During this period, the speed of a disk drive had also been improved by ten times while the IDE controller stayed the same.

In 1983, disk drives had 17 sectors per data track and data was transmitted at 800K per second. In 1994, disk drives have more than 80 to 100 sectors per data track and data is transmitted at 4- to 5MB per second. Hence, the computer processor itself is programmed to move the disk drive data at 800K per second. This is the famous *programmed I/O* (PIO) data transfer scheme of IDE adapters. PIO prevents the processor from completing other useful tasks while data transfer is taking place. In 1994, all IDE adapters still had PIO data transfer.

As the manufacturer of the original IDE controller, Western Digital led a coalition to create an Enhanced IDE standard that improves the maximum IDE data transfer speed from 1- to 2MB per second to 12MB per second. This new standard was promoted as an alternative to SCSI for high-end PC workstations.

Unfortunately, data transfer speed is not the only thing needed for attaching I/O devices to a PC. The most important performance feature needed by an I/O adapter today is multitasking, the capability of a computer or adapter to process many tasks at one time. When a processor capable of 100 MIPS must spend 10 to 20 milliseconds waiting for the completion of an I/O request, it is like driving a racecar in rush hour traffic. You simply cannot get up to 200 miles per hour. Multitasking allows the very fast processor to switch to a different task, which generates new requests to I/O devices.

A popular misconception about Enhanced IDE is that the data transfer is now faster than SCSI. However, to achieve a high data transfer rate, an Enhanced IDE I/O adapter must have a bus master transfer mechanism similar to that of SCSI. A bus master transfer mechanism allows the I/O adapter to become a system bus master, enabling it to initiate a data transfer and thereby freeing up the PC processor to do other processing, such as graphics.

Without bus mastering, even an Enhanced IDE drive must use *programmed I/O* (PIO), a data transfer mechanism, meaning the 100 MIPS processor itself must move the disk drive data. When the processor is moving data, it is not doing other useful work. Unlike bus master data transfer, PIO transfer cannot perform *burst transfer* — the ability to saturate the system local bus at 120MB per second by bursting consecutive data transfers. Bursting 10MB of data on a 120MB bus leaves ninety percent of bus bandwidth to other adapters. The bus master data transfer not only frees the processor from data transfer tasks, but also consumes the minimum bandwidth of the system bus. Using PIO, the Enhanced IDE will consume the system bus at one hundred percent.

An IDE adapter can connect two devices — one Master, and one Slave. Only one of the two can be busy at one time. Remember the single-tasking function of IDE? Two requests to those two drives must be completed sequentially!

We know that data transfer speed is not the only thing needed by today's high-end PC workstations. Multitasking is a much more effective method to match the performance of a very fast processor with multiple I/O devices. A bus master function is needed to free up the fast processor from time-consuming tasks such as transferring data. Having a single adapter for multiple I/O devices can save as much money as buying many cheap, low-performance adapters, not to mention the need for multiple slots to plug in those cheap adapters.

You connect the IDE/EIDE hard drive using ribbon cable. The red stripe of the cable goes closest to Pin 1 on the hard drive and on the controller interface. Then you plug in the power connector; the power connector is keyed so that it will only go in one way.

CD-ROM

CD-ROM is a data storage device. One of the advantages of the CD-ROM is that it can hold a great deal of information on a small portable disk. CD-ROM currently allows up to 650MB of data to be stored on a single disk.

SCSI

Configuring the SCSI CD-ROM is generally an easier task than the IDE CD-ROM. With SCSI devices, there are only two configuration concerns: the SCSI ID and the termination point. With SCSI, devices are assigned a number based on jumpers on the devices themselves. This ID number is how the controller knows where to send information to a device. Termination is done at both ends of the SCSI chain; for example, if you have a SCSI card, a SCSI CD-ROM, and a SCSI hard drive, one of the devices would be terminated, as well as the card. Well-designed SCSI adapters, such as those made by Adaptec, automatically set termination on the card if it is the final device on the SCSI chain. If both internal and external SCSI devices are attached to the same SCSI card, the card is in the middle of the SCSI chain and would not be terminated. The jumpers on a SCSI device are generally self-explanatory — 1 is ID1, 2 is ID2, and so on.

For optimum performance, you should place the least system-resource-intensive device, such as the CD-ROM drive, at the end of the SCSI chain. High-performance hard drives should be the closest devices to the SCSI adapter card. The term *SCSI chain* means all the devices attached to a single SCSI adapter, as shown in Figure 11-3.

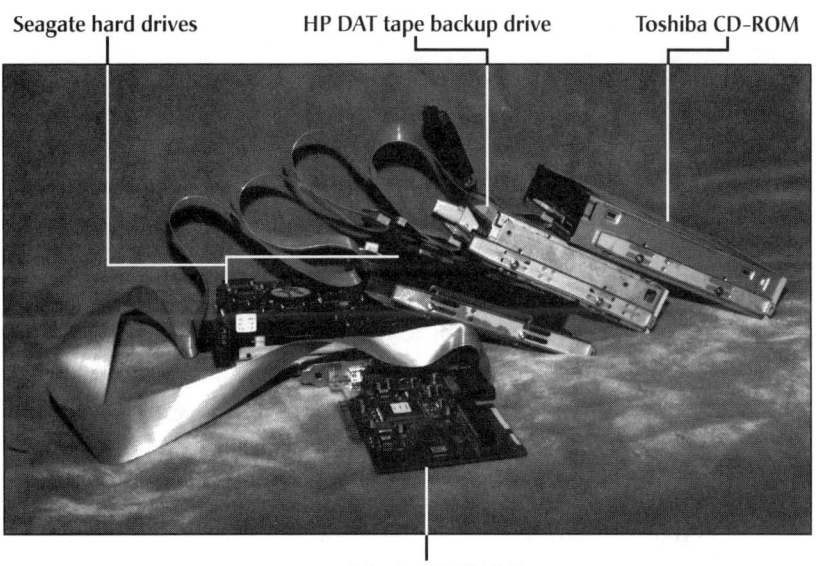

FIGURE 11-3 SCSI chained devices.

With IDE controllers, because they are capable of controlling only two devices, Master or Slave, the chain ends at the Master. This is because the Master is the most resource intensive, and the order in which the system reads is last device first.

IDE/EIDE

When you're configuring the IDE CD-ROM, it is best if you can use the secondary IDE controller exclusively for the CD drive. To configure the CD-ROM to use the secondary IDE, you may need to enable the secondary IDE controller. Normally, you'd do this in the CMOS setup of your system, which you access by restarting your system, then either pressing a specific key (like Del or F1) or booting from a special setup disk. In the CMOS setup, you need to make sure that both IDE controllers are enabled. You may also need to specify whether the drive can be auto-detected or if you need to specify the particular values for accessing your hard drive. Typically, an IDE drive will need values for the following fields:

- Number of cylinders
- Number of heads
- Number of sectors
- Initialization timeout
- IDE translation mode

You can find the values for these fields in your hard drive's documentation. Refer to Chapter 7 for explanations of these concepts.

Once you've set up the CMOS so your computer can recognize the IDE drive, you need to plug the CD-ROM ribbon cable into the secondary IDE controller on the main system board. Normally, the primary and secondary controllers are marked as such on the motherboard itself; however, you may need to check the motherboard's documentation to determine which is which.

The other configuration concerns are the drivers needed for operation of the CD-ROM drive. In DOS-based systems, you need to set up the MSCDEX.EXE. Often, the drivers diskette includes an installation program that makes all of the appropriate settings for you; however, you may need to manually configure the system files. In this case, you should follow the instructions in the drive's documentation. Settings for this driver are in the AUTOEXEC.BAT and the CONFIG.SYS files. Figure 11-4 shows typical IDE CD-ROM settings in the AUTOEXEC.BAT and CONFIG.SYS files. You may also need the drivers provided by the CD-ROM drive manufacturer, depending on the CD-ROM drive type.

```
Sample AUTOEXEC.BAT

PATH=C:\
PATH=C:\DOS;%path%
PATH=C:\WINDOWS;%path%
PATH=C:\CDROM;%path%
SET TEMP=C:\TEMP

C:\CDROM\MSCDEX.EXE /D:MSCD001 /M:08 /L:D

Sample CONFIG.SYS

DEVICE=C:\WINDOWS\HIMEM.SYS
DOS=HIGH, UMB
FILES=50
BUFFERS=50
LASTDRIVE=E
DEVICEHIGH=C:\CDROM\DD250.SYS /D:MSCD001 /C:99 /M:06 /I:5 /P:330
```

FIGURE 11-4 AUTOEXEC.BAT and CONFIG.SYS for IDE CD-ROM

To eliminate the need for a second adapter, some companies build CD-ROM devices with an IDE interface, so that it can share the same adapter with a hard disk drive. However, the average access time of a CD-ROM is considerably slower than a hard disk. Sharing an adapter between a CD-ROM and a hard disk is going to slow data transfer down — way down. For example, if the CD-ROM is spending 100 milliseconds to complete an I/O request, the hard disk drive capable of 10-millisecond access time must wait the full 100 milliseconds. Most of the newer computer systems have gotten around this performance issue by having two IDE/EIDE controllers built in.

Tape Drives

Though it's not an IDE device, tape drives were often connected via floppy disk controller as the last device on the floppy ribbon. You may run across this type of older tape drive in the field, often with a QIC-80 tape format. Their limited capacity and slow performance make them a thing of the past, but if they still work well in their original system and have sufficient capacity for the user's needs, by all means leave them alone. Also, you should be aware that this type of tape backup will not work while the floppy drive is being accessed, nor will the floppy drive work while the tape backup connected to the floppy controller is being accessed. This is because not only do they share the same cable, but they also share the same IRQ. So if a floppy drive is the source of your service call, always look for this floppy-cable connected tape drive as one possible source of problems.

Digital Audio Tape (DAT) is a type of magnetic tape that uses helical scan (a high-speed rotating tape head writes to the tape in diagonal tracks, greatly increasing the amount of data that can be stored) to record data. A DAT cartridge can store from 2- to 24GB of data. It can also support data transfer rates of about 2MB per second, making it a good choice for network backups. The DAT unit is usually installed as a parallel or SCSI device. In either case, the drivers for the device are included with the unit from the manufacturer and must be installed per their instructions.

CONFIGURING PORTS AND OTHER CONNECTIONS

Practically every computer has some type of port allowing data to be passed to and from the computer. Modems, printers, scanners, keyboards, mice, and a great variety of other devices connect through standard ports. This means that you'll need to know how to configure these ports to work properly in your computer. This section describes how to do just that.

LPT or Parallel Ports

Parallel ports are the most common type of port for PC printers. They transfer data 8 bits (1 byte) at a time, using a synchronous transfer method governed by a strobe signal. LPT originally stood for *line printer terminal*. Now LPT is more a computer slang word for any printer or the 25-pin printer port on the back of the computer. Figure 11-5, along with Table 11-1, show the pin configurations, or *pinouts,* for an LPT port.

Parallel Card Interface

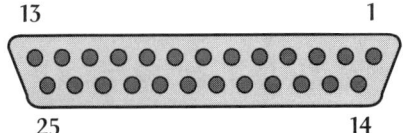

25 PIN D-SUB FEMALE

FIGURE 11-5: 25-pin parallel interface

TABLE 11-1 PARALLEL PIN OUT

PIN	CODE	NAME	DESCRIPTION
1	/STROBE	Strobe	The steady signal that tells the device and the port when data should be transferred.
2	D0	Data Bit 0	The first of the 8 data bits.
3	D1	Data Bit 1	The second of the 8 data bits.
4	D2	Data Bit 2	The third of the 8 data bits.
5	D3	Data Bit 3	The fourth of the 8 data bits.
6	D4	Data Bit 4	The fifth of the 8 data bits.
7	D5	Data Bit 5	The sixth of the 8 data bits.
8	D6	Data Bit 6	The seventh of the 8 data bits.
9	D7	Data Bit 7	The last of the 8 data bits.
10	/ACK	Acknowledge	The printer uses this line to signal the computer that the byte was received correctly.
11	BUSY	Busy	The printer uses this line to tell the computer not to transmit data.
12	PE	Paper End	The printer uses this line to tell the computer that the printer is out of paper.
13	SEL	Select	The computer uses this line to tell the printer that it is selected.
14	/AUTOFD	Autofeed	Paper automatically feeds one line after printing.
15	/ERROR	Error	An error occurred at the printer.
16	/INIT	Initialize	This line instructs the printer to initialize itself.
17	/SELIN	Select In	The printer uses this line to tell the computer that it is online.
18	GND	Signal Ground	The electrical reference ground that all other signals vary from.
19	GND	Signal Ground	The electrical reference ground that all other signals vary from.
20	GND	Signal Ground	The electrical reference ground that all other signals vary from.
21	GND	Signal Ground	The electrical reference ground that all other signals vary from.

continued

		TABLE 11-1 *(continued)*	
PIN	CODE	NAME	DESCRIPTION
22	GND	Signal Ground	The electrical reference ground that all other signals vary from.
23	GND	Signal Ground	The electrical reference ground that all other signals vary from.
24	GND	Signal Ground	The electrical reference ground that all other signals vary from.
25	GND	Signal Ground	The electrical reference ground that all other signals vary from.

When installing a parallel port, you may need to set jumpers or dip switches on the port itself to configure its I/O port address and IRQ. Standard addresses and IRQs for parallel ports are listed in Table 11-2.

	TABLE 11-2 PARALLEL PORT ADDRESSES AND IRQs	
LPT #	*I/O Port*	*IRQ*
LPT1	0x378	7
LPT2	0x278	5

If you have a Plug and Play system, you may have to configure the address and IRQ in the CMOS setup that you access at boot-time. Enter the CMOS setup as described in the "IDE/EIDE Hard Drives" section of this chapter, and locate the section allowing you to configure your parallel port. Because each CMOS setup program is different, I can't provide any clearer direction than that, but it should be fairly obvious, and if necessary you can refer to the system's documentation. Once you've found the parallel port setup section, you should be able to choose between autodetect, disabled, and the values listed in Table 11-2. Normally you'll want to leave these settings on autodetect, but if you need to reserve a particular I/O port or IRQ for some other device, then you can come here and manually specify the settings for your parallel ports.

Async/COM or Serial Ports

Serial ports are sometimes called *asynchronous* or *communication* ports, or COM ports. The standard use for these ports is the connection of external modems. Configuring these ports is done in the same manner as with other ports on the system. These ports may have jumpers or software that configure the IRQ, I/O address, and communication number. For specific information on how to configure a serial port, consult the owners manual for all the hardware it will be connected to, as well as the port itself. Printers can also be hooked up to these ports if the printer is a serial printer, though serial printers are rare these days. It is important that you assign a unique I/O address for each port. If you do not assign a unique address for each of the ports, conflicts will arise. For example, a serial mouse and a modem frequently conflict with one another. If the mouse and modem are configured for the same port, one of the two devices will not work properly. Figure 11-6, along with Table 11-3, shows the pin outs for a 9-pin serial connection. Figure 11-7, along with Table 11-4, shows the pin outs for a 25-pin serial connection.

Serial Card Interface

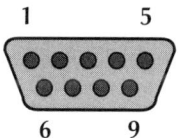

9 PIN D-SUB MALE

FIGURE 11-6 9-pin serial interface

TABLE 11-3 9-PIN SERIAL PIN OUT			
PIN	CODE	NAME	DESCRIPTION
1	CD	Carrier Detect	Tells the computer that the modem is connected to another modem.
2	RXD	Receive Data	This line transmits data from the modem to the computer.
3	TXD	Transmit Data	This line transmits data from the computer to the modem.

continued

TABLE 11-3 *(continued)*

PIN	CODE	NAME	DESCRIPTION
4	DTR	Data Terminal Ready	This line tells the modem that the computer is ready to communicate.
5	GND	System Ground	The electrical reference ground that all other signals vary from.
6	DSR	Data Set Ready	This line tells the computer that the modem is ready to communicate.
7	RTS	Request to Send	The computer uses this line to tell the modem that the computer will be sending data to the modem.
8	CTS	Clear to Send	The modem uses this line to tell the computer that the modem will be sending data to the computer.
9	RI	Ring Indicator	The modem uses this line to tell the computer that the phone is ringing.

Serial Card Interface

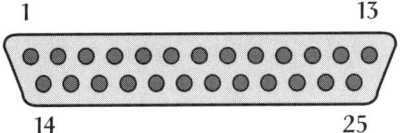

25 PIN D-SUB MALE

FIGURE 11-7   25-pin serial connection

TABLE 11-4 25-PIN SERIAL PIN OUT

PIN	CODE	NAME	DESCRIPTION
1	SHIELD	Shield Ground	This electrical ground acts as a shield against radio wave or electrical interference.
2	TXD	Transmit Data	This line transmits data from the computer to the modem.
3	RXD	Receive Data	This line transmits data from the modem to the computer.

Pin	Code	Name	Description
4	RTS	Request to Send	The computer uses this line to tell the modem that the computer will be sending data to the modem.
5	CTS	Clear to Send	The modem uses this line to tell the computer that the modem will be sending data to the computer.
6	DSR	Data Set Ready	This line tells the computer that the modem is ready to communicate.
7	GND	System Ground	The electrical reference ground that all other signals vary from.
8	CD	Carrier Detect	Tells the computer that the modem is connected to another modem.
9	n/c		Not connected.
10	n/c		Not connected.
11	n/c		Not connected.
12	n/c		Not connected.
13	n/c		Not connected.
14	n/c		Not connected.
15	n/c		Not connected.
16	n/c		Not connected.
17	n/c		Not connected.
18	n/c		Not connected.
19	n/c		Not connected.
20	DTR	Data Terminal Ready	This line tells the modem that the computer is ready to communicate.
21	n/c		Not connected.
22	RI	Ring Indicator	The modem uses this line to tell the computer that the phone is ringing.
23	n/c		Not connected.
24	n/c		Not connected.
25	n/c		Not connected.

You configure serial ports in much the same way that you configured parallel ports, either with jumpers or dip switches on the port itself or through the CMOS setup for Plug and Play ports. Either way, you should be familiar with the port settings and IRQs listed in Table 11-5 when setting up serial ports.

TABLE 11-5 SERIAL PORT ADDRESSES AND IRQs

COM PORT	I/O ADDRESS	IRQ
COM1	0x3F8	4
COM2	0x2F8	3
COM3	0x3E8	4
COM4	x2E8	3

One thing you may notice about the information in Table 11-5 is that COM1 and COM3 share IRQ 4, and COM2 and COM4 share IRQ 3. In practice, you'll find that this does *not* work. When COM3 signals the CPU with IRQ 4, the CPU has no way of knowing whether COM1 or COM3 sent that signal. The hardware of a standard PC is not set up to permit the CPU to check all of the devices registered as using IRQ 4, so it checks only one of them. If that happens to be COM1, then COM3 gets ignored, even though it was the one that sent the signal. Data transfers under these conditions are nearly impossible.

If you truly need to have devices connected to three serial ports on a single computer, then you should consider using a non-standard IRQ for COM3 or COM4. In many cases, I've found that you can use IRQ 5 without causing problems. If you remember from the parallel ports section, IRQ 5 is associated with LPT2, and we've rarely encountered a system with a printer on LPT2 *and* three devices connected to serial ports.

PS/2 Ports

PS/2 ports are a popular alternative for connecting a mouse and keyboard to a computer system. Plugging your mouse into a PS/2 port reduces the chance of IRQ conflicts by using IRQ 12, a normally unused IRQ. This way you can plug your modem into COM1 and leave COM3 empty so that the two don't need to share an IRQ.

PS/2 ports originated on the IBM PS/2 series of computers that were popular in the late 1980s. They are round 6-pin ports, and normally you'll find a matched pair in the back of a computer that has them — one for the mouse and one for the keyboard. The IRQs and port addresses of PS/2 ports are not configurable, except possibly for the ability to disable the port altogether in the CMOS setup. Figure 11-8, along with Table 11-6, shows the pin outs of a PS/2 port.

PS/2 Mouse Interface

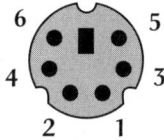

6 PIN MINI-DIN FEMALE
FIGURE 11-8   PS/2 pin out

	TABLE 11-6 PS/2 PIN OUTS		
PIN	**CODE**	**NAME**	**DESCRIPTION**
1	DATA	Key Data	The data is sent between the device and the computer on this line.
2	n/c		Not connected.
3	GND	Gnd	The electrical reference ground that all other signals vary from.
4	VCC	Power, +5 VDC	Electrical power from the computer to the device.
5	CLK	Clock	The timing by which synchronous data is transferred.
6	n/c		Not connected.

Key Point Summary

In this chapter, you learned about the basics of configuration.

- We explained how I/O ports, IRQs, and DMA channels work, and showed you how to interview your customer to find out what type of configuration is necessary.

- We covered basic monitor adjustments and the broader display settings, as well as how to install and configure display adapters.

- You learned how to install and configure hard drives, CD-ROM drives, tape drives, SCSI devices, and ports.

- You learned that there is more to configuration than just dealing with one device — you must take into consideration the total system in which the device is being installed.

- We've also provided pin out references for your use once you become a certified technician.

Applying What You've Learned

This chapter has covered a lot of important material that will help you prepare for the A+ exam and be an excellent computer technician. Take a few minutes and work through the multiple choice questions, then review your notes, and see how you did.

The Hands-on lab will also help you build your comfort level with the hardware as well as reinforce the readings from this chapter.

Instant Assessment

Multiple choice

Choose the best answer(s). There may be more than one correct answer for each question.

1. Monochrome monitors are sometimes referred to as:

A. TTL

B. CGA

C. VGA

D. White

2. Most PCs built after 1995 support a minimum video standard of

_____.

A. SVGA

B. MCGA

C. CGA

D. VGA

3. When configuring Windows 3.*x* displays, the display type can be changed using:

A. The Control Panel

B. The system icon in the Program Manager

C. The DOS driver loaded in the CONFIG.SYS file

D. The Windows Setup

4. When configuring Macintosh displays, the display type can be changed using:

A. The Control Panel

B. The system icon in the Program Manager

C. The DOS driver loaded in the CONFIG.SYS file

D. The OS Setup

5. For optimum performance using SCSI devices, the least resource-intensive device should be located at:

A. The beginning of the chain

B. The middle of the chain

C. LUN #1

D. The end of the chain

6. If a customer complains about their mouse not working, a relevant question to ask would be:

A. Have you changed keyboards

B. Is the CD-ROM still working

C. Have you installed a modem recently

D. Are you using a network

7. For an IDE CD-ROM to function properly in DOS, the MSCDEX.EXE must be loaded in the CONFIG.SYS file.

A. True

B. False

8. A printer on a PC will normally be attached to which of the following ports?

A. LPT

B. COM

C. PS/2

D. ESD

9. If a mouse on a PS/2 port has intermittent failures and you replace it with another mouse and it still doesn't work, the least likely cause of the problem is:

A. The PS/2 connector

B. An internal IRQ conflict

C. The motherboard

D. A second bad mouse

10. The _____ is most susceptible to electromagnetic interference.

A. Monitor

B. Hard drive

C. CD-ROM drive

D. Floppy drive

Hands-on Lab Exercises

For these lab exercises, you will need access to a complete computer system, a set of screwdrivers, and a second hard drive. The purpose of these exercises is to familiarize you with changing configuration settings. This particular lab will walk you through setting up a slaved hard drive on a computer system.

Lab 11-11 *Changing configuration settings*

Getting Organized

tip **When installing an expansion board, consulting the documentation for the board or PC is the best way to determine the required settings.**

Make sure you have a clear work area and can access the computer from all angles. Also, make sure that the computer is not plugged in to eliminate the chance that you'll be electrocuted in the course of this procedure. In this lab, we will be adding a slaved hard drive to a system.

1. Take a preformatted hard drive and change the jumper settings so that it is configured as a Slave, by moving the appropriate jumpers to the location described in the owner's manual for a slave drive.

2. Open the computer and locate an empty bay next to the existing hard drive.

3. Insert the new drive in the empty bay.

4. Insert the signal cable in the new slave drive, making sure that Pin 1 is closest to the red stripe on the cable.

5. Plug in the power connector for the new drive and secure the drive to the case.

6. Replace the case cover and turn on the computer.

7. When the system starts up, enter the CMOS setup by following the onscreen instructions and set the values for the new drive in the CMOS based on the Auto Configure option, or the options described in the owner's manual.

You should now have a computer with two hard drives, one called C: and one called D:. This is useful for separating out files. For example, you could have:

o A server with the operating system (OS) on one drive and application files on another.

o The OS on one drive and shared files on another.

o Development software on one drive and a developed product on another.

Computer Assembly

About Chapter 12

I n this chapter, we will tackle the steps necessary to build a basic computer. In previous chapters, we discussed how to select a computer and defined the specific tasks we wanted our system to perform. Now we will tell you how to choose the components to add to the system, introduce some helpful tools you can use, and then discuss the installation of hardware devices such as floppy drives.

Building a system is a methodical process, and not as difficult as you might think. There are quite a few ways to make expensive mistakes, though, so always make sure to work slowly and methodically, double-checking connections before hitting the power switch. You can use many assembly techniques when you're upgrading specific components on an existing system as well. We'll add a bit of information on why we made our hardware decisions, because purchasing the most cost-effective hardware will help you get the best performance for your needs at the lowest cost. Follow the steps as outlined in this chapter. This step-by-step framework will save you time, and will ultimately help you verify that you've completed each phase of installation successfully.

COMPUTER COMPONENTS

Before you install the various components of your computer system, check that you already have all the parts and components you'll need. In addition to the major components, you'll want to have plenty of screws, plastic risers, and metal risers. You should also make sure your power supply has enough plugs for all your components, and buy splitters (Y-cables that split a single power connector into two) if needed. Since you'll be making repairs and possibly building systems on a fairly regular basis, I recommend that you get several plastic parts boxes for all the odds and ends you'll find you need. We have four plastic divided boxes, bought at a hardware store, so that all the different screws, grommets, clips, and risers are sorted and easy to find.

In this chapter, we will build a basic computer system and verify its functions. You'll need the following parts to build your basic computer system:

- **Computer case with power supply:** We've found that computer cases get in the way on our desks, so we've developed a preference for mid-sized tower cases. They allow plenty of room for adding extra components, they have room for a generous power supply, and they have enough room inside that overheating is not much of an issue. Select a well-made case with an adequate power supply—275 to 300 watts is a good size given the number of goodies we'll be stuffing in this box. We selected the PC Power and Cooling mid-tower case, along with their Silencer 275-watt ATX power supply. The Silencer power supply is ideal for office settings, as it's substantially quieter than comparably sized power supplies. Cases come in two motherboard form factors—AT style, and ATX. Older systems used the AT form factor, but with the advent of the Pentium II, most vendors have switched to the ATX case design because its design leaves room for the substantial footprint of the Pentium II chip, while still permitting full use of the peripheral slots.

- **Motherboard (main system board):** You must match the motherboard form factor to your case, and select a motherboard based on what CPU you plan to use. Given that our case is an ATX and we're choosing an Intel Pentium II CPU, we chose an Intel Seattle motherboard with the 440BX chipset. It supports the full range of available Pentium II speeds and supports both 66MHz and 100MHz bus speed, depending on the CPU chosen (350-, 400-, and 450MHz Pentium II CPUs support the 100MHz bus speed if you use PC100-compliant RAM). Be sure to compare the number of PCI, AT, and AGP slots with what you anticipate needing. Other boards offer a few more peripheral slots, which may appeal to gamers or those involved in video or audio editing.

- **Main system memory (RAM):** RAM has gotten so cheap lately that it's astonishing. The Intel board supports three SDRAM slots, and we bought 64MB of PC100-compliant SDRAM. PC100-compliant RAM is required to capitalize on the 100MHz bus speed of the motherboard. We recall when 64MB of RAM cost $1,200 a little more than three years ago. This time it cost $130!

- **Main system processor (CPU) with fan:** The only Intel processors still on the market are all the flavors of Pentium II. We recommend you buy one version down from the top-of-the-line speed. Because 450MHz Pentium IIs are now available, we opted for the 400MHz, saving a cool $200 for a small performance difference. The 400MHz CPU supports PC100 RAM. You absolutely *must* use a CPU cooling fan. Not using one voids your CPU warranty, in fact. PC Power makes a great one, as does Intel. Several other vendors are out there, but look for a ball-bearing fan for longer life.

- **Video card:** Video cards are available from a wide variety of firms, some new and some old. Because faulty video drivers are among the biggest sources of system problems, learn which video card providers you trust and stick with them. Going with the latest flavor-of-the-month card can cost you a lot of time. The Intel board has an *Accelerated Graphics Port* (AGP) slot, so we chose the ATI All-in-Wonder Pro video card.

- **Floppy drive:** Floppy drives are fairly generic, and disposable when they act up. We use a 3.5-inch floppy drive in each new system.

- **Floppy drive ribbon cable:** One usually comes with the floppy drive, but make sure you get it.

- **Plastic risers:** These hold the motherboard off the bottom of the case. The board is supported with several metal riser nuts for grounding purposes, and plastic risers elsewhere to keep the board from flexing as peripheral cards are installed.

- **Riser nuts:** These metal nuts are threaded male on one side, female on the other. They are screwed into the case in the appropriate spots, then the motherboard is screwed onto them.

- **Screws:** You'll need plenty of 'em! You'll need screws to fasten the motherboard to the riser nuts, screws to hold peripheral cards into the back of the case, and screws to fasten devices into the drive bays.

- **Bootable floppy disk:** Created from a recent version of DOS, like 6.22. Be sure to include the FDISK and FORMAT programs.

- **Hard drive:** Many choices abound here. If you choose an EIDE drive, the hardware you need to run the drive is built right into the motherboard. If you choose SCSI, you'll need a separate SCSI drive controller card.

- **Hard drive ribbon cable:** You'll need one appropriate for your drive type, either SCSI or EIDE.

- **Keyboard:** Don't skimp here if you can help it. The difference between a lousy keyboard and a good one is only a few dollars, and it's a wise investment.

- **Monitor:** 17-inch and 19-inch monitors are coming down drastically in price. The added viewing area offered by the bigger monitor is a huge productivity improvement, allowing more applications to be open and viewable at the same time.

- **Power cords:** You'll need power cords for the monitor and the case.

- **System speaker:** Usually included with the case.

- **Phillips screwdriver:** Insulated and non-magnetic.

- **Standard screwdriver:** Insulated and non-magnetic.

- **Long-nose pliers:** Insulated and non-magnetic.

Owner/user's manuals: You need one for every part you intend to put into the system. A good idea is to hold every manual in a gallon freezer Ziploc bag.

 tip

Before you even touch any of the parts outside their static protection bags, use an *electrostatic discharge* (ESD) wrist strap that is clipped to something grounded. A very small static discharge—one you wouldn't even feel—could be enough to cost you hundreds or even thousands of dollars in destroyed electronic components. We'll discuss wrist straps again later in this chapter.

Visually inspect each part and computer component to make sure it's not physically damaged. Each different motherboard has different setup requirements, such as jumpers for the bus speed or for the CPU voltage. One of the nice benefits of the Intel board we selected is that it has jumperless setup — it detects the CPU speed, and away you go. With your motherboard owner's manual in hand, check the main board to be sure any jumpers are set properly for the type of RAM you are using, as well as CPU voltage and bus speed settings. Make sure the main board and video card have no obvious cracks, and check for burn marks near power connections and on the back of the main board (a sign of a possibly defective returned board). Check the keyboard, mouse, and *universal serial bus* (USB) connectors on the main board to be sure they are securely attached to the motherboard.

Check the case against the main board. Be sure it will line up and fit properly. Examine the CPU for bent or missing pins, cracks in the silicon casing, or glassy-looking edges. Examine the RAM chips individually to make sure they are the same type and speed, and check the individual chips at the solder joints to be sure they have been securely connected to their board at each pin. Check the pins on the monitor cable and on the keyboard cable to be sure they are not bent or broken.

Check the floppy drive by turning it upside down — it should not make clacking sounds. Check the hard drive the same way. Check the hard drive for jumpers, and that the jumpers are set properly. I also recommend that you smell the pieces. Burnt computer components give off a distinct odor, and in time you will recognize it when you deal with overheated and improperly installed components. We will deal with each of these issues later in this chapter.

MECHANICAL AND ELECTRICAL CONNECTIONS

In this section, we will look at the process of installation in detail. Let's begin with the case and power supply. The case should be of adequate size to accommodate the main board (motherboard) and the power supply should be large enough to power all the devices you will be installing — 250 or 300 watts should be adequate for most needs. The power supply has several bundles of electrical wires leading off it, called *leads*. Leads have connectors specifically keyed for the types of devices for which they are intended to be used.

The motherboard has holes in it, and these holes should line up with the system case. Some of these motherboard holes have a metallic ring around them on both the front and back of the board. These holes with the metallic strip are for securing the motherboard to the case using riser nuts and screws. Figure 12-1 shows a motherboard with risers installed. Take care when tightening the screws. You only need to torque the screws enough so that they do not back out—excessive tightening will destroy the motherboard.

FIGURE 12-1 Motherboard with risers installed

Line up the motherboard so that the keyboard, mouse, and USB connectors are in line with the back of the case, as shown in Figure 12-2. Not all motherboards work with all cases, although most case and motherboard manufacturers stick to standard specifications. Keep in mind the AT versus ATX form factor mentioned earlier in the chapter, and don't be afraid to ask questions when you're buying parts. Do not attempt to force-fit a motherboard. If it doesn't fit the case, get a new case, as it's not worth the frustration and possible destruction of the motherboard and case.

FIGURE 12-2 Aligned motherboard

With the motherboard lying in the case and aligned with the keyboard connector, look through the holes in the motherboard. Some will have corresponding holes in the case frame. Some will have threaded insertion points. Locate and identify the corresponding threaded case holes with the metallic lined holes in the motherboard, then remove the board and insert the riser nuts in the threaded holes at the back of the case. You'll need to fiddle with these to be sure the holes in the case you choose are the correct ones to line up with holes in the motherboard. It's easy to make a mistake, but just as easy to correct it. Think of it like a puzzle.

Now you are ready to install the CPU and RAM, as shown in Figure 12-3. You'll want to install the CPU and RAM now because of space limitations inside the case. Sometimes you might have to slide and twist the motherboard to get it to fit into the base of the case.

You should be very careful when installing the CPU and RAM so you don't damage the chips. You might be tempted to install these components later, but we've found that installing them first gives you more room to work in than installing them later. As you gain experience working with different vendors' cases and motherboards, you will be able to tell which areas of the case require riser nuts. It's fairly simple — if there is a hole in the motherboard, try and fill it with a plastic standoff, unless the hole is ringed with metal. These holes get riser nuts. Your goal is to ensure that no area on the back side of the motherboard is unsupported, so that when you install RAM, CPU, or peripheral cards, you don't buckle the board. Even small amounts of flexing can harm the motherboard by creating hairline cracks in its conductive layers, so get it fixed safely in place in the case before installing the CPU and memory. Your next step will be to install the CPU and RAM on the motherboard.

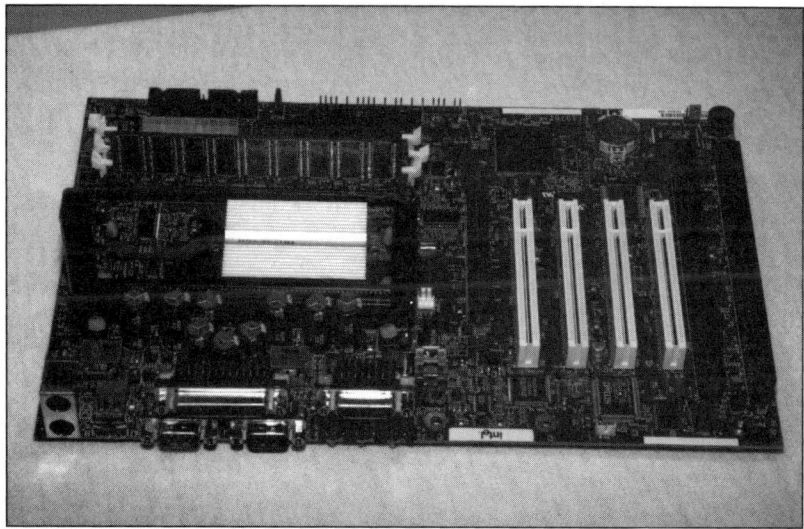

FIGURE 12-3 Motherboard with CPU and RAM

Pull out the user's guide or owner's manual for the motherboard. *Read it!* Well, at least enough to find the jumpers and their location on the motherboard (shown in Figure 12-4). You must configure the motherboard jumpers for the type of CPU and the voltage of the CPU and RAM at a minimum, unless your motherboard (like the Intel 440BX motherboard mentioned previously) automatically configures these settings. Some motherboards provide for bus speed settings and manual priority setting for the expansion slots. You must consult the owner/user's guide.

Before handling *any* electronic components, including the CPU and RAM, you should discharge your body's static electricity. You can do this by grabbing onto any grounded object, like the metal part of a plugged-in PC. The goal is to ensure any static electricity present has a shorter path to the ground — through you and your wrist strap — than through your delicate and as of yet unprotected electronics. Next, affix a wrist strap to yourself so that you remain grounded while handling the static-sensitive components.

You should be aware that many shops do not think the risk of static damage is sufficient to use wrist straps, but we recommend that you always wear one. Separate but equally as important as the static issue, to possibly save your life while working with electricity, we recommend that you remove any jewelry, including necklaces. Remove any items from your shirt pocket.

Now that the motherboard is set up for the CPU and RAM, you need to locate Pin 1 on the RAM and on the motherboard where the RAM will be inserted, as shown in Figure 12-5. If Pin 1 is difficult to find, lay the RAM board alongside the RAM slot and closely examine the shape of the board and the slot. RAM is manufactured so that it can only be inserted one way.

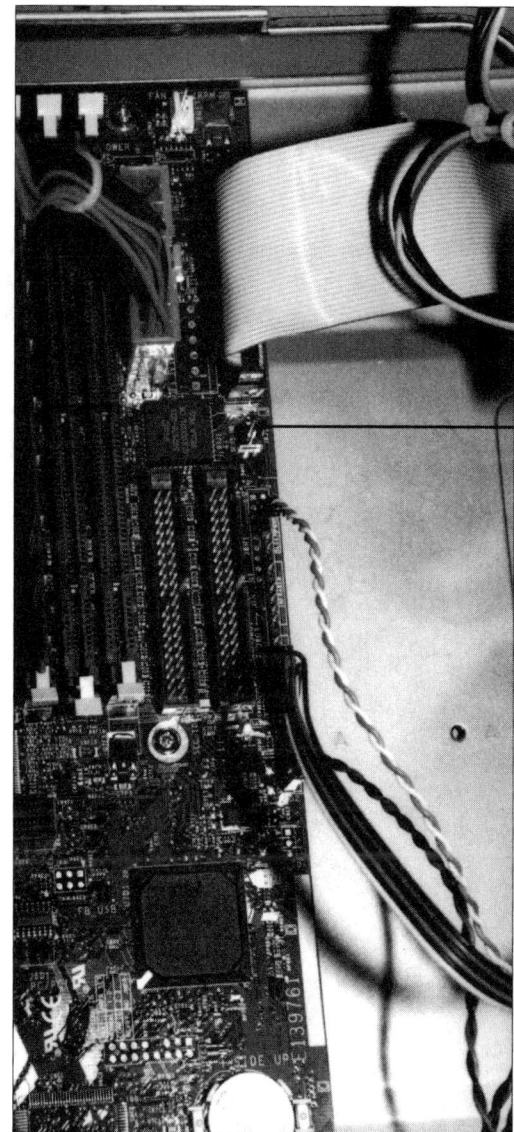

Motherboard jumpers

FIGURE 12-4   Motherboard jumpers

PIN 1

FIGURE 12-5 Pin 1 location

Inserting the Pentium II is easy. Look for the notch on the CPU risers, and line the Pentium II up with it. Ease the CPU into place until the corners latch. For systems with Pentium CPUs, finding Pin 1 on the CPU is an easy process — it will have an obvious dot or corner slot visible from the top of the CPU chip, as shown in Figure 12-6. Examine the insertion socket for the CPU and make sure you are placing it in the right way. If you plug a CPU in wrong and power on the system, it will be destroyed.

FIGURE 12-6   ZIF socket

Next, slide the motherboard into place on the case frame and attach it using screws in the proper holes, as shown in Figure 12-7.

Now you are ready to plug in the leads. Find the power connectors on the motherboard and their corresponding leads. On a Pentium II AGP system, the power connector is a single attachment that can only be attached one way (see Figure 12-8). On other motherboards, the black wires of the P8 and P9 connector are usually together toward the inside. If you power on the system with these connected backward, you will likely destroy the power supply, as well as the motherboard.

FIGURE 12-7 Motherboard attached to the case

FIGURE 12-8 Power connector attached

Never force a connection — steady gentle pressure will do for any component you install.

Now it is time to install the video adapter card, as covered in Chapter 10. Then plug the monitor's connector into the video card.

Plug the keyboard into the motherboard connector, as shown in Figure 12-9.

FIGURE 12-9 Keyboard being plugged in

If you have external speakers, plug them into the motherboard's sound connector, as shown in Figure 12-10.

FIGURE 12-10   Speaker system being plugged in

Plug power into the power supply, as shown in Figure 12-11.

FIGURE 12-11 Power being plugged in

VISUAL CHECKLIST

You can visually check your work by verifying that you've completed the installation items listed here:

- Motherboard is secured to case

- Power supply, with switch off, is set to 110, not 220 volts

- CPU with Pin 1 to Pin 1 or properly slid into risers

- RAM with Pin 1 to Pin 1

- Video card is in proper slot (see Chapter 10)

- Monitor is plugged in

- Keyboard is plugged in

- P8 & P9 have been connected with the black wires together

- System speaker is plugged in

- Power cord is plugged into power supply and monitor

Let's give it a test. Turn the switch on. The monitor should receive a signal from the video card and display information about the system; the system speaker should give one short beep. If it doesn't, check each connector and jumper and verify their settings. If it's still giving you grief, see the Troubleshooting Checklist. That's it — you've put together a basic computer and tested it. Because a basic computer won't do much, let's continue with a floppy and a hard drive.

Next install the floppy drive. Find an open bay, and use the proper-size screws to secure the device to the case frame. Plug in the ribbon cable so that the red stripe is closest to Pin 1 on the device and on the motherboard. Find a lead with the proper type of keyed connector and plug it into the device.

When the floppy drive is properly installed and configured, it will clear the security checks on startup, and you will see the drive indicator light up before your system begins loading the operating system.

 tip **Sometimes Pin 1 is not clearly defined on a device. When this occurs, Pin 1 is usually farthest from the power connection.**

Now to the hard drive. Prior to installing the hard drive, inspect the drive for a label giving the head, cylinder, and track settings, if it's an EIDE drive. SCSI drives are automatically recognized by the SCSI adapter card's BIOS. You'll need this information, and you won't want to pull the drive back out just to see what is written on it.

Now find an open bay and install the hard drive using the proper type of screws. Be careful when securing the hard drive to the case — make sure you are not using screws that are too long. If you use screws that are too long, you will damage the hard drive. When tightening screws, use only enough strength to secure the device. Plug the hard drive ribbon cable into the hard drive, with the red stripe closest to Pin 1, and attach the other end of the ribbon cable to the IDE/EIDE connection on the motherboard or controller as appropriate, again with the red stripe closest to Pin 1. Find a lead with a connector keyed for the hard drive power receptacle and plug it in. That's it. If you completed the installation properly, your hard drive is ready to use. To check your hard drive's installation configuration, you can reboot the computer, press F1, and then check the hard drive settings in CMOS.

One more test: Turn the power on again and listen to the hard drive. You should hear it spin up and there may be an indicator light on the drive that comes on when it first gets power or when it is accessed.

In the next section, we'll discuss the tools and procedures used for running the system setup.

TOOLS AND PROCEDURES FOR SETUP

In this section, we will discuss the basic *complementary metal-oxide semiconductor* (CMOS) settings required to make our basic computer run. First, we need to set up the CMOS, which is the non-volatile memory that stores the system's configuration standards. CMOS is the semiconductor technology used in the transistors that are manufactured in most of today's computer microchips. The CMOS will automatically count the amount of RAM we have, provided that the system is configured for the correct kind of RAM.

Opening the CMOS is generally done on startup. When the system first starts, press Del or F1 to access the CMOS setup screen. Other motherboards may have a different keystroke combination to access CMOS setup. It will either appear onscreen at bootup, or it can be found in your owner's manual.

Now access the Standard CMOS Setup. To change CMOS date and time settings, follow these steps:

1. When booting your computer, press either the Del key or F1 to access the CMOS setup screen.

2. Tab through the options until you see Date and Time highlighted.

3. Press Enter to change the date or time, and then type the information you wish to change.

4. Be sure to save your new settings.

To change CMOS hard drive settings, follow these steps:

1. Tab through the CMOS setting options until you see hard drive type.

2. Select Auto to let the system automatically detect the size and type of your hard drive.

3. Be sure to save your new settings.

 If Auto does not work properly with your hard drive, you will have to set the cylinders, heads, pre comp, landing zone, and sectors. From this, the system will automatically determine the size of the hard drive. To accomplish this, you'll need to refer to your owner's manual to view the specifications. However, for the hard drive, floppy drives, and video types, it's best to set all the CMOS options to Auto to let the system automatically detect each of these devices.

Next, move on to the BIOS setup features:

1. For Intel CPUs where the main board has caching, enable both the internal and external CPU cache.

2. Set the Boot Sequence for the type of adapter you want the system to recognize first, i.e., SCSI or IDE.

3. Set the Boot Search Sequence, i.e., A: C: CD-ROM. This will tell the system the order in which to search for boot information. If you always want to boot from the hard drive, then set the order to C: X: X:, where X is any device other than the hard drive.

4. Set the boot floppy to Enable, which will boot the system from the floppy drive. Booting from the floppy drive is essential for installing your disk operating system. You may want to disable this option so no one can tamper with it. Keep in mind that even if you specify Drive A: in the search order for boot sequence, it will not boot from Drive A: unless this option is enabled.

5. Set the Security option. We recommend setting this option to System, which lets the operating system control the logon security. To ensure that your system settings cannot be changed by the end user, set this option to Login. Login forces the user to log on to the operating system and to specify a password before being able to change any system settings.

6. Where possible, always use the Auto option when configuring a device in CMOS. Most hardware can be automatically detected and configured by CMOS.

7. Select the chipset features next, to configure the main board controllers and ports. This screen is self-explanatory; however, if you want to use the onboard IDE controller, then you must enable it.

Depending on the manufacturer of the CMOS, you may have several selection options. The options above help explain most of the options you'll encounter. For configuring hardware devices such as Plug and Play, PCI configuration, power management, or hard drive detection, consult the owner's manual.

TOOLS FOR CONFIGURATION AND TROUBLESHOOTING

Now we are ready to give the hard disk an operating system. For this, we will need a bootable floppy disk with the following files at a minimum:

- msdos.sys
- io.sys
- FDISK.exe
- command.com
- format.com

You can make a bootable floppy disk from any MS-DOS computer, or from another Windows 95 machine. In DOS from the c: prompt, type **format A: /s**. In Windows 95 Explorer, right-click on the floppy drive and select format. Choose "system files only." This will copy command.com, msdos.sys, and io.sys, and you can find format.com and fdisk.exe in the Windows/command folder. This disk will allow you to start your new system, which doesn't have an operating system yet. Once you start the system with this disk, you can configure your new hard drive and install the operating system, and your system will be ready for use.

Now you are ready to format the hard drive and make it bootable. At the DOS prompt, type **format C: /s**, which specifies to format the C drive and to add the system files. Once this operation is complete, you are ready to boot the hard drive. Remove the floppy disk from the disk drive, power off the system, then power it back on. Your system will now boot from the hard drive.

Troubleshooting Checklist

Now let's talk about things that could go wrong. If your system won't boot from the hard drive, then most likely something has been set incorrectly in the CMOS settings. Just because that is the most likely solution doesn't mean that's where we start our troubleshooting process. In troubleshooting, we start by looking for the most obvious answer, and then work our way toward the likely problem. We do this because if we jump straight to the most likely problem and we are wrong, it will take more time to repair than if we looked at our options step-by-step and tried to eliminate possible causes of the error. Always start by asking yourself these questions:

1. Is the computer plugged into a known good outlet? You can check the outlet with a lamp to make sure it has power.

2. Is it plugged in correctly? If the cable has two ways of attaching to the component, have you tried the other way? Note that this applies to disk drives — floppy and hard drives — and not power connectors.

3. Can you verify that the cable or power cord is functional? If you've checked for power and for cable connections, check with another cable or power cord to verify that the one you started with is good. Spare cables for hard drives and floppy drives as well as spare power cords should be part of your technician's toolbag.

4. Is the component getting power? Check the power connector from the power supply to the component. Is it fully seated? If it is, try another connector from the power supply.

5. Is the component getting signal? Once you've verified power is getting to the component, check to see if the computer is talking to it. For example, is the monitor receiving any video signal? Check for video operation with a known good monitor.

6. Is the component configured correctly? EIDE hard drives must be set to the proper master/slave setting. Drive parameters have to be entered correctly into the CMOS setup. SCSI peripherals must have a SCSI ID set, and termination settings set correctly.

First, check to be sure the computer is plugged in. You'd be surprised how many times the problem is as simple as "It's not plugged in." Next, check the ribbon cable to be sure Pin 1 is closest to the red stripe on the cable. Check that the power lead is plugged securely into the hard drive. Power on the system, look at the power supply to be sure the fan is turning, and listen to the hard drive to be sure it is spinning. Look at the power connectors to the motherboard to be sure they are still secure. Go to the monitor and see that you have signal from the video card. If the computer still doesn't boot, restart the computer and enter the CMOS. This process should have only taken a minute or two.

It's important to run down this checklist *before* entering CMOS setup. It could take a long time to reset the CMOS entries if you changed them before realizing you didn't need to change the settings in the first place. Also, there is a chance that multiple problems could lead you to false conclusions about the systems components. If the ribbon cable is on backwards, no amount of CMOS adjustment would fix it. Now, look at the hard drive settings in the standard CMOS setup and write them down. Escape from there and do an autodetect of the hard drive, checking to be sure the entries match. If they don't, enter the entries from the autodetect in the hard drive configuration table, save the settings, and rerun Fdisk, then reformat the hard drive.

Next, try to boot the hard drive again. If you're still running into problems at this point, the most likely cause is that the hard drive's real parameters are different from what the autodetect finds. Refer to the owner's manual on the hard drive and check to see what settings the manufacturer suggests. Enter those settings in the hard drive configuration table and then perform Fdisk again to reformat the drive. If by this point you are still having problems, you should consider the possibility the hard drive is defective. Attempt the process with a different drive if possible before giving up on the first drive.

Visual Checklist

Before packing and shipping the computer, you'll want to visually check your installation to make sure everything works properly.

When all the components have been properly installed, the computer will sound one short beep on startup, indicating that the hardware has been installed correctly. Other sounds are associated with failures for each of the components. Messages are displayed on the monitor as well when an error occurs. One of my favorite error messages is "System Error: Keyboard not present, Press F1 to continue." Exactly *how* I'm supposed to press F1 on a missing keyboard isn't divulged.

Once the system beeps and all hardware is accounted for, you need to run the system setup, also referred to as setting up the CMOS. In the CMOS, you need to set up the system time and hard drive type and size. You can also configure bus priorities, RAM type and function, floppy drive type, boot order, and a number of other parameters. The exact configuration and options in CMOS setup depends on the motherboard manufacturer and BIOS vendor. BIOS, or *Basic Input and Output Settings*, is the name given for the interface you see when configuring your CMOS. For our purposes, all that you need to set is the floppy drive and hard drive, then verify the system is reading the amount of memory correctly. From this, you can move on to the last parameter of testing.

The last parameter is function. Will the system boot and perform commands? Once you have installed all of the components, the system speaker has returned one short beep, and you have set up the CMOS, you should be able to boot from floppy. To do this, you will need a bootable floppy disk. If the system boots, you are ready to install the other components and software as needed. Once you get the system booting from the hard drive, you are ready to install the final operating system software — Windows, DOS, or NT. And once you've installed the operating system, you are ready to install the applications software for the system.

If all of this has gone a little fast for you, the following sections will break it down in detail.

Preparing Your Computer for Shipment

Now we've built a system, configured it, troubleshot the problems, and it's working according to the specifications the customer requested. If it's for local use, plug it in and fire it up. If you're building a system for delivery elsewhere, however, you've got a few more chores. Most new hard drives automatically park the drive heads away from the hard drive surface in a safe spot as soon as they're powered down. On older drives, you may need to run a drive head parking utility provided by the manufacturer. Make sure that all the internal devices are firmly secured, using all the screws and clamps provided by the manufacturer. Place the case cover on the system and securely fasten it together. Once the cover is in place, restart and test the system again. Be careful — cables often get pulled loose when you're putting covers on. Place the computer and monitor in a padded container, using Styrofoam, newspaper, or whatever you have at your disposal.

Using a checklist, make sure you package the entire system. There is nothing more frustrating to a customer than getting their computer home or to the office and not having all the pieces. Power cords are a big culprit here. It's very easy to forget to pack a power cord or monitor cable, and then the computer won't run. The checklist should include mouse, keyboard, system unit, power cords, monitor cords, and all manuals that came with the components, as well as anything else purchased with the system.

KEY POINT SUMMARY

In this chapter, we discussed the basic procedures, components, and tools required to assemble a computer system.

- Several safety issues are involved in this process, including possible system damage from *electrostatic electricity* (ESD) and the risk of electrical shock when working with electronics.

- System cases come in both AT and ATX form factors. Configuration of motherboards can, but does not always, require setting jumpers for CPU speed and voltage. Hard drive parameters, disk boot order, system time, bus settings, and RAM type and function are among the settings you may see in CMOS setup screens.

- Troubleshooting requires that you verify power and signal to system components, and that you verify your findings with known good components before making a final decision. Hard drive settings should be taken from the drive before installation and written down somewhere convenient, preferably inside the system board manual for later reference.

- Packing a system for shipping requires that you verify its operation before packing, and that you safely protect the system from damage from loosely packed articles such as power and connector cords. A checklist is necessary to ensure you don't forget to ship any crucial parts.

- From what this chapter has taught you, you should be able to assemble a basic computer system and troubleshoot the most common problems associated with new systems. We have discussed settings for the system, testing parameters, and mechanical and electrical connections. We have also discussed packing and shipping a computer system and the related safety issues.

APPLYING WHAT YOU'VE LEARNED

This chapter has covered a lot of important material that will help you prepare for the A+ exam and be a competent technician. Take a few minutes and work through the Instant Assessment questions, review your notes, and see how you did.

The Hands-on lab will also help build your comfort level with the hardware, as well as reinforce the readings from this chapter.

Instant Assessment

Multiple choice

Choose the best answer(s). There may be more than one correct answer for each question.

1. When testing components, the first and simplest test you can perform is:

   A. Visual inspection

   B. Continuity test

   C. Power-on self test

   D. Ohm meter

2. The ultimate test of a computer system is:

   A. It boots from a floppy

   B. It performs the function it was designed to perform

   C. It passes *power-on self tests* (POST)

   D. It is sold for a lot of money

3. When connecting devices that use ribbon cables, it is important that the red stripe is closest to:

   A. Pin 30

   B. Power

   C. Ground

   D. Pin 1

4. When setting up a computer to boot from floppy, the floppy drive must be in the boot sequence and:

   A. Boot from floppy must be enabled in the CMOS

   B. The system must be password-protected at the system level

   C. There must be a bootable floppy in the floppy drive

   D. The hard drive must be configured first

5. The first thing you should do when troubleshooting a computer system is:

   A. Identify the problem

   B. Record the problem

   C. Blame it on someone else

   D. Check to be sure it is plugged in

6. Before a hard drive can be formatted, it must:

   A. Have an operating system on it

   B. Be configured as a Slave drive

   C. Be booted

   D. Be partitioned

7. When troubleshooting a problem, it is usually best to start from the basics and work toward the problem because:

   A. You get paid by the hour, not the job

   B. If you go straight to what you believe the problem is and you're wrong, it takes longer than if you had done it correctly the first time

   C. There is no way of knowing what the problem is without starting with the basics

   D. If you have multiple troubleshooting problems, you might not properly diagnose the problem

8. The main concerns when shipping a computer are (pick all that apply):

   A. That it is packed securely

   B. That all the components are present

   C. That it is always shipped 3-day ground

   D. That it is shipped in separate containers

9. In order to boot from floppy, you must (pick all that apply):

   A. Add the floppy drive to the boot sequence

   B. Enable the Boot from Floppy option

   C. Have a bootable floppy disk

   D. Boot from the hard dive and change to the floppy

10. The files required to boot a floppy or hard disk are (pick all that apply):

    A. `msdos.sys`

    B. `boot.sys`

    C. `io.sys`

    D. `command.com`

Hands-on Lab Exercises

For these lab exercises, you will need access to a complete computer system, a set of screwdrivers, and an unpartitioned hard drive. The purpose of these exercises is to familiarize you with the installation and configuration of a new hard drive. This particular lab will walk you through setting up a new hard drive on a computer system.

Lab 12-12 *Installing and configuring a new hard drive*

Getting organized

Clear your work area of all non-essential items. Make sure you can move the system around without causing an avalanche of miscellaneous computer debris. Unplug the system when you're working inside it. In this lab we will be preparing a new hard drive.

1. Remove the hard drive from its static packing.
2. Check to be sure the jumpers are set to Master on an EIDE drive, or SCSI ID of zero.
3. Set the jumpers on the hard drive.
4. Write the hard drive settings inside the system manual, or somewhere handy.
5. Open the computer case.
6. Find an empty drive bay in the computer and insert the hard drive.
7. Connect the signal cable, being sure that Pin 1 is closest to the red stripe.
8. Connect the power lead to the hard drive.
9. Secure the hard drive to the case.
10. Plug the computer in and power on the system.
11. Insert a bootable system floppy with:

   o format.com

   o fdisk.exe

12. When the computer starts, enter the CMOS setup and configure the CMOS for the drive.

    The system will boot from the bootable floppy; now you need to configure the hard drive so the system can use it to store data.

13. At the command prompt, type **fdisk**.
14. Choose Create a New Partition.
15. Give the volume a name and allow the maximum size for the primary partition.

At this point, you will be prompted to press Escape to continue; do so. Then restart the system using the bootable floppy.

16. When the system starts this time, at the command prompt, type **format C:/s**. This will format the drive and transfer the system files so that it is bootable.

17. When the format operation is complete, remove the floppy and restart the computer.

You have now prepared a drive to be bootable and store data.

Upgrading Systems and Components

About Chapter 13

This chapter deals with issues you'll face when upgrading computer systems and their components. We'll familiarize you with the common drivers, configuration commands, ports, and memory types used when upgrading devices for MS-DOS and Microsoft Windows systems. By becoming familiar with these items, you will be able to configure, install, and upgrade systems software more easily.

We also discuss in this chapter how to replace the motherboard. You should have no trouble replacing a motherboard if you followed the example from the previous chapter. The difference is that in this chapter, we're upgrading the computer's components rather than building a computer from scratch.

COMMON DRIVERS USED BY MS-DOS AND WINDOWS

A program that controls a device is called a *device driver*. A device driver is basically a software program that handles the interface between the device and the operating system or application programs. Whenever a program (including the operating system) wants to access that device, it must talk to the device driver, which then passes the message on to the device itself. Every device, whether it is a printer, disk drive, or keyboard, must have a driver program to communicate between the operating system, the program/software, and the device itself. The operating system has several of the standard, commonly used drivers integrated in it. For most devices that you add to your computer, however, you will need to load a new driver before you can use it.

For a driver to be the interface between the hardware and the operating system, it must be loaded before the operating system starts. In DOS, this means loading from the CONFIG.SYS file. Windows 95/98 needs to have the device installed in the device manager, whereas Windows NT loads device drivers listed in the Devices control panel applet.

MS-DOS Configuration Commands and Drivers

In MS-DOS, drivers are commonly stored in files with a .SYS extension. However, there are exceptions — some of the .EXE and .COM files can be loaded from CONFIG.SYS as drivers to make the device work properly. When you upgrade or troubleshoot a computer, you'll need to be familiar with the following drivers and configuration commands. These drivers and commands may appear in either the CONFIG.SYS or AUTOEXEC.BAT configuration files and you need to be aware of their uses before changing or removing them:

- **Break:** Checks for Ctrl+C or Ctrl+Break key combinations
- **Buffers:** Specifies memory reserved for transferring information to and from disks
- **Country:** Establishes the language for the computer
- **Device:** Installs device drivers

- **DeviceHigh:** Installs device driver into upper memory
- **Doskey:** Memory resident program that recalls previous MS-DOS commands
- **Drivparm:** Sets the characteristics of a disk drive
- **Echo off:** Does not display the commands onscreen when a file executes
- **Lastdrive:** Sets the number of valid drive letters
- **Mode:** Sets the input and output port characteristics
- **Numlock:** Indicates if the Num Lock setting is on or off
- **Path:** Sets the order of the directories to search for executables
- **Prompt:** Defines the appearance of the command prompt
- **Semi-colon(;):** Reserves a line of code as a non-executable comment
- **Set:** Defines the environment variables
- **Shell:** Indicates which command interpreter to use
- **SMARTDrive:** A cache that writes to disk or RAM
- **Stacks:** Specifies how much memory to reserve for data in the CPU register when hardware interrupts demand the CPU's attention
- **Switches:** Specifies special options in MS-DOS
- **TSR:** A utility program designed to remain in the computer's RAM at all times, so it can respond to system events even if another program is in memory
- **Vsafe:** Monitors the computer for viruses

Understanding Windows Drivers

In Windows environments, drivers have a .DRV extension. In Windows, two types of drivers are available that support the two different modes that Windows 3.*x* can run in: Standard and 386-Enhanced. When running in 386-Enhanced mode, Windows is capable of making use of the protected mode of an 80386-SX or better CPU. This enables the use of virtual memory, and also enables you to run DOS applications in a window, rather than full screen. If Windows is running in Standard mode, these features aren't available. Microsoft Windows determines the correct mode for your system's particular configuration and runs that mode automatically. Refer to Table 13-1 to see the differences between Standard and

386-Enhanced modes. You can also force Windows to run in a particular mode, provided the system hardware will support it. In Table 13-1, you can see that adding the /s parameter to the win command will force a 286 or higher processor into Standard mode, and using the /e switch on the Win command line will attempt to force Windows to run in Enhanced mode if the hardware is capable.

The information in Table 13-1 will help you determine how much hardware a system requires to be able to run in 386-Enhanced mode.

TABLE 13-1 STANDARD VERSUS 386 ENHANCED MODE		
SPECIFICATION	*STANDARD MODE*	*386-ENHANCED MODE*
WIN command switch	/s	/e
Computer	80286 or higher	80386-SX or higher
Conventional memory required	256K	256K
Extended memory required	None	2MB
Virtual memory	Not supported	Supported for Windows
DOS applications	Must run full-screen	Can run in a window
Extended memory usage	Through application swap files	

The driver files provide interfaces between the computer's physical devices and the Windows core files. Device drivers are the software you need to install and configure a hardware device. These drivers are what make it possible for Microsoft Windows applications to run independent of the type of device on the computer. Driver files include specifications for device, system, keyboard, mouse, display, printer, network, and multimedia drivers.

Fonts support the display and output devices for the system, Windows and non-Windows applications running in Windows, and clipboard data. The various fonts supported in DOS and Windows often have these file extensions: TTF, FON, or FOT. There are three basic types of fonts: system, fixed, and OEM. Normally, only the TTF (True Type Font) font types are used in Windows applications, but

FON and FOT font types can be substituted when you want to achieve a certain effect.

The Windows initialization files are listed below. These INI files are a critical part of the Windows operation system, because each INI file stores pertinent information about your programs, computer, applications, and your personal settings. To manually change settings in your computer system, you would open one of these INI files with a text editor such as Notepad, then change the settings. However, this is not suggested unless you are a very experienced computer user. Changing one of these settings if you don't know what you're doing could prove damaging to how your computer system runs, even to the point of rendering it temporarily inoperable.

- **WIN.INI:** Defines your customized Windows environment, including things like color settings, programs that run at startup, and port settings.
- **SYSTEM.INI:** Defines how Windows will start, and loads the device drivers Windows needs to communicate with hardware devices.

Windows initialization files contain drivers that are configured by both system and device installation software. The common drivers for the Windows environment are set up during installation, and other drivers are provided by the device manufacturer.

Remember that a driver acts as a translator between the device and programs that use the device. Each device will have its own set of specialized commands that will be translated and acted upon by that device's driver. Drivers accept commands from a program and then translate them into commands specific to that device.

Memory Types

When you upgrade computer components, you will most likely also upgrade your computer's memory capacity. Memory management is critical in MS-DOS environments. The Windows interface, excluding Windows NT, is dependent on MS-DOS for memory resources at startup. Therefore, you must understand the basic architecture of memory and how to best configure it.

The following drivers and their configurations will help you get the most from your DOS-based system with or without the Windows interface:

o Conventional memory is the contiguous physical memory in a computer below the address of the first hardware memory address (normally this refers to the addresses from 0K to 640K). These addresses refer to actual physical memory. The CPU can access memory one byte at a time by reading from or writing to a particular address. All computer programs use memory, both for a place to exist during operation and as a place to store data used during execution.

o Upper memory is the address space between 640K and 1MB that is used as a map space for accessing hardware and the system BIOS. Normally these addresses don't point to actual physical memory, but to the I/O ports of the hardware devices that are accessed by the computer. Device drivers provide the mapping from the memory to the operating system, while jumpers, dip switches, or auto-configuration (in the case of Plug and Play devices) determine which address the device itself will access. This means that the CPU can write data to a particular address in upper memory, and the assigned hardware will receive that data.

o If any addresses in upper memory are not being used by hardware adapters, then special device drivers can map those addresses to actual physical memory if you have enough physical memory installed in the system. This memory is useful for loading other drivers or *terminate and stay resident* (TSR) programs.

o In order to access upper memory, you need to load a memory manager from CONFIG.SYS to handle the remapping of memory. The most popular memory manager for this task is HIMEM.SYS, which comes with DOS version 5.0 and above. You'll also need to include EMM386.EXE, a memory mapping manager, and the command DOS=UMB in the CONFIG.SYS file to enable upper memory support.

o Another use for upper memory that isn't being used by hardware devices is a paging space for expanded memory. Though this style of memory is somewhat outdated, we'll explain it here just in case you run into a customer that uses it. If you have more than the conventional memory installed in a computer (usually more than 640K), then you can load drivers that will use that memory as expanded memory. This memory is never directly accessed by the operating system, but is used a small chunk at a time. These chunks are called *pages*. To access expanded memory, the driver needs to map a chunk of the expanded memory into a page in upper memory. The operating system can then write to the upper memory, and the driver stores that data in the corresponding expanded memory. By quickly changing the chunk of expanded memory that's mapped to the page of upper memory, your expanded memory-aware programs can make use of large amounts of memory previously unavailable to a DOS-based system. This was a common method of expanding the amount of usable memory for early spreadsheet programs, which quickly filled up the conventional 640K memory space.

o If you want to use expanded memory, you'll need to load HIMEM.SYS, as well as the expanded memory manager EMM386.EXE, which allows expanded-memory-aware DOS programs to access pages of expanded memory. Check the DOS user manual for more details on configuring EMM386.EXE.

o If you have more than 1MB of memory installed in your DOS-based system and the processor is an 80286 or better, then you can use 64K of that memory to load part of the operating system. This is because of the obscure method that DOS uses to address a megabyte of memory.

o You see, the hexadecimal addresses of 1MB of memory range from 00000 to FFFFF, which are expressed as 20-bit binary numbers inside the computer. Since the 80386 used 16-bit registers, a single register couldn't address the entire megabyte at once. Therefore, the engineers at Intel came up with an addressing scheme that used two 16-bit registers to map out the megabyte of memory space, calling one register the *segment address* and the other the *offset address*. The segment address corresponds to the most significant 16 bits, whereas the offset corresponds to the least significant 16 bits. This of course means that there are 12 bits of overlap between the two. To arrive at a memory address, the computer needs to multiply the segment address by 16 (0x10), then add the offset. For example, with a segment address of 4E2B and an offset of 09AC, the corresponding memory address is:

```
4E2B0
010AC
4F35C
```

- Therefore, to reach the top of the 1MB memory range supported by the PC, you can use a segment address of FFFF and an offset of 000F, which gives you memory address FFFFF, the highest byte in DOS memory. The trick to reaching the HMA is to use a segment address of FFFF and an offset of 0010, resulting in a memory address of 100000. Therefore, by using a segment address of FFFF and an offset of FFFF, you can reach up to memory address 10FFEF, which is 65,520 bytes (or 64K minus 16 bytes) higher than the standard DOS 1MB limit. However, due to limitations in the operating system that are too detailed to go into here, this memory can be accessed only by special means, so the only practical purpose of this space is to place a portion of the operating system code there. This, however, frees up a good deal of space in conventional memory for use by other programs.

- To access the HMA, you need to load a special driver in the CONFIG.SYS file, specifically HIMEM.SYS. This driver, along with the CONFIG.SYS command DOS=HIGH, instructs your computer to access the HMA and load a portion of the operating system there.

- The other way to make use of memory above 1MB in DOS is to install more physical memory and configure it as extended memory. A majority of this memory is beyond the reach of the standard DOS addressing scheme, so only programs that are specially designed to use this type of memory can access it. Windows 3.1 is just such a program, and in fact it makes heavy use of extended memory. Again, this requires that HIMEM.SYS be loaded from CONFIG.SYS to enable access to the extended memory.

So now that you know about the various forms of memory, you can make informed decisions about how to configure a computer to best make use of the available memory for the situation at hand. If the customer will be using old DOS programs that use expanded memory, you'll need to load an expanded memory manager. And whatever else you do, you should always try to free up as much conventional memory as possible for use by other applications.

In any case, if the customer is using Windows (3.*x*, 95, 98, or NT), then adding memory can only help. You should add as much memory as the customer can afford. Windows 95 really only begins to work properly with 24MB of RAM; Windows NT with 64. If you can push a system above these numbers, then the performance improvements will be dramatic.

Be aware that 486 and Pentium systems normally have either two or four slots for installing memory on the motherboard. Often, four-slot systems require that the memory be installed in matched pairs of SIMMs, so that you can have perhaps two 8MB SIMMs and two 4MB SIMMs, but you can't have a 16MB, an 8MB, and a 4MB SIMM. This limits the memory configurations somewhat, but the real problem is when the customer has two low-megabyte SIMMs installed and wants more memory. Normally this means throwing away the memory that's currently installed, since used, low-megabyte SIMMs have very little if any value. This is an important point to keep in mind when building a system: Buy the highest-megabyte SIMMs available to end up with the memory configuration desired by the user, thereby leaving space to upgrade in the future without throwing anything away.

HIMEM.SYS

HIMEM.SYS is a memory managing device driver that provides access to extended memory and tests the system's memory when the computer is started. HIMEM.SYS coordinates the use of extended memory and *high memory area* (HMA) so that no two applications or device drivers use the same memory at the same time.

To access extended memory, add HIMEM.SYS to the DEVICE= command in CONFIG.SYS. Note that HIMEM.SYS must precede any applications or device drivers that use extended memory. To do this, open CONFIG.SYS with a text editor such as Edit and enter the following text as the first line of the file: **DEVICE=HIMEM.SYS**.

Then save and close CONFIG.SYS and restart the computer to enable that device driver. That's all there is to it!

The advantages of using HIMEM.SYS are:

- It makes extended memory available to programs that use extended memory according to XMS.

- It prevents system errors if requests are issued for conflicting memory.

- It allows portions of MS-DOS to be loaded in the HMA.

- It enables MS-DOS to load device drivers and TSRs in upper memory area, thereby conserving conventional memory.

- Used in conjunction with EMM386 (described next), it allows extended memory to be used as expanded memory.

The disadvantages of using HIMEM.SYS are:

- It uses a small amount of conventional memory.
- It is not compatible with older programs that allocate extended memory directly.

EMM386.EXE

Expanded Memory Manager (EMM386.EXE) is a dual-purpose memory manager that provides access to the *upper memory area* (UMA), and allows extended memory to be used as expanded memory. It does both of these tasks by managing the transfer of information between the upper memory addresses that DOS can access and the extended memory beyond DOS's range.

To activate the extended memory manager, add EMM386.EXE to the DEVICE= command in CONFIG.SYS on the line following HIMEM.SYS. The EMM386.EXE file enables expanded-memory support and upper memory block support when needed.

MemMaker

MemMaker is an MS-DOS memory-optimization program that moves device drivers and memory-resident programs from conventional memory into upper memory. MemMaker modifies the CONFIG.SYS and AUTOEXEC.BAT files to move the installed drivers and programs into UMA. MemMaker is run from the DOS prompt and supports two options: Express and Custom. Express setup is the default choice. It analyzes the memory, makes required changes to the system files, and restarts the computer with the new memory settings.

After MemMaker has analyzed your system, it adds the appropriate DeviceHigh and LoadHigh commands to the CONFIG.SYS and AUTOEXEC.BAT files.

 **Do not use MemMaker when Microsoft Windows is running.**

Figure 13-1 shows the error message MemMaker displays if you attempt to run it while running Windows.

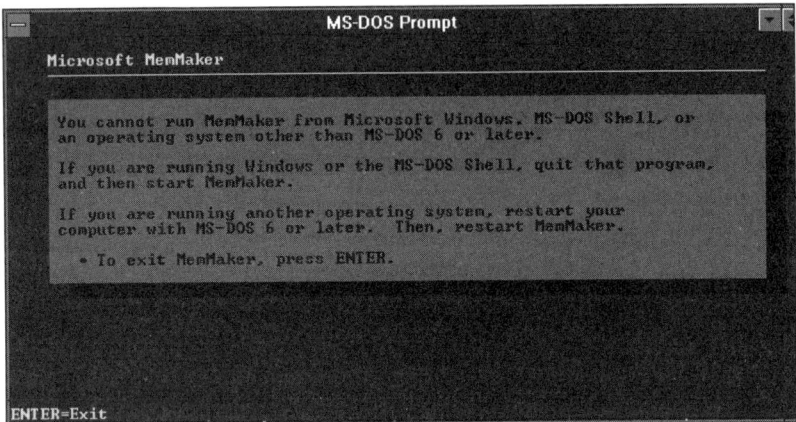

FIGURE 13-1   MemMaker warning message screen

Disk Cache

SMARTDRV.EXE speeds up disk access by using a portion of memory to act as a temporary copy of information recently accessed from a disk. This portion of memory is referred to as *disk cache*. If the data is located in the disk cache, MS-DOS accesses the disk cache rather than reading directly from the disk. The use of a disk cache speeds up the system's performance at the expense of using additional memory. In some cases, systems with SCSI, ESDI or MCA devices won't be able to directly support the SMARTDrive disk cache, so SMARTDrive is capable of using a cache procedure called double-buffering. Double-buffering enables these devices to work with the SMARTDrive disk-caching tool.

In MS-DOS version 6.*x*, SMARTDrive can cache CD-ROM players. To create and use a disk cache, add SMARTDRV.EXE to the DEVICE= command in the CONFIG.SYS file. Figure 13-2 shows the SMARTDRV functions.

```
[drive:][path]SMARTDRV [/X] [[drive[+!-]]...] [/U] [/C!/R] [/F!/N] [/L]
[/U!/Q!/S] [InitCacheSize[WinCacheSize]] [/E:ElementSize]
[/B:BufferSize]
```

FIGURE 13-2   SMARTDrive screen

UPGRADING THE MOTHERBOARD

If you're considering upgrading your PC, you should think about upgrading the motherboard. While this may seem like a daunting task at first, it is really not that difficult. If you were able to install the hard drive back in Chapter 4 and the video adapter cards back in Chapter 10, then you've already won half the battle. Though replacing the motherboard is somewhat more difficult and more expensive than adding an adapter card or replacing the CPU, it does have its advantages.

The motherboard contains the bus, ROM, and main memory. Replacing it with a later revision improves performance of all of these components in addition to adding the ability to add a faster and more powerful CPU. In addition, by replacing the motherboard, you help avoid potential compatibility problems with newer hardware and add-on cards.

Before replacing the motherboard, it's important to verify that replacement motherboards are available that will fit into your system case. Some system manufacturers use a proprietary form factor (or size and shape) for their motherboards to ensure you don't use anything but their motherboards. Additionally, standard form factors change periodically. For example, for quite some time, motherboards have used the *AT form factor*, a standardized size with a few variations like baby AT and full-size AT. This standardization ensures that the motherboard lines up with the openings in the case, and that screw holes all line up. With the advent of the Pentium II, the ATX motherboard was introduced, and the two are not interchangeable. Be sure you're familiar with the form factor of your current motherboard before you go shopping for a replacement. It may be listed in your motherboard's documentation.

To replace the motherboard, you simply remove all the memory, adapter cards, drives, and anything else that's in the way, then you remove the motherboard itself. Normally, the motherboard is held in place by a single screw and several nylon clips. Once you've removed the motherboard, you can place the new one in the case, then reinstall the memory, adapter cards, drives, and anything else you removed. That's all there is to it!

You must take the same precautions you took when installing other items in the computer. First, remove any jewelry and secure any loose-fitting clothing or hair. Next, be sure the system is unplugged — power is supposed to be your friend, but don't get too close to it. Make sure you are free from static charge by putting on an ESD wrist strap.

Your area should be clear of everything except the items you will need for the job. Save yourself a lot of frustration and clean as you go, organizing the components you remove in an orderly fashion. This includes keeping different types of screws together. You may want to use an egg carton or a plastic parts bin to hold the pieces.

The following section describes the replacement of the motherboard in a PC. To remove the case cover from the PC we used, simply remove the screws in the back. Once you have removed the holding screws from the back, slide off the case cover.

Now it's time to remove all the memory, adapter cards, and drives from the system. Refer back to Chapters 3, 4, and 10 if you've forgotten how to do this. After that, you need to remove the power connections and all other wires from the systems motherboard. Figure 13-3 shows the system with all of the drives, adapter cards, and connections removed. The photo shows the CPU and RAM still in place on the motherboard, but remove it before taking out the motherboard.

FIGURE 13-3 Everything's been removed from the motherboard except the CPU and RAM.

Now you're ready to remove the motherboard. The motherboard is held in place with a single metal screw and several nylon tabs. First you need to remove the screw, then squeeze the top of the nylon tabs so the motherboard can lift free from them. Figure 13-4 shows the PC completely disassembled, with motherboard and parts out of the case.

Now all you need to do is reverse that process with the new motherboard, installing all of the components back to their appropriate locations as you go.

FIGURE 13-4 Complete system without the motherboard

KEY POINT SUMMARY

In this chapter, you have learned about the common drivers used in basic computer systems.

- You've learned what a driver is, and how to configure and install it.
- This chapter has covered memory configuration, as well as how to add or upgrade computer hardware.
- You've also learned how to replace and upgrade the motherboard.

APPLYING WHAT YOU'VE LEARNED

This chapter has covered a lot of important material that will help you prepare for the A+ exam and be a competent technician. Take a few minutes and work through the Instant Assessment questions, review your notes, and see how you did.

The Hands-on lab will also help build your comfort level with the hardware, as well as reinforce the readings from this chapter.

Instant Assessment

Multiple choice

Choose the best answer(s). There may be more than one correct answer for each question.

1. A program that controls a device is called a _____.

   A. Driver

   B. Peripheral

   C. Component

   D. System

2. In MS-DOS, drivers are commonly files with a _____ extension.

   A. .DRV

   B. .COM

   C. .INI

   D. .SYS

3. Expanded memory uses a _____ area of memory as pages and is provided by an add-in memory card or through a 386 expanded memory manager.

   A. 512K

   B. 64K

   C. 1024K

   D. 32K

4. Extended memory is an upward extension of conventional memory to 1MB. Extended memory is memory above 1024K and is referred to as:

A. EMS memory

B. XMS memory

C. ROM

D. DOS

5. The high-memory area (HMA) is the first 64K of:

A. EMS

B. XMS

C. CMOS

D. BIOS

6. When working with static-sensitive components, you should always:

A. Wear an ESD wrist strap

B. Wear rubber-soled shoes

C. Wear a static-free cap

D. Touch a metal object to diffuse the static shock before touching anything on the computer.

Hands-on Lab Exercises

Lab 13-13 *Installing new RAM*

To provide experience in installing and configuring components in a computer system, this lab demonstrates the process of installing new RAM. You'll need a computer, new RAM, and a set of screwdrivers. You should also have a clear, well-lit area to work in and a container for screws that you remove from the computer.

Getting organized

 tip To set up an ESD workstation, place the PC on a grounded conductive rubber mat and connect yourself to the mat with an approved wrist strap.

Clear your work area of all non-essential items. You should be able to freely move the computer on the work area without space constraints. For your safety, be sure that the computer is not plugged in while you're replacing internal components. In this lab, we will upgrade the system's RAM.

1. Remove the case cover.

Locate the RAM modules, as shown in Figure 13-5.

FIGURE 13-5   SDRAM module in a PC

2. The SDRAM module is kept in place by two plastic clips, one on each end. To remove RAM, press on the clips. When they release, you can easily remove the module. If you are replacing an existing SDRAM strip, remove it and set it aside in a static-free bag. If you're adding RAM, orient it so that it can be gently inserted into the slot (it only fits one way) until the plastic clips snap onto the ends of the SDRAM strip.

3. Replace the module with the upgrade module, or add the new module if you're simply adding RAM. You will feel the RAM lock into place once it is fully inserted.

4. Replace the case cover and power the system on.

   The PC will automatically generate the memory total of the new RAM configuration when the computer is turned on. In fact, you may (depending on your system BIOS) see the numbers counting onscreen, indicating the total amount of RAM memory you have installed.

Diagnosis and Troubleshooting

About Chapter 14

This chapter discusses diagnosis and troubleshooting concepts and principles. We'll cover the use of basic test equipment, proper repair techniques for computer equipment, and the development of a troubleshooting strategy. And finally, we'll discuss electrostatic discharge (ESD) considerations.

DIAGNOSTIC TOOLS

The use of diagnostic software tools and deduction can save you a great deal of time when you're troubleshooting and diagnosing computer problems. Tools themselves do not identify problems — you do — but you'll need certain items to be able to perform your diagnosis. The basic tools you will require for diagnosing most computer problems will be readily available in repair shop environments. These tools include the following:

- **POST:** The *power on self-test* built into most computer system BIOS
- **MSD:** Microsoft Diagnostics, which is included with MS-DOS and Windows
- **Floppy drive:** Have a working spare on hand
- **Video card:** Have a working spare on hand
- **FDD/HD controller card:** Have a working spare on hand
- **RAM:** Have working spare RAM on hand in the form factors common to the machines you service
- **Keyboard:** Have a working spare available
- **Monitor:** Have a working spare available
- **Power supply:** Have a working spare on hand

Along with these items, you should have a good set of screwdrivers, long-nose pliers, a chip-puller, and storage bins for keeping parts separate and out of the way.

DIAGNOSIS

This chapter covers troubleshooting equipment and methodology. *Troubleshooting* refers to the ability to find and quickly diagnose problems that occur in a system. Troubleshooting is both an art and a skill. Skills can be taught, and will prove useful in almost any situation, but the art aspect of troubleshooting is something that comes with practice and experience. You will take a look at some of the more common methods of troubleshooting in this chapter. Whereas these skills work in most situations, intuition and an analytical mind can fill in the gaps in your training. Your ability to rapidly and accurately determine a problem and develop a course of action to repair the problem is the primary reason that you are needed.

Troubleshooting may include either an involved on-site process, or a simple telephone call. Some things can be diagnosed by the end user, who can run simple tests while talking to you on the phone. The repair may be as simple as Ctrl+Alt+Delete (the so-called "three-finger salute") or significantly more involved, especially in the case of a motherboard failure. Some software problems, especially with operating system components, may appear to be hardware problems. In other cases, where memory may be involved, the problem may appear to be a software problem.

Ideally, troubleshooting occurs on the spot at the time of the problem, in the environment where the error occurs. This is an ideal situation when the error is predictable. The worst types of problems are created when the problem occurs sporadically and for no apparent reason. Most computer systems provide built-in diagnostics and tools to help catch obvious problems, and in most cases they are quite effective. Where they are of little use, however, is when the system is just plain dead, or when it only breaks periodically according to a schedule no one can figure out.

Things you can do to make troubleshooting easier include a little pre-planning and record keeping. For example, if configuration information is kept on file about a system, it may be easy to identify addresses, IRQ, and other problems that might require troubleshooting.

A number of tools can keep this type of information automatically for the environment. For example, Microsoft has a product called *Systems Management Server* (SMS) that maintains a configuration database of all systems under its control. This database is periodically updated and changes to configurations can be noted and recorded. Figure 14-1 shows an example of the equipment inventory on a system under control by SMS. This type of inventory management can simplify the process of troubleshooting and repairing systems, because the configuration is known at a given point in time.

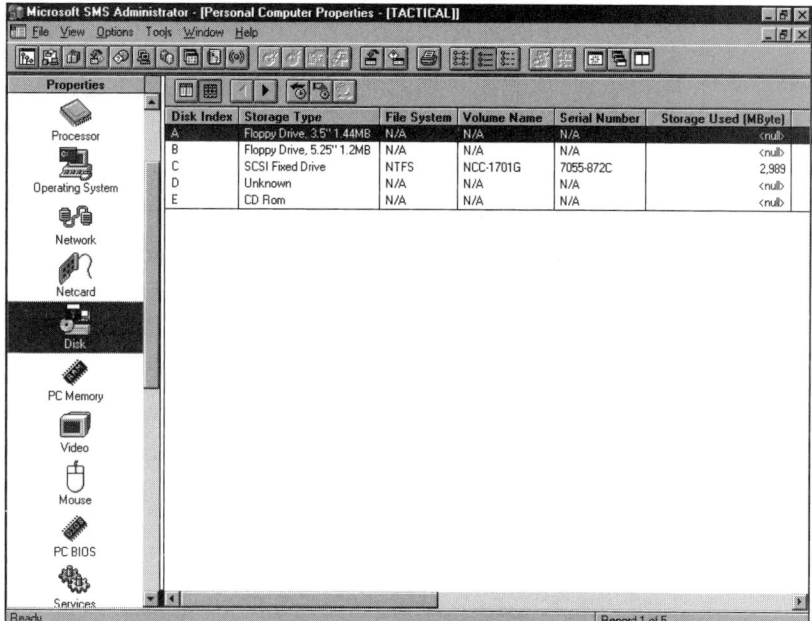

FIGURE 14-1   SMS screen, showing system information available using an inventory management system

The process of troubleshooting may begin with a phone call, personal contact, email, or someone yelling at you from across the room. It's frequently helpful to document each contact, keeping a chart of all corrective action attempts. This information does not have to be elaborate, but may help identify a specific system or component that is repeatedly failing.

The troubleshooting process is what you must engage in to discover the underlying problem with a computer. Often, the device itself cannot tell you what is wrong, so you must rely upon the end user for a description of what's happening. To effectively gather information from the end user (either on the phone or in person), you must stand in their shoes. They are undoubtedly under time pressure and high stress. The description they give you will, in their opinion, be an accurate description of what happened. Most people will realize that the problem has negative consequences for their job.

When you are on the telephone with them, use calm, reassuring tones. This will help them feel secure with you and your knowledge. In most cases, they won't know or care if you are new on the job. They will primarily care about the problem they are dealing with. They will anticipate that they are talking to a professional who can help them. Don't talk yourself out of that perception.

Take notes about what they say, provide feedback, ask questions, and help them understand that you are listening and concerned about their problem. This gives them a feeling of security, knowing that you are listening. Don't be afraid to have them repeat themselves. Jumping to conclusions can have major negative consequences. Based upon the phone conversation, decide on the best course of action. Tell the customer what you are going to do for them and what steps you'll take to repair the problem.

In our opinion, going to the scene is the last or nearly last step you want to take. When you go on site, the customer expects that when you leave, the problem will be repaired. That's why you came, isn't it? Be realistic, both with yourself and your customer. They may not like what you tell them, but in most cases, the truth is the best policy.

Fault Determination and Data Gathering

It is important, when troubleshooting problems, to maintain a log of your activities, the errors and concerns voiced by customers, and the fixes or steps you've come up with. When gathering information about fault, you are trying to troubleshoot a bigger problem, and identify any that are poised to strike. Fault can usually be broken down into three areas: customer-caused, application-caused, and hardware-caused. Let's look at these individually.

Customer-caused faults

Customer-caused faults can be the hardest to track down. Try to avoid looking for customer fault wherever possible — it's not necessary for you to fix blame to fix the problem. It is easy to blame customers, especially after listening to them complain for hours on end, but that's just not good data. You need to determine the real fault based on the facts, not how you feel.

Customer-caused faults are things like not following directions. Now just because they didn't follow the directions doesn't mean you categorize it customer fault and stop there. You need to find out all you can about the implications of the fault — the error messages, the symptoms the system displayed. You do this because if enough customers don't follow directions and you start getting overrun with the same type of calls, then it may be time to see if there is some way that the step customers are having trouble with could be removed from their responsibility. It may be that the step or process could be adjusted so the error doesn't occur. This is why it is important to collect and disseminate the data to the people in your organization so you can make changes and recommendations.

Application-caused faults

Application-caused faults are handled the same way — you collect and record all the information you can. You record the symptoms, the actions leading up to the error, and process you took to correct it. The "Troubleshooting Techniques" section of this chapter will help you deal with Windows faults.

Hardware-caused faults

Hardware-caused faults can be tracked the same way. You will need information on manufacture, as well as the symptoms and steps leading up to the errors. This is useful in determining which components work best with one another. As you will see in "Troubleshooting Techniques," some things work together better than others. This is true of hardware in general, as well as component-level troubleshooting.

What is the best way to deal with a customer when troubleshooting a problem? Try dealing with them the way you would want to be dealt with. Be professional, courteous, and don't waste their time. Listening is important for good customer relations and effective troubleshooting. Customers aren't technicians and can't explain problems in terms a technician understands. Customers will say things like "My computer doesn't start right." What does that mean? We don't know, and it's a good bet that they don't know either. That's why they're calling you. If you can follow that logic, you'll do fine with even the toughest customers.

Fixing the computer is the easy part. Keeping customers happy and making them feel secure in you or your company's ability to help them is what will keep them coming back as repeat customers.

Stick to the interrogatives:

- **Who:** "Who was the last person to use the machine?" (This is simply to verify that it was working at some point in time, so don't say it with an accusing tone of voice — it will make the customer very defensive and less likely to be forthcoming with other information.)

- **What:** "What has changed since the last time it was running?" (Look for obvious or known conflicts.)

- **Where:** "Where are you in relation to the computer now?" (Can the customer see the errors, or are they just telling you from their memory? Validate the facts.)

- **Why:** "Why did you change the settings?" (There may have been an error previously that the customer tried to fix themselves — if you know what it was, it might save you time in solving the problem.)

- **How:** "How did this happen?" (This deals mostly with an accident where the unit was physically damaged, like soda spilled in the key board.)

In addition, if you suspect that you're not getting all the information, try what is called the seventh interrogative — "Hmmmm..." with a long pause. It draws out information they might not otherwise volunteer.

In general, it's a good idea to establish that you're on the customer's side. Agreeing with them as often as possible and letting them hear that you agree helps build a bond. You'll get better information and make them more willing to follow your instructions.

For example, a customer might say something like, "I got this computer home and now it doesn't work right. The packing you people use is ugly, I don't know how you keep customers." Temper your response by realizing the customer is frustrated. "I agree with you completely, that packaging is some of the ugliest packaging I've ever seen. In fact, we wanted to use a different type of packaging, but we just couldn't find any that did the same job of protecting the computer as that one does. I'm sure I can help you with your problem, can you get in front of the computer?"

Some individuals seem to be people pleasers. These are the people who say and do anything they think will please whomever they're dealing with. This would seem like a good way to act when dealing with customers, and you will find lots of this at help desks. However, it's not a good approach. Most people feel patronized when confronted with this type of person, and can spot insincerity very easily. The customer might identify initially, but it wears off quick when results aren't forthcoming. Help the customer the best way you can, don't make false promises, and don't take them down paths that have no chance of fixing the problem just because you don't know what to do. It's okay to say "I don't know." It's even okay to say, "I'm stumped." Customers can identify with that better than being run around in circles for hours just to be told that you will have to call them back later after consulting with your senior tech.

Usually people who buy a product or service know what they're buying and what they will use it for. However, some people really can't be pleased, can't be reasoned with, and will not allow you to help them, no matter how hard you try. When you encounter this kind of person, you need to escalate the process immediately. You need to inform your supervisor that you have a customer you cannot help.

Of course, this customer type won't appreciate anything you do, but it's good practice for you to extend every courtesy possible. Just because that person was not in your market doesn't mean they don't have influence with people or companies that are. The rule is, for every ten people that love your product or service enough to tell a friend, one more will buy. For every one person who dislikes your product enough to tell a friend, ten won't buy. This is because people tend to remember negatives and act on positives.

Once on site, it is sometimes necessary to remove the user from the "scene of the crime," and instead go to a small, quiet office or conference room, so you can effectively listen to their story. It is important that you explain to them that you are not interested in establishing fault, and that you need crucial information to get them back up and going as quickly as possible. Above all, keep in mind that the customer's frame of mind may be less than cordial. They may have been working without a critical tool they need to accomplish their work. It is not unusual for a technician to initially be treated rudely by the customer. Don't take this personally.

Gathering data

Ask questions designed to narrow the scope of your troubleshooting: Did the error occur at bootup or while running? Has the same error occurred before? Does it happen all the time, or just sometimes? Under what circumstances did the problem occur? Were you able to continue working (if so, what steps did you take, if not, did the system lock)? Ask the end user if they duplicated the error. If not, try to duplicate the error in their presence. Of critical importance is whether an error message was displayed and whether the end user recorded the message.

 caution **Whenever possible, you should encourage end users to record error messages before doing anything, even calling for assistance.**

Collecting the information calmly will set an important tone for future contacts. Often, once confidence in your ability develops, you can get to the root of the problem quicker. You should do this without accusations or judgement, as the end user will probably respond more effectively and be more helpful. Do not mention that while you are with them, your phone, pager and email are going crazy. Think of how resentful you feel when the doctor leaves you to handle another patient, only to return and make you repeat the story again.

One of our customers had a large MIS department that had a tendency to leave partially repaired systems lying around in offices. It would not be unusual for the technicians to leave covers open, spare parts lying out for a few days while they waited for parts to arrive. This may have been efficient for them, but many users complained about the mess that they left behind when they left. Even though they understood that parts were not available or on order, it made the users feel that the technicians didn't care enough about them or the job they did to clean up after themselves. This may not seem like a troubleshooting problem, but it created difficulties in the relationships between the technicians and the end users. Always clean up after yourself.

It is important that you appear to be prepared and ready to proceed to resolution, though this may not be possible (depending upon what is wrong). Occasionally, you won't be able to fix a problem on the first visit.

Diagnosing the problem

Do your best to diagnose the problem before you come to the scene by asking questions over the phone. Use the subjective and objective techniques that we've discussed, both on the phone and in person. Usually, you can determine the problem simply by inspecting the system as well as listening and watching the system's behavior. Most systems also provide self-diagnosis tools that can help you quickly identify the subsystem that is causing the problem.

A typical example of a diagnostic used by PC users is the Microsoft diagnostic called `MSD.EXE`. MSD provides information about the systems configuration, devices installed, possible conflicts, and other hardware- and software-related information. Several other tools exist that can be purchased separately both from professional diagnostics companies and from software stores. These utilities can in some cases provide almost instantaneous reports on the system's health. It is worth a visit to a computer store or to the Web sites of these diagnostic tool vendors to evaluate these different software products. Still, in most cases, the diagnostics provided with most operating systems and hardware are adequate to troubleshoot most problems quickly and efficiently.

Fixing the problem

Once you're in front of the malfunctioning equipment, it is important to prepare the environment for a safe and effective remedy to the situation. You can do many things that demonstrate your professionalism. This often pays for itself in many ways. One big benefit is that even if you don't fix the problem right then, you yourself are not the problem. Looking and acting professionally will almost always serve you well.

First, keep all items that you remove from the computer, such as screws, in a container that you use for that purpose only. This ensures that you don't lose anything and will have the necessary pieces to complete the job. A very effective container for the screws and other small parts are plastic 35mm film cases. You can put screws for each component you remove into separate containers. We also recommend that you carry a small box of plastic lunch bags with you. They are useful for holding larger parts and can be used as a disposable glove in a pinch.

Use diagrams to assist your troubleshooting. If you need to, draw a picture of the inside of the box, connections, adapter locations, and any relevant color codes on the cables. If you are dealing with a piece of equipment that is new to you, "label the cables." When you disconnect a cable, use a Post-it note, masking tape, or pieces of floppy disk labels to identify which cable goes where.

If you suspect a disk problem, it is a good idea to back up the hard drives before you start replacing components. Keep the parts together. When you put the system back together, be sure that the case is replaced and fastened together properly. Many systems will vibrate and rattle if they aren't fastened, which is both annoying and undermines your credibility. Finally, when the problem is repaired, it is a good idea to back up the system. It is also a good idea to log all IRQ addresses and DMA information. This is a great time to record any other settings needed to install expansion cards, modems, adapters, and so on. This may seem like a lot of work, but it will save you time, and remember, time is money.

Most operating systems provide a disaster recovery or emergency recovery procedure. Windows 95 provides what is called an *emergency recovery directory* (ERD). This directory can either be on a floppy disk or as a subdirectory on a computer system. Figure 14-2 shows the directory on a Windows 95 system. This directory is updated by a program that should be run after each installation of software and systems configuration. It contains critical information about the registry, directory structure, and critical systems files needed to restore normal operations.

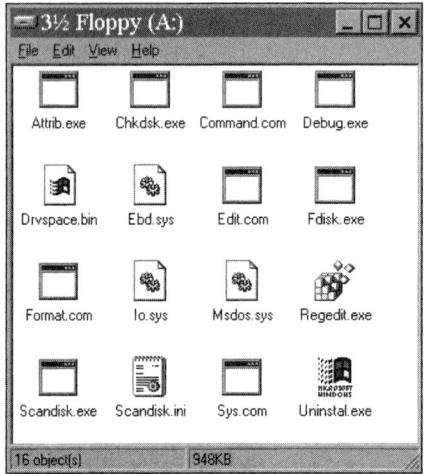

FIGURE 14-2 **The directory listing of the ERD disk for a Windows 95 system**

Older systems such as Windows 3.1 do not provide these capabilities. The best method of maintaining troubleshooting information on those systems may be to print out a few of the .ini files from the Windows subdirectory. This will help reinstall operations and configuration quickly.

Not all technicians share this belief, but we feel you shouldn't leave the site until the end user can restore normal operations. This, though maybe more expensive, can have positive long-term effects on your relationship with customers. Many manufacturers now provide restore CDs that contain all of the operating system and systems files that can be used to recover the system back to the equivalent of new. This provides the technician with a quick way to recover a system and get the end user back into operation.

If you keep proper logs regarding each PC, you'll be able to proceed quickly through a review of any upkeep, maintenance, and swap-outs performed on the target system. For example, the log should tell you who has worked on the system, any recent hardware or software upgrades, and any changed settings in the AUTOEXEC.BAT, CONFIG.SYS, SYSTEM.INI, WIN.INI, or the Windows Registry. Figure 14-3 shows an AUTOEXEC.BAT file used in a Windows 3.1 system. Figure 14-4 shows the CONFIG.SYS on a Windows 95 system, and Figure 14-5 shows the Windows 3.1 SYSTEM.INI file. Figure 14-6 shows a portion of the Windows WIN.INI file. These files are explained in more detail in Chapters 17-20. Because your log contains the last settings, you should be able to compare the log version with the current AUTOEXEC.BAT, CONFIG.SYS, SYSTEM.INI, and WIN.INI, and spot any alterations.

```
@ECHO OFF
PROMPT $P$G
SET MIDI=SYNTH:1 MAP:E
SET VIPERPATH=C:\VIPER
SET TEMP=C:\TEMP
SET TZ=PST8PDT
SET BLASTER=A220 I5 D1 H5 P300 T6
SET SOUND=C:\SB16
C:\SB16\SBCONFIG.EXE /S
C:\SB16\SB16SET /M:220 /VOC:220 /CD:220 /LINE:220 /TREBLE:0
C:\WINDOWS\net start
C:\MOUSE\MOUSE.COM
C:\WINDOWS\MSCDEX.EXE /S /V /D:MSCD001 /M:15
C:\WINDOWS\SMARTDRV.EXE C 2048 128  /1
C:\DOS\DOSKEY /INSERT
C:\DOS\SHARE.EXE /1:500 /F:5100
```

FIGURE 14-3 The AUTOEXEC.BAT file used on a typical DOS computer

```
DEVICE=C:\DOS\HIMEM.SYS
DEVICE=C:\DOS\EMM386.EXE RAM
BUFFERS=40,0
FILES=200
DOS=UMB
LASTDRIVE=Z
FCBS=4,0
DOS=HIGH
REM *************************************************************
device=C:\SB16\DRV\CTSB16.SYS /UNIT=0 /BLASTER=A:220 I:5 D:1 H:5
device=c:\sb16\DRV\CTMMSYS.SYS
devicehigh=c:\sb16\DRV\SBCD.SYS /D:MSCD001 /P:220
device=C:\DOS\ANSI.SYS
device=C:\WINDOWS\IFSHLP.SYS
STACKS=9,256
SHELL=C:\DOS\COMMAND.COM C:\DOS\ /E:1024 /p
set PATH=C:\WINDOWS;C:\DOS;C:\BIN;C:\MOUSE;C:\VIPER;
```

FIGURE 14-4 The CONFIG.SYS file of a typical Windows computer

```
[boot]
386grabber=viper.3gr
oemfonts.fon=vgaoem.fon
fixedfon.fon=vgafix.fon
fonts.fon=vgasys.fon
display.drv=viper_08.drv
shell=progman.exe
network.drv=wfwnet.drv
mouse.drv=mouse.drv
language.dll=
sound.drv=mmsound.drv
comm.drv=comm.drv
system.drv=system.drv
keyboard.drv=keyboard.drv
286grabber=vgacolor.2gr
drivers=mmsystem.dll

[keyboard]
keyboard.dll=
oemansi.bin=
subtype=
type=4

[boot.description]
aspect=100,96,96
display.drv=Viper VLB:  640x480x256 Small font
mouse.drv=Microsoft, or IBM PS/2
language.dll=English (American)
system.drv=MS-DOS System
codepage=437
woafont.fon=English (437)
keyboard.typ=Enhanced 101 or 102 key US and Non US keyboards
network.drv=Microsoft Windows Network (version 3.11)
secondnet.drv=No Additional Network Installed


[386Enh]
display=vipervdd.386
EGA80WOA.FON=EGA80WOA.FON
EGA40WOA.FON=EGA40WOA.FON
CGA80WOA.FON=CGA80WOA.FON
CGA40WOA.FON=CGA40WOA.FON
device=*vpd
mouse=*vmd
woafont=dosapp.fon
COM4Base=02E8
COM4Irq=3
COM3Base=03E8
COM3Irq=4
device=vpmtd.386
device=lpt.386
device=serial.386
```

FIGURE 14-5 The SYSTEM.INI file of a typical Windows machine

```
[windows]
spooler=yes
NetWarn=1
NetMessage=Yes
load=
run=
Beep=yes
NullPort=None
BorderWidth=3
CursorBlinkRate=530
DoubleClickSpeed=452
Programs=com exe bat pif
Documents=
DeviceNotSelectedTimeout=15
TransmissionRetryTimeout=45
KeyboardDelay=2
KeyboardSpeed=31
ScreenSaveActive=0
ScreenSaveTimeOut=120
device=HP LaserJet III,HPPCL5MS,LPT1:

[Desktop]
Pattern=(None)
GridGranularity=0
wallpaper=(None)

[Extensions]
cal=calendar.exe ^.cal
crd=cardfile.exe ^.crd
trm=terminal.exe ^.trm
txt=notepad.exe ^.txt
ini=notepad.exe ^.ini
pcx=pbrush.exe ^.pcx
bmp=pbrush.exe ^.bmp
wri=write.exe ^.wri
```

FIGURE 14-6   The `WIN.INI` file used in
Windows 3.1

TROUBLESHOOTING TECHNIQUES

Troubleshooting is a logical progression for finding problems. That is to say, you start from a given point and you work toward the problem, or, if that is not possible, you start at the problem and work toward the least common denominator. Troubleshooting is an investigation of the facts to determine the cause of a known or unknown problem. In troubleshooting, you should start from the base and work toward the problem.

For example, if the problem is that the computer won't start, check first to see if it is plugged in — don't just go tearing into the computer. If you find it is not plugged in, plug it in. Assumptions can be the most time-consuming element of troubleshooting. When your assumptions are right, what do you really save? Maybe a few screws turned. But when your assumptions are wrong, you often start a lengthy process that will not help you discover the truth about the problem.

Deductions, on the other hand, can save you many hours of unnecessary tests. For example, if you sit down to a computer that appears to be off, but you can see and hear the power supply fan turning, then you can deduce that the power is on.

The Basics (Hardware)

Troubleshooting can be likened to an algebra problem. If you don't follow the order of operations, you don't get the right answer. What is the least common denominator or base for a computer system? Power is the answer — it won't work if it's not plugged in. So first check to see if it is plugged in.

Once power is eliminated as the cause of the problem, it's time to open the system up. We're about to take you through the long method of troubleshooting hardware problems. From experience, we have found this to be the most time-efficient approach because so many different types of computers use the same basic parts. Using a routine and starting at a common point will save you many hours of frustration while you gain experience with the different PCs that are on the market.

With the case cover off and the power disconnected, check to be sure that no obvious electrical connections are disconnected. The power on switch will often have four wires connected to it; check to be sure it is still securely plugged in. The power connection to the motherboard can also come loose if the PC has been handled roughly.

The internal components themselves have power connections. Check them to see that they have not come loose or undone. With poor internal power connections eliminated, remove all the system components other than the motherboard, RAM, CPU, video card, hard drive, floppy drive, and power supply. Keep the keyboard attached, as well as the monitor, then plug in the computer and attempt to boot it. You should hear one short beep as the system comes up.

If you don't find the problem there, start adding cards one at a time. Reboot the system every time you add a card until it fails. When the system has failed, do you think you found the problem? Maybe, maybe not. Remove the offending item and install the next piece. If it works, then reinstall the offending item. See if it still works, then continue this process of next item, offending item until the only time something fails is when the offending item is installed. By doing this, you have the ability to track multiple problems.

Usually only one thing goes out at a time, but that's not always the case. Also, it is important to realize that some of the devices you're plugging in may depend on other items in the system. That's why you complete the total elimination process rather than just stopping at the first thing you find.

On systems that have many devices plugged in, it's a good idea to adopt a labeling system for the items you remove and their original locations. For example, label the sound card as *A*, the DVD card as *B*, the floppy tape controller as *C*, and the network card as *D*. Make a legend on a separate sheet of paper. By doing this, you can easily write down the steps and the results of your troubleshooting and ensure that when you plug the items back in, they're going in the right places.

This is why you don't stop at the first thing you find. Sound cards have no "standard IRQ," although a particular brand of sound card will probably always have the same IRQ setting by default. This is true with many other add-on devices, the network card in our scenario, for example. In the scenario above, we would now check the IRQ settings on the network card and the sound card to see if there is a conflict. That is the most likely cause at this point and we can prove it out with the notation. Because you didn't stop at the first error, you just saved buying a new network card needlessly.

Troubleshooting Microsoft Windows 3.1

Installation problems typically fall under one of the following three categories:

- Failure to detect TSRs — terminate and stay resident programs that run, then on completion stay resident in memory
- Failure to correctly autodetect hardware
- Failure to load Windows properly

Problems can include setup crashes that return the user to the command prompt, or a system that requires rebooting.

Diagnosing setup problems

Try these options to diagnose and fix setup problems when installing Windows 3.1:

- Use Setup /t to check for conflicting TSRs. Do not install them during computer reboot, but wait until Windows is running.
- Use Setup /I to skip autodetection phase. Setup displays standard configuration screen. Select the appropriate settings manually.

- If Windows fails early during Windows Mode Setup, use `Setup /I` to ignore autodetection and specify a basic display adapter.

- If the desktop does not configure, confirm that group (`.grp`) files are correctly specified in `PROGMAN.INI`.

- Disable TSRs that might be incompatible with Windows 3.1.

- For display problems, check that you are running the correct Windows display driver, grabber, and virtual display drivers.

- Avoid program conflicts in EMM386 or other memory management utilities.

Diagnosing printing problems

Typical support printing problems on a non-networked computer are:

- The printer does not print

- Printing works from DOS but not from Windows

- The format is displaying garbled output

- Carriage returns with line feeds are not sent to the printer

- The last page is left in the printer

    To resolve most print problems:

- Read the `README.TXT` file — this document often has supplemental information that wasn't available at the time the documentation was printed

- Test printing through MS-DOS

- Check printer cable connection

- Determine if the correct printer driver is being used

- If the printer has a self-test mode, run the self-test to validate that the printer is working properly

- Check that the COM port or LPT port settings are set correctly in the windows software

Trouble starting Windows

To start Windows, there needs to be sufficient memory, an extended memory manager such as HIMEM.SYS, and processor support for 386 Enhanced mode. When Windows does not load, check to make sure that these two files have not been corrupted or deleted by viewing them through the program manager. If these files are not present or are unreadable by the system, then reinstall them from the original installation diskettes, using these programs:

1. WIN.COM, which checks the machine type, memory configuration, and device drivers

2. WIN386.EXE, which is the program for running Windows in 386 Enhanced mode

   The WIN.COM file looks for and loads these files before loading Windows:

o The core files

o The drivers

o The fonts

o Support files for non-Windows applications

o MS-DOS support and mode-specific files

   If Windows starts, you can make a reasonable deduction that the files listed above are not the source of the problem.

Memory violation error

A *memory violation* error occurs when Windows or a Windows application has attempted to access memory that has not been allocated for use by Windows or the application. When an application writes to unallocated memory space, it may be writing over that used by another application, which corrupts Windows memory. This type of memory violation is called a *general protection fault* (GPF).

   When a GPF occurs, run Dr. Watson, a program provided with Windows to give detailed technical information on the internal state of the computer when the system error occurred. Dr. Watson creates a file, DRWATSON.LOG, in the Windows directory and prompts you for information on how the system error occurred. Dr. Watson can detect and determine that some memory violation errors are not fatal and provide the choice of continuing or closing the application.

Using MSD

The Microsoft Diagnostic (MSD) program that is included with Microsoft Windows provides a detailed report of the computer configuration. This is useful for examining the configuration of the system. Two options are available for viewing the results of running the MSD program: an onscreen report for viewing purposes only, or a report written to a filename to print or save for reference.

When a written report is generated, the user has the option of using switches for specific troubleshooting solutions. Listed below are switches (also called options) available for use with the MSD program. To use the options, simply type, for example, **MSD /b** for the "b" switch functions described in Table 14-1.

TABLE 14-1 OPTIONAL PARAMETERS FOR MSD

SWITCH	Description
/b	This switch displays the MSD report in black and white rather than color.
/f[drive:][path]filename	Creates a report with the filename you specify and prompts the user for the name, company, address, country, phone number, and comments to include.
/i	Runs MSD without initially detecting hardware.
/p[drive:][path]filename	Creates a complete MSD report with a separate filename, without prompting the user for any information.
/s[drive:][path]filename	This creates a summary report with the filename specified without prompting for any information.

MSD menu

MSD is also capable of displaying detailed information on system usage. To review how memory is currently allocated, start MSD and click the Memory button.

The information that MSD provides is detailed in Table 14-2.

TABLE 14-2 FUNCTIONS OF MSD	
BUTTON LABEL	*DESCRIPTION*
COM Ports	Lists communication parameters of installed serial ports with a status of each port.
Computer	Lists the manufacturer, computer and bus type, ROM BIOS manufacturer, version and date, keyboard, DMA controller configuration, and status of a math coprocessor.
Device Drivers	Lists the names of installed drivers.
Disk Drives	Shows the size and bytes free on local and remote drives.
IRQ Status	Displays the hardware configuration.
LPT Ports	Displays the port addresses and the status of each port.
Memory	Displays the upper memory area map, which is the memory region from 640K to 1024K.
Mouse	Lists the mouse driver version, mouse type, IRQ number, and other mouse configuration information.
Network	Displays information regarding the network installed.
Operating System	Displays the version number, location of memory for MS-DOS, the drive the computer was started from, environment settings, and path where MSD was run.
Other Adapters	Lists the status of a game card if used for up to two game devices or joysticks
TSR Programs	Displays the name, memory location, and size of each program loaded in memory.
Video	Indicates the video card used, the model, type, and video BIOS version and date, and the current video mode.

The memory allocation screen is a screen option available in the MSD program. It displays exact memory addresses, as shown in Figure 14-7.

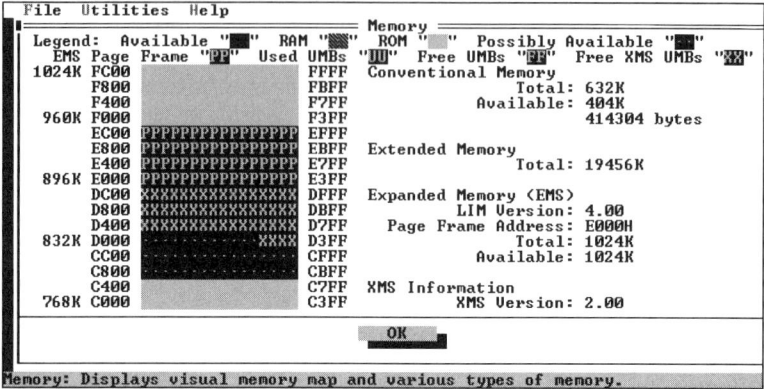

FIGURE 14-7 Memory allocation screen

Troubleshooting Example

If you arrive on the scene and find a dead and lifeless PC, test all the power cords to check that they are plugged in on both ends. Next, with the PC turned on, listen for any kind of noise (e.g., power supply fan, spinning drives) that indicates activity. Do you feel air when you place your hand near the fans?

If the power supply fan is on, then the problem is probably inside the system unit. A good question to ask is whether or not anything new has been added to the system recently. This may help you identify a bad connection somewhere in the power circuitry.

If there is no sign of life from the power supply fan, then the power source is dead, the power supply is dead, or there is a problem with a power cord. Unplug the power cord from the source. You should always verify that power is available on the plug. Use a multimeter, or plug a monitor or some other device into the plug and see if you have power. Check all connections for looseness; if the customer has a surge protector, check the circuit breaker, the wires, and any other possible connection problems. If no power is indicated at the plug, check the breaker switch to make sure that the circuit is active. If tripped, be sure to check and see if the power unit is overloaded. You should now have clearly established that the power is either on or off. Now you can move on to the system.

If the system was working properly and is now dead, the power supply is a likely candidate. You can check this by looking for other indications of life in the system. Do any lights on the keyboard work, do any activity lights on the floppy or hard drive illuminate? You can also use a multimeter to check the power supply output. Is the power switch bad? Are the power connectors plugged in?

If you have arrived at this point and verified that all power supply connections are secure and you still haven't found the problem, you should think about either a blown fuse in the power supply or a short circuit in one of the units attached to it. Start unplugging things from the power supply one unit at a time to see if power comes back on. After you unplug each unit, turn the power off and back on. This allows the circuitry in the power supply to reset. Figure 14-8 shows a typical power supply used in a Pentium-based system. There are four wire peripheral connectors and the larger motherboard power connectors. The connectors marked P8 and P9 are connected to the motherboard on a single large connector. This connector has caused many hours of anguish for technicians. The previous chapter explained P8 and P9 thoroughly. Some power supplies have short circuit protection and do what is called *crowbar*. In short, if a short circuit develops, it will turn off the power to that circuit, until reset. This protects the circuit and the power supply.

FIGURE 14-8 An ATX system power supply

Two popular variations are used in the modern computer system. The AT type (older standard) motherboards use the P8, P9 configuration, whereas newer ATX styles use keyed connectors, as shown in Figure 14-9. The ATX style systems are easier to assemble and present less opportunity for plugging things in backwards. The ATX configuration requires a different case and power supply. Both types of power supplies can be easily replaced and require only a few minutes of service time to be swapped out. Many technicians today merely change the power supply if a power supply problem is detected.

FIGURE 14-9 ATX power supply connector to the motherboard

caution

If you hear bearing noise – a chattering or chirping noise on a power supply fan – you should replace the power supply. Power supplies are field-replaceable units.

Occasionally, you may get a call about monitor problems, because a few normal mistakes that end users make involve adjustments to the monitor. Check the brightness, contrast, and other controls to verify that they are set properly. Many of the newer monitors have a reset button, which sets parameters back to factory original settings. Resetting the monitor may solve many of the monitor problems you will encounter.

Most newer monitors have a two-colored power indicator. A green light indicates that the monitor is synchronized to the motherboard. A yellow light is an indication that the monitor and controller card are not working properly. This may be a configuration problem with the monitor, a bad cable, or a defective video adapter. If the monitor works for awhile and then "as if by magic" it shuts itself off, check the power saver settings on the motherboard and the BIOS power saver settings. Many newer motherboards provide BIOS level power saver capability. Windows 95 also provides this capability. Sometimes these two power savers conflict with each other, causing unpredictable behavior. Try disabling one or both of them and see if the problem persists. The power saver used by Windows 95 is illustrated in Figure 14-10. The options include the amount of time before the screen saver turns on and the amount of time before the monitor is turned off. In general, pressing any key or moving the mouse is supposed to turn the system back on. This power saver system will also control the fans, power supply, and other things that might appear to cause a dead system. We recommend that you only use one of the power saver systems.

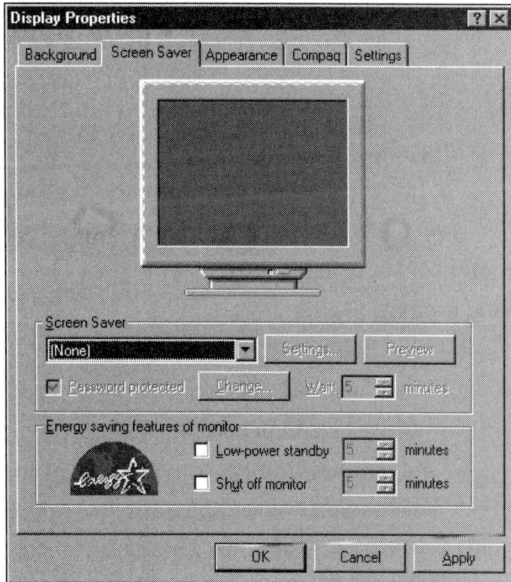

FIGURE 14-10 The power saver screen in the
Display icon under Control Panel

Boot Problems

Boot problems, or a PC that can't complete the booting process, can be caused by a number of things: bad hardware, bad software, bad end user. The next few paragraphs will take you through some of the things you can do to correct boot problems.

If you have had to replace a disk drive, you will have to run FDISK (normally used for partition creation) to re-establish the Master Boot Record. Unfortunately, FDISK can and will completely destroy everything on the target disk unless you are very careful. You must boot from a floppy, and launch FDISK using the following format: **FDISK /MBR** (for Master Boot Record) at the command prompt. You will be able to boot normally if the MBR has been successfully reinstalled.

caution  **The FDISK utility can irrevocably destroy all the data on the hard disk. Be sure all critical data is backed up and that you are working on the correct disk.**

You are confronted with an error message when you boot the system that refers to COMMAND.COM. Most COMMAND.COM errors can be solved by booting from your emergency boot disk and reinstalling COMMAND.COM in its proper directory.

Every now and then a user will complain of the dreaded "Non-system disk or disk error" appearing on their screen at boot. Almost a hundred percent of the time, it results from having a floppy in the floppy drive at boot. Be kind — don't make them feel too bad. If, however, the message appears and there is no disk in the floppy drive, then you likely have either missing or corrupt IO.SYS or MSDOS.SYS files. Simply copy these files from your emergency boot disk by typing **SYS C:** at the command prompt.

Other notable boot errors involve problems with the *File Allocation Table* (FAT) and CMOS. The only way to salvage corrupt FAT is by using a utility program such as Norton Utilities. We recommend that the first couple of times you do this, that you get a second opinion from someone with more experience and have them show you how. Once you start down this path, it is critical that you follow directions. Most of the utility manufacturers provide technical support — use it! Never attempt to recover the FAT unless you are secure in your capability to proceed. Call technical support or consult with more experienced coworkers before proceeding.

CMOS issues typically involve the need to update system settings to take into account the correct amount of RAM, correct video settings, set time, date, and other settings, or errors related to a failing battery backup. Most manufacturers provide detailed information on CMOS settings and you should get that information before getting too involved in changing the settings.

There are times when the installation of new devices results in an errant update of critical system files, such as AUTOEXEC.BAT and/or CONFIG.SYS. The result of this is that the system has trouble booting. To find the lines that are causing the problem, verify the proper settings. You will have to boot the system in such a way as to check each command line, pausing to verify. In non-Windows 95 machines, at the message "Starting MS-DOS," press F8. Press Y to execute, N to bypass. In Windows 95 computers, press F8 at the message "Starting Windows 95" and select option 5 in the boot menu. This process only works in MS DOS version 6.0 and greater and Windows 95 (though the process is different in a Windows 95 machine). This allows you to step through the contents of your startup files one item at a time to identify which line or lines are problematic.

When you reach the line or command that hangs the system, you've likely located your problem. At that point, you can delete, modify, or remark out the problem line. To remark out a line is to place a semicolon or the word *rem* at the beginning of the line. This causes the line to be bypassed in the boot process. Note also that there are times when the memory manager command lines are displaced. The effect of this is that the system might boot during this line-by-line process, but won't boot normally. The cure is placing these lines that load and configure memory first in the configuration files.

At times, it may be prudent to boot the system without using its configuration files. This is another method of examining the CONFIG.SYS and AUTOEXEC.BAT files. Because the system is booted using minimal CONFIG.SYS and AUTOEXEC.BAT files, no device drivers load, thus eliminating potential conflict. This enables editing of the CONFIG.SYS and AUTOEXEC.BAT files to include the proper statements. The commands for these are covered in greater detail in the DOS section of this book.

In Windows 95, *safe mode* is effective in troubleshooting device driver and hardware conflicts. Safe mode bypasses the CONFIG.SYS and AUTOEXEC.BAT files, runs in VGA mode to allow video card assessment, and loads only what is necessary to boot the system. Open Control Panel and proceed accordingly to resolve conflicts, install and/or remove drivers and devices, and change settings (IRQ, DMA).

Electrostatic Discharge Considerations

Electrostatic discharge, or ESD, is a major concern in most computer environments. ESD is a silent killer of components. ESD damage leaves no trace and is very difficult to identify and diagnose. ESD can be caused by things as traumatic as a lightning strike, or as subtle as a spark of static electricity. The difficult and painful part of ESD is that it will frequently destroy many components at once and leave no evidence that anything has occurred.

The heart of the problem with ESD revolves around the technology used to manufacture PC components. For example, a typical memory chip uses some form of metal oxide process to create the electronic circuitry needed to operate. These circuits may be one or two thousands of an inch thick. The density of the components inside a typical integrated circuit is measured in thousands of components. This amounts to little if any margin of error. In the process of manufacturing, a single speck of dust could ruin thousands of chips and render a whole manufacturing run unusable.

These standards require carefully controlled environments as far as dust, temperature, humidity, and all other factors. It is an amazing sight to watch the personnel in these environments get prepared for work. A team of doctors at an ebola outbreak would hardly be more separated from the environment. The point of all of this is simple: The circuits you will be handling are made to the most exacting standards known to man.

The PC is also highly susceptible to permanent damage or destruction from ESD. A single discharge (the term for static electricity leaving your body) will destroy a chip or board. In many cases, you will not even feel this discharge.

There may be no outward or visible signs of this discharge, like smoke, fire, light, heat, or zapping feeling. Static electricity is an unfortunate fact of life, caused by simple acts like rubbing feet under a desk, or walking across carpet.

 caution **You must assume that static electricity is always present; and *never* touch any internal PC component unless you have discharged yourself.**

With regard to the place of work, prepare the surface or work environment by taking anti-static precautions. For example, if necessary, move the device to a better work surface (e.g., away from conducting materials) or bare carpet. Be wary of plastic surfaces such as the popular floor mats that facilitate the average rolling desk chair's ease of motion. Note the ESD potential of tower (mini, mid, and so on) machines that rest on a carpeted floor. You may also want to set the PC on an anti-static mat. Anti-static mats (which look like a placemat) are made from insulating materials that you set on a flat surface and connect to a ground source. Many organizations do not feel that static discharge is a major consideration. Over the last few years, the durability of components has increased greatly. Nevertheless, a typical CPU chip may cost between $300 and $800. Using a wrist guard, described in the following paragraph, seems like good insurance. And always ensure that the AC power cord is removed from the system before opening the case.

caution

Complimentary Metal Oxide Semiconductor chips are most susceptible to ESD damage.

Several actions you can take can effectively neutralize ESD. Foremost is wearing an anti-static bracelet (also called an *earthing* bracelet). The anti-static bracelet is worn around the wrist and is connected to a ground source (like a grounded outlet) so that static charges flow away from the wearer to the ground, and not into the PC. The wrist strap is worn on the wrist of the hand that is making contact with components. Many wrist straps also provide an alligator clip that can be clipped onto the chassis of the system that you are working on. These devices can usually be purchased from electronic supply houses and are very inexpensive.

Be wary of the ESD potential of monitor screens and cases. Use anti-ESD chemicals when you're preparing to work on the affected PC.

As a practical matter, note that PC components are shipped in anti-static containers. The purpose of these bags is to protect the device from ESD damage during shipment. It is a good practice to leave the components in the ESD packaging until you are ready to use them.

Using Basic Test Equipment

Having the proper tools and knowing how to use them makes all the difference in the world in terms of task completion. The PC professional needs certain tools to troubleshoot and resolve PC system issues. You can spend hundreds of dollars for deluxe kits, or you can spend very little. In our opinion, good tools are worth the investment, especially if your income is dependent upon them. For the average home user, a tool set similar to that shown in Figure 14-11 is adequate. However, you can buy custom leather-cased toolkits or tool boxes that have hundreds of tools, many of which you will probably never use. Before you buy tools, talk to your peers about what they need and use. Buy the minimum you need to get started and add to it as you need to. However, make sure that you have two or three sizes of Phillips-head and flat-head screwdrivers. You will also need a good set of Allen wrenches and a Torx head set. Nothing is worse than arriving at a customer site and having one of your tools break. You will be unable to repair the problem and you'll feel like an idiot.

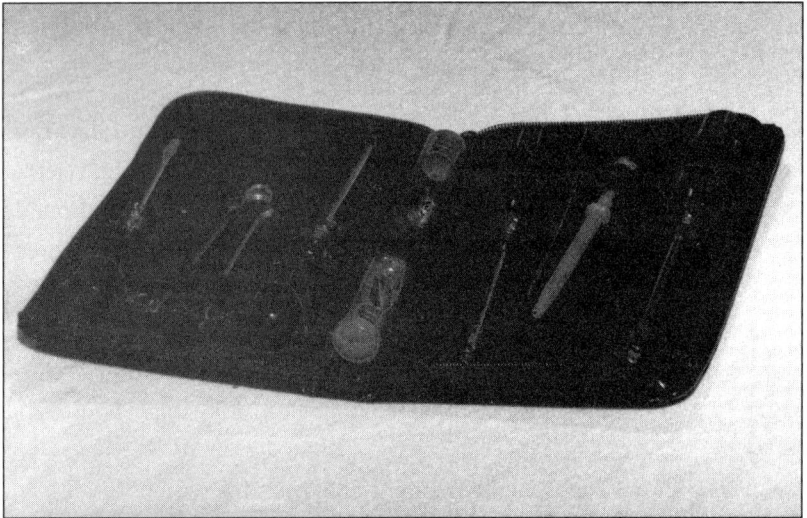

FIGURE 14-11 A minimal toolkit that provides most of the tools you need to repair a system

Commercially available toolkits can be obtained at almost any credible computer supply store. For the most part, these kits contain necessary tools, though not everything needed to be fully prepared. The following tools are essential for hardware troubleshooting and repair. Phillips-head screwdrivers (medium and small bit) are used to open the case and unscrew internal components. If possible, buy insulated handles. Small-blade flat-head screwdrivers are used to remove and install connectors inside the computer. The blade can also remove chips from their sockets.

What seem silly but are truly useful are the small reversible (Phillips on one end, flat-head on the other) screwdrivers passed out at trade shows. You can never have enough of them. Cordless, reversing, rechargeable screwdrivers are essential if you do any volume. They protect you from repetitive use injury to your wrist and are fun to use. It also helps to have a long, flexible Phillips bit to fit in a manually powered driver or the electric driver. Some of the internal screws are hard to reach.

Though not always possible, it is desirable to have a test bench with an adequate electrical supply (featuring grounded plugs), anti-static mats, and floor protection. Bins with necessary parts, screws, and so on readily available should surround the test bench. Extra network connections, analog phone lines, and sufficient extra cables and power cords should be available. Anti-static wristbands should be available and used.

Your test bench should have working, licensed copies of crucial utilities, file-transfer utilities drivers, virus protection, and other software applications that may have to be installed. It is good practice to have boot images and emergency boot disks available as well.

It is important to have a set of needle-nosed pliers and wire cutters. Hobby kits featuring these tools are available at most hardware or home stores. In addition to long-nosed needle-nosed, bent-nosed are quite useful for getting into tight spots. A good pair of wire strippers, a reliable crimping tool (for data and voice), and a pair of long pronged tweezers (for removing jammed floppy disks) is necessary.

Always keep compressed air, clean cotton rags, cleaning materials, mouth and nose protectors, and cleaning supplies available to the test bench. When visiting a client site or end user workstation, remember to bring necessary cleaning supplies along to finish your job.

KEY POINT SUMMARY

This chapter reviewed basic troubleshooting concepts and principles. It is important to have a plan for tracking and keeping records of all client and system contact. The use of a log showing all service and maintenance, who performed the service, and any outstanding issues is necessary to build client confidence and to perform reliably under pressure. When contacting end users, they likely will be defensive and therefore a calm, non-confrontational approach will help you obtain the information you need.

- Ask the end user these questions: Did the error occur at bootup or while running? Has the same error occurred before? Does it happen all the time, or just sometimes? Under what circumstances did the problem occur? Were you able to continue working (if so, what steps did you take; if not, did the system lock)? Ask the end user if they duplicated the error. If not, try to duplicate the error in their presence. Of critical importance is whether an error message was displayed and whether the end user recorded the message. Collecting the information calmly will set an important tone for future contacts. Once confident in your ability to get to the root of the problem, without accusations or judgement, the end user will respond more effectively in the future.

- Every PC professional should encourage end users to record error messages before doing anything, even calling for assistance. Training end users in basic maintenance and troubleshooting assistance techniques (e.g., recording error messages) is critical to the successful performance of the PC professional's duties.

- Safety is a prime consideration, and the presence of high voltage potential warrants the exercise of substantial caution. We reviewed the development of a troubleshooting strategy through the use of scenarios like these: the computer seems lifeless, there are some signs of life but no action, there is some action but basic error messages, and so on. Your approach and response should be systematic to ensure safety and customer satisfaction.

- We also discussed electrostatic discharge (ESD) considerations and safe operating procedures.

APPLYING WHAT YOU'VE LEARNED

This chapter has covered a lot of important material that will help you prepare for the A+ exam and be a competent technician. Take a few minutes and work through the Instant Assessment questions, review your notes, and see how you did.

The Hands-on lab will also help build your comfort level with the hardware, as well as reinforce the readings from this chapter.

Instant Assessment

Multiple choice

Choose the best answer(s). There may be more than one correct answer for each question.

1. To step through each line in the `CONFIG.SYS` and `AUTOEXEC.BAT` files during bootup, which button should you press?

   A. F7

   B. F5

   C. Shift+Insert

   D. F8

2. To recreate only the Master Boot Record on a hard drive, you should use which of the following commands?

   A. Restore from backup

   B. `SYS C:`

   C. `Format C:/s`

   D. `Fdisk/mbr`

3. When troubleshooting Windows 95 after installing a failed device, start Windows 95 in:

   A. Command prompt only

   B. Normal mode

   C. Safe mode

   D. No Network mode

Hands–on Lab Exercises

Lab 14-14 *Identifying a video card*

For these lab exercises, you will need access to a complete computer system and a set of screwdrivers. The purpose of this exercise is to familiarize you with installation and configuration settings. This particular lab will walk you through identifying the type of video card installed in your computer system.

Getting organized

Clear your work area of all non-essential items. You should be able to freely move the computer on the work area without space constraints. For your safety, be sure that the computer is not plugged in while you're replacing internal components. In this lab, we will be identifying the video card manufacturer and type.

1. Start the computer in DOS mode.
2. At the DOS prompt, type **debug** and then press Enter. The system will display a single dash (-).
3. Type the following: **d c000:0010**.
4. Exit debug by typing **q** and then press Enter.

In Figure 14-12, you will see that the information identifying the video card is displayed to the right of the hexadecimal contents of the BIOS.

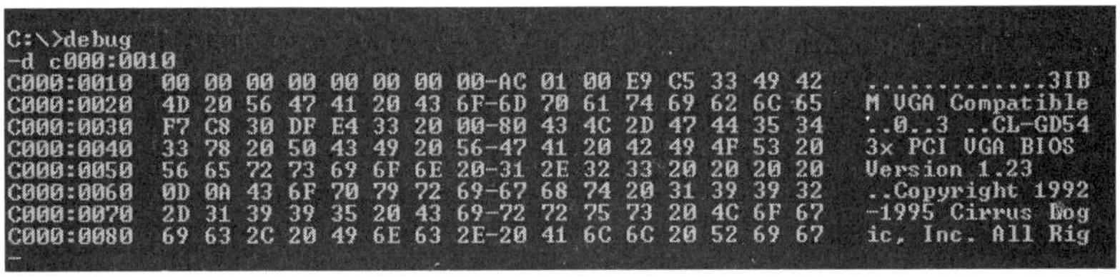

```
C:\>debug
-d c000:0010
C000:0010  00 00 00 00 00 00 00 00-AC 01 00 E9 C5 33 49 42   .............3IB
C000:0020  4D 20 56 47 41 20 43 6F-6D 70 61 74 69 62 6C 65   M VGA Compatible
C000:0030  F7 C8 30 DF E4 33 20 00-80 43 4C 2D 47 44 35 34   ..0..3 ..CL-GD54
C000:0040  33 78 20 50 43 49 20 56-47 41 20 42 49 4F 53 20   3x PCI VGA BIOS
C000:0050  56 65 72 73 69 6F 6E 20-31 2E 32 33 20 20 20 20   Version 1.23
C000:0060  0D 0A 43 6F 70 79 72 69-67 68 74 20 31 39 39 32   ..Copyright 1992
C000:0070  2D 31 39 39 35 20 43 69-72 72 75 73 20 4C 6F 67   -1995 Cirrus Log
C000:0080  69 63 2C 20 49 6E 63 2E-20 41 6C 6C 20 52 69 67   ic, Inc. All Rig
-
```

FIGURE 14-12 The screen output of the debug command

PC Repair

About Chapter 15

Now that you know all about the various parts of your computer, it's time you learned how to repair and replace those components. This chapter is dedicated to teaching you these things. We'll go over how to remove and install many of the common components found in today's computers, and give you some hints on how to tell whether to repair or replace those pieces. We'll also point out some issues you need to keep in mind about personal safety and taking care of the computer components as you're handling them.

Basic Approaches to PC Repair

PC repair can be broken down into four areas:

o **Diagnostics:** Before you start repairing a PC, you need to understand what's wrong. This was covered in Chapter 14.

o **Software:** It's often easier to fix a software problem than a hardware problem, so you should normally start by looking there. For example, if the operating system thinks that COM3 is using IRQ 4, but in reality the hardware is set to use IRQ 5, it makes more sense to tell the operating system which IRQ the hardware is using than to open and disassemble the computer to change the hardware.

o **Hardware:** If you can't fix the problem by changing the software, you may need to repair or replace a hardware component.

o **Replacement or reconfiguration:** Having found the source of the problem, you need to make the appropriate reconfigurations, repairs, or replacements so that the system functions the way the user needs it to.

In addition to the four basic approaches to repairing a PC, you must also consider which brand of PC you are trying to repair. Some PCs use proprietary components that are not interchangeable with other PCs. For example, some companies use SCSI hard drives, instead of less expensive IDE drives. If you suspect a problem with the hard drive of a computer, one way to test it is to use a known working hard drive from another computer; however, if one of the drives is SCSI and the other isn't, you won't be able to perform this test.

Some software applications can mimic hardware problems. For example, a program might instruct the computer to reboot the system based on a condition in the program. If such a program were loaded at startup and it could not get past the condition, then the system would constantly start and reboot. You might be led to believe you had a hard drive or memory problem, when in fact nothing would be wrong with the hardware at all.

Just as software problems can mimic hardware problems, sometimes hardware will mimic software problems. For example, a failing hard drive might appear okay on a diagnostic program, but after running an application for 30 minutes or so, it could fail. If you always use the same program over and over again, you might be led to believe that something is wrong with the software. For example, if the software you use requires you to perform special keystroke combinations, and pressing them results in the system locking or rebooting, you might think that the software is the culprit, when in fact it is nothing more than a hard drive failing. This is not typical, but it has been known to happen.

When this type of error happens, it can be caused by small pieces of the drive's surface dislodging after years of use. As these pieces fly away from their origin on the hard drive's platter, they may destroy other areas of the drive's surface. If these pieces are big enough, they may destroy the entire drive, but not all at once.

A good way to test different components to identify the source of a problem is to try using the same piece of hardware under a different operating system. For example, if you can get a network card to run under DOS but not Windows, the network card is not the problem. Most likely, a bad driver or configuration is the cause of the problem.

IDENTIFYING DEFECTIVE COMPONENTS AND BOARDS

The first, most basic tool you will use to identify defective components or boards is the *Power On Self Test* (POST). The POST is located in the ROM BIOS and automatically runs when you turn on the computer. The first thing the POST does is to initialize the register in the CPU that keeps track of the current program instruction to 0xF000. The purpose of this is so that the flags and registers of the processor are tested first (see Chapter 3 for more information). A checksum is then calculated and checked against the proper value stored in ROM. If the calculated checksum does not match the one stored in ROM, the system will halt, as shown in Figure 15-1.

THE SYSTEM DETECTED AN INTERNAL PROCESSING

ERROR AT LOCATION ## 0160:fff541f8 - 000d:c1f8
60000 , 9084 058604f4

SYSTEM HALTED

FIGURE 15-1 CPU checksum error

The next item the POST checks is the *Direct Memory Access* (DMA) controller. It's difficult to determine which component has a problem at this point, because the error resulting from a defective DMA controller looks the same as the error generated when there is a checksum mismatch within the flags and registers of the CPU. In any event, it still points to problems on the motherboard.

It is important to note that CPUs rarely go bad. Usually when you receive these types of errors, a jumper on the motherboard or the chip has come loose.

After testing the CPU, the POST moves on to the interrupt controller. Once it is tested, the POST advances to the timer. Each of these tests will sound an audible beep if they do not pass. For both the interrupt controller and the timer, if either fail, you'll hear one long beep, then one short beep, then the system will halt. Again, these problems point to the CPU, but rarely is the CPU bad. Most likely, the jumper on the motherboard that controls the clock is not set properly or has come loose.

Expansion slots and ports are checked next. This is just a loop-back test, in which the CPU sends information to the port and the port sends the same information back to be certain that it is getting the signal. On IBM PCs that have a BASIC language ROM chip, a checksum is calculated rather than the loop-back test. Both of these types of tests do the same thing, though a checksum test is more accurate, taking into account more bytes of information than a simple loop-back test. Checksum errors report the errors; for example, you might get a message like this: "Checksum error XXX-yyy failed."

The video card is tested next. In this test, the POST checks to see whether the video card is present and can send and receive a signal. If the video card passes the test, the BIOS of the video card is copied to RAM, in the upper memory area.

System RAM is tested next. This is a test to see if the RAM can be written to and read from. If this test fails, you will receive an onscreen message indicating the memory error — for example, "PARITY Error CHECKSUM Failed." RAM is a lot like the CPU in the sense that memory chips themselves rarely go bad. If you suddenly start getting memory errors after the RAM has been functioning properly in a system for some time, then it's probably because the memory chips are loose, or the CMOS has been improperly reset.

You can mix parity and non-parity memory if you set the CMOS to not have it check the parity. You should not mix speeds, though. For example, if you are using 80ns RAM and mixing it with 60ns RAM, you will likely encounter intermittent memory errors if the system works at all. On most standard SIMMs, you can read the speed by looking at the last two numbers on the chip: -80 is 80 nanoseconds, -70 is 70 nanoseconds, and so on. Figure 15-2 shows the speed of the SIMM.

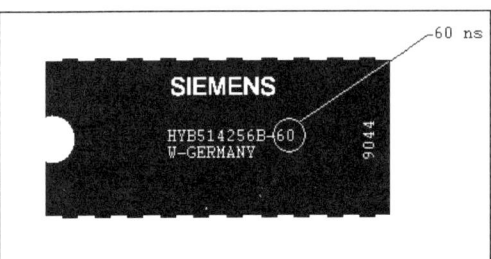

FIGURE 15-2   Reading SIMM speed

The keyboard is tested next. First, the POST checks to see that it is plugged in and then it checks to see if a key was pressed. Many computers allow the user to enter CMOS setup by pressing a key (such as F1 or DEL) at this point; the POST checks for this condition here.

Now drives are tested. In newer systems, if problems are found with either the keyboard or hard drive, the POST produces an error message on the screen and sounds an audible tone.

Other errors that can occur with the hard drive include things like motors not starting or heads not moving. If this type of error occurs, an error code is displayed and one short beep sounds. The most common reason for keyboards and hard drives to fail the POST test is an incorrect connection. Occasionally, hard drives that are autodetected by the CMOS aren't really what the CMOS interprets them to be. Check the user's manual to be sure the basic parameters match what the autodetect has set up for the drive.

The last thing the POST checks for is to see if any other adapters are present. If other adapters are found, their BIOS is copied to RAM, and the system sounds one short beep. In this phase of the test, unless the other adapters have an onboard diagnostic, there is really no way to know if they are working properly until you try to use them. For example, a network card could be bad and the BIOS information copied from it could be bad as well. In this case, you cannot correctly troubleshoot the system until the offending item is removed from the system.

As a guideline, the components tested by the POST rarely fail if they have been in the system and operating correctly for 90 days or more. In other words, if it doesn't fail in the first 90 days, it will probably not fail during the life of the computer, as far as the items the POST tests go. This is true with all of the non-mechanical components of the computer. Things like the hard drive, floppy drive, and CD-ROM player have moving parts that make them more susceptible to failure at any time.

These mechanical parts have a rating called *Mean Time Before Failure* (MTBF). This is usually expressed in *Power On Hours* (POH). MTBF basically refers to the amount of time a mechanical device will operate before you can expect it to start having problems. *Duty cycle* is another important term that pertains to performance and quality of components. Duty cycle refers to the amount of time the component operates at peak performance. For example, an item with a sixty percent duty cycle operates at peak performance sixty percent of the time; the rest of the time it operates below its maximum level. There are other considerations than duty cycle when it comes to determining how long over a given period of time an item will perform at peak levels. This can be influenced by the devices connected to it. For example, if you slave a hard drive to a CD-ROM drive, the hard drive will not likely ever reach its peak performance, because it will always be waiting for the CD-ROM to finish its operations. You can use this information to assess the likelihood that a component has failed, or whether it's more probable that there is some type of configuration problem.

COMPONENT IDENTIFICATION AND REPLACEMENT

This section will help familiarize you with the various components you're most likely to have to repair or replace. We'll explain removing a computer's case, working with power supplies, and understanding motherboards.

Replacing the Power Supply

Power supplies do go bad from time to time. Figure 15-3 shows a power supply mounted in the case. Power spikes or brown outs occasionally destroy a power supply, but most of the time they are destroyed by dust. As dust accumulates in the power supply, more energy is required to turn the fan. Eventually, the fan cannot turn, and the power supply fuse blows out. With new Pentium II systems and high-performance coprocessed video cards, heat buildup is a serious concern.

Whenever possible, such as when replacing a power supply, consider adding additional cooling fans.

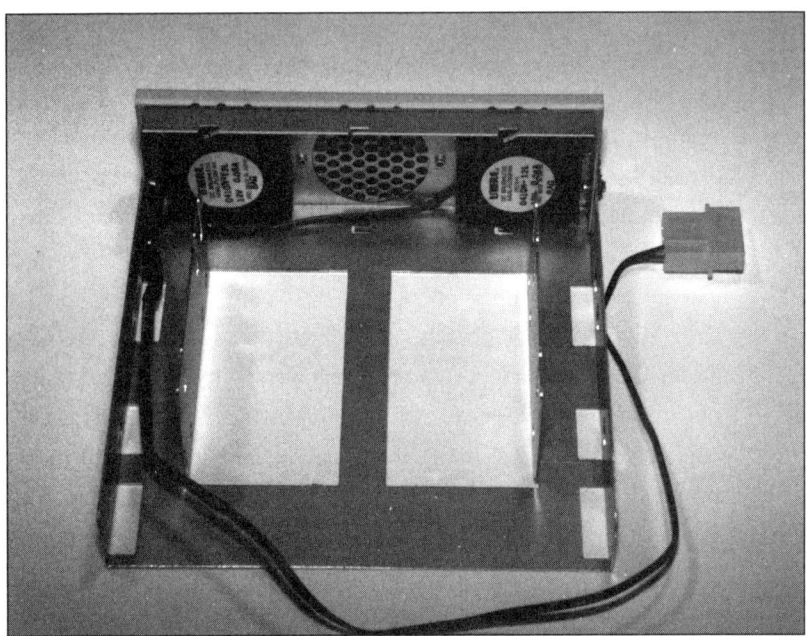

FIGURE 15-3   PC Power and Cooling Silencer 275 power supply

Worse than the fuse going out is heat buildup. Heat building up because a power supply's fan can't turn could destroy other parts of the system, as well as the power supply. Because power supplies are inexpensive, it is usually cheaper to replace the entire power supply rather than take it apart to repair it. Additionally, power supplies don't contain parts that are typically field serviceable.

Most power supplies have a sixty percent duty cycle and 50,000 POH MTFB. This means that they should last more than 5.5 years, providing they are kept free of dust and bad power conditions.

To replace a power supply:

1. Attach an ESD wrist strap.

2. Unplug the computer from its power source.

3. Disconnect the monitor, printer, sound cables, keyboard, mouse, and any other connections so the computer itself has nothing connected to it.

4. Remove the case cover.

5. Remove the screws holding the power supply to the case.

6. Disconnect the power leads to the motherboard and other system components.

7. Remove the unit and replace it with the new power supply.

8. Reconnect all power leads.

9. Secure the power supply to the case with the screws.

10. Replace the case cover and secure it.

There are normally four color-coded leads between the power supply and the on/off switch; take care to connect these properly. Consult the documentation that comes with your power supply and compare it with the previous connections on the system before making these connections. Nothing prevents you from hooking it up wrong besides your own diligence, and hooking it up wrong will destroy the new power supply.

Replacing the Motherboard

Once a motherboard is functioning, the primary reason it would need replacing is to upgrade the system. Figure 15-4 shows the older motherboard and a newer motherboard. (Note that in these photos, the older motherboard is AT form factor, while the newer is ATX, and these two different sizes are not interchangeable. Call it photographic license.)

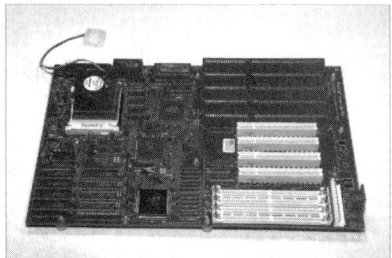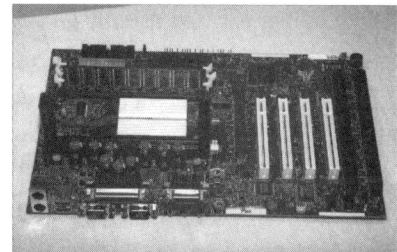

FIGURE 15-4 Comparison of older and newer motherboards

To replace a motherboard:

1. Attach an ESD wrist strap.

2. Unplug the computer from the power source.

3. Disconnect the monitor, printer, sound cables, keyboard, mouse, and any other connections, so the computer itself has nothing connected to it.

4. Remove the case cover.

5. Disconnect the power leads to the motherboard.

6. Remove any cards plugged into the motherboard.

7. Remove the screws holding the motherboard to the case.

8. Slide the motherboard out of the case.

9. Remove the RAM and CPU.

10. Place the RAM and CPU into the new motherboard. (At this point, you will probably have a new CPU to put in the motherboard as an upgrade.)

11. Secure the mounting spacers to the motherboard and slide it in the case.

12. Reconnect all the systems cards and power leads.

13. Secure the motherboard to the case using the proper screws.

14. Double-check all connections and power the system on.

15. Once you verify that the system is booting properly, replace the case cover and secure it.

Replacing a Floppy Drive

Floppy drives usually go bad when dust builds up around the motor and causes the motor to overheat. Figure 15-5 shows a floppy drive prior to installation.

To replace a floppy drive:

1. Attach an ESD wrist strap. (Have you noticed a pattern with Step 1 yet?)

2. Unplug the computer from its power source.

3. Disconnect the monitor, printer, sound cables, keyboard, mouse, and any other connections, so the computer has nothing connected to it.

4. Remove the case cover to access the unit.

5. Disconnect the power leads to the floppy drive.

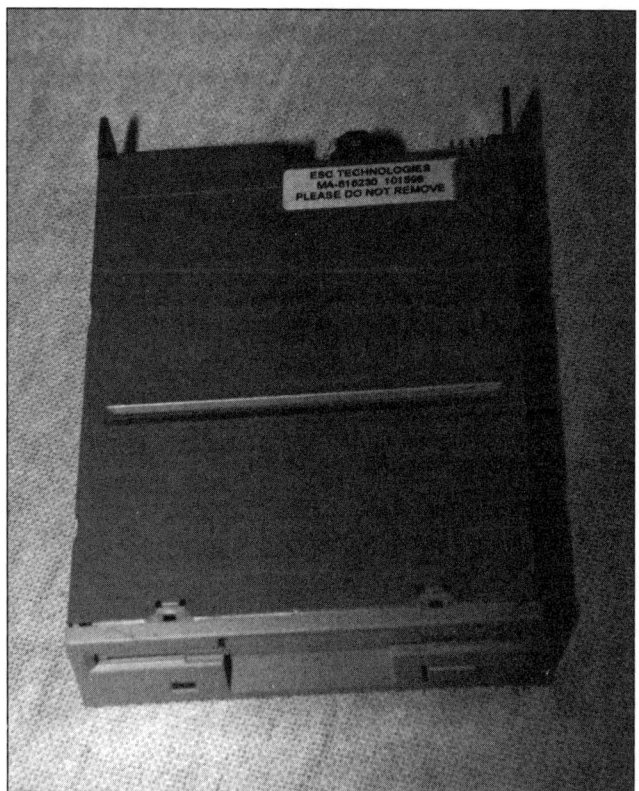

FIGURE 15-5 Floppy drive prior to installation

6. Disconnect the ribbon cable from the floppy drive.

7. Remove the screws holding the floppy drive to the case.

8. Slide the floppy drive out of the case.

9. Insert the new floppy drive in the case.

10. Reconnect the ribbon cable with the red stripe closest to Pin 1.

11. Reconnect the power lead.

12. Secure the unit to the case using the screws and any other mounting hardware required.

13. Replace the case cover and secure it.

Replacing a Hard Drive

A hard drive's worst enemy is a user shutting down the computer and turning it back on. Once the hard drive has spun up to its operating RPM, there is very little friction on the unit. If possible, it is best not to shut off the power to the unit. To save energy, turn off the monitor and leave the computer running. This will add many thousands of hours of life to a system's hard drive. Figure 15-6 shows a hard drive prior to installation.

Hard drive

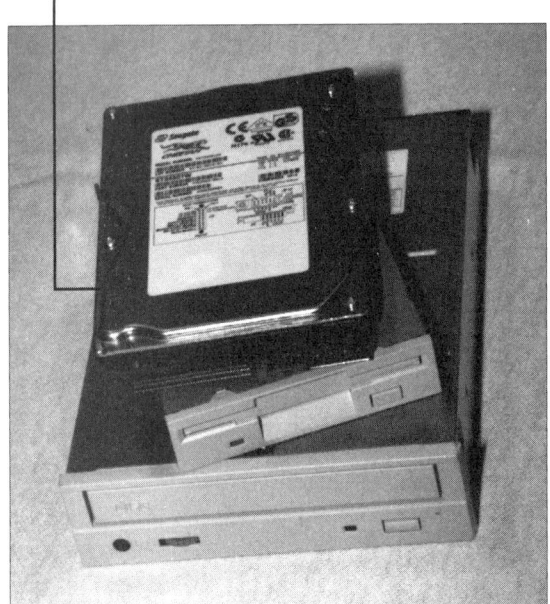

FIGURE 15-6   Hard drive prior to installation

To replace a hard drive:

1. Attach an ESD wrist strap.

2. Unplug the computer from the power source.

3. Disconnect the monitor, printer, sound cables, keyboard, mouse, and any other connections, so the computer itself has nothing connected to it.

4. Remove the case cover.

5. Disconnect the power leads to the hard drive.

6. Disconnect the ribbon cable from the hard drive.

7. Remove the screws holding the hard drive to the case.

8. Slide the hard drive out of the case.

9. Insert the new hard drive in the case.

10. Reconnect the ribbon cable with the red stripe closest to Pin 1.

11. Reconnect the power lead.

12. Secure the unit to the case using the screws and any other mounting hardware required.

13. Replace the case cover and secure it.

14. Attach the peripheral components and restore power to the computer.

15. Power on the computer.

16. Go into the CMOS and set the new hard drive's parameters (IDE only).

Replacing a Video Card

Replacement of a video card generally takes the form of an upgrade. Video cards rarely go bad unless there has been damage from static or a severe power spike.

To replace a video card:

1. Attach an ESD wrist strap.

2. Unplug the computer from the power source.

3. Disconnect the monitor, printer, sound cables, keyboard, mouse, and any other connections, so the computer itself has nothing connected to it.

4. Remove the case cover.

5. Remove the screws holding the video card to the case.

6. Pull the video card out of its slot in the motherboard.

7. Insert the new video card in the slot in the motherboard.

8. Secure the unit to the case using the screws and any other mounting hardware required.

9. Replace the case cover and secure it.

Replacing Memory

In most cases, RAM is replaced when you want to upgrade it. RAM boards and chips come in various sizes and configurations. For most desktop systems, you can get standard SIMMs in 1-, 2-, 4-, 8-, 16-, 32-, 64-, or 128MB sizes. Newer systems use SDRAM modules, which are generally available in 32-, 64-, 128-, 256-, and 512MB sizes. With laptops and some specialized desktops, you need to use special RAM components; check your system's documentation to make sure you're installing the right thing. You also need to be aware that depending on the type of motherboard, you may need to set jumpers for the new RAM, specifying things like the RAM speed, how many SIMMs are installed, and the amount of memory on the chips. Again, you'll need to consult your system's documentation to find out if this is necessary, and if so, where the jumpers are and how they should be set. Finally, you may have to install RAM in *matched pairs*, meaning that if you have four RAM slits on your motherboard, you might be able to fill them with two 8MB SIMMs and two 4MB SIMMs, but your system probably won't work if you try to install one 2-, one 4-, one 8-, and one 16MB SIMM. This is no longer a concern with SDRAM modules, as they can be added one at a time.

To replace RAM:

1. Attach an ESD wrist strap.

2. Unplug the computer from the power source.

3. Disconnect the monitor, printer, sound cables, keyboard, mouse, and any other connections, so the computer itself has nothing connected to it.

4. Remove the case cover.

5. Pull back the holding clamps and let the RAM fall into the unlocked position.

6. Remove the RAM modules.

7. Insert the new RAM modules in the slot and push them into the locked position.

8. Replace the case cover and secure it.

Replacing the Keyboard

The obvious time to replace a keyboard is when the keys fail to work. It is possible in most cases to just clean the keyboard to return it to working order; however, the time required to disassemble the keyboard, clean it, and reassemble it usually costs more than just replacing it. In the field, you will probably not want to disassemble a keyboard on a customer's desk. However, if the customer wants the original keyboard fixed, you can normally pop the keycaps off with a screwdriver, then use compressed air to blow out the connections, hopefully removing any dust. If that doesn't work, you'll need to remove the soldered connections from the board, which is beyond the scope of the A+ certification. Figure 15-7 shows two types of typical keyboards prior to installation.

FIGURE 15-7 Microsoft Natural Elite keyboard and a conventional keyboard

To replace a keyboard:

1. Turn off the computer.
2. Unplug the old keyboard.
3. Plug in the new keyboard.
4. Turn on the computer.

Replacing a Monitor

Monitors are one of the first things to go bad on a computer system. The average monitor, if constantly left on, will only last about 2 years. To save monitor life, turn it off when not in use. Monitors have no internal moving parts and are not susceptible to friction damage that you would notice in your lifetime.

To replace a monitor:

1. Power off the computer.

2. Unplug the old monitor.

3. Plug in the new monitor.

4. Power on the computer.

5. If the monitor is Plug and Play, install the new drivers.

Replacing a CD–ROM Drive and a Sound Card

Most new computer systems have a CD-ROM drive and a sound card. Generally, the CD-ROM drive should be attached to the computer's IDE controller; however, sometimes you may find the CD-ROM attached to the sound card, which could have its own built-in IDE controller. Creative Labs Incorporated has one of the most popular sound cards ever produced for the PC — the Sound Blaster. Most software you purchase today that requires a sound card will state "Sound Blaster or Sound Blaster Compatible."

To replace a CD-ROM attached to a Sound Blaster:

1. Attach an ESD wrist strap.

2. Unplug the computer from the power source.

3. Disconnect the monitor, printer, sound cables, keyboard, mouse, and any other connections, so the computer itself has nothing connected to it.

4. Remove the case cover.

5. Disconnect the power leads to the CD-ROM drive.

6. Disconnect the ribbon cable from the CD-ROM drive.

7. Remove the screws holding the CD-ROM drive to the case.

8. Slide the CD-ROM drive out of the case.

9. Insert the new CD-ROM drive in the case.

10. Reconnect the ribbon cable with the red stripe closest to Pin 1.

11. Reconnect the power lead.

12. Secure the unit to the case using the screws and any other mounting hardware required.

13. Replace the case cover and secure it.

14. Attach the peripheral components and restore power to the computer.

15. Power on the computer.

16. Edit the AUTOEXEC.BAT and CONFIG.SYS files to be sure the CD-ROM drivers are present and configured properly.

The following is an example of setting up a CD-ROM drive in the AUTOEXEC.BAT file (specific switch settings will differ among different systems):

C:\DOS\MSCDEX.EXE /D:MSCD001 /M:08 /L:D /V

The following is an example of setting up the CD-ROM drive in the CONFIG.SYS file (again, specific switch settings may vary):

DEVICE=C:\CDROM \DD250.SYS /D:MSCD001 /C:99 /M:06 /I:5 /P:340

To replace a Sound Blaster sound card:

1. Attach an ESD wrist strap.

2. Unplug the computer from the power source.

3. Disconnect the monitor, printer, sound cables, keyboard, mouse, and any other connections, so the computer itself has nothing connected to it.

4. Remove the case cover.

5. Remove the screws holding the sound card to the case.

6. Pull the sound card out of its slot in the motherboard.

7. Insert the new sound card in the slot in the motherboard.

8. Secure the unit to the case using the screws and any other mounting hardware required.

9. Replace the case cover and secure it.

10. Edit the AUTOEXEC.BAT file to be sure the sound card drivers are present and configured properly.

The following is an example of setting up a Sound Blaster sound card in the AUTOEXEC.BAT file:

SET BLASTER=A220 I5 D1 H5 P330 T6

SET SOUND=C:\SB16

C:\SB16\SB16SET /M:220 /VOC:220 /CD:220 /MIDI:220 /LINE:220
/TREBLE:0

C:\SB16\SBCONFIG.EXE /S

9 /M:06 /I:5 /P:340

Replacing the Computer Case

Different manufacturers use different case types. A computer case is generally chosen based on environmental concerns, such as desk space. The case of the computer is by far the most time-consuming and difficult to replace because all of the components of the computer have already been installed. Normally, you will not need to replace an entire case. However, a computer occasionally is dropped and while the case is badly bent out of shape, yet the innards miraculously survive. When this happens, it's just like building a computer from scratch, only you don't have to purchase all of the parts — they're already there (assuming they're not broken as well).

To replace the case:

1. Attach an ESD wrist strap.

2. Unplug the computer from the power source.

3. Disconnect the monitor, printer, sound cables, keyboard, mouse, and any other connections, so the computer itself has nothing connected to it.

4. Remove the top of the case (for a desktop model) or the side (on a tower model).

5. Remove all the systems components using the procedures you learned in the previous sections.

6. Rebuild the computer in the new case, again using the knowledge you've gained from this chapter.

You will probably need the case manual for this operation. The leads for the system speaker, turbo switch, reset switch, and other functions may have different colors or connectors. Don't throw away the old case before you have completed the operation — you might need some of the internal mounting hardware to secure the systems components inside the new case.

PERSONAL SAFETY AND PROPER HANDLING OF COMPONENTS

As with any endeavor, whenever you are working inside a computer, you need to put safety first. By being careless, not only can you damage the components that you're working with, but you can seriously injure yourself as well. Computers are like any other electrical appliance — not only are they potentially dangerous, but the area around them is also dangerous. In this section we discuss basic safety measures you should take around the computer workshop area.

Safety Tips

Following is a list of safety tips to consider when you're working with a computer:

- Do not place electric cords under rugs or anywhere else they might be walked on — you may not notice right away if they become damaged or the floor becomes just wet enough to be dangerous.

- Check for cords that are broken, frayed, damaged, or tied in knots, or that have melted insulation. Have them repaired or replaced promptly.

- If you must use an extension cord, use the kind with three-pronged plugs that require grounding.

- Insert and remove plugs by grasping the plug, not the cord. Pulling on the cord could damage it. Be careful not to let your fingers touch the metal prongs.

- Don't overload an outlet with too many computers or peripherals.

- Always dry your hands before touching the computer or any other electrical device.

- Keep the floor around your work area clean and dry.

- If an electrical appliance catches fire, *never* use water to try to put it out, because water can conduct the electricity back to you. Unplug the unit or turn off the fuse or circuit to the outlet. It's a good idea to keep an ABC-type fire extinguisher handy for situations like this.

○ If someone receives an electrical shock, use a non-metallic dry object, such as a long board, pole, or wooden broom handle to separate the victim from the power source without touching the victim. Call for medical assistance immediately.

Warnings

caution   **You should follow these safety recommendations before working on any computer. Failing to heed these warnings can lead to data loss, serious damage to the computer, personal injury, or *death*! Use common sense while completing the labs in this book.**

We've made every effort to provide you with the information necessary to be a competent PC technician, but many different computer configurations are out there. It is possible that you may run into a situation that is not covered here or the situation is different enough that the procedures outlined do not apply. If this happens, use your own judgment and common sense to modify the procedures to suit your situation, but only if you feel safe doing so. If the directions that came with your system or components differ from the procedures outlined in this book, use the directions provided by the manufacturer. Do not attempt any operation with electrical equipment if you don't feel comfortable and safe.

This book is designed to give you an overview of common procedures used in the field and computer workshop environments. This information can increase your understanding of the systems and procedures necessary to pass the A+ Certification exams and become a competent certified PC technician. Still, if you feel that any procedure in this book is more then you are ready for, *do not attempt it*. Everyone has a learning curve and a comfort zone; in time, you will gain the confidence and experience required to accomplish whatever task is at hand. Until then, don't rush it.

If the computer is under warranty and you are not doing the warranty service, you should realize that some companies will void the warranty if you open the PC.

Do not work on or open a system under any circumstances while it is plugged in. Don't just turn it off and think that's enough. If the system were to be accidentally turned on while you're working, components could be destroyed and you could be seriously injured.

Power supplies and monitors are the components most likely to shock a careless technician. Do not open either of them unless you're sure you know what you are doing. The PC's power supply and the leads from it to the switch carry a live charge, even when it is turned off. Be very careful working around the power supply — a slip with the screwdriver could cause you serious injury. Monitors carry the highest charge of any of the common PC components — you can even electrocute yourself on a monitor with the power disconnected. Be careful not to leave foreign objects such as screws loose inside any of the PC's components. Dropping a screw inside the case and sealing it up can be like leaving a time bomb behind. Make sure you have an area that is flat and large enough for you to work on comfortably.

Don't use screws that are too long for the component you're securing — anything longer than an eighth of an inch is probably too long. And do not tighten screws too tight, or you may strip them or possibly destroy the component you are securing.

Watch out for sharp edges inside the case. Contrary to popular belief, a blood sacrifice is not required to successfully repair a computer. The frame inside most PCs is made from sheet metal. The edges of these cases can cause some pretty nasty cuts if you aren't careful. Be careful when installing or working with leads and cables — you can also damage them on these sharp edges.

There may be occasions when you'll be unsure if the changes you just made will work. In this case, you could try running the machine before sealing the case. If you need to do this, check and then recheck and check one more time before powering the system on, making sure there are no loose screws, open wires, or improper connections. By the way, did you double check?

Back up data before you do any work on the computer's hard drive or data storage system. The first few times you work on a computer, it would be a good idea to have a backup no matter what the operation, just in case you accidentally damage the hard drive. Sometimes a seemingly simple operation becomes a major disaster because there was no backup prior to starting a repair or maintenance operation. At a *minimum*, make sure you have at least one bootable floppy, and on that floppy have a copy of the `AUTOEXEC.BAT`, `CONFIG.SYS`, `WIN.INI`, `SYSTEM.INI`, and in the case of Windows 95 or Windows NT, another disk with an updated *Emergency Repair Disk* (ERD). Take the time to write down the system's

CMOS settings — you never know what you may be in for if the operation doesn't go as planned. Always exit any open programs such as Windows 3.1, Windows 95, and Windows NT before shutting off the power to the computer. Simply turning off the power while programs are running can cause serious damage to the software program.

Static has always been a major enemy of computer components. Almost every component in a computer system is very static sensitive. The recommended way to avoid this problem is to work at a static-safe station using a commercial grounding wrist strap. Make sure you ground yourself before working on a computer — it's as easy as grabbing onto a grounded object for a couple of seconds. If you're in an environment that does not provide ESD wrist straps, stay conscious of your surroundings — simply walking on a carpet can recharge the static in your body. Commercial grounding straps are specially designed to incorporate a large resistor that protects you in the event that you touch live power while grounded.

Look at a component before even picking it up — handle all components by their edges where there are no obvious electrical connections or designated pickup spots. Avoid touching pins, or anything else made of metal, because you greatly increase the chances that you will damage a component with static electricity if you pick it up by its conductive areas. Components such RAM, CMOS chips, and processors are at the greatest risk of static damage. Leave these types of components in their static-resistant packaging whenever possible.

Finally, around the home and office, children of any age are serious factors to consider from a safety point of view. If you have children in the work area, don't leave open electrical devices lying around. Leaving an open computer running with children around will inevitably draw their curiosity. One of our sons used to think the slot for the floppy drive was a piggy bank. Guess how his father found out!

KEY POINT SUMMARY

In this chapter, we have learned how to identify, replace, and repair the major components of a computer system.

- Sometimes it is better to simply replace a component than attempt a repair. Costs in time versus hardware can make an inexpensive component expendable even if it could be fixed.

o We showed you when and how to replace the power supply, motherboard, floppy drive, hard drive, video card, memory, keyboard, monitor, CD-ROM drive, sound card, and the computer's case. The step-by-step instructions in this chapter apply in the most general terms — you will have to consult your owner's manual/user's guide for each component you repair or replace to ensure proper installation.

o Some components are more static sensitive than others and it is generally a good practice to handle adapter cards and chips by their non-conductive edges. The static protective packaging included with static-sensitive components is not a good insulator — it is conductive.

o Finally, we discussed general safety practices and common sense in dealing with computers in the home or work area.

APPLYING WHAT YOU'VE LEARNED

This chapter has covered a lot of important material that will help you prepare for the A+ exam and be a competent technician. Take a few minutes and work through the Instant Assessment questions, review your notes, and see how you did.

The Hands-on lab will also help build your comfort level with the hardware, as well as reinforce the readings from this chapter.

Instant Assessment

Multiple choice
Choose the best answer(s). There may be more than one correct answer for each question.

1. You should choose a computer case based on:

   A. Cost

   B. Environmental concerns

   C. Appearance

   D. Amount of power it will consume

2. Shutting down the computer and turning it back on is good for the hard drive.

   A. True

   B. False

3. When you work on a computer, it is a good idea to have:

   A. Your hands wet to avoid getting dust in the computer

   B. The computer plugged in to absorb the static electricity

   C. A backup before you do any work

   D. The computer turned on so you can tell immediately if your repairs are working

4. Which two components are you most likely to be shocked by?

   A. The keyboard and the mouse

   B. The mouse and the monitor

   C. The power supply and the monitor

   D. The floppy drive and hard drive

5. What is one of the first things to go bad on a computer system?

   A. The monitor

   B. The keyboard

   C. The power supply

   D. The mouse

6. What do most new multimedia computer systems have that older systems did not?

   A. A motherboard

   B. A keyboard and monitor

   C. A CD-ROM drive and a sound card

   D. A floppy drive

7. When the keys on a keyboard fail, it is most time efficient to:

   A. Replace the keyboard

   B. Rebuild the keyboard

   C. Clean the keyboard

   D. Send it back for warranty service

8. Why do floppy drives usually go bad?

   A. Because the diskettes ruin the floppy drive

   B. Because dust builds up around the motor and causes it to overheat

   C. Because floppy drives are only good for a few years

   D. Because they become obsolete

9. Once a motherboard is functioning, the primary reason it would need replacing is:

   A. To upgrade the system

   B. Because the CPU has gone bad

   C. To keep it from getting old and ruining the system

   D. Because you're changing a case

Lab Exercises

The purpose of this exercise is to familiarize you with installation and configuration settings. For this lab exercise, you will need access to a complete computer system, a set of screwdrivers, and a universal mounting kit that allows you to install a 3.5-inch floppy drive in a bay meant for a 5.25-inch floppy drive. This particular lab will walk you through installing a mounting kit.

Lab 15-15 *Installing a mounting kit*

Getting organized

 The capacity of a 5.25-inch high-density diskette is 1.2MB.

Clear your work area of all non-essential items. You should be able to freely move the computer on the work area without space constraints. For your safety, be sure that the computer is not plugged in while you're replacing internal components. In this lab, we will install a universal mounting kit.

The universal mounting kit is designed for mounting most 3.5-inch disk drives in most standard computers that accept a standard 5.25-inch disk drive. Along with this kit, other standard rails can be used.

The universal mounting kit includes:

- Left rail
- Right rail
- Face plate
- Mounting screws of various sizes

To install the mounting kit:

1. Attach the left rail to the face plate by inserting the bottom tab first.

2. Attach the right rail to the face plate by inserting the bottom tab first.

3. Slide the disk drive into position in the frame you just created.

4. Align the bottom holes of the disk drive with posts of the bracket assembly.

5. Inspect the assembly to ensure there are no gaps between the face plate and the drive.

6. Locate the bay into which you will insert the mounted drive.

7. Secure the mounted drive to the case using the screws provided in the kit.

Maintaining PCs, Monitors and Printers

About Chapter 16

This chapter explores the techniques necessary for performing ongoing maintenance to PCs, monitors, and printers. Preventive maintenance is a proactive strategy employed by the PC professional designed to maximize a system's useful life. Our primary focus is on the PC, but we'll also discuss basic monitor and printer adjustments that will enable maximum user effectiveness. In addition, we'll present ways for the PC professional to keep a baseline on these devices for life cycle and warranty purposes. A strategy of systematic proactive maintenance will preserve the device and ensure the best possible system performance.

PREVENTIVE MAINTENANCE

When you are called on to repair a system, you can take simple preventative maintenance steps for system parts unrelated to the original service call. These steps, in addition to possibly adding to the system's ultimate longevity, demonstrate to clients that you are serious about their needs and value their time enough to try and derail problems even before they occur. A strategy of systematic proactive maintenance is a very cost-effective way to improve system performance.

This chapter takes into account market conditions and the nature of the components and techniques involved in installing or upgrading PCs and peripheral parts. Given the modular nature of PCs, you should expect that parts may need to be exchanged, replaced, or upgraded, thereby ensuring the repaired system continues to perform for its originally intended useful life, or even beyond. A system that is well maintained may help to justify additional upgrades even when the system is approaching the end of its expected service life.

The PC technician is not the only person who should keep systems clean and operating as smoothly as possible. Given proper instruction, end users can save substantial amounts of technician time by properly maintaining and protecting the PC from dust, liquids, power surges (e.g., knowing safe procedures during lightning storms), and so on.

Laser printers are, by their very design, notoriously dusty machines. This is partially because the laser printing process involves the generation of large amounts of static electricity. The corona wires create high voltages, which ionize the air and attract dust. Though it is not likely that much dust will become attached to the paper, dust is by nature gritty and can age mechanical parts.

Ink jet cartridges must be handled properly, and the ink jet heads need to be cleaned to maintain acceptable print quality. Some companies choose to re-ink cartridges rather than replace them. This may save money, but it can cause premature printer failures, high wear, and other maintenance-related problems. The savings earned by re-inking will quickly disappear if you have to replace a printer before its time.

Monitor maintenance usually involves cleaning and adjusting the controls of the monitor for optimum display. In most cases, this can be handled by the end user, though some older monitors have focus controls that require a special alignment tool.

PC SYSTEMS MAINTENANCE STRATEGY

An important part of our strategy is to realize that many factors affect our ability to perform preventive maintenance on a PC. Financial constraints, unrealistic scheduled service life, and an unwillingness to take a working machine out of service, even briefly and just for preventative maintenance are among the factors conspiring against solely preventative maintenance calls.

It is imperative to keep current documentation on each system you may be called on to maintain. At a minimum, *Microsoft Systems Diagnostics* (MSD) information, either electronic or hard copy, should be kept on file. In some ways, the maintenance style of an auto mechanic's chart will serve you and your client well. Charting each item of maintenance is important for billing, warranty, and potential liability purposes. Some end users will swear that nothing was wrong until you came along and "messed up" the machine. Sound record-keeping practices will protect you and your client. Show the client the service log and make it mandatory that whoever touches the machine must make proper entries in the log or work order for verification. In short, if you are charging for your services, you must provide a detailed report of the work provided and parts used.

Knowing the cost of talent and the reliability of machines, rarely will outside PC professionals be called in merely to perform maintenance tasks. Use every opportunity you can to perform preventive maintenance on equipment you have been brought in to work on. It only takes a few minutes to clean a system and check a few routine items.

When servicing a system, perform basic maintenance and clean up anything you can. You may also want to show the customer some maintenance tasks they can do on their own. Distribute tip sheets listing basic cleaning procedures. This makes both your job and their life easier. Working on a clean machine is much easier, and it also tells you a little bit about the end user. Users who follow instructions and keep their machines clean are less likely to abuse machines and more likely to take pride in their work environment.

If the environment is dry or prone to static, let the client know about preferred humidity levels (e.g., around fifty-five percent) and the consequences that static may have on the PC equipment. In short, a sound maintenance strategy involves sound record keeping, effective use of your time, and end user training.

BASIC PC MAINTENANCE

The PC professional should focus first on airflow when performing maintenance on a PC system. The internal components of a PC generate tremendous amounts of heat, which necessitates good air circulation. Air circulates into and out of the case, not only by fan, but also through vents built into the casing. These must be free of dust and obstruction. Dry, static-prone environments, or environments with electric baseboard heat seem to have higher levels of dust accumulation. It is not unusual to look at the power supply fan and see dust blocking the flow of air. Dust is an insulator. It tends to trap heat below it. By removing the dust, you reestablish airflow over the components.

If you haven't taken the cover off a PC for a while, don't be dismayed if a large amount of dust and lint has accumulated. Use disposable cans of compressed air to clean it out. It only takes a few minutes and makes the environment much easier to work on. Be sure to clean up the mess you blow out of the system onto the floor — carry a Dustbuster portable vacuum for dirt outside the PC. Ordinarily you won't open the case just to clean up dust, but this might be the first thing you do when troubleshooting demands that the lid be lifted.

When blowing the dust out of a PC, do it in a well-ventilated area where you can control the spread of the dust, or take it outside. Never, ever, blow out a PC while it is running. If you use compressed air or gas, a little goes a long way.

Any time you open the case, carefully inspect all cables, drives, connectors, adapters, expansion card fasteners, and the motherboard's attachment to the case. You might find loose ICs that you'll need to reseat in their socket. This is a great time to fix this type of problem. In fact, it may also eliminate phantom problems that the user has with the machine.

Preventive maintenance involves more than simply cleaning dust from critical parts. It might be a good idea to clean the floppy drive using a cleaning floppy, available in most computer stores. Be very careful with cleaners and solvents. Electronic components tend to be delicate and it is easy to damage them by using the wrong chemicals. Make a trip to a local computer store and see what types of chemicals are available. You may need to visit a store that caters to technicians and repair people, as opposed to a retail store. Your client will be more likely to authorize the expense of a drive replacement if you can demonstrate that the failing drive has been maintained to manufacturer's standards. The floppy drive contains read/write heads that can be cleaned using floppy disk drive cleaners. These types of cleaner use an alcohol-based cleaning solution on the drive heads, and should only be used if the drive is filthy or causing errors. If cleaning it does not fix the drive, replace it.

It is always a good idea to back up hard disk drives before you perform any maintenance on a PC. There may be circumstances where you cannot get a backup — for example, if the hard drive is inoperable and can't be backed up. If this is the case, it may be impossible to recover data from it in the field. Several companies specialize in recovering data from a hard drive. You can find them in the classified ads in the back of most PC magazines. These companies have special laboratories and environments that may be able to help you recover the data. Though these services are expensive, the cost of recreating lost data may be much higher. You may never need these types of services, but it is good to know who can assist you in data recovery should you need it. If no backup is possible or available, be sure the client knows this and approves your efforts before proceeding. It may be helpful to put it in writing.

Less serious maintenance includes things like defragmenting the disk drives. This can improve data access speeds and give new life to older disk drives. Defragging is a method of reorganizing data so that it becomes "contiguous," one record after another. Most operating systems use a model of data storage that places information in the next available blank space. Over time, as files of varying size are deleted and new files are written into available spaces, this can leave data sprawled all over the disk. Windows 95 provides a utility called Disk Defragmenter — click Start ⇒ Programs ⇒ Accessories ⇒ System Tools ⇒ Disk Defragmenter to start it. Figure 16-1 shows the Disk Defragmenter program reporting about a disk.

The defrag procedure is covered in more detail in Chapter 20, but the concept of disk fragmentation is almost universal in computer systems. As disk files are added and deleted, areas of the disk are marked available. Most operating systems use this free space to place files. Consequently, as files grow and expand, the operating system will look for the next available free space to which data can be written. Heavily fragmented disks can greatly reduce system performance, because the disk read and write operations are occurring all over the disk drive, requiring continuous head repositioning.

Defragmentation programs are also available for Windows 3.1 and Windows for Workgroups 3.11 that perform the same basic functions as the Windows 95 Disk Defragmenter. Numerous software vendors also offer software utility packages that can defrag systems and perform other maintenance functions. Whichever method you choose, running a defrag process on a regular basis will help keep system performance optimal.

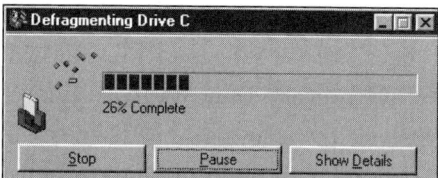

FIGURE 16-1   **A report from the Windows 95 Disk Defragmenter**

Hard drive maintenance can include defragmentation, inspection of the air vents and airflow around the drive, and checking cable connections. It is important not to perform any software enhancements on the system without your client's prior approval. Why? Many times older versions of software are needed to access ancillary, yet important applications. Though installing the latest version of DOS might be helpful, don't do it unless someone with appropriate supervisory authority preapproves the installation.

Do not do "favors" by installing screensavers and games. Not only do such installations raise serious licensing issues, but they also may compromise the system resources in given applications. Never assume that such a favor will stay a secret. Everyone will want the cool application, and soon bootlegged copies will propagate throughout the client's environment like wild rabbits.

Maintaining Peripherals

PC-based CD-ROM drives (internal or external) should be maintained, as any other CD-ROM drive would be. You can also blow out the drive if necessary. Encourage the end user to maintain CDs by storing them properly, handling them properly, and if necessary, cleaning them with a manufacturer-approved solution.

Tape drives are popular and effective backup mechanisms. They also accumulate dirt on the read/write heads. Typically, a cleaning schedule is included with the tape drive documentation. Be sure your client has the proper cleaning kit and uses it regularly. If necessary, provide them with a tape rotation and cleaning schedule.

With other peripherals, such as modems, not much in the way of maintenance is required. External modems need proper ventilation, so be sure the vents aren't blocked. When working on a system, test all external cabling.

The Mouse

The mouse tends to collect debris in the ball area. This eventually causes it to become unusable or to perform erratically. Often it can be easily cleaned using a dental pick or other sharp device to remove grunge from the inner surfaces. Examine the underside of a mouse and the cavity in which the mouse ball resides. Inside this area are several rollers that track the movement of the mouse. Over time, these can become clogged with residue. If you periodically clean those areas, the mouse will continue to operate reliably.

Check the mouse ball and replace it if it's damaged. Clean it with alcohol or soapy water. Check the mouse pad. If it is ragged, dirty, or sticky, we recommend you replace it. Given the low price of a new mouse, it may be more cost effective to replace the mouse rather than repair it. Clean the outside cover of the mouse with a cloth lightly dampened with warm water. Do not allow water to invade the mouse itself.

Keyboards

Another area of preventive maintenance involves the keyboard. The most common types of maintenance involve cleaning the keycaps or unjamming a stuck key. Normally you can clean keycaps with a damp rag and cleaner. It is not uncommon in a home system for children to spill things into the keyboard. Many of these types of keyboards can be cleaned and repaired using special keyboard cleaners. It may be useful from time to time to take a cotton swab and clean under the keycap to dislodge solid debris such as food, or pencil eraser scraps. Check the keyboard manufacturer supplier to see what cleaning methods are approved for that keyboard.

Maintaining Monitors and Displays

 caution

Before touching a monitor, remember that it houses enough electrical power to kill or severely injure you. Safety first! Power the monitor off before performing even the simplest maintenance on it.

Most of the preventive maintenance requirements for monitors involve cleaning either the screen or case or making adjustments to video display controls. Monitors tend to gather dust along the back vents and on the front screen. Many monitor owners seem to keep their fingerprint collections on the screen. Fingerprints and glare can be quite distracting when you're trying to write the Great American Novel.

Well-meaning end users often clean the screen with glass cleaner or other chemicals, not realizing that in the process, they can destroy the coating that protects them from eye damage.

Teach users to use a clean cloth lightly dampened by warm water. Never let water run down the screen, because if it does, it can potentially cause damage. Follow up with a dry cloth to remove any damp residue before powering up.

Most monitors also provide a series of adjustments that allow the geometry of the monitor to be adjusted. Older monitors provide a focus adjustment that can help clear the picture. These monitors can be focused using a non-metallic alignment tool. Most of the newer monitors feature automatic focus. The alignment tool is included in many more expensive toolkits, or can be purchased for a few dollars at an electronics supply house.

The more common adjustments featured on most monitors include vertical and horizontal positioning and sizing, contrast, brightness, and symmetry. We will briefly demonstrate these adjustments on a ViewSonic G790 monitor. This monitor is representative of the more sophisticated monitors that allow for adjustment by front panel control.

First, we will look at the adjustment for vertical and horizontal height and positioning. With these adjustments, the viewable area on the monitor can be sized and positioned all over the screen.

The other adjustments involve advanced symmetry of the monitor. These adjustments include pincushion adjustment, which affects the shape of the screen's edges. The other adjustment that we will look at is the trapezoidal adjustment that affects the geometry of the top and bottom of the monitor. The trapezoidal adjustment helps keep the top and bottom widths the same. These four adjustments are somewhat interdependent and when you adjust one, you may need to adjust the others. We have always found it helpful to adjust them in increments. Fix one, then fix the other, then go back, and so on. It takes a little patience to do this, but it will provide the customer with a distortion-free image.

One last control worth mentioning is the *degauss* adjustment. This adjustment demagnetizes the front of the screen. This frequently clears up distortion problems caused by normal usage.

Most modern monitors permit these types of adjustments and it is worth a few minutes to become familiar with the types of adjustments. Whenever you help set up new monitors, you should discuss these adjustment features with the end user and help them make these adjustments the first time. If they later switch to a different video resolution, they have the ability to fine-tune their monitor for this resolution change.

Maintaining Printers

caution   **Before servicing a laser printer, remember that it houses enough electrical power to kill or severely injure you. Safety first! Power the laser printer off before performing even the simplest maintenance on it.**

Printers operate in an environment that contains paper dust, ink, and oils from mechanical parts. They must be allowed to breathe, especially laser printers. Otherwise paper jams, slide rails that resist print head movement, and other problems can result. A thorough cleaning can solve most printer problems. Follow all recommended steps in the printer service manuals.

Laser Printers

Most printer manuals include a comprehensive cleaning and servicing section that should be referred to whenever possible. The laser printer we will demonstrate this on is a Hewlett-Packard HP4L, a light duty printer. The preventive maintenance of this printer is fairly straightforward. It involves cleaning the case and cleaning the ribs inside the printer. Most printers have self-test programs that can be activated from the front panel of the printer (see the printer manual for exact commands to activate the self test). Self-test printouts typically show printer settings, as well as the print quality available. Should the printer be malfunctioning and print quality is substandard, the printer self-test output can determine whether the problem lies with the printer, or if instead the printer is getting garbled input.

Ink Jet Printers

Ink jet printers have become quite popular recently due to their relatively low cost, good performance, and color capability. The ink is stored in up to four cartridges — a black cartridge, and either one containing three colors, or three separate color cartridges — that also contain the print heads. The *print head* is a series of small nozzles that direct the ink as commanded by the PC. Typical problems involve messy printing (a bad cartridge, wrong paper, or misaligned print heads) or poor paper feeding.

The preventive maintenance on an ink jet printer is fairly straightforward. On most ink jet printers, the printer jets can be aligned using software provided with the printer, the cartridges can be changed, or the print areas cleaned. Beyond these adjustments, about the only thing you can do is to send them out to be repaired by a factory-authorized repair center. In our experience, these types of printers operate for years and when they break, they may not be cost effective to repair.

The preventive maintenance for ink jet printers involves exterior washing with a damp, lint-free cloth to clean dust. The interior maintenance on this printer involves cleaning ink accumulation and replacing the cartridges if a cartridge malfunctions.

Dress for Success

For those of us old enough to have seen washing machines with ringers attached, we remember the admonition not to get our hands, clothes, or hair anywhere near the ringer's moving parts. Like these old washing machines, printers have rollers and other moving devices. The unfortunate person who gets a tie anywhere near these devices will be in for a rude awakening and potential injury.

Dress for printer repair success, even if it means tucking in your shirt, or putting your tie inside your shirt, or wearing outer wear to protect your clothes from the toner or the dust created by daily operations. We have found that a set of coveralls is extremely helpful when working with printers. You may also want to invest in a box of disposable gloves, as ink jet ink is sometimes hard to get off your hands.

If you vacuum a printer, use a vacuum dedicated for that purpose alone. Printer toner will ruin the vacuum over time, and some toner will remain in the bag. Local environmental or hazardous waste laws may control disposal of toner.

KEY POINT SUMMARY

Preventive maintenance is a proactive strategy that maximizes a system's useful life, extending the original life of the PC and peripherals. It is imperative that a regular maintenance routine be employed to preserve the customer's technology investment and maintain end user effectiveness.

- o PC professionals aren't the only ones who should keep systems clean and operating as smoothly as possible. Properly trained end users can save substantial amounts of time by properly maintaining and protecting the PC from dust, liquids, power surges, and other potential sources of damage.

- o Monitor maintenance is usually limited to cosmetic adjustments of screen parameters. The primary effort is directed at keeping the monitor free from obstructions that block air from the internal components, and properly cleaning the screen.

- o If something beyond preventive maintenance on a printer is required, we suggest you remove the printer from the environment and repair it in your work facility. This will prevent any unfortunate accidents with toner cartridges or ink cartridges being witnessed by the end user.

- o Most manufacturers provide comprehensive service manuals beyond those provided as end user documentation. You may find these manuals helpful in troubleshooting advanced problems, but in most cases, the installation guide or user's guide will provide all you need in the field.

APPLYING WHAT YOU'VE LEARNED

This chapter has covered a lot of important material that will help you prepare for the A+ exam and be a competent technician. Take a few minutes and work through the Instant Assessment questions, review your notes, and see how you did.

The Hands-on lab will also help build your comfort level with the hardware, as well as reinforce the readings from this chapter.

Instant Assessment

Multiple choice

Choose the best answer(s). There may be more than one correct answer for each question.

1. Before performing any type of hard drive maintenance, you should
_____.

    A. Make a backup

    B. Vacuum the inside of the computer

    C. Get authorization to replace the dive

    D. Reformat and partition the drive

2. When performing even routine maintenance on a laser printer or monitor, you should _____.

    A. Unplug it from its power source

    B. Get permission

    C. Only attempt it in the presence of another qualified technician

    D. Make sure you are grounded

3. When cleaning surfaces that record or read data, you should use
_____.

    A. Approved cleaners that do not contain residual materials or abrasives

    B. Rubbing alcohol

    C. Any abrasive cleaner

    D. A fine-grit sandpaper or emery cloth

4. When testing a printed page from a printer you have just performed maintenance on, you should _____ (pick all that apply).

    A. Send the test page from the DOS prompt

    B. Send the test page from the printer's software

    C. Send the test page from the printer's hardware

    D. Not send a page to print

5. When disposing toner from a laser printer, you may _____.

   A. Throw it in any available trash can

   B. Be required to dispose of it in accordance with local environmental laws

6. It is not important to dress properly for maintaining a printer.

   A. True

   B. False

7. A computer monitor does not contain enough electricity to kill or seriously injure the average person.

   A. True

   B. False

8. Most printers have a self-test program built into them.

   A. True

   B. False

9. Using glass cleaner to clean a monitor can remove protective coatings designed to protect your eyes.

   A. True

   B. False

10. From a maintenance point of view, there is not much that can be done to a modem other than ensure it is well seated and free from dust.

   A. True

   B. False

Hands-on Lab Exercises

For these lab exercises, you will need access to an HP laser printer and new toner cartridge. The purpose of this exercise is to familiarize you with the essential skills required to replace a toner cartridge.

Lab 16-16 *Replacing a toner cartridge*

Getting organized

Clear your work area of all non-essential items. You should be able to freely move the laser printer on the work area without space constraints. For your safety, be sure the printer is not plugged in while you're replacing internal components.

1. Locate the release points on the side or top of the printer.

2. Disengage the release and lift the cover.

3. Grasp the pull point with your thumb and forefinger and gently pull the cartridge up and out.

4. Remove the new toner cartridge from the bag.

5. Rotate the cartridge until the insertion arrows are visible. Because the cartridge may have been shipped or stored on its side, gently shake the cartridge side to side to evenly distribute the toner inside the cartridge.

6. Grasp the tape along the side of the cartridge and pull firmly until it is completely free of the cartridge. This tape is designed to keep the toner from spilling from the cartridge during shipping. However, do not trust that it will always work — keep the cartridge horizontal at all times after removing it from its storage bag. Insert the toner cartridge back into the laser printer and close the access door.

Operating Systems

About Chapter 17

Threads his chapter explores Microsoft Windows 3.1, Microsoft Windows 95, and Microsoft Windows 98 operating systems. Although Windows 98 is the next evolutionary step beyond Windows 95, Windows 95 and Windows 98 are functionally interchangeable for the purposes of this chapter. You can assume that all references to Windows 95 in this chapter apply to Windows 98 as well. An operating system is a collection of software that directs a computer's operations, schedules the execution of other programs, and manages storage, input/output, and communication resources.

Architecture, file and print manipulation, hardware configuration, and system optimization are covered in this chapter. First, we will cover the components of each user interface, and describe how each is different. Next, the chapter explores the architecture for each system—how each system handles file and print capabilities, hardware, and system performance. Finally, we have provided several exercises that reinforce the contents of this chapter, and will help you prepare for the A+ Certification exam.

MICROSOFT WINDOWS 3.1 AND WINDOWS 95 OPERATING SYSTEMS

The Windows environment replaces the MS-DOS text-based user interface with a graphical approach in which users can see icons on the screen and use a pointing device to select commands rather than typing them in. In this chapter, we will explore the differences between Windows 3.1 and Windows 95.

Command-line functionality refers to a character-based system where you tell your computer to perform functions by typing commands from your keyboard. From the Start button, click Programs, and then choose MS-DOS Prompt. This opens a window that lets you type commands at the C: prompt. For example, you can list all the files on your C drive and view them one screen at a time by typing **DIR C: | more**. A *graphical user interface* lets you use your mouse to point to an object, and then click it to perform a basic task.

To begin, this chapter will compare Windows 3.1 functionality to that of Windows 95. You will see comparisons in the graphical user interface, and be able to quickly understand how Windows 95 emerged.

Windows 3.1 Desktop

Microsoft Windows 3.1 uses a graphical user interface to display computer and application information. The Windows 3.1 graphical interface groups applications together, and displays them in a single group window. The operating system applications enable you to:

- Manage files and directories.
- Maintain disk inventory and integrity in a visual presentation mode rather than requiring the user to know and execute programming language commands. For example, the visual display of your files' inventory can be viewed by using File Manager, which shows you all the files that are stored on your computer. Maintaining disk integrity means you can run special Windows programs such as ScanDisk for finding and fixing errors on your hard drive that you might not normally be aware of, and which could slow down your system's performance and functionality.
- Configure hardware.
- Optimize memory inside the computer if possible through configuring your swap file and CONFIG.SYS files. For example, you can load some programs in upper memory, while allowing other programs to run in conventional memory. Windows 95 uses your hard disk as an extension of internal memory, moving data to a swap file on disk when memory becomes full and restoring it from disk to memory as needed. The Virtual Memory option for 386 Enhanced mode lets you establish a file that can emulate memory. This file is called a *swap file*, and you can make it permanent to improve performance. *Conventional memory* is the first 640K of RAM in a PC and is the memory that MS-DOS controls.
- Improve application performance.

In the Windows 3.1 operating system, you can manage all system tasks and user functions by using a mouse, which supports the point-and-click functionality of the software. Even MS-DOS commands are executed in the Windows interface.

Windows 95 Desktop

Like Windows 3.1, Windows 95 also uses a graphical user interface for the operating system. The initial screen displayed on the desktop is called a *shell*. When

Windows 3.1 was upgraded to Windows 95, a new shell was created for the desktop that replaced the Windows 3.1 manager programs such as Program Manager, File Manager, Task Manager, and Print Manager. Windows 95 consolidates all these functions into a single program called Windows Explorer. In addition, Windows 95 permits the use of long filenames when saving a file. Previously, Windows 3.1 had a naming length maximum of eight characters. With the enhancement of long filenames, users can put names to files that are easily recognized. This helps the user more easily identify what is contained in the file or document.

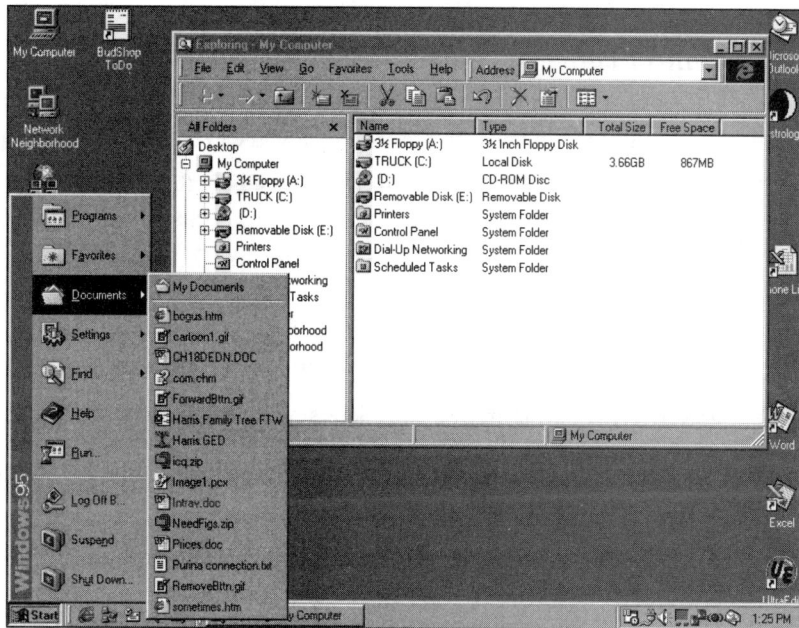

FIGURE 17-1 Windows 95 Desktop user interface

OPERATING SYSTEM MODULES

Each operating system has its own special components that enable users to find, work with, and display information. As you compare Windows 3.1 and Windows 95 operating systems with other products on the market, you will see differences in the operating system *modules*. These modules provide features such as ease of use, improved system performance, compatibility of device and application support, support for networking and connectivity, support for communications and messaging, and support for mobile services and remote access. In addition, after studying this chapter, you will learn that several components are common to both Windows 3.1 and Windows 95 operating systems.

Common Components of Windows 3.1 and Windows 95

The components that are common to both Windows 3.1 and Windows 95 are the Control Panel, Print Manager, Task Manager, and Task Switching.

Control Panel

The Control Panel exists in both Windows 3.1 and Windows 95. From within the Control Panel window (see Figure 17-2), you can change the desktop and file settings, appearance of how your files display, and even set preferences for how your computer will perform in various circumstances. Specifically, some of the components that you can configure with the Windows 95 Control Panel are shown here:

- **Printers:** Add and remove printers and modify their properties
- **Modems:** Add and remove modems and modify their properties
- **Networks:** Configure the parameters of your network
- **Mouse:** Configure various settings of your mouse
- **Internet:** Modify settings of Internet Explorer
- **Hardware:** Add, remove, and configure drivers for hardware attached to your computer
- **Date/Time:** Set the computer's date and time
- **Passwords:** Modify passwords used to access resources on your computer and the network
- **Sounds:** Specify sounds that play when various events occur

FIGURE 17-2   The Control Panel

Print Manager

The Print Manager window (see Figure 17-3) shows you the documents that are queued or printing and lets you pause or cancel printing for individual documents. With Print Manager, you can view the size, filename, and date and time the document was sent to the printer. In addition, you can drag a file (indicated by its filename) and drop it onto the printer icon to print the document.

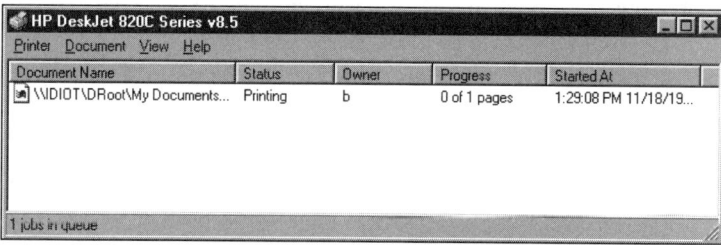

FIGURE 17-3   Print Manager

Task Manager

Task Manager is a special feature that enables you to switch between two or more programs that are running at the same time (see Figure 17.4). For example, if you were typing a letter in Microsoft Word, and then wanted to switch to your email program, you could call up Task Manager to change to the next program. In the world of computer terminology, this is known as *multitasking*, or working in more than one application at the same time.

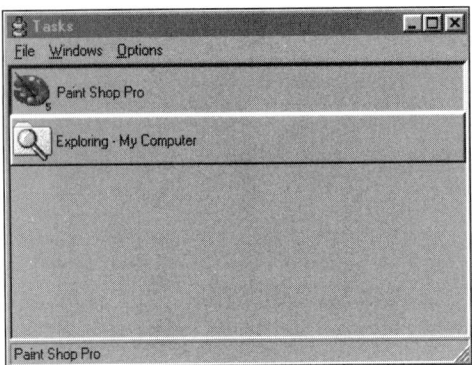

FIGURE 17-4   Task Manager

Task switching

You can use the Taskbar to switch between open windows. Just click the button on the Taskbar (represented with text and/or an icon) that represents the window you want to switch to. You can also use Alt+Tab to switch between various applications or documents. Or, in Windows 95, click Start, select Documents, and then choose a previous document you want to work with (see Figure 17-5).

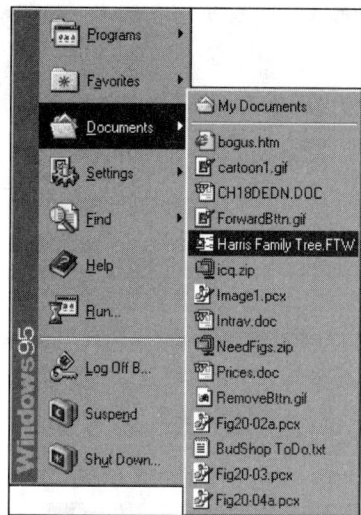

FIGURE 17-5 Start an application by choosing a document from the Start menu

Windows 3.1 Modules

The default components on the Windows 3.1 desktop are Program Manager, Control Panel, File Manager, Print Manager, Task Manager, and the Windows Initialization Files. *Default modules* are those modules that are automatically installed through a normal setup routine. To change the default modules and how they are displayed, you would use the Control Panel.

Program Manager

Figure 17-6 shows the Program Manager for Windows 3.1, with icons inside the window. If you double-click your left mouse button over a component, the component opens up another window, which presents you with choices on working with, or configuring that individual component. For example, if you are connected to a network, you can open up Program Manager and then double-click on another network drive to view its contents.

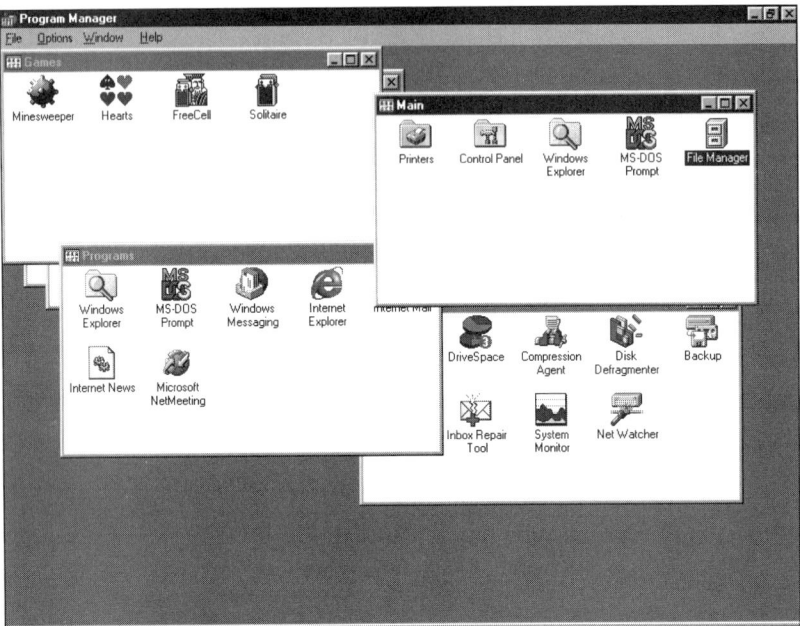

FIGURE 17-6 Program Manager

The Program Manager's function is to manage settings and groups. The PROGMAN.INI file is the initialization file for the Program Manager that is located in the Windows subdirectory. This file identifies which programs are shown in the Program Manager window when a user launches Microsoft Windows. Furthermore, Program Manager defines the appearance of each group. For example, the items within a group can be displayed as text only, or as large or small icons. Then within that category, you can determine whether you want to view filenames by name only, or whether to include details such as date and time stamping, or size of the file.

File Manager

The File Manager, as shown in Figure 17-7, is found only in Windows 3.1. It enables you to see all the files that are stored on your personal computer. With File Manager, you can create, save, move, and copy files to another location on your hard drive.

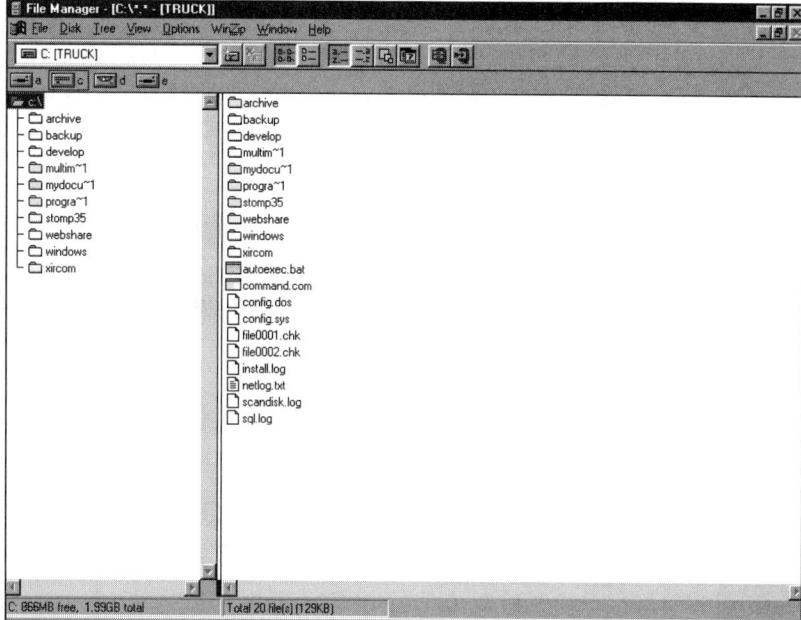

FIGURE 17-7 File Manager

Modes for running Windows 3.1

Windows 3.1 can run in either of two modes: Standard mode or 386 Enhanced mode. In both operating systems, the computer's processor runs in protected mode, which enables multitasking, data security, and virtual memory. The proper mode for each computer is automatically configured on startup. However, if you want to force Windows to start in a particular mode, you can use one of these switches when you start Windows from the command line:

- `win /s:` Start Windows 3.1 in Standard mode
- `win /e:` Start Windows 3.1 in 386 Enhanced mode

Windows 95 Components

The default components, which are installed automatically with a "Normal" install routine for Windows 95 are My Computer, Network Neighborhood, Recycle Bin, and the Microsoft Network. Each of these default components that appear as icons on the Windows 95 desktop are defined in the following sections.

My Computer

My Computer, as shown in Figure 17-8, is a Windows 95 component that helps the user get started by displaying as icons all the drives available to that desktop — Control Panel, printers, and dial-up networking.

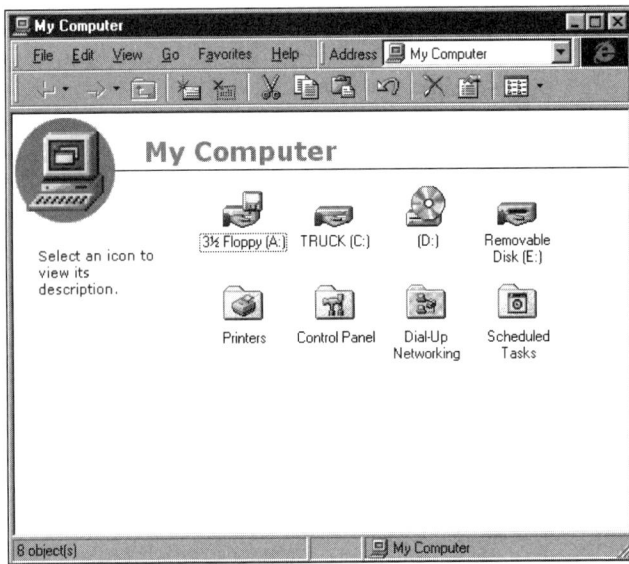

FIGURE 17-8   My Computer

Network Neighborhood

In Windows 95, the Network Neighborhood icon appears only if Setup detects a network connection. The user can explore local systems and files by clicking the icons.

Recycle Bin

In Windows 95, the Recycle Bin is a temporary storage area for deleted files. After dumping files into the Recycle Bin, you can later right-click on it and either retrieve the files, or select Empty Recycle Bin, which deletes all traces of the files after you're sure you're done. Most accidental deletions are discovered immediately after the user hits the Delete key, and after a few days, most users are safe emptying the bin. Deleted files continue to occupy disk space until the Recycle Bin is emptied.

Microsoft Network

The Microsoft Network is available if the option is selected during installation. The purpose of this component is to enable the user to access the Microsoft Network online service.

Start Button

The central point of access to Windows 95 is through the Start button (see Figure 17-9), which is located in the lower left corner of the screen unless the Taskbar has been moved elsewhere on the desktop (see the next section). From this Start button, users have access to various programs and files available within the Windows 95 operating system.

FIGURE 17-9 Access to Windows 95 through the Start button on the desktop

Taskbar

The bottom portion of the screen is called the *Taskbar*, as shown in Figure 17-10. The Taskbar is a common storage point for active programs that the user has opened. Also, the Taskbar gives you access to startup system functions as defined in programs at installation. Although the objects on the Taskbar are not configurable, the Taskbar can be moved to another location on the edge of the screen and can also be resized in height. For example, if you prefer to work with your Taskbar on the right side of your screen rather than along the bottom, just move your mouse pointer on top of the Taskbar, then hold down and click your left mouse button. Drag the Taskbar to the right side of your screen and release the mouse button. Your Taskbar will now be located on the right side of your screen, on the desktop.

FIGURE 17-10 Windows 95 Taskbar located at the bottom of the screen

Explorer

With Explorer, you can browse through your list of files like you did in Windows 3.1 with File Manager.

The Windows 95 desktop is where all the action in Windows originates, so the top of the naming hierarchy is called *Desktop*. At the next organizational level are three folders: My Computer, Network Neighborhood, and Recycle Bin. My Computer is the parent folder for all disks attached to your own computer, including hard disks, floppy drives, and CD-ROM drives. Network Neighborhood is a folder comprising all network servers in your immediate workgroup. Through Network Neighborhood, you can also view and work with network servers beyond the immediate workgroup. The Recycle Bin is where deleted folders, files, and shortcuts go until you empty the trash, at which point such items are gone for good and deleted from your computer.

Folders

A *folder* is a bin for storing files and other folders. To move from one point to another within the Windows 95 structure, you simply double-click My Computer and then double-click each subfolder in turn. Depending on how you've set Windows browsing options, your screen might then display a proliferation of folder windows (see Figure 17-11).

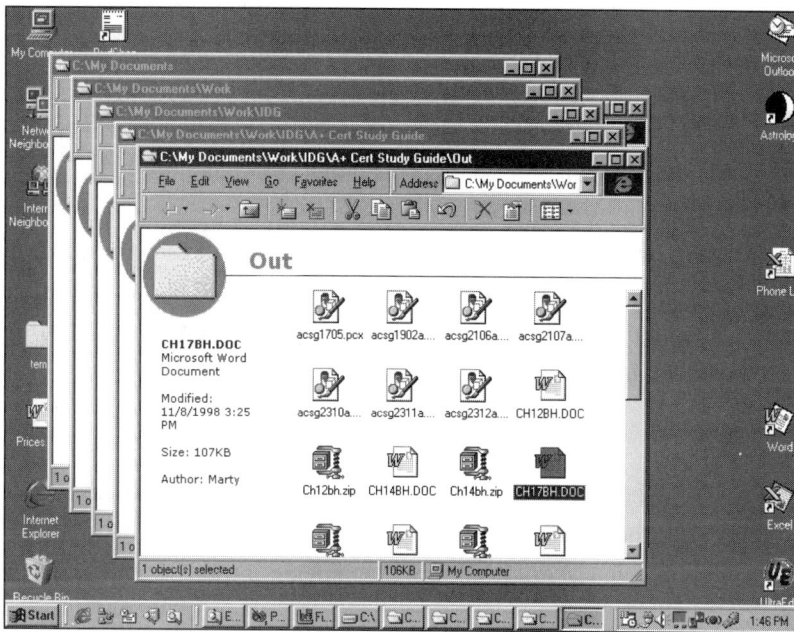

FIGURE 17-11   Windows 95 folders

By default, when you double-click a folder icon in a folder window, the newly opened folder appears in a separate window, and the window for the parent folder (the one containing the newly opened folder) remains open. This separate-window browsing mode is shown in Figure 17-11.

The advantage of the separate-window mode is that it lets you see the parent folder and the new folder at the same time. To return to the parent folder, you simply click back to that folder window or press the Backspace key. You can also reselect the parent window by pressing Alt+Tab.

The disadvantage of this mode is that it tends to clutter your screen when you search through several layers of subfolders. However, you can switch to the single-window browsing mode, and then a newly opened folder window replaces its parent window.

MS-DOS prompt

In Windows 95, you can open an MS-DOS window by clicking the Start button, pointing to Programs, and then clicking the MS-DOS prompt (see Figure 17-2). You would use the MS-DOS prompt when you want to view or access MS-DOS-based programs or for performing command-line commands outside the Windows shell. Also, many games are run in MS-DOS mode, and must be run in a DOS shell, because they are not programmed to work in a Windows environment. Also, for those users who grew up using MS-DOS as their first computer operating system, they are more familiar with command-line programming than working within the Windows interface. However, as users have become more familiar with the Windows operating system, they are less likely to use command-line commands.

For example, to view and delete all the .TMP files from the temporary directory on the hard disk of your computer, you would type this MS-DOS command at the MS-DOS prompt:

```
DIR C:\Windows\Temp
```

When all of the files are displayed on your screen, then type: **DEL *.TMP** to delete the unneeded .TMP files from your computer. By deleting the .TMP files, you free up disk space on your computer.

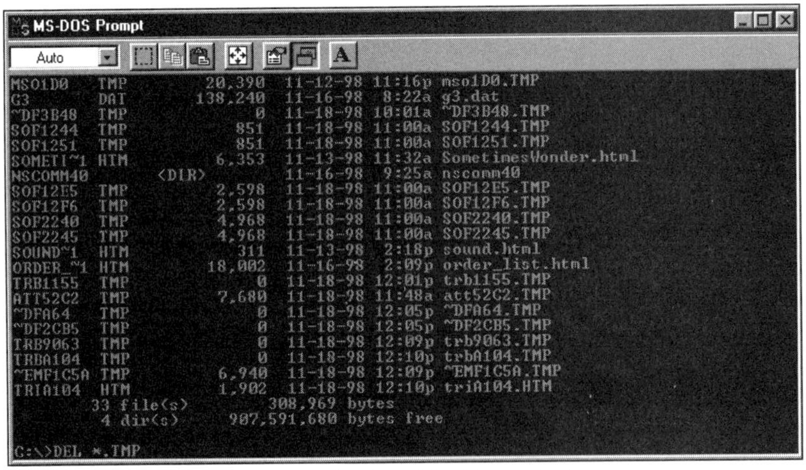

FIGURE 17-12 MS-DOS prompt displayed inside a window

Run command

To use the Run command (see Figure 17-13), you click the Start button, and then click Run. You can run MS-DOS-based and Windows-based programs, open folders, and connect to network resources by using the Run command.

For example, you can type **Setup.exe** or **Install.exe** to create or modify your existing programs.

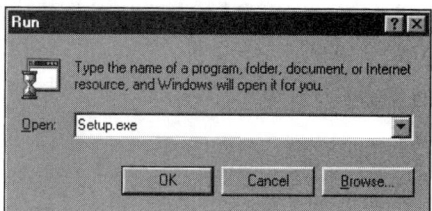

FIGURE 17-13 Run command

Close button

To close a window in Windows 95, you click the large "x" button located in the upper-right corner of the window. The Close button is located next to the Minimize and Maximize buttons. Or, another way of closing a program is to double-click on the left-most top corner of the application window.

ARCHITECTURE

Windows 3.1 architecture is based on a 16-bit operating system, whereas Windows 95 is based on a 32-bit operating system. The 32-bit system is fully integrated, has a protected mode operating system that eliminates the need for MS-DOS, and provides multitasking and multithreading support that improves system response time and background processing.

Real mode is an operating mode of Intel microprocessors in which a program is given a definite storage location in memory and direct access to peripheral devices. *Protected mode* is an operating mode that supports virtual memory (which uses space on your hard drive to simulate memory and accesses other memory using techniques such as paging) and enables multitasking, in which two or more programs can run and use the computer's memory simultaneously without conflict.

Multitasking means running several applications at the same time, whereas *multithreading* enables different tasks in a single application to execute concurrently. When properly implemented, these features can enable multiple tasks to occur simultaneously with minimal impact on the performance of the foreground application. Response time is improved with Windows 95 because of the faster Win32 operating system, which allows users to more quickly access, save, and retrieve their files. Background processing allows applications to run while users are working on other files. For example, if you are saving a large file in Microsoft Word, you can switch to an email program to view your incoming mail without either program slowing down. With Windows 3.1, you could only work in one application at a time.

Core Windows Files

Three files in the system directory of Windows 3.1 define the core of the Windows environment. These files are located in the `C:\Windows\System` subdirectory. The core Windows files are:

- The kernel files (`KRNL286.EXE` or `KRNL386.EXE`), which manage the computer's memory, load applications, and schedule program execution and other tasks.

- The user file (`USER.EXE`), which executes all requests to create, move, size, and delete a window or an icon. Commands are executed mainly through the keyboard or mouse.

- The graphics file (`GDI.EXE`), which executes all graphic operations so those images can be created.

Driver Files

The Windows 3.1 driver files provide hardware-specific interfaces between your computer's physical devices and the core files. Driver files include specifications for device, system, keyboard, mouse, display, printer, network, and multimedia files.

Fonts

Fonts support the display and output devices for the system, Windows and non-Windows applications running in Windows, and clipboard data. Font files often have filename extensions of `.TTF`, `.FON`, or `.FOT`. The four basic types of fonts are system, fixed, TrueType, and OEM.

Installable File Systems for Windows 95

Windows 95 uses a layered file system architecture, which supports a multiple file system, including VFAT and CDFS. A layered file system architecture that supports a multiple file system is one that enables the operating system to work with several configurations, including MS-DOS, Win16, and Win32 environments. VFAT is the 32-bit file allocation table that keeps track of all the files maintained on your computer. CDFS stands for the *CD-ROM File System*. The input/output performance in Windows 95 is dramatically improved over Windows 3.1. File system drivers are low-level components of the operating system, which provides support for:

o The 32-bit FAT (VFAT) driver, which is a virtual file allocation table driver that works in the Windows 95 environment.

o The 32-bit CD-ROM file system (CDFS) driver, which is installed automatically by Windows 95 for automatically configuring the virtual file allocation systems.

o The 32-bit network redirector, for connection to the Microsoft Network servers like Windows NT Server, and a 32-bit network redirector to NetWare servers.

VFAT is compatible with the existing DOS file allocation system. All DOS disks that were partitioned and formatted as FAT partitions can be read and written to by VFAT. This includes hard disks and removable media, including diskettes. FAT16 drivers operate in the Windows 3.1 operating system. The 32-bit VFAT driver interacts with the block I/O (input/output) subsystem to provide access to more device types than are supported by Windows 3.1. Windows 95 also supports mapping to any real-mode disk drivers that might be installed.

The Windows 95 file system architecture is made up of these components:

- *Installable File System* (IFS) Manager, which is responsible for giving access to different file system components.

- File system drivers layer that gives access to FAT-based disk devices, CD-ROM file system, and redirected network device support.

- Block I/O subsystem, which interacts with the physical disk device.

Microsoft Windows Swap File

A *swap file* is a large, hidden system file created by Microsoft Windows that stores program instructions and data that won't fit in the computer's RAM. Swap files can be either temporary (`WIN386.SWP`) or permanent (`SPART.PAR` and `386PART.PAR`). (Warning: Do not delete, move, or rename these files.) The *permanent swap file* is a disk file composed of contiguous disk sectors that are set aside for the rapid storage and retrieval of program instructions or data in the program's 386 Enhanced mode. Because storage areas used in a permanent swap file are contiguous, storage and retrieval operations exceed the normal speed of hard disk operations, which usually distribute data here and there on the disk. The permanent swap file, however, consumes a large amount of space on the disk. A *temporary swap file* is a disk file that's created only while Windows is running and is used for the storage and retrieval of program instructions or data in the program's 386 Enhanced mode. This storage space is used for virtual memory, which uses disk space as a seamless extension of RAM.

A swap file is set aside for exclusive use by the *Virtual Memory Manager* (VMM). The VMM transfers information from memory to the swap file to free physical memory for other applications. Swap files are supported only on disks that use 512-byte sectors. Windows 3.1 uses virtual memory to enable an application to address more memory than the computer actually has.

Virtual memory is known as a swap file that exchanges data on your computer system as it is being read and written to the disk. The swap file in Windows 95 is dynamic and can shrink or grow, based on the operations performed on the system. In Windows 3.1, you had to set the file size of the swap file (see Figure 17-14). The swap file can occupy a fragmented region of the hard drive and it can be located on a compressed disk volume.

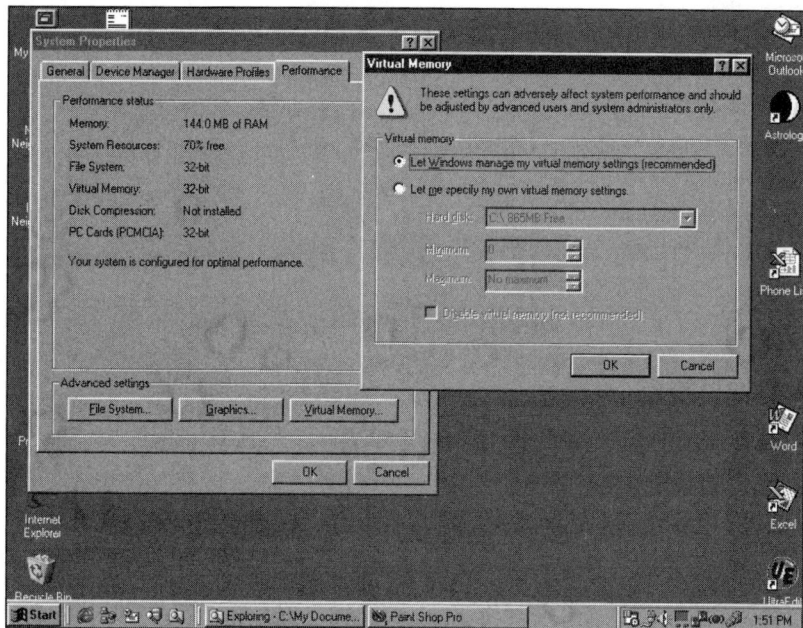

FIGURE 17-14 Virtual memory and swap file configuration

In 386 Enhanced mode, Windows makes optimal use of memory by swapping, which moves those pages that have not been recently referenced. In Standard mode, an application swap file is created each time a non-Windows application starts. When task switching, Windows moves some or all of the application to the temporary swap file to make more memory available to the new task. Application swap files are created in the directory specified by the Swapdisk setting in SYSTEM.INI.

Assuming that the same application is being run, a computer with 8MB of memory performs more swapping than a computer with 16MB of memory. The computer with the 16MB performs fewer memory management operations than the computer with 8MB.

Windows 3.1 Memory Architecture

The paging system is part of the Windows architecture and implements a virtual memory technique where the memory is divided into fixed-sized blocks called *pages*. A page is a fixed-size block of RAM. There are two kinds of pages: physical and virtual.

Memory Paging for Windows 95

Windows 95 uses a demand-paged virtual memory system, which is based on a flat, linear address space accessed using 32-bit addresses. Each 32-bit application can access up to 2GB of addressable memory space. In demand paging, code and data are moved in pages from physical memory to a temporary paging file on disk. When the information is requested again by an application or a process, it is paged back into physical memory.

Picture a two-drawer file cabinet. When you open a file folder inside one of the file drawers, you can take out a document to review at your desk, and you can put a paper placeholder inside the folder telling you that you temporarily removed some of its contents. This lets you return your papers back to their designated place when you're finished with them. The same is true with paging. Basically, it moves information from a permanent, physical memory position to a temporary paging file so you can work with the data. When you are finished working with the data, it is paged or moved back into physical memory.

As the application is executed, virtual pages of the application are assigned to physical memory and referenced. The *Virtual Memory Manager* (VMM) page table maps the process's virtual addresses to physical addresses. When the application executes, only the required pages of the application are read from the disk into memory. A *page fault* is an interruption that results when software requests a memory location that is not already in physical memory. Virtual memory lets an application address more memory than the computer actually has. Thus, paging enables the computer to store only those application pages into physical memory locations that are currently being used (see Figure 17-15).

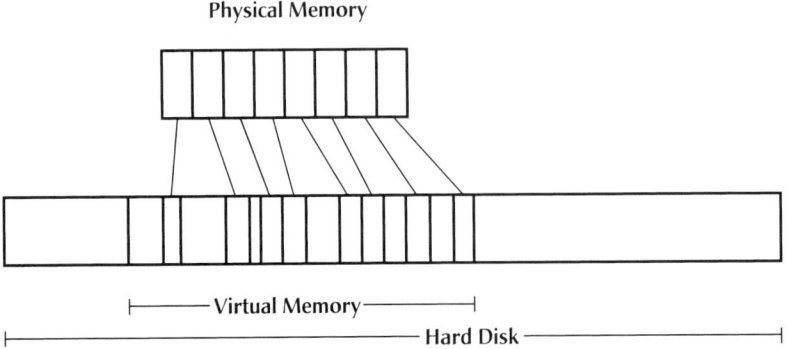

FIGURE 17-15 Virtual memory enables you to use space on your hard drive as an extension of memory.

To recap, paging implements a virtual memory technique where the memory is divided into fixed-size blocks called pages. The two types of pages are physical and virtual. To determine the amount of physical pages on a computer, divide the amount of physical memory by four. For example, a computer with 8MB of memory has 2,046K pages of physical memory. When an application is compiled, the compiler assigns addresses within the program to virtual pages.

Windows 95 Redirectors

A network redirector provides a way to locate, open, read, write, and delete files and print jobs that exist on computers other than your own. Some examples of redirectors are application services like named pipes and mail slots. Named pipes provide backward compatibility with existing LAN manager installations and applications (common on Windows NT 3.51). Named pipes provide an easy-to-access conduit for a one-to-one, reliable, connection-oriented data transfer between two processes. These two processes are normally differentiated as a server process (the one that creates and manages the named pipe) and a client process (the one that connects to the named pipe). Windows 95 supports client-side named pipes for Microsoft networks, allowing you to connect to named-pipes applications on a Windows NT server or workstation. Server-side named pipes are not supported on Windows 95.

The named-pipe server process creates the pipe and manages access to it. The resources that make up the pipe are owned by the server process and physically exist on the workstation where the server process is running. The named-pipe client process uses the services of the underlying network protocols to access the remote pipe resources. Although named pipes are usually used bidirectionally, the pipe can be configured to allow communication in only one direction, such as from server to client.

Mailslots provide backward compatibility with existing LAN manager installations and applications. Mailslot *application programming interfaces* (APIs) in Windows 95 and Windows NT are a subset of the APIs in Microsoft OS/2 LAN Manager. Clients for Microsoft Network make the Mailslots API available for applications that use mailslots for interprocess communication.

Mailslots can be used for one-to-one or one-to-many communications. A mailslot can be created on any network workstation. When a message is sent to a mailslot, the sending application specifies in the mailslot message structure whether the message is to be sent using first-class or second-class delivery.

First-class delivery is a session-oriented, guaranteed data transfer for one-to-one or one-to-many communication. Messages designated as first-class delivery can only be sent to a mailslot that was created on the server. Note: Windows 95 does not use first-class messaging.

Second-class delivery is a datagram-based, unguaranteed data transfer for one-to-one and many-to-one communication. Messages designated as second-class delivery can be sent to a mailslot that was created on any workstation, or even on multiple workstations, if the message size is 400 bytes or less.

Windows 95 and Windows NT implement only second-class mailslots, which are most useful for identifying other computers or services on a network and for wide-scale identification of a service. Windows 95 uses second-class mailslots for WinPopup messages and browsing.

The following two files are the redirectors included in Windows 95 network client software as file system drives:

- `VREDIR.VXD:` This driver supports all networks based on Microsoft networking and uses the *Server Message Block* (SMB) file-sharing protocol.

- `NWREDIR.VXD:` This driver is the redirector that supports NetWare networking products, which use the *NetWare Core Protocol* (NCP) file-sharing protocol.

Plug and Play Devices

A Plug and Play device is one that automatically configures itself to use available resources on the computer, then reports which resources it is using to the operating system. Plug and Play devices free the user from having to manually configure hardware resources. To use Plug and Play features, the operating system, BIOS, motherboard, and device must all support Plug and Play. Windows 95 is a Plug and Play aware operating system. For more information about Plug and Play, refer back to Chapter 7.

When the Plug and Play BIOS is installed on the computer, Windows 95 Setup performs an inventory of all devices on the computer and records information about those devices in the Registry. To add new Plug and Play devices, follow these steps:

1. From the Start menu, select Settings, and then select Control Panel.

2. Choose Add New Hardware, and let the wizard guide you through the process of installing new hardware.

Types of Memory

The Windows 3.1 and Windows 95 operating systems require a minimum amount of memory to run and process operating system requests. Although this type of memory is physical hardware, when we refer to types of memory, we are talking about how memory is used within the operating system itself. To better understand the various memory types and how each is used, we've defined them here:

- **Conventional memory:** The first 640K of memory available on your computer.

- **Extended memory:** An upward extension of the original 1MB address space available on 286 and 386 computers. Extended memory starts at 1,024K, where the upper memory area ends.

- **Expanded memory:** Can be installed as an expanded memory card or through EMM as an extended memory manager.

FILE AND PRINT MANAGEMENT

File management is the process of organizing files and directories on your computer. In Windows 3.1, the program that handles file management is called File Manager. In Windows 95, it is Explorer. Both File Manager and Explorer can move, copy, delete, rename, and search for files or directories on your personal computer or a computer on the network.

Printing is managed through the Print Manager in both Windows 3.1 and Windows 95. You can find the Print Manager under Control Panel. In Windows 95, you can also find it from My Computer, from the Start Menu under Settings, and from Control Panel.

The Print Manager can print files and documents in the background while you continue to work on other applications. When multiple files are sent to the printer, they are stored in a print queue.

With both file and print management, you can click and drag filenames to any desired location. For example, if Explorer was open, you could click on a filename to highlight it, and then you could drag it to the printer icon and drop it on the icon. Your document would automatically start to print.

File and Print Sharing

Windows 95 supports file and print sharing for Microsoft networks and for NetWare networks. If you installed file and printer sharing for Microsoft networks or NetWare networks, you could then share your resources with other people on the network. Resources include programs, documents and other files, and printers. When you share resources, you make them available to other network users to connect to and use. To share files, you share the folder they are in.

OLE Capabilities

Object linking and embedding (OLE) supports the transferring and sharing of information between applications. The information that is shared is referred to as an *object*, and objects are considered encapsulated data and must be created in a Windows application that supports OLE.

An *embedded object* is an object located in a destination document that is an exact copy of information created in another application. Because an embedded object is only a copy, any modifications made to the embedded object are not reflected in the source document. Therefore, if you want to update all embedded objects, you must change the source document.

Both Windows 3.1 and Windows 95 support OLE capabilities. Linking and embedding objects are similar to cut and paste, except that the item being pasted is not just plain text or graphics, but rather it is an object that contains information that can be updated transparently and automatically each time the application is started.

For example, you can link data from two documents and store it in a third document that just shows the results to your users.

The following is the process you would use to link and embed objects:

1. Create the object in a source document.

2. Open the destination document, move the cursor to the location where you want to insert the object, and then choose the Insert Object, Cut, Copy, or Paste From command. (These options are visible when you right-click your mouse button.)

3. Specify the filename of the source document where the object is located, or choose the name of the application you used to create the object.

4. Choose the command to embed or link the object: Update, Insert Object, or Paste Link.

In Windows 95, OLE information used in Windows and OLE applications is stored as a Class subkey in the Windows Registry. The Windows Registry is arranged in a hierarchical format (see figure 17-16), and can be accessed by clicking Start ⇒ Run, and then typing **regedit.exe**.

 caution **Do not tamper with or alter any settings in the Windows Registry unless you are an advanced user. Changing settings in the Registry could result in an inoperable system.**

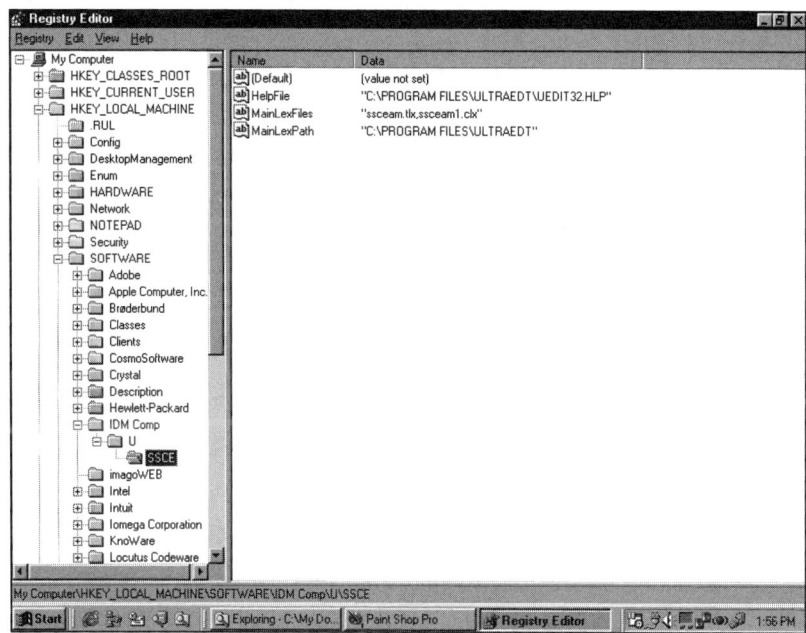

FIGURE 17-16   **Registry trees**

A *subkey* is a second-level heading, or grouping, in the Registry's hierarchical structure. The HKEY_CLASSES_ROOT section of the Registry lists all the subkeys (filename extensions) that you could possibly ever need for running an application. For example, one of the subkeys is .DOC, the filename extension for Word documents.

The Classes subkey has two types of subkeys:

- Filename-extension subkeys that specify the class definition associated with files that have a selected extension.
- Class-definition keys that specify the shell and OLE properties of a class or type of document.

OPTIMIZATION AND PERFORMANCE

System performance refers to the speed and efficiency of a system while a broad set of tasks is being carried out. For example, you might measure the performance of a system while running a group of applications and programs that are normally run simultaneously. The term *performance* also refers to the capability of individual system components or subsystems to perform a more narrow set of tasks such as file input/output (I/O) operations. When these programs and systems are optimized, it means that they are running at their most efficient and fastest rate possible for that operating system.

Windows 3.1

To achieve optimum performance in Windows 3.1, you should do the following:

- Modify virtual memory by enlarging the swap file and making the permanent file larger than what is currently shown. You can access the virtual memory windows through the Control Panel.
- Eliminate unnecessary files from your hard drive.
- Load device drivers and the operating system into the correct memory location. With Windows 3.1, you can type **MEM** at the MS-DOS prompt to see how the memory allocations are distributed and where your files are located. Viewing this information will allow you to change memory settings in your computer's files.
- Set up swap files large enough to handle the tasks you perform normally. If you find that your computer applications are running extremely slow, and your operating system is having an extremely hard time saving and recalling information, it's very possible that your swap file is too small.

Enlarging the amount of disk space dedicated to your swap file can sometimes increase performance.

o Run MS-DOS in high memory and not in conventional memory by specifying DOS=HIGH in your CONFIG.SYS file.

o Streamline CONFIG.SYS and AUTOEXEC.BAT by removing unnecessary files and batch files.

o Set the buffers to 30 when using MS-DOS 5 or later by typing **BUFFERS=30** in your CONFIG.SYS file.

o Free extended memory and run HIMEM.SYS or another extended-memory manager.

o Use Smartdrive as a disk-caching program.

You can find more information about the last four items on this list in Chapter 13.

Windows 95

Optimization is set up automatically when you install Windows 95. The only tweaking you really should do on a frequent basis is to defragment your hard drive. Defragmenting your hard drive improves your computer's performance and processing speed for retrieving documents.

Defragmention is a procedure in which all the files on a hard drive are rewritten on disk so that all parts of each file are written to contiguous sectors. The result is an up to seventy-five percent improvement in speed during retrieval operations. During normal operations, the files on a hard disk eventually become fragmented, so that parts of a file are written all over the disk, which slows down retrieval operations.

To defragment your hard drive in Windows 95, follow these steps:

1. Click Start, then select Programs ⇒ Accessories ⇒ System Tools ⇒ Disk Defragmenter.

2. Choose a drive to defragment, and then click OK.

You can also execute the defragmentation process from the MS-DOS prompt. At the MS-DOS prompt, type **DEFRAG** and then press Enter.

Modifying the System Settings File for Windows 3.1

The system settings are modified in the SETUP.SHH file. Table 17-1 describes each section.

TABLE 17-1 SYSTEM SETTINGS	
[sysinfo]	Specifies whether System Configuration screen should appear during Setup.
[configuration]	Specifies various system devices.
[windir]	Indicates where Windows files are located.
[userinfo]	Displays the user and company name.
[dontinstall]	Indicates which components not to install.
[options]	Specifies Setup options such as README.
[printers]	Displays printers to set up.
[endinstall]	Indicates if CONFIG.SYS and AUTOEXEC.BAT are modified and if the system is rebooted.

Windows 3.1 Initialization Files

Following are the names and descriptions of each initialization file. These files make up the Windows 3.1 system. You can modify them by opening them in a text editor and saving each file, but it's especially important that you make a backup copy of the file before you begin altering it.

- WIN.INI: Defines your customized Windows environment
- SYSTEM.INI: Defines how Windows will work
- CONTROL.INI: Defines the icons in the Control Panel window
- WINFILE.INI: Defines the look and behavior of the File Manager
- APPLICATION.INI: A specific Windows application initialization file
- PROGMAN.INI: Identifies which programs are part of the Program Manager window

System Directory Files

The Windows system directory is filled with files that Windows uses to handle its normal operations. Several system directory files are necessary for Windows to operate correctly. Though you should be aware of the general purpose of these files, you'll rarely have occasion to work with them because they're such low-level files. Generally, only Microsoft will modify these files, and then only when they release a new version of the operating system.

Kernel files

KRNL286.EXE or KRNL386.EXE are kernel files that manage the computer's memory, load applications, and schedule program execution.

User file

The user filename is USER.EXE. It manages all requests to create, move, size, and delete a window or icon.

Graphics file

The GDI.EXE file runs all graphic operations to create images.

Swap file

A swap file is an area on your hard disk that's used exclusively for *Virtual Memory Manager* (VMM). The VMM transfers data from memory to the swap file, which then frees physical memory for other applications.

Paging system

When memory is divided into fixed-sized blocks, these are called pages. There are two types of pages — physical and virtual.

A page fault is an interrupt that results when software requests a memory location that is not already in physical memory.

Virtual memory

Virtual memory allows an application to address more memory than the computer actually has.

Protected mode

This is an operating mode that supports multitasking, data security, and virtual memory for the Intel 80286 and higher processors. Backfilling designates memory on an expanded memory card.

VCPI

Virtual Control Program Interface (VCPI) allows applications using MS-DOS extenders to run simultaneously with expanded memory manager.

LIM

Lotus/Intel/Microsoft expanded memory manager.

DPMI

DOS Protected Mode Interface (DPMI) provides a standard method for applications to switch the 80286 to protected mode and to allocate extended memory.

KEY POINT SUMMARY

This Chapter covered Microsoft Windows 3.1, Microsoft Windows 95, and Microsoft Windows 98 operating Systems.

- Windows 3.1 was an early and highly successful attempt to create a graphical user interface, or GUI. This interface allowed the user to manage files, configure some hardware settings, and manage systems resources from a screen or dialog box. Windows 95 was a significant upgrade in capability that largely simplified the capabilities of the end user to manage systems resources.

- Windows 3.1 operated in two modes: Standard mode or 386 Enhanced mode. 386 Enhanced mode allowed the system to fully utilize virtual memory and other advanced capabilities of the system. Windows maintained a set of files that indicated given parameters for the environment. These files were called .INI files. To change parameters of the system, these files had to either be edited by applications under Windows or by the end user using a text editor.

- Windows 95 represents a significant improvement over the Windows 3.1 environment, because the end user can almost completely configure the system using the Settings dialog box.

- Windows 95 stores files in folders. These folders can be managed using either Explorer or the My Computer window. Explorer manages files simply and easily. All of the capabilities for management are provided on the Explorer tool bar. Explorer is accessed either from the Start tab or by right-clicking the mouse over the resource you want to explore in the My Computer tab.

- The traditional MS-DOS prompts are available by running the command prompt from the Start bar. Programs can be run directly using the DOS subsystem by using the Run command from the Start bar.

- Both Windows 3.1 and Windows 95 use files called driver files. Driver files interface hardware devices to the operating system. Windows 3.1 requires that the drivers be installed manually for each device. Windows 95 provides a capability called Plug and Play that automatically checks for hardware devices, and then attempts to install the devices automatically. For most common devices, Windows 95 will have a driver already available. If that is the case, Windows 95 will automatically install the driver. If the driver is not available, it will prompt the user for the driver files.

- Windows 95 provides support for all of the major PC buses in use today. This includes PCI, ISA, EISA, VLB, MCA, and SCSI. Windows 95 systems are generally much easier to integrate and install hardware on than are comparable Windows 3.1 systems.

- A key feature of the Windows environment is the capability to allow programs to communicate to each other. This is called an *object linking and embedding* (OLE). OLE lets you link and embed data within your applications, so that when information changes, the object it's linked to will be automatically updated. OLE tools are used extensively in the Office environment to link data from one application into another.

APPLYING WHAT YOU'VE LEARNED

This chapter has covered a lot of important material that will help you prepare for the A+ exam and be an excellent computer technician. Take a few minutes and work through the questions in the Instant Assessment, then review your notes and see how you did.

The Hands-on lab will also help you build your comfort level with the hardware as well as reinforce the readings from this chapter.

Instant Assessment

Multiple choice

1. To check for upper memory conflicts at system startup, which of the following commands would you use?

   A. `win /d:x`

   B. `win d:/f`

   C. `win /d:v`

   D. Press F8

2. Is it possible to set up a shortcut to launch an application from the Windows 95 desktop?

   A. No

   B. Yes

   C. Only if you're running `AUTOEXEC.BAT` on startup

   D. Only if you right-click the application's icon

3. To use all Plug and Play features, your system must include which of the following:

   A. Plug and Play BIOS

   B. A modem Microsoft Windows backup software

   C. A PCCARD sound card

4. Which mouse action copies an object to another location?

   A. Ctrl+drag and drop

   B. Shift+drag and drop

   C. Shift+Ctrl+drag and drop

   D. Click+drag and drop

5. Which box in the Property sheet would you check to allow other applications to run concurrently with an MS-DOS based application?

   A. Advanced

   B. Memory

   C. Screen

   D. Miscellaneous

6. Which remote administration tool would you use to manage computers remotely in the local workgroup?

   A. Network Neighborhood

   B. Net Watch

   C. Performance Monitor

   D. File and Printer Sharing Manager

7. How many subtrees of keys are contained in the Registry structure?

   A. 6

   B. 4

   C. 10

   D. 27

8. Which of the following is not part of memory management?

   A. Physical addresses

   B. Page faults

   C. Swap files

   D. Multitasking

9. The dynamic link library that handles the base operating system functions of Windows is (choose all that apply):

   A. GDI.EXE

   B. USER.EXE

   C. HEAP.EXE

   D. KRNLxxx.EXE

Fill in the blank

1. To establish network connections to start every time with Windows 3.1, you would modify the _____ file.

2. To set up a server on a Windows 3.1 network, you must type this command to expand and copy all the files to a named directory and set attributes to "read only" — _____.

3. A technical term for simulating additional memory for an application is

   _____.

4. A physical address in the upper memory where a page of expanded memory can be mapped is called _____.

5. To create packages, you would use the _____ to create an icon that represents the object.

6. Which core system component provides base operating system functionality such as file I/O services, virtual memory management, and task scheduling? _____.

7. If you want to update data in a report without retyping information, you would _____.

8. The purpose of safe mode in Windows 95 is

   _____.

9. _____ is the file you would use to have direct access to the Registry for a local or remote computer.

Hands-on Lab Exercises

These labs focus on some of the capabilities of the Windows 95 environment. The labs will identify the hardware characteristics, as well as the OLE capabilities of a Windows 95 system.

Lab 17-17 *Working with Explorer*

In this lab, we will use Explorer to examine the Windows folder. The first step in this lab will be to open the My Computer icon and right-click on drive C. Figure 17-17 illustrates this. As you can see, this system has several drives and resources, each identified by a symbol. The options are displayed by right-clicking the mouse on the drive we want to examine.

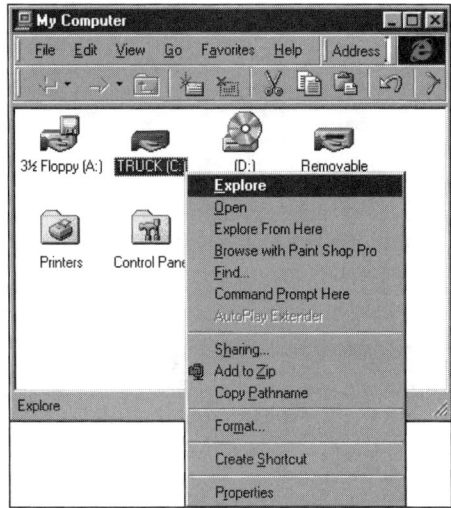

FIGURE 17-17   **The disks and folders under the My Computer folder**

When the Explore option is selected, the Explorer window opens. Figure 17-18 illustrates the Explorer window. Notice that two areas are displayed below the tool bar. The left side of the screen displays the folders on the drive, while the right side shows the files and folders that are under the selected option. In this example, we are displaying the files that exist under the Commands subfolder. These commands are the standard DOS commands that can be accessed using the Run command on the Start bar.

Explorer can then be used to add, delete, or otherwise alter the characteristics of the files. For example, we can add a folder by right-clicking in the large window. This opens up a bar that provides several options. Figure 17-19 shows this happening. The right-click also enables several other options to manipulate files. Try some of the other options to see what happens.

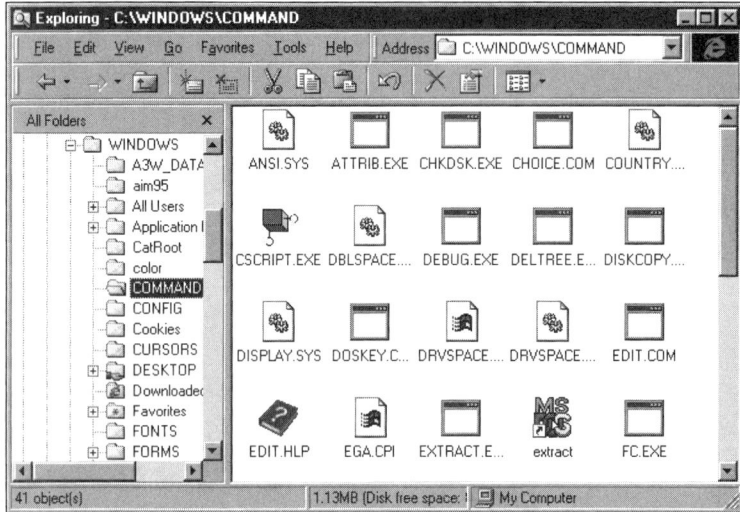

FIGURE 17-18   The files that exist under the Commands subdirectory under the Windows folder

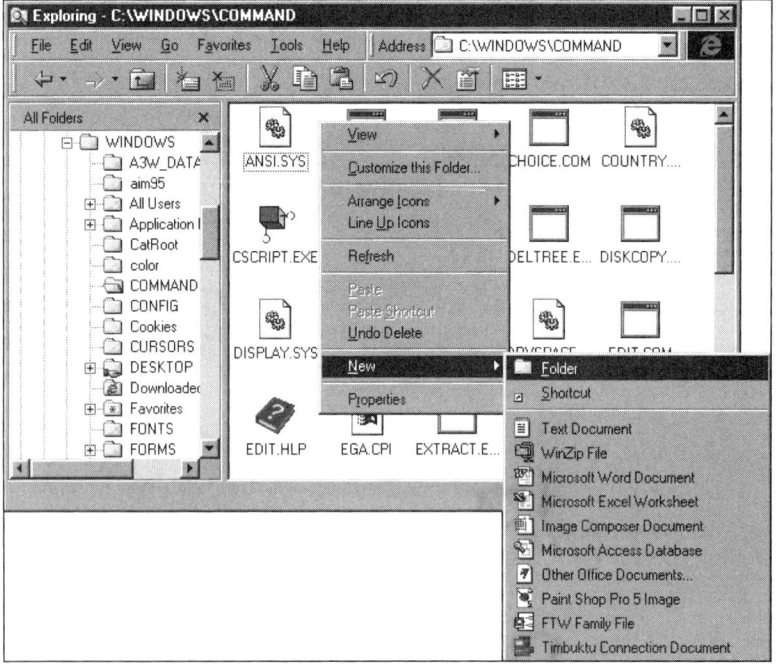

FIGURE 17-19   Creating a new folder in Explorer.

Lab 17-18 *Working with OLE objects*

This lab demonstrates the OLE capabilities of Word and Excel. We will create a graph in Excel and link it to Word. Then we will change the graph in Excel and see the values change in the document. When we double-click the graph, the OLE container or frame opens, giving us the ability to change the data on the graph. When we click out of the graph, the data changes back to the presentation mode. This enables the integration of text, graphics, and spreadsheets to be fairly easy for the end user to accomplish. Windows 3.1 supported some of this capability, but it is much more fully developed in the Windows 95 and Windows NT environments.

DOS/Windows Systems

Configuring Windows 95 Systems

About Chapter 18

This chapter explores the various ways you can configure Windows 95 systems. We'll cover some aspects of working with hardware, software, the file system, system analysis and optimization, and the Registry. Each of these components is important for management and system administrators in any computer environment.

First, this chapter will explore hardware components and software interaction. Then we'll cover how to use software configuration tools such as the Registry Editor, and explain how to work with the file system. Finally, we'll tell you about system optimization and how to make Windows 95 systems perform more efficiently.

HARDWARE COMPONENTS

In this section, we'll explain some of the basics about how Windows 95 interacts with a system's hardware. We'll show you the minimum hardware requirements for running Windows 95, explain how it works with Plug and Play devices, introduce you to the Device manager, and explain how Windows 95 works with PC Cards.

Before you can install Windows 95 on a computer, the computer needs to meet some basic hardware requirements. The following table outlines the requirements necessary for this operating system. The actual requirements are somewhere north of this. The best way we've heard it described is if you were happy with the way the system below ran Windows 3.1, then you'll be happy with it running Windows 95. The requirements shown in Table 18-1 are bare minimums.

TABLE 18-1 HARDWARE COMPONENTS FOR RUNNING WINDOWS 95

COMPONENT	MICROSOFT WINDOWS 95 REQUIREMENT
Computer	386 or higher processor with a mouse, high-density floppy disk drive, and a hard disk drive
Disk Space	30MB of free hard disk space
Memory	8MB of RAM minimum; 12MB recommended
Video Display	VGA minimum, Super VGA recommended

Partition Requirements

Microsoft Windows 95 is designed for computers that use Intel x86-based processors; a *file allocation table* (FAT) partition is required and must exist on the hard disk. If a FAT partition does not exist on the computer, then you cannot install Microsoft Windows 95. Some other common file systems are *High-Performance File System* (HPFS), which is used primarily with IBM's OS/2 and *NT File System* (NTFS), the secure file system used with Windows NT. Windows 95 cannot read disks formatted with either of these file systems, so any data that you want to use in Windows 95 must be stored on a FAT partition.

Microsoft Windows 95 can be installed over existing MS-DOS FAT partitions if the partition is large enough to include swap files and accommodate Microsoft Windows 95 files. In addition, the partition can recognize a removable media drive such as Zip drives, or Iomega Jaz drives. The FAT system has existed since the early days of DOS. This system has a maximum space allocation of 2GB. In 1997, Microsoft released a new version of the FAT called FAT-32. The previous version of FAT is now referred to as FAT-16. The FAT-32 system allows for partition sizes beyond the 2GB limit of FAT-16.

If you are using Windows NT, Microsoft Windows 95 cannot be installed on the NTFS partition. You must configure your computer with a multiple-boot system option because Microsoft Windows 95 cannot recognize information on an NTFS partition.

If you plan to use OS/2 or Windows NT, then Microsoft Windows 95 must be run from MS-DOS, and you must configure the computer as a dual-boot system between MS-DOS and OS/2, and MS-DOS and Windows NT.

Plug and Play

Plug and Play is designed to aid in the configuration of ISA devices under the Windows 95 operating system. Given the difficulty of configuring multiple peripheral cards manually, the Plug and Play BIOS standard was established to make the configuration process easier.

When you use Plug and Play, it improves the use of multimedia devices by automatically recognizing and configuring hardware and software for you. For example, it would recognize a CD-ROM drive, or a new modem, once it's installed.

Requirements for Plug and Play

To use Plug and Play features with Microsoft Windows 95, you must have a system with a Plug and Play BIOS and the Windows 95 operating system.

When you have Plug and Play compliant devices, you can:

- Add a new hardware device by plugging it in and turning it on.
- Insert and remove Plug and Play compliant devices such as PCMCIA cards with automatic configuration.
- Connect your computer to a docking station or network without restarting your computer or changing configuration parameters.

Plug and Play Devices

The following is a more detailed list of Plug and Play devices that you can use with Windows 95.

ISA devices   ISA stands for *Industry Standard Architecture* bus design and is the architecture specified for IBM-type computers. Plug and Play ISA devices can run on existing computers because the specification does not require any changes to ISA buses.

To automatically configure Plug and Play ISA devices, the system performs the following actions:

- Identifies and configures the devices using I/O ports, which enable Plug and Play logic on the card.
- The ISA devices isolate each card and it is assigned a unique device ID and serial number.
- Resource requirements are read and stored on each card.
- Resources are allocated to each device.
- It activates the Plug and Play ISA cards.

PC card devices   A PC Card is a credit card-sized device that slides into a slot on notebook computers. These devices are often called PCMCIA cards because they are built to a standard developed by the Personal Computer Memory Card

International Association. These devices are supported by Microsoft Windows 95 and let you use real-mode and protected-mode PC Card system software drivers from other vendors. It also supports *hot* or *warm docking*. This means that you can insert and remove PC Cards from the computer without having to restart Windows 95.

VESA local bus and PCI devices   The *Video Electronic Standards Association* (VESA) local bus standard enables high-speed connections to peripherals. When you take the A+ Certification exam, remember that the VESA local bus devices are not totally Plug and Play compliant, because a VESA local bus device is an ISA child bus, and VESA local bus devices can work similarly to ISA devices.

The *Peripheral Component Interconnect* (PCI) local bus is a standard used in most Pentium and above computers and in the Apple PowerPC Macintosh. Note that if Plug and Play is not the primary bus, then the PCI bus cannot use Plug and Play functions.

LPT ports   Parallel ports, or LPT ports, can also take advantage of Plug and Play options, and the most common type is the Centronics interface.

It's important to remember that Plug and Play parallel ports meet Compatibility and Nibble model protocols defined in IEEE P1284. To understand this, note that the compatibility mode provides a byte-wide channel from the computer to the peripheral. When your peripheral isn't working properly, you will see that there is a compatibility problem noted when you look at Device Manager/Performance for your LTP port. Nibble mode provides a channel from the peripheral to the host through which data is sent as 4-bit nibbles using the port's status lines.

The IEEEP1284 is a committee that was established in 1993 to define the chipsets supported in personal computers that first appeared in 1994.

Device Manager

You can use Device Manager, shown in Figure 18-1, by clicking Start ⇒ Settings ⇒ Control Panel, and then clicking the System icon. Device Manager provides a graphical presentation of all the devices configured in Windows 95.

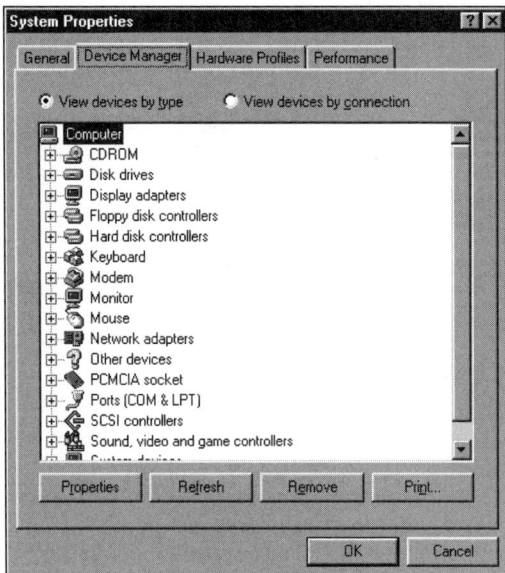

FIGURE 18-1   Device Manager window

Device Manager also shows allocated resources for each configured device. Windows 95 automatically identifies and resolves device resource conflicts, but sometimes you need to delete a device and have Windows 95 reconfigure it.

Follow these steps to use the Device Manager:

1. Double-click the System icon in the Control Panel, or right-click the My Computer icon on your desktop, then select Properties, then the Device Manager Property Page.

2. Double-click the device type shown in the list.

3. Double-click the device or select the device, then choose Properties to view or change a device's settings.

Using the PC Card Wizard

To determine whether a PC Card socket is supported, follow these steps to activate the wizard shown in Figure 18-2:

1. In Control Panel, double-click Add New Hardware.

2. From the Add New Hardware wizard, click Next.

3. Click No, then Next to select from a list of hardware types.

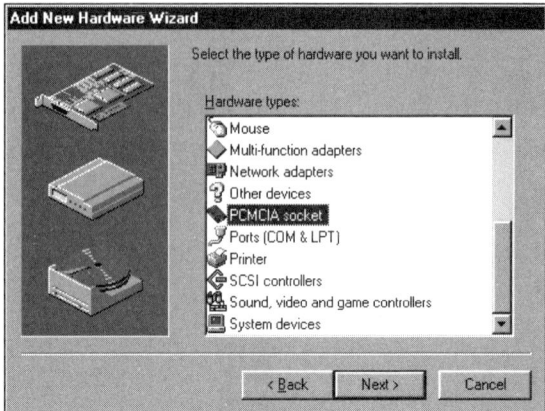

FIGURE 18-2   PC Card wizard window

Remember that Microsoft Windows 95 automatically disables enhanced PC Card support when it detects the presence of previous drivers. It does this because it cannot remove these drivers automatically. Running the PC Card wizard removes old PCMCIA drivers from the CONFIG.SYS file and other configuration files.

VIRTUAL MEMORY MANAGER

The Virtual Memory Manager is located inside the System properties. You can choose between letting Windows 95 manage your virtual memory settings, or you can configure them manually. If you let Windows 95 automatically configure your virtual memory settings, you are assured that the system will assign the correct amount of space, and that it will work correctly. If you configure the virtual memory settings manually, you stand a good chance of having the system fail if it isn't configured correctly. Again, the advanced graphic settings are configured through the System property pages. When you choose Advanced Graphic settings, you can set the hardware accelerator from None to Full. This tells Windows 95 how to use your graphics hardware. Changing this setting can help you troubleshoot display-related problems. You would set the range to Full if you were not experiencing any graphic settings difficulties.

VIRTUAL DEVICE DRIVERS

A virtual device driver (VxD) is a 32-bit, protected mode driver that manages system resources like hardware devices and software so more than one application can use the memory resource at the same time. The x in VxD stands for the type of device driver. Windows 95 loads the VxDs only as they are needed at any given time, and then they are loaded into memory.

Virtual device drivers support the disk controller, serial and parallel ports, keyboard and display devices, and other types of hardware configured for your computer.

WINDOWS 95 FILE SYSTEM

Unlike Windows 3.1 file systems, Windows 95 furnishes a layered file system architecture that supports multiple file systems, including VFAT and CDFS. This file system makes the computer easier to use, and adds a new feature for the user. With Windows 95, users are not limited to an eight-character alphanumeric filename. In Windows 95, users can specify up to 255 characters in a filename, making it easier to remember the contents of a file.

The Windows 95 file system comprises the following components:

- An *Installable File System* (IFS) manager that is responsible for giving the user access to different file system components.

- A file system drivers layer that provides access to FAT-based disk devices, CD-ROM devices, and redirected network device support.

- A block I/O subsystem, which interacts with the physical disk drives.

WINDOWS 95 REGISTRY

The Registry simplifies a system administrator's job tasks by providing a unified database that stores configuration data in a hierarchical form.

With the introduction of Windows 95 and the Registry database, AUTOEXEC.BAT and CONFIG.SYS files are no longer needed. The Registry stores both binary and text values in its hierarchical form, and supports keys that have more than one value, as well as different types of data. The Registry is made up of two files: SYSTEM.DAT, which contains computer-specific information, and USER.DAT, which contains user-specific information.

The following list describes some of the ways Windows 95 uses the Registry:

- Nearly all of the configuration information for the computer is stored in the Registry.

- It keeps track of hardware, applications, device drivers, and operating system control parameters and configurations.

- All user preferences and settings (the user profile) are stored in the Registry.

- If the system crashes, you may be able to restore most of your settings by restoring the Registry.

Registry Editor

The Registry Editor is a tool you can use to directly edit the Registry. It displays the Registry as a hierarchy of keys, much the same way Explorer displays your file system as a hierarchy of folders (see Figure 18-3). Just as keys are analogous to folders on your disk drive, so Registry values are similar to files in the file system. Also, just as a file contains information, a Registry value contains Registry data.

 caution

Only an experienced PC user should modify Registry entries in the Windows 95 operating system. Failure to make the correct changes could result in an inoperable system.

To run the Registry Editor, follow these steps:

1. From the Start menu, select Run and type **regedit**.

2. When the Registry Editor starts, double-click any folder icon for a Registry key to display the contents.

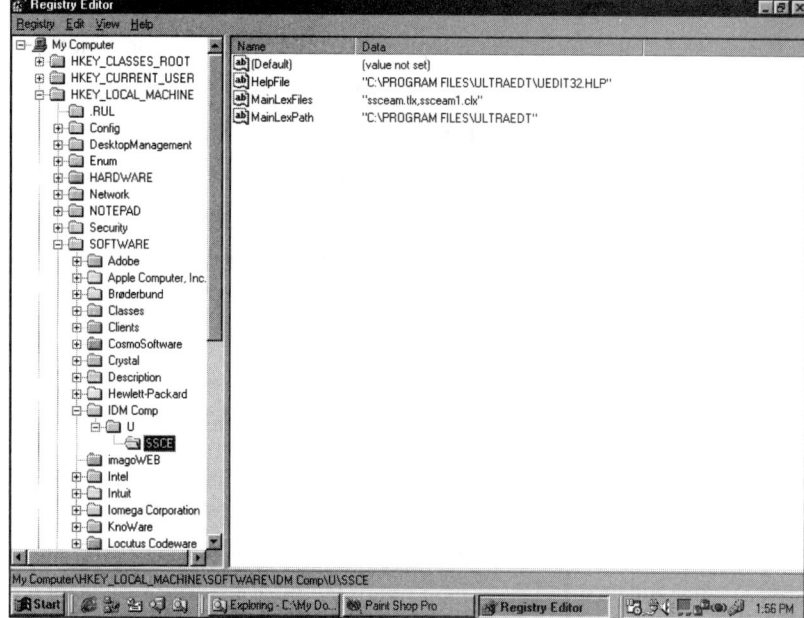

FIGURE 18-3 The hierarchical tree of the Registry

The entries edited most often are found in `Hkey_Local_Machine\System\CurrentControlSet`.

To change settings in the Registry, it's important to understand the key names, and the purpose and functions of the Registry itself. The subtree keys in the Registry are listed here:

- **Hkey_Local_Machine:** Contains information for the computer, drivers, system settings, hardware, port mapping, software configurations, and user information.

- **Hkey_Classes_Root:** Contains OLE information, association mappings, and shortcuts that are OLE links and core aspects of the Windows 95 user interface.

- **Hkey Users:** Logging information for users and default settings for applications, event schemes, desktop configurations, and much more.

- **Hkey_Dyn_Data:** Information for devices used as part of the Plug and Play subsystem. Also included are associate hardware information, associated problems, status, and subkeys for each user who logs into that computer.

- **Hkey_Current_Configuration:** This key points to a branch of Hkey_Local_Machine\Config with information about the current configuration of the hardware attached to the computer.

- **Hkey_Current_User:** Points to a branch of the key Hkey_Users for the user who is currently logged on.

Configuring the Save and Recovery Options in the Registry

You can save Registry information by using the Export Registry feature in the Registry Editor. Choose between saving the entire Registry or a specific branch to a text file format. One reason you might want to save a specific branch to a text file is if you are going to change the Registry and you want to remember the previous settings. Saving a branch guarantees that you'll be able to return to the previous configuration quite easily.

Remember that all changes you need to make to settings for the network adapters and support software should be made through the Network option in Control Panel, not by directly editing the Registry. Figure 18-4 shows the export option of the Registry Editor. The import dialog box is similar to this. We highly recommend that you save the section or key that you plan to change before you make any changes. This will enable a speedy recovery in the event of an error.

You can restore the Registry by using the Import Registry feature. This command rebuilds a branch or the entire Registry from an exported Registry file. However, if a Registry becomes corrupted, or the system doesn't start for some reason, you can run the Registry Editor from real mode to diagnose and correct the problem.

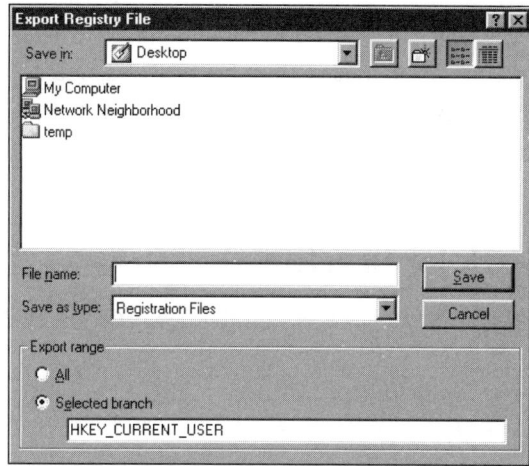

FIGURE 18-4 Saving Registry entries to disk

FILE SYSTEM DRIVERS

The *Installable File System* (IFS) manager is a low-level component of the operating system that manages access to the file systems on the drives of the local computer, and network access to other file systems. This includes the following drivers:

o 32-bit FAT (VFAT) driver

o 32-bit *CD-ROM file system* (CDFS) driver

o 32-bit network redirector for connectivity to the Microsoft Network servers

For more information about these concepts, please see Chapter 17.

VFAT File System Driver

This is a 32-bit, protected mode code path that manages the file system stored on a disk; it also enhances multitasking performance.

VFAT works with a 32-bit protected mode cache driver (VCACHE). VCACHE automatically increases its disk caching size and allocates or deallocates memory for the cache based on system usage.

CD-ROM File System Driver

This driver is a 32-bit, protected mode CDFS that provides better CD-ROM access and performance than previous versions. CDFS conforms to the ISO 9660 standards.

32-Bit Network Redirector

A network redirector enables you to locate, open, read, write, and delete files and print jobs.

Following are the two redirectors included in the Microsoft Windows 95 network client software as file system drivers:

- VREDIR.VXD is the client for Microsoft networks, a redirector that supports all networks based on Microsoft networking. It uses the *Server Message Black* (SMB) as a file-sharing protocol.

- NWREDIR.VXD is the redirector that supports NetWare networking products, which use the *NetWare Core Protocol* (NCP) file-sharing protocol.

Block I/O Subsystem

The block I/O subsystem enhances performance for the entire file system in Microsoft Windows 95 and provides an array of device support. This subsystem is a real-mode-mapping layer that is compatible with real-mode, MS-DOS-based device drivers where a protected model counterpart does not exist.

Following are the components of the block I/O subsystem:

- **Input/Output Supervisor (IOS):** This component provides services and drivers and is responsible for queuing file service requests and routing the request to a file system driver.

- **Port Driver:** This 32-bit driver communicates with a disk device like a hard disk controller.

- **SCSI Layer:** This is a 32-bit, protected-mode universal driver that communicates with SCSI devices.

- **Miniport Driver:** This is a Microsoft Windows 95 driver that helps hardware vendors write device drivers for Windows 95.

WINDOWS 95 SHORTCUTS

In the Program Manager of Windows 3.1 you could create icons that pointed to programs and documents on your hard drive. By double-clicking these icons you could start the program or open the document. Since Windows 95 no longer makes use of the Program Manager, Microsoft came up with the concept of *short-cuts*, providing a new way of linking to files on your computer (or even across the network).

A shortcut is a small file with the extension .LNK. It contains just enough information to tell the operating system which file it's pointing to and the para-meters to use when opening that program or document. Shortcuts can reside any-where on your hard drive, but the most common places for them are the Windows 95 desktop and the Start menu. By double-clicking a shortcut on the desktop (or selecting a shortcut on the Start menu) you can open the program or document that it points to.

You can create new shortcuts in several ways. The easiest way is to use the Windows Explorer to find the file you want to make a shortcut to, then right-drag (right-click and hold, then drag) the file to the place that you want the shortcut to be. When you release the right mouse button a small menu appears. One of the items on the menu is Create Shortcut(s) Here; select that item. Windows 95 cre-ates the shortcut in the location you right-dragged the file to.

OPTIMIZING WINDOWS 95 COMPONENTS

This section is devoted to helping you learn how to optimize various components of Windows 95. We'll explain some of the concepts that affect the overall perfor-mance of a Windows 95 system and show you how to manipulate the system to maximize the user's productivity. In particular, we'll discuss these components:

- Swap file
- Disk cache
- Printing
- Network performance
- CD-ROMs

Swap File

Microsoft Windows 95 provides the virtual memory swap file. Its intended purpose is to enable the system to use some space on the hard disk as though it were memory. This means you can run more applications simultaneously, and can do more memory-intensive tasks without having to install more physical memory. The swap file can shrink or grow based on system operations, and can occupy a fragmented region of the hard disk with little performance detriment. Normally, Windows 95 does a good job of managing the swap file on its own, but if you want to manipulate it yourself, you can.

To determine how well your swap file is performing, open System Monitor by choosing Run from the Start menu, typing **sysmon** in the Run box, then clicking OK. In System Monitor (see Figure 18-5), choose Edit ⇒ Add Item to open the Add Item dialog box, then choose Memory Manager from the Category list. This brings up a series of choices on the Item list; choose Swapfile In Use and Swapfile Size, then click OK. This gives you a graphical representation of how Windows 95 is using the swap file.

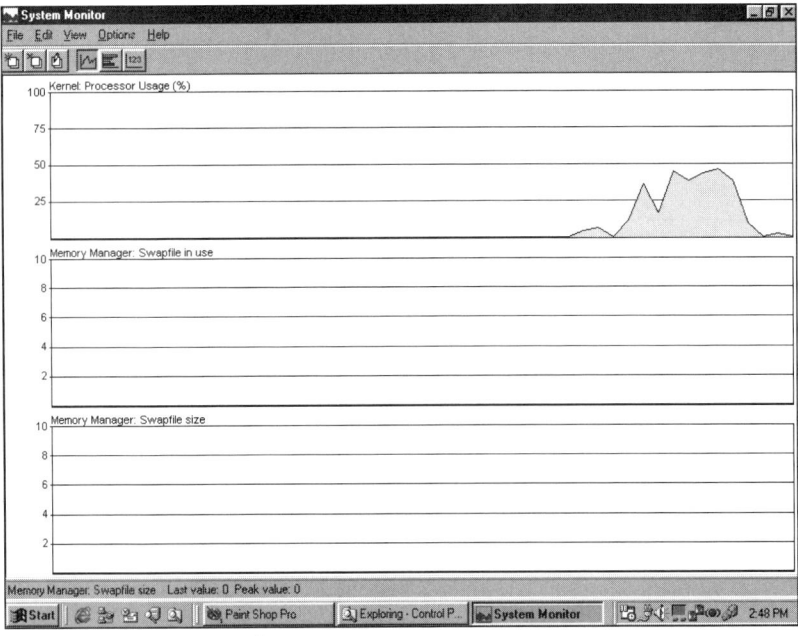

FIGURE 18-5 System Monitor

If you decide you need to modify the default swap file settings, you can do so by double-clicking the System icon in the Control Panel to open the System Properties dialog box. Switch to the Performance tab (see Figure 18-6), and click the Virtual Memory button to open the Virtual Memory dialog box shown in Figure 18-7. Here you need to select the Let Me Specify My Own Virtual Memory Settings radio button, then you can select which drive you want the swap file to reside on and the minimum and maximum amount of space you want it to occupy on that drive. You can also disable virtual memory if you want to, but Microsoft strongly advises against doing so as it can cause serious problems if you need more memory than is physically installed on your computer.

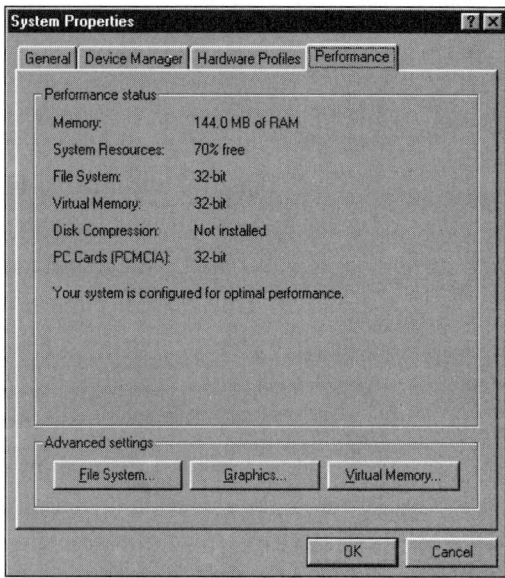

FIGURE 18-6   Click the Virtual Memory button in the System Properties dialog box

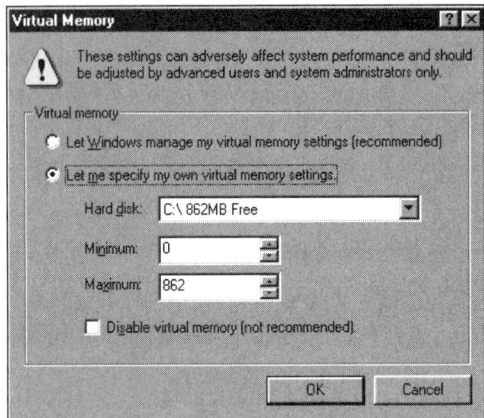

FIGURE 18-7   Specify the settings you want Windows 95 to use for virtual memory

Disk Cache

Because reading from a hard drive is rather slow compared to reading information from memory, the computer industry has come up with a way to minimize disk reads by reserving some memory for use as a *disk cache*. A disk cache is basically an area of memory that holds the most recently accessed information from the disk. If that information is needed again, then the computer can read it from fast memory, rather than having to get it from the hard drive again. Another way a disk cache can be used is as a read-ahead buffer: Whenever an application reads from the disk, Windows 95 can read the next few sectors from the disk and store them in the disk cache in anticipation of the application requesting them. Since most data is stored sequentially on the disk, this can improve performance by resulting in one longer disk read rather than several short disk reads that require seeking, starting, and stopping the reading process.

Using a disk cache can dramatically improve the overall speed of the system, assuming you have enough physical memory installed to handle both the disk cache and provide for the needs of running applications. Obviously, keeping a disk cache in a swap file is not appropriate, because the swap file is stored on the disk and takes just as long to read as the original file.

Optimizing File System Performance

To optimize hard disk performance, follow these steps:

1. From Control Panel, choose System, and then choose Performance.
2. Click the File System button.
3. On the Hard Disk tab, select the list named Typical Role of This Machine.
4. Select the most common use for the computer, then choose OK.
5. Use the Read-Ahead optimization slider to specify the amount of cache you want Windows 95 to use for the read-ahead buffer.

You should optimize your file system's performance when your applications appear to run slowly when accessing or saving information that is stored on the hard drive.

Print Optimization

Windows 95 supports a print spooling device driver that consolidates the spooling functionality into a single architecture. This spooler enables you to print a document (in the background) while you continue working in the same, or another application.

If you print to a server running Microsoft Windows 95, the rendering from the *Enhanced Metafile Format* (EMF) to the printer-specific language happens on the server computer. You need to make a choice between disk use or return-to-application time. For example, if you want to return to your application quickly after sending a document to the printer, you would choose the Return-To-Application Time option. If you'd rather have your document print faster and you're not concerned about working in your existing document right away, then you would choose Disk Use.

You can change or configure a printer's settings by displaying the Printer Properties page shown in Figure 18-8, which lists categories for:

o Fonts
o General
o Details
o Device Options
o Paper

○ PostScript

○ Graphics

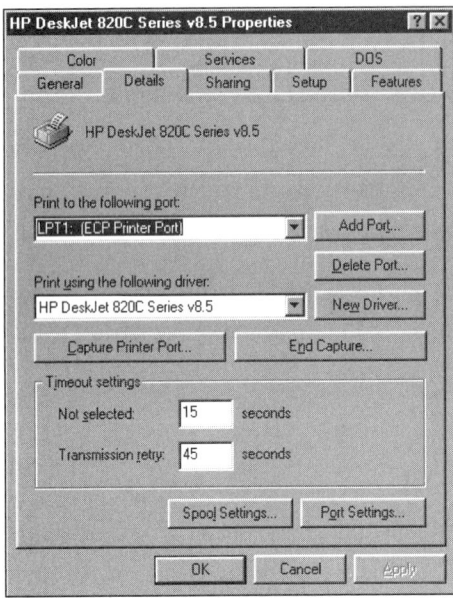

FIGURE 18-8 Printer properties

Sharing a Printer

To share a locally installed printer with other users, follow these steps:

1. From the Printers folder, right-click the printer icon to share, then click Sharing in the context menu.

2. From the Sharing property sheet, you can configure the options you want.

When File and Printer Sharing services are enabled, other users can connect to shared printers, volumes, CD-ROM drives, and directories on that computer.

Using Point and Print to connect to a NetWare printer:

1. From Network Neighborhood, double-click the NetWare server icon.

2. Drag and drop the print queue from the NetWare server window to the Printers Folders window.

3. Follow the online instructions where the Add Printer Wizard prompts you to type a name for the printer.

Follow these steps to set the spool settings for good print performance:

1. In the printer's property sheet, click Details, then click Spool Settings.

2. In the Spool Settings dialog box, you must determine whether you want spooling to start after the first page is spooled, or after the last page is spooled.

Optimizing CD-ROM Drives

Just as a disk cache can improve performance of a hard drive, it can also make reading from a CD-ROM much faster than it would be without the cache. Because CD-ROMs are normally much slower than hard drives, though, the performance gain of using a cache is markedly greater. Figure 18-9 illustrates this on a system that has a 20x CD-ROM player.

To set the CD-ROM cache, follow these steps:

1. From the Control Panel, choose System.

2. Select the Performance tab.

3. Select the File System button.

4. Select the CD-ROM tab.

5. Drag the Settings slide to the desired size.

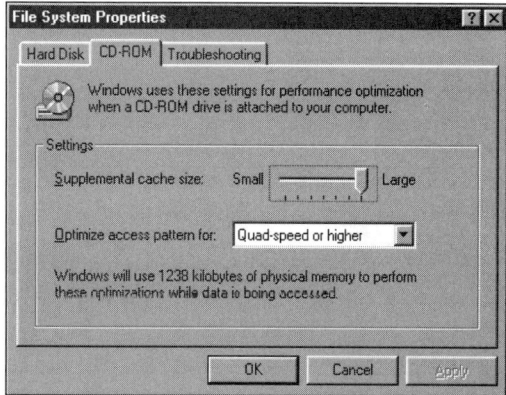

FIGURE 18-9 The buffering for a Windows 95 system with a 20x CD-ROM player

The recommended settings for your CD-ROM drive are:

- For a 1x CD with 8MB or less of physical memory, use 64K cache.
- For a 2x CD with 8- to 12MB of physical memory, use 626K cache.
- For a 4x CD with 12MB or more of physical memory, use 1238K cache.

Using System Monitor for Optimum Performance

System Monitor is especially useful when you're connecting to another computer remotely. The System Monitor monitors real-time performance of several computer components, functions, and behaviors, and displays the results in graphs or charts. System Monitor can also be used over the network to track performance of remote computers. Figure 18-10 shows a Windows 95 system running a Pentium 233MHz with 64MB of RAM.

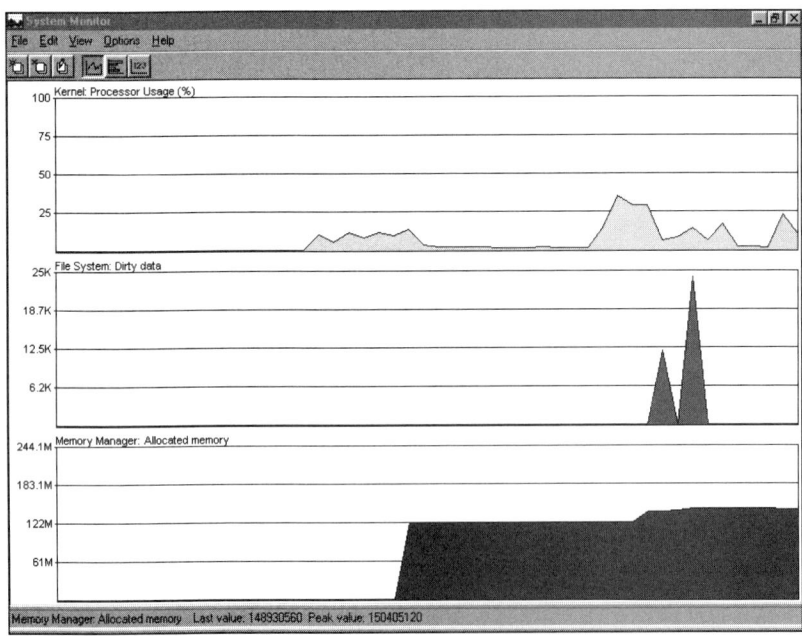

FIGURE 18-10 Output from System Monitor. The parameters represent memory, CPU, and disk performance on a well-performing Windows 95 system.

System Monitor can report on the performance of a wide variety of system components. When you first start System Monitor, it shows a line chart of the percentage of the overall processing power of the CPU that's currently in use. To display a different graph in the System Monitor window, choose Edit ⇒ Add Item to open the Add Item dialog box, then select the item in the category list that you want to know about. Each of the categories has a series of items that you can choose from. Select the ones you want to see and click OK to display them in the System Monitor window.

To remotely view performance data with System Monitor, follow these steps:

1. From the Start button, click Run, then type **sysmon** and press Enter.

2. From the File menu in System Monitor, click Connect, type the name of the computer you wish to monitor, and then click OK.

3. From the Edit menu, click Add Item, then click Category to monitor it.

4. Click the item, and finally, click OK.

KEY POINT SUMMARY

In this chapter we covered several of the ways you can configure the Windows 95 operating system. We explained the types of partitions that Windows 95 can use, and went over many of the concepts of Plug and Play, including the requirements for its use and many of the devices you can use with this technology. We explained how you can use Device Manager to see a graphical representation of all the devices installed on a Windows 95 system and determine what resources each device is using, and then showed you how to install PC Card devices with the PC Card Wizard. Next we showed you how to use Virtual Memory Manager to let Windows 95 configure virtual memory, and we told you what a virtual device driver is.

- We showed you the basics of the Windows 95 Registry, describing how it is a hierarchical type of database where all actions and file specs are stored, and explained how to back up the registry and restore it in case it became corrupt.

- Next we taught you how the Windows 95 file system works, discussing the VFAT and CD-ROM file system drivers, the 32-bit network redirector, and the block I/O subsystem. Here block I/O capabilities supported under Windows 95 provide 32-bit access and speed enhancements over older file processing methods. This improvement is seen in the 32-bit FAT, CD file system, and the 32-bit network redirector.

Microsoft Windows 95 supports three types of drivers. They are:

- 32-bit FAT (VFAT) driver
- 32-bit *CD-ROM file system* (CDFS) driver
- 32-bit network redirector for connectivity to the Microsoft Network servers

- Finally, we discussed the optimization of various Windows 95 Components, including the swap file, disk cache, file system, printing, and CD-ROM drives. We rounded out the chapter with a description of the System Monitor, showing you how it monitors real-time performance of several computer components, functions, and behaviors, and displays the results in graphs or charts. System Monitor can also be used over the network to track performance of remote computers.
- Shortcuts, introduced in Windows 95, enable you to create a reference to an object for quick access without making a copy of the object. Shortcuts can either be displayed on the desktop or in the Start bar.

APPLYING WHAT YOU'VE LEARNED

This chapter has covered a lot of important material that will help you prepare for the A+ exam and be a competent technician. Take a few minutes and work through the Instant Assessment questions, review your notes, and see how you did.

The Hands-on lab will also help build your comfort level with the hardware, as well as reinforce the readings from this chapter.

Instant Assessment

Multiple choice

Choose the best answer(s). There may be more than one correct answer for each question.

1. What is the extension of files used as shortcuts?

    A. .DAT

    B. .INF

    C. .LNK

    D. .SCT

2. Which of the following contains the database of system settings and configurations?

    A. Hardware tree

    B. Registry

    C. Taskbar

    D. Resource system

3. The bus allows for the transfer of information:

    A. Between the computer and the device

    B. Between the computer and the swap file

    C. Between the computer and the network

    D. Between the computer and GDI

4. How many subtrees of keys are contained in the Windows 95 Registry?

    A. 6

    B. 4

    C. 10

    D. 27

5. Which of the following key names contains dynamic status information for devices such as Plug and Play?

    A. HKEY_CURRENT_CONFIG

    B. HKEY_CLASSES_ROOT

    C. HKEY_USERS

    D. KEY-DYN_DATA

6. Which tool enables a user to diagnose a problem remotely, rather than having to be onsite?

   A. System Policy Editor

   B. System Monitor

   C. Net Watcher

   D. Register Editor

7. What is the recommended setting for a 4X CD-ROM with 12MB or more?

   A. 64K

   B. 626K

   C. 1238K

   D. 800K

8. Which of the following components is part of the block I/O subsystem (pick all that apply)?

   A. Port driver

   B. Input/Output supervisor

   C. SCSI layer

   D. Miniport driver

9. To use Plug and Play functionality, your computer system must include which of the following:

   A. Plug and Play BIOS

   B. A Plug and Play bus

   C. Microsoft Windows 95 operating system

   D. A PCMCIA sound card

Fill in the blank

1. CDFS stands for _____.

2. VFAT stands for _____.

3. What does EMF stand for? _____.

4. What is the name of the file where the user's profile is stored?

_____.

5. To locate a collection of files with information for a particular device, you would need to view what types of files? _____.

Hands-on Lab Exercises

In this lab, you will be doing several things to tune and customize a Windows 95 system. To become familiar with manipulating the Registry, you'll change the computer's name within `regedit`. You'll also use the Windows 95 Add Printer Wizard to add a new printer driver to the system.

Lab 18-19 *Registry entry*

First, let's change a parameter in the Registry, the name of the computer system. We will verify this under the Networking panel and then set the Registry back to the original settings. Follow these steps:

1. Select Run from the Start menu, type **regedit** in the Open field, and click OK to run `regedit`.

2. To change the name of the computer, we need to edit the data in the ComputerName value, which is in the
`HKEY_LOCAL_MACHINE\System\CurrentControlSet\control\`
`ComputerName\ComputerName` key. To find this value, click on the + sign beside the `HKEY_LOCAL_MACHINE` entry to expand that branch of the tree. Similarly, you need to expand the System, CurrentControlSet, control, ComputerName, and ComputerName branches. Finally, click on the second ComputerName key to see the values it contains. One of these values is ComputerName, and the data it contains is "Mike," which is currently the computer's name. Figure 18-11 shows this parameter and the hierarchy that was opened to show that parameter.

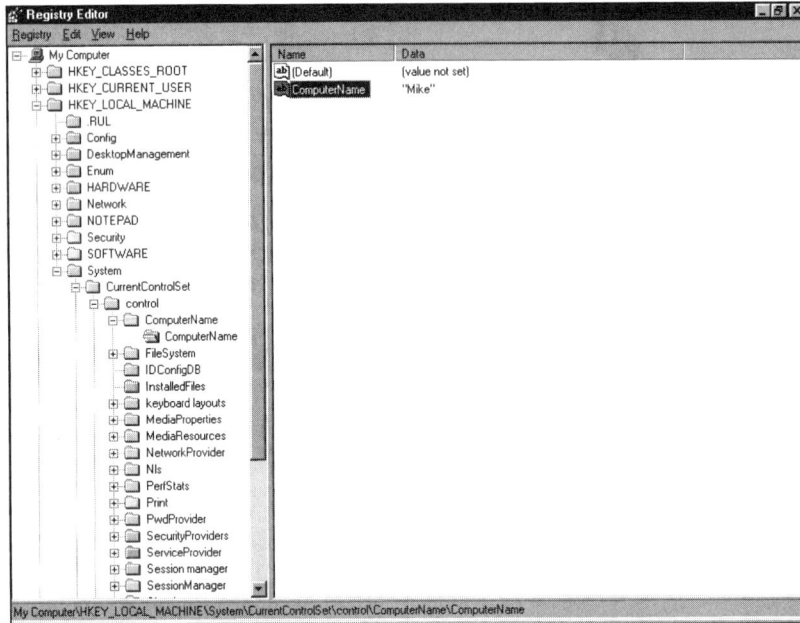

FIGURE 18-11 The Registry entry for computer name under the
HKEY_LOCAL_MACHINE key

3. Double-click on the ComputerName value. An editing window opens up
that looks like Figure 18-12. Type a new name (Mark) for the computer in
this dialog box.

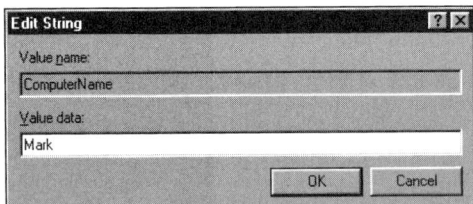

FIGURE 18-12 The Registry Editor changing the value of
ComputerName to "Mark" from "Mike"

4. In the Control Panel, double-click the Network icon to open the Network
dialog box. Switch to the Identification tab, shown in Figure 18-13, to see
the changed value of the computer name.

5. Click OK to close the Network dialog box.

6. Repeat these steps to revert to the computer's original name.

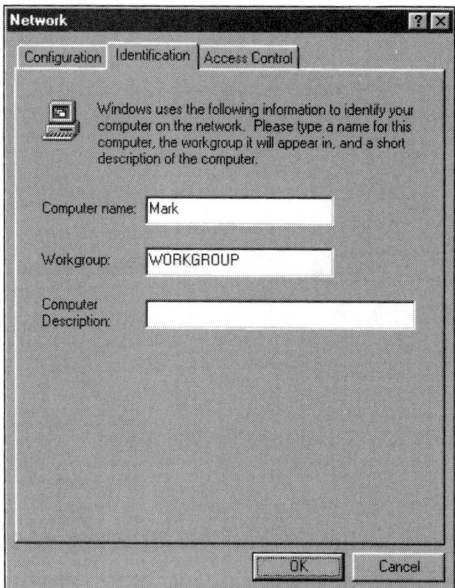

FIGURE 18-13 The changed name under the
network panel

Lab 18-20 *Adding a printer*

In this lab, we will add a printer to our computer system. For the purpose of our
discussion, we will add an HP DeskJet 500 printer. To accomplish this, follow these
steps:

1. Choose Settings ⇒ Printers from the Windows 95 Start menu.

2. Double-click the Add Printer icon to start the Add Printer Wizard shown in
Figure 18-14.

3. Click Next on the introductory screen to move on.

4. If this printer is attached to your computer, select Local Printer, or if this
printer is attached to another computer on your network, select Network
Printer. For this example, we'll select Local Printer. Click Next to continue.

5. Select the manufacturer and model of the printer you want to install — in
this case, the HP DeskJet 500 — then click Next.

6. Select the port that this printer is attached to. Normally this will be LPT1.
Click Next to continue.

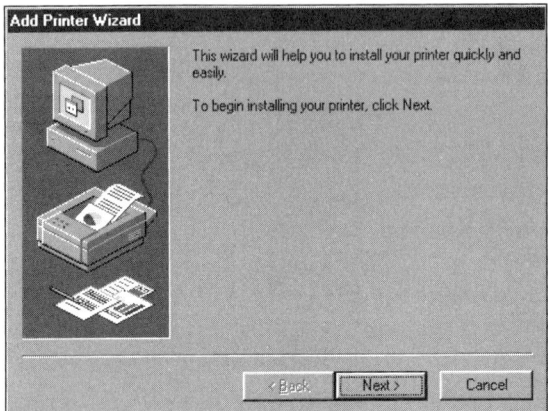

FIGURE 18-14   Adding a printer to a Windows 95 system

7. Type a name for this printer in the Printer Name field, and select Yes or No to specify whether you want Windows-based programs to use this as their default printer, then click Next.

8. Finally, select Yes to have Windows 95 print a test page on your printer to verify that it's working properly. Click Finish when you're ready.

   Figure 18-15 shows the printer dialog box with the HP 500 added as the default printer.

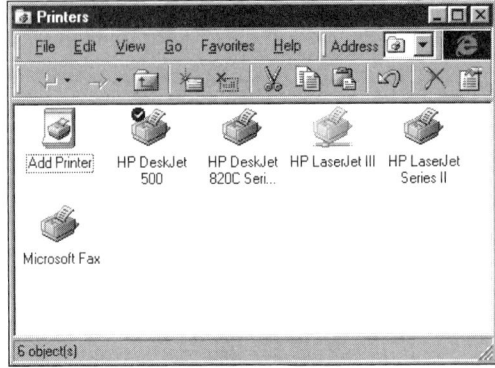

FIGURE 18-15   The Printers dialog box

Installing and Upgrading Windows

About Chapter 19

This chapter explores how to install and upgrade Windows. We'll discuss setup programs, system drivers, and upgrades, along with Windows and DOS software components that you will need to install and upgrade Windows systems.

First, this chapter will explain the new Microsoft Windows 95 and Windows 98 Setup features. (For convenience, we will refer to both Windows 95 and Windows 98 as simply Windows 95, unless a specific difference needs to be highlighted.) Next we'll describe the installation requirements for Windows 95, and show you how to determine when you should run Windows 95 Setup from MS-DOS or Windows. Then this chapter describes the steps for starting Windows 95 Setup, and alternative setups you may want to consider in various scenarios.

WINDOWS 95 SETUP FEATURES

Before you begin to install or upgrade your Windows system, it's important that you be familiar with the setup features in Windows 95. These setup features include wizards and other options that offer easy and quick installation. Setup routines take the guesswork out of installing individual components. For example, if you want to install Microsoft Word, but you don't want to install Help files or the conversion files that enable you to read documents from other word processing programs, you can choose these options during the installation process.

Furthermore, users now have greater control over which components of Windows 95 are installed during the setup process, because they can select the options that Windows 95 will install for the given functionality that they desire.

Wizards to Guide You

Windows 95 features wizards to take all the guesswork out of the process of installation and upgrading. These wizards help you through the configuration process, and permit you to return to a previous screen to make changes to options you've already selected. This is a good feature, because if you change your mind about which options to install or upgrade, you don't have to repeat the entire process from scratch.

Microsoft Windows 95 installs the disk operating system, graphical user interface elements, and networking functionality all at the same time. The user has very little to do, because Microsoft has incorporated safe defaults for automatic configuration and installation of components. However, if you are an experienced and knowledgeable user, you can customize the installation and upgrade to meet your needs.

Automatic Hardware Detection

When you install new hardware, the hardware device is automatically detected; Windows 95 supports the configuration by finding the correct driver, or prompting you to insert a disk containing the new driver.

The installation of Windows 95 is more flexible than it was in earlier versions. Administrators have greater control over configuration options for desktop settings, network adapters, and other hardware devices.

Failure Recovery

In addition, an invaluable feature is an improved recovery mechanism for setup failure. Now you can refer to a log that is maintained each time setup operations are performed and hardware devices are detected. When Windows 95 was being introduced, a common demonstration by Microsoft product evangelists was to unplug a computer right in the middle of the installation process. Windows 95 recovered when the system was restarted, smoothly picking up where it left off.

Automatic Log Maintenance

During setup and maintenance operations, Windows 95 automatically creates and maintains a log of installed components that can be detected, recovered, and verified. So when you initially install the software, you can skip the extra features if you're not sure you'll need them, but you can always go back and reinstall the options you want, when you want them. This feature saves on hard disk space, giving you the option to start with a bare minimum install.

Batch Installation

Finally, you have an automated batch installation option that uses setup scripts. The system administrator can define the settings for various installation setup routines, and then specify defaults for installing and configuring devices. In this way, the process is completed only once for all future installations or upgrades.

INSTALLATION REQUIREMENTS FOR MICROSOFT WINDOWS 95

Before we look at how to install Microsoft Windows 95, you should be aware of several types of installation requirements. When you install Windows 95, you should be aware of:

- Operating system requirements
- Installed memory, disk space, and user information requirements
- Hardware, disk space, partition, and other requirements

Operating System Requirements

The upgrade package of Windows 95 must be installed over an existing operating system. A full package, designed to be installed on a brand new system, is also available, but if you have a previous version of DOS or Windows, the upgrade version will save you money. The minimum operating system software required to install Microsoft Windows 95 is any of the following:

- MS-DOS version 3.2 or higher
- Windows 3.x
- Windows for Workgroups 3.1x

Disk Space and Memory Requirements

Listed here are Microsoft's official minimum system requirements, and following each is our interpretation of what you really need if we disagree with the party line.

- At least 417K of conventional memory. This is accurate, but is really only an issue if you have lots of network drivers loaded in memory.

- 40MB of hard disk space for a new installation. Hard drive space is dirt cheap, and you'll need 100MB of free space to have a smooth installation. This applies regardless of what you're upgrading from.

- 30MB of hard disk space for an upgrade for Windows 3.1.

- 20MB of hard disk space for an upgrade for Windows for Workgroups 3.*x*.

Hardware Requirements

You need to meet these basic hardware requirements to run Microsoft Windows 95 from the hard drive of a local computer:

- The computer must be a 386DX or higher processor with a keyboard, mouse, high-density floppy disk drive, and a hard disk drive. We've run Windows 95 on a 386-33DX with 8MB of RAM, but it was more useful as a proof of concept than as a business tool. Fast 486 chips or Pentiums are much more useful as a Windows 95 platform.

- You must have a bare minimum of 30MB of free hard disk space, but realistically, you'll need more like 100MB for optimal performance. Windows 95 uses a swap file on your hard drive to enhance its performance, and you need to have enough free space for it to be established.

- For memory, 8MB is recommended; however, you can use 4MB as a minimum, but the system will run slowly. In reality, though, a minimal Windows 95 system should have no less than 16MB of memory. Memory is ludicrously cheap right now, so this shouldn't be a serious constraint—we just bought 64MB of memory for a system we put together for this book, and it only cost $135.

- Optionally, you can add a modem, CD-ROM drive, network adapter, a sound card, and any other hardware necessary to perform your job. These days, CD-ROMs are just about indispensable, because almost all software is distributed on them. You can get an adequate CD-ROM drive for under $50.

- The video display must be a minimum of VGA, and SVGA is recommended to bring out the full spectrum of colors and graphics built into Windows 95.

Partition Requirements

To begin a Microsoft Windows 95 installation, you must install over an existing MS-DOS FAT16 (16-bit file allocation table, the standard disk format for Windows and DOS) partition. One limitation to note, however, is that if you have a hard disk drive bigger than 2GB, you must partition your hard drive into 2GB segments, because Windows 95 will not operate on a hard drive partitioned larger than 2GB. This isn't an issue for most people, because the FAT-16 format is widespread. The only people affected by this are those running OS/2 on an HPFS (high-performance file system, the OS/2 disk format) partition, or those running Windows NT on an NTFS (NT file system) partition.

The newest interim release of Windows 95, called OSR2 or Windows 95B, is available to systems integrators and manufacturers, and can optionally be configured to use a new file system called the FAT32 system. Windows 98 also supports FAT32. FAT32 partitions enable more efficient file storage, with less disk space wasted to file allocation table inefficiencies. FAT32 also permits much larger partitions than does FAT-16.

SETUP OPTIONS

Once your hardware is correctly installed and configured, you'll need to know the setup options available to you when installing Microsoft Windows 95. Four different types of installation setups are available (see Figure 19-1):

○ **Typical Setup** is the default option. This choice performs installation steps automatically for standard Windows 95 installation, with minimal user intervention.

○ **Portable Setup** is an option if you are using a portable computer or laptop computer. This choice includes options for Briefcase synchronization between desktop and laptop, and installs software for direct cable connection to swap files back and forth.

○ **Compact Setup** is an option for computers with limited disk space. Only a minimum set of files for Windows 95 is installed. In other words, you will be able to run Windows 95, but extra files like Help, and enhancements are not installed, to conserve disk space.

- **Custom Setup** gives the experienced user several choices and is recommended only for those familiar with Windows 95 who want to control various elements of setup.

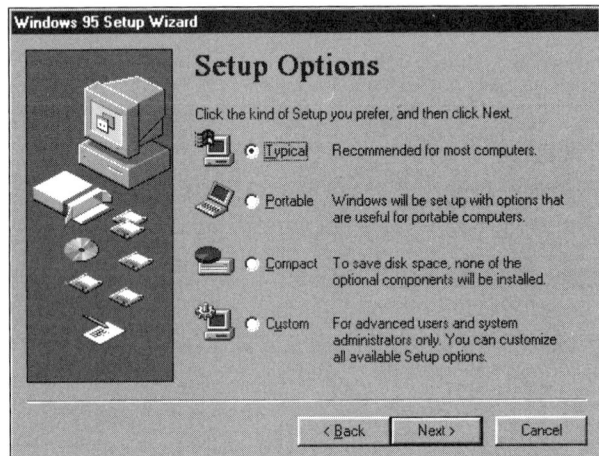

FIGURE 19-1   Windows 95 Setup options

Installing for Various Setup Situations

When you first install Microsoft Windows 95, look on the CD-ROM or installation disks for a file called SETUP.EXE. If by some chance Windows 3.1 is not already installed, the Setup program will ask for you to insert installation disks from Windows 3.1 or Windows 3.0 into the floppy drive for the installation of the Windows 95 upgrade version to continue.

Installing Windows 95 over Windows 3.1 or Windows for Workgroups

You'll need to complete the following steps when installing Microsoft Windows 95 on top of Windows 3.1 or Windows for Workgroups:

1. Start your computer and start Windows.

2. If you are installing from floppy disks, insert Disk #1 into the drive, and make sure it's the active drive in File Manager.

3. If you're installing from a CD-ROM, put the compact disk in the drive, and make sure that the drive is selected in File Manager.

4. Double-click the SETUP.EXE file on either the disk or the CD-ROM. This file is located in the Windows 95 directory on the CD.

5. Instead of double-clicking on the SETUP.EXE file from File Manager, you can also go to the File menu, choose Run, type **SETUP**, then press Enter.

6. From this point, follow the installation instructions, choosing only the default options. You can always customize your settings and choices later.

Installing Microsoft Windows 95 from MS-DOS

If you are installing Microsoft Windows 95 for the first time from a non-Windows environment, you will need to install the operating system from MS-DOS. Follow these steps for a successful installation:

1. Start the computer.

2. When the C prompt appears, insert Disk #1 of the Windows 95 installation program into your floppy disk drive, and make it active.

3. At the command prompt, type **SETUP**, and then press Enter.

4. The Windows 95 installation will begin; follow the setup instructions as you are prompted.

Installing Microsoft Windows 95 from a script to a network computer

If you are installing Microsoft Windows 95 from a network computer, you can use a script to complete the setup process. Follow these steps:

1. Log onto the network and run the existing network client.

2. Connect to the server that contains the Windows 95 distribution files for installation and setup.

3. Run Microsoft Windows 95 setup at the command line by specifying the batch file with the installation settings using this syntax: **SETUP MSBATCH.INF**.

Installing Microsoft Windows 95 to a network server

You can install Microsoft Windows 95 on a network server. First, you would use the server-based setup utility NETSETUP.EXE. Following are the various configurations you can choose from:

- Install and run a shared copy of Microsoft Windows 95 on a computer with a local hard disk, with all system files except the startup files stored on and running from the server.

- Install and run a shared copy of Microsoft Windows 95 on a computer with only a floppy disk drive, with all system files except startup files stored on and running from the server.

- Install and run a shared copy of Microsoft Windows 95 from a Novell NetWare server to support diskless workstations that boot remotely from a Microsoft Windows 95 boot image on the server.

Network protocols

You can have Microsoft Windows 95 Setup automatically install the appropriate protocol for the network client you have selected. It accepts these protocols:

- IPX/SPX-compatible protocol

- Microsoft NetBEUI

- Microsoft TCP/IP

Creating a Startup Disk

Whenever you install or upgrade your operating system, it is wise to create a startup disk in case of failures. The startup disk enables you to start Windows 95 if the normal boot procedure doesn't work, which could happen if the system files loaded on your hard drive are somehow corrupted. You can use this disk to start Microsoft Windows 95 when you cannot start the operating system from the hard disk, and proceed from that point to diagnose the system.

Follow these steps to create your startup disk:

1. Click the option named Yes, I Want A Startup Disk.
2. Click the Next button.

Windows 95 will look for all the basic system files and add them to your floppy disk, and it will make the floppy disk bootable. This is extremely helpful when you cannot load your operating system because of some type of failure.

Server–Based Setup

If you want to install Microsoft Windows 95 source files on a server, follow these steps:

1. In the server-based Setup dialog box, choose the Change Path button and specify the server path in the Source Path dialog box.

2. Click Install. A dialog box appears.

3. Set the server path where the source files will be installed.

4. Decide and specify if you want to create a default setup script, and then define the settings in the script.

5. Decide how your users will install Microsoft Windows 95 from the server. Your options are install to a local hard disk, or use Windows 95 as a shared copy. You might also want to let the user specify where they want it installed.

6. Provide a product identification number.

7. Install Microsoft Windows 95 source files in the shared directory.

How to Add a Driver or Protocol after Completing Setup

You can choose to add a network adapter, and then let Microsoft Windows 95 display a list of supported network adapters for you. Follow these steps to add a driver for a network adapter:

1. From Control Panel (click Start ⇒ Settings ⇒ Control Panel), choose Network, then select the Configuration tab.

2. Click Add, and then double-click Adapter.

3. In the manufacturer's list in the Select Device dialog box, select a network adapter manufacturer.

4. In the Network Adapters list, select the appropriate model, and then click OK.

5. If your network adapter is not listed, you can still add it if you have a disk containing Windows 95 drivers for the adapter. From this previous dialog box, click Have Disk... and point to your installation disk. Click OK.

Installing Windows 95 on Multiple Computers

After you've installed Windows 95 on one or more servers using server-based setup, you can create setup batch scripts as a custom installation for your users. There are three ways you can customize a script for installations:

- You can use a logon script to run Setup with a setup batch script that automatically installs Microsoft Windows 95 when each user logs on.

- You can insert an object in an electronic mail message that starts Setup with a setup batch script when the user clicks the object.

- You can use Microsoft Systems Management Service to run Microsoft Windows 95 Setup with a setup batch script as a mandatory job.

INSTALLING AND UPGRADING FONTS IN WINDOWS 95

Windows 95 does not check the `fonts` section of the `WIN.INI` file when it wants to load fonts, because the fonts are stored in the Registry and are automatically moved when an application installs a new font.

Both Raster and TrueType fonts are loaded from the Registry when Windows 95 starts. Raster fonts are listed in the Registry key like this: `Hkey_Current_Config\Display\Fonts`.

The master list of all resolutions for Raster fonts are stored in the Registry as:
`Hkey_Local_Machine\Software\Microsoft\Windows\CurrentVersion\Fontsize`.

TrueType fonts are loaded from a location specified in the key like this:
`Hkey_Local_Machine\Software\Microsoft\Windows\CurrentVersion\Fonts`.

There is no limit to the number of TrueType fonts that can be installed. About 1,000 fonts can be used and printed simultaneously from the same document.

Installing New Fonts with Windows 95

Follow these steps to install new fonts:

1. From the Control Panel, double-click the Fonts icon.

2. From the File menu, choose Install New Font.

3. Point to the drive containing the new fonts, select a font to install, and then click OK.

Installing Cartridge Fonts for Windows-Based Applications

You can use either the installation program from the cartridge manufacturer, or you can follow these directions to install cartridge fonts:

1. Right-click the printer icon and then click Properties in the menu if you are using an HP LaserJet or DeskJet PCL printer. Other printers will have similar steps.

2. From the printer's Fonts Property sheet, click the Install Printer Fonts button.

3. In the HP Font Installer dialog box, choose the cartridge fonts to install, then click Exit and OK.

   When the cartridge fonts are installed, insert the font cartridge into the printer. Then right-click the printer's icon and click Properties in the menu. From the printer's Fonts Property page, choose the cartridge fonts you want to use.

Font Types

Raster and vector font files have .FON filename extensions, and TrueType fonts have .TTF filename extensions. The vector font collection in Microsoft Windows 95 consists of only one font: Modern.

The TrueType fonts included with Windows 95 are Arial, Courier New, Symbol, and Times New Roman font families.

The Raster fonts included in Windows 95 are MS Serif, MS Sans Serif, Courier, System, and Terminal.

Installing NetWare PServer Print Options

For you to use Microsoft Windows 95 print services for NetWare's PServer capability, a filename MSPSRV.EXE is included with Windows 95. PServer can de-spool print jobs from NetWare queues to printers connected to servers that are running Windows 95.

Print Server for NetWare runs in the background of your applications, and uses no resources except for data packet polling at a set interval. It uses the *queue management services* (QMS) API by logging onto the NetWare printer server and attaching itself to the print queue. The PServer capability can be found on the compact disk in the ADMIN\NETTOOLS\PRTAGENT directory.

Here are the steps to install NetWare PServer:

1. In the Select Network Component Type box, click Service, and then click Add.

2. Click Have Disk, and then type the drive and path to this file: ADMIN\NETTOOLS\PRTAGENT.

3. Check the NetWare print server and the MS-DOS computer configured as the PServer to make sure they are both working properly.

4. From the Printer Server property page, click Enable Microsoft Print Server for NetWare.

5. From the list of servers provided, select the NetWare server where the queue resides.

6. Adjust the time interval for polling the print queue by adjusting it as high as 15 seconds for maximum printer server performance, or as low as 3 minutes for increased local performance. (The default is 30 seconds.)

7. Click OK.

Installing Printer Drivers on a Network

Microsoft Windows 95 supports Point and Print to any Windows 95 printer as well as printers managed by Windows NT, NetWare, or other network servers.

To automatically install a printer driver over the network, drag the network printer icon from the server's shared resource window to the Printer window or to the desktop.

Windows 95 automatically determines the printer name and then loads the driver over the network to the local hard disk and configures the printer on the user's system.

Installing File and Printer Sharing after Windows 95 Setup

In the Network option of Control Panel (click Start ⇒ Settings ⇒ Control Panel ⇒ ⇒ Network), click File and Print Sharing on the Configuration property page.

Enabling File and Printer Sharing in Custom Setup Scripts

In the `Network` section of `MSBATCH.INF`, specify one of the following values:

- `service=nwserver` (for file and printer sharing on NetWare networks)
- `service=vserver` (for file and printer sharing on Microsoft networks)

Installing a Printer

When upgrading to Windows 95 from earlier versions of Windows, Setup can automatically migrate your printer selections to Windows 95. And if no previous printers were installed, you can use the Add Printer wizard. All printer installations take place in the Printers folder.

To set up a new printer, from the Printers folder (click Start ⇒ Settings ⇒ Printers), double-click the Add Printer icon and the wizard guides you through the process to configure and add a printer.

KEY POINT SUMMARY

This chapter dealt with the specifics of installing Windows 95 on a computer system.

- Windows 95 provides four setup options: Typical, Portable, Compact, and Custom. Portable is optimized for notebook systems, whereas Compact is used for machines with limited available disk space. The Typical installation would normally be used to install Windows 95 on a desktop computer, and Custom enables advanced users to specify exactly what components they want installed.

- Windows 95 can be installed as an upgrade from MS-DOS 3.31 or higher, Windows 3.0, Windows 3.1, Windows for Workgroups 3.11, or OS/2 2.0 or higher. The installation will attempt to preserve and convert as much of the older environment as possible. Windows 95 can also be installed over a network using a script.

- Printer fonts can be installed using the utilities provided by most printer manufacturers, as well as from the Setup program for Microsoft-provided fonts. Printer drivers can be installed over a network. If another Windows 95 user has configured the drivers for that system, the installing system can utilize that driver during installation.

APPLYING WHAT YOU'VE LEARNED

This chapter has covered a lot of important material that will help you prepare for the A+ exam and be an excellent computer technician. Take a few minutes and work through the questions in the Instant Assessment, then review your notes and see how you did.

The Hands-on lab will also help you build your comfort level with the hardware as well as reinforce the readings from this chapter.

Instant Assessment

Multiple choice
Choose the best answer(s). There may be more than one correct answer for each question.

1. A Custom setup performs these actions:

    A. Offers several options that are limited for use by only experienced users who want to control certain elements of the Windows 95 setup.

    B. This is the default option.

    C. This option is only for portable computers or laptops.

    D. This type of setup is used only by computers with limited disk space.

2. What is the filename found on the Microsoft Windows 95 installation disks or on a shared network resource for installing Microsoft Windows 95?

    A. SETUP.EXE

    B. NETSETUP.EXE

    C. INSTALL.EXE

    D. STARTUP.EXE

3. The bus enables the transfer of information which way?

    A. Between the computer and the GDI

    B. Between the computer and the swap file

    C. Between the computer and the device

    D. Between the computer and the network

Fill in the blank

1. The reason for making a Startup Disk is

_____.

2. The operating systems that Microsoft Windows 95 can be installed with as an upgrade are:

_____.

3. To save and recover data in the Registry, you would use

_____.

4. To restore a badly corrupted Register, you should

_____.

5. How many times are you allowed to upgrade to Microsoft Windows 95 on the same computer? _____.

6. If you wanted to create a reference to an object without having to make a copy of the object, you would _____.

Hands-on Lab Exercises

In these labs, you will examine the disk partitions of a Windows 95 system and install Windows 95.

Lab 19-21 *FDISK*

FDISK is a program that enables you to divide your disk drives into partitions. In a 16-bit file system like FAT16 (the DOS and Windows 95 standard), the maximum limit of a disk partition is 2GB. In this lab, we will examine and change the partition information on a disk.

The FDISK program is a DOS-based utility that was introduced by MS-DOS. This program has continued to be the primary method of creating partitions. Figure 19-2 shows the startup screen of FDISK. The program has five parameters that can be used to maintain disk partitions.

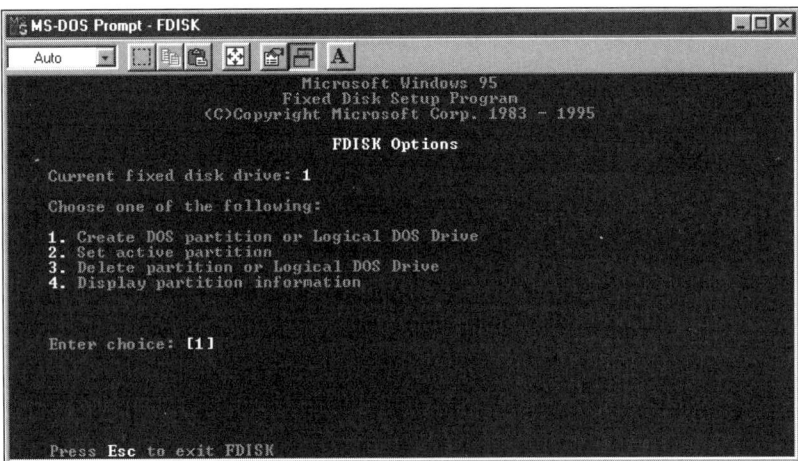

FIGURE 19-2 The FDISK **main menu**

We will select the fourth option, which brings up the screen shown in Figure 19-3. Notice that the drive we are examining is a 4GB drive that has been broken into two partitions, each one 2GB.

 caution **It is important to remember that once you make a change with FDISK, it will permanently erase whatever data was previously stored on that drive.**

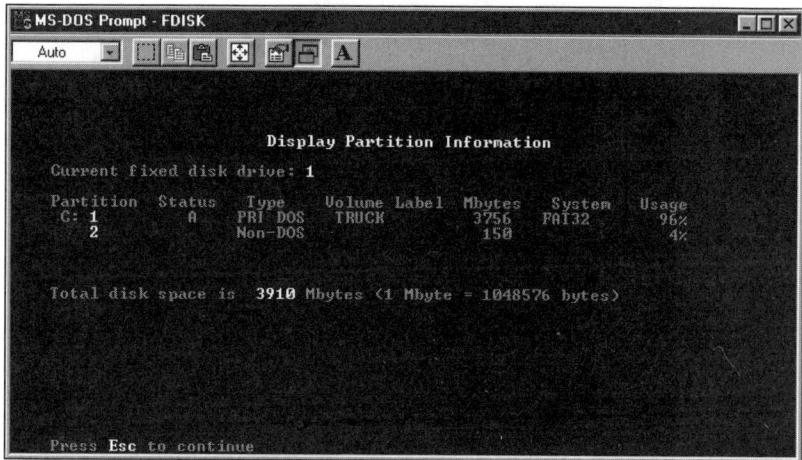

FIGURE 19-3 The partition information for the first drive on the system

Lab 19-22 *Installing Windows 95*

In this lab, we will highlight the important points of a Windows 95 setup. In this application, we will install a version of Windows 95 over an existing version of Windows 95. This type of situation may be necessary if for some reason your Windows 95 system suddenly develops a problem immediately following the installation of a new software package. These problems most commonly arise when setup programs for new software packages overwrite Windows 95 DLLs with their own files of the same name.

The first step would be to insert the CD-ROM into the system and start the Setup program. Given that your system is already running Windows 95, the CD may auto-start and take you directly to the Windows 95 installation screen. If not, double-click SETUP.EXE. This will take you through a series of setup options that will reinstall Windows 95 over itself.

The next step in the process involves choosing which installation option to use (see Figure 19-4). In this case, we will use the Typical installation. The system will then proceed into an installation and query us about the installation directory and other necessary parameters. In general, the installation is fairly straightforward and requires a minimum of planning and installation support. The Custom option is very useful for installing additional components after a previous installation.

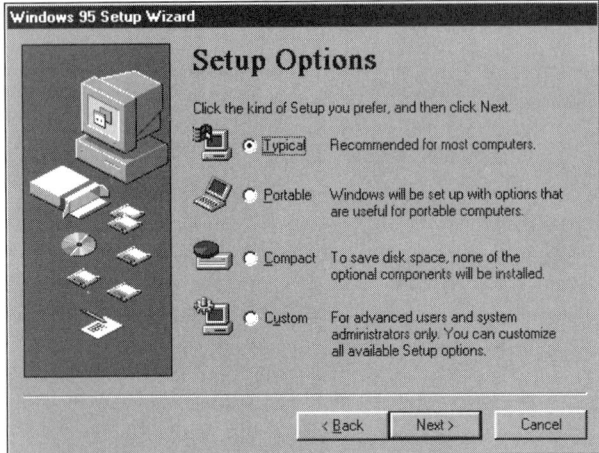

FIGURE 19-4   Setup Options under the Windows 95 Setup Wizard

After a brief installation process, Windows 95 will verify the configuration that it has determined for your computer, shown in Figure 19-5. It is critical that you verify these parameters before proceeding. You can change them using the Change button if they are inaccurate.

If everything is going well, Windows 95 will display splash screens proclaiming the value and wisdom of your purchase. A favorite is "Windows 95 makes everything you do better!" Strange — it has yet to lower any golf handicaps. Many applications programs also use splash screens to quickly explain features of the software.

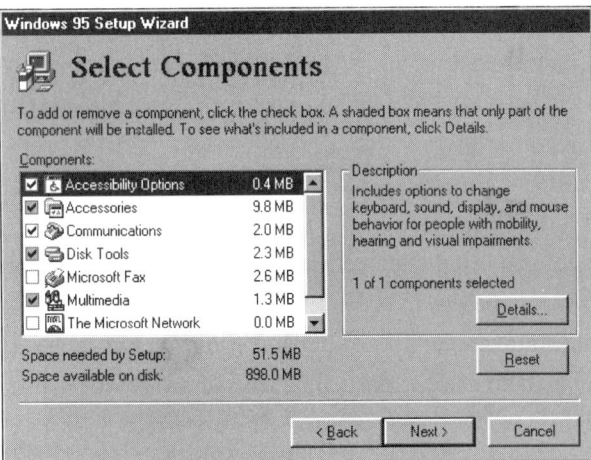

Figure 19-5   Windows 95 Setup Wizard screen showing
Select Components dialog box

Occasionally, you might get a message identifying a version conflict in a file. This type of error message indicates that the version on your hard drive is newer than the one on the distribution media. If you were having difficulties with systems components, you are probably better off installing the older version and answering no to the question. If, on the other hand, you are sure that the file is not the problem, you can leave it alone by selecting yes.

The system will continue through its installation process, which should be successful if you are getting these types of messages.

Good luck with your Windows 95 installation!

Software Tools and Troubleshooting

About Chapter 20

This chapter explores how to solve hardware and software problems when working with Microsoft Windows 95. We'll explain how to use the Install Wizards to add new hardware drivers to your system, how to remove unneeded drivers, and how to replace drivers when they become corrupt. We'll show you specifically how you can add a variety of devices to your computer. You'll learn how to troubleshoot and remove device resource conflicts and how to use the Hardware Conflict Troubleshooter.

We'll also explain how to handle common software problems, including system startup problems. We'll guide you through selecting the mode that Windows 95 starts in and help you use safe mode when your computer crashes. You'll discover how to associate file types with an application of your choice and how to restart your system when an application crashes. Finally, we'll give you some tips on troubleshooting problems with Windows 95 applications.

OPTIMIZING CURRENT RESOURCES

This section explains the basic concepts for making the best possible use of currently available resources in the Windows 95 environment, resolving software problems, and removing and replacing hardware and device drivers.

A basic strategy for optimizing your current resources includes the following:

- Let Windows 95 manage your swap file (virtual memory), as explained in Chapter 18.

- Run ScanDisk regularly to repair file system errors and to mark damaged areas of the disk as unusable.

- Run Disk Defragmenter regularly to keep your files on contiguous sectors of the disk, thereby improving disk access performance.

- Empty the Recycle Bin regularly so that it doesn't eat up too much disk space.

- Consider using DriveSpace as a disk compression tool if you continually run short of hard disk space.

- Check for and eliminate device conflicts or other device problems, as described in Chapter 14.

o Don't ask for background processing of MS-DOS applications unless you really need it.

o Evaluate printing performance trade-offs, as described in Chapter 18.

o Remove those programs that you don't need anymore to free extra space on your hard drive.

o Use the Install Wizard in the Control Panel whenever possible to add hardware or software so that you can properly remove those items if necessary.

Windows 95 has added a dialog box (shown in Figure 20-1) that will help you add and remove programs. However, only programs that were designed for Windows 95 can be removed with Add/Remove Programs. For all other programs, check the program's documentation to determine which files should be removed.

To use the Add/Remove Programs feature, follow these steps:

1. From the Start menu, choose Settings, then select Control Panel.

2. Choose Add/Remove Programs. The Add/Remove Programs Properties dialog box appears.

3. Select the Install/Uninstall property page tab.

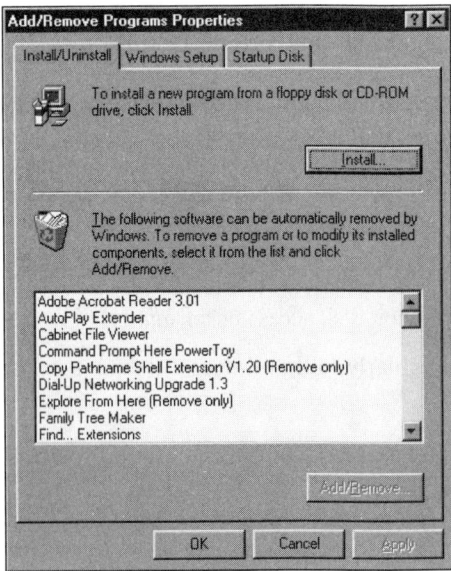

FIGURE 20-1 The Add/Remove Programs
Properties dialog box

The Add/Remove Programs Properties dialog box feature is excellent for adding and removing new software programs where you've allowed Windows 95 to monitor the installation of that software.

However, if you wish to add software for the new hardware you're installing, you will need to select the Add New Hardware icon, rather than Add/Remove Programs.

ADDING NEW HARDWARE

As you purchase new hardware such as printers or modems to use with your computer system, you will need to add these hardware devices to your computer's configuration so they are recognized and work properly. To make it easy to install or add new software, Windows 95 has a special module called Add New Hardware. To add new hardware to your computer system, follow these steps:

1. From the Start menu, choose Settings, then select Control Panel.

2. Choose Add New Hardware.

3. The Add New Hardware Wizard dialog box appears (see Figure 20-2).

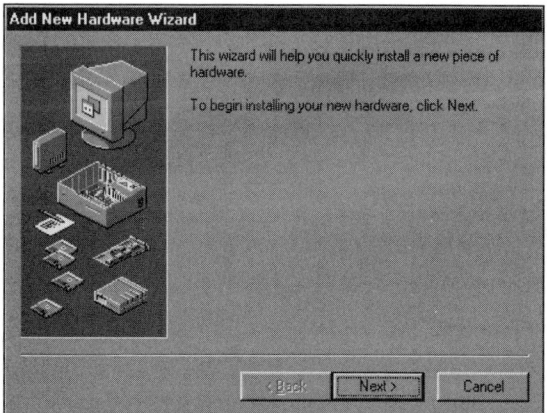

FIGURE 20-2 The Add New Hardware Wizard dialog box

4. Select the Next button to begin installing your new hardware.

5. In the next window that appears (see Figure 20-3), you are asked whether you want Windows to detect your hardware. If you don't know the name of the hardware you are installing, then you can let Windows detect the hardware for you by checking the Yes radio button. However, if you do know the filename and location of the software for the hardware you want to install, then select No.

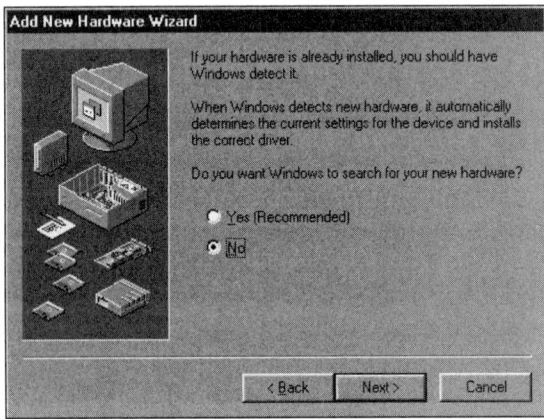

FIGURE 20-3 The second screen in the Add New Hardware Wizard

6. When you select No, the dialog box shown in Figure 20-4 appears, showing you the type of hardware to install.

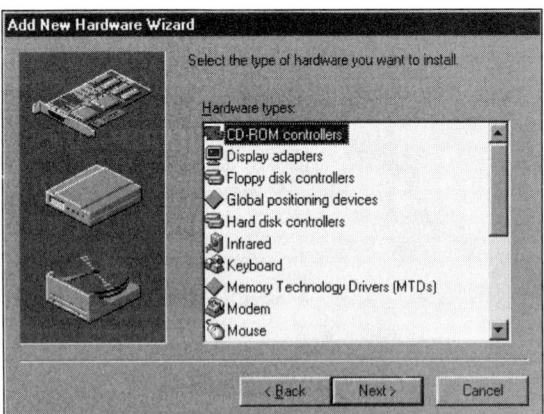

FIGURE 20-4 The third screen in the Add New Hardware Wizard

For example, let's say you wanted to install a driver for your video card. You would select that manufacturer under the display adapter choices and follow the installation wizard from that point on.

7. Then just follow the wizard's prompts until you find the name of the hardware you want to install (see Figure 20-5).

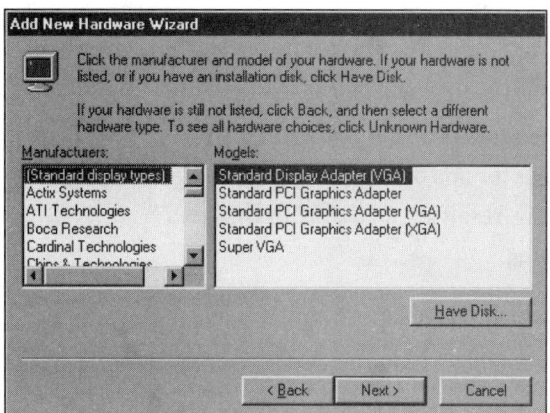

FIGURE 20-5 The next window in the Add New Hardware Wizard

You don't have to use the Install Wizard to add new software, or to set up a new application. Any technique that runs your program's Setup or Install routine will accomplish the same thing. However, the principal benefit of the Install Wizard is not that it saves you time when looking for the SETUP.EXE or INSTALL.EXE file on the CD-ROM or floppy disk — the wizard's real value is that it saves you time and trouble later if you need to remove your new program.

If your software program comes with an uninstall feature, the Install Wizard will register it — that is, add it to the list of programs that the wizard knows how to remove. It's possible you will not know whether your software program has an uninstall program, so it's a good idea to let the Install Wizard handle this option for you. If you need to remove a program, you'll be glad you used the Install Wizard.

If you're thinking that using the Install Wizard is unnecessary, consider this: Most software programs do not install all their files into one folder or subdirectory. Most programs will also install files into various parts of your Windows subdirectories. In addition, it's next to impossible to write down all the filenames and their locations; the Install Wizard keeps track of everything for you. The bonus is that you don't need to remember where all the files are located when you want to delete or remove a software program.

REMOVING AND REPLACING DEVICE DRIVERS

Hardware devices typically compete for a limited number of *input-output* (I/O) addresses, memory addresses, *interrupt request* (IRQ) lines, and *direct memory access* (DMA) channels. For your computer system to work properly, all of these pieces must work together without stepping on each other's toes. If your new modem wants the same IRQ line as your existing network adapter, you'll need to change the settings for one device or the other.

Until recently, resolving a conflict of this kind has entailed some combination of the following:

- Determining which resource is in contention
- Finding a non-conflicting alternative setting for the new peripheral
- Making a physical adjustment to the hardware, like moving a jumper, for example
- Modifying some aspect of the software that uses the new peripheral

To get rid of these difficulties, Microsoft and other vendors developed the Plug and Play specifications.

Achieving Maximum Benefits from Plug and Play

To achieve maximum benefits from Plug and Play support in Windows 95, follow these three policies:

- Whenever possible, try to buy Plug and Play peripherals rather than legacy peripherals.
- When buying a new computer, look for one that uses a Plug and Play BIOS.
- Do not use the Windows 95 Device Manager to adjust IRQ, DMA, I/O, or memory assignments for Plug and Play devices.

If you manually set a resource assignment for a Plug and Play device, Windows can no longer adjust those settings dynamically, and you'll give up one of the principal benefits of Plug and Play technology.

Disabling Hardware Using the Device Manager

After permanently removing a hardware device or driver from your computer system, you should let Windows know the device is gone so that the resources it used can be reassigned as needed. You'll do this through Device Manager. Follow these steps:

1. From the Start menu, choose Settings, then select Control Panel.

2. Choose System, then select the Device Manager tab (see Figure 20-6).

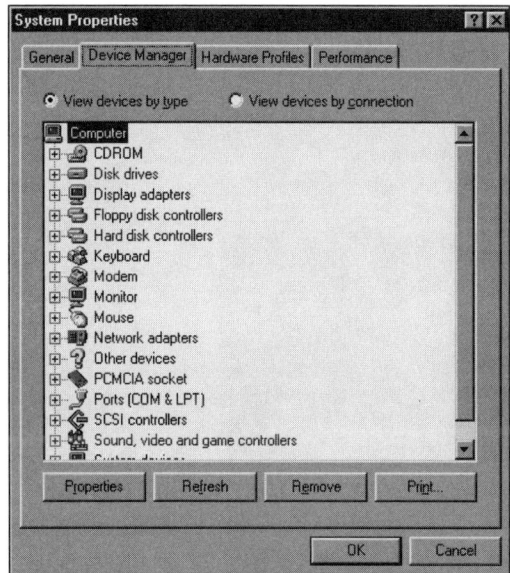

FIGURE 20-6 The Device Manager window

3. Click the plus sign next to the hardware type, and then double-click the hardware.

4. In the Device Usage area, make sure the check box next to the current configuration is empty. If more than one configuration is listed in the Device Usage area, clear the check boxes next to each configuration where you want to disable or remove the device.

The device will be disabled, but the resource settings may not be freed unless you have Plug and Play hardware.

Replacing Device Drivers and Adding New Hardware

You can use the Add Hardware Wizard to install any type of new device; however, you can also manually install other hardware devices. To make sure that the new hardware device you've just installed is working properly, view the Device Manager in Control Panel.

To install a new monitor

Installing a new monitor in Windows 95 is a simple matter of picking it from a list of supported monitors. Just follow these steps:

1. Double-click the Display icon in Control Panel, or right-click the desktop and choose Properties.

2. Click the Settings tab in the Display Properties sheet (see Figure 20-7), and then click the Change button.

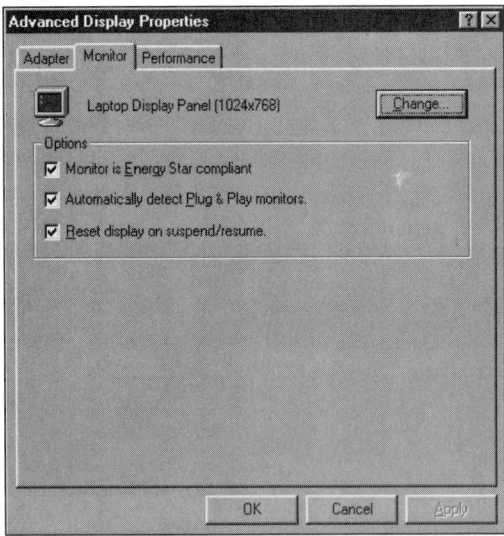

FIGURE 20-7 Changing the display type

To install a new modem

Like the monitor installation procedure, adding a modem can be as simple as choosing it from a list of available modems. Follow these steps:

1. Double-click the Modems icon in Control Panel.

2. Click the Add button in the Modems Properties sheet (see Figure 20-8).

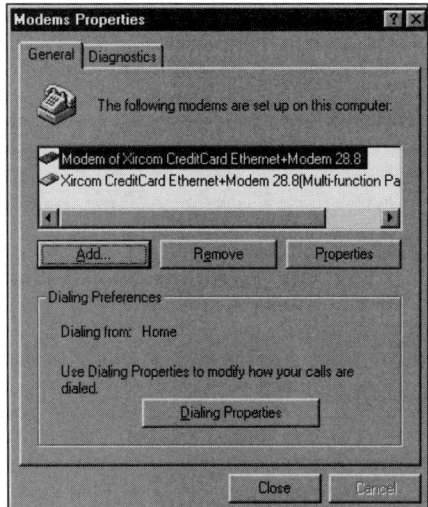

FIGURE 20-8   **Modem installation**

To install a new mouse

Windows 95 makes setting up a new mouse as simple as choosing it from the list of mouse drivers, as shown in the following steps:

1. Double-click the Mouse icon in Control Panel.

2. Click the General tab in the Mouse Properties sheet, and then click the Change button.

3. Select the Show All Devices option button to see the mouse make-and-model list.

To install a new keyboard

Likewise, you can tell Windows 95 to use a different keyboard by following these steps:

1. Double-click the Keyboard icon in Control Panel.

2. Click the General tab in the Keyboard Properties sheet, then click the Change button.

3. Select the Show All Devices option button to see the keyboard make-and-model list.

To install a new printer

Adding a printer in Windows 95 is a simple matter of using the Add Printer Wizard, as described in these steps:

1. Double-click the Printers icon in Control Panel. (Or double-click the Printers icon in your My Computer folder.)
2. Then, in the Printers folder, double-click the Add Printer icon.

Removing Hardware and Device Drivers

To inform Windows that a device is no longer present, follow these steps:

1. Right-click the My Computer icon on your desktop, then choose Properties from the object menu. Alternatively, you can double-click the System icon in Control Panel.
2. Click the Device Manager tab.
3. Select the View Devices By Type option button. The Device Manager displays a list of your hardware devices organized by type, as shown in Figure 20-9. Like the left pane in a Windows Explorer window, the Device Manager list is organized as an outline.
4. Click the plus sign next to the category that describes the hardware you want to remove.
5. Select the name of the item you want to remove.
6. Click the Remove button.

 **Device Manager is not the place to carry out casual experimentation. If you're unsure which entry to remove, get help from your organization's support staff, your vendor's technical support service, or a knowledgeable colleague.**

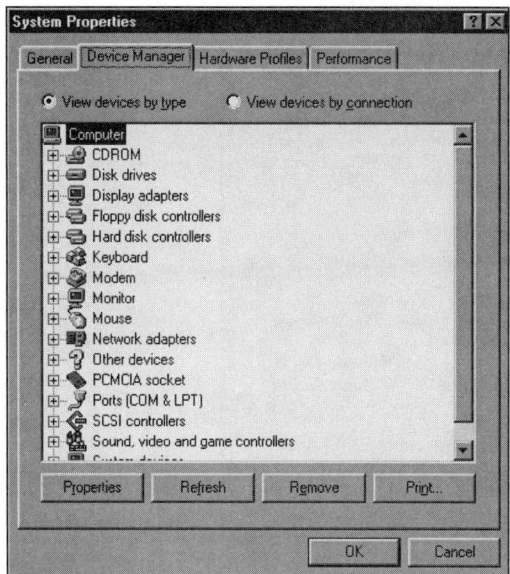

FIGURE 20-9   System Properties on the Device Manager tab

ELIMINATING DEVICE CONFLICTS

To eliminate hardware device conflicts, you can use the Hardware Conflict Troubleshooter. This troubleshooter helps you identify and resolve hardware conflicts. Just click to answer the questions, and then follow the step-by-step instructions to fix the problem.

Using the Hardware Conflict Troubleshooter

First, you'll want to follow the previous instructions that show you how to get to the Device Manager. Once you've launched the Device Manager, make sure that the View Devices By Type option is selected.

If the hardware that has the conflict isn't visible in the list, click the plus sign next to the type of hardware (see Figure 20-10).

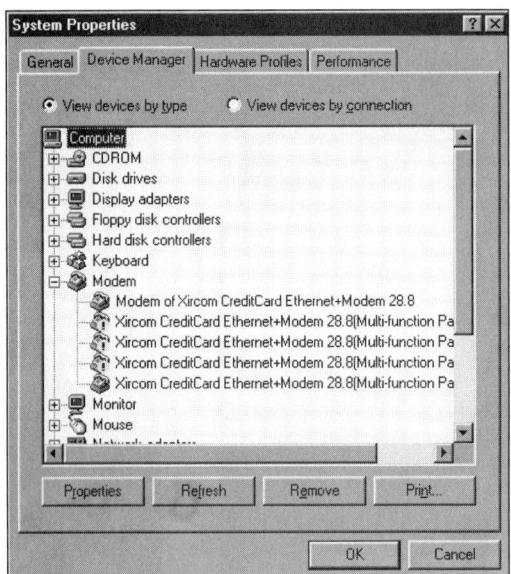

FIGURE 20-10 Find the device with a conflict in the Device Manager

Is the device you were installing (or that had the conflict) listed twice? You should have three options to choose from at this point:

- No, the device is listed only once.

- Yes, it is listed twice. I have only one of this kind of device.

- Yes, it is listed twice, but I have two of this kind of device.

If you chose Option #1 above, you should view resource settings for the device. Here's how:

1. Double-click the hardware that has a conflict to open its Properties sheet.

2. In the Device Usage area of the General tab (see Figure 20-11), make sure that the Disable In This Hardware Profile checkbox is disabled. If the box is checked, click it.

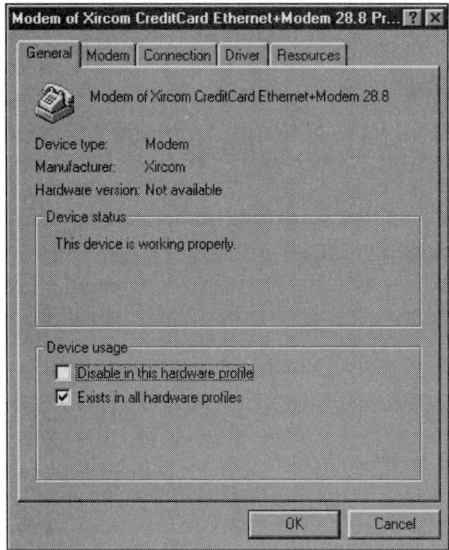

FIGURE 20-11 Make sure the Disable In This Hardware
Profile checkbox is disabled

3. Click the Resources tab (see Figure 20-12).

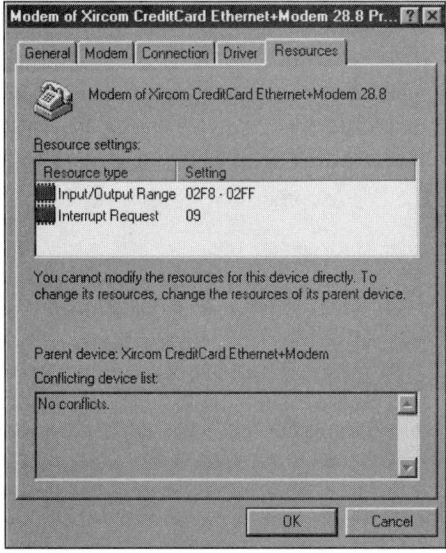

FIGURE 20-12 Check for resource conflicts on the Resources tab

Do you see a box with resource settings? If you said yes, then you must identify which resources are causing the conflict. In the Conflicting Device List box, identify the hardware that is using conflicting resources. Is more than one resource conflict listed? If so, then you must determine how many devices are listed as conflicting. If only one device is causing all the conflicts, you must decide if you want to disable the device that is causing all the conflicts. If you choose yes, then you must determine how to disable the hardware. Here's how:

1. On the hardware list, double-click the hardware that you want to disable.

2. If you do not see the hardware list, click Cancel until you return to it.

3. In the Device Usage area, click the box next to the configuration marked "Current" to remove the check mark.

4. Click the Resources tab.

5. If there is a Set Configuration Manually button, Windows can disable and free up resources used by this hardware without your removing its card from your computer.

However, rather than disabling the conflicting device, you can alternatively look for a resource setting that doesn't conflict with the device you're trying to fix. Follow these steps to do so:

1. In the Resource Settings box, double-click the icon next to the resource setting that is conflicting.

2. If you see a message that says you must clear the Use Automatic Settings box before you can change a resource setting, click OK to close the message, and then clear the Use Automatic Settings box.

3. Scroll through the available resource settings.

4. For each setting, look in the Conflicting Device List box to see if it conflicts with any other hardware.

5. If you find a free setting, click OK.

6. When you find a setting that doesn't conflict with any other hardware, set the new value. First make a note of the old and new settings to refer to later. Click OK. If you see a message prompting you to restart your computer, click No.

Changing Hardware Jumpers

Depending on the type of hardware you have, you may have to change the jumpers on your hardware card to match the new setting, or you may have to run a configuration utility provided by your hardware manufacturer. If the device you're working with isn't Plug and Play compatible, then you need to manually specify which IRQ, I/O port, and DMA channel the device should use. You do this with the jumpers on the device itself.

If the jumper settings on your card aren't set properly, your hardware will not work, even if you resolved the conflict correctly in the operating system. The hardware and software need to be set the same for the device to work. In the next procedure, you will shut down your computer so that you can open it up and work with the hardware. Refer to your hardware documentation for instructions on changing jumpers.

Whenever you make changes to the devices you've installed or removed, you must restart your computer for the changes to take place. Follow the steps below to restart your computer to make the new changes you've made effective.

1. Click OK when you're prompted to restart your computer.
2. When Windows says it is safe to do so, turn off your computer so you can configure the devices that changed. For more information about how to do this, see your hardware documentation.

Correcting Conflict Settings

If you can't find a setting that doesn't conflict with any other hardware, then you must identify the hardware you no longer need. Follow these steps to correct conflicting settings:

1. Scroll through the available resource settings.
2. When a conflict appears in the Conflicting Device List box, determine whether you still need to use the device that is causing the conflict.
3. Did you identify a hardware device that you no longer need to use? If you choose yes, then you must determine whether the hardware you want to disable is Plug and Play.

4. Select each resource setting that conflicts with the hardware you will disable, and then click OK.

5. When the message appears, saying the setting conflicts with another device, click Yes to continue.

6. Click OK until you return to the hardware list.

7. Click the plus sign next to the type of hardware that you want to disable.

8. Double-click the hardware that you want to disable.

9. In the Device Usage area, click the box next to the configuration marked "Current" to remove the check mark.

10. Click the Resources tab.

If there is a Set Configuration Manually button, Windows can disable and free up resources used by this hardware without removing its card from your computer.

Printing a Report for Each Device You Changed

To keep an accurate record of the changes you've made to your computer system and its settings, it's wise to print a report for each device you changed. In this way, you always have a log to refer to if you want to recover the steps you followed. Here's how to print a report:

1. In the hardware list, click a device whose resource settings you changed while resolving the conflict.

2. If you do not see the hardware list, click OK until you return to it.

3. Click Print.

4. Click the second option to print the selected class or device.

5. Click OK.

6. Repeat Steps 1 through 4 for each device you changed during this troubleshooting process.

Solving Common Software Problems

From time to time, you will encounter software problems when using Windows 95. Before you can solve any problems, though, you first need to identify the problem. This section will help you troubleshoot some common software problems and show you how to resolve them.

While taking your A+ Certification exam, you will need to know many of these secrets, tips, and techniques for solving common software problems. This section will better enable you to pass the A+ Certification exam.

Recognizing System Startup Problems

If you're using the CONFIG.SYS and AUTOXEC.BAT startup files, you should verify the accuracy of both files' contents. This includes the device drivers you're using, settings, and path entries. Use Notepad to open these files and make sure they point to valid drivers and programs, and verify the accuracy of settings for those items.

Troubleshooting Options when Using Startup Mode

When you turn on your computer, it runs through various tests, then, while it's still in text mode, the message "Starting Windows 95" appears on the screen. At this point, you can press F8 to bring up the startup menu, which permits you to choose the mode in which you want to run Windows 95. The following table illustrates the options available to you on this menu. Each startup menu option is described, along with the purpose of the option.

TABLE 20-1 STARTUP MENU OPTIONS

STARTUP MENU OPTIONS	DESCRIPTION
Normal	Starts Windows loading all normal startup files and Registry values.
Logged (BOOTLOG.TXT)	Runs system startup, which creates a startup log file.

continued

TABLE 20-1 *(continued)*

STARTUP MENU OPTIONS	DESCRIPTION
Safe Mode	Starts Windows, but bypasses startup files and uses only the basic system drivers. (This is the same as pressing F5 or typing **Win/d:m** at the command prompt.)
Safe Mode with Network Support	Starts Windows and bypasses startup files using basic system drivers. (This is the same as typing **win/d:n** at the command prompt.)
Step-by-Step Confirmation	Starts Windows, and confirms startup files line by line (This is the same as pressing F8 when the Startup menu is displayed.)
Command Prompt Only	This option starts the operating system and displays only the command prompt.
Safe Mode Command Prompt Only	Starts the operating system in Safe Mode and displays only the command prompt, bypassing startup files. (This is the same as pressing Shift+F5.)
Previous Version of MS-DOS	Only available if BootMulti=1 is contained in the MSDOS.SYS file. It starts the previously installed version of MS-DOS. (This is the same as pressing F4.)

Using Safe Mode

Safe mode enables you to run Windows 95 even if certain devices are causing conflicts that prevent you from running the computer in normal mode. For example, if you've set your video adapter to a mode that your monitor doesn't support, you won't be able to see the desktop to set it back to a useable state. Safe mode always runs with the Video adapter set to standard VGA, so any Windows 95-compatible monitor should work properly, letting you gain access to the settings you need to fix the problem. Safe mode starts up automatically immediately after a system crash. When you have finished the repair, you can restart your system and a normal start will occur.

The following conditions would lead Windows 95 to automatically launch you into safe mode:

o Your computer suddenly slows down, creating an overload effect on your system and memory

- An intermittent error condition needs to be tested
- The video display doesn't work properly
- You cannot print to a local printer
- Windows 95 doesn't work correctly, or has unexpected results
- Windows 95 stalls for an extended period of time
- Windows 95 fails to start after the Starting Windows 95 message appears

Associating a File Type with a Program

In Windows 95, you can double-click a file to open the associated application. For example, if you've typed up a report in Microsoft Word and saved it, then you can find that file in Windows Explorer and double-click it to automatically open Word and load that file into it. This happens by associating a file type with a program. File types are determined by the extension (the last three characters following the period) of their filename. In Windows 95, you can associate a file type with any program you want, though it's generally a good idea to associate file types with programs capable of reading or editing them. Here's how to associate a file type with a program:

1. In My Computer or Windows Explorer, click View, and then click Options.
2. Click the File Types tab. Then click the file type you want to associate with that program.
3. Click the Edit button to display the Edit File Type dialog box.
4. Select Open in the action list, and then click the Edit button.
5. In the Editing Action For File Type dialog box, type the name of the program to use to open files with this extension. Include the path pointing to the executable file. You can also use the Browse button to locate the program, and then click OK.

Correcting Applications That Fail

If a software application fails by stalling, crashing, or when the keyboard, mouse, or display does not function correctly, the process of running the application can be closed without quitting Windows 95 or ending other applications.

Press Ctrl+Alt+Del. You're presented with a list of all the running applications, and you can decide which applications to end or stop. An error message "not responding" appears to indicate that the application has failed.

In the Close Program dialog box shown in Figure 20-13, you can choose which application you want to close or end, and then you can click End Task.

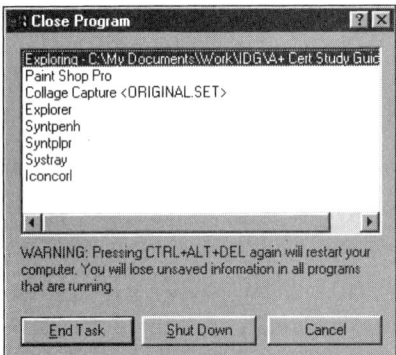

FIGURE 20-13   The Close Program and Quit Windows option

To Quit Windows 95

It is best to use the Shut Down button in the Close Program dialog box, or the Shut Down command on the Start menu. Otherwise, all of the operating system commands and changes will not be made to the hidden files. For example, if you installed a new driver and you failed to shut Windows down properly, your settings could be lost and would not take effect the next time you started Windows.

Troubleshooting Windows 95 Applications

Following are various troubleshooting mechanisms to use when you are having trouble with software applications. Keep in mind that there are many, many troubleshooting options available to you in the Windows 95 Help file, but for now, these will assist your certification requirements.

The Windows 95 README.TXT file

A README.TXT file was shipped with your Windows 95 software. This file lists applications that have been known to have problems when running under Windows 95, and includes descriptions of the problems that arise. Check this list to see if the application you're working with has a known problem on this operating system.

Fixing shortcuts that don't launch an application

A Windows 95 shortcut is basically a pointer to an application program, along with an icon to identify it. You can create a shortcut on your desktop that points to your favorite program; when you double-click the shortcut, the associated program should run. However, if you double-click a shortcut and the associated application doesn't execute, you can right-click the shortcut icon and then choose Properties to open the shortcut's Properties dialog box. Click the Find Target button to have Windows 95 search for the actual application file. If it can't find it, you'll be presented with a Browse dialog box in which you can search for the application on your hard disks. Find the appropriate application executable and click OK. Then the next time you click that application's shortcut, it will launch properly.

Fixing a corrupted or missing Start Menu directory

The items on the Windows 95 Start menu are actually contained in the Windows\Start Menu directory on your hard drive. If this directory becomes corrupt or gets deleted, you'll find that the Start Menu doesn't work anymore. You can fix a corrupted or missing Start Menu directory by following these steps:

1. Shut down Windows 95 properly, and then restart the computer to create a new Start Menu folder.

2. If the Start menu still does not perform properly, delete the entire Start Menu directory, and recreate a new Start Menu folder by opening Explorer to the Windows folder, and clicking File ⇒ New ⇒ Folder. Name the folder Start Menu.

Checking disk corruption in Windows 95

Sometimes your hard disk drive can become corrupted (files are damaged and inaccessible or the drive becomes physically damaged) or fragmented (the files aren't stored in contiguous sectors on the disk). To correct this problem, follow these steps:

1. In Windows Explorer, right-click the drive icon and select Properties from the context menu.

2. Click the Tools tab.

3. In the Error-Checking Status box, click the Check Now button. If the disk is corrupted, you may need to replace system files and structures.

Before performing any disk repair operations, make sure your data is properly backed up, in case you need to restore essential files. You can back up your data by copying it to another disk (preferably a removable disk like a floppy or a Zip disk) or by using the Backup program that comes with Windows 95.

Using ScanDisk

You can use ScanDisk to check your hard disk for logical and physical errors, and then repair the damaged areas. Logical errors are problems with files that are stored improperly and can't be accessed by the operating system; physical errors are actual physical damage to the hard drive.

1. From the Start menu, choose Programs, and then select Accessories.

2. From Accessories, choose System Tools, and then select ScanDisk to open the ScanDisk dialog box, shown in Figure 20-14.

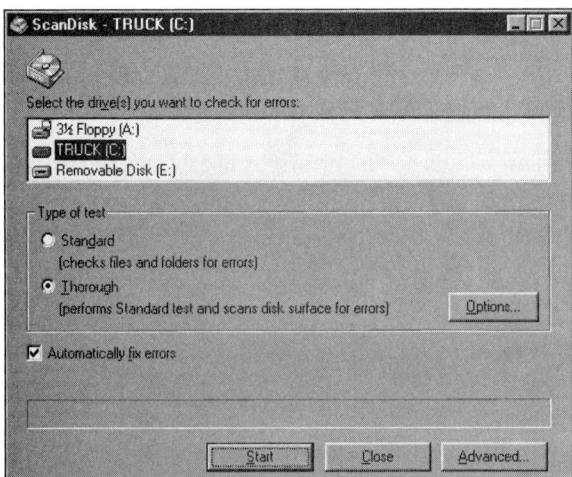

FIGURE 20-14 The ScanDisk dialog box

3. After the ScanDisk dialog box appears, select the Advanced button to reveal the ScanDisk Advanced Options window (see Figure 20-15).

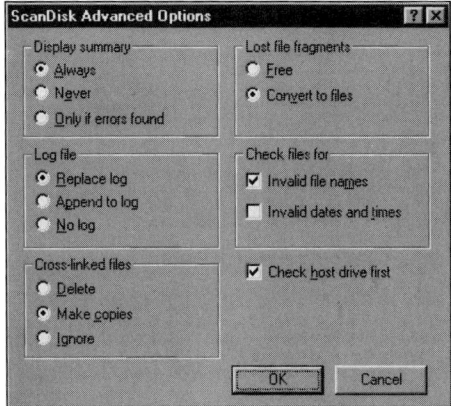

FIGURE 20-15 The ScanDisk Advanced Options choices

ScanDisk finds and fixes the following kinds of logical errors:

- Problems with the *file allocation table* (FAT), in which the description of the file in the FAT doesn't match the actual location of the file on the drive (see Chapter 4 for more information).

- Problems involving long filenames in which the filename isn't stored properly in the directory and doesn't point to an actual file on the disk.

- Lost clusters, which are clusters on the disk that aren't associated with any file in the directory system, but aren't marked as unused in the FAT.

- Cross-linked files. This occurs when two or more files are using the same area of the disk.

- Problems involving the directory structure, meaning that the directories aren't defined correctly and point to invalid areas of the disk.

- On disks compressed with DriveSpace or DoubleSpace, problems involving the volume header, volume file structure, compression structure, or volume signature. This prevents Windows 95 from accessing the information stored on the compressed drive.

Optimizing Disk Performance with Disk Defragmenter

When you store files on a hard disk, Windows writes each file's data in a set of adjacent disk clusters. As you use software applications, the files you create through that application are added and removed from the hard disk. Over time, these disk clusters can become fragmented. Fragmentation does not affect data integrity, but it does reduce the efficiency of your hard disk.

Fragmentation occurs when pieces of your file are saved to different positions on your hard drive. When you have less and less space, and more and more files, or when you delete large groups of files, the new files you create are written to many different spaces on your hard drive. When you defragment your hard drive, you are letting the program regroup your file pieces into one location. Fragmented files take longer to read and write than contiguous ones. To eliminate disk fragmentation and enhance Windows's performance, you can use a defragmentation utility furnished with Windows 95 software.

A quick and simple way to run Disk Defragmenter is as follows:

1. Open My Computer, and right-click the icon for the disk drive you want to defragment.
2. Choose Properties from the object menu.
3. Click the Tools tab, shown in Figure 20-16.
4. Click Defragment Now.

Using DETCRASH.LOG

The DETCRASH.LOG file is a file that Setup uses to determine why an installation failed. Basically, the computer might stop or stall at three points during Windows 95 Setup: before, during, or after hardware detection. If Setup fails before hardware detection, Windows 95 Setup recovers by reading SETUPLOG.TXT to determine where the system stalled, what to redo, and what to skip.

If Setup fails during hardware detection, the DETCRASH.LOG file is created, containing information about the detection module that was running and the I/O port or memory resources it was accessing when the failure occurred.

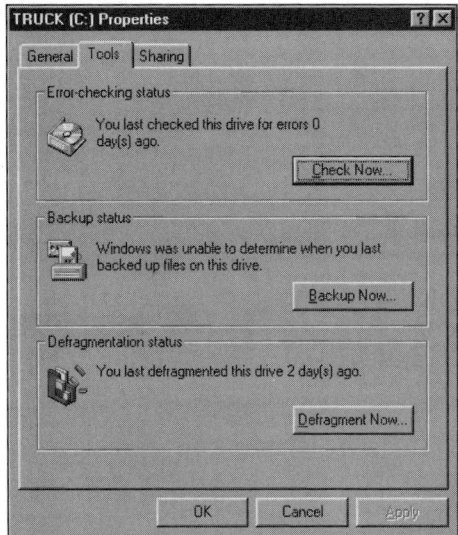

FIGURE 20-16 The Defrag tool

If your computer crashes during one of these stages of Setup, you need to restart it. Upon restarting, Setup will check to see if one of these files exists, and if it finds one of these files, the computer automatically runs in Safe Recovery mode. It verifies all the devices already in the Registry and then skips all detection modules up to the failed module, in effect skipping the action that caused the failure. Then, Safe Recovery or Safe Mode continues the detection process, starting with the next module. If the detection process is completed successfully, DETCRASH.LOG is deleted. DETCRASH.LOG can only be read by Setup, so you won't actually need to work with this file.

KEY POINT SUMMARY

This chapter has addressed troubleshooting software problems, removing and replacing device drivers, eliminating device conflicts, and removing and installing new hardware and software.

o The major tools that you can use to add devices and programs to your computer are found in the Control Panel.

- You can add hardware using the Hardware Wizard, and you can add or remove software by using the Add/Remove Software wizards.

- You can disable devices, and refresh drives using the System program.

- ScanDisk helps find and repair errors on the disk drives.

- Defragment is a utility that optimizes the disk drives by reorganizing the data. Disks become fragmented when parts of files are spread out over the disk. Defrag regroups the data into contiguous files.

- The Windows 95 README.TXT files provide a great deal of information for troubleshooting and repairing software configuration issues. Microsoft Tech-Net as well as the Microsoft Web site (www.microsoft.com) can provide invaluable troubleshooting information.

- The Windows 95 Resource Kit is a valuable investment for technicians who support Windows 95 systems.

APPLYING WHAT YOU'VE LEARNED

This chapter has covered a lot of important material that will help you prepare for the A+ exam and be an excellent computer technician. Take a few minutes and work through the questions in the Instant Assessment, then review your notes and see how you did.

The Hands-on lab will also help you build your comfort level with the hardware as well as reinforce the readings from this chapter.

Instant Assessment

Multiple choice

Choose the best answer(s). There may be more than one correct answer for each question.

1. To check for upper memory area conflicts at system startup, which of the following commands would you use?

    A. `win /d:x`

    B. `win / d:f`

    C. `win /d:v`

    D. Press F8

2. Which of the following examples would qualify for using safe mode?

    A. To test an intermittent error condition

    B. When you cannot print to a local printer

    C. When the video display does not work properly

    D. When a NetWare client is not recognized

3. Which file does Setup read to verify the installed components in Windows 95?

    A. VMM32.VXD

    B. PRTUPD.INF

    C. BOOTLOG.TXT

    D. SETUPLOG.TXT

4. Is it possible to set up a shortcut to launch an application from the Windows 95 desktop?

    A. Yes

    B. No

    C. Only if you're running `AUTOEXEC.BAT` on startup

    D. Only if you right-click the application's icon

5. Under what circumstances would you use Device Manager?

    A. To install a new hardware device

    B. To remove a software application

    C. To resolve hardware conflicts

    D. To load an MS-DOS game

6. The purpose of ScanDisk is to:

    A. File a file quickly

    B. Find and correct hard disk errors

    C. Defragment the file allocation tables

    D. Prepare for a Disk Defrag program

7. How many ways can you install new software and hardware?

   A. One — through a CD-ROM or floppy disk SETUP.EXE file.

   B. Two — running the INSTALL.EXE file from a disk or from your hard drive.

   C. Three — You can use the Add/Remove Program utility, or you can use the Run command from the Start menu, or you can install the program from your hard disk or CD-ROM.

   D. You don't have a choice. You must follow the software or hardware vendor's instructions.

8. If you are running Windows 95, can you use AUTOEXEC.BAT and CONFIG.SYS files?

   A. Yes

   B. No

   C. Maybe

   D. Depends on the software you are using and on which type of computer you are running it on

9. When you are having problems with a software application, and you cannot print, where would you look first to resolve the problem?

   A. You would look at the printer to make sure it's plugged in

   B. You would check in the Printers folder to make sure you have configured a printer

   C. You would check the settings in the software application you are using

   D. You would call your Help Desk and have them figure it out

Fill in the blank

1. If you want to update data in a report without retyping the information, you would use _____.

2. If you want to view a graphical representation of devices configured in Windows 95 so you could see the allocated resources for each device, you would use this program: _____.

3. _____ defines extensions to the existing PC hardware architecture that, with new BIOS and device driver capabilities, facilitates hardware setup and configuration.

4. A _____ that's included with an operating system's utility programs routes printer commands to a file on disk or in RAM instead of to the printer, until the printer is ready to accept the job.

5. The _____ switch is used when starting Windows 95 from the command prompt to isolate an error condition.

6. _____ bypasses the startup files to give access to the Windows 95 configuration files when the operating system fails to start normally.

7. To verify the accuracy of the system startup drivers, settings, and path entries, you would press the _____ key when using the AUTOEXEC.BAT and CONFIG.SYS files.

8. To automatically install new software or hardware that Windows 95 can track and help report errors about later, you would use
_____.

9. To add or remove programs the safe way in Windows 95, you should use this program: _____.

10. If you cannot resolve a software conflict, or cannot figure out how to repair a problem, you should look in this file for help:_____.

Hands-on Lab Exercises

These two labs will provide you with experience in troubleshooting hardware and software problems. The first one demonstrates using the Install Wizard to add a new hardware device driver to the system, and in the second, you'll refresh a device driver from the setup files to restore it to proper working order.

Lab 20-23 *Installing a device driver*

When you want to install a new hardware device driver in Windows 95, you should use the Install Wizard. Follow these steps:

1. Open the Control Panel and double-click the Add New Hardware icon to open the Add New Hardware Wizard shown in Figure 20-17.

2. Click Next on the introductory screen to begin.

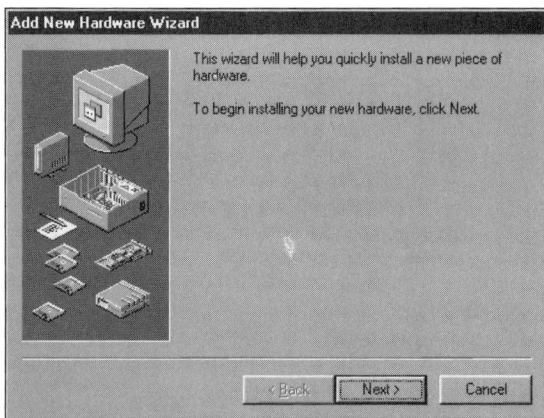

FIGURE 20-17   The Add New Hardware screen that will be
used to change the video adapter

3. Assuming you've already installed the actual device, select Yes and click
   Next to let Windows 95 detect it.

4. Windows 95 will automatically find the device and install the appropriate
   driver for it.

Lab 20-24 *Refreshing a device driver*

Sometimes a device driver becomes corrupt or no longer works. In this case, you can
use the Device Manager to refresh the driver. We would do this if a device that was working suddenly started malfunctioning. In some cases, it may be a hardware problem, but
in as many cases, the software driver may have become corrupted. This often happens
when you have just gone through a series of upgrades in software or hardware.

In this case, the scanner attached to this system has become unknown to the
system. We are going to remove the driver from the system and let the system
restart to automatically find the new hardware. Follow these steps:

1. Delete the driver by selecting it under Device Manager and clicking the
   Remove button.

2. Restart the computer to make sure the changes have taken place.

3. After the system restarted, it discovered the new hardware. The Install
   Wizard asks for driver information.

4. Follow the instructions provided by the Add New Hardware Wizard to
   complete the installation of the scanner.

Resources

Exam Objectives

About Appendix A

For A+ certification, you must pass both the Core and DOS/Windows examinations. The objectives for each are listed here. Although these objectives were current at the time of printing, you should check out www.comptia.org for the most up-to-date infor-mation. And for more information on A+ certification, see Appendix D of this book.

The Core Objectives

1.1 Identify basic terms, concepts, and functions of system modules, including how each module should work during normal operation.

Examples of concepts and modules:

- System board
- Power supply
- Processor /CPU
- Memory
- Storage devices
- Monitor
- Modem
- Firmware
- Boot process
- BIOS
- CMOS

1.2 Identify basic procedures for adding and removing field replaceable modules.

Examples of modules:

- System board
- Storage device
- Power supply
- Processor /CPU
- Memory
- Input devices

1.3 Identify available IRQs, DMAs, and I/O addresses and procedures for configuring them for device installation.

Content may include the following:

- Standard IRQ settings
- Modems
- Floppy drives
- Hard drive

1.4 Identify common peripheral ports, associated cabling, and their connectors.

Content may include the following:

- Cable types
- Cable orientation
- Serial versus parallel
- Pin connections

Examples of types of connectors:

- DB-9
- DB-25
- RJ-11
- RJ-45
- BNC
- PS2/MINI-DIN

1.5 Identify proper procedures for installing and configuring IDE/EIDE devices.

Content may include the following:

- Master/slave
- Devices per channel

1.6 Identify proper procedures for installing and configuring SCSI devices.

Content may include the following:

o Address/Termination conflicts

o Cabling

o Types (example: regular, wide, ultrawide)

o Internal versus external

o Switch and jumper settings

1.7 Identify proper procedures for installing and configuring peripheral devices.

Content may include the following:

o Monitor/Video Card

o Modem

o Storage devices

1.8 Identify concepts and procedures relating to BIOS.

o Methods for upgrading

o When to upgrade

1.9 Identify hardware methods of system optimization and when to use them.

Content may include the following:

o Memory

o Hard Drives

o CPU

o Cache memory

THE DOS/WINDOWS OBJECTIVES

1.1 Identify the operating system's functions, structure, and major system files.

Content may include the following:

- Functions of DOS, Windows 3.*x* and Windows 95
- Major components of DOS, Windows 3.*x* and Windows 95
- Contrasts between Windows 3.*x* and Windows 95

Major system files: what they are, where they are located, how they are used and what they contain:

- System, Configuration, and User Interface files
- DOS
- Autoexec.bat
- Config.sys
- Io.sys
- Ansi.sys
- Msdos.sys
- Emm386.exe
- HIMEM.SYS
- Command.com (internal DOS commands)
- Windows 3.*x*
- Win.ini
- System.ini
- User.exe
- Gdi.exe
- win.ini
- Win.com
- Progman.ini

- progMAN.exe
- Krnlxxx.exe
- Windows 95
- Io.sys
- Msdos.sys
- Command.com
- regedit.exe
- System.dat
- User.dat

1.2 Identify ways to navigate the operating system and how to get to needed technical information.

Content may include the following:

- Procedures (for example, menu or icon-driven) for navigating through DOS to perform such things as locating, accessing, and retrieving information
- Procedures for navigating through the Windows 3.*x*/Windows 95 operating system, accessing, and retrieving information

1.3 Identify basic concepts and procedures for creating, viewing and managing files and directories, including procedures for changing file attributes and the ramifications of those changes (for example, security issues).

Content may include the following:

- File attributes
- File naming conventions
- Command syntax
- Read Only, Hidden, System, and Archive attributes

1.4 Identify the procedures for basic disk management.

Content may include the following:

- Using disk management utilities
- Backing up
- Formatting
- Partitioning
- Defragmenting
- ScanDisk
- FAT32
- File allocation tables (FAT)
- Virtual file allocation tables (VFAT)

Mini–Lab Manual

We've pulled together this Mini–Lab Manual from all the lab exercises that appear in this book to help prepare you for the certification exam. These lab exercises are extremely important and you should not skip them. There's no substitute for using these labs to prepare for the A+ Certification exam.

Lab 3.1 *Assembling a PC system*

Getting organized

The system we are building will be based on an Intel 440BX motherboard. Many manufacturers, including ASUS, SuperMicro, and Micronics, make motherboards.

Our system will have the following components installed in it:

- Systems unit (which typically includes the power supply and disk cables)
- Intel Seattle motherboard with integrated sound (440BX chipset)
- 400MHz Pentium II processor
- Mid-tower case
- 275-watt Silencer ultra-quiet power supply
- CPU-Cool K1 Pentium II cooling fan
- Bay-Cool extra cooling fan kit (previous four items from PC Power and Cooling Corp.)

- 64MB of PC100-compliant SDRAM
- Toshiba DVD-ROM Player
- Toshiba 32X SCSI CD-ROM drive
- 4.5GB UW SCSI hard drive
- 3.5-inch floppy disk
- ATI All-in-Wonder Pro AGP video card
- Adaptec 2940U2W SCSI Controller card
- Microsoft IntelliMouse
- Microsoft Natural Keyboard Elite
- ViewSonicG790 19-inch monitor

All of these components can be ordered from mail order in the back of most computer magazines, or from computer stores that specialize in computer components. Competitive pricing information can be found at www.pricewatch.com.

With the exception of the DVD player, this is a high-end machine that you may encounter in offices this year. In most office settings, you will find a CD-ROM player instead of a DVD player.

Tools required

- A Static Strap, available from most electronic supply houses or by mail order.
- A screwdriver (probably a #2 Phillips head is all you will require).

These tools can be purchased at electronic supply houses such as Radio Shack.

We will be using a table to lay all of the components out. This will help us build this system with a minimum of fuss and aggravation. As you can see in Figure 3-14, we have pretty well taken over the table.

FIGURE 3-14 The computer system laid out in pieces

 tip **Always use a fan on the CPU chip. This will prevent the premature destruction of the chip. The surface temperature of a Pentium II CPU can exceed 200 degrees without a fan.**

General procedures

The following paragraphs briefly explain the steps we will be performing during the installation. The specific steps we will take are shown later in the lab.

The first step in this process is mounting the motherboard to the systems unit. The PC Power and Cooling mid-tower case opens from both sides, but only the left side (looking at the case from the front) needs to be removed to mount the motherboard. Later, when we're installing drives in the drive bays, the right side of the case can be removed to mount the right side of the drives. Figure 3-15 shows the motherboard mounted into the case. Notice that in the middle right of the motherboard is the Pentium II CPU chip with a clip-mounted fan. Pentium II chips generate a great deal of heat and require a fan. If you forget this, then in all probability, your CPU chip will melt itself and you will have to get a new one. Failure to use a CPU fan voids nearly all CPU warranties.

FIGURE 3-15 The motherboard being mounted into the systems case

Mounting the Intel motherboard requires a series of metallic and plastic standoff spacers. The metallic standoffs are used on the holes in the motherboard that are ringed with metal — in this case, all but two of the mounting holes. In addition to serving as a sturdy base for the motherboard, these metallic standoffs also act as a ground and ensure that the board will be shielded. Shielding is important to help ensure the motherboard does not generate *electromagnetic interference* (EMI) in nearby electronic equipment.

This motherboard is designed to support Pentium II CPUs in a wide range of speeds, from the early 233MHz models up to the current fastest model, the 450MHz. Many boards require jumper settings to adjust the board's operating speed and CPU voltage to the levels for a particular CPU speed. The Seattle automatically senses the CPU's speed and adjusts itself accordingly. Be sure to read the manual that comes with your motherboard *before* powering anything up!

Notice also that the memory chips have been inserted into the board in the top right. The connectors to the left are for the keyboard, mouse, and *Universal Serial Bus* (USB) devices. Below these connectors are the PCI slots, and finally the ISA slots. To the right of the memory are the onboard drive connectors, for EIDE drives as well as the floppy drive. Through the course of assembling this system, we will also be connecting wires to power the speaker, fan, and other indicators and controls.

As you can see, most of the motherboards today accomplish a great deal with very few parts. There are really only a half-dozen or so chips on the motherboard. Older PCs might have had thirty or forty chips on the motherboard. The chip in the middle is the ROM that contains the BIOS. The battery (the round object in the lower right corner) provides power to the motherboard, which enables it to remember the date and firmware or permanent systems settings.

The advantage of this type of design (from a technical support perspective) is that very few things can be replaced in the field. Most of the time, a technician will carry a motherboard, a spare CPU chip, and just a few other parts.

Part 1: Installing the motherboard

By mounting the motherboard against the wall of the case, we've accomplished our first step — to mount the motherboard into the system unit. Notice in Figure 3-16 that the expansion slots are close to the openings on the left side of the picture (or back of the systems unit). In the upper left-hand corner of the motherboard is a connector into which the keyboard is plugged. The U-shaped brackets above the motherboard are used for mounting disk drives. These brackets can be easily removed and reinstalled, making access to the motherboard simple. At this time, you will want to install the CPU and fan and check and configure systems jumpers (if needed) per your installation manual.

Mate the connectors with the openings in the back of the case

FIGURE 3-16 Motherboard and systems unit mating ritual

Part 2: Installing cables and jumpers

The next step in our process is to install cables. The first cable we are going to install is very easy to identify because it's the biggest, longest cable in the system. This cable connects the motherboard to the power supply. On our motherboard, it plugs into the motherboard in the top right corner (Figure 3-17).

FIGURE 3-17   Power connector connected to the motherboard

Part 3: Installing systems unit cables

The next step is to plug all of the case wires into the motherboard. Figure 3-18 shows the area that these wires are plugged into. Typically, the disk activity light, power light, the reset button, and system speaker are plugged into these jumpers. Some cases provide a turbo light on the case and a jumper for it. This is a carry-over from the 80486 and earlier systems, which frequently had a switch that allowed for the clock speed to be reduced in the event of applications timing problems. Thankfully, most systems manufacturers have figured out how to have things work at one speed.

Front panel control and light wiring

FIGURE 3-18   The front panel's controls and lights are connected to the
motherboard

Part 4: Installing keyboard, monitor, and video card

At this point, we are almost ready to apply power and test the motherboard. To do
this, we will have to connect the keyboard, a video card, and the power cord. The
video card goes into the AGP slot on this system. On the Intel 440BX motherboard,
the AGP slot (to be explained in Chapter 7) is the first slot below the CPU. The keyboard plugs into the connector on the back of the system unit.

With the monitor, keyboard, and power cord all connected, it is time to turn
the machine on for the first time. Turn your monitor on first to give it a few seconds to warm up.

Part 5: Powering on the system

Turning on the power is a real treat. If everything is working, the system will beep
and the screen will display information on its BIOS. At this point, if everything is
working, you can turn the machine off and continue installation.

Congratulations, break open the champagne! A new computer is born! Anybody got a cigar?

If for some reason you have encountered a problem with your machine, only a few things could be wrong:

1. Check your power cables (both ends).
2. Check all of the jumpers on the motherboard to verify they are configured correctly.
3. Replace the CPU chip.
4. Replace the motherboard.
5. Check the power supply voltage settings.
6. Replace the power supply.

In most cases, you can take the system and CPU back to the place you purchased them and ask for a replacement. Most reputable computer shops will gladly do this for you. If that does not solve the problem, it may be worth it to have them repair the system and show you what you might have done wrong.

Lab 4.2 *Installing a hard drive*

We are going to be installing a hard drive with an Adaptec 2940U2W controller card and a floppy drive onto the motherboard's floppy interface.

Tools required

- Phillips Head screwdriver
- Static strap

Operating system

Decide where to mount the drive. As a convention, the floppy drive gets mounted in the topmost available bay that it will fit, which in our case is the top of the 3.5-inch bays in the lower part of the case. We will mount the hard drive in the lowest 3.5-inch bay, leaving space between it and the floppy drive to help airflow and cooling. Figure 4-12 shows the Adaptec SCSI card. The Adaptec card is slid gently into the top available PCI slot, and its bracket screwed down. We will connect the cables with the red stripe being on Pin 1. This is a convention that we will follow from here on out.

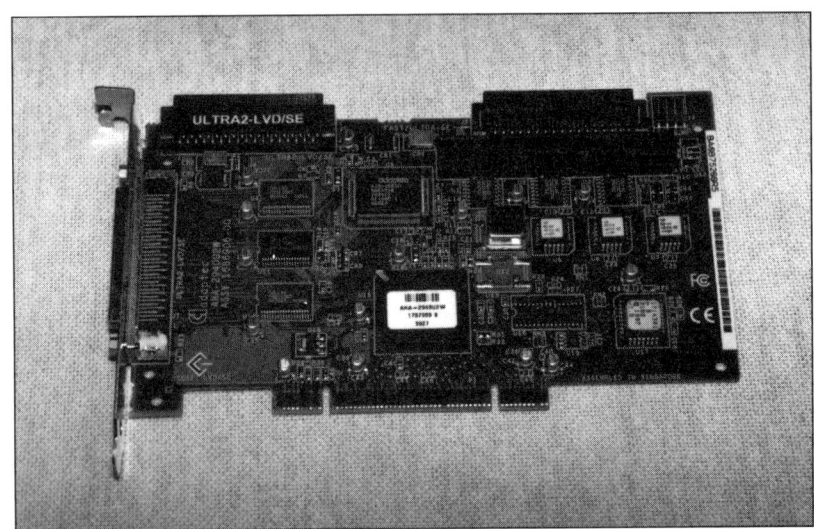

FIGURE 4-12 Adaptec 2940U2W SCSI controller card

The floppy drive connector is immediately next to the power connector shown in Chapter 3.

We will be connecting the hard drive to the Adaptec card. The power supply for the hard drive must also be connected to the drive. The power cord is a four-wire connector that plugs into the back of the drive. You will have your choice of two different types of connectors. Pick the one that works with each device and plug them in.

The hard drive will also require some configuration in order to work properly. First we have to ensure that the SCSI ID jumpers on the back of the drive are configured properly. We will configure this drive to be SCSI ID 0, which is reserved for boot drives. The Seagate Cheetah drive is shipped set to ID 0 as a default, so no change was needed.

Figure 4-13 is a photo of the back of the Seagate Cheetah drive. As you can see, you must connect the power supply, the SCSI cable, and the jumper for the configuration. The jumper configurations for your drive will be explained in the instruction manual that comes with the drive. If you get stuck with this, don't be afraid to ask the person you purchased it from.

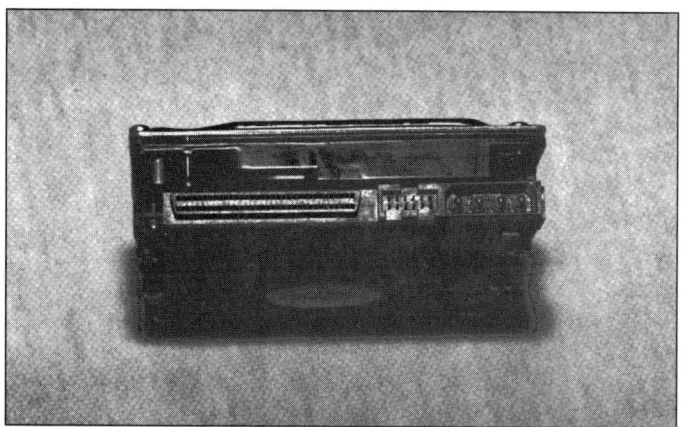

FIGURE 4-13 The back of a disk drive for configuration and cables

Earlier in this chapter you saw a floppy disk drive being mounted into one of the slots, so we won't waste your time by showing you again.

At this point, your system should have a floppy disk, a hard disk, a keyboard, memory, and a video board connected to it. You have a system that should be functionally ready to be powered up and the hard disk formatted.

When you turn your system on, the start screen should indicate what devices are present on your computer. After a moment, the light on the floppy drive should go on. It should then go off, as no operating system is loaded.

We are going to go ahead and put the boot floppy in drive A. This will bring up the setup and installation program for Windows 95. We will need to perform an FDISK on our hard drive to partition it and make it ready. FDISK is the disk utility program that partitions and allocates storage units on Windows 95 systems. This is explained in the DOS sections in greater detail in Chapters 17 through 19 of this book.

We will also need to format the hard disk to get it ready for installation. The format program prepares the disk for the storage of data on a Windows 95 system. This is covered in greater detail in Chapters 17 through 19 of this book.

If for some reason you are having problems with your system, check the most common and obvious areas:

1. Are all the cables plugged in and oriented correctly? Remember, Pin 1 will always be what you orient your cables with. The red stripe or band on your cable should always be on Pin 1.

2. Check the SCSI ID jumpers on the hard drive. Are they set to zero?

If you are still having problems, review your BIOS manual and ensure that all of the parameters are configured properly. Again, don't be afraid to call the place where you bought the motherboard and ask for their help.

Good luck and congratulations on completing this lab!

Lab 5-3 *Installing a DVD drive*

In the last two lab exercises, you installed the motherboard and peripherals, and verified the operation of the system unit. You also installed the hard drives and floppy disk drive. In this lab, we will install the DVD board and connect it to the DVD. The process of installing a DVD is virtually identical to the installation of a CD-ROM device. We will also install a multimedia board. This lab is a fairly short one.

The configuration will include the ability to listen to audio from the DVD through the sound system built into the Intel motherboard. DVD movies will be viewable on the monitor. The DVD will also operate as the system's CD-ROM player.

Materials required

- Static strap
- Phillips Head screwdriver
- DVD kit, including DVD drive and DVD board
- Multimedia card

Part 1: Laying out the DVD, controller, and cables

First, let's lay the pieces we will be installing on the table. The DVD drive looks exactly like a CD-ROM from the outside. The two boards we will be installing are the multimedia card — in this case an AWE64 Sound Blaster card — and a DVD DXR2 card. Figure 5-6 shows these cards and devices.

For the sake of this lab and to demonstrate the capabilities of this system, we are going to assume that we have already installed Windows 95. The specifics of how to install and configure this system will be covered later in the book, but for now assume that this system has Windows 95 installed on it.

DVD card   DVD drive   Connecting cables

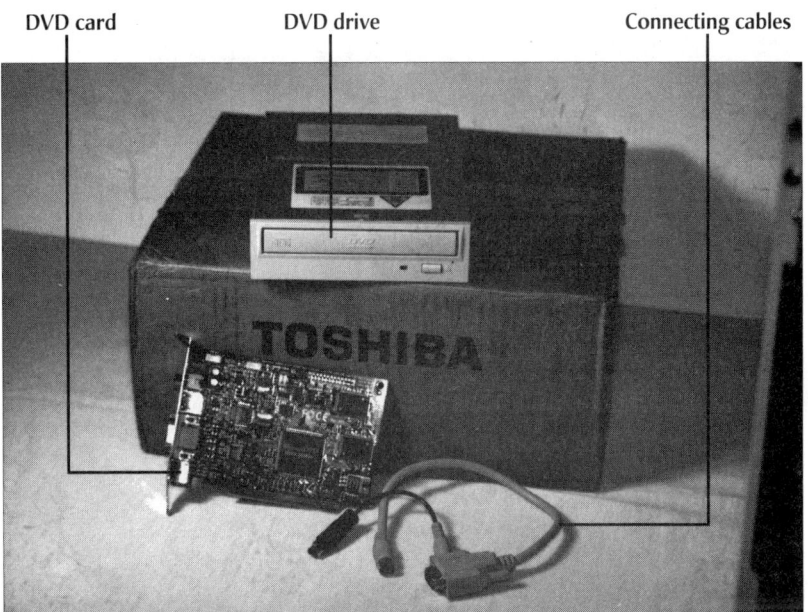

FIGURE 5-6 The components that will be installed into the systems unit

Part 2: Attaching cables

First, we are going to plug the IDE cable for the DVD into the secondary IDE port on the motherboard. Normally, the secondary IDE port will be a 50-pin connector near the disk drive cable on the motherboard. This gives us the primary port for the systems disk drive and the secondary port for the DVD. According to most manufacturers, this configuration provides the fastest access for both devices.

Part 3: Configuring the DVD drive

Configure the DVD drive as a Master. This is accomplished by ensuring that the jumper on the back of the DVD is set to Master. On an IDE port, one of the devices must be configured as a Master, while the other units must be configured as Slaves. This affects how the devices are accessed by the controller. If more than one device is configured as a Master on the motherboard, the IDE bus may hang, and all devices attached to that port will not work.

Part 4: Mounting the DVD

We will mount the drive (shown in Figure 5-7) onto the mounting rails provided for a large expansion slot. The DVD and rails can now be mounted and secured into the drive bay selected for it. The DVD cables will be connected between the DVD unit, the DVD card, and the Sound Blaster card. We will connect the power plug to the power cable. Most systems provide a few extra connectors for power supplies. If you run out of power supply cables, you can usually purchase power extender cables from a computer supply store. As an A+ technician, it is probably good to have a few extra splitter power cables in your toolbox. Connect a power cable to the drive.

IDE Connector   Sound Connector

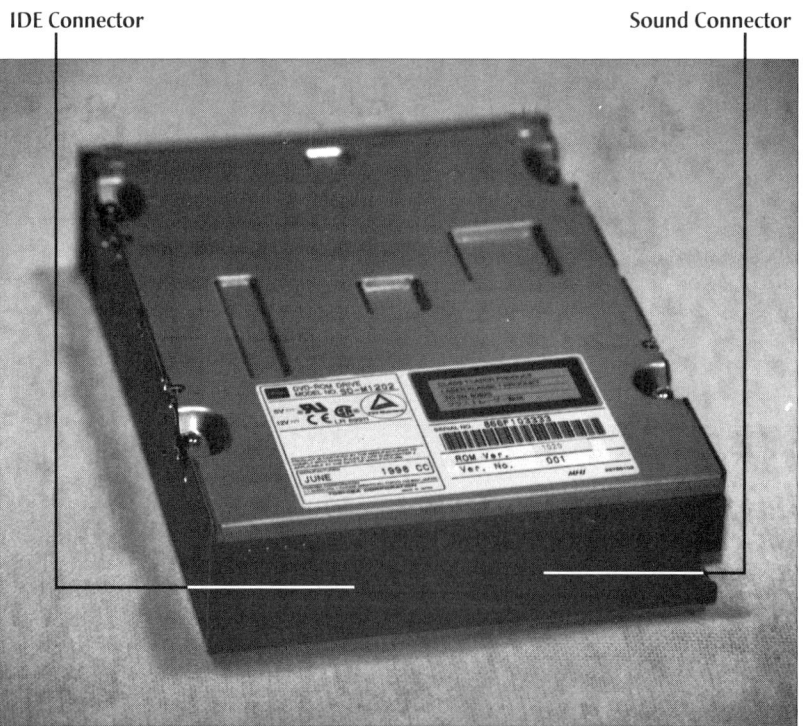

FIGURE 5-7   Installing the DVD drive into the systems unit

Part 5: Cabling the DVD cables to the motherboard

The signal and audio cable that comes with the DVD unit has a small notch in it that will not allow for an incorrect installation. Occasionally, you may encounter a cable without a notch or other type of keying mechanism — in these cases, a good rule of thumb is that the wire with the red marker is always installed closest to the power connector. At this point, we have the drive installed, the cables between the motherboard and the DVD connected, the power cable, and the audio connector on the DVD connected.

Part 6: Installing the DVD controller

The DVD board will be installed into one of the PCI slots closest to the disk connectors. The PCI slots are very fast and this subsystem will need it. After plugging in the card, we will connect the audio cable from the DVD to the connector on top of the board marked *In*.

Part 7: Attaching sound connections

Now move on to the sound system, built into the motherboard. All of the data transfer, with the exception of the analog or music cable, is handled through the IDE connector. Music is handled through that small cable connecting to the DVD card. This process is simple. Just connect the cable between the DVD and the sound port.

At this point, we are ready to power on the system and verify that devices are working. Installation and configuration are covered in more detail in Chapters 11,12, and 13.

After installing the software per the manufacturer's instructions, we should be ready to rock and roll. The DVD comes with a number of demo programs and games designed to show the capabilities of this technology.

This device, when coupled with a good monitor and sound system, create an awesome workstation that can play movies and music, as well as accomplish meaningful work (almost all at the same time).

Lab 6-4: *Installing serial and parallel port cables, the mouse port, modem card, and network card*

In the last three lab exercises, you installed the motherboard and peripherals, and verified the operation of the system unit. You also installed the hard drives, and if you were industrious, you read ahead into the later chapters about how to configure your hard drives and your CD-ROM player. In this lab, you are going to install the serial and parallel port cables, the mouse port, modem card, and a network card.

Materials required

- Static strap
- Phillips head screwdriver
- Parallel/serial connector kit
- Modem card
- Network card

In this lab, we will install a modem. The network card we are going to use is a 3Com 10BaseT NIC.

Laying the system on its side, we will choose an available ISA slot for the modem. We will also choose a PCI slot for the network card. The modem we will be installing is a 56K modem and the network card we are installing is a 100/10Mbit network card.

Let's get the modem card installed into the computer system.

This modem is Plug and Play, and will be configured by the operating system on startup. We will also install the NIC into an available PCI slot.

You will need to connect the modem into a modular telephone jack. For that, you will use what is called an RJ-11 connector. The RJ-11 is a four-wire system that most houses and offices have upgraded to. Several companies sell adapters for the wired wall plug to RJ-11 connector. If you have questions about how these work, take your phone jack apart and study how the wires are connected to the wall plate.

The network connector we will be connecting to is called a *CAT-5 network*. CAT-5 refers to the bandwidth capabilities of a network. This network uses an STP eight-wire connector that is connected via an eight-wire jack called an *RJ-45*. These are standard cables and can be purchased at virtually any computer store.

These systems are fairly simple to work with. Most residences have one- or two-wire cables pulled into a wiring jack. This allows for connection of multiple telephones to the Telco system.

Now it is time for you to take a field trip. Your organization, school, or church probably has a network and a complicated phone system. Go and ask one of the systems managers to give you a tour. Have them explain how the network functions, and the technologies used in that environment. You will probably find this to be fascinating and it will give you a chance to network with groups you may be interested in joining.

When you finish your field trip, write down the things you saw and answer these questions:

1. What type of network technology are they using?
2. Was the network I looked at part of a bigger network, such as the Internet, and how did they connect?
3. What type of network adapters and standards are they using?
4. How is network troubleshooting accomplished?
5. How many workstations are connected to the network?
6. Does the company allow end users to use modems on their computers?
7. How does their data communications system work and is it integrated with the voice system?
8. What was the most interesting thing I saw on the tour?
9. What did I learn about the industry?

Lab 7-5 *Configuring and pricing computer systems*

Part 1

Configure and price a system for a customer. This system will be used by a graphic designer with several years of experience with PCs. She is very discerning about quality and wants a machine that will provide her with two or three years of service.

Her specifications for a system include:

- Pentium-II 450MHz
- Full-size case

- Keyboard and mouse
- Minimum 96MB RAM
- 12GB minimum Ultra SCSI disk drive configuration, minimum three disks
- 100MB Zip drive
- DAT tape backup unit
- CD-RW recorder
- Windows NT Workstation software
- Video card with minimum of 8MB of RAM
- Minimum 17-inch monitor
- Sound card, high-end with speakers
- Minimum 600 DPI flatbed scanner
- Floppy disk drive
- Laser printer

Research and price this system using top-of-the-line components, such as Sound Blaster Live sound card, HP laser printer, and so on. Which devices will be PCI, which will be ISA, and which will be SCSI? What IRQs must these components use to function correctly? Pick a case from the units available in the store and spec out where each device will go and how it will be mounted.

What components could be replaced with lower-cost components and still provide comparable performance? What would that system cost?

Part 2

Your manager has asked you to help him build a computer system. He has asked you to prepare pricing for a system that he can use at home. He is thinking about getting involved in digital photography, Web surfing, and other tasks such as home finance. He doesn't want to spend a lot of money, but wants a system that will hold up for two or three years. He would be comfortable spending between $600 and $1,000. Can you help him out?

Most cities have computer stores that specialize in selling individual components and parts for builders. Visit a couple of those shops and do your shopping there. You should plan on building both of these systems.

Have fun and happy shopping!

LAB 8-6 *Changing the toner cartridge*

This lab involves replacing a toner cartridge in a laser printer.

Step 1: Opening the printer

On this printer, the release is on the front, as shown in Figure 8-14.

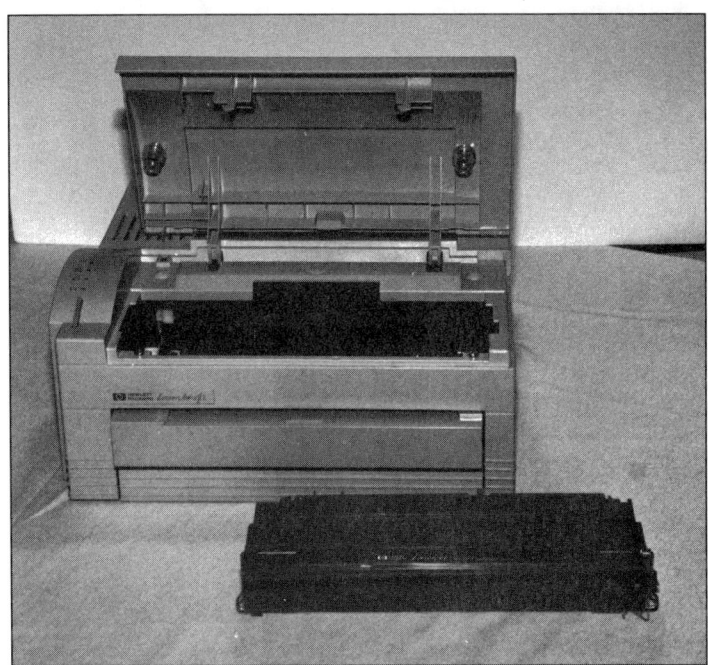

FIGURE 8-14   A laser printer with the cover open and the toner
cartridge removed

Step 2: Removing the toner cartridge

The next step involves removing the toner cartridge and replacing it with a new one. Figure 8-15 shows the toner cartridge being replaced. Remember to follow the directions from the manufacturer regarding how to shake the toner in the cartridge before inserting it. This shaking ensures an even distribution of toner across the toner transfer area.

Release button

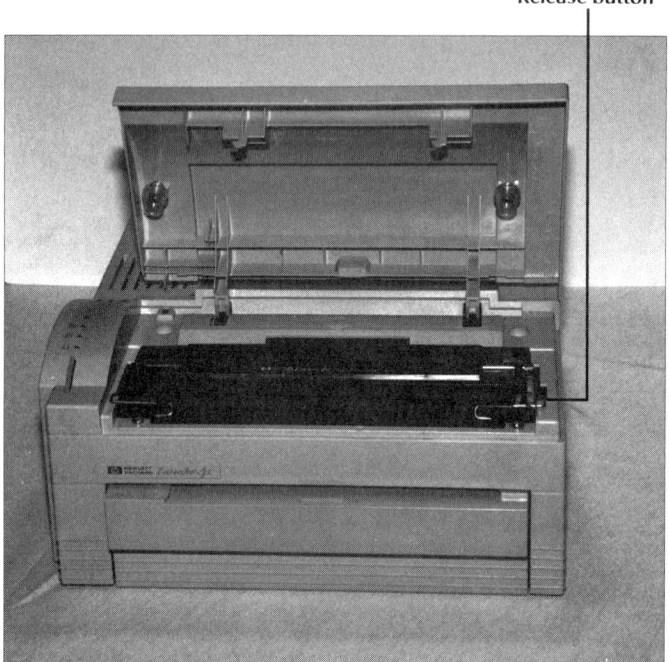

FIGURE 8-15 The new toner cartridge in the printer

Lab 9-9: *Adjusting a monitor*

Getting organized

Clear your work area of all non-essential items. You should be able to freely move the computer monitor on the work area without space constraints. For your safety, be sure that the computer and monitor are plugged in using three-prong power cords and that there is no water in or immediately around the work area. Also, as a point of general computer safety, keep soft drinks and coffee away from the computer and its peripherals. The computer and monitor will need to be turned on for these exercises.

tip **On a wall outlet, the smaller of the two vertical slots is considered hot.**

Using a VGA or SVGA monitor, adjust the vertical and horizontal size of the screen using the controls on the monitor itself.

note 📝 **Modern monitors can derive their power from the PC's power supply.**

In Figure 9-3, you can see a properly sized display area. In the following illustrations, we will show you that it is possible to change both the horizontal and vertical display areas.

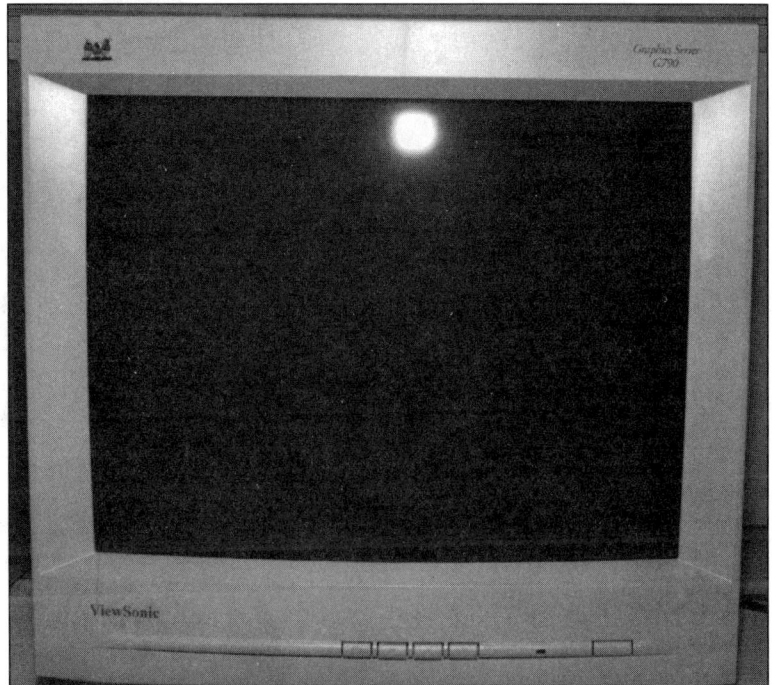

FIGURE 9-3 Monitor with normally sized picture

In Figure 9-4, we have changed the vertical viewing size of the monitor. This is an essential skill to have when you're setting up a monitor for the first time. Not all monitors are preset with their optimum configuration from the factory. Each monitor is different, but the settings can be adjusted from the monitor's front panel. Throughout this exercise, try and set your monitor to match the figures, then reset it back to normal. You may need to refer to a monitor manual to ascertain exactly how each monitor is adjusted.

In Figure 9-5, we have changed the horizontal viewing size of the monitor. Again, this is an essential skill when you're setting up a monitor for the first time. In addition to first-time setups, it is often the case that a customer having display problems actually has a problem with the adjustments of the monitor. The CRT can fail, but it is a rare occurrence within the first two years of a monitor's life.

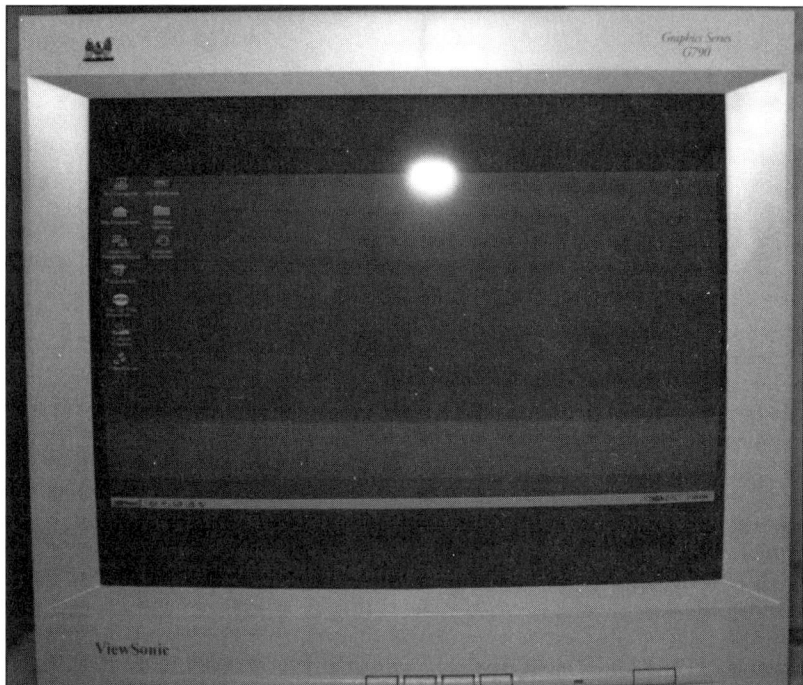

FIGURE 9-4   Monitor with improperly sized vertical image

Manual controls for the adjustment of the horizontal and vertical sizing can be in different places. Some monitors use knobs located at the base of the monitor in the front. Other monitors use push buttons, and still other monitors may need to be accessed from the back. These adjustments are the first thing you should check when diagnosing a monitor. Always check to be sure that the sizing adjustments are set before assuming there is something wrong inside the monitor itself.

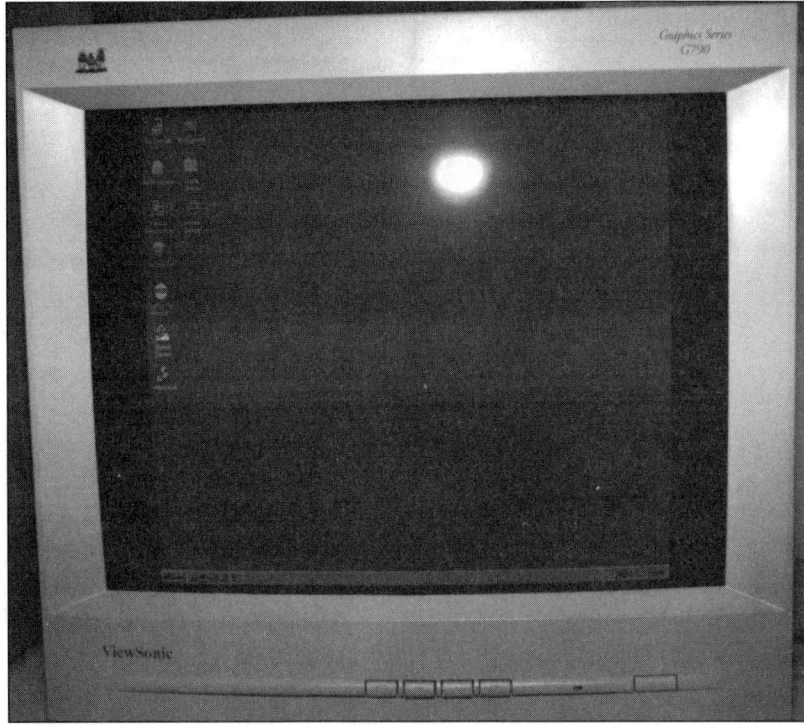

FIGURE 9-5 Monitor with improper horizontal sizing

Lab 10-10 *Replacing a video card*

Getting organized

Clear your work area of all nonessential items. You should be able to freely move the computer around on the work area without space constraints. For your safety, unplug the system.

1. Remove the system cover for access to internal computer components. Certain screws on the back of the case enable removal of the cover, and others hold the power supply in place. Be sure to remove the right ones, which are typically right alongside the edge of the case cover.

   In Figure 10-5, you can see that the system boards are held in place with screws and pressed into bus slots. The center card in this figure is the video card.

2. Remove the video card. Now unscrew the adapter card back plate. Once the back plate is free, pull up with just enough force to remove the adapter card. When you have finished, it will look like Figure 10-6.

Mounting hardware   Video card

FIGURE 10-5 Video card with mounting hardware

AGP slot

FIGURE 10-6 Empty bus slot

3. Insert a video card. In Figure 10-7, notice that the back plate is straight—this is important for proper seating of the card. Insert the card flush along the slot and apply only as much gentle force as is necessary to seat the card in the slot. Secure the card in the computer by screwing the back plate to the case.

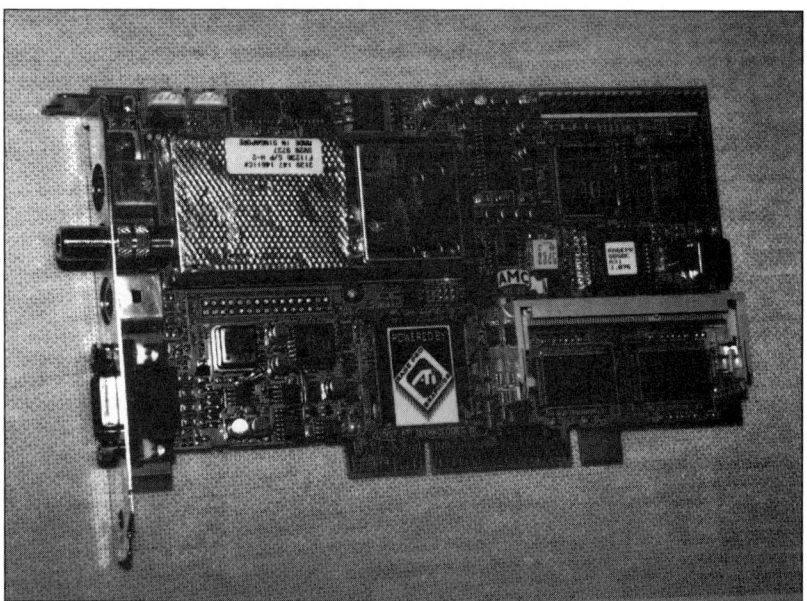

FIGURE 10-7 Side view of a video card

4. Replace the case cover. Be sure to line up the screw holes properly before tightening the case down, and be careful not to scratch the case with your screwdriver.

Lab 11-11 *Changing configuration settings*

Getting organized

 tip When installing an expansion board, consulting the documentation for the board or PC is the best way to determine the required settings.

Make sure you have a clear work area and can access the computer from all angles. Also, make sure that the computer is not plugged in to eliminate the chance that you'll be electrocuted in the course of this procedure. In this lab, we will be adding a slaved hard drive to a system.

1. Take a preformatted hard drive and change the jumper settings so that it is configured as a Slave, by moving the appropriate jumpers to the location described in the owners manual for a slave drive.

2. Open the computer and locate an empty bay next to the existing hard drive.

3. Insert the new drive in the empty bay.

4. Insert the signal cable in the new slave drive, making sure that Pin 1 is closest to the red stripe on the cable.

5. Plug in the power connector for the new drive and secure the drive to the case.

6. Replace the case cover and turn on the computer.

7. When the system starts up, enter the CMOS setup by following the onscreen instructions and set the values for the new drive in the CMOS based on the Auto Configure option, or the options described in the owners manual.

You should now have a computer with two hard drives, one called C: and one called D:. This is useful for separating out files. For example, you could have:

o A server with the operating system (OS) on one drive and application files on another.

o The OS on one drive and shared files on another.

o Development software on one drive and a developed product on another.

Lab 12-12 *Installing and configuring a new hard drive*

Getting organized

Clear your work area of all non-essential items. Make sure you can move the system around without causing an avalanche of miscellaneous computer debris. Unplug the system when you're working inside it. In this lab we will be preparing a new hard drive.

1. Remove the hard drive from its static packing.

2. Check to be sure the jumpers are set to Master on an EIDE drive, or SCSI ID of zero.

3. Set the jumpers on the hard drive.

4. Write the hard drive settings inside the system manual, or somewhere handy.

5. Open the computer case.

6. Find an empty drive bay in the computer and insert the hard drive.

7. Connect the signal cable, being sure that Pin 1 is closest to the red stripe.

8. Connect the power lead to the hard drive.

9. Secure the hard drive to the case.

10. Plug the computer in and power on the system.

11. Insert a bootable system floppy with:

   o format.com
   o fdisk.exe

12. When the computer starts, enter the CMOS setup and configure the CMOS for the drive.

    The system will boot from the bootable floppy; now you need to configure the hard drive so the system can use it to store data.

13. At the command prompt, type **fdisk**.

14. Choose Create a New Partition.

15. Give the volume a name and allow the maximum size for the primary partition.

    At this point, you will be prompted to press Escape to continue; do so. Then restart the system using the bootable floppy.

16. When the system starts this time, at the command prompt, type **format C:/s**. This will format the drive and transfer the system files so that it is bootable.

17. When the format operation is complete, remove the floppy and restart the computer.

You have now prepared a drive to be bootable and store data.

Lab 13-13 *Installing new RAM*

To provide experience in installing and configuring components in a computer system, this lab demonstrates the process of installing new RAM. You'll need a computer, new RAM, and a set of screwdrivers. You should also have a clear, well-lit area to work in and a container for screws that you remove from the computer.

Getting organized

 tip **To set up an ESD workstation, place the PC on a grounded conductive rubber mat and connect yourself to the mat with an approved wrist strap.**

Clear your work area of all non-essential items. You should be able to freely move the computer on the work area without space constraints. For your safety, be sure that the computer is not plugged in while you're replacing internal components. In this lab, we will upgrade the system's RAM.

1. Remove the case cover.

Locate the RAM modules, as shown in Figure 13-5.

The SDRAM module is kept in place by two plastic clips, one on each end. To remove RAM, press on the clips. When they release, you can easily remove the module. If you are replacing an existing SDRAM strip, remove it and set it aside in a static-free bag. If you're adding RAM, orient it so that it can be gently inserted into the slot (it only fits one way) until the plastic clips snap onto the ends of the SDRAM strip.

3. Replace the module with the upgrade module, or add the new module if you're simply adding RAM. You will feel the RAM lock into place once it is fully inserted.

4. Replace the case cover and power the system on.

The PC will automatically generate the memory total of the new RAM configuration when the computer is turned on. In fact, you may (depending on your system BIOS) see the numbers counting onscreen, indicating the total amount of RAM memory you have installed.

FIGURE 13-5 SDRAM module in a PC

Lab 14-14 *Identifying a video card*

For these lab exercises, you will need access to a complete computer system and a set of screwdrivers. The purpose of this exercise is to familiarize you with installation and configuration settings. This particular lab will walk you through identifying the type of video card installed in your computer system.

Getting organized

Clear your work area of all non-essential items. You should be able to freely move the computer on the work area without space constraints. For your safety, be sure that the computer is not plugged in while you're replacing internal components. In this lab, we will be identifying the video card manufacturer and type.

1. Start the computer in DOS mode.

2. At the DOS prompt, type **debug** and then press Enter. The system will display a single dash (-).

3. Type the following: **d c000:0010**.

4. Exit debug by typing **q** and then press Enter.

In Figure 14-12, you will see that the information identifying the video card is displayed to the right of the hexadecimal contents of the BIOS.

```
C:\>debug
-d c000:0010
C000:0010  00 00 00 00 00 00 00 00-AC 01 00 E9 C5 33 49 42  .............3IB
C000:0020  4D 20 56 47 41 20 43 6F-6D 70 61 74 69 62 6C 65  M VGA Compatible
C000:0030  F7 C8 30 DF E4 33 20 00-80 43 4C 2D 47 44 35 34  ..0..3 ..CL-GD54
C000:0040  33 78 20 50 43 49 20 56-47 41 20 42 49 4F 53 20  3x PCI VGA BIOS
C000:0050  56 65 72 73 69 6F 6E 20-31 2E 32 33 20 20 20 20  Version 1.23
C000:0060  0D 0A 43 6F 70 79 72 69-67 68 74 20 31 39 39 32  ..Copyright 1992
C000:0070  2D 31 39 39 35 20 43 69-72 72 75 73 20 4C 6F 67  -1995 Cirrus Log
C000:0080  69 63 2C 20 49 6E 63 2E-20 41 6C 6C 20 52 69 67  ic, Inc. All Rig
```

FIGURE 14-12   The screen output of the debug command

Lab 15-15 *Installing a mounting kit*

Getting organized

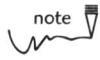 note **The capacity of a 5.25-inch high-density diskette is 1.2MB.**

Clear your work area of all non-essential items. You should be able to freely move the computer on the work area without space constraints. For your safety, be sure that the computer is not plugged in while you're replacing internal components. In this lab, we will install a universal mounting kit.

The universal mounting kit is designed for mounting most 3.5-inch disk drives in most standard computers that accept a standard 5.25-inch disk drive. Along with this kit, other standard rails can be used.

The universal mounting kit includes:

○ Left rail

○ Right rail

○ Face plate

○ Mounting screws of various sizes

To install the mounting kit:

1. Attach the left rail to the face plate by inserting the bottom tab first.

2. Attach the right rail to the face plate by inserting the bottom tab first.

3. Slide the disk drive into position in the frame you just created.

4. Align the bottom holes of the disk drive with posts of the bracket assembly.

5. Inspect the assembly to ensure there are no gaps between the face plate and the drive.

6. Locate the bay into which you will insert the mounted drive.

7. Secure the mounted drive to the case using the screws provided in the kit.

Lab 16-16 *Replacing a toner cartridge*

Getting organized

Clear your work area of all non-essential items. You should be able to freely move the laser printer on the work area without space constraints. For your safety, be sure the printer is not plugged in while you're replacing internal components.

1. Locate the release points on the side or top of the printer.

2. Disengage the release and lift the cover.

3. Grasp the pull point with your thumb and forefinger and gently pull the cartridge up and out.

4. Remove the new toner cartridge from the bag.

5. Rotate the cartridge until the insertion arrows are visible. Because the cartridge may have been shipped or stored on its side, gently shake the cartridge side to side to evenly distribute the toner inside the cartridge.

6. Grasp the tape along the side of the cartridge and pull firmly until it is completely free of the cartridge. This tape is designed to keep the toner from spilling from the cartridge during shipping. However, do not trust that it will always work — keep the cartridge horizontal at all times after removing it from its storage bag. Insert the toner cartridge back into the laser printer and close the access door.

Lab 17-17 *Working with Explorer*

In this lab, we will use Explorer to examine the Windows folder. The first step in this lab will be to open the My Computer Icon and right-click on drive C. Figure 17-17 illustrates this. As you can see, this system has several drives and resources, each identified by a symbol. The options are displayed by right-clicking the mouse on the drive we want to examine.

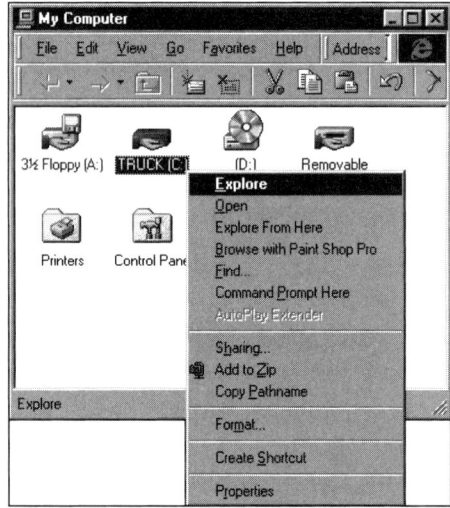

FIGURE 17-17 The disks and folders under the My Computer folder

When the Explore option is selected, the Explorer window opens. Figure 17-18 illustrates the Explorer window. Notice that two areas are displayed below the tool bar. The left side of the screen displays the folders on the drive, while the right side shows the files and folders that are under the selected option. In this example, we are displaying the files that exist under the Commands subfolder. These commands are the standard DOS commands that can be accessed using the Run command on the Start bar.

Explorer can then be used to add, delete, or otherwise alter the characteristics of the files. For example, we can add a folder by right-clicking in the large window. This opens up a bar that provides several options. Figure 17-19 shows this happening. The right-click also enables several other options to manipulate files. Try some of the other options to see what happens.

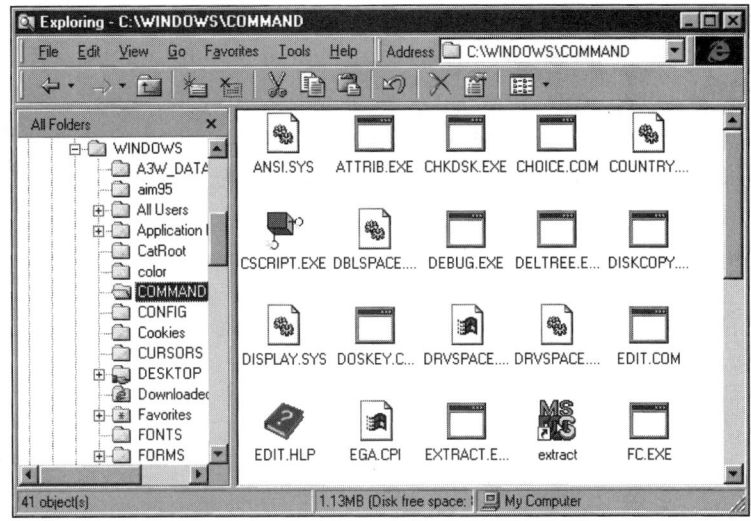

FIGURE 17-18 The files that exist under the Commands subdirectory under the Windows folder

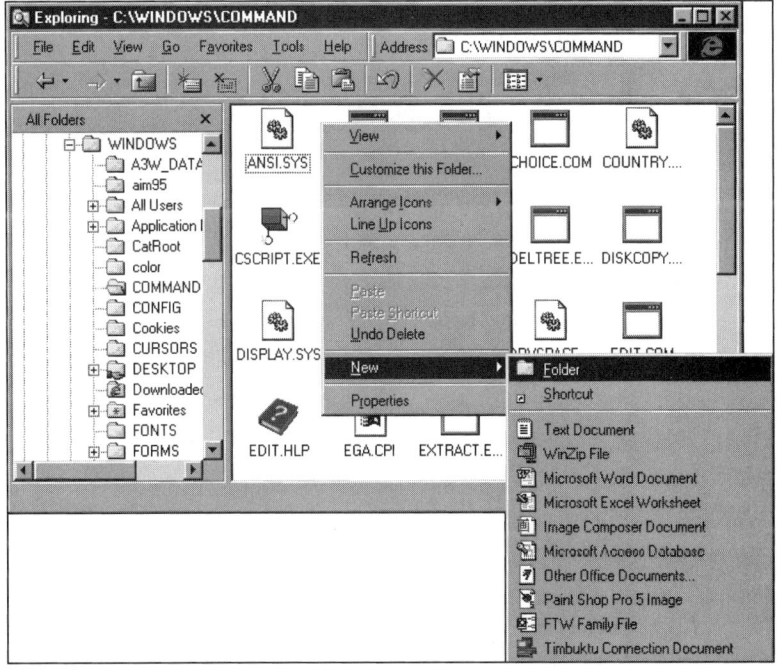

FIGURE 17-19 Creating a new folder in Explorer

Lab 17-18 *Working with OLE objects*

This lab demonstrates the OLE capabilities of Word and Excel. We will create a graph in Excel and link it to Word. Then we will change the graph in Excel and see the values change in the document. When we double-click the graph, the OLE container or frame opens, giving us the ability to change the data on the graph. When we click out of the graph, the data changes back to the presentation mode. This enables the integration of text, graphics, and spreadsheets to be fairly easy for the end user to accomplish. Windows 3.1 supported some of this capability, but it is much more fully developed in the Windows 95 and Windows NT environments.

Lab 18-19 *Registry entry*

First, let's change a parameter in the Registry, the name of the computer system. We will verify this under the Networking panel and then set the Registry back to the original settings. Follow these steps:

1. Select Run from the Start menu, type **regedit** in the Open field, and click OK to run `regedit`.

2. To change the name of the computer, we need to edit the data in the ComputerName value, which is in the `HKEY_LOCAL_MACHINE\System\CurrentControlSet\control\ComputerName\ComputerName` key. To find this value, click on the + sign beside the `HKEY_LOCAL_MACHINE` entry to expand that branch of the tree. Similarly, you need to expand the System, CurrentControlSet, control, ComputerName, and ComputerName branches. Finally, click on the second ComputerName key to see the values it contains. One of these values is ComputerName, and the data it contains is "Mike," which is currently the computer's name. Figure 18-11 shows this parameter and the hierarchy that was opened to show that parameter.

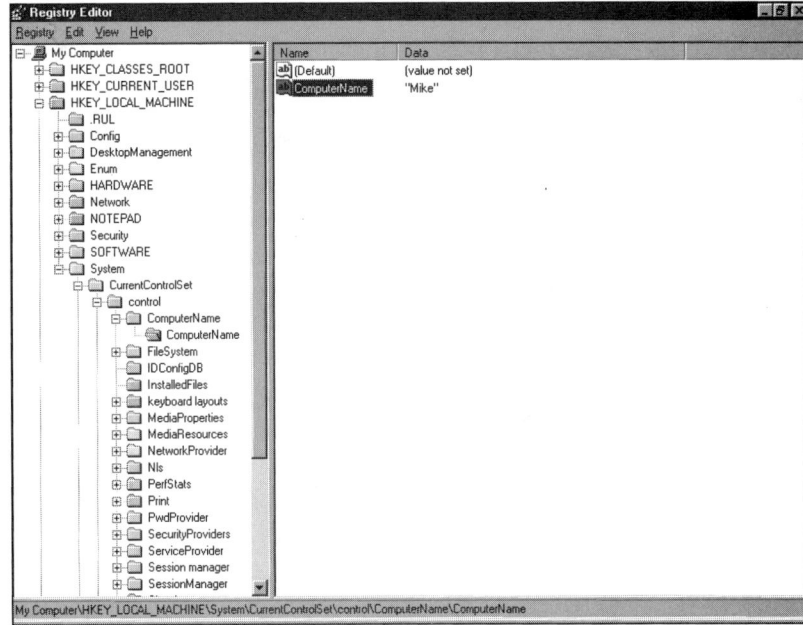

FIGURE 18-11   The Registry entry for computer name under the
HKEY_LOCAL_MACHINE key

3. Double-click on the ComputerName value. An editing window opens up
that looks like Figure 18-12. Type a new name (Mark) for the computer in
this dialog box.

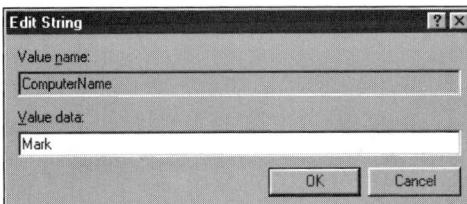

FIGURE 18-12   The Registry Editor changing the
value of ComputerName to
"Mark" from "Mike"

4. In the Control Panel, double-click the Network icon to open the Network dialog box. Switch to the Identification tab, shown in Figure 18-13, to see the changed value of the computer name.

5. Click OK to close the Network dialog box.

6. Repeat these steps to revert to the computer's original name.

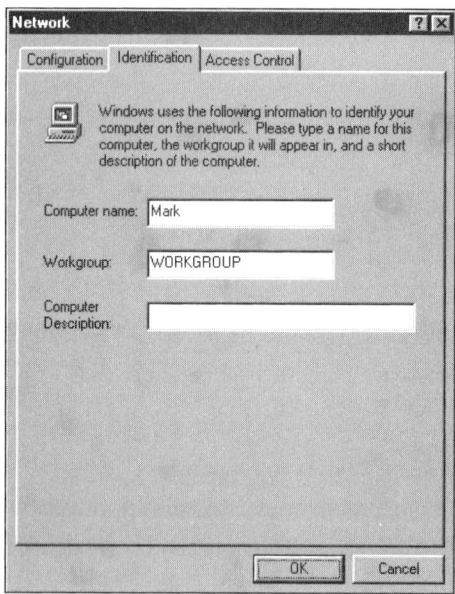

FIGURE 18-13 The changed name under the network panel

Lab 18-20 *Adding a printer*

In this lab, we will add a printer to our computer system. For the purpose of our discussion, we will add an HP DeskJet 500 printer. To accomplish this, follow these steps:

1. Choose Settings ⇒ Printers from the Windows 95 Start menu.

2. Double-click the Add Printer icon to start the Add Printer Wizard shown in Figure 18-14.

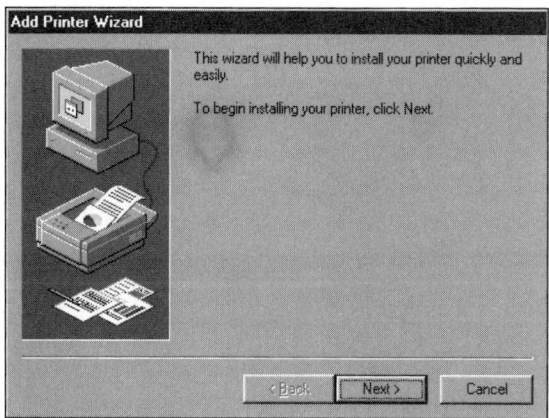

FIGURE 18-14 Adding a printer to a Windows 95 system

3. Click Next on the introductory screen to move on.

4. If this printer is attached to your computer, select Local Printer, or if this printer is attached to another computer on your network, select Network Printer. For this example, we'll select Local Printer. Click Next to continue.

5. Select the manufacturer and model of the printer you want to install — in this case, the HP DeskJet 500 — then click Next.

6. Select the port that this printer is attached to. Normally this will be LPT1. Click Next to continue.

7. Type a name for this printer in the Printer Name field, and select Yes or No to specify whether you want Windows-based programs to use this as their default printer, then click Next.

8. Finally, select Yes to have Windows 95 print a test page on your printer to verify that it's working properly. Click Finish when you're ready.

Figure 18-15 shows the printer dialog box with the HP 500 added as the default printer.

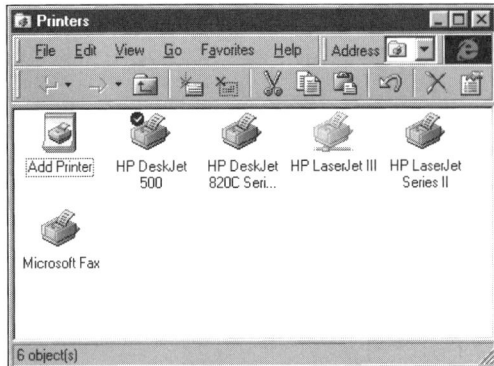

FIGURE 18-15 The printer dialog box with the
HP 500 printer installed

Lab 19-21 *FDISK*

FDISK is a program that enables you to divide your disk drives into partitions. In a
16-bit file system like FAT16 (the DOS and Windows 95 standard), the maximum
limit of a disk partition is 2GB. In this lab, we will examine and change the partition information on a disk.

The FDISK program is a DOS-based utility that was introduced by MS-DOS.
This program has continued to be the primary method of creating partitions.
Figure 19-2 shows the startup screen of FDISK. The program has five parameters
that can be used to maintain disk partitions.

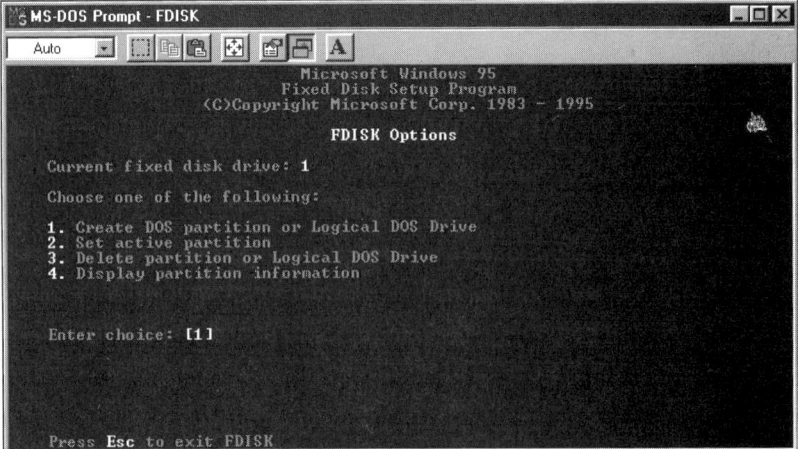

FIGURE 19-2 The FDISK **main menu**

We will select the fourth option, which brings up the screen shown in Figure 19-3. Notice that the drive we are examining is a 4GB drive that has been broken into two partitions, each one 2GB.

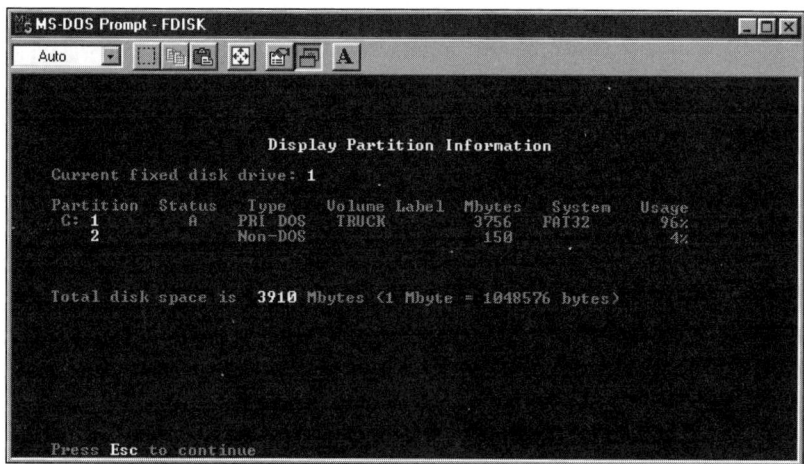

FIGURE 19-3 The partition information for the first drive on the system

 It is important to remember that once you make a change with FDISK, it will permanently erase whatever data was previously stored on that drive.

Lab 19-22 *Installing Windows 95*

In this lab, we will highlight the important points of a Windows 95 setup. In this application, we will install a version of Windows 95 over an existing version of Windows 95. This type of situation may be necessary if for some reason your Windows 95 system suddenly develops a problem immediately following the installation of a new software package. These problems most commonly arise when setup programs for new software packages overwrite Windows 95 DLLs with their own files of the same name.

The first step would be to insert the CD-ROM into the system and start the Setup program. Given that your system is already running Windows 95, the CD may auto-start and take you directly to the Windows 95 installation screen. If not, double-click SETUP.EXE. This will take you through a series of setup options that will reinstall Windows 95 over itself.

The next step in the process involves choosing which installation option to use (see Figure 19-4). In this case, we will use the Typical installation. The system will then proceed into an installation and query us about the installation directory and other necessary parameters. In general, the installation is fairly straight forward and requires a minimum of planning and installation support. The Custom option is very useful for installing additional components after a previous installation.

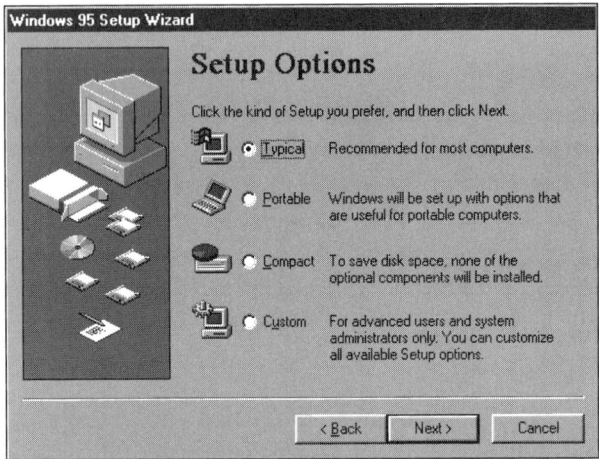

FIGURE 19-4 Setup options under the Windows 95 Setup Wizard

After a brief installation process, Windows 95 will verify the configuration that it has determined for your computer, shown in Figure 19-5. It is critical that you verify these parameters before proceeding. You can change them using the Change button if they are inaccurate.

If everything is going well, Windows 95 will display splash screens proclaiming the value and wisdom of your purchase. My favorite is "Windows 95 makes everything you do better!" Strange — it has yet to lower my golf handicap. Many applications programs also use splash screens to quickly explain features of the software.

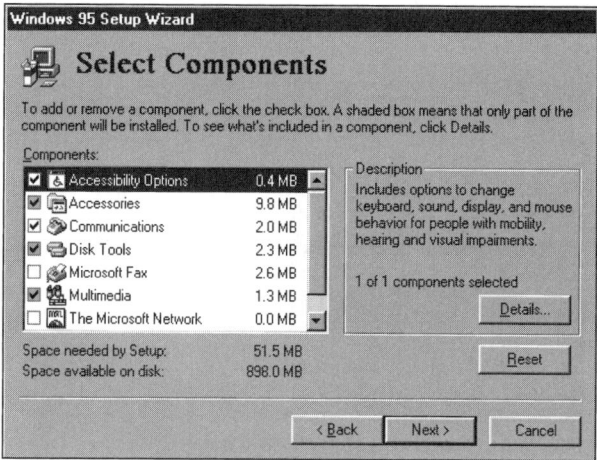

FIGURE 19-5 The Setup Wizard screen, showing the configuration that Windows 95 has determined for your computer

Occasionally, you might get a message identifying a version conflict in a file. This type of error message indicates that the version on your hard drive is newer than the one on the distribution media. If you were having difficulties with systems components, you are probably better off installing the older version and answering no to the question. If, on the other hand, you are sure that the file is not the problem, you can leave it alone by selecting yes.

The system will continue through its installation process, which should be successful if you are getting these types of messages.

Good luck with your Windows 95 installation!

Lab 20-23 *Installing a device driver*

When you want to install a new hardware device driver in Windows 95, you should use the Install Wizard. Follow these steps:

1. Open the Control Panel and double-click the Add New Hardware icon to open the Add New Hardware Wizard shown in Figure 20-17. \

2. Click Next on the introductory screen to begin.

3. Assuming you've already installed the actual device, select Yes and click Next to let Windows 95 detect it.

4. Windows 95 will automatically find the device and install the appropriate driver for it.

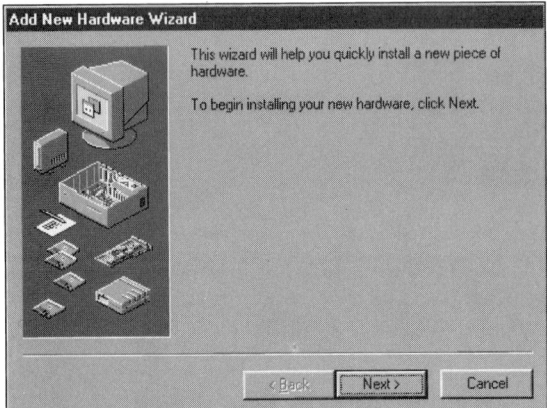

FIGURE 20-17 The Add New Hardware screen that
will be used to change the video adapter

Lab 20-24 *Refreshing a device driver*

Sometimes a device driver becomes corrupt or no longer works. In this case, you
can use the Device Manager to refresh the driver. We would do this if a device that
was working suddenly started malfunctioning. In some cases, it may be a hardware problem, but in as many cases, the software driver may have become corrupted. This often happens when you have just gone through a series of upgrades
in software or hardware.

In this case, the scanner attached to this system has become unknown to the
system. We are going to remove the driver from the system and let the system
restart to automatically find the new hardware. Follow these steps:

1. Delete the driver by selecting it under Device Manager and clicking the
   Remove button.

2. Restart the computer to make sure the changes have taken place.

3. After the system restarted, it discovered the new hardware. The Install
   Wizard asks for driver information.

4. Follow the instructions provided by the Add New Hardware Wizard to
   complete the installation of the scanner.

Answers to Instant Assessment Questions

CHAPTER 3: SYSTEM COMPONENTS

The following are the answers to the Instant Assessment questions in Chapter 3:

Multiple Choice

1. B
2. A
3. C
4. B
5. C
6. D
7. C
8. B
9. C
10. B

Fill in the Blank

1. Virtual memory
2. RISC
3. L1
4. ALU

5. RAM

6. 8

7. 64

8. 256K or 512K

9. motherboard

10. Memory Management

CHAPTER 4: DISK AND TAPE STORAGE COMPONENTS

The following are the answers to the Instant Assessment questions in Chapter 4:

Multiple Choice

1. D

2. A

3. B

4. D

5. C

6. D

7. C

8. B

9. A

10. C

Fill in the Blank

1. Northern and Southern

2. spindle

3. tracks

4. FAT or File Allocation Table

5. DAT or Digital Audio Tape

6. 1.44MB

7. MFM, RLL, or Modified Frequency Modulation and Run Length Limited

8. ST506

9. MTBF or Mean Time Between Failure

10. Multiple

CHAPTER 5: OPTICAL STORAGE, CD-ROMs, AND MULTIMEDIA COMPONENTS

The following are the answers to the Instant Assessment questions in Chapter 5:

Multiple Choice

1. B

2. A

3. C

4. C

5. A

6. D

7. C

8. A and D

9. A

10. B

Fill in the Blank

1. WORM or Write Once Read Many

2. Spiral

3. Dye

4. Yellow

5. 30

6. slower

7. 4.7

8. multimedia

9. Roland, Sound Blaster

10. four

CHAPTER 6: CONNECTIVITY

The following are the answers to the Instant Assessment questions in Chapter 6:

Multiple Choice

1. B

2. A

3. D

4. A

5. A, C, and D

6. B

7. B and C are correct

8. A

9. A

Fill in the Blank

1. higher

2. DIN

3. scanned

4. DB-9 9-pin connector and the DB-25 25-pin connector

5. digital

6. ECP

7. tree

CHAPTER 7: COMPUTER BUSES

The following are the answers to the Instant Assessment questions in Chapter 7:

Multiple Choice

1. A and C
2. B
3. D
4. C
5. B and C
6. A
7. B
8. B
9. A, B, and C
10. C

Fill in the Blank

1. VESA or VL Bus
2. 10MHz
3. PCI
4. I/O, storage
5. IBM PC
6. 16
7. IRQ 4
8. 50
9. termination
10. 25

CHAPTER 8: PRINTERS

The following are the answers to the Instant Assessment questions in Chapter 8:

Multiple Choice

1. C
2. B and C
3. D
4. C and D
5. A
6. A
7. D
8. C
9. B
10. A, B, and D

Fill in the Blank

1. ECU or electronic control unit
2. electrophotographic printer
3. Opacity
4. shed fibers
5. near
6. laser
7. piezoelectric, bubble jet
8. LED bars
9. negatively charges
10. heat

CHAPTER 9: COMPUTER MONITORS

The following are the answers to the Instant Assessment questions in Chapter 9:

Multiple Choice

1. D
2. B
3. C
4. A
5. D
6. B
7. D
8. C
9. B
10. C

Fill in the Blank

1. video information and AC power
2. diagonally
3. red, green, blue
4. shadow-mask
5. liquid-crystal display
6. vertical
7. interlacing
8. deguass
9. horizontal position

CHAPTER 10: VIDEO CARDS

The following are the answers to the Instant Assessment questions in Chapter 10:

Multiple Choice

1. C
2. A
3. D
4. A
5. D
6. B
7. B
8. A
9. C
10. D

CHAPTER 11: CONFIGURATION

The following are the answers to the Instant Assessment questions in Chapter 11:

Multiple Choice

1. A
2. D
3. D
4. A
5. D
6. C
7. A
8. A

9. D

10. A

CHAPTER 12: COMPUTER ASSEMBLY

The following are the answers to the Instant Assessment questions in Chapter 12:

Multiple Choice

1. A

2. B

3. D

4. A

5. D

6. D

7. B

8. A and B

9. A, B, and C

10. A, C, and D

CHAPTER 13: UPGRADING SYSTEMS AND COMPONENTS

The following are the answers to the Instant Assessment questions in Chapter 13:

Multiple Choice

1. A

2. D

3. B

4. B

5. B

6. A

CHAPTER 14: DIAGNOSIS AND TROUBLESHOOTING

The following are the answers to the Instant Assessment questions in Chapter 14:

Multiple Choice

1. D

2. D

3. C

CHAPTER 15: PC REPAIR

The following are the answers to the Instant Assessment questions in Chapter 15:

Multiple Choice

1. B

2. B

3. C

4. C

5. A

6. C

7. A

8. B

9. A

CHAPTER 16: MAINTAINING PCs, MONITORS, AND PRINTERS

The following are the answers to the Instant Assessment questions in Chapter 16:

Multiple Choice

1. A
2. A
3. A
4. B and C
5. B
6. B
7. B
8. A
9. A
10. A

CHAPTER 17: OPERATING SYSTEMS

The following are the answers to the Instant Assessment questions in Chapter 17:

Multiple Choice

1. A
2. B
3. A
4. A
5. A
6. A
7. A
8. A
9. A, B, and D

Fill in the Blank

1. `WIN.INI`

2. `SETUP /a`

3. virtual memory

4. page frame

5. Object Packager

6. Kernel

7. Link an object in that report to another document where the data is currently updated.

8. To bypass the startup files and use only the basic system drivers so you can use Windows 95 and correct the settings or conflicts in the system.

9. Registry Mode in System Policy Editor

CHAPTER 18: CONFIGURING WINDOWS 95 SYSTEMS

The following are the answers to the Instant Assessment questions in Chapter 18:

Multiple Choice

1. C

2. B

3. A

4. B

5. A

6. B

7. C

8. All of them

9. A

Fill in the Blank

1. Compact Disk File System

2. Virtual File Access System

3. Enhanced Metafile Format

4. USER.DAT

5. VxD

CHAPTER 19: INSTALLING AND UPGRADING WINDOWS

The following are the answers to the Instant Assessment questions in Chapter 19:

Multiple Choice

1. A

2. B

3. C

Fill in the Blank

1. To be able to boot the system in case a problem, such as file corruption, interferes with the boot process.

2. MS-DOS 3.2 or higher, Windows 3.x, or Windows for Workgroups 3.x.

3. REGEDIT.EXE

4. Use the Restore feature from REGEDIT.EXE, or if the system is not bootable, physically copy your backup Registry files (USER.DAT and SYSTEM.DAT) to the Windows folder.5.

5. You can reinstall the Windows 95 upgrade an unlimited number of times on the same machine.

6. Create a shortcut.

CHAPTER 20: SOFTWARE TOOLS AND TROUBLESHOOTING

The following are the answers to the Instant Assessment questions in Chapter 20:

Multiple Choice

1. D
2. C
3. D
4. A
5. C
6. B
7. C
8. A
9. C

Fill in the Blank

1. OLE
2. Device Manager
3. Plug and Play
4. Spooler
5. WIN.COM
6. Safe mode
7. F8
8. Install Wizard
9. Add/Remove Programs Utility
10. Help Files for Windows 95

Exam Preparation Tips

EXAM PREP GUIDE

The A+ exams are designed to test knowledge on computer- and support-related issues. These exams measure your ability to grasp and retain critical information you will need to be successful in this field. The A+ Certification exam has been designed by numerous industry experts to be challenging.

If you are new to the computer field, this exam may be difficult for you. If you have been in the field, certification will help you assure your customers that you are competent and have the right to bear the title "computer technician."

About the Exam

A great help to passing this exam is to understand how the test was developed. A panel of industry experts who surveyed and evaluated the skills needed in the field developed the tests. These skills and job functions were broken down into two exams: the core exam and the DOS/Windows exam.

Each of the tests were further broken down into domains of knowledge. These are indicated as Domains 1 through 8 in the core exam and Domains 1 through 5 in the DOS/Windows exam. The skill sets were further broken down into finite and measurable objectives. The phases of the exam-development process in the following list will help you understand how this works:

1. **Job analysis.** A job analysis defines specific job functions, as well as knowledge, skills, and abilities needed to perform the job of computer technician.

2. **Objective domain definition.** The job analysis provides a framework that is used to develop objectives. These objectives include the translation of job functions into a comprehensive set of tasks and skills performed by a computer technician. The list of objectives, or objective domain, forms the basis for the development of the certification exams.

3. **Blueprint survey.** The objective domain document is converted into a survey in which technology professionals rate the importance of each objective. These professionals or contributors are selected from past certification candidates and other technical professionals.

   The results of the survey are prioritized and weighted. The exam questions are then written, based on the results of this survey process. The percentage scores presented in Appendix A are a result of this survey process.

4. **Item development.** A pool of items is developed to measure the blueprinted objective domain. The number and type of test items needed are based on the results of the blueprint survey. The items are reviewed to ensure they are:

   - Technically accurate
   - Clear, unambiguous, and plausible
   - Not biased for any population or subpopulation

- Not misleading or tricky
- Based on a method of learning called *Bloom's Taxonomy*
- Testing for useful knowledge

5. **Alpha review and item revision.** This phase includes technical and job function reviews by experts. Each item is verified for technical accuracy and correctness. The panel of experts is charged with reaching consensus on all technical issues. The questions are then further edited to ensure accuracy and clarity.

6. **Beta exam.** The Beta exam is given to test candidates and certified technicians to verify that the test questions are clear and understandable. At the completion of the Beta exam, a statistical analysis is performed to verify the validity of exam items.

7. **Item selection and cut-score setting.** The Beta exam results are analyzed to determine which items should be used and which rejected. This phase evaluates the difficulty and relevancy of the questions. The minimum passing score is decided at this level.

8. **Exam Live.** CompTIA exams are administered by Sylvan Prometric, an independent testing company. The exams are then made available at Sylvan Prometric Centers.

EXAM ITEMS AND SCORING

The CompTIA exams are multiple-choice. You will be asked a question and told to select the best answer. Your answer is either right or wrong—you will not receive partial credit. You will be required to get at least 70% correct to pass the exam.

PREPARING FOR A COMPTIA EXAM

The best way to prepare for an exam is to study and learn the job functions. Your goal must be to master abilities on the functions that you will be tested on. The process is fairly easy if you follow these preparation steps:

1. Identify the objectives you'll be tested on.

2. Assess your current knowledge on these objectives.

3. Practice the tasks using the skills you are learning.

REGISTERING FOR AND TAKING THE A+ EXAM

This section contains information about registering for and taking the exam. This will include information needed to register and complete the exam at a Sylvan Prometric Testing Center.

How to Register for an Exam

Candidates may take the exams at one of more than 700 Sylvan Prometric testing centers around the world. You can get testing information by calling Sylvan Prometric at (800) 755-EXAM (755-3926). Contact your local Sylvan Prometric Registration Center to locate international centers.

Determine which exam you want to take, then register with the Sylvan Prometric Registration Center nearest you. You will be required to pay for the test when you register. Most centers accept credit cards. You will be able to schedule your exam when you call in most cases. You will receive registration confirmation from Sylvan.

The registration center will send you instructions regarding appointment times, cancellation procedures, and ID requirements. They can also send you information about the test center location. You must take the exam within one year of payment. You can schedule the exam up to six weeks in advance. You can usually reschedule with two days notice. Contact Sylvan Prometric if you have questions about these procedures.

What to Expect at the Testing Center

Knowing what to expect at the testing center will help you prepare and lower your anxiety.

When you enter, you will be asked to sign a log book noting your arrival time. You will need two forms of identification, including an acceptable picture ID. In most cases, a driver's license and credit card are adequate. The test administrator will give you information about rules and requirements that you must follow during the test. Failure to comply with these rules may result in the immediate termination of your test. The test administrator should accompany you to your test system and perform any logon instructions necessary for you to get started.

You will either be provided scratch paper or a small erasable board to use for writing. This will be collected from you at the end of the test. You will not be allowed to bring any materials into the test area. You may be provided with a supplemental booklet that may be used for the test. The test administrator will tell you what you must do when you complete the exam. Don't be afraid to ask if you have any questions or don't understand the instructions.

You are entitled to a quiet place with adequate room to work. If you are not being given fair treatment, do not be afraid to speak up. If the center does not provide you with what you need, don't be afraid to complain. They take your complaints seriously and will do whatever they can to help you. You are entitled to the following things specifically:

- A quiet, uncluttered test environment.
- Scratch paper or other similar writing material.
- A tutorial of the testing tool. You have plenty of time to take the tutorial.
- A knowledgeable and professional test administrator.
- The opportunity to submit comments about the test center or the staff.
- The opportunity to submit comments about the test.

You can get information on how to submit feedback about your exam in the "If You Have Exam Concerns or Feedback" section later in this appendix. The certification team will investigate any problems you may have and attempt to resolve them quickly and fairly.

TEST-TAKING TIPS

Here are some tips that may be helpful as you prepare to take an exam.

Before the Exam

- Be sure to read "What to Expect at the Testing Center" in this appendix for information about the sign-in and test-taking procedures you will likely encounter on your exam day.

- Complete the hands-on labs and review activities for each chapter in this book as you read them. You will need to perform the labs for them to be effective. If you don't have the equipment shown in the lab, use your own PC and experiment on taking it apart and putting it back together.

- Review the Key Point Summary sections and answer the Instant Assessment questions at the end of each chapter in the book. Do this during your study process, and immediately before you take the exam.

- Throughout the book you'll find exam pointers—write these down and memorize them, as they will assist you greatly in taking the test.

- When you've finished reading all of the chapters, go through the questions and answers at the end of each chapter.

- This exam is fairly challenging and very difficult if you are not prepared. So prepare for this exam in a serious manner and don't cut corners, and you will pass with flying colors.

- Research new technologies and information on the Web to get the latest thoughts in the business to prepare for both the exam and the field. Information is plentiful, and it is a powerful ally.

- Subscribe to technical magazines to learn the vocabulary and understand the issues in your field. Join CompTIA and other professional associations and become an active member in local users' groups. This will help you prepare for the exam and build a network of contacts that will be useful for you in your career.

- Think about the times when you are most mentally alert and schedule your exam for that time. As hard as it may be to believe, most people have the highest mental energy first thing in the morning. We always recommend that you take the exams as early as you can.

- Check around in your area and find a testing center that you want to work with before you call for an appointment. This will help you overcome any anxiety you may have about taking the test.

- Take a few minutes and create a mental image of you passing the exam. In fact, take a minute every morning and visualize how you will feel and act as a competent computer technician. Most people will assume you know what you are talking about unless you prove otherwise.

- Get a good night's sleep before the exam. If you are tired, you won't do as well. Relax — if you have prepared and studied, you are ready!

On Exam Day

- Arrive at the test site 10 to 15 minutes early; make sure you bring picture ID.

- Dress comfortably. You will probably be in a fairly small room when you take the test — you should take a sweater with you in case it is cold.

- If you have any questions about the testing procedure, ask them before you start the test. These tests are timed — your time is valuable, so don't waste it.

- Some people recommend that you don't drink a lot of liquid before you take the exam; if you have to go to the restroom during the test, you will lose valuable time.

During the Exam

- Answer the easy questions first. The software is designed to help you move around in the exam. Go through all the items first and answer the ones you know. Then go back through again and answer the hard questions. Keep doing this until you finish the exam. In some cases, answering an easy question will trigger your memory about a harder question.

- There are no trick questions, but read them carefully, as the answers may at times be confusing.

- In most cases, you can eliminate the obvious answers almost immediately; this makes it easier to choose the right answer.

- Make sure you answer all of the questions in the exam. If you are running out of time, give the questions that you don't know the answer to your best shot. You miss the question whether you get it wrong or don't answer.

- Relax—you have enough time to finish the exam. Don't rush—instead, look at each question and answer it. When you go back through the questions, don't change an answer unless you are absolutely positively certain that you answered it wrong. It is human nature for people to analyze themselves out of the right answer.

- Don't forget to breathe—if you pass out because you are stressing out, all they can do is call a medic for you. Take frequent and regular deep breaths. Besides, the oxygen will raise your intelligence level.

After the Exam

- If you didn't pass, take a few minutes and evaluate what questions and areas were difficult for you, then go back and study those areas thoroughly.

- There is no shame in not passing the exam—it just means you need to improve your knowledge and try again. It is hard not to be discouraged, but use it as feedback and try again. In some certifications, it is not uncommon for people to have to take the exams three or four times.

- If you passed the exam, congratulations! Well done! Now, get to work!

YOUR EXAM RESULTS

Once you have completed an exam, you will be given immediate, online feedback on your pass or fail status. You will also receive an examination score report print-out, indicating your status and results by section. If you pass the exam, you will receive a confirmation letter from CompTIA in a few weeks.

If you do not pass the exam, immediately call Sylvan Prometric and schedule another exam. Give yourself a few days to study the areas you had difficulty with. In most cases, people do very well in all but one or two areas, which cause them to fail. Here are some specific ways you can prepare to retake an exam:

- Go over the section-by-section scores on your exam results, not just the areas where you can improve.

- Review the guide with special focus on the areas that correspond to the exam sections with scores that can be improved.

- Get more experience hands-on with the areas you are weak in and reread the relevant sections in the book.

- If you don't understand a specific area, get some outside advice, talk to another computer professional, take a class, do whatever you need to feel comfortable with the material. In most cases, it is probably a minor detail that you didn't understand. When you learn that concept, your understanding of the whole field will increase dramatically.

- Go back over the summaries, retake the review questions, and review the materials.

- Then go take the exam and pass it!

IF YOU HAVE EXAM CONCERNS OR FEEDBACK

CompTIA and Sylvan make every effort to ensure that your exam experience is a positive one. If any problems occur with your testing process, inform Sylvan Prometric through your test administrator immediately. The Sylvan Prometric people are there to make the logistics of your exam work smoothly.

Technical and testing experts developed CompTIA exams. Input was solicited from professional organizations, certified professionals, and technology experts. They have been through an exhaustive process to ensure the test is fair and accurate. If you feel that an exam question is inappropriate, or if you feel the answer shown is incorrect, write or send a fax to the CompTIA development team. Your information will be evaluated and any needed changes will be made.

Sylvan Prometric testing centers are accredited by Sylvan; they try to be very responsive to customer concerns. If you have a concern about the exam or the test center, contact Sylvan and lodge your concerns; they will listen and try to resolve the situation.

FOR MORE INFORMATION

To find out more information about the A+ certification, you can contact one or more of the resources listed below:

- CompTIA at (630) 268-1818: They can provide you with up-to-date information on the status of the exam or any late-breaking news on A+ certification. The CompTIA Web site also contains a wealth of information on the certification process. The Web site is www.comptia.org.

- Sylvan Prometric Testing Centers at (800) 755-EXAM: Call to register to take an exam or for information about the exam process.

- IDG Online at www.idgbooks.com: IDG Books provides a wealth of relevant materials on its Web site that will help you prepare for the exam. Not only does IDG provide an extremely comprehensive series of computer books, but also books on other high-level certification programs and resource materials.

- Microsoft TechNet Technical Information Network at (800) 344-2121: TechNet is a comprehensive resource that provides a wealth of information for technical professionals. The Web site is www.microsoft.com.

- IBID Publishing at (800) 752-9816: IBID Publishing provides a series of links and information on A+ certification and technical resources. The Web site is www.ibidpub.com.

Computer Vendors

MANUFACTURERS OF COMPUTER, PERIPHERALS, AND COMPONENTS

1st Tech Corporation

12201 Technology Boulevard, Suite 160

Austin, TX 78727

(800) 533-1744

Memory products

3Com Corporation

5400 Bayfront Plaza

Santa Clara, CA 95052-8145

(800) 638-3266, (408) 764-5000

3DTV Corporation

P.O. Box Q

San Rafael, CA 94913-4316

(415) 479-3516

Hardware and software for 3D (steroscopic) video, computer graphics, and virtual reality

4Q Technologies

18563 Gale Avenue, Unit A
City of Industry, CA 91748
(818) 935-1999
Speakers

A4 Tech Corporation

20256 Apseo Robles
Walnut, CA 91789
(909) 468-0071
Scanners

ABS Computer Technologies, Inc.

1295 Johnson Drive
City of Industry, CA 91745
(800) 876-8088, (800) 685-3471, (818) 937-2300
fax (818) 937-2322

Absolute Battery Co.

50 Tannery Road, Suite 2
Somerville, NJ 08876
(800) 829-8294
Laptop/notebook computer batteries and charging systems

Abstract R&D, Inc.

120 Village Square, Suite 37
Orinda, CA 94563
(510) 253-9588
Palmtop PCs

Acecad, Inc.

2600 Garden Road, Suite 121
Monterey, CA 93940
(408) 655-1900
Acecat III mouse replacement

Acer American Corporation

2641 Orchard Parkway
San Jose, CA 95134
(408) 432-6200

Acer Sertak Inc.

926 Thompson Place
Sunnyvale, CA 94086
(408) 733-3174
CD-ROMs, MPEG cards, sound cards

Achme Computer Inc.

A Micro Star Co.
4059 Clipper Court
Fremont, CA 94538
(510) 623-8818

ACL/Statcide

1960 E. Devon Avenue
Elk Grove Village, IL 60007
(708) 981-9212
Anti-static equipment and cleaning kits

Acom Inc.

46600 Landing Parkway

Fremont, CA 94538

(510) 353-1600

Patriot multimedia notebooks

ACS Computer Group

100 San Lucar Court

Sunnyvale, CA 94086

(408) 481-9988

ACT-RX Technologies Corporation

10F, 525, Chung Cheng Road

Hsin Tien, Taipei, Taiwan ROC

(886) 2-218-8000 Booth I9025

CPU coolers

Action Electronics Co., Ltd.

198, Chung Yuan Road

Chung Li, Taiwan, ROC

(886) 3-4515494

Axion monitors

Action Well Development Ltd.

Rm. 1011, 1103 and 4 Star Center

443-451 Castle Peak Road

Kwai Chung, NT, Hong Kong

(852) 2422-0010

Fax modems, sound products, controller and VGA cards, and computer cases

ActionTec Electronics, Inc.

750 N. Mary Avenue
Sunnyvale, CA 94086
(408) 739-7000

Actix Systems, Inc.

3350 Scott Boulevard, Building 9
Santa Clara, CA 95054
(408) 986-1625

Actown Corporation

8F, 827, Chung Cheng Road
Hsin Tien, Taipei, Taiwan ROC
(886) 2-2184612 Booth S2050E

Adaptec, Inc.

691 S. Milpitas Boulevard
Milpitas, CA 95035
(800) 934-2766, (408) 945-8600

Addonics Technologies

48434 Milmont Drive
Fremont, CA 94538
(510) 438-6530

Addtronics Enterprise Co.

No.66, Chen-The road
Taipei, Taiwan ROC
(886) 2-5591122

ADI Systems, Inc.

2115 Ringwood Avenue
San Jose, CA 95131
(800) 228-0530, (408) 944-0100
fax (408) 944-0300

Adobe Systems Inc.

1585 Charleston Road
Mountain View, CA 94043
(415) 961-4400

ADPI (Analog and Digital Peripherals, Inc.)

P.O. Box 499
Troy, OH 45373
(513) 339-2241
Backup devices

Adroit Systems, Inc.

9225 Chesapeake Drive, Suite G
San Diego, CA 92123
(619) 627-1888
CCD color video cameras, including OmniCam

Advanced Digital Systems

13909 Bettencourt Street
Cerritos, CA 90703
(800) 888-5244
Multimedia specialty audio/video hardware

Advanced Gravis Computer Technology Ltd.

101-3750 N. Fraser Way
Burnaby, BC V5J 5E9, Canada
(604) 431-5020
PC game interfaces

Advanced Integration Research, Inc.

2188 Del Franco Street
San Jose, CA 95131
(408) 428-0800

Advanced Matrix Technology, Inc.

747 Calle Plano
Camarillo, CA 93012-8598
(805) 388-5799
Dot matrix, laser, and ink jet printers and plotters

Advantage Memory

25A Technology Drive, Building 2
Irvine, CA 92718
(800) 266-0488

Agfa (Bayer Corporation)

200 Ballardvale Street
Wilmington, MA 01887
(508) 658-5600
Scanners, film recorders, color management software, digital cameras

Ahead Systems, Inc.

44244 Fremont Boulevard
Fremont, CA 94538
(510) 623-0900
3D-multimedia surround-sound, accelerator, and 3D stereo vision products

AITech International Corporation

47971 Fremont Boulevard
Fremont, CA 94538
(510) 226-8960
Multimedia and desktop video products

Aiwa America, Inc.

800 Corporate Drive
Mahwah, NJ 07430
(800) 920-2673
Tape backup products

Alaris Inc.

47338 Fremont Boulevard
Fremont, CA 94538
(510) 770-5700
Graphics acceleration and scalable full motion video playback products

Alfa Infotech Co.

46600 Landing Parkway
Fremont, CA 94538
(510) 252-9300
Multimedia and communication products

ALi (Acer Laboratories Inc.)

4701 Patrick Henry Drive, Suite 2101
Santa Clara, CA 95054
(408) 764-0644
ICs for personal computers and embedded systems

Alpha & Omega Computer

101 S. Kraemer Boulevard, Suite 116
Placentia, CA 92670
(714) 577-7688
486/Pentium CPU coolers

Alphacom Enterprises Inc.

1407 Englewood Street
Philadelphia, PA 19111
(215) 722-6133
Joysticks, mice, trackballs, CPU cooling fans with built-in heat sink, and
removable hard disk drive kits

ALPS

3553 N. First Street
San Jose, CA 95134
(408) 432-6000
GlidePoint input devices, drive products

AMCC (Applied Micro Circuits Corporation)

6195 Lusk Boulevard
San Diego, CA 92121
(800) 755-2622

AMD (Advanced Micro Devices)

1 AMD Place
Sunnyvale, CA 94086
(800) 222-9323, (408) 732-2400
CPUs

American Cover, Inc.

102 W. 12200 S
Draper, UT 84092
(801) 553-0600
Computer accessory products

AMI (American Megatrends, Inc.)

6145F Northbelt Parkway
Norcross, GA 30071
(770) 263-8181
Motherboards

Amptron International, Inc.

1028 Lawson Street
City of Industry, CA 91748
(818) 912-5789
System boards

Amquest Corporation

1650 Manheim Pike
Lancaster, PA 17601
(717) 569-8030
Multimedia/communications add-on products for PCs

Amrel Technology Inc.

11801 Goldring Road
Arcadia, CA 91006
(800) 882-6735
Modular notebook computers

AMS, Inc.

12881 Ramona Boulevard
Irwindale, CA 91706
(800) 886-2671

Ana Precision Co., Ltd.

Suite 694, Kumjung-Dong, Kunp'O-shi
Kyunggi-Do, 435-050, Korea
(0343) 53-0813
Ink jet and dot matrix printers

Angia Communications

441 East Bay Boulevard
Provo, UT 84606
(800) 877-9159
fax (801) 373-9847
PCMCIA fax modem

AOC International

311 Sinclair Frontage Road
Milpitas, CA 95035
(408) 956-1070
Visual display products

APC (American Power Conversion)

132 Fairgrounds Road

West Kingdom, RI 02892

(800) 800-4APC

fax (401) 788-2797

UPSes, phone line surge protectors

Apex Data, Inc./SMART Modular Technologies, Inc.

4305 Cushing Parkway

Fremont, CA 94538

(800) 841-APEX, tech support (510) 249-1605

fax (510) 249-1600, tech support fax (510) 249-1604

BBS (510) 249-1601 (8 data bits, 1 stop bit, and no parity)

Apple Computer, Inc.

1 Infinite Loop

Cupertino, CA 95014

(408) 996-1010

APS Technologies

6131 Deramus, Suite 4967

Kansas City, MO 64120

(800) 235-2735, (816) 483-1600

fax (816) 483-3077

Arcada Software

37 Skyline Drive
Lake Mary, FL 32746
(407) 333-7500
Data protection and storage management software products

Archtek America Corporation

18549 Gale Avenue
City of Industry, CA 91748-1338
(818) 912-9800
Voice/data communications and network products

Arco Computer Products, Inc.

2750 N. 29th Avenue, Suite 316
Hollywood, FL 33020
(305) 925-2688
IDE busless, slotless, operating system-independent mirroring adapter

Arkenstone, Inc.

1390 Borregas Avenue
Sunnyvale, CA 94089
(800) 444-4443
Products to aid individuals who are blind, visually impaired, or learning
disabled to better access written information.

Artek (Asicom, Inc.)

46716 Fremont Boulevard
Fremont, CA 94538
(510) 354-0900
High-end PC subsystems

Artisoft, Inc.

2202 N. Forbes Boulevard

Tucson, AZ 85745

(520) 670-7100

Networking products suited to small businesses and workgroups

ArtMedia

2772 Calle del Mundo

Santa Clara, CA 95050

(408) 980-8988

ASK LCD, Inc.

1099 Wall Street W, Suite 396

Lyndhurst, NJ 07071

(201) 896-8888

fax (201) 896-0012

LCD presentation products

Ask Technology Ltd.

Unit 1,4/F., Henley Ind. Ctr., 9-15 Bute Street

Mongkok, Kowloon, Hong Kong

(852) 2398-3223

Systems boards, VGA cards, and sound cards

Askey Communications USA

162 Atlantic Street

Pomona, CA 91768

PCMCIA, external, and internal modem cards and pocket models

ASM (Automated Systems Methodologies, Inc.)

16100 Fairchild Drive

Boatyard 105

Clearwater, FL 34622

(800) 992-0120

4x and 6x Gator Audio CD-ROM for parallel port and SCSI

Asolid Computer Supply, Inc.

(Biostar Manufacture Group)

4044 Clipper Court

Fremont, CA 94538

(510) 226-6678

Motherboards

Aspen Systems Inc.

4026 Youngfield Street

Wheat Ridge, CO 80033-3862

(303) 431-4606

RISC systems

Aspen Technologies

400 Rogers Street

Princeton, WV 24740

(304) 425-1111

Internal, external, and PCMCIA fax modems

Assmann Data Products

1849 W. Drake Drive, Suite 101

Tempe, AZ 85283

(602) 897-7001

Ergonomic mice

AST Computer

16215 Alton Parkway

Irvine, CA 92718

(714) 727-4141

ATI Technologies

33 Commerce Valley Drive East

Thornhill, Ontario, Canada L3T 7N6

(905) 882-2600

fax (905) 882-2620

faxback (905) 882-2600 (press #2)

CompuServe: GO ATITECH

Graphics accelerators

Atlantic Technology

343 Vanderbilt Avenue

Norwood, MA 02062

(617) 762-6300

Speakers

ATronics International, Inc.

45635 Northport Loop E

Fremont, CA 94538-6415

(510) 656-8400

Advanced external storage products

ATTO Technology, Inc.

40 Hazelwood Drive, Suite 106

Amherst, NY 14228

(716) 691-1999

Vantage PCI-Multi Channel SCSI accelerator card

AuraVision Corporation

47865 Fremont Boulevard
Fremont, CA 94538
(510) 252-6800
Multimedia IC devices

Autumn Technologies

11705 69th Way N
Largo, FL 34643
(800) 837-8551
Test Bed Pro, a commercial PC testing, assembly, and repair workbench

AVerMedia, Inc.

47923A Warm Springs Boulevard
Fremont, CA 94538
(510) 770-9899
PC-Video multimedia hardware

AVM Technology, Inc.

9774 S. 700 East
Sandy, UT 84070
(810) 571-0967
Professional MIDI wavetable modules

Avnet Technology Co., Ltd.

6F-1, No.102, Sung Lung Road
Taipei, Taiwan ROC
 (886) 2-7607603
Audio-Visual Network Card

Award Software International

777 E. Middlefield Road

Mountain View, CA 94043

(415) 968-4433

Desktop plug-and-play BOIS for 486, 586, Pentium, and P6-based PC platforms

Axonix Corporation

844 S. 200 East

Salt Lake City, UT 84111

(801) 521-9797

CD-ROMs

Axxon Computer Corporation

3979 Tecumseh Road E

Windsor, ON N8W 1J5, Canada

(519) 974-0163

Jumperless I/O cards

Aztech labs, Inc.

47811 Warm Springs Boulevard

Fremont, CA 94539

(510) 623-8988

6x CD-ROM drive

Belkin Components

1303 Walnut Parkway

Compton, CA 90220

(310) 898-1100

Standard and custom computer cables, printer-sharing devices, surge protectors, and LAN cabling-related products

Benwin Inc.

345 Cloverleaf Drive, Suite B
Baldwin Park, CA 91706
(818) 336-8779
Multimedia products, specializing in speakers

Best Data Products

21800 Nordhoff Street
Chatsworth, CA 91311
(818) 773-9600

Best Power

General Signal
P.O. Box 280
Necedah, WI 54646
(800) 356-5794
UPSes and shutdown software

BIS Technology

13111 Brooks Drive, Suite A
Baldwin Park, CA 91706
(818) 856-5800
High-speed voice/fax/data modems

Boca Research

1377 Clint Moore Road
Boca Raton, FL 33478
(407) 997-6227
fax (407) 994-5848

Borland International

100 Borland Way
Scotts Valley, CA 95066
(831) 431-1000
Products and services for software developers

Bose Corporation

The Mountain
Framingham, MA 01701
(800) 444-BOSE

Brooks Power Systems Inc.

1400 Adams Road
Bensalem, PA 19020
(800) 523-1551
Power Systems's SurgeStopper surge and noise suppressors

Brother International Corporation

200 Cottontail Lane
Somerset, NJ 08875
(908) 356-8880
Multifunctional products and laser printers

BRYSiS Data, Inc.

17431 Gale Avenue
City of Industry, CA 91748
(818) 810-0355
Touch screen monitors

BSF Components Inc.

420 Third Street
Oakland, CA 94607
(510) 893-8822
Molded and assembled computer cables

Bus Logic Inc.

4151 Burton Drive
Santa Clara, CA 95054
(408) 492-9090
fax (408) 492-1542
SCSI host adapters

C-Cube Microsystems

1778 McCarthy Boulevard
Milpitas, CA 95035
MPEG and JPEG decoders and encoders for personal computers

California PC Products

205 Apollo Way
Hollister, CA 95023
(408) 638-9460
Computers chassis and power supplies

Calluna Technology Ltd.

1 Blackwood Road
Eastfield, Glenrothes
Fife KY7 4NP, Scotland, UK
(44) 1592-630-810
PC card hard disk drives

Canon Computer Systems

2995 Redhill Avenue

Costa Mesa, CA 92626

(800) 848-4123, (714) 438-3000

Canon U.S.A., Inc.

1 Cannon Plaza

Lake Success, NY 11042-1113

(516) 488-6700

Bubblejet CJ10 desktop color copiers, scanners, and printers

Canopus

2010 N. First Street, Suite 510

San Jose, CA 95131

(408) 467-4000

High-performance multimedia products for PCs

Cardinal Technologies, Incorporated

1827 Freedom Road

Lancaster, PA 17601

(800) 775-0899 ext.656, (717) 293-3124

Fax modems

Casco Products, Inc.

375 Collins Road NE, Suite 115

Cedar Rapids, IA 52402

(319) 393-6960

LightLink infrared, cordless keyboard

CD Technology, Inc.

766 San Aleso Avenue
Sunnyvale, CA 94086
(408) 752-8500
CD-ROMs

Centon Electronics, Inc.

20 Morgan
Irvine, CA 92718
(714) 855-9111
Manufacturer of memory upgrades for desktops, workstations, laptops, notebooks, portables, and printers

Cerwin-Vega, Inc.

555 E. Easy Street
Simi Valley, CA 93065
(805) 584-9332
Digital audio-quality multimedia speaker systems

CH Products

970 Park Center Drive
Vista, CA 92038
(619) 598-2518
Joysticks, F-16 sticks, throttles, rudder pedals, flight yokes, trackballs, and game cards

Chaintech Computer U.S. Inc.

12880 Lakeland Road
Santa Fe Springs, CA 90670
(310) 906-1698
Main boards, VGA cards, multi I/O cards, SCSI interfaces, and sound cards

Chaplet Systems USA, Inc.

252 N. Wolfe Road
Sunnyvale, CA 94086
(408) 732-7950
Notebook computers

Chartered Electronics Industries

210A Twin Dolphin Drive
Redwood City, CA 94065
(415) 591-6617
PC PrimeTimeTV add-on board

Chase Advanced Technologies

500 Main Street
Deep River, CT 06417
(203) 526-2400
Computer peripheral products

Cheer Electronics (U.S.A.)

9740 N. Seymour
Kansas City, MO 64153
(816) 891-0050
Monitors

Cheery Electrical Products

3600 Sunset Avenue
Waukegan, IL 60087
(708) 662-9200
PC/POS keyboards, low-cost 101-key data entry keyboards

Chinon America Inc.

615 Hawaii Avenue
Torrance, CA 90503
(310) 533-0274
Digital cameras, CD-ROM drives

Cirque Corporation

433 W. Lawndale Drive
Salt Lake City, UT 84115
(800) 454-3375, (801) 467-1100
GlidePoint trackpad

Cirrus Logic, Inc.

3100 W. Warren Avenue
Fremont, CA 94538
(510) 623-8300

Citizen America Corporation

2450 Broadway, Suite 600
Santa Monica, CA 90404
(310) 453-0614
Printiva 600C near-photo-quality color printer

Clary Corporation

1960 S. Walker Avenue
Monrovia, CA 91016
(800) 442-5279
UPSes

CMD Technology, Inc.

1 Vanderbilt
Irvine, CA 92718
(714) 454-0800
SCSI RAID and PC host adapters

Colorgraphic

5980 Peachtree Road
Atlanta, GA 30341
(770) 455-3921

COM2001 Corporation

4350 La Jolla Village Drive, Suite 930
San Diego, CA 92122
(619) 638-2001
Video and audio conferencing software

ComByte, Inc.

4424 Innovation Drive
Fort Collins, CO 80525
(970) 229-0660
Doubleplay dual-mode drives, reads and writes both floppy disks and minicartridge

Comdial Corp.

1180 Seminole Trail
Charlottesville, VA 22906-7266
(800) 347-1432, (804) 978-2200
faxback: (800) COMDIAL
PC and telephone interfaces

Command Software Systems

1061 E Indiantown Road, Suite 500
Jupiter, FL 33477
(800) 423-9147
F-Prot Professional anti-virus software

Compaq Computer Corporation

P.O. Box 69200
Houston, TX 77269
(800) 345-1518, (713) 518-1518
http://www.compaq.com

Computer Connections America

19A Crosby Drive
Bedford, MA 01730
(617) 271-0444
Peripheral equipment for backup and data storage

Computer Fun

8250 Valdosta Avenue
San Diego, CA 92126-2130
email garyo@computerfun.com
Manufacturer of mouse pads and computer toys

Connectix Corporation

2655 Campus Drive
San Mateo, CA 94403
(800) 950-5880, (415) 571-5100
fax (415) 571-5195
Quickcam video camera

Conner Peripherals, Inc

1650 Sunflower Avenue
Costa Mesa, CA 92626
(800) 4-CONNER

Copam Dynamics Systems, Inc.

46560 Fremont Boulevard, Suite 409
Fremont, CA 94538
(510) 770-0149
CPU cooling kits and memory-related components

Copper Leaf Technology

2233 Paragon Drive
San Jose, CA 95131
(408) 452-9288
Motherboards

Cornerstone Imaging, Inc.

1710 Fortune Drive
San Jose, CA 95131
(408) 435-8900

Creative Labs, Inc.

1901 McCarthy Boulevard
Milpitas, CA 95035
(800) 998-1000, (408) 428-6660
fax (408) 428-6631

Creatix Polymedia, L.P.

3945 Freedom Circle, Suite 670
Santa Clara, CA 95054
(408) 654-9300
Multimedia products, high-speed modems, and PCMCIA cards

Crystal Semiconductor

3100 W. Warren Avenue
Fremont, CA 94538
(510) 623-8300

CTX International, Inc.

20530 Earlgate Street
Walnut, CA 91789
(909) 598-8094
Monitors

CyberMax Computer, Inc.

133 North 5th Street
Allentown, PA 18102
(800) 443-9868, from Canada (800) 695-4991
(610) 770-1808

Cyrix Corporations

P.O. Box 853923
Richardson, TX 75085-3923
(800) 462-9749, (800) 340-7971
email tech_support@cyrix.com
BBS (214) 968-8610

Daewoo Electronics

120 Chubb Avenue
Lyndhurst, NJ 07071
(201) 460-2000
Monitors

DarkHorse Systems, Inc.

1st Tech Corporation
12201 Technology Boulevard
Suite 135
Austin, TX 78727
Memory test systems

Data Depot Inc.

1710 Drew Street, Suite 1
Clearwater, FL 34615
(813) 446-3402
PC diagnostic test products, including hardware and software products

DataLux Corp.

155 Aviation Drive
Winchester, VA 22602
(800) DATALUX, (703) 662-1500
fax (540) 662-1682
faxback: (540) 662-1675
Space-saving PC hardware

Datasonix Corporation

5700 Flatiron Parkway
Boulder, CO 80301
(303) 545-9500
Peros portable gigabyte storage device

Dell Computer Corporation

2112 Kramer Lane
Austin, TX 78758
(800) 545-7141, (512) 728-3431

Delrina Corporation

6320 San Ignacio Avenue
San Jose, CA 95119-1209
(800) 268-6082
PC fax, communications, and electronic forms software

Delta Products Corporation

3225 Laurelview Court
Fremont, CA 94538
(510) 770-0660
Video display products

Deltec

2727 Kurtz Street
San Diego, CA 92110
(619) 291-4211
Uninterruptible power systems and power management software

Denon Electronics

222 New Road
Parsippany, NJ 07054
(201) 575-7810
CD-ROM jukebox that houses 200 discs

DFI (Diamond Flower, Inc.)

135 Main Avenue

Sacramento, CA 95838

(916) 568-1234

Motherboards, video cards, notebooks, desktop systems, and multimedia components

DiagSoft, Inc.

5615 Scotts Valley Drive, Suite 140

Scotts Valley, CA 95066

(831) 438-8247

Diagnostic software

Diamond Multimedia Systems, Inc.

2880 Junction Avenue

San Jose, CA 95134-1922

(408) 325-7000

fax (408) 325-7070

Digital Equipment Corporation (DEC)

Digital Semiconductor

77 Reed Road

Hudson, MA 01749

(508) 568-6872

Digital Equipment Corporation (DEC)

Computer Systems Div.

111 Powdermill Road

Maynard, MA 01754-1499

(800) DIGITAL

PCs, servers, and workstations for 32- and 64-bit computing

Disctec

925 S. Semoran Boulevard, Suite 114
Winter Park, FL 32792
(407) 671-5500
Parallel port products including CD-ROM drives, hard drives, floppy drives, and rewriteable optical drives

DPT–Distributed Processing Technology

140 Candace Drive
Maitland, FL 32751
(407) 830-5522
SmartCache SCSI host adapters

DTC Data Technology, Inc.

1515 Centre Pointe Drive
Milpitas, CA 95035
(408) 942-4000, technical support (408) 262-7700
fax (408) 942-4027
faxback: (408) 942-4005
BBS (408) 942-4010
Drives and SCSI devices

DTK Computer Inc.

770 Epperson Drive
City of Industry, CA 91745
(818) 810-0098
Pentium-based systems

Edek Technologies, Inc.

Div. of Elite Computer, Taiwan

1212 John Reed Ct.

City of Industry, CA 91745

(818) 855-5700

Manufacturer and distributor of computer mainboard and VGA products

ELSA Inc.

2041 Mission College Boulevard, Suite 165

Santa Clara, CA 95054

(408) 565-9669

2D and 3D graphics accelerators and ISDN products

Enhance Memory Products, Inc.

18730 Oxnard Street, Suite 201

Tarzana, CA 91356

(818) 343-3066

Memory systems

Ensoniq

155 Great Valley Parkway

Malvern, PA 19355

(610) 647-3930

EPS Technologies

10069 Dakota Avenue

Jefferson, SD 57038

(800) 447-0921, (800) 526-4258, (609) 966-5586

fax (605) 966-5482

Epson America

20770 Madrona Avenue
Torrance, CA 90509
(800) 463-7766, (301) 782-0770

ESS Technology, Inc.

46107 Landing Parkway
Fremont, CA 94538
(510) 226-1088
ES689 Wavetable Music Synthesizer, ES938 3D Audio Effects Processor

Evergreen Technologies, Inc.

915 NW 8th Street
Corvallis, OR 97330
(503) 757-0934
CPU upgrades for 386- and 486-based computers

Exabyte Corporation

1685 38th Street
Boulder, CO 80301
(800) 445-7736, (3030 417-7511, (303) 417-7792
fax (303) 417-7890
EXAFAX (fax-on demand system): (201) 946-0091

EXP Computer Inc.

141 Eileen Way
Syosset, NY 11791
(516) 496-3703
Memory and PCMCIA products for notebooks and palmtops

Expert Computer International, Inc.

129 166th Street
Cerritos, CA 90703
(310) 407-1740
Generic and name-brand VGA cards in DRAM/VRAM ISA, VL-bus, and PCI
configurations

Fast Electronics U.S., Inc.

393 Vintage Park Drive
Foster City, CA 94404
(650) 345-3400
FPS60 video compression board for multimedia production

Focus Computer Products, Inc.

35 Pond Park Road
Hingham, MA 02043
(617) 741-5008
Anti-glare glass screen filters, anti-radiation glass screen filters, wraparound
screen filters, cleaning products for screen filters

Focus Electronic Corporation

21078 Commerce Pointe Drive
Walnut, CA 91789
(909) 468-5533
Signature Series keyboards

Formosa USA, Inc.

9400 Lurline Avenue Suite B
Chatsworth, CA 91311
(818) 407-4956
MPEG decoding cards, video capture boards, TV tuners, video conference
products, 16-bit sound cards, wavetable modules

Fujitsu

Fujitsu Personal Systems, Inc.
5200 Patrick Henry Drive
Santa Clara, CA 95054
(408) 982-9500

Fujitsu Computer Products of America

2904 Orchard Parkway
San Jose, CA 95134
(408) 432-6333
Peripherals including hard disk drives, optical disk drives, tape drives, laser
and dot matrix printers, document imaging scanners

Fujitsu Microelectronics, Inc.

3545 N. First Street
San Jose, CA 95134
(408) 922-9000
Memory cards, LAN cards, multimedia, and communications cards

Gateway2000

610 Gateway Drive
N. Sioux City, SD 57049-2000
(888) 888-0244, from Canada (800) 846-3609, (605) 232-2000
fax (605) 232-2023
faxback (800) 846-4526

GVC Technologies

376 Lafayette Road

Sparta, NJ 07871

(800) 289-4821

Modems

Hayes Microcomputer Products, Inc.

P.O. Box 105203

Atlanta, GA 30348-5203

(800) 377-4377, (770) 840-9200

fax (770) 441-1213

http://www.hayes.com

Modems

HEI

Fast Point Light Pens

1495 Steiger Lake Lane

P.O. Box 5000, Victoria, MN 55386

(612) 443-2500

Fast Point light pens

Hercules Computer Technology, Inc.

3839 Spinnaker Court

Fremont, CA 94538

(800) 323-0601, (510) 623-6030, (501) 623-6050

fax (510) 623-1112

tech support fax; (510) 490-6745

faxback: (800) 711-HERC (800-711-4372)

CompuServe; GO HERCULES, 71333,2532

BBS (510) 623-7449

Hewlett-Packard

Personal Information Products Group

5301 Stevens Creek Boulevard

Santa Clara, CA 95052

(800) 762-0900

Hewlett-Packard Co.

Information Storage Group

800 S. Taft Avenue

Loveland, CO 80537

(970) 679-6000

HP Colorado tape products, HP DAT tape products, and HP optical products, disk drives, and disk array systems

Hewlett-Packard Co.

North American Hardcopy Marketing

16399 W. Bernardo Drive

San Diego, CA 92127

(800) 752-0990

Printers

Hilgraeve Inc.

111 Conant Avenue, Suite A

Monroe, MI 48161

(313) 243-0576

32-bit communications software, including HyperTerminal

Hitachi America, Ltd.

50 Prospect Avenue

Tarrytown, NY 10591-4698

(800) 448-2244

Computer peripherals and components, including storage products

HTP International

1620 South Lewis Street

Anaheim, CA 92805

(714) 937-9300

Hyundai Electronics America

510 Cottonwood Drive

Milpitas, CA 95035

(408) 232-8000

Components including memory devices for DRAM, SRAM

I/Omagic Corporation

9272 Jeronimo Street, Building 122

Irvine, CA 92718

(714) 727-7466

IBM PC Co.

1 Orchard Road

Armonk, NY 10504

(800) 772-2227, (914) 766-1900

fax (800) 426-4323

Iiyama North America, Inc.

650 Louis Drive, Suite 120
Warminster, PA 18974
(215) 957-6543

Integrated Technology Express, Inc.

1557 Centre Pointe Drive
Milpitas, CA 95035
(408) 934-7330
PC core logic sets, I/O peripheral chips, and custom ASIC design services on x86 and PowerPC architectures

Intel Corporation

2200 Mission College Boulevard
Santa Clara, CA 95052
(408) 765-1703

Intel Corporation

2111 NE 25th Avenue
Hillsboro, OR 97124-5961
(800) 538-3373, (503) 264-1007

Interact Accessories, Inc.

(formerly STD Entertainment)
10945 McCormick Road
Hunt Valley, MD 21031
(410) 785-5661
Multimedia gaming products such as joysticks, control pads, game cards, speakers, woofers, mice, storage cases, and cleaning kits

Iomega Corporation

1821 West Iomega Way

Roy, UT 84067

(800) MY-STUFF, (810) 778-3010

IPC Technologies, Inc.

Austin Computer Services, Inc.

10300 Metric Boulevard

Austin, TX 78758

(512) 339-3500

J–Mark Computer Corporation

13111 Brooks Drive, Suite A

Baldwin Park, CA 91706

(818) 856-5800

Motherboards, fax modems, SVGA cards, PCMCIA devices, and network cards for notebooks and PCs

Jazz Speakers

1217 John Reed Court

Industry, CA 91745

(818) 336-2689

JBL Consumer Products Inc.

Harmon Consumer Group

80 Crossways Park W.

Woodbury, NY 11797

(516) 496-3400

Multimedia speakers, both satellites and subwoofers

Joss Technology Ltd.

No 20, Lane 84, San Min Road
Hsin Tien City
Taipei Hsien, Taiwan ROC
(886) 2-9102050
Motherboards, 4MB/16MB 72-pin SIMM modules

JVC Information Products of America

17811 Mitchell Avenue
Irvine, CA 92714
(714) 261-1292
CD-ROM products and software

KeySonic Technology Inc.

A Div. of Powercom America
1040A S. Melrose Street
Placentia, CA 92670-7119
(714) 632-8887
MPEG video and audio decoding cards

Kinesis Corporation

22121 17th Avenue SE, Suite 107
Bothell, WA 98021-7404
(206) 402-8100
fax (206) 402-8181
Ergonomic keyboards

Kingston Technology Corporation

17600 Newhope Street

Fountain Valley, CA 92708

(800) 259-9370, (714) 437-3334

fax (714) 435-2699

http://www.kingston.com/b.htm

Konica Business Machines U.S.A., Inc.

500 Day Hill Road

Windsor, CT 06095

(203) 683-2222

Multifunctional printers

Koss Corporation

4129 N. Port Washington Boulevard

Milwaukee, WI 53212

(800) USA-KOSS, (414) 964-5000

Stereo audio accessories for computers

Labtec Enterprises, Inc.

3801 109th Avenue, Suite J

Vancouver, WA 98682

(360) 896-2000

Lava Computer Mfg. Inc.

LSMI Division

28A Dansk Court

Rexdale, ON M9W 5V8, Canada

(800) 241-5282

Manufactures high-speed I/O boards

Lefthanded Computer Keyboards, Inc.

354 Eisenhower Parkway
Livingston, NJ 07039
(800) 50-LEFTY

Leverage International, Inc.

46704 Fremont Boulevard
Fremont, CA 94538
(510) 657-6750
Manufacturer of memory modules and other semiconductor products for
IBM, Compaq, PC compatible, and other computers

Lexmark International, Inc.

2275 Research Boulevard
Rockville, MD 20850
(301) 212-5900

LG Electronics

1000 Sylvan Avenue
Englewood Cliffs, NJ 95131
(201) 816-2000
Goldstar monitors

Liberty Systems, Inc.

375 Saratoga Avenue, Suite A
San Jose, CA 95129
(408) 983-1127
CD-ROMs, hard drives, backup devices

Lion Optics Corporation (Likom SdnBhD)

1751 McCarthy Boulevard

Milpitas, CA 95035

(408) 954-8089

CD-ROM drive products

Logicode Technology, Inc.

1380 Flynn Road

Camarillo, CA 93012

(800) 735-6442, (800) 388-9000

Logitech, Inc.

6505 Kaiser Drive

Fremont, CA 94555

(510) 795-8500

Pointing devices

MAG InnoVision Co., Inc.

2801 South Yale Street

Santa Ana, CA 92704

(800) 827-3998, (714) 751-2008

fax (714) 751-5522

Monitors

Magnavox

Philips Consumer Electronics Company

One Philips Drive

Knoxville, TN 37914-1810

(800) 531-0039, (423) 521-4316

Matrox Graphics, Inc.

1025 St-Regis Boulevard
Dorval, Quebec, Canada H9P 2T4
(514) 969-6320
Video boards

Maxell Corporation of America

Multi-Media Division
22-08 Rt.208
Fair Lawn, NJ 07410
(800) 533-2836
Data storage media

Maxi–Switch

2901 East Elvira Road
Tucson, AZ 85706
(520) 294-5450
Keyboards

Maximus Computers

710 East Cypress Avenue, Unit-A
Monrovia, CA 91016
(800) 888-6294, (818) 305-5925
fax (818) 357-9140

MaxTech Corporation

400 Commons Way
Rockaway, NJ 07866
(800) 9-FORMAX
fax (201) 586-3308

Maxtor Corporation

510 Cottonwood Drive
Milpitas, CA 95135
(800) 2-MAXTOR, (408) 432-1700
fax (408) 922-2050
tech support fax (303) 678-2260

McAfee Associates

2710 Walsh Avenue
Santa Clara, CA
(408) 988-3832
VirusScan anti-virus software

Media Vision

47900 Bayside Parkway
Fremont, CA 94538
(510) 770-8600
Semiconductor products, audio products

Mediatrix Peripherals Inc.

4229 Garlock Street
Sherbrooke, PQ J1L 2C8 Canada
(819) 829-8749
Audiotrix Pro 16-bit sound board

Megahertz Corporation

605 North 5600 Way
Salt Lake City, UT 84116
(800) 517-8677

Memory Card Technology

141 Duesenberg Drive, Suite 12
Westlake Village, CA 91362
(805) 494-1395
Memory upgrades and PCMCIA products

Micro 2000, Inc.

1100 E. Broadway, Suite 301
Glendale, CA 91205
(818) 547-0125
Universal Diagnostics Toolkit

Micro Accessories, Inc.

6086 Stewart Avenue
Fremont, CA 94538
(510) 226-6310
Computer interface cables and terminators

Micro Solutions

132 West Lincoln Highway
DeKalb, IL 60115
(815) 754-4500
fax (815) 756-4986
faxback (815) 754-4600
BBS (815) 756-9100

MicroClean, Inc.

2050 S. Tenth Street
San Jose, CA 95112
(408) 995-5062
Computer care cleaning products

Microcom, Inc.

500 River Ridge Drive

Norwood, MA 02062

(800) 822-8224, (617) 551-1000

faxback (800) 285-2802

Data/fax modem for laptops

MicroData Corp.

3001 Exec. Drive

Clearwater, FL 34622

(813) 573-5900

PC diagnostic hardware and software products for technicians, system integrators, and computer service professionals

Microlabs

204 Lost Canyon Court

Richardson, TX 75080

(214) 234-5842

Micron Electronics, Inc.

900 East Karcher Road

Nampa, ID 83687

(800) 214-6674, Canada (800) 708-1758,

(208) 893-3434

fax (208) 893-3424

Computer systems, WinBook notebook computers

Micron Technology, Inc.

8000 S. Federal Way
Boise, ID 83707-0006
(208) 368-3850
DRAMs, fast SRAMs, and modules, including EDO and Burst EDO (BEDO)
DRAMs

Micronics Computers

221 Warren Avenue
Fremont, CA 94539
(800) 767-2443
Orchid series graphics accelerators

Microsoft Corporation

One Microsoft Way
Redmond, WA 98052-6399
(206) 882-8080

Microtek Lab, Inc.

3715 Doolittle Drive
Redondo Beach, CA 90278
(800) 654-4160, (310) 297-5000
tech support (310) 297-5100
fax (310) 297-5050
BBS (310) 297-5102
AutoTech fax-back: (310) 297-5101
CompuServe: GO GRAPHSUP, library 6

Mindflight Technology Inc.

4-608 Weber Street North
Waterloo, Ontario N2V 1K4
(519) 746-8483
fax (519) 746-3317
Portable data products that connect to a PC parallel port or a SCSI port

Minolta Corporation

101 Williams Drive
Ramsey, NJ 07446
(201) 825-4000
Graphics-specific input and output devices

Miro Computer Products, Inc.

955 Commericial Street
Palo Alto, CA 94303
(415) 855-0940
Multimedia products

Mita Copystar America, Inc.

225 Sand Road
P.O. Box 40008
Fairfield, NJ 07004-0008
(800) ABC-MITA
Multifunctional printers

Mitsuba Corporation

1925 Wright Avenue
Laverne, CA 91750
(800) 648-7822
http://www.mitsuba.com
Custom file servers, PCs, and notebooks

Mitsubishi Chemical America

Optical Storage & Software Systems Group
99 W. Tasmania Drive, Suite 200
San Jose, CA 95134-1712
(408) 954-8484
Magneto-optical storage technologies

Mitsubishi Electronics America

5665 Plaza Drive
Cypress, CA 90630
(800) 828-6372, (714) 220-2500

Mitsumi Electronics Corporation

6210 N. Beltline Road, Suite 170
Irving, TX 75063
(800) 648-7864, (800) 801-7927, (214) 550-7300
BBS (415) 691-4469
Keyboards, mice, floppy disk drives, and CD-ROM drives

Motorola ISG

5000 Bradford Drive
Huntsville, AL 35805
(205) 430-8000
Modems

Motorola PCMCIA Products Division

50 East Commerce Drive

Shaumburg, IL 60173

(800) 4A-PCMCIA

MP Computer Parts Supply Co., Ltd.

150 Commercial Street

Sunnyvale, CA 94086

(408) 738-3388

Cables, switches, connectors, computer accessories, and data communication accessories

MTC America, Inc.

2500 Westchester Avenue, Suite 110

Purchase, NY 10577

(800) MTC-CDRS

Mitsui Gold CD-R device

Multi–Tech Systems, Inc.

2205 Woodale Drive

Mounds View, MN 55112

(800) 328-9717

fax (612) 785-9874

Multiwave Technology, Inc.

15318 Valley Boulevard

City of Industry, CA 91746

(800) 234-3358, (800) 587-1730, (818) 330-7030

fax (818) 333-4609

Mustek, Inc.

1702 McGaw Avenue
Irvine, CA 92714
(800) 468-7835, (714) 247-1300
BBS (714) 247-1330
faxback (714) 247-1340
Scanners

Nanao USA Corporation

23535 Telo Avenue
Torrance, CA 90505
(800) 800-5205, (310) 325-5202
Monitors

National Semiconductor

Personal Systems Division
2900 Semiconductor Drive
Santa Clara, CA 95052
(408) 721-5000
Silicon products and systems for personal computers and peripherals

NCE Storage Solutions

9717 Pacific Heights Boulevard
San Diego, CA 92121
(619) 658-9720
Emerald Systems backup devices

NCR Corp.

(800) 774-7406
fax (803) 939-7824

NEC Technologies, Inc.

1414 Massachusetts Avenue

Boxborough, MA 01719

(508) 264-8000

NEC Technologies, Inc.

NEC RISC Systems

339 N. Bernardo Avenue

Mountain View, CA 94043

(415) 528-6000

RISC-based servers

New Media Corporation

One Technology Park, Bldg. A

Irvine, CA 92718

(714) 453-0100

fax (714) 453-0114

NewCom, Inc.

311666 Via Colinas

Westlake Village, CA 91362

(818) 597-3200

Internal and external fax modems, high-fidelity stereo sound cards, and multimedia kits

NexGen Inc.

1623 Buckeye Drive

Milpitas, CA 95035

(800) 8NEXGEN

Designer of the Nx586 processor

Nokia Display Products

1505 Bridgeway Boulevard
Sausalito, CA 94965
(800) 396-6541, (415) 331-0322

Nokia Mobile Phones

2300 Valley View Lane, Suite 100
Irving, TX 75062
(214) 257-9800

NSA/Hitachi

100 Lowder Brooke Drive
Westwood, MA 02090
(800) 441-4832, (617) 461-8300

Number Nine Computer Corporation

18 Hartwell Avenue
Lexington, MA 02173
(617) 674-0009

Ocean Information Systems Inc.

(Ocetek)
688 Arrow Grand Circle
Covina, CA 91722 USA
(818) 339-8888
fax (181) 859-7668

PC computer systems, motherboards, cases, power supplies, multimedia products, and peripherals

Okidata Corporation

532 Fellowship Road
Mt. Laurel, NJ 08054
(609) 235-2600

Olivetti Office USA

765 US Highway 202
Bridgewater, NJ 08807
(908) 526-8200

Orchestra MultiSystems, Inc.

12300 Edison Way
Garden Grove, CA 92841
(800) 237-9988, (714) 891-3861
fax (714) 891-2661

Orchid Technology

221 Warren Avenue
Fremont, CA 94539
(800) 577-0977, (510) 651-2300, (510) 661-3000
fax (510) 651-6692
fax on demand (510) 661-3199
CompuServe: GO ORCHID

Orevox USA Corporation

248 N. Puente Avenue
P.O. Box 2655
City of Industry, CA 91746
(818) 333-6803
Computer cases and multimedia speakers

Pacom Data Inc.

1257 B Tasman Drive
Sunnyvale, CA 94089
(408) 752-1590
Monitors and multimedia products

Padix Co., Ltd.

Rockfire
18F-3, No.75, Sec. 1 Hsin Tai Wu Road
Hsih-Chih, Taipei, Taiwan ROC
(886) 2-6981478
PC-compatible game controllers and joysticks

Panasonic Communications & Systems Co.

2 Panasonic Way
Secaucus, NJ 07094
(201) 348-7000

Pantex Computer Inc.

10301 Harwin Drive
Houston, TX 77036
(713) 988-1688
Motherboards, bare-bones systems

Pathlight Technology Inc.

767 Warren Road
Ithaca, NY 14850
(607) 266-4000
Storage I/O and networking interface technologies and products

PC Concepts, Inc.

10318 Norris Avenue
Pacoima, CA 91331
(800) 735-6071

Computer accessories including color-coded cables, manual and data switches, printer network devices, surge protectors, and multimedia products

PC Power & Cooling, Inc.

5995 Avenida Encinas
Carlsbad, CA 92008
(619) 931-5700
CPU cooler for Intel P6 processor

PCMCIA (Personal Computer Memory Card Int'l. Association)

4529 Lillian Court
La Canada, CA 91011
(408) 433-2273

Pengo Computer Accessories

15612 First Street
Irwindale, CA 91706
(800) 447-3646
Floppy diskettes, dust covers, keyboard drawers, diskette file boxes, tool kits, and various workstation accessories

Philips Consumer Electronics Co.

1 Philips Drive
Knoxville, TN 37914
(423) 521-4316
http://www.philips.com

Phoenix Technologies, Ltd.

2770 De La Cruz Boulevard
Santa Clara, CA 95050
(408) 654-9000
PhoenixBIOS for desktops, NoteBIOS for notebook computers, and
PhoenixPICO for handheld and embedded systems

Pioneer New Media Technologies, Inc.

Multimedia & Mass Storage
2265 E. 220th Street
Long Beach, CA 90810
(800) 444-6784
CD-ROM and CD-R products for multimedia and mass storage applications

Pionex Technologies, Inc.

3 Riverview Drive
Somerset, NJ 08873
(908) 563-9809

Pixie Technologies

46771 Fremont Boulevard
Fremont, CA 94538
(510) 440-9721
Monitors

PKWare, Inc.

9025 N. Deerwood Drive
Brown Deer, WI 53223
(414) 354-8699
PKZIP compression utilities

Play Inc.

2890 Kilgore Road
Rancho Cordova, CA 95670-6133
(916) 851-0800
Snappy Video Snapshots software

Plextor USA

4255 Burton Drive
Santa Clara, CA 95054
(800) 886-3935, (408) 980-1838
CD-ROM drives

Portrait Display Labs

6665 Owens Drive
Pleasanton, CA 94588
(510) 227-2700
Monitors

Powercom America, Inc.

1040A S. Melrose Street
Placentia, CA 92670-7119
(714) 632-8889
Modems and UPSes

PowerQuest Corporation

1083 North State Street

Orem, UT 84057

(800) 379-2566

Manufacturer of Partition Magic, a software utility for creating and managing disk partitions

Practical Peripherals

P.O. Box 921789

Norcross, GA 30092-7789

(770) 840-9966

Princeton Graphic Systems

2801 South Yale Street

Santa Ana, CA 92704

(800) 747-6249, (714) 751-8405

fax (714) 751-5736

Monitors

Procom Technology

2181 Dupont Drive

Irvine, CA 92715

(714) 852-1000

hard drives, backup devices

Professional Technologies

21038 Commerce Pointe Drive

Walnut, CA 91789

(800) 949-5018, (909) 468-3730

fax (909) 468-1372

Computer systems

ProLink Computer

2530 Corporate Place, Suite A-100

Monterrey Park, CA 91754

(213) 780 7978

Quadrant International, Inc.

269 Great Valley Parkway

Malvern, PA 19355 USA

(800) 700-0362, (610) 521-9999

tech support (610) 251-9999

fax (610) 695-2592

Video editing and capture products

Quantex Microsystems, Inc.

400B Pierce Street

Somerset, NJ 08873

(800) 836-0566

Quantum Corporation

500 McCarthy Boulevard

Milpitas, CA 95053

(800) 624-5545, (408) 894-4000

Quarterdeck Select

5770 Roosevelt Boulevard #400

Clearwater, FL 34620

(800) 683-6696

fax (813) 523-2391

Troubleshooting tools

Quatech, Inc.

662 Wolf Ledges Pkwy.
Akron, OH 44311
(800) 553-1170
Communication, data acquisition, industrial I/O, and PCMCIA products

QuickPath Systems, Inc.

46723 Fremont Boulevard
Fremont, CA 94538
(800) 995-8828, (510) 440-7288
fax (510) 440-7289

QuickShot Technology, Inc.

Milpitas, CA
(408) 263-4005
http://www.quickshot.com

QVS, Inc.

2731 Crimson Canyon Drive
Las Vegas, NV 89128
(800) 344-3371
Computer cables, computer electronic products

Regal Electronics, Inc.

4251 Burton Drive
Santa Clara, CA 95054
(408) 988-2288
Plug-and-Play CD-ROM changers and multimedia speakers

Relisys (Teco)

320 S. Milpitas Boulevard

Milpitas, CA 95035

(408) 945-9000

http://www.relisys.com

Video monitors, scanners, and multifunctional facsimile products

Repay Trading, Inc.

3345 Wilshire Boulevard, Suite 901

Los Angeles, CA 90010

(213) 385-2580

CD-ROMs and CD-R drives

Reveal Computer Products, Inc.

6045 Variel Avenue

Woodland Hills, CA 91367

(800) REVEAL2, (818) 702-6564

fax (818) 340-2379

faxback (800) 4REVEAL (800-473-8325)

Rockwell Telecommunications

Multimedia Communications Division

4311 Jamboree Road

Newport Beach, CA 92658

(714) 833-4600

Modems

Roland Corporation U.S.

Desktop Media Production
7200 Dominion Circle
Los Angeles, CA 90040
(213) 685-5141
Sound cards, PCMCIA cards, MIDI keyboards, powered speakers, and music
software

Rose Electronics

10707 Stancliff
Houston, TX 77099
(713) 933-7673
Keyboard and video control products, print servers, and data switches

S & S Software International

17 New England Executive Park
Burlington, MA 01803
(617) 273-7400
Dr. Solomon's Anti-Virus Toolkit

S.T. Research Corp.

8419 Terminal Road
Newington, VA 22122
(703) 550-7000
Palmtop computers

S3, Inc.

2770 San Tomas Expressway
Santa Clara, CA 95051
(408) 980-5400
Graphics acceleration products

Sager Computer

18005 Courtney Court
City of Industry, CA 91748
(800) 669-1624, (818) 964-8682
fax (818) 964-2381
Notebook computers

Sampo Technology, Inc.

5550 Peachtree Ind. Boulevard
Norcross, GA 30071
(770) 449-6220
Monitors

Samsung America, Inc.

14251 E. Firestone Boulevard
La Mirada, CA 90638
(310) 802-2211
CPU cooler for the Pentium and P6

Samsung Electronics America, Inc.

Information Systems Div.
105 Challenger Road
Ridgefield Park, NJ 07660
(800) 933-4110, (210) 229-4000
Notebook PCs, color monitors, hard disk drives, and laser printers

Samtron

A Div. of Samsung Electronics America
18600 Broadwick Street
Rancho Dominguez, CA 90220
(310) 537-7000
Monitors

Sanyo Energy (U.S.A.) Corporation

Office Automation Products
21350 Lassen Street
Chatsworth, CA 91311
(818) 998-7322
Multifunctional fax machines, CD-ROM drives, notebooks, desktop personal computers, and monitors

Seagate Technology

920 Disc Drive
Scotts Valley, CA 95066-6550
(831) 438-6550
Hard drives

Seattle Telecom & Data, Inc.

18005 NE 68th, Suite A115
Redmond, WA 98052
(208) 883-8440
Manufacturer of PS/2-compatible accelerator boards for most Micro Channel models

Sempro L.L.C.

2459 SE T.V. Highway, Suite 133
Hillsboro, OR 97123
(503) 693-7894
PC gaming peripherals

Sharp Electronics Corporation

Sharp Plaza
Mahwah, NJ 07430
(201) 529-8200
LCDs and LCD-based products

Shining Technology, Inc.

10533 Progress Way, Suite C
Cypress, CA 90630
(714) 761-9598
Parallel I/O products to EIDE (supporting HDD and CD-ROMs)

Shuttle Computer International Inc.

1161 Cadillac Court
Milpitas, CA 95035
(408) 945-1480
Pentium 75- to 180MHz PCI motherboards with pipeline SRAM, EDO, and
DRAM support

Shuttle Technology

43218 Christy Street
Fremont, CA 94538
(510) 656-0180
Parallel port interfacing technology

Sigma Interactive Solutions Corporation

46515 Landing Parkway
Fremont, CA 94538
(510) 624-4928

Simple Technology

3001 Daimler Street
Santa Ana, CA 92705
(714) 476-1180
Memory and PC card products

SL Waber

520 Fellowship Road
Mount Laurel, NJ 08054
(800) 634-1485, (609) 866-8888
Uninterruptible power supplies

Smart and Friendly

20520 Nordhoff Street
Chatsworth, CA 91311
(800) 542-8838, (818) 772-8001
fax (818) 772-2888
CD recording devices

SMART Modular Technologies, Inc.

45531 Northport Loop W

Fremont, CA 94538

(510) 623-1231

DRAM, SRAM, and Flash memory modules and upgrade cards

Smile International, Inc.

175 Sunflower Avenue

Costa Mesa, CA 92626

(714) 546-0336

Sony Corporation

1 Sony Drive

Park Ridge, NJ 07645

(201) 930-1000

Digital technologies for computers, communications, audio, and video

Spider Graphics, Inc.

580 Charcot Avenue

San Jose, CA 95131

(408) 526-0535

Graphics and multimedia accelerators

SRS Labs, Inc.

2909 Daimler Street

Santa Ana, CA 92705

(714) 442-1070

3D sound technology

Stac Electronics

12636 High Bluff Drive
San Diego, CA 92130-2093
(619) 794-4300
Backup and disaster recovery products

STB Systems, Inc.

1651 North Glenville, Suite 210
Richardson, TX 75085
(214) 234-8750, (214) 669-0989
fax (214) 234-1306
tech support fax (214) 669-1326
BBS (214) 437-9615

Storage Technology Corporation

2270 S. 88th Street
Louisville, CO 80028-4341
(303) 673-5151
StorageTek storage products

Stracon, Inc.

1672 Kaiser Avenue
Irvine, CA 92714
(714) 851-2288
Memory upgrades for PCs, laptops, and workstations

Summagraphics Corporation

8500 Cameron Road
Austin, TX 78754-3999
(800) 444-3425, (512) 835-0090
fax (512) 873-1329

Supra Corporation

7101 Supra Drive
Albany, OR 97321
(800) 717-8772
Modems

Swan Instruments

Drive Division
3000 Olcott
Santa Clara, CA 95054
(408) 727-9711
Ultra high-Capacity (UHC) flexible disk drives

Symantec Corporation

10201 Torre Avenue
Cupertino, CA 95014-2132
(408) 253-9600
Norton Utilities, Norton Anti-Virus software

Synnex Information Technologies, Inc.

3797 Spinnaker Court
Fremont, CA 94538
(510) 656-3333

SyQuest Technology

47071 Bayside Parkway
Fremont, CA 94538
(800) 245-2278, (510) 226-4137
Removable storage products

Tagram System Corporation

1451-B Edinger Avenue
Tustin, CA 92680
(800) TAGRAMS, (714) 258-3222
fax (714) 258-3220

Tahoe Peripherals

999 Tahoe Boulevard
Incline Village, NV 89451
(800) 288-6040
fax (702) 832-3611

Tandberg Data

2685-A Park Center Drive
Simi Valley, CA 93065
(805) 579-1000
SCSI QIC tape backup drives and kits

Tatung Company of America, Inc.

2850 El Presidio Street
Long Beach, CA 90810
(213) 979-7055
Monitors

TDK Electronics Corporation

12 Harbor Park Drive
Port Washington, NY 11050
(800) TDK-TAPE
Optical and Magnetic recording media

TEAC America, Inc.

Data Storage Products Division

7733 Telegraph Road

Montebello, CA 90640

(213) 726-0303

CD-ROM, tape, and floppy drives

Techmedia Computer Systems Corporation

7345 Orangewood Avenue

Garden Grove, CA 92641

(800) 379-0077, (714) 379-6677

fax (714) 379-6688

Monitors

Tektronix, Inc.

P.O. Box 7000 MS 63-580

Wilsonville, OR 97070

(800) 835-6100, (503) 682-7377

fax (503) 682-2980

Tempest Micro

375 N. Citrus Avenue #611

Azusa, CA 91704

(800) 818-5163, (800) 848-5167, (818) 858-5163

fax (818) 858-5166

Texas Instruments, Inc.

P.O. Box 650311

M/S 3914

Dallas, TX 75265

(800) 848-3927, (214) 917-6278

ThristMaster, Inc.

7175 NW Evergreen Parkway, #400
Hillsboro, OR 97124
(503) 615-3200
fax (503) 615-3300

Thunder Max Corporation

15011 Parkway Loop, Suite A
Tustin, CA 92680
(714) 259-8800

TMC Research Corporation

631 S. Milpitas Boulevard
Milpitas, CA 95035
(408) 262-0888
Windows 95-compatible motherboards and SCSI host adapters

Toshiba America Information Systems, Inc.

9740 Irvine Boulevard
Irvine, CA 92718
(800) 457-7777, (714) 583-3000
CD-ROMs, hard drives

TouchStone Software Corporation

2124 Main Street
Huntington Beach, CA 92648
(800) 531-0450, (714) 969-7746
CheckIt Pro, WinCheckIt 4.0 diagnostic software

Trend Micro Devices

20245 Stevens Creek Boulevard
Cupertino, CA 95014
(408) 257-1500
PC-cillin anti-virus software

Trident Microsystems, Inc.

189 N. Bernardo Avenue
Mountain View, CA 94043
(415) 691-9211
32- and 64-bit integrated graphics and multimedia video processing
controllers for PC compatibles

Truevision, Inc.

2500 Walsh Avenue
Santa Clara, CA 95051
(800) 522-TRUE, (408) 562-4200
fax (408) 562-4200
tech support fax (317) 576-7770
CompuServe: GO TRUEVISION
BBS (317) 577-8777

Tseng Labs, Inc.

6 Terry Drive
Newton, PA 18940
(215) 968-0502
Graphics and video controllers

Turtle Beach Systems

5690 Stewart Avenue

Fremont, CA 94538

(510) 624-6200, tech support (510) 624-6265

fax (510) 624-6291, tech support fax (510) 624-6292

faxback (510) 624-6296

BBS (510) 624-6279

CompuServe: GO TURTLE, GO TBMIDI

Tyan Computer

1645 S. Main Street

Milpitas, CA 95035

(408) 956-8000

High-end motherboards and add-on cards

U&C AMERICA

5931 N. Reno Avenue

Temple City, CA 91780

(818) 287-4488

fax (818) 287-4499

Makers of SuperPen

U.S. Robotics Corp.

8100 North McCormick Boulevard

Skokie, IL 60076-2999

(800) DIAL-USR, (800) USR-CORP, (708) 982-5001

Modems

UMAX Technologies

3353 Gateway Boulevard

Fremont, CA 94538

(800) 562-0031, (510) 651-9488

fax (510) 651-8834

Unisys Corporation

Personal Computer Division

2700 N. First Street

San Jose, CA 95134-2028

(800) 448-1424

Notebook and desktop systems

Valitek

100 University Drive

Amherst, MA 01102

(413) 549-2700

Backup devices

Verbatim Corporation

1200 W.T. Harris Boulevard

Charlotte, NC 28262

(704) 547-6500

Optical disks, tape products, floppy disks, CD-R and CD-ROM, imaging products

Video Electronics Standards Association (VESA)

2150 N. First Street, Suite 4400

San Jose, CA 95131

(408) 435-0333

ViewSonic Corporation

20480 East Business Parkway

Walnut, CA 91789

(800) 888-8583, (909) 869-7976

ViewSonic and Optiquest Monitors

VLSI Technology, Inc.

8375 S. River Parkway

Tempe, AZ 85284

(602) 752-8574

64-bit+graphics controller supporting SGRAM

Voyetra Technologies

5 Odell Plaza

Yonkers, NY 10701

(914) 966-0600

Multimedia sound products

WACOM Technology Corporation

501 SE Columbia Shores Boulevard, Suite 300

Vancouver, WA 98661

(800) 922-9348, (360) 750-8882

fax (360) 8924

BBS (360) 750-0638 (300 to 14400 baud, 8-bit, no parity, 1 stop bit)

Pen tablets

Weitek Corporation

1060 E. Arques Avenue
Sunnyvale, CA 94086
(408) 738-8400
Processors

Western Digital

8105 Irvine Center Drive
Costa Mesa, CA 92718
(714) 932-5000
http://www.wdc.com
IDE hard drives, integrated circuits, and board-level products for the microcomputer industry

Wetech Electronics Inc.

11807 E. Smith Avenue
Santa Fe Springs, CA 90670
(310) 810-9818
Monitors

Willow Peripherals

(800) 444-1585, (718) 402-0203
fax (718) 402-9603
BBS (718) 993-2066
Manufacturer of video output and video capture products

Winner Products (U.S.A.) Inc.

21128 Commerce Pointe Drive
Walnut, CA 91789
(909) 595-2490
Joysticks and other peripherals

Wyse Technology

3471 N. First Street
San Jose, CA 95134
(408) 473-1200
Advanced video display terminals

Xerox Corporation

80 Linden Oaks Parkway
Rochester, NY 14625
(800) 349-3769, (716) 442-4028
Printers

Xircom

2300 Corporate Center Drive
Thousand Oaks, CA 91320-1420
(800) 438-4526
fax (805) 376-9311

Yamaha Corporation of America

CBX Group
6600 Orangethorpe Avenue
Buena Park, CA 90630
(714) 522-9011
Computer sound products

Zenith Data Systems

2455 Horse Pen Road, Suite 100

Herndon, VA 22071

(703) 713-3000

Desktops and wireless technology

Zoom Technologies

207 South Street

Boston, MA 02111

(800) 631-3116

fax (617) 423-3923

Data Recovery Vendors

AA Computech

28170 Avenue Crocker #105

Valencia, CA 91355

(800) 360-6801, (805) 257-6801

fax (805) 257-6805

AMS (American Micro Solutions)

15461 Redhill Avenue, Suite E

Tustin, CA 92680

(800) 580-2525, (714) 258-8818

fax (714) 258-8918

email ams@calypso.com

Aurora Electronics

1101 National Drive
Sacramento, CA 95834
(800) 767-9281, (916) 928-1107
fax (916) 928-1106

Data Recovery Labs

1315 Lawrence Avenue East, Unit 502-503
Don Mills, Ontario, Canada M3A 3R3
(800) 563-1167, (416) 510-6990
fax (416) 510-6992

Data Recovery Labs, Inc.

24705 US 19 North, Suite 312
Clearwater, FL 34623
(813) 725-3818
fax (813) 712-0800

Data Retrieval Services

1040 Capp Drive
Clearwater, FL 34625
(813) 461-5900
fax (813) 461-5668

Disk Drive Repair, Inc.

863 Industry Drive, Building 23
Seattle, WA 98188
(206) 575-3181
fax (206) 575-1811

Disktec

5875 W. 34ᵗʰ Street
Houston, TX 77092
(713) 681-4691
fax (713) 681-5851

Drive Service Company

3303 Harbor Boulevard, Suite E-7
Costa Mesa, CA 92626
(714) 549-DISK, (714-549-3475)
fax (714) 549-9752

DriveSavers Data Recovery

400 Bel Marin Keys Boulevard
Novato, CA 94949
(800) 440-1904, (415) 382-2000
fax (415) 883-0780

Electric Renaissance

105 Newfield Avenue
Edison, NJ 08837
(908) 417-9090
fax (908) 471-9099

Excalibur Data Recovery, Inc.

101 Billerica Avenue, Building #5
N. Billerica, MA 01862-1256
(800) 466-0893, (508) 663-1700
fax (508) 670-5901

Micro Com

19011 Ventura Boulevard
Tarzana, CA 91356
(800) 469-2519, (818) 881-7417
fax (818) 881-8015

OnTrack Data Recovery, Inc.

6321 Bury Drive
Eden Prairie, MN 55346
(800) 872-2599, (612) 937-5161
fax (612) 937-5750

Total Peripheral Repair

(A division of Technical Parts, Inc.)
4204 Sorrento Valley Boulevard, Suite A
San Diego, CA 92121-1412
(800) 890-0880, (619) 552-2288
fax (619) 552-2290

Valtron Technologies, Inc.

28309 Avenue Crocker
Valencia, CA 91355
(800) 2VALTRON, (805) 257-0333
fax (805) 257-0113

VANTAGE Technologies, Inc.

4 John Tyler Street, PO Box 1570
Merrimack, NH 03054
(800) ITS-LOST (800-487-5678), (603) 429-3019
(603) 883-6249
fax (603) 883-1973

MEMORY VENDORS

Avalon Micro

688 #D Wells Road
Boulder City, NV 89005
(800) 610-1215, (702) 293-2300
fax (702) 293-4453

DMS (Data Memory Systems)

24 Keewaydin Drive
Salem, NH 03079
(800) 662-7466, (603) 898-7750
fax (603) 898-6585

H&J Electronics International, Inc.

2700 West Cypress Creek Road
Ft. Lauderdale, FL 33309
(800) 275-2447, (954) 971-7750
fax (954) 979-9028
Laptop, printer, and PC memory for name brand computers

McDonald and Associates: The Memory Place

2544 South 156th Circle
Omaha, NE 68130
(800) 694-1307, (800) 306-8901, (402) 691-8548
fax (402) 691-8548

Memory 4 Less

2622 West Lincoln, Suite 104
Anaheim, CA 92801
(800) 821-3354, (714) 826-5981
fax (714) 821-3361

Memory and CPU Warehouse

8361 East Evans Road, Suite 105
Scottsdale, AZ 85260
(800) RAM-7091, (602) 443-0696
fax (602) 443-0918

The Memory Man

7225 NW 25th Street
Miami, FL 33166
(800) 854-0067, (305) 418-4149
fax (305) 418-4277

Worldwide Technologies

437 Chestnut Street
Philadelphia, PA 19106
(800) 457-6937, (215) 922-0050
fax (215) 922-0116

BIOS Upgrade Vendors

Alltech Electronics Co.

1300 E. Edinger Avenue, Suite D

Santa Ana, CA 92705

(714) 543-5011

fax (714) 543-0553

email allelec.com

TTli Technologies, Inc.

1445 Donlon Street #9

Ventura, CA 93003

(800) 541-1943

Unicore Software

1538 Turnpike Street

N. Andover, MA 01845

(800) 800-2467, (508) 686-6468

fax (508) 683-1630

Storage Device Vendors

AA Computech

28170 Avenue Crocker #105

Valencia, CA 91355

(800) 360-6801, (805) 257-6801

fax (805) 257-6805

Hard drives and data recovery

Ashtek, Inc.

2600-B Walnut Avenue
Tustin, CA 92680
(800) 801-9400
fax (714) 505-2693
Buy and sell hard drives and memory SIMMs

Bason Hard Drive Warehouse

(800) 238-4453, (818) 727-9054
fax (818) 727-9066

Dirt Cheap Drives

3716 Timber Drive
Dickinson, TX 77539
(800) 786-1170, (713) 534-4140
fax (713) 534-6452
Hard drives, CD-ROMs, optical drives, tape backup units

Drive Outlet Center

3412 Milwaukee Avenue #445
Northbrook, IL 60062
(800) 260-5930
fax (847) 419-0705
Hard drives, CD-ROMs, optical drives, tape backup units

MegaHaus Hard Drives

2201 Pine Drive
Dickinson, TX 77539
(800) 786-1185, (713) 534-3919
fax (713) 534-6580
Drives, controller cards, drive accessories

Storage USA

101 Reighard Avenue
Williamsport, PA 17701
(800) 538-DISK, (717) 327-9200
fax (717) 327-1217

MISCELLANEOUS COMPUTER PRODUCTS VENDORS

1st Compu Choice

740 Beta Drive - Unit G
Cleveland, OH 44143
(800) 345-8880, (216) 460-1002
fax (216) 460-1066

A Matter of Fax

65 Worth Street
New York, NY 10013
(800) 433-3FAX, (212) 941-8877
Fax machines, printers, scanners, other components, and peripherals

A+ Factory Outlet

526 S. Coralridge Pl.
City of Industry, CA 91746
(800) 717-7060, (818) 937-3090
fax (818) 937-3091
Computers and parts; a liquidator of computer products

A2Z Computers

701 Beta Drive, Unit 19

Mayfield Village, OH 44142

(800) 983-8889, (216) 442-9028

fax (216) 442-8891

Computer components and peripherals

ABC Drives

8717 Darby Avenue

Northridge, CA 91325

(818) 885-7157

Specializes in the sale and service of most major storage devices, including hard-to-find or obsolete drives

ACIS Corporation

2381 Philmont Avenue, Suite 219

Huntingdon Valley, PA 19006

(800) 223-9493, (215) 938-4288, tech support (215) 938-6482

fax (215) 938-4290

Motherboards, sound cards, video cards, RAM, hard drives, CPUs, CD-ROMs

AllMicro, Inc.

18820 U.S. Hwy 19 N, #215

Clearwater, FL 34624

(800) 653-4933, (813) 539-7283

fax (813) 531-0200

BBS (813) 535-9042

http://www.allmicro.com

Many computer products, including the AlertCard (power supply and temperature monitoring card)

Allsop Computer Accessories

4201 Meridian
Bellingham, WA 98226
(800) 426-4303
Ergonomic enhancements (drawers and glare filters)

Alpha Systems, Inc.

47000 Warm Springs Blvd, #455
Fremont, CA 94539-7467
(510) 249-9280
fax (510) 259-9288

American Computer Products (ACP)

(503) 526-3551
fax (503) 646-7631

American Computer Resources, Inc.

155 Research Drive
Stratford, CT 06497
(203) 380-4600

American Micro Professionals

Corporate Center, 5351 Naiman Parkway
Solon, OH 44139
(800) 857-3223, (216) 498-9564
fax (216) 349-6170

American Ribbon and Toner Co.

2895 West Prospect Road
Ft. Lauderdale, FL 33309
(800) 327-1013
Printer ribbons, toner cartridges, etc.

American Wholesale Center

817 New Churchman's Road
New Castle, DE 19720
(302) 845-4962

AMP Tech (American Micro Products Technology)

5351 Naiman Parkway
Solon, OH 44139
(800) 619-0508, (216) 498-9499
fax (216) 349-6170
email amptech@icgroup.net
Computers, motherboards, cases, drives, memory

Arlington Computer Products

851 Commerce Court
Buffalo Grove, IL 60089
(800) 548-5104, (847) 541-6583
fax (847) 541-6881

ARM Computer Inc.

1637 South Main Street
Milpitas, CA 95035
(800) 765-1767, (408) 935-9800
fax (408) 935-9192
email arm@armcomputer.com

ASI

48289 Fremont Boulevard

Fremont, CA 94538

(510) 226-8000

Distributor of computer hardware, peripherals, and private-label Nspire personal computers and multimedia kits

Aspen Imaging International, Inc.

1500 Cherry Street, Suite B

Louisville, CO 80027-3036

(800) 955-5555, (303) 666-5750

fax (303) 665-2972

Computer printer supplies including printer ribbons, printbands, and laser toner and ink jet supplies

Associate Computer Supply Co., Inc.

275 West 231st Street

Riverdale, NY 10463

(718) 543-8686

fax (718) 548-0343

Motherboards, cases, video cards, hard drives, keyboards, memory, CD-ROMs

Astra Computer Corporation

7786 Metric Drive

Mentor, OH 44060

(800) 800-6047, (216) 974-7933

fax (216) 974-7939

Atlantic Logic

41 Canfield Road
Cedar Grove, NJ 07009
(201) 857-7878

Atronics International Inc.

44700-B Industrial Drive
Fremont, CA 94538
(800) 488-7776, (510) 656-8400
fax (510) 656-8560
Parallel port CD-ROM adapter, BIOS enhancement card for IDE hard drive
controllers

Aura Industries, Inc.

6352 N. Lincoln Avenue
Chicago, IL 60659
(312) 588-8722
CPUs, hard drives, memory, multimedia products, and computer accessories

Automated Tech Tools

851B Freeway Drive
Macedonia, OH 44056
(800) 413-0767

Autotime Corporation

6605 SW Macadam Avenue
Portland, OR 97201
(503) 452-8577
Memory recycling services and products

Barnett's Computers

417 Fifth Avenue
New York, NY 10017
(212) 696-4777

Battery Network

50 Tannery Road, Unit 2
North Branch, NJ 08876
(800) 653-8294
Assembly, sales and service of rechargeable batteries

Battery Technology Inc.

5700 Bandini Boulevard
Commerce, CA 90040
(213) 728-7874
Battery products for laptop computers and portable peripherals

Battery-Biz Inc.

31352 Via Colinas
Suite 104
Westlake Village, CA 91362
(800) 848-6782, (818) 706-2767
Distributes batteries for desktops, laptops, and notebooks, as well as for UPS systems and utility meters

Black Box Corporation

1000 Park Drive
Lawrence, PA 15055
(412) 873-6564
Networking and data communications products

BNF Enterprises

134R Rt.1 South Newbury Street
Peabody, MA 01960
(508) 536-2000
fax (508) 536-7400

Bulldog Computer Products

851 Commerce Court
Buffalo Grove, IL 60089
(800) 438-6039, (847) 541-2394
fax (847) 541-6988

Cable Connection

102 Cooper Court
Los Gatos, CA 95030
(408) 395-6700
Manufacturer of cable products and interconnect accessories

Cables America

(800) 348-USA4
fax (800) FAX-USA4

Cables To Go

1501 Webster Street
Dayton, OH 45404
(800) 225-8646, (800) 826-7604
Cables, test equipment, toolkits

CAD & Graphics Warehouse

8515-D Freeway Drive
Macedonia, OH 44056
(216) 487-0485

CAD Warehouse

1939 East Aurora Road
Twinsburg, OH 44087
(216) 487-0485

Century Microelectronics, Inc.

4800 Great America Parkway, Suite 308
Santa Clara, CA 95054
(408) 748-7788
Memory upgrades, with products raging from industry-standard SIMMs and DIMMs to proprietary modules and memory cards

Chemtronics

8125 Cobb Centre Drive
Kennesaw, GA 30144
(800) 645-5244, (404) 424-4888
fax (800) 243-6003, (404) 423-0748
Ozone-safe compressed gas for cleaning inside PCs

CIRCO Technology Corporation

222 South 5th Avenue
City of Industry, CA 91746
(800) 678-1688
Cases, power supplies, removable hard drive kits, motherboards

CMO Corporation

101 Reighard Avenue
Williamsport, PA 17707
(800) 417-4580, (717) 327-9200
fax (717) 327-1217

Compaq DirectPlus

PO Box 692000
Houston, TX 77269-2000
(713) 888-5831

ComUSA Direct

15167 Business Avenue
Addison, TX 75244
COMP-USA

ComputAbility

PO Box 17882
Milwaukee, WI 53217
(800) 554-9950, (414) 357-8181
fax (414) 357-7814

Computer City

PO Box 2526
Tempe, AZ 85280-2526

Computer Discount Warehouse (CDW)

1020 East Lake Cook Road
Buffalo Grove, IL 60089
(800) 726-4239
fax (847) 465-6800
Computers, parts, memory, monitors, printers

Computer Gate International

2960 Gordon Avenue
Santa Clara, CA 95051
(408) 730-0673
fax (408) 730-0735
Tester, cleaning products, cables, switches, computer assembly products

Computer Parts Outlet, Inc.

33 SE First Avenue
Delray Beach, FL 33444
(800) 475-1655
Buys all types of memory, including large or small quantities of working or non-working modules

Computer Products Corporation

1431 South Cherryvale Road
Boulder, CO 80303

Computer Things

2608 Mountain Road, Suite #2
Pasadena, MD 21122
(410) 661-8613
Ink jet printer supplies

Computers Direct

3613 Lafayette Road
Portsmouth, NH 03801

CompuWorld

24441 Miles Road
Cleveland, OH 44128
(800) 666-6294, (216) 595-6500
fax (216) 595-6565

Core Components

9728 Alburtis Avenue
Santa Fe Springs, CA 90670
(888) 267-3266, (310) 654-2866
fax (310) 801-5630
Motherboards, controllers, video boards, memory

Corporate Raider

1449 39th Street
Brooklyn, NY 11218
(718) 453-3555

Dalco Electronics

275 S. Pioneer Boulevard
Springboro, OH 45066
(800) 445-5342, (513) 743-8042
fax (513) 743-9251
BBS (513) 743-2244
CompuServe: GO DA

Data Impressions

13180 Paramount Blvd.

South Gate, CA 90670

(310) 634-5033

Computer supplies, printer supplies

DataVision

445 Fifth Avenue

New York, NY 10016

(800) 771-7466

Computers and multimedia components

DC Drives

1110 NASA Road One, Suite 304

Nassau Bay, TX 77058

(800) 473-0960, (713) 333-9602

Dee One Systems

1550 Centre Pointe Drive

Milpitas, CA 95035

(408) 262-8938

DellWare Direct

2214 West Baker Lane, Building 3

Austin, TX 78758-4053

Digital Micro, Inc.

901 S. Fremont Avenue, Suite 118

Alhambra, CA 91803

Diskette Connection

PO Box 1674
Bethany, OK 73008
(800) 654-4058, (405) 789-0888
fax (405) 495-4598
Diskettes, tapes, drive cleaning kits

Diskettes Unlimited

6206 Long Drive
Houston, TX 77087
(713) 643-9939
fax (713) 643-2722
Diskettes

DTP & Graphics

1175 Chess Drive, Suite C
Foster City, CA 94404
(415) 387-9945

Edmund Scientific Corporation

101 E. Gloucester Pike
Barrington, NJ 08007
(609) 573-6250
fax (609) 573-6295
Dual Function Digital Lab Thermometer

ELEK-TEK

7350 North Linder Avenue
Skokie, IL 60077
(800) 395-100, (708) 677-7660

Envisions Solutions Technology, Inc.

47400 Seabridge Drive
Freemont, CA 94538
(800) 365-SCAN, (510) 661-4357
fax (510) 438-6709
Scanners, printers, graphics/OCR software

Expert Computers

2495 Walden Avenue
Buffalo, NY 14225
(716) 681-8612

FairFax

145 West 45th Street, Suite 1010
New York, NY 10036
(800) 932-4732, (212) 768-8300

First Computer Systems, Inc.

6000 Live Oak Parkway, Suite 107
Norcross, GA 30093
(800) 325-1911, (770) 441-1911
fax (770) 441-1856
email sales@fcsnet.com

Motherboards, computers, peripherals

First Source International

7 Journey
Aliso Viejo, CA 92656
(800) 348-9866, (714) 448-7750
fax (714) 448-7760

Galaxy Computers, Inc.

423 South Lyndhaven Road, Suite 109
Virginia Beach, VA 23452
(814) 486-8389
Motherboards

GIFI Inc.

20814 Aurora Road
Cleveland, OH 44146
(216) 662-1910

Global Computer Supplies

2318 East Del Amo Boulevard, Department 73
Compton, CA 90220
(800) 829-0785, (800) 227-1246
fax (516) 625-6683

Global MicroXperts

6230 Chochran Road
Solon, OH 44139
(800) 676-0311, (216) 498-3330

Graphics Warehouse

8515 Freeway Drive, Unit C & D
Macedonia, OH 44087
(216) 487-0485

Harmony Computers

1801 Flatbush Avenue
Brooklyn, NY 11210
(800) 441-1144, (718) 692-3232

Hartford Computer Group, Inc.

1610 Colonial Parkway
Inverness, IL 60067
(800) 617-4424, (847) 934-3380
fax (847) 934-9724

HDSS Computer Products

2225 El Camino Real
Santa Clara, CA 95050

Hi Tech USA

1562 Centre Pointe Drive
Milpitas, CA 95035
(800) 831-2888, (408) 262-8688

Hi-Tech Component Distributors, Inc.

59 S. La Patera Lane
Goleta, CA 93117
(800) 406-1275, (805) 967-7971
fax (805) 681-9971

Hi-Tech USA

1582 Centre Pointe Drive
Milpitas, CA 95035
(800) 831-2888, (408) 262-8688, (408) 956-8285
fax (408) 262-8772
BBS (408) 956-8243

HyperData Direct

809 South Lemon Avenue
Walnut, CA 91789
(800) 786-3343, (800) 380-1899, (909) 468-2933
fax (909) 468-2954
BBS (909) 594-3645
Laptops, accessories

Insight Computers

1912 West 4th Street
Tempe, AZ 85281
(602) 902-1176

InterPro Microsystems, Inc.

46560 Fremont Boulevard, Suite 417
Fremont, CA 94538
(800) 226-7216, (510) 226-7226
fax (510) 226-7219

Jade Computer

18503 Hawthorne Boulevard
Torrance, CA 90504
(800) 421-5500, (310) 370-7474
fax (310) 371-4288
Parts and peripherals

Jinco Computers

5122 Walnut Grove Avenue
San Gabriel, CA 91776
(800) 253-2531, (818) 309-1108
fax (818) 309-1107
Cases and power supplies

Kahlon, Inc.

22699 Old Canal Road
Yorba Linda, CA 92687
(800) 317-9989, (714) 637-5060
fax (714) 637-5597
email kahlonmem@aol.com
IBM and Compaq parts and memory

Kenosha Computer Center

2133 91st Street
Kenosha, WI 53143
(800) 255-2989, (414) 697-9595
fax (414) 697-0620

KREX Computers

9320 Waukegan Road
Morton Grove, IL 60053
(800) 222-KREX, (847) 967-0200
fax (847) 967-0276

Laitron Computer

1550 Montague Expressway
San Jose, CA 95131
(408) 888-4828

Lamberth Computer Services

3837 Northdale Blvd, #113
Tampa, FL 33624
fax (800) 876-0762

Legend Micro

5590 Lauby Road, Suite 70B
N. Canton, OH 44720
(800) 366-6333
fax (330) 497-3156
Motherboards and components

M.B.S.7466 Early DriveMechanicsville, VA 23111(804) 944-3808Macro Tech Inc.

23151 Verdugo Drive, Suite 102
Laguna Hills, CA 92653
(714) 580-1822
http://www.electiciti.macrot

Magic PC

5400 Brookpark Road
Cleveland, OH 44129
(800) 762-4426, (216) 661-7218
fax (216) 661-2454
http://www.magicpc.com
Motherboards, systems, components

Main Street Computer Co.

1720 Oak Street

Lakewood, NJ 08107-9885

(800) 333-9899

fax (908) 905-5731

Marine Park Computers

3126 Avenue U

Brooklyn, NY 11229

(719) 262-0163

Megacomp International, Inc.

261 NE 1st Street, #200

Miami, FL 33132

(888) 463-4226, (305) 372-0222

fax (305) 374-5040

Megatech Inc.

3070 Bristol Pike

Bensalem, PA 19020

Merritt Computer Products, Inc.

5565 Red Bird Center Drive, Suite 150

Dallas, TX 75237

(800) 627-7752, (214) 339-0753

fax (214) 339-1313

SafeSkin keyboard cover

Micro Assist

50 Harrison Street
Hoboken, NJ 07030
(888) 97-MICRO, (201) 459-0233
fax (201) 459-0283

Micro Pro, Inc.

5400 Brookpark Road
Cleveland, OH 44129
(800) 353-3003, (216) 661-7218
fax (216) 661-2454
BBS (216) 661-7431
http://www.magicpc.com
Computers, parts, accessories, motherboards

MicroTime, Inc.

35375 Vokes Drive, Suite 106
Eastlake, OH 44095
(800) 834-0000, (216) 954-9640
fax (216) 954-9648
CPUs, memory, motherboards, peripherals

Micro x-Press

5646-48 West 73rd Street
Indianapolis, IN 46278
(800) 875-9737, (317) 328-5780

Micronix USA, Inc.

23050 Miles Road
Cleveland, OH 44218
(800) 580-0505, (216) 475-9300
fax (216)475-6610
Motherboards, memory, and other hardware

Micro Sense, Inc.

370 Andrew Avenue
Leucadia, CA 92024
(800) 544-4252, (800) 246-7729, (909) 688-2735
fax (619) 753-6133
email docdrive@microsense.com

MicroSupply, Inc.

(800) 535-2092

Midland ComputerMart

5699 West Howard
Niles, IL 60714
(800) 407-0700, (847) 967-0700
fax (847) 967-0710
CompuServe: 102404,327

Midwest Computer Works

180 Lexington Drive
Buffalo Grove, IL 60089
(800) 86-WORKS, (847) 459-9410
fax (847) 459-6933

Midwest Micro

6910 US Route 36 East
Fletcher, OH 45326
(800) 537-1426, (513) 368-2309
fax (513) 368-2306

Midwestern Diskette

509 West Taylor
Creston, IA 50801
(800) 221-6332
fax (515) 782-4166
Bulk diskettes

Millennium Technologies

35 Cherry Hill Drive
Danvers, MA 01923
(800) 251-3448
Motherboards, additional components

MMI Corporation

2400 Reach Road
Williamsport, PA 17701

Motherboard Discount Center

1035 N. McQueen, Suite 123
Gilbert, AZ 85233
(800) 486-2026, (602) 813-6547
fax (602) 813-8002
Motherboards, video boards, other hardware

Motherboard Express

333-B West State Road
Island Lake, IL 60042
(800) 560-1195, (847) 487-4639
fax (847) 487-4637
Motherboards and drives

Motherboards International (Shambis Corporation)

8361 East Evans Road, Suite 107

Scottsdale, AZ 85260

(800) 574-4000, 499-3970

(602) 596-5226

fax (602) 596-1554

Motherboards and cases

Nationwide Computers Direct (NWCD)

110A McGaw Drive

Edison, NJ 08837

(800) 747-NWCD, (908) 417-4455

fax (800) 329-6923

Notebook computers, PCMCIA cards, printers, modems, scanners

NCA Computer Products

1202 Kifer Road

Sunnyvale, CA 94086

(800) NCA-1115, (408) 522-5066

fax (800) NCA-1666

NECX Direct

4 Technology Drive

Peabody, MA 01960

(800) 961-9208

Network Express

1720 Oak Street
PO Box 301
Lakewood, NJ 08701-9885
(800) 333-9899
fax (908) 905-5731
Computers, peripherals, and test equipment

Next Generation

6230 Cochran Road
Solon, OH 44139

Next International

13622 Neutron Road
Dallas, TX 75244
(800) 730-NEXT, (214) 404-8260
fax (214) 404-8263

North American CAD Company

4A Hillview Drive
Barrington, IL 60010
(800) 619-2199, (847) 381-8834
fax (847) 381-7374
Graphics-related peripherals, including printers, monitors, video boards, digitizers, and scanners.

Nova Computers, Inc.

1420 Lloyd Road
Wickliffe, OH 44492
(800) 461-5535, (216) 516-3035
fax (216) 516-3040
Computers, parts, accessories, motherboards

Odyssey Technology

5590 Lauby Road, Suite 70B
Canton, OH 44720
(800) 683-2808, (330) 497-2444
fax (330) 497-3156

PC Connection

6 Mill Street
Marlow, NH 03456
(603) 800-1111

PC Impact

(800) 853-9337, (800) 698-3820
fax (216) 487-5242

PC Importers

290 Lena Drive
Aurora, OH 44202
(800) 886-5155
fax (216) 487-5242

PC Importers

8295 Darrow Road
Twinsburg, OH 44087

PC International

290 Lena Drive
Aurora, OH 44202
(800) 458-3133
fax (216) 487-5242
Parts, systems, and components

PC Universe

2302 North Dixie Highway
Boca Raton, FL 33431
(800) 728-6483, (407) 447-0050
fax (407) 447-7549
Computers, peripherals, accessories

PCL Computer Inc.

636 Lincoln Highway
Fairless Hills, PA 19030
(215) 736-2986
Cases

PComputer Solutions

130 West 32nd Street
New York, NY 10001
(212) 629-8300

PCS Compleat

34 St. Martin Drive
Marlborough, MA 01752-3021
(800) 210-8323, (508) 624-6400

Peripherals Unlimited, Inc.

1500 Kansas Avenue, Suite 4C
Longmont, CO 80501
(303) 772-1482
Supplies computer-related hardware and software products, specializing in
mass storage and connectivity

Power Pros, Inc.

105 Cromwell Court

Raleigh, NC 27614

(800) 788-0070, (919) 782-9210

http://www.powerpros.com

Power protectors, UPSes

Price Pointe

3 Pointe Drive

Brea, CA 92621

(800) 840-7860

fax (800) 840-7861

Computers, peripherals, and software

Publishing Perfection

PO Box 307, Dept. CS9608

Menomonee falls, WI 53052-0307

(800) 716-500, (414) 252-2502

Digital cameras, scanners, multimedia hardware

Quark Technology

5275 Naiman Parkway

Solon, OH 44139

(800) 443-8807, (216) 498-7387

fax (216) 498-8857

Quick-Line Distribution

26001 Miles Road, Unit 8
Warrensville Heights, OH 44128
(800) 808-3606, (216) 514-9800
fax (216) 514-9805

Royal Computer

1208 John Reed Court
Industry, CA 91745
(800) 486-0008, (818) 855-5077
fax (818) 330-2717
Multimedia/graphics monitors

Seattle Data Systems

746 Industry Drive
Seattle, WA 98188
(206) 575-8123
fax (206) 575-8870
email sdsinc@seadat.com

Sky 1 Technologies

437 Chestnut Street
Philadelphia, PA 19106
(800) 294-5420, (215) 922-2904
fax (215) 922-6920
Motherboards, memory, drives, peripherals

Starquest Computer

4491 Mayfield Road
Cleveland, OH 44121
(800) 945-0202, (216) 691-9966
Systems, parts, peripherals

Sunshine Computers

1240 East Newport Center Drive
Deerfield Beach, FL 33442
(305) 422-9680

Sunway Inc.

(715) 483-1179
fax (715) 483-1757
Ergonomically designed computer accessories

Swan Technologies

3075 Research Drive
State College, MA 01680

TC Computers

PO Box 10428
New Orleans, LA 70181-0428
(800) 723-8282, (504) 733-2527
http://www.tccomputers.com
Motherboards, cases, peripherals

Technology Depot

Parsippany, NJ
(800) 882-8682
email techdepot@gti.net
http://www.techdepot.com

Technology Distribution Network

1000 Young Street, Suite 270
Tonawanda, NY 14150
(800) 420-3636, (716) 743-0195
fax (716) 743-0198
Motherboards and components

The PC Zone

15815 SE 37th Street
Bellevue, WA 98006-1800
(206) 258-2088

Tiger Software

800 Douglas, Executive Tower
Coral Gables, FL 33134

Top Data

574 Wedell Drive, #5
Sunnyvale, CA 94089
(800) 888-3318, (408) 734-9100

Tri-State Computers

650 6th Avenue
New York, NY 10011
(800) 433-5199, (212) 633-2530
fax (212) 633-7718

USA Flex

444 Scott Drive
Bloomingdale, IL 60108
(800) 944-5599, (708) 582-6206
fax (708) 351-7204

Older PC Repair and Exchange

Computer Commodity, Inc.

1405 SW 6th Court, Suite B
Pompano Beach, FL 33069
(305) 942-6616
fax (305) 946-7815
A full-service dealer/broker/distributor of new, used, and refurbished computer hardware

Computer Recycle Center Inc.

303 East Pipeline
Bedford, TX 76022
(817) 282-1622
fax (817) 282-5944
email recycles@spindle.net
www.spindle.net/recycles/
A worldwide trading site and recycling center for used and surplus computer equipment and materials; provides upgrades for users of older equipment

Computer Recycler

670 West 17th Street
Costa Mesa, CA
(714) 645-4022
email maurer44@wdc.net
www.coolsville.com/recycler
Buyer, seller and trader of new and preowned Mac and PC equipment

Computer Recyclers

4119 Lindberg Road
Addison, TX 75244
(214) 774-0366
fax (214) 774-1161

CPAC (Computers, Parts, and Commodities)

22349 La Palma Ave, #114
Yorba Linda, CA 92687
(800) 778-2722, (714) 692-5044
fax (714) 692-6680
email cpac@wavenet.com
http://remarketing.com/broker_html/cpac/

Crocodile Computers

240 West 73rd Street
New York, NY 10021
(212) 769-3400

DakTech

4025 9th Ave. SW
Fargo, ND 58103
(800) 325-3238, (717) 795-9544
fax (717) 795-9420
email daktech@ix.netcom.com
Specializing in IBM and COMPAQ parts

Data Exchange Corporation

3600 Via Pescador

Camarillo, CA 93012

(800) 237-7911, (805) 388-1711

fax (805) 482-4856

http://www.dex.com/dexhome/

A leading full-service company specializing in contract manufacturing, end-of-life support, depot repair, logistics services, and worldwide inventory management services for all high technology industries; has an extensive inventory of spare parts for sale.

Eritech International, Inc.

(800) 808-6242, (818) 244-6242

fax (818) 500-7699

Buyers of old CPUs and memory

NIE International

3000 E. Chambers

Phoenix, AZ 85040

(602) 470-1500

fax (602) 470-1540

email nie@nieint.com

http://www.onsale.com/vendors/nie.htm

A leading supplier of microcomputer parts and systems to companies that maintain and support PC installations

Northstar

7101 31st Avenue North

Minneapolis, MN 55427

(800) 969-0009, (612) 591-0009

fax (612) 591-0029

A complete PC repair service

Oak Park Personal Computers

130 South Oak Park Avenue, Suite #2

Oak Park, IL 60302

(708) 848-1553

fax (708) 524-9791

OnLine Computing

3550-L SW 34th Street

Gainesville, FL 32608

(352) 372-1712

fax (352) 335-8192

email online@gnv.fdt.net

The Used Computer Marketplace(part of the Affiliated ReMarketing Web)

A place where you can list for-sale or wanted items for free in their confidential classifieds, which are then accessed by subscribing dealers.

United Computer Exchange

2110 Powers Ferry Road, Suite 307

Atlanta, GA 30339

(800) 755-3033, (770) 612-1205

fax (770) 612-1239

FaxInfo Line (770) 955-0569

email united@uce.com

CompuServe: 73312,1224

America Online: UnCoEx

Info on Demand: uce-info@uce.com

A global clearinghouse for buyers and sellers of new and used microcomputer equipment

Computer Recycling Centers

Computer Re-use Network (CoRN)

PO Box 1078

Hollywood, SC 29449

(803) 889-8247

email jas@awod.com

Computer Recycling Project, Inc.

email dale@wco.com

www.wco.com/~dale/list.htm

A listing of additional organizations that accept old computers and funnel them to nonprofit groups/individuals in need

Lazarus Foundation, Inc.

East Coast

10378 Eclipse Way

Columbia, MD 21044

Donald Bard, President

(410) 740-0735

email Ebard@aol.com

West Coast

30 West Mission Street, #4

Santa Barbara, CA 93101

Kenneth M. Wyrick, Western Regional Director

(805) 563-1009

email Recycle@west.net

This is a computer recycling center that accepts donated computers which they, in turn, refurbish. These computers are then donated to individuals, schools, and other nonprofit organizations.

Support Sites

MAJOR HARDWARE VENDOR SUPPORT SITES

Company	Web Site
3Dfx	http://www.3dfx.com/download/
Acer	http://www.aceramerica.com/aac/support/index.htm
Advanced Logic Research (ALR)	http://www.alr.com/service/service.htm
Apple	http://support.info.apple.com/tso_home.html
AST	http://www.ast.com/support/support.htm
ATI	http://support.atitech.com/
Boca Research	http://www.bocaresearch.com/support/
Creative Labs	http://www-nt-ok.creaf.com/wwwnew/tech/support/support.html

Company	Web Site
CTX	http://www.ctxintl.com/ techsup.htm
Diamond Multimedia	http://207.1.65.7/vweb/
Digital Equipment Corp.	http://www.dec.com/info/services/mcs/ mcs hardware.htm
DTK	http://www.dtkcomputer.com/ tech.html
Epson	http://www.epson.com/connects/
ESS Technology	http://www.esstech.com
Fujitsu	http://www.8fujitsu.com/
Gateway 2000	http://www.gw2k.com/corp/support/cs techdocs/
Hayes	http://www.hayes.com/support/index.htm
Hewlett-Packard (HP)	http://hpcc923.external.hp.com/ wcso-support/Services/services.html
IBM	http://www.ibm.com/Support
Leading Edge	http://www.pirmenet.com/'fwagner/le/
Logitech	http://support.logitech.com/support.nsf/ support/OpenView
Matrox	http://www.matrox.com/mgaweb/techsupp/ ftp.htm
Media Vision	http://www.svtux.com/new/new.html
Megahertz	http://www.mhz.com/intransit/support/ index.html
Micron	http://www.micronpc.com/support/support.html
Midwest Micro	http://www.mwmicro.com/support
Multi-Tech	http://www.multitech.com/servsupp.htp
NCR	http://www.ncr.com/support/
NEC	http://www.nec.com/support.html

Company	Web Site
Okidata	`http://www.okidata.com/services/`
Packard Bell	`http://support.packardbell.com/`
Panasonic	`http://www.panasonic.com/host/support/index.html`
PNY Technologies	`http://www.pny.com/Tech/index.stm`
Power Computing	`http://support.powercc.com/service.html`
Practical Peripherals	`http://www.practinet.com/support.htm`
Quantum	`http://support.quantum.com/`
S3	`http://www.s3.com/bbs/0main/topindex.htm`
Samsung	`http://www.sec.samsung.co.kr/Support/support.html`
Seagate	`http://www.seagate.com/support/supporttop.shtml`
Sony	`http://www.ita.sel.sony.com/support`
Sun Microsystems	`http://www.sun.com/service/`
Supermac	`http://www.supermac.com/service/index.html`
Toshiba	`http://www.toshiba.com/tais/csd/support/`
US Robotics	`http://infodeli.3com.com/`
Viking Components	`http://www.vikingmem.com/support/index.html`
Vision Tek	`http://www.visiontek.com/htdocs/services/support.html`
Western Digital	`http://www.wdc.com/support/`
Zenith Data Systems	`http://support.zds.com/default.asp`

COMPUTER SOFTWARE SUPPORT SITES

Company	Web Site
Adobe	`http://www.adobe.com/supportservice/main.html`
Caldera	`http://www.caldera.com/tech-ref/`
Claris	`http://www.claris.com/support/support.html`
Corel	`http://www.corel.com/support/index.htm`
Lotus	`http://www.support.lotus.com/`
Microsoft	`http://www.microsoft.com/support/`
Netscape	`http://home.netscape.com/comprod/products/supportprograms/index.html`
Novell	`http://support.novell.com/`

OTHER TECHNICAL SUPPORT SITES

Company	Web Site
HealthyPC.com	`http://www.zdnet.com/hpc/`
HelpMeNow.com	`http://www.HelpMeNow.com/`
CMP Techweb	`http://www.techweb.com/`
PC Week	`http://www.pcweek.com/`
Help Desk Institute	`http://www.HelpDeskInst.com/`
The Computer Technology Industry Association	`http://www.comtia.org/`
Ask a Geek	`http://www.flash.net/~cge/java/ask.htm`
Software.net	`http://www.software.net/directory.htm`
Software Support Professionals Association	`http://www.sspa-online.com/`

Company	Web Site
The Technical Support Nightmare	http://www.geocities.com/
Scott's page o'Computer Literacy	http://www.center-net/8888/
Association of Support Professionals	http://www.asponline.com
SupportHelp.com	http://www.supporthelp.com

ASCII Character Set

ASCII Character Text

Dec	Hex	Char	Dec	Hex	Char	Dec	Hex	Char
0	00	NUL (Null)	45	2D	–	90	5A	Z
1	01	SOH (Start of heading)	46	2E	.	91	5B	[
2	02	STX (Start of text)	47	2F	/	92	5C	\\
3	03	ETX (End of text)	48	30	0	93	5D	]
4	04	EOT (End of transmission)	49	31	1	94	5E	^
5	05	ENQ (Enquiry)	50	32	2	95	5F	–
6	06	ACK (Acknowledge)	51	33	3	96	60	`
7	07	BEL (Bell)	52	34	4	97	61	a
8	08	BS (Backspace)	53	35	5	98	62	b
9	09	HT (Horizontal tab)	54	36	6	99	63	c
10	0A	LF (Linefeed)	55	37	7	100	64	d
11	0B	VT (Vertical tab)	56	38	8	101	65	e
12	0C	FF (Formfeed)	57	39	9	102	66	f
13	0D	CR (Carriage return)	58	3A	:	103	67	g
14	0E	SO (Shift out)	59	3B	;	104	68	h
15	0F	SI (Shift in)	60	3C	<	105	69	I
16	10	DLE (Data link escape)	61	3D	=	106	6A	j
17	11	DC1 (Device control 1)	62	3E	>	107	6B	k
18	12	DC2 (Device control 2)	63	3F	?	108	6C	l
19	13	DC3 (Device control 3)	64	40	@	109	6E	m
20	14	DC4 (Device control 4)	65	41	A	110	6E	n
21	15	NAK (Negative acknowledge)	66	42	B	111	6F	o

DEC	HEX	CHAR	DEC	HEX	CHAR	DEC	HEX	CHAR
22	16	SYN (Synchronous idle)	67	43	C	112	70	p
23	17	ETB (End transmission block)	68	44	D	113	71	q
24	18	CAN (Cancel)	69	45	E	114	72	r
25	19	EM (End of medium)	70	46	R	115	73	s
26	1A	SUB (Substitute)	71	47	G	116	74	t
27	1B	ESC (Escape)	72	48	H	117	75	u
28	1C	FS (File separator)	73	49	I	118	76	v
29	1D	GS (Group separator)	74	4A	J	119	77	w
30	1E	RS (Record separator)	75	4B	K	120	78	x
31	1F	US (Unit separator)	76	4C	L	121	79	y
32	20	<space>	77	4D	M	122	7A	z
33	21	!	78	4E	N	123	7B	{
34	22	"	79	4F	O	124	7C	:
35	23	=	80	50	P	125	7D	}
36	24	$	81	51	Q	126	7E	~
37	25	%	82	52	R	127	7F	DEL (delete)
38	26	&	83	53	S			
39	27	'	84	54	T			
40	28	(	85	55	U			
41	29	)	86	56	V			
42	2A	*	87	57	W			
43	2B	+	88	58	X			
44	2C	'	89	59	Y			

IBM Character Set

IBM Extended Character Set

Dec	Hex	Char	Dec	Hex	Char	Dec	Hex	Char	Dec	Hex	Char
128	80	Ç	156	9C	£	184	B8	•	212	D4	□
129	81	ü	157	9D	¥	185	B9	•	213	D5	□
130	82	é	158	9E	•	186	BA	•	214	D6	□
131	83	â	159	9F	ƒ	187	BB	•	215	D7	□
132	84	ä	160	A0	á	188	BC	•	216	D8	□
133	85	à	161	A1	í	189	BD	•	217	D9	□
134	86	å	162	A2	ó	190	BE	•	218	DA	□
135	87	ç	163	A3	ú	191	BF	•	219	DB	□
136	88	ê	164	A4	ñ	192	C0	•	220	DC	□
137	89	ë	165	A5	Ñ	193	C1	□	221	DD	□
138	8A	è	166	A6	a̲	194	C2	□	222	DE	□
139	8B	ï	167	A7	o̲	195	C3	□	223	DF	□
140	8C	î	168	A8	¿	196	C4	–	224	E0	α
141	8D	ì	169	A9	•	197	C5	□	225	E1	β
142	8E	Ä	170	AA	¬	198	C6	□	226	E2	Γ
143	8F	Å	171	AB	1/2	199	C7	□	227	E3	π
144	90	É	172	AC	1/4	200	C8	□	228	E4	Σ
145	91	æ	173	AD	¡	201	C9	•	229	E5	•
146	92	Æ	174	AE	«	202	CA	•	230	E6	µ
147	93	ô	175	AF	»	203	CB	•	231	E7	•
148	94	ö	176	B0	•	204	CC	•	232	E8	Φ
149	95	ò	177	B1	•	205	CD	•	233	E9	Θ
150	96	û	178	B2	•	206	CE	•	234	EA	Ω
151	97	ù	179	B3	•	207	CF	•	235	EB	δ
152	98	ÿ	180	B4	•	208	D0	•	236	EC	∞
153	99	Ö	181	B5	•	209	D1	•	237	ED	•
154	9A	Ü	182	B6	•	210	D2	•	238	EE	•
155	9B	¢	183	B7	•	211	D3	•	239	EF	∩

DEC	HEX	CHAR	DEC	HEX	CHAR	DEC	HEX	CHAR	DEC	HEX	CHAR
240	F0	•	244	F4	•	248	F8	•	252	FC	η
241	F1	±	245	F5	•	249	F9	•	253	FD	²
242	F2	≥	246	F6	÷	250	FA	'	254	FE	•
243	F3	≤	247	F7	≈	251	FB	√	255	FF	

EBCDIC Character Set

Dec	Hex	Name	Character	Meaning
0	00	NUL		Null
1	01	SOH		Start of heading
2	02	STX		Start of text
3	03	ETX		End of text
4	04	SEL		Select
5	05	HT		Horizontal tab
6	06	RNL		Required new line
7	07	DEL		Delete
8	08	GE		Graphic escape
9	09	SPS		Superscript
10	0A	RPT		Repeat
11	0B	VT		Vertical tab
12	0C	FF		Form feed
13	0D	CR		Carriage return
14	0E	SO		Shift out
15	0F	SI		Shift in
16	10	DLE		Data length escape
17	11	DC1		Device control 1
18	12	DC2		Device control 2
19	13	DC3		Device control 3
20	14	RES/ENP		Restore/enable presentation
21	15	NL		New line
22	16	BS		Backspace
23	17	POC		Program-operator communication
24	18	CAN		Cancel
25	19	EM		End of medium
26	1A	UBS		Unit backspace
27	1B	CUI		Customer Use 1
28	1C	IFS		Interchange file separator
29	1D	IGS		Interchange group separator

DEC	HEX	NAME	CHARACTER	MEANING
30	1E	IRS		Interchange record separator
31	1F	IUS/ITB		Interchange unit separator/intermediate transmission block
32	20	DS		Digit select
33	21	SOS		Start of significance
34	22	FS		Field separator
35	23	WUS		Word underscore
36	24	BYP/INP		Bypass/inhibit presentation
37	25	LF		Line feed
38	26	ETB		End of transmission block
39	27	ESC		Escape
40	28	SA		Set attribute
41	29	SFE		Start field extended
42	2A	SM/SW		Set mode/switch
43	2B	CSP		Control sequence prefix
44	2C	MFA		Modify field attribute
45	2D	ENQ		Enquiry
46	2E	ACK		Acknowledge
47	2F	BEL		Bell
48	30			(not assigned)
49	31			(not assigned)
50	32	SYN		Synchronous idle
51	33	IR		Index return
52	34	PP		Presentation position
53	35	TRN		Transparent
54	36	NBS		Numeric backspace
55	37	EOT		End of transmission

continued

Dec	Hex	Name	Character	Meaning
56	38	SBS		Subscript
57	39	IT		Indent tab
58	3A	REF		Required form feed
59	3B	CU3		Customer use 3
60	3C	DC4		Device control 4
61	3D	NAK		Negative acknowledgment
62	3E			(not assigned)
63	3F	SUB		Substitute
64	40	SP		Space
65	41	RSP		Required space
66	42			(not assigned)
67	43			(not assigned)
68	44			(not assigned)
69	45			(not assigned)
70	46			(not assigned)
71	47			(not assigned)
72	48			(not assigned)
73	49			(not assigned)
74	4A		¢	
75	4B		.	
76	4C		<	
77	4D		(	
78	4E		+	
79	4F		•	Logical OR
80	50		&	
81	51			(not assigned)
82	52			(not assigned)
83	53			(not assigned)
84	54			(not assigned)

Dec	Hex	Name	Character	Meaning
85	55			(not assigned)
86	56			(not assigned)
87	57			(not assigned)
88	58			(not assigned)
89	59			(not assigned)
90	5A		!	
91	5B		$	
92	5C		*	
93	5D		)	
94	5E		:	
95	5F		¬	
96	60		-	
97	61		/	
98	62			(not assigned)
99	63			(not assigned)
100	64			(not assigned)
101	65			(not assigned)
102	66			(not assigned)
103	67			(not assigned)
104	68			(not assigned)
105	69			(not assigned)
106	6A		•	Broken pipe
107	6B		`	
108	6C		%	
109	6D		-	
110	6E		>	
111	6F		?	
112	70			(not assigned)

continued

Dec	Hex	Name	Character	Meaning
113	71			(not assigned)
114	72			(not assigned)
115	73			(not assigned)
116	74			(not assigned)
117	75			(not assigned)
118	76			(not assigned)
119	77			(not assigned)
120	78			(not assigned)
121	79		`	Grave accent
122	7A		:	
123	7B		#	
124	7C		@	
125	7D		'	
126	7E		=	
127	7F		"	
128	80			(not assigned)
129	81		a	
130	82		b	
131	83		c	
132	84		d	
133	85		e	
134	86		f	
135	87		g	
136	88		h	
137	89		i	
138	8A			(not assigned)
139	8B			(not assigned)
140	8C			(not assigned)
141	8D			(not assigned)

DEC	HEX	NAME	CHARACTER	MEANING
142	8E			(not assigned)
143	8F			(not assigned)
144	90			(not assigned)
145	91		j	
146	92		k	
147	93		l	
148	94		m	
149	95		n	
150	96		o	
151	97		p	
152	98		q	
153	99		r	
154	9A			(not assigned)
155	9B			(not assigned)
156	9C			(not assigned)
157	9D			(not assigned)
158	9E			(not assigned)
159	9F			(not assigned)
160	A0			(not assigned)
161	A1		~	
162	A2		s	
163	A3		t	
164	A4		u	
165	A5		v	
166	A6		w	
167	A7		x	
168	A8		y	
169	A9		z	

continued

DEC	HEX	NAME	CHARACTER	MEANING
170	AA			(not assigned)
171	AB			(not assigned)
172	AC			(not assigned)
173	AD			(not assigned)
174	AE			(not assigned)
175	AF			(not assigned)
176	B0			(not assigned)
177	B1			(not assigned)
178	B2			(not assigned)
179	B3			(not assigned)
180	B4			(not assigned)
181	B5			(not assigned)
182	B6			(not assigned)
183	B7			(not assigned)
184	B8			(not assigned)
185	B9			(not assigned)
186	BA			(not assigned)
187	BB			(not assigned)
188	BC			(not assigned)
189	BD			(not assigned)
190	BE			(not assigned)
191	BF			(not assigned)
192	C0		{	Opening brace
193	C1		A	
194	C2		B	
195	C3		C	
196	C4		D	
197	C5		E	
198	C6		F	

Dec	Hex	Name	Character	Meaning
199	C7		G	
200	C8		H	
201	C9		I	
202	CA	SHY		Syllable hyphen
203	CB			(not assigned)
204	CC			(not assigned)
205	CD			(not assigned)
206	CE			(not assigned)
207	CF			(not assigned)
208	D0		}	Closing brace
209	D1		J	
210	D2		K	
211	D3		L	
212	D4		M	
213	D5		N	
214	D6		O	
215	D7		P	
216	D8		Q	
217	D9		R	
218	DA			(not assigned)
219	DB			(not assigned)
220	DC			(not assigned)
221	DD			(not assigned)
222	DE			(not assigned)
223	DF			(not assigned)
224	E0		\	Reverse slash
225	E1	NSP		Numeric space
226	E2		S	

continued

DEC	HEX	NAME	CHARACTER	MEANING
227	E3		T	
228	E4		U	
229	E5		V	
230	E6		W	
231	E7		X	
232	E8		Y	
233	E9		Z	
234	EA			(not assigned)
235	EB			(not assigned)
236	EC			(not assigned)
237	ED			(not assigned)
238	EE			(not assigned)
239	EF			(not assigned)
240	F0		0	
241	F1		1	
242	F2		2	
243	F3		3	
244	F4		4	
245	F5		5	
246	F6		6	
247	F7		7	
248	F8		8	
249	F9		9	
250	FA			(not assigned)
251	FB			(not assigned)
252	FC			(not assigned)
253	FD			(not assigned)
254	FE			(not assigned)
255	FF	EO		Eight ones

Numeric Equivalents

Numeric Equivalents

Decimal	Hexadecimal	Octal	Binary
(Base 10)	(Base 16)	(Base 8)	(Base 2)
1	01	001	00000001
2	02	002	00000010
3	03	003	00000011
4	04	004	00000100
5	05	005	00000101
6	06	006	00000110
7	07	007	00000111
8	08	010	00001000
9	09	011	00001001
10	0A	012	00001010
11	0B	013	00001011
12	0C	014	00001100
13	0D	015	00001101
14	0E	016	00001110
15	0F	017	00001111
16	10	020	00010000
17	11	021	00010001
18	12	022	00010010
19	13	023	00010011
20	14	024	00010100
21	15	025	00010101
22	16	026	00010110
23	17	027	00010111
24	18	030	00011000
25	19	031	00011001
26	1A	032	00011010
27	1B	033	00011011
28	1C	034	00011100
29	1D	035	00011101

DECIMAL	HEXADECIMAL	OCTAL	BINARY
30	1E	036	00011110
31	1F	037	00011111
32	20	040	00100000
33	21	041	00100001
34	22	042	00100010
35	23	043	00100011
36	24	044	00100100
37	25	045	00100101
38	26	046	00100110
39	27	047	00100111
40	28	050	00101000
41	29	051	00101001
42	2A	052	00101010
43	2B	053	00101011
44	2C	054	00101100
45	2D	055	00101101
46	2E	056	00101110
47	2F	057	00101111
48	30	060	00110000
49	31	061	00110001
50	32	062	00110010
51	33	063	00110011
52	34	064	00110100
53	35	065	00110101
54	36	066	00110110
55	37	067	00110111
56	38	070	00111000
57	39	071	00111001
58	3A	072	00111010
59	3B	073	00111011

continued

NUMERIC EQUIVALENTS *(continued)*			
DECIMAL	*HEXADECIMAL*	*OCTAL*	*BINARY*
60	3C	074	00111100
61	3D	075	00111101
62	3E	076	00111110
63	3F	077	00111111
64	40	100	01000000
65	41	101	01000001
66	42	102	01000010
67	43	103	01000011
68	44	104	01000100
69	45	105	01000101
70	46	106	01000110
71	47	107	01000111
72	48	110	01001000
73	49	111	01001001
74	4A	112	01001010
75	4B	113	01001011
76	4C	114	01001100
77	4D	115	01001101
78	4E	116	01001110
79	4F	117	01001111
80	50	120	01010000
81	51	121	01010001
82	52	122	01010010
83	53	123	01010011
84	54	124	01010100
85	55	125	01010101
86	56	126	01010110
87	57	127	01010111
88	58	130	01011000
89	59	131	01011001

DECIMAL	HEXADECIMAL	OCTAL	BINARY
90	5A	132	01011010
91	5B	133	01011011
92	5C	134	01011100
93	5D	135	01011101
94	5E	136	01011110
95	5F	137	01011111
96	60	140	01100000
97	61	141	01100001
98	62	142	01100010
99	63	143	01100011
100	64	144	01100100
101	65	145	01100101
102	66	146	01100110
103	67	147	01100111
104	68	150	01101000
105	69	151	01101001
106	6A	152	01101010
107	6B	153	01101011
108	6C	154	01101100
109	6D	155	01101101
110	6E	156	01101110
111	6F	157	01101111
112	70	160	01110000
113	71	161	01110001
114	72	162	01110010
115	73	163	01110011
116	74	164	01110100
117	75	165	01110101
118	76	166	01110110
119	77	167	01110111

continued

DECIMAL	HEXADECIMAL	OCTAL	BINARY
	NUMERIC EQUIVALENTS *(continued)*		
120	78	170	01111000
121	79	171	01111001
122	7A	172	01111010
123	7B	173	01111011
124	7C	174	01111100
125	7D	175	01111101
126	7E	176	01111110
127	7F	177	01111111
128	80	200	10000000
129	81	201	10000001
130	82	202	10000010
131	83	203	10000011
132	84	204	10000100
133	85	205	10000101
134	86	206	10000110
135	87	207	10000111
136	88	210	10001000
137	89	211	10001001
138	8A	212	10001010
139	8B	213	10001011
140	8C	214	10001100
141	8D	215	10001101
142	8E	216	10001110
143	8F	217	10001111
144	90	220	10010000
145	91	221	10010001
146	92	222	10010010
147	93	223	10010011
148	94	224	10010100
149	95	225	10010101

DECIMAL	HEXADECIMAL	OCTAL	BINARY
150	96	226	10010110
151	97	227	10010111
152	98	230	10011000
153	99	231	10011001
154	9A	232	10011010
155	9B	233	10011011
156	9C	234	10011100
157	9D	235	10011101
158	9E	236	10011110
159	9F	237	10011111
160	A0	240	10100000
161	A1	241	10100001
162	A2	242	10100010
163	A3	243	10100011
164	A4	244	10100100
165	A5	245	10100101
166	A6	246	10100110
167	A7	247	10100111
168	A8	250	10101000
169	A9	251	10101001
170	AA	252	10101010
171	AB	253	10101011
172	AC	254	10101100
173	AD	255	10101101
174	AE	256	10101110
175	AF	257	10101111
176	B0	260	10110000
177	B1	261	10110001
178	B2	262	10110010
179	B3	263	10110011

continued

NUMERIC EQUIVALENTS *(continued)*			
DECIMAL	*HEXADECIMAL*	*OCTAL*	*BINARY*
180	B4	264	10110100
181	B5	265	10110101
182	B6	266	10110110
183	B7	267	10110111
184	B8	270	10111000
185	B9	271	10111001
186	BA	272	10111010
187	BB	273	10111011
188	BC	274	10111100
189	BD	275	10111101
190	BE	276	10111110
191	BF	277	10111111
192	C0	300	11000000
193	C1	301	11000001
194	C2	302	11000010
195	C3	303	11000011
196	C4	304	11000100
197	C5	305	11000101
198	C6	306	11000110
199	C7	307	11000111
200	C8	310	11001000
201	C9	311	11001001
202	CA	312	11001010
203	CB	313	11001011
204	CC	314	11001100
205	CD	315	11001101
206	CE	316	11001110
207	CF	317	11001111
208	D0	320	11010000
209	D1	321	11010001

DECIMAL	HEXADECIMAL	OCTAL	BINARY
210	D2	322	11010010
211	D3	323	11010011
212	D4	324	11010100
213	D5	325	11010101
214	D6	326	11010110
215	D7	327	11010111
216	D8	330	11011000
217	D9	331	11011001
218	DA	332	11011010
219	DB	333	11011011
220	DC	334	11011100
221	DD	335	11011101
222	DE	336	11011110
223	DF	337	11011111
224	E0	340	11100000
225	E1	341	11100001
226	E2	342	11100010
227	E3	343	11100011
228	E4	344	11100100
229	E5	345	11100101
230	E6	346	11100110
231	E7	347	11100111
232	E8	350	11101000
233	E9	351	11101001
234	EA	352	11101010
235	EB	353	11101011
236	EC	354	11101100
237	ED	355	11101101
238	EE	356	11101110
239	EF	357	11101111

continued

NUMERIC EQUIVALENTS *(continued)*			
DECIMAL	*HEXADECIMAL*	*OCTAL*	*BINARY*
240	F0	360	11110000
241	F1	361	11110001
242	F2	362	11110010
243	F3	363	11110011
244	F4	364	11110100
245	F5	365	11110101
246	F6	366	11110110
247	F7	367	11110111
248	F8	370	11111000
249	F9	371	11111001
250	FA	372	11111010
251	FB	373	11111011
252	FC	374	11111100
253	FD	375	11111101
254	FE	376	11111110
255	FF	377	11111111

What's on the CD-ROM

CD-ROM CONTENTS

The CD-ROM included with this book contains the following materials:

- Adobe Acrobat Reader
- An electronic version of this book, *A+ Certification Study System* in .pdf format
- BeachFront Quizzer exam simulation software
- *Micro House Technical Library* (evaluation copy)
- Microsoft Internet Explorer Version 4.0

INSTALLING AND USING THE SOFTWARE

The following sections describe each product and include instructions for installation and use.

Adobe Acrobat Reader

Adobe's Acrobat Reader is a helpful program that will enable you to view the electronic version of this book in the same page format as the actual book.

TO INSTALL AND RUN ADOBE'S ACROBAT READER, AND VIEW THE ELEC-TRONIC VERSION OF THIS BOOK, FOLLOW THESE STEPS:

1. Start Windows Explorer (if you're using Windows 95/98) or Windows NT Explorer (if you're using Windows NT), and then open the `Acrobat` folder on the CD-ROM.

2. In the `Acrobat` folder, double-click `ar32e30.exe` and follow the instructions presented onscreen for installing Adobe Acrobat Reader.

3. To view the electronic version of this book after you have installed Adobe's Acrobat Reader, start Windows Explorer (if you're using Windows 95/98) or Windows NT Explorer (if you're using Windows NT), and then open the `Books\MCSE TCPIP` folder on the CD-ROM.

4. In the `MCSE TCPIP` folder, double-click the chapter or appendix file you want to view. All documents in this folder end with a `.pdf` extension.

Micro House Technical Library (Evaluation Copy)

Micro House Technical Library is a useful CD-ROM-based set of encyclopedias that contains hardware-configuration information. This evaluation copy of *Micro House Technical Library* includes only the Encyclopedia of I/O cards. Use this evaluation copy to determine whether or not you want to purchase the full version of the *Micro House Technical Library*.

**TO INSTALL AND ACCESS THE MICRO HOUSE
TECHNICAL LIBRARY, FOLLOW THESE STEPS:**

1. Start Windows Explorer (if you're using Windows 95/98) or Windows NT
Explorer (if you're using Windows NT), and then open the `Micro House`
folder on the CD-ROM.

2. In the `Micro House` folder, double-click `Install.exe` and follow the
instructions presented onscreen for installing the *Micro House Technical
Library*.

3. To run the *Micro House Technical Library*, select Start ⇨ Programs ⇨
MH Tech Library ⇨ MTL Demo Edition.

BeachFront Quizzer

The version of BeachFront Quizzer software included on the CD gives you an
opportunity to test your knowledge by taking simulated exams. The BeachFront
Quizzer product has many valuable features, including:

- Study session
- Standard exam
- Adaptive exam
- New exam every time
- Historical analysis

If you want more simulation questions, you can purchase the full retail version of the BeachFront Quizzer software from BeachFront Quizzer. See the
BeachFront Quizzer ad in the back of the book.

TO INSTALL AND RUN BEACHFRONT QUIZZER, FOLLOW THESE STEPS:

1. View the contents of the BeachFront folder.
2. Execute `ExamName.exe`, where `ExamName` is the name of the exam you wish to practice.
3. Follow the directions for installation.

Microsoft Internet Explorer Version 4.0

This is a complete copy of Microsoft Internet Explorer. With Internet Explorer, you can browse the Internet if you have an Internet connection, and view the contents of the Microsoft Training and Certification Offline CD-ROM (included on this CD-ROM).

TO INSTALL AND RUN MICROSOFT INTERNET EXPLORER, FOLLOW THESE STEPS:

1. Start Windows Explorer (if you're using Windows 95/98) or Windows NT Explorer (if you're using Windows NT), and then open the `\Msie40` folder on the CD-ROM.
2. In the `\Msie40`, double-click `Setup.exe` and follow the instructions presented onscreen for installing Microsoft Internet Explorer.
3. To run Microsoft Internet Explorer, double-click the Internet Explorer icon on the desktop.

Glossary

6502 An 8-bit microprocessor chip manufactured by Rockwell International. This microprocessor was used in Apple II computer systems.

6800 An 8-bit microprocessor chip manufactured by Motorola Corporation. This microprocessor was used in several microcomputer systems in the 1970s.

68000 A 32-bit microprocessor chip introduced in the late 1970s by Motorola. The first Apple Macintosh used this microprocessor.

680x0 The Motorola family of 32-bit microprocessors.

80286 A 16-bit microprocessor introduced by Intel in the early 1980s. First used in the IBM PC AT type computers.

80386 Also referred to as an *80386DX microprocessor*. The 80386 is a 32-bit microprocessor that was introduced in the mid-1980s by Intel.

80386DX *See* 80386.

80386SX A low-cost version of the 80386DX processor introduced by Intel. The 80386SX used a 16-bit data bus, which enabled usage of lower-cost peripherals.

80387   This is a *floating-point processor* (FPP) designed for use with 80386 microprocessors.

80486   Also referred to as the *i486DX*. A 32-bit microprocessor introduced by Intel in the late 1980s. The 80486 includes an internal floating-point coprocessor.

8080   An early 8-bit microprocessor introduced by Intel in the early 1970s. The basic architecture of this chip served as a blueprint for the Intel 80xx family of microprocessors.

8086   A 16-bit microprocessor introduced by Intel in the late 1970s.

8087   A floating-point processor for use with 8086 and 8088 microprocessors.

8088   The 8-bit microprocessor manufactured by Intel that was used by the original IBM PC systems.

A connector   A common connector for SCSI application. The A connector uses 50 pins.

A+   A certification supported by CompTIA for computer technicians.

ablative WORM   A storage technology that uses optical technology for storage, instead of magnetic technology. *See also* WORM.

AC (Alternating Current)   Electronic current that reverses its direction of flow according to a frequency measured in Hertz. U.S. Standard AC alternates at 60Hz. Many other countries use a 50Hz standard.

acknowledge (ACK)   A signal sent from the receiver to the sender acknowledging successful reception of a message.

Add New Hardware   A wizard used in Windows 95 to install hardware on a computer system.

Add/Remove Programs   A wizard used in Windows 95 and Windows NT to install or remove software from a computer system.

Ad Lib A maker of one of the first sound cards for PCs. Most sound cards used on PCs today are Ad Lib compatible.

Advanced SCSI Programming Interchange A specification developed by Adaptec to send commands to SCSI host adapters. This interface isolates the programmer from the host adapter. Also called *ASPI*.

Advanced Technology The first 80286 systems introduced by IBM. Also known as *AT*.

Alternating Current *See* AC.

ALU An acronym for the *arithmetic logic unit*, the part of a microprocessor chip that specializes in mathematical and arithmetic processes.

AM Acronym for *amplitude modulation*. A method of encoding information into a transmission medium. Frequently used in radio communications. The audio signal is imposed onto the carrier wave, causing the carrier amplitude to vary.

AMD K6 A 64-bit microprocessor manufactured by AMD Corporation. This process is considered to be roughly comparable to a Pentium II microprocessor.

American Standard Code for Information Interchange Also known as *ASCII*. This is a coding system that uses 7 or 8 bits to encode the alphabet, numbers, and punctuation. Early ASCII devices used a 7-bit format that represents 128 characters (0-127). Most IBM PC systems use an 8-bit version of ASCII that represents a total of 255 characters.

Amplitude Modulation *See* AM.

Analog The nature of a signal to have the ability to have varying signal strength and frequency. Examples of analog signals include speech and music.

Anode The term used in electronics that refers to a positively charged terminal or electrode that attracts electrons.

ANSI   An acronym for the *American National Standards Institute*. This institution is involved in the development and support of communications standards in the United States.

`ANSI.SYS`   A driver used by MS-DOS that enables enhanced characters to be displayed on the monitor. ANSI codes are typically accessed using ESC sequences.

aperture grill CRT   A method of CRT manufacturing in which a series of vertical slits stretch from the top to the bottom of the CRT screen. This technology, according to Sony, allows for superior resolution and the reduction of distortion on the CRT.

Apple II   The Apple II computer system was one of the first microcomputers introduced in high-volume retail in the late 1970s. The Apple II had a maximum of 48KB of RAM and used a 6502 processor.

application program   An application program is a program designed to help someone perform specific tasks. These tasks might include word processing or accounting.

arithmetic logic unit   *See* ALU.

Arm   The moving part of a disk drive unit that contains the reading and writing heads. The arm moves the heads across the media.

ASCII *See* American Standard Code for Information Interchange.

Aspect ratio   Computer displays and graphics use this measurement to indicate the ratio of the width and height. An aspect ratio of 2:1 means that a unit is twice as tall as it is wide.

ASPI *See* Advanced SCSI Programming Interface.

Asynchronous   A type of communications method where data is sent intermittently or one character at a time. Asynchronous transmissions usually rely on a start and stop bit included with the character for validation.

AT *See* Advanced Technology.

ATA An acronym for *Advanced Technology Attachment*. Also known as *Integrated Drive Electronics* (IDE) and AT Attachment. A common disk drive interface used in PC systems.

ATX A type of PC motherboard. ATX boards usually include USB and built-in audio and video capabilities.

`AUTOEXEC.BAT` A file used by MS-DOS to load basic startup commands into the operating system. This file can be modified by the end user to permit the addition of special commands for multimedia, TSR programs, and other utilities.

B connector A common connector used for parallel printers. The B connector is a 36-pin connector.

band printer A printer that uses a band to print characters onto the paper. Band printers are generally used in high-volume environments.

base 2 Also called *binary*. The number system that counts from 0 to 1.

base 8 Also called *octal*. The number system that counts from 0 to 7.

base10 Also called *decimal*. The number system that counts from 0 to 9.

base16 Also called *hexadecimal*. The number system that counts from 0 to F.

BASIC Acronym for *Beginners All Purpose Symbolic Instruction Code*. A high-level programming language. It is considered by many to be one of the easiest programming languages to learn.

basis weight The weight of a ream (normally 500 sheets) of paper cut to its basis size (17 inches by 22 inches).

Baudot code A coding system that uses 5 bits. Baudot was an early coding scheme used primarily for telex types of transmissions.

binary   A number system based on the power of two. Digits in binary are limited in value to either a zero or a one.

BIOS   Acronym for *Basic Input/Output System*. The BIOS is essential software that tests computer hardware and starts the operating system. The BIOS is stored in Read Only Memory, or ROM, and is executed automatically when the hardware is first turned on.

Bit   Short for *binary digit*. A bit is the smallest unit of information that can be handled by a computer. A bit is a single binary number (1 or a 0). A 1 bit is also sometimes referred to as *true,* while a 0 bit is referred to as *false*. A bit that is *set* will contain the value of 1, while a bit that has been *cleared* has been set to 0.

Block   A collection of characters that can be read from or written to a disk drive. A contiguous grouping of information that is treated as a single unit.

Boot   The process of loading the microcomputer with the operating system. This occurs either by turning the power on, which is called a *cold boot*, or by pressing the Restart button, which is called a *warm boot*.

BPI   Acronym for *Bits Per Inch*, a measure of storage capacity. Usually refers to the number of bits that can be stored or fit onto a single inch of space on tape or disk media.

break   A key or command that tells the computer to halt what it was doing. IBM PCs can send a break to a program by pressing the Pause/Break key.

brightness   The quality of luminosity or radiance a visible object displays. On computer monitors, the brightness control adjusts the amount of information displayed on the screen.

buffer   A region of memory in which information is temporarily stored. Buffers are used extensively in input/output devices and adapters to hold information until it can be processed by the device on the other side of the buffer.

bus   A collection of hardware lines that are used to convey data and commands between devices in a computer system. Buses can be thought of as a street that can be used by a number of different vehicles to accomplish transportation of people from place to place.

bus controller   A device that manages or controls the flow of information on a bus system. In computer systems, a bus controller is usually a chip dedicated to the process of managing a bus.

bus master   A device that takes control of an expansion bus.

bus slave   A device that receives information from a bus master.

busy line   The busy line is a signal or control line that tells the transmitter or originator that the receiver is busy performing some process and is unable to receive the message, thus controlling the flow of the message.

byte   Short for *By Itself*. A byte is a small unit of data that is usually 8 bits. A single byte can usually store a single character or number with a value of up to 255 base 10.

C connector   A 36-pin connector that is an upgrade to the B connector, used in some of the newer parallel devices. The C connector is also referred to as a *1284-C (IEEE 1284-C Standard)* connector.

cache   A special high-speed memory that is used to store frequently accessed information.

caching   A process whereby frequently accessed information can be stored in fast memory for access by a system. Most modern microprocessors provide some form of caching to access information quickly.

caliper   In computer paper, this refers to the thickness of a sheet of paper measured in thousandths of an inch.

capacitance   A device that can store a charge is said to have capacitance. Capacitance is the measure of the ability to store a charge. The measurement used in capacitance is the Farad. Most capacitors used in computer circuits are thousandths or millionths of farads.

capacitor   An electronic component that can store a small charge. Capacitors block DC or Direct Current voltages, but pass AC or Alternating Current voltages.

Caps Lock key   The key on a keyboard that sets the keyboard to type all-uppercase letters.

card   A printed circuit board or adapter that is typically plugged into a computer expansion slot.

carriage   A part or assembly that holds the platen next to the print area in a typewriter or printer.

carrier   A specified frequency that can be modulated to contain information.

carrier detect   A special signal used in modem communications that tells the modem that a carrier has been detected from the other end of a circuit.

cartridge   A device that usually contains either a disk, tape, or media. Typically, a cartridge is either plastic or metal.

case   The outer cover of a computer or other hardware system.

cassette   A unit that typically contains magnetic tape. Cassettes are usually used for data storage applications such as backup.

cathode   The negatively charged terminal or electrode that provides the source of electron flow in cathode ray tubes.

cathode ray tube   Also referred to as a *CRT*. The primary display device in a television or monitor. CRTs are usually large vacuum tubes that use electronic voltages to shoot electrons at the front screen of the tube. The electrons hit the front part of the tube and cause the illumination of a phosphorescent coating on the inside of the tube. This coating glows when hit by electrons, thus illuminating the front of the screen.

CD   An acronym for *carrier detect* or *change directory*, or an abbreviation for CD-ROM. *See* carrier detect, CD-ROM.

CD-R   An acronym for *CD-ROM Recordable*.

CD-Recordable   A type of CD-ROM that can be recorded using a CD-ROM recorder.

CD-RW   A type of CD-ROM that can be recorded or erased using a CD-RW recorder.

CDFS   An acronym for *CD file system*. The file system used in Microsoft operating systems on CD-ROMs.

CD-ROM   An acronym for *Compact Disk Read-Only Memory*. A type of high-capacity storage that uses laser optic technology. CD-ROMs are strictly read-only.

central processing unit   Also known as the *CPU*, it provides the computational and control unit of the computer. The Pentium, 80486, and other microprocessors are examples of the CPU.

CGA   An acronym for *Color/Graphics Adapter*. The CGA is an early color standard used for computers. CGA was capable of 40- or 80-column display by 25 lines. CGA was also capable of 640x200 pixels, with two colors or 320x200 pixels, with four colors.

Characters per Second   Measurement of speed in non-laser printers. The speed that data is transferred between two devices.

charging stage   One of the six stages of the laser printer process. The charging phase applies a uniform electrostatic charge on the Optical Photo Conductor Drum.

chassis ground   The ground connection made on the metal frame or chassis of an electronic device.

cleaning stage   The cleaning stage removes any unused toner from the OPC drum and prepares the drum for the next printing operation.

clear to send   Also known as *CTS*. A signal sent from one device to another, indicating that transmission can proceed. Usually CTS is used in modem and other serial type connections.

Clock   The electronic signal in a computer that generates timing information for operation. Clock speed is typically measured in Millions of Cycles or Hertz per second, or MHz.

Cluster   In disk storage, a fixed number of sectors. A cluster is usually between two and eight sectors.

CMOS   Acronym for *Complementary Metal-Oxide Semiconductor*. A type of integrated circuit manufacturing technology used extensively in RAM technology. CMOS is also referred to as the area in which systems information is kept. CMOS is extremely fast and consumes relatively little power. A small battery is used by the CMOS to keep systems information when systems power is off.

CMOS Setup   A configuration utility that stores systems information that is used at startup. CMOS setup parameters typically include systems disk information, memory configuration, bus speeds, and port settings.

coaxial cable   A type of cable that uses a center conductor enclosed in an insulation and then isolated by an outer wire shield. The outer shield prevents electronic interference from entering the center cable. Coaxial cable is used extensively in high-speed networks and cable television installations.

COBOL   An acronym for *Common Business-Oriented Language*. A computer programming language used extensively in mainframe and business applications programming.

color graphics adapter   *See* CGA.

COM1   The first serial port in a computer system. Usually the address of COM1 is 03f8H, the IRQ is usually 4. COM ports are usually connected using the RS232 protocol.

COM2   COM2 usually has the address of 02f8h and IRQ 3. See *COM1*.

`COMMAND.COM`   A computer file used in MS-DOS that provides the command interpreter.

Compact Disk Read Only Memory   *See* CD-ROM.

Compiler   A program that converts or transforms one set of symbols, or programming languages, into another. Usually compilers are used to translate programming languages such as BASIC, C, or COBOL into a machine-readable form. A compiler is usually followed by a link or loader stage that adds additional information necessary for the code to be executed by the computer.

composite video   A video standard that encodes all information about the video signal on a single line. Composite Video is used extensively in entertainment systems. Composite video is less readable than other video standards.

`CONFIG.SYS`   A text file used by MS-DOS that controls some aspects of systems behavior. The `CONFIG.SYS` file can contain information about drivers, buffer parameters, and other control information for MS-DOS. The `CONFIG.SYS` file is user editable.

contrast   The difference between the light and dark extremes on a computer monitor or printout.

Control Panel   In the Windows environment, a utility that allows for the configuration and management of the key aspects of the operating system. The Control Panel can manipulate devices, change systems settings such as date and time, and configure network components.

control unit   A circuit that arbitrates and controls functions, typically in the CPU.

`CONTROL.INI`   In Windows, this file defines the icons in the Control Panel window.

conventional memory   The RAM addressable in an IBM PC in real mode. Typically, this is 640K.

corona wire   Used in laser printers to generate electrostatic charges. High voltage is passed through the corona wire to prepare the OPC drum.

CP/M   Acronym for *Control Program/Monitor*. An early operating system used on 8080-based machines.

CPU   *See* central processing unit.

CRT   *See* cathode ray tube.

CU   *See* control unit.

cylinder   A vertical stack of tracks on a disk drive.

daisy wheel   A print element where each character is on the end of a separate type bar, and each bar is attached to a center hub.

daisy-wheel printer   A printer that uses a daisy wheel for printing. This type of printer is considered a *character printer*, because a separate impact is required for each character. Daisy-wheel printers provide typewriter-quality output.

DAT   *See* Digital Audio Tape.

data carrier detected   A signal used in serial communications, typically with modems, indicating that the modem or data device is ready to transmit.

DB connector   A type of connector used for connecting data bus type devices, such as serial ports. Usually a number follows the DB number, such as DB-25, indicating the number of pins in the connector. DB-25 is a standard connector used for serial communications.

DB-9   A standard 9-pin data bus connector used for serial communications.

DB-25   A standard 25-pin data bus connector used for serial communications and printer connectors.

DCD   *See* data carrier detected.

decimal   The base-10 number system.

decoding   The process or method used to convert a message from one format into another.

deflection coil   The yoke or component of a CRT system that deflects the particle beam from the cathode to the screen.

defrag   *See* defragmentation.

defragmentation   The process of rewriting files into single contiguous blocks instead of being fragmented all over the disk. Defragmentation improves data access efficiency.

degauss   The process of removing the magnetic charge from a device such as a magnetic tape or CRT.

desktop   The onscreen area where icons and menus are presented in the Windows environment.

developing   The process in which toner is transferred onto the OPC drum in a laser printer.

device   A computer subsystem, such as a disk drive, floppy drive, serial port, or printer.

device address   The location in address space used by a device such as a port or peripheral. Device addresses can be altered only by the microprocessor or device.

device driver   A software program that permits the computer to communicate with a device. Device drivers are typically loaded during boot-up of the operating system.

Device Manager   A Windows 95 function in the System Properties utility that allows configuration settings to be changed by the user.

dialog box   In a graphical user interface, or GUI, a special window that is displayed by the operating system or application that enables a user to respond to a program or problem.

digital   The technology type in which information is represented in 1s and 0s.

Digital Audio Tape   A magnetic tape that uses digital encoding to store information.

digital voltage meter   A type of electronic test instrument that represent electronic voltage and other measurements using a digital display.

digital versatile disk   Also known as *DVD*. A type of optical disk technology. DVD technology allows for storage of 5GB or more of data in a device that looks like a CD-ROM.

DIMM   An acronym for *Dual In-line Memory Module*. A type of memory package scheme that uses a two-sided edge connector. Current technology utilizes 168-configuration. DIMM memory is almost always used in Pentium-based processors.

Din connector   A type of connector used to connect mice and keyboards to computer systems.

direct connect   In data communications, a type of connection where the two devices are physically connected using a wire or other connection scheme.

Direct Memory Access   Memory access that does not involve the CPU. Typically, Direct Memory Access involves data transfer between disk drives or other intelligent peripherals and memory.

directory   A catalog or organizing scheme that shows the files stored on a disk. PCs use a hierarchical storage structure with directories and subdirectories. The top-most directory is called the *root directory*.

DIR   The MS-DOS command that displays the contents of a directory.

disk   A physical media, typically magnetic or optical, that is used to store data.

disk controller   An adapter or chip set that controls disk access and control. The disk controller is responsible for physically moving the disk heads between locations under control of the operating system.

disk crash   The failure of a disk. In the past, a disk crash meant that a R/W head physically crashed into the magnetic media.

disk directory   An index of the files on a disk drive. Information about the access rights, size, location, and creation are usually stored in a disk directory.

disk drive   The physical device that contains all of the components of a disk.

disk driver   The software that manages the disk controller and access to the disk on behalf of the operating system.

disk format   The method by which storage allocation is created on a disk drive.

diskette   A floppy disk.

disk operating system   The master control program and utilities that interface between the computer hardware and the end user. MS-DOS is an example of a disk operating system.

display   The visual output of a computer system, such as a computer monitor.

DMA   *See* Direct Memory Access.

DONTINSTALL   A section in the Windows 3.1 and Windows 3.11 SETUP.SHH shell that tells the installation procedure which programs not to install.

DOS   *See* disk operating system.

DOS Protected Mode Interface   A software interface that allows MS-DOS-based applications programs to run in protected mode on 80286 processors.

dot matrix printer   Also known as a *DMP*. A printer that produces characters using a wire-pin print head.

dot pitch   The distance between dots in a dot-matrix printer. The measure of clarity in a video display. Generally, the smaller the number, the better the quality.

DPMI   *See* DOS Protected Mode Interface.

DRAM   *See* Dynamic RAM.

drawing tablet   A type of user interface that is designed to let end users draw illustrations and figures for use in computer applications.

drive bay   A special area, usually rectangular, designed to hold a disk drive.

driver   A hardware program or device that controls the operation of a hardware device on a computer.

.DRV   The file extension type that identifies a file as a driver. Used by the MS-DOS and Windows operating systems.

duplex   The ability of a device to communicate simultaneously in both directions. A device that can communicate simultaneously in both directions is said to be *full-duplex*. A device that can only communicate in one direction at a time is said to be *half-duplex*.

duty cycle   The percentage of time that a device is able to operate due to design limitations. A device that has a one hundred percent duty cycle is able to operate continuously, whereas a device with a fifty percent duty cycle is able to operate only fifty percent of the time. This may be caused by heat generation or other factors.

DVD   *See* digital versatile disk.

DVM   *See* digital volt meter.

Dvorak keyboard   A keyboard layout developed by August Dvorak and William Dealey in 1936. This keyboard is supposed to provide better input capabilities than a standard keyboard.

Dynamic Random RAM A type of semiconductor RAM that use electronic circuits to dynamically or regularly refresh its memory contents. Dynamic RAM is the most common RAM memory used in computer systems today.

ECP *See* extended capabilities port.

EDO RAM *See* Extended Data Out Dynamic Random Access Memory.

EEPROMS *See* Electronic Erasable Programmable Read Only Memory.

EGA *See* Enhanced Graphics Adapter.

EISA *See* Extended Industry Standard Architecture.

Electronic Erasable Programmable Read Only Memory A type of Read-Only Memory that can be erased and reprogrammed using an electronic signal.

extended capabilities port A capability in parallel ports that enables the exchange of data between two parallel devices.

Extended Data Out Dynamic Random Access Memory A type of RAM memory that keeps data available for use while other memory is being initialized. This type of memory is very fast compared to other RAM technologies and is used extensively in Pentium class computers.

Extended Industry Standard Architecture A PC bus standard for the connection of add-on cards. EISA has 32-bit data path.

electrophotographic printer Printer technology that includes LED, LCD, and laser type printers.

electrostatic discharge Also called *ESD*. The discharge of static electricity generated from an outside source. Typical sources of ESD include human hands, atmospheric conditions, and certain fabrics and rugs.

emergency recovery disk A floppy disk or other media used to recover a system in the event of data loss or disk hardware failure.

EMM386   A file that allows MS-DOS to emulate *expanded memory*. This file is included in the `CONFIG.SYS` file.

enhanced graphics adapter   A video display adapter with the capability of 320x200 to 640x400 pixel resolution in color or black and white.

enhanced parallel port   A connection between parallel devices that enables high-speed connections. Usually used for printers.

enhanced small device interface   A device that enables disks to communicate with a PC at high speeds.

EPP   *See* enhanced parallel port.

EPROM   See Erasable Read-Only Memory.

Erasable Read-Only Memory   A type of memory storage technology that permits memory to be programmed or reprogrammed after manufacturing.

ERD   See emergency recovery disk.

ESD   *See* electrostatic discharge.

ESD wrist strap   A physical connection that reduces the risk of ESD damage by a technician. The wrist strap is usually attached to the technician's wrist, and the other end connected to the device being serviced.

ESDI   *See* Enhanced Small Device Interface.

expanded memory   A type of memory in PCs, up to 8MB. This memory is not normally accessible by applications programs. The Expanded Memory Manager segments this memory into pages to make it accessible for use.

expanded memory manager   A driver that implements a memory management process to make expanded memory available to the PC.

expansion board   A circuit card that is plugged into an expansion slot on the computer bus to expand the functionality or capability of the system. Expansion boards include disk controllers, video adapters, and other types of devices.

Extended Binary Coded Decimal Interchange Code   An IBM standard coding system used in mainframe computer systems.

extended capabilities port   A capability that enables data to be exchanged between two parallel ports.

extended memory   The memory in PCs above 1MB.

Fast SCSI   A type of SCSI-2 interface that can transfer 8-bit data at speeds up to 10MB. The connector for Fast SCSI is 50 pins.

FAT   *See* file allocation table.

FAT16   *See* file allocation table.

FAT32   *See* file allocation table.

fault   A physical malfunction, such as a failed component or loose connection. This prevents the system from performing as it should.

FCC   Federal Communications Commission, the US agency responsible for all regulation and administration of rules and regulations in the communications industry.

FDISK   An MS-DOS program used to create and manage disk partitions on a PC.

Fiber Optics   A technology that uses light beams along a special cable for data communications.

file allocation table   A table or list used by some operating systems (such as MS-DOS) to manage disk information. Microsoft supports a number of file systems, including FAT, FAT16, and FAT32. FAT was the original file system used in PCs. The limit of a FAT file system was originally 521MB. The FAT file system was upgraded to the FAT16 file system, which has a maximum storage limit of 2.1GB.

The FAT32 file system was released with Windows 95 Service Release and has a limit of storage in the terabyte range (very, very big).

File Manager   A module in an operation system that controls the placement and access of files.

file system   The overall structure in which files are stored and accessed by the operating system.

file   A collection of information, such as a program or set of data, that is stored under a name in a file system.

flash memory   A type of memory similar to EEPROM. This memory can be programmed in the field using an electrical system.

floppy disk   A round, plastic disk treated with ferric oxide particles. This disk is then used for storage of information. Original floppy disks were 8 inches and could store 360K of information. Another standard floppy disk is the 5.25-inch floppy disk. The most current floppy disk is a 3.5-inch disk, which can store 1.44MB of data.

floppy disk controller   The controller for floppy disk drive units.

floating point processor   A coprocessor or special-purpose processor that performs high-speed arithmetic computations.

FM   *See* Frequency Modulation.

focus   The control used to adjust the electron beam on a CRT for maximum clarity.

folder   In the Windows 95 environment, a graphical representation of a subdirectory.

font   A set of characters used by a computer to represent information.

format   To prepare a disk for the storage of data.

`FORMAT.COM`   The program used to format a disk drive.

Fortran   Short for *Formula Translation*. A programming language used to solve complex mathematical problems.

FPU   *See* floating point processor.

frame   A unit of transmission that is measured in either time or frequency.

frequency   The measure of a periodic event. In the case of radio frequency, the measure is in millions of cycles per second, or Hertz (Hz).

Frequency Modulation   A method of encoding information onto a single center carrier. FM modulates the frequency depending on the modulating frequency.

frequency shift keying   A method of modulating a carrier. A positive or binary 1 is converted into a mark, and a binary 0 is converted to a space. Marks apply one tone to the carrier, and spaces apply another. In this manner, digital transmissions can be superimposed on an FM signal and data transmission is possible.

FSK   *See* frequency shift keying.

full-duplex   A method of communication between two devices that enables the simultaneous transmission of information in both directions.

fusing   The step in a laser printer where the toner is melted onto the paper using high heat.

GDI   *See* graphical device interface.

`GDI.EXE`   The program that manages the graphical user interface for Windows systems.

General Protection Fault   An error condition that occurs in Windows 3.1 systems and beyond. A GPF is usually caused by a program attempting to access memory outside of its authorized memory access area.

gigabyte   One billion bytes.

graphical user interface   A type of environment where programs communicate with the end user using boxes, icons, and other devices. Windows 95 is an example of an operating system that uses a graphical user interface.

GPF   *See* general protection fault.

grey scale   A method using black and white to allow monitors and printers to represent various shades. This is accomplished by interspersing white and black together in varying intensities.

groups   A section in the Windows 3.1 and Windows 3.11 `PROGMAN.INI` that identifies what groups are created by the Program Manager.

GUI   *See* graphical user interface.

half-duplex   A method of managing two-way communications where only one end can communicate at a time.

HDD   *See* hard disk drive.

hard disk drive   A device containing the components of a hard disk. This typically includes all of the media and electronics necessary for the drive to connect to a power supply and operate.

head   The mechanism that performs the read/write operations on a disk or tape drive.

heat sink   A device typically used on power supplies and microprocessor chips to remove heat. This enables the component to operate cooler and last longer.

hub   A central device that connects network components together.

I486   The Intel 80486 microprocessor chip.

I487   The math coprocessor for the 80486.

IDE   *See* Integrated Device Electronics.

IEEE   Acronym for *Institute of Electrical and Electronics Engineers*, a non-profit organization of engineering and electronics professionals.

IEEE 1284   A standard parallel interface specification. The 1284 standard has several modes. The most common modes are Enhanced Parallel Port, or EPP, and Enhanced Capabilities Port, or ECP.

IFS   *See* installable file system.

impact printer   A printer such as a wire-pine dot matrix printer. The printer operates by physically impacting the print wires through an inked ribbon onto the paper.

index file   A file that assists in the storage and retrieval of data in an information system.

information   Data that has been organized and can be used by an end user.

installable file system   A component of the file system architecture that is responsible for access to the different file systems components.

ink jet printer   A type of printer in which ink is either vibrated or heated and sprayed onto the paper through tiny holes or nozzles in the print head.

Input/Output address   *See* I/O address.

interlace   A technique used by some types of computer monitors that scans odd lines in one pass and even line in the next pass.

interleaving   A way to arrange the sectors on a disk drive so that one sector is read after another. Interleaving is usually established at an optimal interval by the disk controller and manufacturing recommendations.

Interrupt Request   Also called an *IRQ*. A hardware interrupt on a PC. 80486 and Pentium chips support 16 IRQs.

I/O address   The address used to access peripheral devices. In PC systems, the I/O address is a three-digit hexadecimal address.

IO.SYS   A hidden file installed by MS-DOS that contains device drivers for peripherals. *See also* MSDOS.SYS.

IPX/SPX   An acronym for *Internet Packet Exchange/Sequenced Packet Exchange*. The protocols developed by Novell in Netware used to transport information across a network. Windows 95 supports IPX/SPX for connection to NetWare networks.

IRQ   *See* Interrupt Request.

ISA   An acronym for *Industry Standard Architecture*. A bus design specification for connection of expansion cards to standard IBM Compatible PCs. ISA is an 8- or 16-bit specification, depending upon the connectors used.

keyboard   The input device used to provide alphanumeric data to a PC. Two standards exist for keyboard format: QWERTY (the most common) and Dvorak.

laptop   A small portable computer system. Laptops are usually battery powered and have LCD displays.

laser printer   An electrophotographic printer that uses laser technology for printing.

LCD   An acronym for *Liquid Crystal Display*. LCD is a type of display that uses a liquid compound sandwiched between two electrodes. The LCD is illuminated by passing electricity between the electrodes. LCD displays are used extensively in laptop computers.

L1 Cache   The high-speed cache memory that is integrated inside the microprocessor.

L2 Cache   The memory that serves as a buffer between the microprocessor L1 Cache and the systems memory.

LIM   Acronym for *Lotus/Intel/Microsoft*. A memory standard for expanded memory.

line printer   A printer that prints one line at a time. Usually line printers are very large and designed to print hundreds or even thousands of lines per minute. Band printers are a very common form of line printer.

local bus   A bus designed for high-speed access by peripherals and the microprocessor. PCI is an example of a local bus architecture.

low-level format   A process where the sectors are located on a hard disk drive.

Macintosh   A family of computer systems introduced by Apple Computer.

magnetic tape   A type of magnetic storage media that uses a polyester or Mylar film coated with magnetic material. Magnetic tape is usually stored in reels or cartridges.

magneto-optical   A technology usually used in optical disk technology. Magneto-optical disks are re-recordable.

MB   Megabyte, one million bytes.

MCA   An acronym for *Micro Channel Architecture*. MCA is a 32-bit bus that was used in certain models of IBM PS/2 computers.

MDA   *See* Monochrome Display Adapter.

media   Physical material, used for storage of information.

Megahertz   A million hertz or cycles. A standard measurement of frequency.

MEMAKER   An MS-DOS utility designed to optimize memory allocation and storage on a PC.

memory   A device used to store information. Typically, memory refers to RAM memory in the systems unit.

Memory Management Unit   The physical hardware that supports memory access.

MFM   An acronym for *Modified Frequency Modulation*. An encoding method that is used on floppy disks and some smaller disk drives.

MGA   *See* Monochrome Graphics Adapter.

microchip   An integrated circuit. A device that contains a large number of transistors and other components in a very small package.

microprocessor   A microchip that contains the central processing unit on a single chip.

MIDI   An acronym for *Musical Instrument Digital Interface*. A serial interface that enables connection of music synthesizers, musical instruments, and music components.

MIPS   An acronym for *Millions of Instructions Per Second*. MIPS is used in the measurement of computer performance.

MMU   *See* Memory Management Unit.

MMX   An acronym for *Multi-Media Extensions*. An extension of the Intel 808X instruction set designed to optimize multimedia capabilities.

modem   Short for Modulator/demodulator. A communications device that enables two computers to transfer information over a standard telephone line.

mode   An operational state of a computer or program.

Monochrome Display Adapter   A video adapter used in early IBM PC systems.

Monochrome Graphics Adapter   MGA is an adapter introduced by Hercules Graphics.

motherboard   The main circuit board of a computer. The motherboard contains the processor, memory, and other support chips necessary for a computer to function.

mouse   A common pointing device used in computer systems.

mouse port   The input port that a mouse is connected to.

Moving Pictures Expert Group   Also known as *MPEG*. A standard for video compression. MPEG is used in CD-ROMS and video CDs.

MPC   A standard for PCs specified by the Multimedia PC Marketing Council.

Multimedia PC Marketing Council   The association that created a set of multimedia standards for computer systems. The standard specifies three different standard configurations for multimedia applications.

MPEG   *See* Moving Pictures Expert Group.

MPU-401   A MIDI standard from the Roland Corporation.

MSCDEX.EXE   A set of CD-ROM extensions that are loaded into MS-DOS to use a CD-ROM.

MSD   An acronym for *Microsoft Diagnostics*. MSD is useful in helping display system configuration information.

MS-DOS   An operating system created by Microsoft that is used extensively in PC systems.

MTBF   An acronym for *Mean Time Between Failure*. MTBF is used to measure the reliability of electronic and mechanical components.

multi-meter   A testing device that can be used to measure voltage or resistance in electronic circuits.

Multi-scan   A monitor that can adjust itself to operate on a number of different scanning frequencies.

MultiSync   A family of monitors manufactured by Sony that uses Multi-scan technology.

multitasking   A mode of operation in an operating system where the computer works on more than one program at a time. This can be accomplished by switching between programs rapidly, making the system appear that they are running simultaneously.

My Computer   An icon in Windows 95 systems that identifies and enables access to systems resources.

near letter quality   Also known as *NLQ*. A print quality usually referring to dot matrix printers. NLQ print quality is said to be near the printing quality of a typewriter.

NetBEUI   NetBIOS *Extended User Interface*. An enhancement to NetBIOS.

NetBIOS   A protocol for network operating systems for PC computer systems.

NetWare   A family of network operating systems manufactured by Novell. A number of versions of NetWare provide capabilities to large and small networks.

NLQ   *See* near letter quality.

NTFS   An acronym for *NT File System*. A high-performance file system used in Windows NT computer systems.

Numlock   The key that activates the numeric keypad on a keyboard.

`NWREDIR.VXD`   A driver file used in Windows 95 and NT for networking. *See also* driver.

Octal   A base-8 number system that uses only, 0, 1, 2, 3, 4, 5, 6, and 7. Octal format is used primarily because it is easy to read and translate into binary format. In octal format, each digit represents three binary digits. For example, the octal number 3456 is 011 100 101 110 in binary.

OEM   A version of someone else's product that has been customized and sold under another name. Confusing, but just remember if it's an OEM, it's not made by the company whose brand appears on it.

ohm meter   An instrument for measuring electrical resistance.

OLE   Object Link Embedding is a compound document standard developed by Microsoft Corporation. It enables objects within an application to be linked or embedded in a second application.

opacity   A term generally associated with pixels, indicating the degree of transparency. *See also* pixel.

OPC   OLE Process Control is a non-proprietary standard that enables applications to be available in a network environment without the developer having to write a custom interface. OPC may also be referred to with laser printers, in which case the acronym stands for *Optical Photo Conductor*. *See also* Optical Photo Conductor.

OPCODE   Hardware-level instructions similar to software programs. OPCODE is primarily referred to as the code that controls the order of available operations within an integrated circuit (IC) or microprocessor.

operating system   The software that translates user input into commands the computer can operate on. The operating system may also translate the computer results of an operation into language the user can understand.

operation code   The steps of an operation written in a language the computer can utilize. A program can also be called operation code. *See also* OPCODE.

optical media   Media that uses light to encode or decode the information contained on it.

Optical Photo Conductor   The light-sensitive coating on the surface of the drum in a laser printer. *See also* OPC.

Orange book   Technical papers outlining the specifications for writable CDs.

oscilloscope   Device used to graphically display an electrical signal over time on three axes — X, Y, and Z.

P5 Pentium   The fifth generation of Pentium microprocessors and the first released to the public by the Intel Corporation in 1993. This microprocessor contains 3.3 million transistors, about triple that of a 486 microprocessor. *See also* 80486.

page   A virtual memory area of fixed length that the system uses like physical memory. *See also* RAM.

paging system   The software and/or hardware used to translate and manage data in the virtual memory page. *See also* page.

paper empty error   A message displayed on either the computer monitor and/or the printer when the user attempts to print from a printer that has no paper loaded.

parallel   A bidirectional signal.

parallel ports   Physical ports located on systems that use parallel communication protocols. *See also* protocol, parallel.

partitions   Spaces that have been designated as separate storage areas within the same hard drive.

path   A system variable that lets the operating system or programs know where to look for files on the computer system.

PC Card   A broad term for any card device that plugs into a computer. Examples of a PC Card can include video display adapters, hard drive controllers, serial and parallel port adapters, and so on. *PC Card* can also refer to a miniature device that plugs into a laptop computer that looks like a card.

PCI *Peripheral Component Interface* is a bus standard developed by Intel. The PCI bus is a 32-bit bus that supports extensions for 64-bit processors.

PCI bus The physical connection of a device where the device has been manufactured to conform to the PCI bus standard. *See also* PCI.

PCMCIA *Personal Computer Memory Card International Association* originally designed PC Cards for memory modules that plug into laptop computers. Now the standards have been expanded into a broad range of devices for laptops. *See also* PC Card.

Pentium The name of the microprocessor currently manufactured by the Intel Corporation. *See also* P5 Pentium.

Pentium II The latest design in Pentium microprocessors manufactured by the Intel Corporation. This microprocessor includes an additional two million transistors more than its predecessor, the Pentium Pro *See also* P5 Pentium, Pentium Pro.

Pentium Pro The name of the sixth generation of the Pentium microprocessor manufactured by the Intel Corporation. Also known as the P6. *See also* P5 Pentium, Pentium.

Peripheral Component Interconnect Bus standard capable of data transfer speeds of 100MHz. *See also* PCI.

PGA *Professional Graphics Adapter* designed by the IBM Corporation; this adapter was soon superseded by VGA because of its cost and extensive setup requirements.

phase modulation An operation where the intensity of electrical current is changed at the same time the signal it carries changes. *See also* modem.

pincushion A common type of distortion with monitors where the vertical and horizontal lines bend inward.

PIO   *Programmed Input/Output*, a method of transferring data between two devices, using the CPU as part of the data path.

pixel   Smallest visible element of a picture.

picture element   Smallest visible element of a picture, often referred to as *pixel* in computer terminology. *See also* pixel.

planar board   Term for a computer motherboard or mainboard. This term's popularity has significantly dropped since the late 1980s. *See also* motherboard.

platter   The media surface of a hard drive, called *platter* because of its similarity to a disk/platter.

Plug and Play   Term for the technology that allows devices to automatically configure themselves without the user having to change systems settings. The philosophy is you plug it in and it plays.

PNP   Abbreviation for Plug and Play. *See also* Plug and Play.

port   A physical connection area on the PC for attaching devices.

POST   *Power On Self Test*. A built-in diagnostic on IBM-compatible computers that checks the basic components of the system each time the computer is turned on.

Power PC   The name of Macintosh's line of high-performance personal computers.

power supply   A device in the computer system that provides power to the internal components.

Print Manager   A software application found in Windows 95 and NT operating systems that allows the user control over the printers attached to the computer system.

PROGMAN.INI A configuration file found in Windows for detailing to the Windows interface how the Program Manager will look and function.

WIN.INI A configuration file for Windows that outlines the overall appearance and functionality of the Windows interface.

program A set of instructions written so that a computer can follow and execute them in a prescribed order.

Program Manager A software application found in Windows used to display files, folders, and detailed information about them.

PROM *Programmable Read Only Memory* is an integrated circuit that has been programmed to perform a specific function. Once the program is loaded, this is the only function this IC will perform. *See also* program.

prompt A term generally associated with DOS for an area where the user inputs information, as though the computer were "prompting" the user.

protected mode The process of accessing extended memory and virtual memory simultaneously.

Protocol Manager Software used by Windows to manage network protocols.

protocol A set of rules defining communication between two devices.

PS Short for *Post Script*, a font type. *See also* font.

QIC Short for *Quarter Inch Cartridge*, this term is associated with tape backup cartridges and defines the nomenclature of the cartridge to be used on a specific tape device, i.e., QIC-80, QIC-120, and so on.

QWERTY The arrangement of keys on a standard English keyboard.

RAID *Redundant Array of Independent Disks*, this term is most commonly associated with networks and pertains to the security of data, i.e. fault tolerance.

RAID 0   A *Redundant Array of Independent Disks* that spreads out file blocks across many disks. This increases system file access performance, but provides no fault tolerance.

RAID 3   A *Redundant Array of Independent Disks* that spreads out file blocks across many disks and reserves one disk to keep all files for error correction.

RAID 5   A *Redundant Array of Independent Disks* that provides data striping and stripe error correction information across the RAID.

RAM   *Random Access Memory*, the memory most often referred to as a feature of computer performance.

random access   The ability to access information in a non-sequential order.

raster   The rectangular area of a display monitor, the area actually being used to display images.

RDRAM   Type of computer memory developed by the Rambus Corporation. This type of RAM has the capability of operating at speeds up to 600MHz. *See also* RAM.

README.TXT   A file containing information that the software or hardware manufacturer wants you to know before using their product.

real mode   A CPU that emulates the 8088 processor — no multitasking is available and no access to extended memory is available. *See also* CPU, 8088.

ream   A unit of measurement, generally associated with printer paper.

Recycle Bin   A feature of Windows 95 and NT that acts as a temporary storage area for deleted files.

Red book   The standard for the manufacturing audio CDs, developed by Sony and Philips Corporations.

redirectors   A term for software or hardware that sends information to another device for routing.

REGEDIT   A software program found in Windows 95 and NT that allows the user to edit the system registry; the system registry takes on many of the functions of the previous WIN.INI and SYSTEM.INI configuration files.

register   A CPU's storage area containing logical information, for instance, True or False.

Registry   The database found in Windows 95 and NT that holds the information that determines the function and layout of the operating system. The Registry performs similar functions to the WIN.INI and SYSTEM.INI files found in Windows versions 3.*x*.

REM   A command notation used with files read by MS-DOS dealing with the startup configuration of the computer system. REM indicates that the line is a remark and is not to be executed.

request to send   A block of information sent by a modem asking another modem permission to send information. *See also* modem.

resistance   The opposition to the electrical current in a circuit; resistance is measured in ohms. *See also* ohm.

ring indicator   The signal a modem receives when the phone rings. This is useful in determining if the line is open as opposed to busy.

RISC   Short for *Reduced Instruction Set Chip*, this term is used to identify an integrated circuit (IC) that uses the reduced instruction set. The reduced instruction set allows the IC to perform tasks faster because it has fewer instructions to deal with.

riser nut   A nut that incorporates a spacer; this type of nut serves two purposes — to secure the hardware and to physically provide space between two pieces of hardware. These types of nuts are often used to secure motherboards to the base of the computer case because they provide enough space to keep the exposed solder joints off of the metal case plate.

RLL   Short for *Run Length Limited*. This is a term for the encoding of data on newer hard drives.

ROM   *Read Only Memory*, as in CD-ROM. This is a term for a data storage that can only be read from, not written to, by the user.

RS232C   Recommended Standard-232C, this term is often used to describe the standard interfaces for Serial Ports on PCs.

safe mode   A startup configuration found in Windows 95 that starts the Windows environment with minimal drivers. This is useful for troubleshooting because you can determine if the Windows operating system is working independent of add-on peripherals.

safe recovery   A feature of the Windows 95 setup that allows users to continue an interrupted installation of the operating system.

ScanDisk   A Microsoft utility program that checks the system's hard disk for faults and repairs common problems.

scanner   A peripheral that allows users to transfer images such as photographs into a format that can be displayed and manipulated on a computer.

scripts   Scripts are similar in function to programs — they are a set of instructions that the computer executes in a set order, and the difference is that a script usually does not require compiling to run.

SCSI   Short for *Small Computer Serial Interface*, SCSI is one of the fastest available data transfer interfaces available for computer peripherals.

SCSI chain   More than one SCSI device on a single SCSI controller. *See also* SCSI, controller.

SCSI 1   A SCSI device or controller that supports an 8-bit bus and data transfer rates of 4MB per second. *See also* bit, bus.

SCSI II   Same as SCSI I, except that it uses a 25-pin connector to attach external peripherals. *See also* connector, SCSI I, peripheral.

SDRAM   Term for the RAM, used in computers, that synchronizes its data transfer rates with the system's bus speed. *See also* RAM, bus speed.

sectors   The areas on a hard drive in which the data is stored. *See also* hard drive.

Sequential Access   The order in which data is read on a computer, i.e. FIFO (First in First Out) or FILO (First in Last Out).

serial   A method of transferring one sequential bit of information after the other — as opposed to parallel, where several bits are transferred at a time.

SET   A DOS command that assigns a value to a variable, i.e., X=1 would read "SET X=1". The SET command when issued alone will also return the value of the variables that have been set, i.e., SET "X=1".

settings   A section of the Windows 3.1 and Windows 3.11 PROGMAN.INI that defines the settings that Program Manager will use for appearance.

SETUP.SHH   Configuration file used by Setup.

SGRAM   Short for *Synchronous Graphic Random Access Memory*, this is a type of RAM that works much like SDRAM in that it synchronizes to the CPU bus; this type of RAM also uses techniques that allow for more data to be transferred at one time. *See also* RAM, SDRAM.

Shadow Mask CRT   The technology used in computer monitors to display images using elongated pixels. *See also* pixel.

Shell   An interface where there are no controls, i.e., the desktop of Windows 95 without any icons. *See also* interface.

Shugart Associates Standard Interface   *SASI*, the predecessor of SCSI.

Signal Ground   A path for the signal to return on.

SIMM   *Single Inline Memory Module;* this component incorporates several memory chips on one board and is usually referred to when talking about RAM. *See also* RAM.

SIP   *Single Inline Package*; a memory board much like the SIMM, with the distinguishing feature being that it has pins that protrude from it to connect to its socket. *See also* socket, SIMM.

SMARTDrive   A disk-caching program provided with MS-DOS that allows zaster access to data from a storage device. *See also* cache.

Sound Blaster   An adapter card that allows the PC to produce sounds. Sound Blaster is a brand name of a sound card manufactured by Creative Labs Inc. *See also* adapter card.

speed ball   Sometimes referred to as a *track ball*, this is a type of interface used with pointing devices where the user runs their hand along a ball to move the cursor on the screen.

SRAM   *Static Random Access Memory* is a type of RAM that is commonly used in PCs — it requires less refreshing of information, making it faster than its predecessor DRAM. *See also* RAM, DRAM.

STACKS   A setting in the CONFIG.SYS file of a DOS-based PC that allows data to be accessed in reverse order.

standard mode   The default operation mode of the PC, on an 8088 the standard mode would be real mode. On a 486 or higher, the standard mode would be protected mode. *See also* real mode, protected mode.

SVGA   *Super Video Graphics Adapter* is a video display adapter based on IBM's VGA Standards; however, SVGA is capable of displaying more colors at higher resolutions. *See also* VGA.

swap file   A file created by the computer's operating system where information is exchanged between the RAM and the file as though it were one device. *See also* page file.

switches   Parameters or variables that can be assigned to a command.

synchronous   One after the other, one at a time.

SYS   An MS-DOS command that transfers the files required to boot from one disk to another; i.e., issuing the command SYS A: would transfer the system boot files to drive A.

SYSINFO   This section specifies whether systems configuration information will appear during setup. It is contained in the SETUP.SHH file.

SYSMON   A software utility included with Windows 95 and NT that allows the user to see what resources are being used on the system in a graphical display.

Taskbar   A shell included with Windows 95 and NT that allows the user to switch between running applications without exiting the application first.

TCP/IP   *Telecommunications Control Protocol/Internet Protocol* is the default protocol used on the Internet. *See also* protocol.

Temp   A directory on the computer's hard drive where working files for the running applications are stored until the task is finished.

terminator   A device that tells the SCSI controller that this is the last place on the SCSI chain to look for devices. *See also* controller, SCSI chain.

thermal printer   A printer that uses heat to affix ink or wax to paper.

toner cartridge   A field-replaceable unit in copiers and laser printers, this cartridge holds the toner that is used to create the image on paper.

Transistor Transistor Logic   Also referred to as *TTL*, this term is used to describe digital monitors.

Ultra SCSI   A SCSI standard supporting up to 20MBps data transfer. *See also* SCSI.

upper memory   The area or RAM above the first 640K and up to the first 1024K. *See also* RAM.

USB   *Universal Serial Bus* is a bus that automatically configures the devices attached to it.

USERINFO   This section specifies the user and company name in the SETUP.SHH file.

VCPI   Short for *Virtual Control Program Interface*, this is the standard that allows access to memory about the first 1MB on 80386 and greater Intel processors.

vertical position   The height of an image on a display monitor.

vertical refresh rate   The number of times the vertical lines on a monitor are redrawn, this rate is measured in Hertz.

vertical scan rate   The amount of time between checking to see if the vertical lines on the monitor need to be redrawn.

vertical size   The actual height of the image being displayed on the computer monitor.

VESA   *Video Electronics Standards Association* was the consortium of manufacturers who developed the standards by which greater resolutions and color depths display on a SVGA monitor.

VFAT   Short for *Virtual File Allocation Table*, VFAT is a copy of the File Allocation Table kept in memory so that applications software can find files quickly without having to read it from the hard drive.

VGA   *Video Graphics Adapter* is the de facto standard for IBM-compatible PCs currently being manufactured. This standard allows for resolution of 640x480 pixels and 256 colors.

video accelerators   Video adapters with their own coprocessor. *See also* coprocessor.

Video Graphics Adapter   A device that plugs into the computer's bus and allows display information to display on the computer's monitor.

Video Random Access Memory   RAM used by the video adapter to hold and manipulate the data to be sent to the display monitor. *See also* RAM.

Virtual Memory Manager   Software that controls the way Virtual Memory is used in the system. *See also* page file.

VLB   Short for *VESA local bus*, this is a bus standard used primarily with the 80486 processor — it is a 24-bit bus standard that is compatible with 32-bit processors.

VSAFE   An MS-DOS utility that checks for and removes common computer viruses.

.WAV   The file extension associated with a Windows sound file, i.e., STARTUP.WAV, a file that is played when Windows is started.

White book   The written specifications covering video CDs.

Wide SCSI   SCSI that uses a 16-bit bus. *See also* SCSI.

WINDIR   This section specifies where Windows files are located. WINDIR is contained in the SETUP.SHH file.

Windows 95   Operating system developed by Microsoft Corporation.

Windows NT   Operating system that integrates networking developed by Microsoft Corporation.

wizard   An application that automates configuring of software or hardware.

word processor   A software application that is used to write documents on a computer.

WORM   An acronym for *Write Once Read Many*, usually associated with CD-Recorders, where the data is transferred to the CD media in one session, then can be read many times.

write protect   A term generally used with floppy disks referring to the tab that prevents users from overwriting the data on the disk.

WYSIWYG   Acronym for *What You See Is What You Get*, this term refers to print quality from the computer monitor to the printer. If the quality is WYSIWYG, then what you see on the screen is what the printed document will look like.

XMS   A memory manager for accessing the first 64K above 1MB.

Yellow book   General specifications for manufacturing CDs.

ZIF   Acronym for *Zero Insertion Force*, a term for a socket that does not require the chip installer to apply a great deal of force to seat it; instead, a ZIF socket incorporates a locking lever.

Index

Numbers

A

Continued

Continued

Continued

Continued

Continued

Continued

Y

Yahoo!, users groups search, 22

Yellow Book, CD-ROM drive standards, 125

Z

ZIF (Zero Insertion Force) socket,
    described, 38

Zilog Computers, Zilog Z80 CPU, 48

Zilog Z80 CPU, development history, 48

ZIP drives, described, 99
    standards, 125

IDG BOOKS WORLDWIDE, INC.
END-USER LICENSE AGREEMENT

<u>READ THIS</u>. You should carefully read these terms and conditions before opening the software packet(s) included with this book ("Book"). This is a license agreement ("Agreement") between you and IDG Books Worldwide, Inc. ("IDGB"). By opening the accompanying software packet(s), you acknowledge that you have read and accept the following terms and conditions. If you do not agree and do not want to be bound by such terms and conditions, promptly return the Book and the unopened software packet(s) to the place you obtained them for a full refund.

1. <u>License Grant</u>. IDGB grants to you (either an individual or entity) a nonexclusive license to use one copy of the enclosed software program(s) (collectively, the "Software") solely for your own personal or business purposes on a single computer (whether a standard computer or a workstation component of a multiuser network). The Software is in use on a computer when it is loaded into temporary memory (RAM) or installed into permanent memory (hard disk, CD-ROM, or other storage device). IDGB reserves all rights not expressly granted herein.

2. <u>Ownership</u>. IDGB is the owner of all right, title, and interest, including copyright, in and to the compilation of the Software recorded on the disk(s) or CD-ROM ("Software Media"). Copyright to the individual programs recorded on the Software Media is owned by the author or other authorized copyright owner of each program. Ownership of the Software and all proprietary rights relating thereto remain with IDGB and its licensers.

3. <u>Restrictions On Use and Transfer</u>.

 (a) You may only (i) make one copy of the Software for backup or archival purposes, or (ii) transfer the Software to a single hard disk, provided that you keep the original for backup or archival purposes. You may not (i) rent or lease the Software, (ii) copy or reproduce the Software through a LAN or other network system or through any computer subscriber system or bulletin-board system, or (iii) modify, adapt, or create derivative works based on the Software.

 (b) You may not reverse engineer, decompile, or disassemble the Software. You may transfer the Software and user documentation on a permanent basis, provided that the transferee agrees to accept the terms and conditions of this Agreement and you retain no copies. If the Software is an update or has been updated, any transfer must include the most recent update and all prior versions.

4. <u>Restrictions On Use of Individual Programs</u>. You must follow the individual requirements and restrictions detailed for each individual program in the About the CD-ROM appendix of this Book. These limitations are also contained in the individual license agreements recorded on the Software Media. These limitations may include a requirement that after using the program for a specified period of time, the user must pay a registration fee or discontinue use. By opening the Software packet(s), you will be agreeing to abide by the licenses and restrictions for these individual programs that are detailed in the About the CD-ROM appendix and on the Software Media. None of the material on this Software Media or listed in this Book may ever be redistributed, in original or modified form, for commercial purposes.

5. <u>Limited Warranty</u>.

(a) IDGB warrants that the Software and Software Media are free from defects in materials and workmanship under normal use for a period of sixty (60) days from the date of purchase of this Book. If IDGB receives notification within the warranty period of defects in materials or workmanship, IDGB will replace the defective Software Media.

(b) IDGB AND THE AUTHORS OF THE BOOK DISCLAIM ALL OTHER WARRANTIES, EXPRESS OR IMPLIED, INCLUDING WITHOUT LIMITATION IMPLIED WARRANTIES OF MERCHANTABILITY AND FITNESS FOR A PARTICULAR PURPOSE, WITH RESPECT TO THE SOFTWARE, THE PROGRAMS, THE SOURCE CODE CONTAINED THEREIN, AND/OR THE TECHNIQUES DESCRIBED IN THIS BOOK. IDGB DOES NOT WARRANT THAT THE FUNCTIONS CONTAINED IN THE SOFTWARE WILL MEET YOUR REQUIREMENTS OR THAT THE OPERATION OF THE SOFTWARE WILL BE ERROR FREE.

(c) This limited warranty gives you specific legal rights, and you may have other rights that vary from jurisdiction to jurisdiction.

6. <u>Remedies</u>.

(a) IDGB's entire liability and your exclusive remedy for defects in materials and workmanship shall be limited to replacement of the Software Media, which may be returned to IDGB with a copy of your receipt at the following address: Software Media Fulfillment Department, Attn.: *A+ Certification Study System*, IDG Books Worldwide, Inc., 7260 Shadeland Station, Ste. 100, Indianapolis, IN 46256, or call 1-800-762-2974. Please allow three to four weeks for delivery. This Limited Warranty is void if failure of the Software Media has resulted from accident, abuse, or misapplication. Any replacement Software Media will be warranted for the remainder of the original warranty period or thirty (30) days, whichever is longer.

(b) In no event shall IDGB or the authors be liable for any damages whatsoever (including without limitation damages for loss of business profits, business interruption, loss of business information, or any other pecuniary loss) arising from the use of or inability to use the Book or the Software, even if IDGB has been advised of the possibility of such damages.

(c) Because some jurisdictions do not allow the exclusion or limitation of liability for consequential or incidental damages, the above limitation or exclusion may not apply to you.

7. <u>U.S. Government Restricted Rights</u>. Use, duplication, or disclosure of the Software by the U.S. Government is subject to restrictions stated in paragraph (c)(1)(ii) of the Rights in Technical Data and Computer Software clause of DFARS 252.227-7013, and in subparagraphs (a) through (d) of the Commercial Computer — Restricted Rights clause at FAR 52.227-19, and in similar clauses in the NASA FAR supplement, when applicable.

8. <u>General</u>. This Agreement constitutes the entire understanding of the parties and revokes and supersedes all prior agreements, oral or written, between them and may not be modified or amended except in a writing signed by both parties hereto that specifically refers to this Agreement. This Agreement shall take precedence over any other documents that may be in conflict herewith. If any one or more provisions contained in this Agreement are held by any court or tribunal to be invalid, illegal, or otherwise unenforceable, each and every other provision shall remain in full force and effect.

my2cents.idgbooks.com

Register This Book — And Win!

Visit **http://my2cents.idgbooks.com** to register this book and we'll automatically enter you in our fantastic monthly prize giveaway. It's also your opportunity to give us feedback: let us know what you thought of this book and how you would like to see other topics covered.

Discover IDG Books Online!

The IDG Books Online Web site is your online resource for tackling technology — at home and at the office. Frequently updated, the IDG Books Online Web site features exclusive software, insider information, online books, and live events!

10 Productive & Career-Enhancing Things You Can Do at www.idgbooks.com

- Nab source code for your own programming projects.

- Download software.

- Read Web exclusives: special articles and book excerpts by IDG Books Worldwide authors.

- Take advantage of resources to help you advance your career as a Novell or Microsoft professional.

- Buy IDG Books Worldwide titles or find a convenient bookstore that carries them.

- Register your book and win a prize.

- Chat live online with authors.

- Sign up for regular e-mail updates about our latest books.

- Suggest a book you'd like to read or write.

- Give us your 2¢ about our books and about our Web site.

You say you're not on the Web yet? It's easy to get started with IDG Books' *Discover the Internet*, available at local retailers everywhere.

CD-ROM INSTALLATION INSTRUCTIONS

Each software item on the *A+ Certification Study System* CD-ROM is located in its own folder. To install a particular piece of software, open its folder with My Computer or Internet Explorer. What you do next depends on what you find in the software's folder:

1. First, look for a ReadMe.txt file or a .doc or .htm document. If this is present, it should contain installation instructions and other useful information.

2. If the folder contains an executable (.exe) file, this is usually an installation program. Often it will be called Setup.exe or Install.exe, but in some cases the filename reflects an abbreviated version of the software's name and version number. Run the .exe file to start the installation process.

3. In the case of some simple software, the .exe file probably is the software—no real installation step is required. You can run the software from the CD to try it out. If you like it, copy it to your hard disk and create a Start menu shortcut for it.

The ReadMe.txt file in the CD-ROM's root directory may contain additional installation information so be sure to check it.

For a listing of the software on the CD-ROM, see Appendix K.